KERUX COMMENTARIES

NUMBERS

A Commentary for Biblical Preaching and Teaching

JOEL BARKER
STEVEN D. WEST

Numbers: A Commentary for Biblical Preaching and Teaching

© 2023 by Joel Barker and Steven D. West

Published by Kregel Ministry, an imprint of Kregel Publications, 2450 Oak Industrial Dr. NE, Grand Rapids, MI 49505-6020.

All rights reserved. No part of this book may be reproduced, stored in a retrieval system, or transmitted in any form or by any means—electronic, mechanical, photocopy, recording, or otherwise—without written permission of the publisher, except for brief quotations in printed reviews.

Unless otherwise indicated, the translations of the Scripture portions used throughout the commentary are the authors' own English rendering of the original biblical languages.

Scripture quotations marked CEB are from the COMMON ENGLISH BIBLE. © Copyright 2011 COMMON ENGLISH BIBLE. All rights reserved. Used by permission. (www.CommonEnglishBible.com).

Scripture quotations marked CSB have been taken from the Christian Standard Bible®, Copyright © 2017 by Holman Bible Publishers. Used by permission. Christian Standard Bible® and CSB® are federally registered trademarks of Holman Bible Publishers.

Scripture quotations marked ESV are taken from The Holy Bible, English Standard Version. Copyright © 2001 by Crossway Bibles, a publishing ministry of Good News Publishers.

Scripture quotations marked HCSB are from the Holman Christian Standard Bible®. Copyright © 1999, 2000, 2002, 2003 by Holman Bible Publishers. Used by permission.

Scripture quotations marked KJV are from the King James Version.

Scripture quotations marked NASB are taken from the New American Standard Bible® (NASB), Copyright © 1960, 1962, 1963, 1968, 1971, 1972, 1973, 1975, 1977, 1995 by The Lockman Foundation. Used by permission. www.Lockman.org

Scripture quotations marked NEB are from The New English Bible. Copyright © 1961, 1970 Oxford University Press and Cambridge University Press. All rights reserved.

Scripture quotations designated (NET) are from the NET Bible® copyright ©1996, 2019 by Biblical Studies Press, L.L.C. http://netbible.com All rights reserved

Scripture quotations marked NIV are taken from the Holy Bible, New International Version®, NIV®. Copyright © 1973, 1978, 1984, 2011 by Biblica, Inc.™ Used by permission of Zondervan. All rights reserved worldwide. www.zondervan.com

Scripture quotations marked NKJV are taken from the New King James Version®. Copyright © 1982 by Thomas Nelson, Inc. Used by permission. All rights reserved.

Scripture quotations marked NLT are taken from the *Holy Bible*, New Living Translation, copyright © 1996, 2004, 2015 by Tyndale House Foundation. Used by permission of Tyndale House Publishers, Inc., Carol Stream, Illinois 60188. All rights reserved.

Scripture quotations marked NRSV are from the New Revised Standard Version Bible, copyright © 1989 by the National Council of the Churches of Christ in the U.S.A. Used by permission. All rights reserved.

Scripture quotations marked RSV are from the Revised Standard Version of the Bible, copyright © 1946, 1952, and 1971 by the National Council of the Churches of Christ in the U.S.A. Used by permission. All rights reserved.

Italics in Scripture quotations indicate emphasis added by the authors.

The Hebrew font, NewJerusalemU, and the Greek font, GraecaU, are available from www.linguistsoftware.com/lgku.htm, +1-425-775-1130.

All photos and images are under Creative Commons licensing, and contributors are indicated in the captions of the photos.

Map on page 47 is by A. D. Riddle. Used by permission.

ISBN 978-0-8254-5852-1

Printed in China

23 24 25 26 27 / 5 4 3 2 1

Contents

Publisher's Preface to the Series / 7

Preface to Numbers / 9

Exegetical Author's Acknowledgments / 10

Preaching Author's Acknowledgments / 11

Overview of All Preaching Passages / 13

Abbreviations / 41

Introduction to Numbers / 43

SHAPING THE COMMUNITY AT SINAI (1:1–10:10)

Numbering Israel (1:1–54) / 55

The Arrangement of Israel's Camp (2:1–34) / 67

The Census of the Levites and Their Responsibilities (3:1–4:49) / 75

Maintaining Purity in the Camp (5:1–10) / 85

The Test for Infidelity (5:11–31) / 95

The Nazirite Vow (6:1–21) / 105

The Priestly Blessing (6:22–27) / 115

Gifts for the Sanctuary (7:1–89) / 123

Ministering in God's Holy Presence (8:1–26) / 131

Celebrating the Passover (9:1–14) / 141

Following Where God Leads (9:15–10:10) / 151

THE TRAVELS AND TRAVAILS OF THE FIRST GENERATION (10:11–19:22)

Israel Begins Its Journey to the Promised Land (10:11–36) / 163

Grumbling and the Giving of the Spirit (11:1–35) / 171

Miriam and Aaron's Complaint (12:1–16) / 183

Fear and Faith at the Borders of the Promised Land (13:1–14:4) / 193

Israel's Rebellion and Its Consequences (14:5–45) / 203

Regulations for Sacrificial Offerings (15:1–21) / 215

Remediation for Sin (15:22–36) / 225

Remembering God's Commands (15:37–41) / 235

Rebellions in the Wilderness (16:1–35) / 243

A Failure to Learn: The Aftermath of Korah's Rebellion (16:36–50) / 255

Aaron's Staff Blossoms (17:1–13) / 263

Duties and Benefits of the Priests and Levites (18:1–32) / 271

Cleansing from Corpse Impurity (19:1–22) / 281

SIN AND REDEMPTION FOR THE SECOND GENERATION (20:1–25:18)

Water from the Rock (20:1–13) / 293

Israel in Transition (20:14–21:3) / 303

Internal and External Challenges (21:4–35) / 313

Balak Summons Balaam (22:1–41) / 323

Balaam's First Two Oracles (23:1–26) / 335

Balaam's Remaining Oracles (23:27–24:25) / 345

Idolatry and Zealotry at Baal Peor (25:1–18) / 357

SHAPING THE COMMUNITY ON THE PLAINS OF MOAB (26:1–36:13)

The Census of the Second Generation (26:1–65) / 369

The Promise of a Legacy (27:1–23) / 379

The Sacral Calendar (28:1–29:40) / 389

Making Vows to God (30:1–16) / 401

War with the Midianites (31:1–54) / 411

The Transjordanian Tribes (32:1–42) / 425

The Wilderness Journey (33:1–49) / 435

The Promised Land (33:50–34:29) / 445

Cities of Refuge (35:1–34) / 453

Inheritance and Marriage: The Daughters of Zelophehad (36:1–13) / 463

References / 471

PUBLISHER'S PREFACE TO THE SERIES

Since words were first uttered, people have struggled to understand one another and to know the main meaning in any verbal exchange.

The answer to what God is talking about must be understood in every context and generation; that is why Kerux (KAY-rukes) emphasizes text-based truths and bridges from the context of the original hearers and readers to the twenty-first-century world. Kerux values the message of the text, thus its name taken from the Greek *kērux*, a messenger or herald who announced the proclamations of a ruler or magistrate.

Biblical authors trumpeted all kinds of important messages in very specific situations, but a big biblical idea, grasped in its original setting and place, can transcend time. This specific, big biblical idea taken from the biblical passage embodies a single concept that transcends time and bridges the gap between the author's contemporary context and the reader's world. How do the prophets perceive the writings of Moses? How does the writer of Hebrews make sense of the Old Testament? How does Clement in his second epistle, which may be the earliest sermon known outside the New Testament, adapt verses from Isaiah and also ones from the Gospels? Or what about Luther's bold use of Romans 1:17? How does Jonathan Edwards allude to Genesis 19? Who can forget Martin Luther King Jr's "I Have a Dream" speech and his appropriation of Amos 5:24: "No, no, we are not satisfied, and we will not be satisfied until 'justice rolls down like waters, and righteousness like a mighty stream'"? How does a preacher in your local church today apply the words of Hosea in a meaningful and life-transforming way?

WHAT IS PRIME IN GOD'S MIND, AND HOW IS THAT EXPRESSED TO A GIVEN GENERATION IN THE UNITS OF THOUGHT THROUGHOUT THE BIBLE?

Answering those questions is what Kerux authors do. Based on the popular "big idea" preaching model, Kerux commentaries uniquely combine the insights of experienced Bible exegetes (trained in interpretation) and homileticians (trained in preaching). Their collaboration provides for every Bible book:

- A detailed introduction and outline
- A summary of all preaching sections with their primary exegetical, theological, and preaching ideas
- Preaching pointers that join the original context with the contemporary one
- Insights from the Hebrew and Greek text
- A thorough exposition of the text
- Sidebars of pertinent information for further background
- Appropriate charts and photographs
- A theological focus to passages

- A contemporary big idea for every preaching unit
- Present-day meaning, validity, and application of a main idea
- Creative presentations for each primary idea
- Key questions about the text for study groups

Many thanks to Jim Weaver, Kregel's former acquisitions editor, who conceived of this commentary series and further developed it with the team of Jeffrey D. Arthurs, Robert B. Chisholm, David M. Howard Jr., Darrell L. Bock, Roy E. Ciampa, and Michael J. Wilkins. We also recognize with gratitude the significant contributions of Dennis Hillman, Fred Mabie, Paul Hillman, Herbert W. Bateman IV, and Shawn Vander Lugt who have been instrumental in the development of the series. Finally, gratitude is extended to the two authors for each Kerux volume; the outside reviewers, editors, and proofreaders; and Kregel staff who suggested numerous improvements.

—*Kregel Publications*

PREFACE TO NUMBERS

The book of Numbers shows us Israel at a pivotal moment. Through God's miraculous deliverance and under the leadership of Moses, the people have left behind slavery and bondage in Egypt but have not yet reached the anticipated rest of the Promised Land. Numbers tells the story of this in-between period. Throughout Numbers we see Israel learning about God's character and what it means to be in covenant relationship with him. Unfortunately, Numbers is also home to the stories of Israel's rebellion and rejection of God's commands. On the brink of seeing the fulfillment of God's promises, the people succumb to fear and disbelief. However, their failure is not the final word. Though judgment falls, hope remains as God confirms his promises to a new generation whom he brings to the borders of the Promised Land.

Numbers resists simplistic categorization. It gives us some of the Bible's best known and tragic narratives. It also calls upon Israel to heed God's instructions for a covenant relationship, to offer appropriate worship, and to remember what God has done. It further contains odd literary forms such as censuses, itineraries of travel, and geographical surveys. Holding it all together is the constancy of God's presence despite Israel's sin and rebellion. Studying Numbers thus invites the people of God to bear witness to his covenant fidelity and to respond in worship and faithful obedience.

EXEGETICAL AUTHOR'S ACKNOWLEDGMENTS

*To my parents who instilled in me a love of Scripture and study,
and to my wife Karen whose patient love and support is my sustaining strength.*

It is a privilege to contribute to the Kerux series. The need for commentaries that make the Bible accessible and available to preachers is unending. I believe that all biblical truth can speak into the life of God's people, even through books that may seem strange or impractical. Working through the book of Numbers yields rich treasure concerning the nature of God and the call that he places upon the lives of his people.

I greatly appreciate the support I have received from the leadership of Heritage College and Seminary in Cambridge, Ontario. I had the opportunity to teach Numbers during the writing process and received a well-timed sabbatical that allowed me to complete it. I hope that this commentary echoes the school's commitment to serve God with passion and excellence. I would also like to thank Heritage Baptist Church in Ancaster, Ontario, for giving me multiple opportunities to preach on Numbers, including some of its more obscure and challenging passages. I am grateful for the faithful diligence of this congregation to hear and respond to the proclamation of Scripture.

Further, I am grateful to Herb Bateman IV for taking me on as an author, and to Shawn Vander Lugt and the rest of Kregel's editorial team for their diligence and expertise in improving this work in innumerable ways. I also want to thank Steve West for jumping in as the homiletical author. Writing can be a lonely endeavor and having such an encouraging companion for this journey has been invaluable.

To you, the reader, I pray that in your engagement with Numbers, you may experience a taste of the blessing God gave to his people: "The LORD bless you and keep you; the LORD make his face to shine on you and be gracious to you; the LORD turn his face toward you and give you peace" (Num. 6:24–26 NIV).

—Joel Barker

PREACHING AUTHOR'S ACKNOWLEDGMENTS

Dr. Adam Brown
Too different to be twins,
Too similar not to be brothers.
You're a treasured friend and a great colleague.

When Dr. Joel Barker asked me to partner with him in writing this commentary, I was honored but also keenly aware of my limitations. I still feel inadequate as a guide for preaching through the book of Numbers, but Joel provided such solid exegetical work that my task was made much easier. Every component in the preaching sections is offered as a suggestion, a hint, or as one possible way of approaching the text. In this work I am a preaching practitioner wrestling with the meaning of the text and with ways to communicate it to God's people, rather than an expert insisting that these are the best observations and the best approach for preaching the text.

I have had the incalculable blessing of growing up immersed in environments of expository preaching. Until becoming a preaching pastor myself, I sat under the preaching ministries of Warren Charlton, Kirk Wellum, and Les Clemens Jr. All three men were faithful preachers of the Word, and because of their example when I was asked to preach my very first sermon, all I knew was that I needed to find a text and exposit it. From those men I learned preaching by example, rather than in a classroom. Classes in homiletics can be valuable, but there is no substitute for listening to excellent preaching year in and year out. In many ways I learned preaching through osmosis. Not only did my pastors open God's Word; they provided me with a methodology for approaching and teaching the text. When I was growing up I didn't recognize that my pastors were modeling to me what faithful preaching looks like, but now that I'm a preacher and teacher myself, I'm incredibly thankful for their example.

As a preacher, I have had the tremendous blessing of preaching and teaching in churches that value God's Word. Not every preacher has a receptive congregation where people want to hear the whole counsel of God. Not every preacher has taught in churches where people are kind, gracious, and encouraging. Like everyone who opens God's Word week by week, I have made mistakes, I have mixed human wisdom with God's truth, I have had wrong attitudes, and I have used wrong words. The pulpit can testify to both my fallibility and my sin. As much as the preacher proclaims grace to the congregation, the preacher needs grace as well. Over and over again, I have been met with support, encouragement, and mercy. As much as a congregation is blessed by a faithful preacher, a preacher is blessed by a faithful congregation. In my life, I have benefited from both sides of that equation.

Preaching Author's Acknowledgments

When I was starting out in ministry, I would not have guessed that one day I'd contribute to a commentary on the book of Numbers. Ministry is surprising sometimes, and the Lord sometimes opens doors we never would have imagined. From the perspective of an author, my work was made much easier by the competence and support of all of the staff at Kregel. Thank you for your help in shepherding and improving this work at every stage.

—Steven D. West

OVERVIEW OF ALL PREACHING PASSAGES

Numbers 1:1–54

EXEGETICAL IDEA
Enumerating Israel reveals God's faithfulness and prepares the nation to worship him.

THEOLOGICAL FOCUS
God knows and names his people and consecrates them for his service.

PREACHING IDEA
God knows every individual, and he redeems, gathers, and organizes people together into his covenant community for worship and service.

PREACHING POINTERS
Although to us the people in these tribes are nameless, faceless numbers, to God they were his special, chosen people. He knew everything about every one of them. Sheep may look generic to the passerby, but to the shepherd they are all known by name. God knows all that there is to know about each one of his children, and he loves them perfectly. This chapter shows us that God is fulfilling his covenant promises with Abraham. From one man—and he as good as dead—has come this enormous multitude.

God redeemed this people out of slavery in Egypt, and he formed them into his covenant community. When the Lord God redeems, he does not call his people to walk with him in isolation from others. On the contrary, God puts his beloved children into the church, where they exist together with other believers as part of one body. The body is properly ordered, since effective service and good health require it. The same is true of the church. God organizes his people so that they are prepared for the battles they will face and also for moving forward in their pilgrimage in this world. The new covenant community is organized for edification, service, worship, and spiritual warfare. We do not need uniformity in every detail, but we do need unity and organization in the body. We also need the Spirit of God: without the Spirit, no amount of organizing will be sufficient for what we are called to do. God knows every individual, and he redeems, gathers, and organizes people together into his covenant community for worship and service.

Numbers 2:1–34

EXEGETICAL IDEA
God provides specific direction for how the Israelites should encamp around his presence.

THEOLOGICAL FOCUS
God is to be the center of his people's life.

PREACHING IDEA
Both individually and corporately, God is to be the absolute center of our lives.

PREACHING POINTERS
In incredible grace, the holy Creator God of the universe camps in a tent in the middle of the community of his people. He puts his royal presence in the center of his covenant community. The community's whole life was to be organized around him. Everything Israel did had YHWH as the literal center. This physical reality was an object lesson of basic, fundamental moral and spiritual principles. There were to be no competing gods in the camp; there were to be no gods before the Lord God. Only he could be the center of the people's existence.

Even when the people rebelled, God remained enthroned at the center of their camp. He could not be dislodged from his place in the universe, or uprooted from his place in the midst of his people. God remained there because he is holy, just, and good. In covenant grace, he redeemed his people and took them to himself. Human beings were designed and created to flourish only when they build their lives around God in all things. In sin, we try to put other things at the center of our lives and societies, but without God, there is no center that will hold. Unless we acknowledge his reign, we will be lost. It is a high and awesome thing to stand in this relation to a holy God, and it is only by his redeeming grace that we can joyfully live our lives fully for him. Through the work of the triune God, we can love and honor God, submitting to his place at the center of all things. Both individually and corporately, God is to be the absolute center of our lives.

Numbers 3:1–4:49

EXEGETICAL IDEA
God selected and commissioned the Levites to preserve the holiness of his sanctuary.

THEOLOGICAL FOCUS
God's holiness establishes his authority over his people.

PREACHING IDEA
Through Christ the High Priest, there is now a holy priesthood of all believers.

PREACHING POINTERS
It was an unimaginable privilege for the tribes of Israel to have God dwell in the middle of their community. To know God this way was an awesome thing. But, as in other areas of Israel's religious life, there were spheres of holiness and unique roles accorded to those whom God sovereignly set aside for his purposes. God provided redemption through substitution, and in doing so he freed up the Levites to discharge special responsibilities in his service. As a subset of the Levites, the priests were allowed to minister in the tabernacle itself. Although every Israelite could walk with the Lord, only the priests and Levites could minister in the sacred precincts.

One of the significant—and beautiful—developments from the old covenant to the new covenant is that now the priests of the covenant are not a subset of the covenant community.

In the church, the priesthood is coextensive with the covenant membership. In other words, there really is a priesthood of all believers. Gone are the days of setting out the bread of the presence or keeping the lamp burning, but there are still holy tasks to be performed by the people of God. Every believer is a priest, and every believer is to worship God and serve him with all of their heart, mind, soul, and strength. We bring different sacrifices in this era: we bring the sacrifice of praise. Every believer is a holy priest, serving a holy God in the age of new covenant fulfillment in Jesus Christ, through the power of God's Spirit. The church can rejoice that through Christ the High Priest, there is now a holy priesthood of all believers.

Numbers 5:1–10

EXEGETICAL IDEA
Living with a holy God requires a commitment to be separate from both physical and moral imperfections.

THEOLOGICAL FOCUS
God provides the means through which his people can dwell in his holiness.

PREACHING IDEA
We are sanctified in Christ, so act like it!

PREACHING POINTERS
God organized his people, established his presence in the middle of the community, and set aside the Levites for special service. However, whether or not someone was a priest or Levite, every member of the community was to be holy and clean. These ten verses establish the principles of being holy in God's presence and faithful toward our neighbor. The physical reality in 5:1–4 points to the spiritual principle of holy moral purity. Those who are unclean cannot remain in the camp of his people. When people sin against each other, justice must be done. In some cases, what is required is not only confession and forgiveness, but also restitution. These verses teach us that we must be holy toward God, and that there are both divine and civil consequences for sin.

In the covenant community, we have responsibilities to both God and our fellow covenant members. Only through the blood of Jesus Christ can we be purified and made clean, and only through his righteousness can we be numbered among his people. Having been redeemed, we must take care not to sin against those who bear his image. When we do, we must make restitution. This is a warning to help keep us from sinning in the first place. Ultimately, the law is fulfilled by Christ, and Paul tells us that love is the fulfillment of the law (Rom. 13:8–10). If we loved God and our neighbor perfectly, we would never sin against them. God reminds us that we are sanctified in Christ, and then tells us to act like it!

Numbers 5:11–31

EXEGETICAL IDEA
God alone is a suitable judge of cases of suspected adultery.

THEOLOGICAL FOCUS
Marital fidelity among God's people reflects his holiness.

PREACHING IDEA
God designs, creates, sustains, and protects covenant relationships.

PREACHING POINTERS
If we do not understand the divine design and sacredness of the marriage covenant, we will not be able to grasp the significance of this passage. Marriage was created by God, and he alone has the right to set its covenant parameters. Idolatry is often depicted as spiritual adultery, and that analogy helps us understand the significance of both. It is a terrible thing for the people of God to pursue other gods, and since Christ is the bridegroom of the church, it is unthinkable that his bride would engage in illicit relations with others. God is faithful to the covenant, and God's people are called to be faithful in their covenants, too.

This text must be handled with sensitivity and tact. There is a lot of pain in marriages. Some have been divorced, and others are working through confessed adultery. Some people are married to irrationally jealous spouses and face false accusations. In this passage, a guilty spouse is cursed, but an innocent one is exonerated. Nevertheless, in either case, there is no doubt that by the time things had reached the stage of this trial, the damage in the home was already incalculable. Look to Christ for forgiveness and reconciliation, and thank God that he is perfectly faithful to his covenant promises. Given the theological and practical ramifications of marriage dynamics, we need to remember that God designs, creates, sustains, and protects covenant relationships.

Numbers 6:1–21

EXEGETICAL IDEA
The Nazirite vow permitted any Israelite to mark a period of special devotion to God.

THEOLOGICAL FOCUS
God provides the means for all of his people to express the fullness of their dedication.

PREACHING IDEA
When you dedicate yourself to God, actions speak louder than words.

PREACHING POINTERS
Only a fraction of the Israelites could serve the Lord as priests or Levites, but any Israelite could dedicate themselves to the Lord in a special way by taking the Nazirite vow. A Nazirite had to give up some of the normal pleasures of life, as well as voluntarily place themselves under certain restrictions. People were not forced to make this vow, but if they did, it was binding. Actions speak louder than words, and what counted in God's sight was not a person saying they would uphold a vow, but rather the follow-through and fulfilment of the vow that had been made.

It may sound to us like the restrictions in the Nazirite vow were quite limiting, but what was given up was more than compensated for by the opportunity to live in self-conscious awareness of being specially dedicated to the Lord. The joy and Spirit of the Lord amply repaid the faithful Nazirite. In the new covenant era, we do not have Nazirites, but every follower of Christ has made an even more serious, binding commitment when they put their faith in Jesus. Jesus does not call us to give up grapes, haircuts, and funerals: he calls us to pick up our cross, die to self daily, and follow him. To the world, this looks like a terrible sacrifice, but the ones who love Jesus wouldn't take the entire world in exchange for the riches they have in him. These things are matters of eternal significance, and God holds us accountable for every word we utter, so remember that when you dedicate yourself to God, actions speak louder than words.

Numbers 6:22–27

EXEGETICAL IDEA
God desires to bless and preserve the Israelites.

THEOLOGICAL FOCUS
Pronouncing God's blessing shapes the identity of God's people.

PREACHING IDEA
In Scripture, there is a beautiful spiral between God's benediction and our response in doxology.

PREACHING POINTERS
This benedictory blessing is a gem that has biblical, theological, and literary beauty. It is crafted to be beautiful, and the blessing it conveys is life-giving. To bask in the glowing, holy, and gracious countenance of the Lord, and to feel his love and grace, is an experience that is too definite for words; it is literally inexpressible. For God's representative to stand before the people and pronounce this blessing is a wonder of God's grace and mercy. He truly, truly loves his people.

Throughout Scripture, there are numerous ways that God blesses his people, and numerous ways that his people respond by blessing his name in praise. God pronounces his benediction on his people, and his people break into doxology, worshipping him and extoling all that he is and all that he has done. The more God blesses his people, the more they are drawn into praise. This spiral is beautiful, as benediction leads to doxology, and doxology leads to the outpouring of even greater blessing. It is impossible to be blessed more richly than God's children are blessed in Jesus Christ, and so every believer ought to live a life of praise, thanksgiving, and rejoicing in the Lord. The greater our blessings, the greater our praise ought to be. In Scripture, there is a beautiful spiral between God's benediction and our response in doxology.

Numbers 7:1–89

EXEGETICAL IDEA
Israel obeyed God's command to bring gifts to mark the dedication of the tabernacle.

THEOLOGICAL FOCUS
God's people should be generous in their gifts to him.

PREACHING IDEA
In Christ, the gifts we bring are not identical, but every believer should have a heart for giving.

PREACHING POINTERS
It is easy for contemporary Christians to miss how much disunity and tribal tension often existed among the tribes of Israel. However, this text gives a welcome example of tribal unity. Each tribe of Israel contributed its share, and its shares in the dedication of the tabernacle were identical. This is more than pedantic record-keeping: it is a witness to the inclusion of all of God's people on equal terms. No tribe owned the ministry, neither was any tribe excluded. The repetition of the gifts, reported in their identical details, ensured that no tribe could claim a greater stake than another. It was a testimony to the unity of the covenant community as it prepared to head for the Promised Land. This was what God desired of his people.

In the new covenant assembly, there is unity but also diversity. At this time, we do not all bring the same gifts when we come into the Lord's holy presence. We are all members of one body, but we are different parts of it and each is to function in their own role, using the special gifts that God has given them. Yet, there is another fundamental unity: every believer is to give God their entire heart through Jesus Christ their Lord. No believer is to hold back or give God less than their best. The gifts in our hands are diverse, but every believer should rejoice in giving to the Lord and working to edify his saints. In Christ, the gifts we bring are not identical, but every believer should have a heart for giving.

Numbers 8:1–26

EXEGETICAL IDEA
Setting up the lampstand and dedicating the Levites reflects the holiness of God's presence.

THEOLOGICAL FOCUS
God's holy presence is worthy of reverence by his chosen and holy people

PREACHING IDEA
Come into the light! Be washed, be consecrated, and serve the Lord with reverent awe.

PREACHING POINTERS
Part of the symbolism found in the tabernacle depicts the shining of God's light upon his people, which illustrates the grace of the benediction in Numbers 6:24–26. When the priest blesses the people, it is only because God has already sovereignly determined to make his face shine upon them. No priest or prophet must cajole a reluctant God to bless his people. God is a God of light and life, not darkness and death.

When God's light shines upon his people, they must be purified and cleansed. Having been made holy, they are consecrated to the service of the Lord. In Numbers 7, Israel brought offerings for the tabernacle, but God selects the Levites to be offerings in themselves. When the light dawns, we are called into life, love, and holy service. This chapter is filled with sacred, symbolic details. In God's plan of redemption, it is his Son the Lord Jesus Christ who is the light of the world. It is also the Son who provides the blood needed for washing, purification, and atonement. Levites had to retire, but the Son lives forever and so his priestly office never ends. Hebrews reveals in exquisite detail how the old covenant forms were fulfilled by the new covenant mediator. There were lessons in this text for Israel in their own day, but the fullness and richness are only seen in Jesus Christ. So, since God's light is shining in Jesus, come into the light! Be washed, be consecrated, and serve the Lord with reverent awe.

Numbers 9:1–14

EXEGETICAL IDEA
Everyone who is part of the community of Israel must celebrate the Passover.

THEOLOGICAL FOCUS
The people of God should commemorate God's gracious acts of deliverance.

PREACHING IDEA
Our purpose in the present requires us to remember our origins and look toward our future hope.

PREACHING POINTERS
Without question, the Passover is one of the most important and well-known events in the Bible. Its significance as a redemptive event is paradigmatic. As with its greater fulfillment in the cross of Christ, numerous lines of biblical-theological importance run up to it, intersect within it, and flow out from it. God called Israel to continually look back on the covenant with Abraham and to continue to look back in awe at his mighty work of redemption on that first Passover night in Egypt. Christ is the fulfillment of everything Passover represented: he is the lamb who takes away the sin of the world, and it is his blood that shields his people from the angel of death. Jesus frees us from slavery to Satan, the world, and sin; Jesus redeems us into eternal life.

In order to live well in the present, we need to be able to simultaneously look back and look ahead. Human meaning, purpose, and dignity require meaningful origins, and they also require a significant, future *telos* (i.e., an ultimate goal, purpose, or end). As Christians, our orientation in life comes from being created in the image of God, being redeemed by Christ (in fulfillment of Passover), and looking forward to eternal, eschatological glory in the new heaven and new earth. Our purpose in the present requires us to remember our origins and look toward our future hope.

Numbers 9:15–10:10

EXEGETICAL IDEA
The Israelites were to obey God's instructions as they went where he directed.

THEOLOGICAL FOCUS
The people of God must follow where God leads.

PREACHING IDEA
The call of discipleship has always been, "Come, follow me."

PREACHING POINTERS
After redeeming his people at the first Passover, God led them out of Egypt, across the Sea, and into the desert. This unit shows us that after God redeems his people, he continues to act as their Sovereign Lord, King, and Guide. God does not redeem his people and then let them go off merrily in all directions. He is not a liberator who lets people out of jail and then watches them disappear into the night. God is the covenant Lord of his people, and he redeems them so that they can follow him in holy obedience. He is our Redeemer, but he is also our Master.

There is never a time in Scripture when God is pleased with those who refuse to obey him or follow his law. The importance of following God's decrees is an extremely important theme all through the Bible. Time after time, human characters are challenged to follow God by faith, and the consequences of both obedience and disobedience are clearly revealed. The incarnate Son of God called his disciples to leave everything and follow him. In the gospel, the call for discipleship still goes out, and everyone with ears to hear is to leave their sin and follow Jesus. This passage in Numbers help us see how gracious God is to lead us and guide us, but it also reminds us that he is the holy God, and he rules with infinite authority. Its central theme resonates with the rest of Scripture, where the call of discipleship is always, "Come, follow me."

Numbers 10:11–36

EXEGETICAL IDEA
Israel's journey to the Promised Land begins with obedience to God's commands and evidence of God's presence.

THEOLOGICAL FOCUS
God rewards his obedient people with signs of his presence.

PREACHING IDEA
Obey and be led, or disobey and be scattered.

PREACHING POINTERS
The themes of chapters 9 and 10 continue to build. God redeems his people and then, as their sovereign Lord, he commands them to be obedient to his holy law and follow him wherever he takes them. As we see in this passage, God leading his people is compatible with gifted, knowledgeable human beings helping out along the way. Yet the accent is on the covenant God who has full authority over the movements and direction of his people.

It was an incredible blessing to be led by YHWH. Having been redeemed from bondage, having experienced Sinai, and having lived through numerous manifestations of God's power and holy love, it is hard to believe that any would be so hard-hearted as to not joyfully follow God. Security and peace rested upon those who followed him, but those who persisted in rebellion were scattered. God led his people, scattering their enemies before them. Then God set up camp with his people again, dwelling in the middle of their community. There is no greater safety than the safety found in following God in obedience and faith. Since this safety is available, make sure you are numbered among those who obey and are led, rather than those who disobey and are scattered.

Numbers 11:1–35

EXEGETICAL IDEA
Israel's failure to be satisfied with God's provision brings judgment that is only removed by God's mercy.

THEOLOGICAL FOCUS
The failure to appreciate God's provision reflects a selfish and distorted view of reality that damages our relationship with God.

PREACHING IDEA
Internal grace, not external law, is what makes the heart thankful to God.

PREACHING POINTERS
Those who are familiar with the Pentateuch cannot help but notice parallels between this chapter and Exodus 16, even though the events are not identical. Far from simply being a recast of an old event, Numbers 11 has its own color and nuance. Tragically, it also occurs after the exodus, after Sinai, after the tabernacle was constructed, and after God's glory took up residence in the middle of their camp. Now, they are led forward by the glory cloud. Immediately—as their first recorded act after breaking camp from the base of Sinai—the people grumble and complain against God. After all that they have witnessed and experienced, they continue to repeat their patterns of sin. Greater light, and even the awesome power of Sinai that stands behind the law, does not remove the heart of stone.

At first, this passage leaves the reader utterly discouraged. There are also eerie parallels in our own lives, with how slow we are to learn our lessons and how frequently we fall into the same patterns of sin. Nevertheless, this passage cries out for a greater reality, where we will be moved to obey God's law from the inside out. We need the law written not on tablets of stone, but on the tablets of our heart. Gloriously, in the new covenant, this is exactly what the Spirit does. In Christ, we are given a new heart, and the will and word of the Lord are internalized. Standing under the law will never move us to obey from our heart, but the marvelous, matchless grace of God in Jesus Christ changes our heart and reorients it. The new covenant reality to come is glimpsed in the elders who are filled with the Spirit. This text clearly shows us that internal grace, not external law, is what makes the heart thankful to God.

Numbers 12:1–16

EXEGETICAL IDEA
God rejects Miriam and Aaron's challenge to Moses's leadership.

THEOLOGICAL FOCUS
Humility is an essential quality for those whom God chooses to lead his people.

PREACHING IDEA
Leaders are not perfect and sometimes sin against each other, but there can be intercession, reconciliation, and renewed partnership.

PREACHING POINTERS
Anyone who has long experience in pastoral or other kinds of Christian ministry knows that many, many times there are terrible tensions and divisions among leaders. Sometimes there is open animosity in the office. This passage shows us that such problems are not new. Here, there is a collocation of personal, prejudicial, and professional antagonism. Even today, the pain in the text comes through. The events described here are both very sad and very sinful. Unfortunately, many Christian leaders can identify with the general scene. But if we are honest, we must also remember that we have sometimes been the attackers as well as the target.

There are consequences for this arrogant attack on Moses, but there is also an incredible note of grace and forgiveness. This is a bitter squabble that brings personal family and social issues into the wider sphere of public ministry among the people of God. It challenges God's own decisions about leadership. Nevertheless, there is mercy and restoration. They remain brother and sister, and they are all still to fulfill their roles in the covenant community. Sadly, leaders can fight against each other, and there may be consequences for doing so, but in God's grace there can be forgiveness, reconciliation, and restoration. We need to recognize that leaders are not perfect and sometimes sin against each other, but there can be intercession, reconciliation, and renewed partnership

Numbers 13:1–14:4

EXEGETICAL IDEA
The spies' fearmongering triumphs over the call to faithfully trust God when the time comes to enter the Promised Land.

THEOLOGICAL FOCUS
God's people are called to respond in faith and obedience rather than succumb to fear.

PREACHING IDEA
We are to respond in faith to God's promises, trusting his word more than those who incite fear and disbelief.

PREACHING POINTERS
This is a familiar story, and one that connects well with our experiences. It is a pivotal moment in the Pentateuch and is used as a warning lesson throughout the canon. Israel's failure in that particular historical moment cannot be repeated (since nobody else will ever stand in that epoch facing that exact decision), but the underlying reason for their failure to enter the Promised Land is one that people face day after day. When we stand on the brink of momentous, life-changing decisions, or as we make our countless daily choices, we will either choose to put our faith in God's promises, or we will give way to fear and abandon our trust in God.

There are many frightening realities in this world, and our strength indeed is small. Yet, the Lord is our covenant God, and we are called to trust in him. In the Gospels, this dichotomy between fear and faith recurs over and over again. If we trust Jesus, we will not give way to fear. If we give way to fear, we are not exercising proper faith in Jesus. God's Word must be taken over every lie, piece of propaganda, and alternative opinion. We must not look to our own wisdom, strength, and goodness, but to God's. Only by faith can we be saved and enter the Promised Land. We are to respond in faith to God's promises, trusting his word more than those who incite fear and disbelief.

Numbers 14:5–45

EXEGETICAL IDEA
Israel's failure to trust God yields fatal consequences as God decrees that the generation rescued from slavery in Egypt will die in the wilderness. However, evidence of God's grace and mercy is found in his continued presence among his sinful people.

THEOLOGICAL FOCUS
God's great mercy redeems human sinfulness but does not eliminate all of the consequences of sin.

PREACHING IDEA
Although there can be enormous consequences for sin, God is forgiving and merciful to fulfill his redemptive promises.

PREACHING POINTERS
This chapter reveals the consequences of walking in fear rather than in faith. Having come so far and having experienced so much of God's redeeming grace and power, the Israelites now turn away from him. On the brink of having one of God's significant promises fulfilled, their faith fails. Instead of going into the Promised Land, they talk about going back to slavery in Egypt. In saying this, they are literally contemplating a total rejection of God's redemption and covenant promises. Given their response, God threatens to destroy the people totally and start a new nation with Moses. However, Moses intercedes on the basis of God's glory and name.

After numerous examples of hard-hearted stubbornness and high-handed rebellion, the amazing thing about this passage is that God decides to bear patiently with his people. Yes, this generation will die in the wilderness, but the next generation will enter the land. God will not swerve from his covenant loyalty, and he will not cast aside his people or his plan. There are real consequences for those who rebel, but God is filled with covenant mercy, grace, and kindness. God has a plan, and he is going to bring it to fruition. If we put our faith in him, we will be blessed and enter into salvation. If we turn from him in lack of faith, we will be lost. Although there can be enormous consequences for sin, God is forgiving and merciful to fulfill his redemptive promises.

Numbers 15:1–21

EXEGETICAL IDEA
The sacrificial system requires both obedience to God's commands and generosity on the part of the worshippers.

THEOLOGICAL FOCUS
Offerings remind God's people to show gratitude for what he has done for them.

PREACHING IDEA
God's rich, infinite grace is the best motive for joyful giving.

PREACHING POINTERS
Coming out of the previous chapter, Numbers 15:1–2 should stop you in your tracks. God says, "After you enter the land I am giving you as a home . . .". What just happened? Despite the continued grumbling about food, despite the infighting, and despite the colossal failure of faith and the rejection of God in the previous two chapters, God still promises that one day he will give them the land. It would be difficult to find a text that showcases the covenant faithfulness and love of God more clearly than this. After all of this provocation—and in his eternal omniscience God knows that more is coming, even in this book—the Lord God is still operating to bless the children of Abraham.

The details of the offerings and sacrifices that will be offered in the land may not strike the contemporary Christian as having immediate interest or value, but the underlying principle is incredible: God will not only bring his people into the Promised Land, but he also will bless them abundantly. He has redeemed them and will bless them with superabounding grace.

God's grace is necessary for us every step of the way. Without his grace and power, we would not be redeemed, and without it we would not be able to worship him as he deserves. He is so good to us that he gives to us so that we have something to return to him. It is in Jesus Christ where we see how richly we are blessed, and it is God's rich, infinite grace that is the best motive for joyful giving.

Numbers 15:22–36

EXEGETICAL IDEA
The sacrificial system can remediate sin classified as unintentional; however, defiant or high-handed sin stands outside of this process.

THEOLOGICAL FOCUS
Remediation of sin requires a repentant heart.

PREACHING IDEA
Our new covenant mediator can forgive all of our sins, but if we reject Christ no forgiveness is possible.

PREACHING POINTERS
There can be no doubt about the kindness, mercy, and grace of God, but there must also not be any doubt about his holiness and justice. Everyone falls short and everyone sins, but where there is sin there needs to be confession and repentance. There are also sins that constitute a fundamental, total rejection of God and his ways. In this passage, we find that people who sin that way against God were to be put to death. The man violating the Sabbath command was symbolically rejecting the entire covenant, and as a result he died. There is no life outside of a saving relationship with the God of Abraham.

The author of Hebrews is at pains to show his readers that there is no salvation outside of Jesus Christ. If Christ is rejected, there can be no salvation. The Son of God is the covenant mediator of the new covenant, and it is only in this mediator that we can find forgiveness for sins, and the gift of eternal life. Like the man in this text who died for rejecting the covenant, if we reject the new covenant in Christ we will experience the second death. There is no atonement and forgiveness outside of Jesus Christ. Do not reject him. Come to him and be saved. Take seriously the truth that our new covenant mediator can forgive all of our sins, but if we reject Christ no forgiveness is possible.

Numbers 15:37–41

EXEGETICAL IDEA
The requirement of placing tassels on garments provides Israel with a tangible reminder to obey God and to not follow their own desires.

THEOLOGICAL FOCUS
Remembering what God has commanded is crucial to the life of faith.

PREACHING IDEA
"Thy word have I hid in mine heart, that I might not sin against thee" (Ps. 119:11 KJV).

PREACHING POINTERS
Most Christians today do not put tassels on their garments to remind themselves of the words of God. We do, however, live in a society filled with reminders, alarms, notifications, calendars, day planners, and memory aids. Consequently, the principle of jogging our memories is one that resonates with people in our contemporary society. Everyone knows that when you get a notification reminding you of a meeting in fifteen minutes, the point isn't the notification—it's *the meeting*. Similarly, the point in this passage wasn't a fashion accessory; it was remembering and obeying *the commands of God*.

More importantly, the notification to go to the meeting is of no help unless you actually go to the meeting. Knowing there's a meeting and attending the meeting are not the same thing. Likewise, knowing the commands of God is not the same as obeying the commands of God. Memorization and knowledge have their place, but God wants us to put his words into practice. We are to be doers of the word, not hearers only. We must be able to say with the psalmist, "Thy word have I hid in mine heart, that I might not sin against thee" (Ps 119:11 KJV).

Numbers 16:1–35

EXEGETICAL IDEA
Dissatisfaction with their allotted roles fuels some of Israel's leaders to rebel against God by attempting to undermine Moses and Aaron.

THEOLOGICAL FOCUS
Jealousy and envy at what God has given others can motivate rebellion against God.

PREACHING IDEA
Pastors are not Moses, and Christians must not act like Korah, Dathan, and Abiram.

PREACHING POINTERS
Even this far removed from the events described in this passage, it is difficult to read this account without feeling the stress of the situation. These accusations against Moses are incredibly unfair. Those who rise up against Moses slander him, make false accusations, and rebel against God. The very ones who refused Moses's pleading and God's commands are now blaming Moses for the outcome of their own sinful failure. It is rare to find so much hypocrisy and intransigence.

Faced with this onslaught, Moses placed himself in the hands of the Lord, and the Lord defended and vindicated him. The rebellion was crushed by a supernatural act of God (for which Moses is also blamed in the next section). Today, no pastor or Christian leader has the role or authority of Moses, but this passage does serve as a strong warning against rebelling against the authorities that have been instituted by God. Every one of us needs to guard our attitudes and hearts. It is easy to be willfully blind to our own sin, as well as willfully blind to the plan of God in appointing certain people to the offices that they hold. Pastors need to remember that they are not in the position of Moses, and Christians who are members of a church must not act like Korah, Dathan, and Abiram.

Numbers 16:36–50

EXEGETICAL IDEA
God uses Korah's rebellion to further instruct Israel about his holiness. However, Israel's refusal to learn necessitates intercession to avert God's wrath.

THEOLOGICAL FOCUS
Sinful humanity requires an intercessor to dwell with a holy God.

PREACHING IDEA
Ultimately, there is only one priestly mediator and intercessor, but he is sufficient for all of our needs.

PREACHING POINTERS
Immediately following God's supernatural vindication of Moses and his swallowing up of the rebellion, the people are accusing Moses of murder. Rather than learn their lesson, they actually want to imitate and follow the example of Korah. God is angry and strikes the people with a plague. Ironically, the only way for the people to be saved is for Aaron as high priest to intercede for them. The people rebelled against Moses and Aaron—and in so doing rebelled against the Lord God—and now it is Aaron who will save their lives through priestly intercession.

In this passage we see the incredible blindness and folly of sin, but we also see the grace of God in providing a means for forgiveness. One of the major lessons to learn in this text is that sinners need a priestly mediator and intercessor or they will die. This is not merely an Old Testament principle; it is a typological one that is fulfilled in the high priestly ministry of the Lord Jesus Christ. In Christ, God provides the high priest, covenant mediator, and intercessor that we so desperately need. Those who trust him will be saved and forgiven, but those who refuse him will be irrevocably lost. Ultimately, there is only one priestly mediator and intercessor, but he is sufficient for all of our needs.

Numbers 17:1–13

EXEGETICAL IDEA
God provides a miraculous sign to confirm Aaron's consecrated status and to quell Israel's spirit of rebellion.

THEOLOGICAL FOCUS
Only the one whom God has chosen can mediate between humanity and God.

PREACHING IDEA
The great High Priest is chosen by God, bears spiritual fruit, and makes his followers fruitful in the Spirit.

PREACHING POINTERS
Although the context for this passage is God's response to the unspeakable wickedness of the previous chapter, it is somewhat refreshing. Here, God takes the initiative to settle the matter once and for all. He will not wait for the next wave of rebellious grumbling before he vindicates his chosen priest. This chapter proves that it is God who selects the high priest and it is God who makes him bear spiritual fruit. The miracle of the staff that blossoms and bears almonds points beyond the physical miracle to these spiritual principles. God elects, and then God makes his chosen ones bear fruit.

This principle finds its highest fulfillment in Jesus Christ. He is the great high priest, and the only high priest the church will need both now and through eternity. Not only is Christ maximally fruitful in the spiritual realm—he is so powerful that he makes his followers fruitful too. By the Spirit of God, and in union with Christ, God's children are able to see spiritual fruit grow in their lives. In the same way that Aaron was identified through the fruitfulness of the staff, now Christ's disciples are known by the fruit of their lives. Incredibly, the great high priest is not only chosen by God and bears spiritual fruit, but he is powerful enough to make his followers fruitful in the Spirit.

Numbers 18:1–32

EXEGETICAL IDEA
God confirms the calling of Aaron and the Levites and directs the whole community to support them.

THEOLOGICAL FOCUS
Faithful ministers merit the support of God's people.

PREACHING IDEA
There is a relationship between spiritual responsibility, true prosperity, financial support, and generous giving.

PREACHING POINTERS
The staggering importance of the roles of the priests and Levites in the wider Israelite community runs through Numbers. Here, coming out of Numbers 16–17, God provides detailed, clear instructions so that there will not be any confusion about proper role delineation in the community. Each group has their own responsibilities and obligations. The special privileges and service to which the Levites are called brings with it an accompanying responsibility and high stakes; how they perform their service is literally a matter of life and death. Their lives are on the line in the holy spheres in which they minister.

In the nation of Israel, the non-Levites had the responsibility of providing the Levites with food and the essentials of life. God arranged the nation's economy so that the tribes were blessed so abundantly that they not only had all that they needed but had more than enough to share. As a result, the Levites could be fully supported out of the bounty given to the other tribes. This arrangement set up a virtuous spiral. Those with spiritual responsibility ministered for the glory of God and the good of the people, and the people were blessed. The people responded by joyfully giving back to God and the Levites. Material blessings, spiritual responsibilities, financial support, and generous giving all intersected and fed into one another. This text helps illustrate the wider biblical principle that there is a relationship between spiritual responsibility, true prosperity, financial support, and generous giving.

Numbers 19:1–22

EXEGETICAL IDEA
Impurity from contact with a dead body can be remedied through the ritual of the red cow.

THEOLOGICAL FOCUS
God provides the means for his holy presence to remain among his people.

PREACHING IDEA
God gives us rituals to increase our appreciation of the realities found in Christ.

PREACHING POINTERS
The details of this text are very foreign to the contemporary reader. In our churches, we do not use this water of cleansing, and we do not go through with these rituals. Even at the level of rationality, it seems doubtful that anyone could ever have thought that the ashes of a dead bovine mixed with water could make someone clean. Since God's instructions are not absurd, the obvious explanation is that there is a deeper, abiding principle that is being illustrated by the production and application of the water of purification.

Christian readers should know that these types of symbolic acts point forward to Jesus Christ. It is by his shed blood and sacrificial death that we are made clean; it is by being washed in the water and the blood that we are made pure. Christ's death brings about the ultimate purification that this text in Numbers can only hint at. The water of purification in this text is the shadow, but Christ is the substance and fulfillment. Today in the church, we still enact religious rites when we follow the ordinances of our Lord. Baptism and the Lord's Supper are divinely appointed rituals of worship for the new covenant community. It is important for us to understand that God gives us rituals to increase our appreciation of the realities found in Christ

Numbers 20:1–13

EXEGETICAL IDEA
Moses and Aaron's failure to show God as holy disqualifies them from leading Israel into the Promised Land.

THEOLOGICAL FOCUS
God's servants must reflect God's character.

PREACHING IDEA
Moses was an imperfect servant, but Christ is the perfect Son of God.

PREACHING POINTERS
According to the divine verdict, we know that Moses and Aaron sinned in what they did in this pericope. Most Christian leaders, however, can probably look at times in their lives when they have said and done things that seem worse in the face of much less provocation. It's natural that our hearts go out to Moses: he was human, just like us, and this was the straw that broke his back. Nevertheless, God's holy standards are not lowered for any of his servants, and there were real consequences for his and Aaron's sin.

One of the marks of the honesty and trustworthiness of the biblical witness is that it is unflinching when it comes to reporting both the successes and failures of its main characters.

This deep honesty is all the more remarkable when it comes to the presentation of Jesus Christ. In a book that depicts the sins of the heroes of the faith, Jesus alone is depicted as sinlessly perfect. No sin is reported of him, because there was no sin to report. Moses and Aaron were servants of God, and they were imperfect—like all of us—but Jesus is the Son of God, and he is infinitely perfect and matchless in every way. Moses's sin prevented him from going into the Promised Land, but Jesus leads his redeemed people into eternal glory in the new heaven and earth. Moses was an imperfect servant, but Christ is the perfect Son of God.

Numbers 20:14–21:3

EXEGETICAL IDEA
Israel's progression toward the Promised Land is marked by hostility from foreign enemies and a transition in leadership.

THEOLOGICAL FOCUS
God remains sovereign over both the nations and his people.

PREACHING IDEA
God is sovereign over every nation and every person, and he is sovereign over *you*.

PREACHING POINTERS
God is sovereign over all things. He rules the macro-level and the micro-level. He is sovereign over the nations and sovereign over every individual. This passage draws the past into the present and then looks into the future. Israel was a relatively small and weak nation, but God has already shown that he is faithful to his covenant people and more powerful than superpowers like Egypt. No gods can oppose him, and no human armies can defeat him. These lessons of the past are essential for Israel to take to heart as they move toward the Promised Land.

Yet even though God is moving in the large events of world history, and he is sovereign over the nations, he is intimately aware of every detail in the lives of every one of his children. He knows each one of us by name. The King of the Universe is also a personal God who delights in relationship with each individual in his family. Nations are composed of individuals, and God does not lose the individual in the crowd or the mass. His track record is one of holy, steadfast faithfulness, and no power can resist him. Nations should call on him, and every person on earth should trust in him. If he is your heavenly Father, trust his sovereign will and know that he cares for you as he directs the affairs of the world. God is sovereign over every nation and every person, but he is also sovereign over *you*.

Numbers 21:4–35

EXEGETICAL IDEA
Israel's journey to the Promised Land is marked by God's discipline and God's provision.

THEOLOGICAL FOCUS
God sustains his people in the face of their own failings and external challenges.

PREACHING IDEA
Our victory is secure through God's provision of atonement and Christ's victory over every evil power.

PREACHING POINTERS
Jesus refers to this passage in John 3, and in doing so ensures that it will be one of the best-known events in Numbers. The incarnate Christ himself tells us the prophetic significance of this event: the bronze serpent lifted up on the pole symbolizes his own atoning death when he is lifted up on the cross. People cannot control what their external enemies do, but even more frighteningly, apart from grace they also cannot control their internal, deadly enemy (i.e., their sin nature). Human beings stand in absolute need of forgiveness and atonement for sin, but we also need a conquering champion to win a victory over enemies we cannot defeat. Biblically speaking, we need a Savior to save us from ourselves.

Numbers 21 shows us that God provides atonement for his people, and then he leads them on in victory over their enemies. Christ's substitutionary atonement is multifaceted, and one vital element of it is that in his death and resurrection he is the victor over sin, death, hell, and all the powers of darkness (*Christus victor*). Only in Christ can we find atonement for our sins, and only in Christ can we be led forth in victory. In order to defeat our spiritual enemies, we must first bow our knee and look to Christ as he is lifted up on the cross. Thanks be to God, our victory is secure through God's provision of atonement and Christ's victory over every evil power.

Numbers 22:1–41

EXEGETICAL IDEA
Balaam cannot curse Israel because God alone controls the spiritual realm.

THEOLOGICAL FOCUS
God is sovereign over all creation: material and spiritual.

PREACHING IDEA
The more we see, the more we see that our God reigns.

PREACHING POINTERS
Everyone enjoys the story of Balaam's donkey, but just as with Jonah and the big fish, it is vitally important to see beyond the surface details and understand what God is doing and communicating in these texts. If all people remember about Balaam is the story with the donkey, they simply did not understand these chapters. As a preacher, do not major on the minor details: bring out the point of the text. What we have in the Balaam narrative is an attempt to destroy Israel and control the Lord God through occultic means. Human military power alone will not avail, so Balak looks to magic and spiritual manipulation.

This is a test of the power of God, as well as a test of his faithfulness. Will God change his mind about Israel, or will he fulfill all of his covenant promises to Abraham? Does divination work? Does God truly reign over both the heavens and earth, and all that is within them? Westerners may only have a vague, general sense of this, but for many people in history and for many people in various cultures around the world today, the power of God over evil spirits is a vital truth they cling to. The witchdoctor, shaman, or magician cannot control the Lord God, and this provides incredible comfort and security. In this passage, we see that God cannot be manipulated, challenged, or thwarted. He remains absolutely faithful, and his will *will* be done. No one can make him change his mind or his plan, and none can coerce him. The more we see, the more we see that God is sovereign and immutable. Pray that God will open the eyes of our hearts—because the more we see, the more we see that our God reigns.

Numbers 23:1–26

EXEGETICAL IDEA
Israel is a nation that God has chosen to bless.

THEOLOGICAL FOCUS
God's blessing provides protection for his people.

PREACHING IDEA
The people of God are blessed both in life and in death.

PREACHING POINTERS
The first message delivered by Balaam immediately proves that God, not Balak, is going to prevail. Far from having power over God, Balak's chosen prophet is helpless to say anything outside of what the Lord allows him to say. Balak wants to turn the gods against Israel, but the living God has determined to fulfill his covenant promises to Abraham, and he will not change his mind. God will not only *not* allow his people to be cursed; he is going to ensure that they are blessed superabundantly. God's word of promise and blessing cannot be defeated, no matter what people try to do to oppose him.

In this message, God emphatically shows Balak and Balaam that he will fulfill his previous promises. He is steadfast in his resolve and infinite in his power, so what he said he would do will be accomplished. Balaam knows this is true, and Balaam extols the blessed nature of belonging to God's covenant people. God's people are so deeply and richly blessed that Balaam confesses that in the end, nothing could be better than dying as a righteous member of God's covenant community. Because of the infinite grace and goodness of God, nothing can be better than living and dying in his loving care. As Christians, living in union with Christ, we are prepared for both life, death, and the life to come. It is a profound and solemn truth, yielding to joy, that the people of God are blessed both in life and in death

Numbers 23:27–24:25

EXEGETICAL IDEA
God's blessing of Israel means that it will triumph over hostile foreign nations.

THEOLOGICAL FOCUS
God reigns over the nations.

PREACHING IDEA
There is no greater kingdom than the kingdom of God, and no greater king than King Jesus.

PREACHING POINTERS
Throughout these oracles and messages, the themes of God's sovereignty and authority and his faithfulness to his covenant promises are often repeated. Vibrant language is used to describe the rich blessings that are going to rest upon Israel. As a nation, they will prosper under God's hand, but all of their enemies will be destroyed. These messages speak comfort to Israel but warning to Balak and all those nations which will oppose God's chosen people or try to interfere with God's plans to bless.

This section contains the famous prophecy in 24:17. Scholars debate its exact significance, question how much Balaam could know or understand of it, and look for figures who may be possible fulfillments of it. Living this side of Christ, however, this prophecy is connected with the Messiah, king, and conqueror, and even if there is a typological stop along the way, the ultimate fulfillment is found in Jesus Christ. It is through Jesus that God's enemies are destroyed, and it is through Jesus that God's people are blessed. Christ the Lord is prophet, priest, and king, and his reign will never cease. Of the increase of his government there be no end. The oracles of Balaam had direct application in his original context, but they also point forward to an era and figure of greater fulfillment. There is no greater kingdom than the kingdom of God, and no greater king than King Jesus.

Numbers 25:1–18

EXEGETICAL IDEA
Israel succumbs to the temptations of idolatry, and God's wrath is averted only by the zealous actions of Phinehas.

THEOLOGICAL FOCUS
Appropriate worship of God requires zealous commitment.

PREACHING IDEA
Zeal is important in living for God, but sincerity and passion are not enough on their own.

PREACHING POINTERS
Having failed to gain control over Israel by controlling Israel's God, a new plan for Israel's destruction is hatched. Since they cannot manipulate the spiritual realm, they will attempt to manipulate Israel through physical seduction. There is a great meal provided (very tempting, given the complaints of the Israelites about their food supply), and an opportunity for unbridled sexual indulgence in pagan revelry. Many Israelites fall into this trap, and as a result many are killed in a plague of judgment. Phinehas's action may shock modern sensibilities, but God approves of it and calls it righteous (Ps. 106:30–31). Moab and the Midianites were engaged in a subtle war against Israel, and Phinehas's act was an act of war.

Phinehas's zeal is commendable, and his action was righteous given the circumstances, but zeal and sincerity alone are not enough to please God. In our contemporary society, many people insist that as long as a person is sincere, they are justified in almost anything they think or do. Scripture, however, takes a very different view. We ought to be filled with zeal for the Lord, but zeal is only as good as the end it is directed toward. Jesus was filled with zeal for his Father's house, but Paul was filled with zeal to destroy the church, until he met the risen Lord and was converted. Zeal is important in living for God, but sincerity and passion are not enough on their own.

Numbers 26:1–65

EXEGETICAL IDEA
Israel's second generation inherits God's covenant promises.

THEOLOGICAL FOCUS
God's faithfulness endures despite human frailty.

PREACHING IDEA
God blesses his people through covenant grace, but we all need to take warning.

PREACHING POINTERS
The second census is important both historically and theologically. After all that Israel had done, it was a testimony to grace that the nation still existed. The generation that refused to enter the Promised Land has died off, and the new generation was being prepared to go in. As a result, even the historical context is charged with both grace and judgment. Then, throughout the chapter, there are multiple reminders of the danger of rebelling against the Lord. God has proven that he will remain faithful to his covenant, and he has proven that no power in the physical or spiritual realm can challenge him. He has also proven that he will punish whole generations for their sin. He is a great and good God, but he is also holy, righteous, and just. No one in any generation can trifle with him.

As the people prepare to approach the Promised Land, they are given necessary reminders of God's covenant grace and his covenant wrath. The new generation needed hope, but they also needed warning. None may presume on God's grace. He is a God of love, but he is also holy, holy, holy. It was an awesome privilege for the Israelites to have God encamped at the center of their community, and he was with them to guide and to bless. He would not, however, tolerate rebellion, idolatry, and wickedness. Every generation needs to know of God's grace, love, mercy, kindness, faithfulness, and covenant promises, but every generation also needs to know the fear of the Lord. Every generation needs to know that God blesses his people through covenant grace, but we all still need to take warning.

Numbers 27:1–23

EXEGETICAL IDEA
The daughters of Zelophehad preserve their father's name, and Joshua inherits Moses's legacy.

THEOLOGICAL FOCUS
God responds graciously to the concerns of his people.

PREACHING IDEA
God takes care of his flock and gives them a good shepherd.

PREACHING POINTERS
There can be no doubt that a modern interpreter needs to exercise due tact and sensitivity in a text like this one. Given that the problem is generated on the basis of sex and gender, contemporary hearers may be prone to miss what the text is actually saying, as well as anachronistically read back into it all kinds of modern debates and concerns. Of the utmost importance to see is that God considers the needs of each one of his children, and he ensures that justice will be done.

From the level of concern for individuals to the level of concern for the entire nation, this chapter moves from Zelophehad's daughters to the need of a shepherd over all of God's people. Moses will die outside of the Promised Land, and Joshua is appointed to take over as leader of the people. In terms of biblical theology, this shepherding motif carries forward in all kinds of ways and then is fulfilled in Jesus the Good Shepherd. It is only because of Christ that God's flock is not left scattered like sheep without a shepherd. Psalm 23, Psalm 100, and John 10 give us a beautiful picture of what it means to have the Lord as our shepherd. In the end, we are able to live and have a name because our shepherd laid down his life for the sheep, only to take it up again in resurrection power and glory. As a loving heavenly Father, God takes care of his flock and gives them the ultimate Good Shepherd.

Numbers 28:1–29:40

EXEGETICAL IDEA
God establishes required sacrifices and festivals for Israel to sustain its relationship with him.

THEOLOGICAL FOCUS
Life should be oriented around worshipping God.

PREACHING IDEA
We need regular times of worship, but we also need special times of worship.

PREACHING POINTERS
These two chapters contain a theological feast. The expositor can approach these daily, weekly, monthly, and yearly sacrifices, feasts, and special occasions from a variety of angles. It is worthwhile zooming in for a close-up view of each element, but it is also richly rewarding to pull back and take in the progression and sweep of these chapters in a panoramic way. It is essential to understand both the immediate context and the importance of these things for the original audience, but also to chart out the biblical-theological fulfillment that is found in Christ.

There really is a wide assortment of lessons that can be learned in these chapters, but one macro-level lesson is that the time-horizons set up a spiral of worship. The daily prepares for the weekly, and the special feasts and special days feed back into the excitement of daily, regular worship. At its best, our regular lives of worship prepare us for special times of worship, and the special times enrich and encourage us in our daily walk with God. Do not miss all the varied elements in these chapters, but do not fail to help the church see their interconnections and biblical fulfillment. These chapters have immense practical value, as they engender worship of Christ, and remind us that we need both regular and special times of worship

Numbers 30:1–16

EXEGETICAL IDEA
Vows and pledges sworn to God must be upheld, but those offered by women are subject to the approval of their father or husband.

THEOLOGICAL FOCUS
Speech invoking God must be considered carefully.

PREACHING IDEA
Because God's Word is trustworthy, our words should be trustworthy.

PREACHING POINTERS
For the contemporary Western expositor, this text bristles with potential obstacles. Cultural issues always need to be handled with sensitivity, but the preacher must be faithful to the message of every text in God's Word. The concern of the passage is with social cohesion and harmony in its variety of interpenetrating relationships, and that unity requires a profound commitment to truth. In our contemporary society—as in ancient ones—if human communication cannot be trusted, human community breaks down. Words matter. Anyone who makes a vow to God will be held accountable for their words. As a result, this passage underscores the vital importance of truthfulness in speech, especially when it comes to making special vows to the Lord. Religious vows could be overridden if they disrupted God's design and order for interpersonal relationships, but if they didn't, the vows were binding and could not be annulled.

We know what it is like to live in a society where words are cheap and where lies and propaganda are part of the common milieu in which we all live. Scripture is very clear that our words are to be honest, transparent, and true. When we tell someone we will do something, we must honor our word. When we tell God we will do something, we must fulfill our commitment. Our example and standard for our speech is God himself. Because God's Word is trustworthy, our words should be trustworthy.

Numbers 31:1–54

EXEGETICAL IDEA
At God's command, Israel seeks vengeance against the Midianites and shares the spoils of conquest with him.

THEOLOGICAL FOCUS
Vengeance and victory belong to God.

PREACHING IDEA
"Unless you repent, you too will all perish" (Luke 13:3, 5).

PREACHING POINTERS
Anyone who teaches the Old Testament knows that there are hard texts and difficult themes, and some passages raise ethical issues that do not sit well with modern sensibilities and intuitions. Sometimes a careful, nuanced, sensitive, and duly humble apologetic is needed to place a hard text in context so that it can be preached faithfully. It is essential to see that this is not genocide. God already punished Israel for their sin in the event of Baal Peor, and now the Midianites receive the consequences for their sin. Moab and the Midianites had tried to destroy Israel, and thus now they experience reciprocal justice. They had proclaimed war on Israel through subtle seduction and idolatry, and now they reap the bitter fruit of their attempt to kill the souls of the Israelites.

It may be somewhat uncomfortable for us today, but Jesus used tragic events to warn his hearers that they all needed to repent and be prepared to stand before God. When we see the death of 24,000 Israelites because of this event, and see the death of the Midianites, one of the lessons we are to learn is that *we* need to repent. If we remove ourselves from God, we will die. In many churches today, the pendulum has swung so far from hellfire and brimstone preaching that one might be in church services for years without hearing that there is a day of judgment coming. An honest exposition of Scripture, however, requires dealing with the truth that God blesses and gives life, but also judges sin and punishes those who reject him. Scripture is filled with sober warnings that drive people to Christ. As the preacher deals with the historical, ethical, and theological principles of the text, one thing to tell the congregation is that, in the words of our Lord Jesus Christ, "Unless you repent, you too will all perish" (Luke 13:3).

Numbers 32:1–42

EXEGETICAL IDEA
Tribes that wish to claim an inheritance in the Transjordan region must help their fellow Israelites conquer the Promised Land.

THEOLOGICAL FOCUS
God's people should sacrificially serve their community.

PREACHING IDEA
God's people must be united and work in harmony.

PREACHING POINTERS
In the lens of biblical history, this text marks an important transition. Incredibly, what seems like a threat to the unity of the nation is turned into a unifying event, and what seems like a potential division actually turns into an expansion of their territory. This chapter represents a wise leadership handling a sensitive situation, and an amazing gift of the grace of God. Even

though the tribes of Israel will occupy unique geographic locations, they must all work together, serving and helping each other in the conquest of the land. They may be spread out in one way, but they must be united in their God-given tasks.

When we receive the gifts of God's grace, they are not to be used to promote laziness or self-indulgence. Spiritual gifts are given to individuals so that they can work hard to edify others. In the church, the unity of the body of Christ is essential, and maintaining and strengthening that unity must be a priority. We must serve others and ride together side by side along the paths where God calls us to go. Until we all receive our inheritance, God's people must be united and work in harmony.

Numbers 33:1–49

EXEGETICAL IDEA
Moses preserves the account of Israel's journey.

THEOLOGICAL FOCUS
God's people endure because of his sustaining presence.

PREACHING IDEA
Every believer has a path on which God leads them through their pilgrimage.

PREACHING POINTERS
Having nearly completed their entire time in the wilderness, the Israelites are now told to look back on the places they have been and the things they have experienced. Some of the locations evoke the most significant events in Israel's redemptive history up to that point, whether they were good or bad. Aaron dies and is gathered to his people, ending the era of the first high priest and bearing witness to the fact that God will allow no exceptions to his decree about who would enter the Promised Land.

Remembering what happened at these locations (at least the ones we can collate with recorded events in Scripture), provides us with an extremely important hermeneutical lens for interpreting the important events in Israel's journey. Although we are not aware of the significance of many of these places, they were stopping places in Israel's wilderness wandering, and the names meant something to the people who camped there. Today, believers pass through a variety of experiences and live in a variety of places, and every person has their own life's journey. As believers, it can be very helpful to look back on the key events of our lives, to see what God has brought us through, and to prepare ourselves for his continued leading in the future. We will not recapitulate the route of Israel, but every believer has a path on which God leads them through their pilgrimage.

Numbers 33:50–34:29

EXEGETICAL IDEA
Israel is commanded to drive out the Canaanites so that it can receive its full inheritance.

THEOLOGICAL FOCUS
God intends to give his people a place where they can flourish.

PREACHING IDEA
Hear the word of the Lord, rid yourselves of idols, and live in the boundaries established by God.

PREACHING POINTERS
This preaching unit is built around the word of the Lord to Moses and the necessity of following his commands. Once again, Israel is called to faithful obedience to the word of the Lord, and once again they are faced with challenges beyond their own strength. They have to trust that God will empower them to take the land, and they have to trust in him exclusively. TheyABY going into an environment that is filled with snares and pitfalls, and their track record is abysmal. Nevertheless, their faithful covenant God is determined to fulfill his promises, and he will not swerve from his divine plan.

When the people of God moved into the Promised Land, they were commanded to uproot and destroy every false god and every type of idol. This spiritual principle applies today just as much as it applied then. If we are going to flourish in the land of blessing, we must be a people marked by deep, rigorous obedience. Now is a time to recommit ourselves to faithful and full obedience to every word that proceeds from the mouth of God. It is also a time to identify the false gods, idols, and religious practices of our society, and search our own hearts for the same. We must surrender everything to God and follow him alone. Only then will we excel in the glory of his blessings. Now is the time to hear the word of the Lord, rid ourselves of idols, and live in the boundaries established by God.

Numbers 35:1–34

EXEGETICAL IDEA
Upon entry into the Promised Land, the Israelites must assign cities to the Levites, six of which will become cities of refuge.

THEOLOGICAL FOCUS
Human life is sacred in the eyes of the God who created it.

PREACHING IDEA
God is a God of life, and the standard of justice comes from his nature.

PREACHING POINTERS
Contemporary judicial systems have quite different organizational structures than what we find in this text, but there are abiding principles that teach us about how God views justice, mercy, life, and death. Life is sacred, and life cannot be taken without due penalty. No human court is infallible, however, and there are times when it is difficult to know if a killing was premeditated or a tragic accident. In the ancient world, cycles of revenge killing could quickly escalate into blood feuds, and this text guards against that possibility.

At a fundamental level, this passage can be used to remind people that God is a God of justice, and that human laws are to reflect his character. Many cultures have been rightly described as cultures of death, but God desires every society to have a culture of life. God's image-bearers are precious to him, and he cares for their lives. As a result, his image-bearers are to have their lives protected from murderers, but they are also to be protected against execution if they accidentally kill someone. Deep down, at the heart of this text, is the principle that God is a God of life, and the standard of justice comes from his nature.

Numbers 36:1–13

EXEGETICAL IDEA
To preserve their tribe's full allotment, God instructs the daughters of Zelophehad to marry within the tribe of Manasseh.

THEOLOGICAL FOCUS
God responds to his people's concerns about his promises.

PREACHING IDEA
"For the Lord is good and his love endures forever; his faithfulness continues through all generations" (Ps. 100:5).

PREACHING POINTERS
This last chapter in the book of Numbers ties up some loose ends but is transparently oriented to the future rather than the past. After all of this time and after all of the things Israel did and failed to do, God has remained a God of steadfast love and covenant faithfulness. His people *will* enter the Promised Land, and he *will* take care of them; he *will* bless them and fulfill all of his covenant promises. This book is not a record of human faithfulness, but an incredible testimony to the gracious and holy character of the living God. No reader can reach this finishing chapter without the conviction that it is only because of the patience and longsuffering of God that the story can continue.

The last verse of the book points the reader to the commands and regulations of the Lord. Numbers is part of God's inspired Word, and it self-referentially directs the reader's gaze to the law of the Lord. There are times when stepping back to observe the contours and development of God's entire special revelation in the Bible is worth doing, and this chapter provides an opportunity not only to unfold the significance of this particular text but also to connect it to God's unfolding plan of redemption. In other words, this passage can be located as the fitting conclusion to Numbers, but also as a springboard for expositing the flow of revelation from the beginning of the Bible to the end. From creation to the new heaven and new earth, it is only because of God's character, and only because of the redemption that was accomplished through Jesus Christ our Lord, that we can be saved. This message will echo down to the end of time, so surely with the psalmist we can joyfully exclaim: "For the Lord is good and his love endures forever; his faithfulness continues through all generations" (Ps. 100:5 NIV).

ABBREVIATIONS

GENERAL ABBREVIATIONS

A.D.	*anno Domini* (in the year of our Lord)
B.C.	Before Christ
LXX	Septuagint
MT	Masoretic Text
OT	Old Testament
NT	New Testament

TECHNICAL ABBREVIATIONS

cf.	*confer*, compare
e.g.	*exemplum gratia*, for example
i.e.	*id est*, that is
vol(s).	volume(s)

BIBLICAL SOURCES

Old Testament

Gen.	Genesis
Exod.	Exodus
Lev.	Leviticus
Num.	Numbers
Deut.	Deuteronomy
Josh.	Joshua
Judg.	Judges
Ruth	Ruth
1 Sam.	1 Samuel
2 Sam.	2 Samuel
1 Kings	1 Kings
2 Kings	2 Kings
1 Chron.	1 Chronicles
2 Chron.	2 Chronicles
Ezra	Ezra
Neh.	Nehemiah
Esther	Esther
Job	Job
Ps./Pss.	Psalm(s)
Prov.	Proverbs

Old Testament (continued)

Eccl.	Ecclesiastes
Song	Song of Songs
Isa.	Isaiah
Jer.	Jeremiah
Lam.	Lamentations
Ezek.	Ezekiel
Dan.	Daniel
Hos.	Hosea
Joel	Joel
Amos	Amos
Obad.	Obadiah
Jonah	Jonah
Mic.	Micah
Nah.	Nahum
Hab.	Habakkuk
Zeph.	Zephaniah
Hag.	Haggai
Zech.	Zechariah
Mal.	Malachi

Abbreviations

New Testament

Matt.	Matthew
Mark	Mark
Luke	Luke
John	John
Acts	Acts
Rom.	Romans
1 Cor.	1 Corinthians
2 Cor.	2 Corinthians
Gal.	Galatians
Eph.	Ephesians
Phil.	Philippians
Col.	Colossians
1 Thess.	1 Thessalonians
2 Thess.	2 Thessalonians

New Testament (continued)

1 Tim.	1 Timothy
2 Tim.	2 Timothy
Titus	Titus
Philem.	Philemon
Heb.	Hebrews
James	James
1 Peter	1 Peter
2 Peter	2 Peter
1 John	1 John
2 John	2 John
3 John	3 John
Jude	Jude
Rev.	Revelation

EXTRABIBLICAL SOURCES

Dead Sea Scrolls

CD — Cairo Geniza copy of the Damascus Document

PUBLISHERS

IVP — InterVarsity Press

REFERENCE

ANET — Pritchard, James B. ed. *Ancient Near Eastern Texts Relating to the Old Testament*. 3rd edition. Princeton, NJ: Princeton University Press, 1969.

CHALOT — Holladay, William L. *A Concise Hebrew and Aramaic Lexicon of the Old Testament*. Leiden: Brill, 2000.

BIBLE TRANSLATIONS

CEB	Common English Bible
CSB	Christian Standard Bible
ESV	English Standard Version
HCSB	Holman Christian Standard Version
KJV	King James Version
NASB	New American Standard Bible
NET	New English Translation
NIV	New International Version
NKJV	New King James Version
NLT	New Living Translation
NRSV	New Revised Standard Version
RSV	Revised Standard Version

INTRODUCTION TO NUMBERS

> ## OVERVIEW OF NUMBERS
>
> **Author:** Primarily Moses
>
> **Provenance:** With Israel in the wilderness
>
> **Readers:** The wilderness generation and Israel's subsequent generations
>
> **Historical Setting:** After God's deliverance of Israel from Egyptian slavery and prior to Israel's entry into the Promised Land
>
> **Occasion for Writing:** Providing a record of Israel's sojourn in the wilderness and instructions for being God's covenant people
>
> **Genre:** Multiple: census, legal commentary, cultic instructions, historical narrative, diplomatic correspondence, travel itinerary
>
> **Structure of Numbers:**
>
> A (1:1–10:10): Shaping the Community at Sinai
>   B (10:11–19:22): The Travels and Travails of the First Generation
>   B' (20:1–25:18): Sin and Redemption for the Second Generation
> A' (26:1–36:13): Shaping the Community on the Plains of Moab
>
> **Theological Emphasis:** Despite Israel's doubt and complaints, God faithfully upholds his covenant promises and brings the nation to the borders of the Promised Land. Israel also learns what it means to dwell with a holy God in their midst, including facing the consequences of sin and rebellion.

INTRODUCTORY COMMENTS

The book of Numbers poses unique challenges for readers and expositors of Scripture. It is home to some well-known stories such as Balaam and his talking donkey (Num. 22:21–41), the bronze snake to which Jesus refers in John 3 (Num. 21:4–9), and the devasting effects of the report of the faithless spies (Numbers 13–14). It also contains many passages that appear to be dense, impenetrable, and have limited relevance for the life of the Christian. And yet, as Paul reminds us in 2 Timothy 3:16, Numbers is part of God-breathed, Spirit-inspired Scripture which is essential for Christian formation. Paul even makes multiple allusions to Numbers in his instructions to struggling believers in 1 Corinthians 10:6–12 (Sprinkle 2015, 187).

The opening of the book is particularly challenging, as it begins with four chapters that seem like an endless parade of strange names being assigned to strange tasks. Many have remarked on its challenges, with the church father Origen referring to Numbers as "heavy and burdensome food,"[1] while a more recent commentator notes that Numbers will never supplant books like Psalms, John, or Romans in terms of Christian devotion and theology (Ashley 1993, ix). And yet, a study of Numbers can yield great insight into the character of God, his relationship with his covenant people, and his commitment to fulfill his promises. Numbers demonstrates the overwhelming holiness of God as he establishes the requirements to be in his presence. It reveals that God shows grace in the face of failure, even as he disciplines and corrects his people. Further, Numbers has much to say to God's people as they live in a place that is not their final home. It is a book of anticipation, longing for the fulfillment of God's promises, and yet learning to live in the time and space in between. Although the challenges cannot be minimized, expositors who shepherd their congregations through this book will find that it yields rich rewards.

A challenge in writing a commentary on Numbers is finding the balance between comprehensiveness and readability. This is even more necessary in a commentary geared toward the practical work of exposition. Some of the preaching units in this commentary cover more text than is plausible in a traditional half-hour sermon, especially if the preacher is accustomed to reading the entire text. This is true for parts of the book that do not lend themselves to verse-by-verse exposition such as the census lists (Numbers 1, 26), the responsibilities of the Levites (Numbers 3–4), dedicatory offerings at the tabernacle (Numbers 7), and the sacral calendar (Numbers 28–29). These are treated as one preaching unit with the expectation that the expositor will work with representative elements of the text to illustrate its larger themes and message.

AUTHORSHIP OF NUMBERS

The question of authorship in Numbers is inextricably linked to the wider context of the Pentateuch. The traditional understanding is that Moses is the primary author. Indeed, on multiple occasions the New Testament uses Moses as a metonymy for this body of literature (Luke 16:29, 31; 24:27, 44; John 1:17, 5:45, 46; Acts 13:39; 26:22; 28:23). Following the trajectory of the biblical narrative, Moses's presumed education in a sophisticated Egyptian court along with his roles as lawgiver, prophet, and leader in Israel make him uniquely qualified to have written this material (Cole 2000, 29).

Over the past two centuries, critical scholarship has more or less eliminated Moses's direct authorial connection to the Pentateuch. Instead, it posits a lengthy period of development for different source documents that lie behind it. Though scholarship has moved on from Wellhausen's classic formulation of the Documentary Hypothesis (known colloquially as JEDP), it still casts a long shadow. According to this approach, most of the material in Numbers is assigned to either a largely narrative document dating from the monarchic period known as JE (a combination of the so-called "Yahwist" and "Elohwist" sources), or to the P ("Priestly") source that is thought to be mostly postexilic (Levine 1993, 48–49).[2] Speaking broadly, this approach holds that JE material dominates

---

1 Origen, *Homilies on Numbers*, Homily 27, 1.3–1.4.
2 Arguments abound for the dates of these sources. For example, see Milgrom 1990, xxiii–xxv, for arguments putting the P source much earlier than traditionally supposed. For an evangelical survey of this issue see Cole 2000, 31–33.

Introduction to Numbers

Moses Breaking the Tablets of the Law (1659) by Rembrandt. Public domain.

Numbers 11–25, while Priestly material governs the legal and cultic regulations found in Numbers 1–10, 26–36 (Olson 1996, 2–3). Critical commentaries identify further substrata of these sources and discuss the situations that could give rise to this material.

In response, there remain strong reasons to continue to associate Moses with the creation of the Pentateuch and the book of Numbers in particular. Moses is instructed to write down the phases of Israel's journey in Numbers 33:2. Further Moses (or occasionally Moses and Aaron) frequently receive direct communication from God to disseminate to the entire congregation. The phrase "YHWH said to Moses" (וַיְדַבֵּר יהוה אֶל־מֹשֶׁה) occurs more than sixty times in Numbers alone and is intended to be viewed not merely as a literary convention but as an established fact (Ashley 1993, 3). In addition to identifying Moses as a writer, Harrison attributes to him the status of "supervising author," overseeing the collection of legal decisions, cultic regulations, and other material brought together by a small group of literate officials (Harrison 1990, 23).[3] In this view, Moses retains a preeminent position in the creation and distribution of this material, and Numbers thus provides a near-contemporaneous account of Israel's experiences in the wilderness.

The perspective adopted in this commentary is that Numbers is "essentially Mosaic, but not purely Mosaic" (Sprinkle 2015, 3). Moses's presence is indelibly imprinted on the entire book. His role as the recipient and disseminator of God's regulations and instructions should not be discounted. However, even conservative commentators will note that there are later explanatory glosses (Harrison 1990, 23). In the same vein, many would acknowledge that the attribution to Moses of "unparalleled humility" in Numbers 12:3 was likely not written by Moses himself (Gane 2004, 473).[4] Other evidence of updating can be found in things like geographic and ethnic terms in the Pentateuch that would have been unknown in the time of Moses (Sprinkle 2015, 3). There is also evidence of other sources brought into Numbers, possibly with Moses's oversight, such as administrative lists, victory songs, and even the explicitly cited "Book of the Wars of the LORD" in Numbers 21:14 (Gane 2004, 473). Consequently, Moses can be viewed as the originator of much of Numbers. However superintended

---

3   Harrison identifies this group as the שֹׁטְרִים first mentioned in Exodus 5:19. For their proposed development and functions within ancient Israel see Harrison 1990, 18–23.

4   This verse reminds me (Joel) of a joke that the father of one of my high school friends use to tell: a "world's humblest man" competition was held in which the winner received a pin marking the victory. As soon as he tried to wear it, the organizers took it away from him!

by the Holy Spirit, the material that comprises this book was preserved, transmitted, and finalized throughout Israel's history (Cole 2000, 34). Moses remains the authority figure at the heart of the Pentateuch: the "principal, dominant, and determinative voice" whom Jesus and the New Testament writers could associate with it (Walton and Sandy 2013, 65). Consequently, this commentary situates Numbers against the historical backdrop of Israel's sojourn in the wilderness and concentrates on the received form of the text.

DATE AND SETTING

Working from the perspective that Moses is the primary authority behind Numbers, the date of the initial composition of the book falls in the time of Israel's sojourn in the wilderness.[5] Traditionally, this is thought to be in the middle of the fifteenth century, a date that can be identified by working backwards from 1 Kings 6:1, which places the beginning of Solomon's temple construction 480 years after Israel left Egypt. This date cannot be confirmed through archaeological data, which has led to the suggestion that it is schematic rather than literal (Walton 2003, 269). Others prefer a date sometime in the thirteenth century, citing greater congruence with the history of the ancient Near East. They suggest that this era accords more naturally with other evidence of migratory people groups (Stone 2014, 138–42).[6] Certain biblical data can be read to support this date, if for example, Jacob's journey to Egypt took place in the seventeenth century during the period when a people known as the Hyksos dominated northern Egypt (Stone 2014, 136). Exodus 12:40–41 then states that Israel departed Egypt 430 years later, aligning it with this later date.

Certainty on this topic is impossible and unnecessary for understanding the message of the book. There is sufficient historical and biblical data to support the idea of an Israelite exodus out of Egypt in antiquity whether one places it in the fifteenth or thirteenth centuries (Falk 2018, 194–200). The background for the book of Numbers is God's great deliverance of his people from slavery and his continued preservation of them in the period before their entry into Canaan.

This setting of the book is crucial. The traditional Hebrew title of the book (בְּמִדְבַּר) translates as "In the Wilderness," which is more fitting. Although there are multiple census accounts along with other lists and divisions of responsibilities, "numbering" or counting is only a very small part of the book. Instead, this book is a record of Israel's time in transition: between Egypt and Canaan, slavery and promise. The wilderness is where Israel enters into covenant relationship with God at Sinai and learns what it means to serve a holy God. It is where Israel learns of the need for sacrifice along with the reorientation of one's own heart. In the wilderness, Israel experiences God's great power to provide for their needs, though complaint rather than gratitude is the typical response. The wilderness is also a place of anticipation and delay. Just over the horizon is the hoped-for fulfillment of God's promises, yet Israel's inability to see beyond the immediate context results in the duration of this period being prolonged for an entire generation. The setting of Numbers thus establishes a liminal experience for Israel: they have come so far from where they started, yet they continue to anticipate who they will become.

There is a progression in the geographical setting of the book. It is provided in detail in Numbers 33, but in broad strokes the book begins with Israel at Sinai where they have been since Exodus 19. They remain there for the first census and to receive further divine instruction

---

5   See Harrison 1990, 14, for an exploration of the types of writing material available at the time.
6   A more thorough discussion of the "early date" and "late date" theories of the Exodus and their relevance to Numbers can be found in Cole 2000, 30, and Walton 2003, 258–72.

through Numbers 10:10. Beginning in Numbers 10:11 they begin to move toward Canaan, arriving on its border in a place called Kadesh in chapters 13–14. However, Israel's refusal to enter the land leads to their return to the wilderness where they wander according to God's direction while the rebellious generation meets its fate. In Numbers 20, Israel returns to Kadesh and proceeds to the Plains of Moab where they remain as Moses gives further instruction in this book followed by his farewell address in Deuteronomy.

Israel's travels through the wilderness cannot be mapped with precision. Many of the place names mentioned are unknown, though one can establish the general boundaries of the Sinai wilderness. As with the date, not knowing the exact geographical setting for every passage does not detract from the message. Every step of the way, Israel's existence is preserved by the presence of God in their midst. They move through an inhospitable land and face foreign enemies, along with the consequences of their own rebellion. Through it all, God is with them, and his daily provision anticipates the fulfillment of his promises.

LITERARY GENRES AND STRUCTURE

The literary character and structure of Numbers is also challenging to determine. Previous generations of critical scholarship, more interested in determining the hypothetical sources of the book, considered it to be an unorganized hodgepodge.[7] More recent study has corrected this perspective, but it is true that Numbers contains more distinct styles of literature than any other biblical book. Readers encounter multiple genres including narratives (4:1–3; 11:1–3, 4–35; 12:1–16, etc.), cultic instructions (7:1–89; 15:1–36; 28:1–29:40), census lists (1:1–43; 26:1–51), prophecy (24:3–9), diplomatic correspondence (21:14–19), victory song (21:27–30), travel itinerary (33:1–49), and priestly blessing (6:24–26; Milgrom 1990, xiii). All of these genres require care to interpret. However, each thread of this rich tapestry contributes to the complex picture of Israel's developing relationship with God. Laws and cultic instructions provide guidance for what it means to be the people of God. Narratives reveal how they fail to live up their calling. Priestly blessing and prophetic utterance provide hope that God will be with them, even amid their failures.

The variety of genres also makes it a challenge to discern an overarching structure. One possibility is to use the geographical setting as a

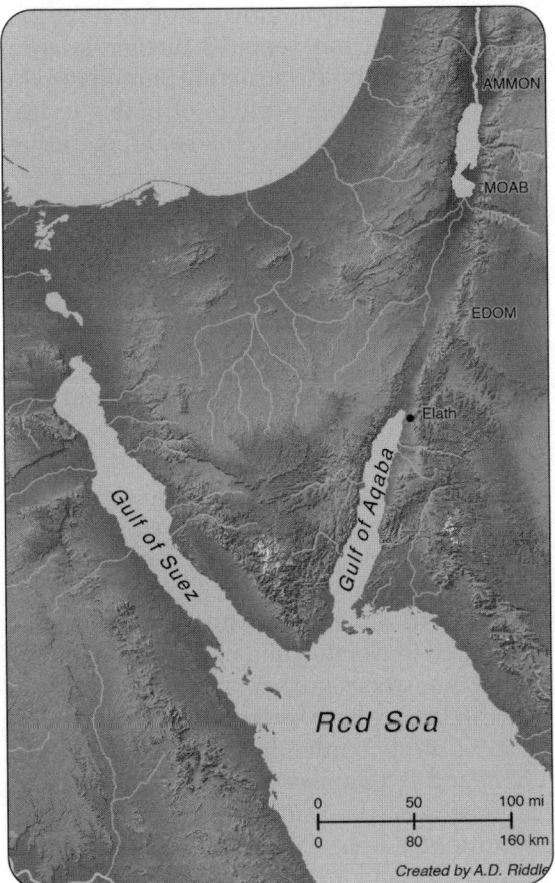

Created by A.D. Riddle

---

7   One of the leading scholars of an earlier generation referred to it as "an unsystematic collection of innumerable pieces of tradition of very varied content, age, and character" (Noth 1968, 3).

guide, setting up a tripartite structure situated first at Sinai (1:1–10:10), through the wilderness (10:11–19:22), and on the plains of Moab (20:1–36:13; Ashley 1993, 2). Another approach is to consider the thematic significance of the two generations in Numbers: the one rescued from Egypt but did not see the Promised Land because of their unbelief (Numbers 1–25), and their children through whom God fulfilled his promises (Numbers 26–36). In support of this approach, Olson notes a number of parallels between these sections including: lists of tribal leaders (Numbers 1; 34), censuses of the tribes and Levites (Numbers 1; 3; 26), legal discourse concerning women (Numbers 5; 27), lists and laws concerning sacrificial offerings (Numbers 7; 15; 28–29), and Passover celebrations (Numbers 9; 28:16–25; Olson 1996, 5–6). This is an important insight that helps the reader to see how God renews his people through his gracious discipline and brings them to brink of his promises being fulfilled.

A difficulty with this approach is determining the point of transition between the two generations. The second census in Numbers 26 is a notable marker, but there is compelling evidence that the second generation is the focus of the narrative prior to that. Numbers 20 is a transitional chapter as it records the death of Miriam (Num. 20:1), the disqualification of Moses and Aaron from entering the land (Num. 20:2–13), and the death of Aaron himself (Num. 20:22–29; Lee 2003a, 261–62). The primary leaders of the first generation are thus either dead or diminished. Further, Aaron's death is placed in the fortieth and final year of the wilderness wandering (cf. Num. 33:38), which suggests that the events of Numbers 20–25 take place toward the end of those forty years and feature the second generation. From this perspective, the reader learns that the second generation complains in the same manner as their parents in 20:1–13 and 21:4–9 and succumbs to temptation and idolatry in 25:1–9 (Schnittjer 2006, 400–401). A division of Numbers between a "sinful" first generation and a "faithful" second generation is an oversimplification.

Stubbs modifies Olson's proposal by noting that the section before the second census (Numbers 1–25) can be further subdivided: a vision of who Israel was to be (Numbers 1–10) and accounts of its failure to live up to that calling (Numbers 11–25). He thus creates an ABA' structure in which the outlook of A (Numbers 1–10) and A' (Numbers 26–36) are generally positive while that of B (Numbers 11–25) is generally negative (Stubbs 2009, 23). This is helpful but requires further nuance. The B element of the structure should also be subdivided into the exploits of both the first and second generations. The resulting outline is thus:

A (1:1–10:10):[8] Shaping the Community at Sinai
    B (10:11–19:22): The Travels and Travails of the First Generation
    B' (20:1–25:18): Sin and Redemption for the Second Generation
A' (26:1–36:13): Shaping the Community on the Plains of Moab

As mentioned above, the A (Num. 1:1–10:10) and A' (Numbers 26–36) sections have significant parallels. Both begin by enumerating the people and provide examples of Israel following God's commands while they learn what is required to worship him properly. The A' section demonstrates greater anticipation of entry into the land, which makes sense given Israel's location on its border. In the B (Num. 10:11–19:22) and B' (Numbers 20–25) sections Israel demonstrates fear, faithlessness, and a propensity to forget what God has done. The refusal to enter the land in Numbers 13–14 and God's

---

8   It is better to mark the division between the A and B sections at 10:10, rather than the end of the chapter. Numbers 10:11 details Israel's departure from Sinai, thus establishing that a new phase of the book has begun.

subsequent judgment reveals that a second generation must arise. Even though this generation is not morally superior, God demonstrates the depths of his grace as he disciplines, protects, and preserves his people. Recognizing that the second generation is also guilty of sin and rebellion prevents the expositor from engaging in simplistic moralizing. Israel continued to rebel against God, but because he is great in covenant loyalty (Num. 14:18), he remained faithful to the promises he made to Israel's forebearers (Gen. 15:12–16).

More complex structural patterns can be proposed but this broad ABB'A' arrangement provides guardrails to keep the expositor on track. Discussions of the preaching units will highlight further interrelationships within the major movements of the book.

THEOLOGICAL EMPHASES

Worship of a Holy God

A key emphasis of Numbers is what is required to worship God. Although a sinful people can never fulfill the command to "be holy as I am holy" (Lev. 19:2), Numbers continues in the vein of Leviticus in articulating how Israel was to approach God. Numbers 3–4 focuses on the role of the Levites in reflecting God's holiness by tending and carrying the tabernacle, its furnishings, the altar, and the sacred implements. The Levites were set aside for this purpose, chosen

The Tabernacle in the Wilderness by the Illustrators of the 1890 Holman Bible. Public domain.

by God to express his holiness throughout the entire community. The cleansing of the Levites in Numbers 8 consecrates them for that purpose. All Israel received the opportunity to demonstrate special devotion toward God through the Nazirite vow (Numbers 6). Instructions to maintain purity in the camp further express the sanctity of being in God's presence (Num. 5:1–10; 15:22–36; 18:1–7; 19:1–22). The list of dedicatory offerings in Numbers 7 demonstrates Israel's commitment to revere God. God also commands Israel to perform sacrifices and celebrate festivals in worshipful response to him (Numbers 28–29). This is such a serious requirement that there are even instructions for what Israelites must do if they are ceremonially unclean at the time of the Passover (Num. 9:1–14). God's holiness is even expressed in the gruesome story of Phinehas's execution of an Israelite man and a Midianite woman whose liaison threatened the fragile sanctity of the community (Num. 25:6–18). As readers work through Numbers, they cannot avoid coming face to face with a God who is holy, sanctified in his very essence, and who calls his chosen people to worship him faithfully.

Disobedience and Grumbling

An overarching theme of Numbers is whether or not Israel lives up to the commitments it made with God at Sinai. On several occasions Israel declares "all that God has said, we will do" (Exod. 19:8; 24:3, 7). Unfortunately, in keeping with the fallen human condition, disobedience is far more prevalent in the narratives of Numbers (Num. 10:11–25:18). Israel's travels begin with an expression of obedience in which Israel moves when directed by the cloud that signifies God's presence (Num. 10:11–36). However, the refrain that Israel obeyed what God commanded quickly disappears, and instead readers encounter example after example of Israel succumbing to the allure of grumbling. The Israelites are afflicted with chronic amnesia, unable or unwilling to remember God's provision for them in the journey thus far. Instead, hunger and thirst bring them to look back fondly at slavery and servitude in Egypt (Num. 11:4–34; 20:1–5). Complaints about Moses's leadership spring up from even his siblings (Num. 12:1–16) along with resistance led by individuals who desire greater position and responsibility (Num. 16:1–40). The specter of idolatry haunts the people, rearing its head at Baal Peor where Israel succumbs to physical and spiritual seduction (Num. 25:1–5). Most terribly, the grumbling spirit even delays the fulfillment of God's promises as the first generation of Israelites listens to the counsel of fearful spies while ignoring the faith-filled pleas of Caleb and Joshua (Numbers 13–14).

Judgment and Restoration

The character of God and Israel's sinful nature interact in fascinating ways throughout the book. God called Israel to be a kingdom of priests and a holy nation (Exod. 19:6). As a result, Israel's disobedience carried heavy consequences. Israel faced fire, plague, disease, natural disasters, and even attacks from serpents as signs of God's displeasure. On several occasions, individual Israelites experienced the deadly weight of what it meant to reject God's law (Num. 15:32–36; 25:6–15). God even threatened the nation with utter destruction when they refused to enter the Promised Land (Num. 14:10–12). In response to Moses's intercession, the punishment was mitigated so that it required only the death of the first generation (Num. 14:22–23) and a lengthy extension of Israel's time in the wilderness. However, ultimately God fulfilled his promises through the next generation. These warnings and punishments must be read alongside God's continuing grace and mercy. God's penalties do not sever his covenant with Israel. Instead, God's steadfast commitment to his people continued even when they rejected him (Num. 14:17–20). He continually provided for their needs, sustaining them through their sojourn in the wilderness. He also gave them victory over foreign nations

(Num. 21:1–3, 21–35) and subverted the attempt by Balak, the king of Moab, to curse them in the spiritual realm (Numbers 22–24). As the book enters its final section (Numbers 26–36), readers see the preparations of Israel to enter the Promised Land, a sign that punishment is not the final word: God will continue to restore his sinful people.

Anticipation of Fulfilled Promises

As Numbers details the experience of Israel in the wilderness, it also looks forward with hope. God had promised to Abraham that he would have many descendants, that he would be in relationship with them, and that they dwell in the land that he promised (Gen. 17:3–8). Numbers reveals that the seventy members of Jacob's family who went down to Egypt have now become numerous (Numbers 1, 26) and that their relationship with God endures despite sin and failure. The promise of the land remains unfulfilled, but Numbers provides reasons for hope. There are laws and regulations that anticipate entry into Canaan (Num. 15; 18:8–32), instructions for celebrating festivals that require the produce of the land (Num. 28:16–29:40), discussions of inheritance and property (Num. 27:1–11; 36:1–13), and cities set aside for the landless Levites and for those requiring refuge (Numbers 35). Further, God's blessing of land is extended into the Transjordan region in Numbers 32 after the tribes who wish to settle there commit to aiding their brothers in claiming the land God promised to Abraham. Though hired to curse Israel, Balaam discovers that he cannot curse those whom God has chosen to bless. Balaam is compelled to highlight God's steadfast character and his commitment to fulfill his promises (Num. 23:19–20). When discussing Numbers, Israel's sin and rebellion can threaten to overwhelm the entire narrative. It is important to see where hope emerges. It is not through any great turnaround on the part of Israel, but rather on account of God's continued faithfulness.

Leadership

Another important theme of Numbers is leadership. God chose Moses to lead Israel out of slavery and through the wilderness to the Promised Land. He spoke with him in a manner unlike anyone else (Num. 12:6–8). And yet on many opportunities the people sought to reject his leadership. On those occasions the text contrasts Moses's humility with the self-serving nature of his opponents. Numbers 12:3 attributes to Moses a spirit of unmatched humility while his siblings sought to undermine his position. When two elders began to prophesy outside the allotted place which could have been viewed as a potential threat, Moses replied that he wished that all of God's people would share in the prophetic spirit (Num. 11:26–30). Later, a disgruntled Levite named Korah attempted to usurp Moses's authority, only to be met with unmistakable confirmation of Moses's position (Numbers 16). Through it all, Moses continued to intercede for Israel, reminding God of his essential character (Num. 14:18) and falling on his face to avert outpourings of judgment (Num. 14:5; 16:4, 22, 45; 20:6). Of course, Moses himself failed to live up to his calling. This culminates in Numbers 20:1–13 when Moses strikes the rock to provide Israel with water. This act prevented him from seeing his commission fulfilled: he would die outside of the Promised Land. However, God continued to provide the leadership that his people required. He ordained Joshua to succeed Moses (Num. 27:12–23), providing Israel with a faithful leader to follow Moses.

OUTLINE

SHAPING THE COMMUNITY AT SINAI (1:1–10:10)

- Numbering Israel (1:1–54)
- The Arrangement of Israel's Camp (2:1–34)
- The Census of the Levites and Their Responsibilities (3:1–4:49)
- Maintaining Purity in the Camp (5:1–10)
- The Test for Infidelity (5:11–31)
- The Nazirite Vow (6:1–21)
- The Priestly Blessing (6:22–27)
- Gifts for the Sanctuary (7:1–89)
- Ministering in God's Holy Presence (8:1–26)
- Celebrating the Passover (9:1–14)
- Following Where God Leads (9:15–10:10)

THE TRAVELS AND TRAVAILS OF THE FIRST GENERATION (10:11–19:22)

- Israel Begins Its Journey to the Promised Land (10:11–36)
- Grumbling and the Giving of the Spirit (11:1–35)
- Miriam and Aaron's Complaint (12:1–16)
- Fear and Faith at the Borders of the Promised Land (13:1–14:4)
- Israel's Rebellion and Its Consequences (14:5–45)
- Regulations for Sacrificial Offerings (15:1–21)
- Remediation for Sin (15:22–36)
- Remembering God's Commands (15:37–41)
- Rebellions in the Wilderness (16:1–35)
- A Failure to Learn: The Aftermath of Korah's Rebellion (16:36–50)
- Aaron's Staff Blossoms (17:1–13)
- Duties and Benefits of the Priests and Levites (18:1–32)
- Cleansing from Corpse Impurity (19:1–22)

SIN AND REDEMPTION FOR THE SECOND GENERATION (20:1–25:18))

- Water from the Rock (20:1–13)
- Israel in Transition (20:14–21:3)
- Internal and External Challenges (21:4–35)
- Balak Summons Balaam (22:1–41)
- Balaam's First Two Oracles (23:1–26)
- Balaam's Remaining Oracles (23:27–24:25)
- Idolatry and Zealotry at Baal Peor (25:1–18)

SHAPING THE COMMUNITY ON THE PLAINS OF MOAB (26:1–36:13)

- The Census of the Second Generation (26:1–65)
- The Promise of a Legacy (27:1–23)
- The Sacral Calendar (28:1–29:40)
- Making Vows to God (30:1–16)
- War with the Midianites (31:1–54)
- The Transjordanian Tribes (32:1–42)
- The Wilderness Journey (33:1–49)
- The Promised Land (33:50–34:29)
- Cities of Refuge (35:1–34)
- Inheritance and Marriage: The Daughters of Zelophehad (36:1–13)

SHAPING THE COMMUNITY AT SINAI (1:1–10:10)

Numbers begins with Israel at Mount Sinai, waiting for God's command for the nation to begin its journey to the Promised Land. The guiding theme of this section is community formation: God shaping Israel into a nation that can remain in his presence. This is accomplished by counting the community and giving them guidelines for encamping around the central sanctuary (1:1–2:34), selecting and consecrating the priests and Levites to serve God (3:1–4:49; 7:1–8:26), and giving instructions to maintain the purity of the nation (5:1–31). All Israelites are invited and encouraged to respond by devoting themselves to him (6:1–21) and remembering what he has done (9:1–14). The relationship between God and Israel is harmonious, with numerous affirmations that Moses and the people did what God instructed. This paints a hopeful picture as Israel prepares to depart for the Promised Land.

Numbers 1:1–54

EXEGETICAL IDEA
Enumerating Israel reveals God's faithfulness and prepares the nation to worship him.

THEOLOGICAL FOCUS
God knows and names his people and consecrates them for his service.

PREACHING IDEA
God knows every individual, and he redeems, gathers, and organizes people together into his covenant community for worship and service.

PREACHING POINTERS
Although to us the people in these tribes are nameless, faceless numbers, to God they were his special, chosen people. He knew everything about every one of them. Sheep may look generic to the passerby, but to the shepherd they are all known by name. God knows all that there is to know about each one of his children, and he loves them perfectly. This chapter shows us that God is fulfilling his covenant promises with Abraham. From one man—and he as good as dead—has come this enormous multitude.

God redeemed this people out of slavery in Egypt, and he formed them into his covenant community. When the Lord God redeems, he does not call his people to walk with him in isolation from others. On the contrary, God puts his beloved children into the church, where they exist together with other believers as part of one body. The body is properly ordered, since effective service and good health require it. The same is true of the church. God organizes his people so that they are prepared for the battles they will face and also for moving forward in their pilgrimage in this world. The new covenant community is organized for edification, service, worship, and spiritual warfare. We do not need uniformity in every detail, but we do need unity and organization in the body. We also need the Spirit of God: without the Spirit, no amount of organizing will be sufficient for what we are called to do. God knows every individual, and he redeems, gathers, and organizes people together into his covenant community for worship and service.

NUMBERING ISRAEL (1:1–54)

LITERARY STRUCTURE AND THEMES

Numbers begins with its titular event: a census of Israel's fighting force. This is the first of two censuses since the process is repeated with the next generation (26:1–4). The censuses reflect God's ongoing care for Israel, revealing that the small family that went down to Egypt in Genesis 50 is now a nation. This passage has three overarching units. Numbers 1:1–16 provides God's command to take the census and lists those who are to assist Moses and Aaron. Then, 1:17–46 provides the account and the results of the census. This unit is highly repetitive once the counting of the individual tribes begins in 1:20. Numbers 1:47–54 concludes the census with a transition to the realm of divine holiness and worship. It details why Moses and Aaron were not to count the Levites and what responsibilities they were to have instead. There is a census of the Levites in 3:14–39 but it uses different criteria and performs a strictly religious function.

Thematically, this first census blends military and cultic concerns as Aaron participates in the counting (Num. 1:3), suggesting that Israel is preparing to engage in holy war, under the guidance and direction of God (Gane 2004, 495). The command not to include the Levites in this census (Num. 1:47–54) further emphasizes the sacral nature of Israel. Showing proper reverence and devotion to God is so important that the Levites must devote themselves to that task exclusively. Their purpose is to keep Israel in communion with God, who ultimately provides the military victories.

- *God's Instructions for the Census (1:1–16)*
- *The Results of the Census (1:17–46)*
- *A Culmination to the Census: The Levites (1:47–54)*

EXPOSITION

Preaching a census is not for the faint of heart. It is easy to get lost in monotonous rhythm of names and numbers. The expositor should look at this chapter with a broad lens. Taking the time to count Israel reveals the depths of God's faithfulness to them, even during their time in slavery. When God remembered Israel in Exodus 2:24 it marked the beginning of their liberation. However, the numerical growth detailed here reveals that God had never abandoned them. Further, the census notes Israel's obedience to God's command (Num. 1:19, 54), which sets an example that unfortunately Israel will not follow in the upcoming chapters. In this passage, we see that enumerating Israel reveals God's faithfulness and prepares the nation to worship him.

God's Instructions for the Census (1:1–16)

1:1a. Numbers commences with divine instruction that also orients the reader to the time, place, and leading characters of Numbers. It begins, "The LORD spoke with Moses in the wilderness of Sinai, in the Tent of Meeting," (1:1a ESV). Numbers thus begins with the word of God communicated to the rest of Israel through Moses. This intermediary role for Moses persists throughout the book. Following this, the text provides two spatial modifiers. First, this occurs "in the wilderness of Sinai." Although the precise location of Mount Sinai has been debated for centuries, the traditional location somewhere in the southern region of what is now called the Sinai peninsula is quite defensible (Hoffmeier 2014, 82–85). Identifying it as a "wilderness" further shapes the reading of the text. It implies a location that cannot sustain life (Job 24:5; Isa. 42:11; Jer. 2:31; Ashley 1993, 45). Israel's existence is attributable only to God's continued provision and protection. Secondly, God addressed Moses "in the Tent of Meeting" (בְּאֹהֶל מוֹעֵד), which this chapter also calls "the Tabernacle" (1:50, 51) and the "Tabernacle of the Testimony" (1:50, 53). These phrases are best understood as stylistic variants, focusing on different elements of God's relationship with Israel (Allen 2012, 81).[1] Here, the emphasis is on divine disclosure, where God meets with his people in "revelatory communion" mediated through Moses (Cole 2000, 67). It reflects the heart of the Israelite community, the place which God commanded be constructed for his presence to dwell.

1:1b. This half-verse provides temporal orientation, setting this event on the first day of the second month of the second year after their departure from Egypt. More colloquially, about thirteen months have passed since the events of the first Passover. Israel is nearing the end of its time at Sinai since 10:11 declares that they departed on the twentieth day of the same month. This indicates that the timeframe of 1:1–10:10 is approximately three weeks during which God prepared Israel for the next phase of their journey (Ashley 1993, 47).

1:2–3. God's specific command to Moses follows in 1:2–3. He is to "take a census" (שְׂאוּ אֶת־רֹאשׁ) of the entire community, who are then subdivided into their clans (מִשְׁפְּחֹתָם) and their families (בֵּית אֲבֹתָם).[2] Numbers 1:2b uses multiple descriptions of the counting, indicating that this is to be a thorough process, registering the "number of the names, every male, head by head" (ESV). The following verse gives the census its military framing. Those men "twenty years old and upward" (ESV) are to be counted, with the further declaration that they are the ones who can go out and fight for Israel.[3] Further, Moses and Aaron are to number them "by their divisions" (NET), which is a military arrangement.

1:4. Moses and Aaron do not have to do this task alone, which is why it can be completed expeditiously. Each tribe could be counted simultaneously with Moses and Aaron then receiving the collected results (Gane 2004, 494). Their assistants are categorized as "the head of the house of his father" in 1:4, which suggests high standing in Israel's tribal arrangement. This understanding is confirmed by the reoccurrence of these same names in the instructions for the arrangement of the camp (2:3–31), the list of offerings presented to God (7:12–83), and the order of march (10:14–28; Allen 2012, 85). God thus provides leading figures from each tribe to assist Moses and Aaron.

1:5–15. The list of assistants consists of the tribal identification, name, and patronymic of these twelve men. The order of the tribes is roughly the same as the birth order of their namesakes, but further grouped according to the wives of Jacob (Milgrom 1990, 6). Thus, the Leah tribes (minus Levi) are

---

1 Exodus 25–40 describes in great detail the process of constructing and furnishing this place.
2 The phrase שְׂאוּ אֶת־רֹאשׁ is typically translated "take a census" (ESV, NASB, NET). It literally means "lift up the head," but its colloquial association with census-taking is attested elsewhere in Scripture (Exod. 30:12; Lev. 5:24).
3 The Hebrew idiom for twenty years old is literally "a son of twenty years" (מִבֶּן עֶשְׂרִים שָׁנָה).

listed first (1:5–9), followed by the Rachel tribes (1:10–11), concluding with the tribes descended from the concubines (1:12–15).[4] Numbers 1:10 lists two tribes who are the descendants of Joseph's sons Ephraim and Manasseh. This confirms Joseph's ascension over his brothers as he receives a double portion of Israel's inheritance. Further, many of the names point to the antiquity of the list as they are built upon appellations like אֵל (*el*, "God"), שַׁדַּי (*shaddai*, "Almighty"), עַמִּי (*ammi*, "my people"), and אָב (*ab*, "father") rather than the covenantal name YHWH revealed to Moses in Exodus 3 (Allen 2012, 85; Cole 2000, 72; Milgrom 1990, 6).[5] These appellations give the names theological resonance, although one's name is not necessarily reflective of one's character. These elders must also have participated in Israel's rebellions against God since they are not spared the punishment of the first generation.

1:16. This first unit concludes with a summary statement highlighting the status of these individuals. They are "the ones chosen from the community, leaders of their ancestral tribes. They were the heads of the thousands of Israel" (NET). These three statements indicate God has selected appropriate figures to help Moses and Aaron with their work.

The Results of the Census (1:17–46)

1:17–19. Numbers 1:17–19 gives a general introduction that indicates that Moses and Aaron immediately did what YHWH commanded. According to 1:18, Moses and Aaron gather Israel on the same day they received God's command. Vocabulary from 1:2–3 also recurs such as "by their clans and families," "according to the number of names," and "twenty years old and upward" (ESV). This introduction concludes in 1:19 with the affirmation that it was done "just as the LORD commanded Moses" (NASB, NET). The book of Numbers thus begins with God giving detailed instructions and his servants responding in obedience.

1:20–43. The results of the census for each tribe follow a formula consisting of: 1) the name of the tribe, 2) the specifics of those who were counted (by generation, clan, family, etc), 3) a restatement of the tribe's name, and 4) the total (Allen 2012, 89). The order is similar to that of the chosen elders in 1:5–15, arranged according to the mother of the tribal namesake (Leah, Rachel, the concubines), although Gad is listed third (1:24–25).[6] This mirrors the arrangement of the tribal camp in which Gad is part of the group headed by Reuben (2:10–16). Given that Israel will be divided into four groups of three tribes camped around the central sanctuary, pushing Gad forward in the order creates two Leah groups (Reuben-Simeon-Gad and Judah-Issachar-Zebulun), a Rachel group (Ephraim-Manasseh-Benjamin), and a concubine group (Dan-Asher-Naphtali; Ashley 1993, 52). Listing the results tribe by tribe reveals that God has been faithful to all Israel: each tribe has grown substantially during Israel's sojourn in Egypt (cf. Exod 1:1–7).

---

[4] The tribes originating with the concubines are mixed together here since Dan and Naphtali are descended from Bilhah (Rachel's servant), while Asher and Gad are descended from Zilpah (Leah's servant). A different order is used for the census itself as Gad is listed third (1:24–25).

[5] The italicized English in this sentence is not formal transliteration but rather an approximation of English spelling so that the reader can connect the appellations to the appropriate name.

[6] Interestingly, the Septuagint moves the Gadites among the tribes of the concubines, placing 1:24–25 after 1:37. This may reflect the translator trying to harmonize the order of the census with the order of the elders in 1:5–15 (Harrison 1990, 42–43).

Reading the Numbers of the Census

At this point it is necessary to address the challenging question of how one ought to read the numbers of the census. Do they refer to the literal population of Israel in the wilderness or is there another approach? This question defies simple resolution. The first thing to note is the final census tally of 603,550 men twenty years and older (Num. 1:46). Extrapolating from that, the projected Israelite population is likely 2.5 million or higher (Allen 2012, 54). This is an incredibly large number of people. For the sake of comparison, I live outside of Toronto, Ontario, which has an estimated population of around 3 million.[7] The logistics of preserving, shepherding, and directing that many people for a generation through the inhospitable Sinai wilderness boggles the mind. Of course, it is not beyond God's capabilities. We must also consider that similar numbers are found in other presentations of Israel's population, including the number who escaped from Egypt (600,000 men according to Exod. 12:37), the account of the sanctuary tax (603,550 men in Exod. 38:26), and the second census of Numbers 26 (601,730 men). These passages all appear to present the numbers in a straightforward manner.

However, other biblical data complicates the picture. Most crucial is Deuteronomy 7:1, which claims that Canaan contains seven nations stronger and more numerous than Israel. Indeed, the same passage states that Israel is "the least numerous of all the peoples" (Deut. 7:7 NET). If multiple nations outnumbered Israel, then the ancient population of that land quickly outstrips its modern equivalent, which is problematic given the restrictions of Bronze Age agriculture and technology. Another challenge is Numbers 3:43, which identifies 22,273 firstborn Israelite males. To link this number of family units with the number of fighting men would require family sizes of thirty males, likely exceeding fifty total children per family (Cole 2000, 79). This is unlikely, even if there were widespread polygamy.[8] Others difficulties include the fact that only two midwives are named as serving the Israelites in Exodus 1:15, while Israel's terror at six hundred of Pharaoh's chariots (Exod. 14:7) seems overstated if they had the capability to amass more than 600,000 fighting men (Sprinkle 2015, 197). Further, when all Israel (including the Transjordanian tribes) prepares to assault Jericho, Joshua 4:13 lists a total of forty thousand fighting men, which reflects a serious decrease (Goldstein 2012, 100).

Multiple alternative arrangements have been proposed with varying degrees of persuasiveness. An earlier generation of scholarship proposed that the figures from this census actually reflected the time of David (Albright 1957, 253). This creates

---

7   Information drawn from the 2016 census, found at https://www12.statcan.gc.ca/census-recensement/2016/dp-pd/prof/details/Page.cfm?Lang=E&Geo1=CSD&Code1=3520005&Geo2=PR&Data=Count&B1=All.
8   In a delightfully wretched pun, Allen calls these figures "unbearable" (Allen 2012, 66).

more problems than it solves.⁹ Others have looked to different forms of gematria, in which the numerical totals have symbolic value (Bailey 2005, 388–91). These are speculative at best, and the text gives no indications that these numbers point to something beyond themselves.

Another approach builds on the fact that in compiling numbers in Hebrew, there are no digits, but rather each word must be spelled out.¹⁰ This leads to potential confusion since the word translated "thousand" (אֶלֶף) can also mean "group," or "troop," or another kind of unit without a specific number attached (Josh. 22:14; Judg. 6:15; 1 Sam. 10:19; 23:23). Consequently, a number like 46,500 for Reuben in 1:21 could indicate forty-six "units" (אֶלֶף) comprising five hundred men in total. Following this procedure for the remaining tribes would drastically reduce the number of fighting men and with it, the population of the whole nation (Waite 2010, 490–91). The issue with this approach is the sum of 603,550 in 1:46. One proponent of this theory suggests that during the process of transmission the "unit" meaning of אֶלֶף was lost and scribes instead substituted a literal meaning of "thousand," and added up the twelve figures accordingly (Humphreys 1998, 207).

A final approach to consider is that the numbers are intentionally hyperbolic, reflecting an ancient Near Eastern literary convention in which rulers employed inflated numbers of their own soldiers or of casualties inflicted for purposes of self-aggrandizement (Fouts 1997, 383–86).¹¹ This has the advantage of reading אֶלֶף as "thousand" and avoids the issue of an interpretive error in textual transmission. In this context, the exceedingly vast numbers instead redound to the glory of God as they reflect his commitment to make Abraham's descendants more numerous than the stars in the sky (Gen. 15:5) or grains of sand along the shore (Gen. 22:7). One common suggestion is to reduce the total by a factor of ten, yielding a fighting force of around sixty thousand, which also aligns better with the total of firstborn in Numbers 3:43 (Allen 2012, 65; Sprinkle 2015, 197). This also preserves the text of Numbers without requiring emendations. Presumably the audience would understand this literary convention and not view it as deceitful or misleading (Goldstein 2012, 108).

Ultimately, this question does not have a conclusive resolution. Expositors will need to exercise their own judgment concerning the degree to which they wish to address it. Given the challenges brought about by the biblical data outside of the census chapters, I (Joel) maintain a slight preference for the hyperbolic approach, but a literal reading certainly fits the text as we have it.

---

9   See the critique in Harrison 1990, 46. He points out that by the time of David, the tribe of Simeon had been more or less incorporated into Judah, yet in the Numbers 1 census, it is listed as one of the largest.
10 A very literal rendering of the Hebrew figure in Numbers 1:46 would be "six hundred thousand and three thousands and five hundreds and fifty."
11 Fouts points to several examples drawn from Akkadian and Assyrian literature in which large numbers reflect the stature of the ruler. The *Keret* epic found in Ugarit (a city along the coast of the Mediterranean, north of Phoenicia) even suggests an army exceeding three million. See Fouts 1997, 386.

1:20–43. (continued). Repetition characterizes the presentation of the census figures in 1:20–43. Reuben and Simeon show some slight variation, adding the phrases "head by head" and "every male" (1:20, 22 ESV) to the stock report of the other tribes. The total attributed to Judah and the Joseph tribes is also noteworthy regardless of whether the numbers are literal or hyperbolic. At 74,600 (1:27), Judah is the most populous tribe by a significant margin. This anticipates the leading role that the Judahites play in the biblical narrative, providing Israel with David, the king after God's own heart, and ultimately being the lineage that leads to the Messiah. Jacob even foretells Judah's preeminence in his farewell to his son, declaring that the other tribes will bow before Judah and that his tribe will wield the ruler's scepter (Gen. 49:8–12). Similarly, combining Ephraim and Manasseh yields the second highest number of 72,700 (40,500 in Ephraim [1:33] + 32,200 in Manasseh [1:35]). This is appropriate since 1:32 introduces them first as the people of Joseph. As mentioned above, this reflects Joseph's status as the ranking heir of Jacob. It also preserves the traditional number of twelve tribes even though the Levites are excluded from the count of fighting men (Allen 2012, 89–90). Thus, the census figures provide hints as to the way God will pour out certain blessings among the Israelites.

1:44–46. These verses provide a summary of the census, restating that Moses and Aaron performed it with the assistance of the twelve men listed in 1:5–15. Their names are not listed again, but 1:44b notes that they represented each of Israel's twelve tribes of fighting men. Thus, the Israelites have completed the task that God assigned. Numbers 1:46 then provides the cumulative total of 603,550 fighting men. The excursus provides a more detailed presentation of the debate around this figure, but its exegetical significance is apparent in light of the unfolding story of Israel. God is fulfilling his promise to Abraham to make him into a great nation (Gen. 12:1; 15:5; 17:2).

The Culmination of the Census: The Levites (1:47–54)

The final subunit of this first chapter addresses the Levites. It summarizes the instructions that God will give in much greater detail in Numbers 3–4.

1:47–51. This section begins by acknowledging that the Levites were omitted from the census at God's command (1:47–49). Numbers 1:49 provides God's specific instruction, beginning with the Hebrew adverb אַךְ, which typically places restrictions upon preceding clauses (Arnold and Choi 2018, 141). Here, what is being limited are God's prior instructions to count the other tribes. Numbers 1:50–51 then provides a brief account of what the Levites are to do instead. They are to serve at the "Tabernacle of the Testimony" (1:50), which likely has the Ten Words (Commandments) as its backdrop (Allen 2012, 92–93). The tablets were found inside the ark of God (Exod. 25:16; Deut. 10:5). Thus, the Levites receive the charge to care for the most visible representation of God's covenant relationship with Israel. In the wilderness, this involves transporting the tabernacle and its furnishings, encamping around it, and assembling and disassembling it at the appropriate times. The Levites also provide a buffer of consecrated servants between the manifest holiness of God and the rest of the Israelites. This is necessary since 1:51b declares that if any "unauthorized person" (NET) approaches, they will be put to death.[12]

---

12 The Hebrew word here is זָר, which often refers to foreigners or those not part of the Israelite community (Isa. 1:7; 25:2; Jer. 5:19; 30:8; 51:2; Ezek. 7:21; Obad. 11). Here it points to non-Levitical Israelites who are excluded from the religious duties of caring for this sanctuary (Allen 2012, 93).

1:52–53. The instructions to the Levites conclude by reinforcing the distinction between the Levites and the other tribes. The other tribes camp in their military units but the Levites camp around the Tabernacle "so that there may be no wrath on the congregation of the people of Israel" (1:53b ESV). This refers to divine wrath for violations of his holiness. In order to dwell among sinful human beings, God designed layers of sacred space which require greater and greater ceremonial purity to enter. This of course culminates with the Holy of Holies which only the high priest can enter once a year. Every Levite is thus a visual reminder that a holy God dwells among the Israelites even as they make their way through the wilderness.

1:54. The chapter concludes with a summary statement which declares that the Israelites did what God commanded Moses. This is the second declaration of obedience along with 1:19. Similar statements occur throughout the early chapters but disappear once Israel departs Sinai.

THEOLOGICAL FOCUS

The exegetical idea (Enumerating Israel reveals God's faithfulness and prepares the nation to worship him) leads to this theological focus: *God knows and names his people and consecrates them for his service.* The census reveals that God has been with Israel as it has grown from an extended family to a nation. This account of God's provision makes the failure of this generation in Numbers 13–14 even more tragic, but the second census in Numbers 26 reveals that God continues to know and number his people (Allen 2012, 91). The detail and repetition reinforce the idea that every Israelite is known to God and has a place within the community. This sense of belonging is incredibly powerful. Even lists that consist of the simplest information such as names and numbers have tremendous value, recognizing that those mentioned are worthy of commemoration.[13]

The census in Numbers stands in stark contrast to another one that took place more than a millennium later. A very different lord, Caesar Augustus, required a census of the Roman world to lay a tax burden upon conquered peoples (Luke 2:1–3). Caesar had achieved his lordship through Rome's brutal displays of power rather than through faithful presence among an oppressed people. However, in his sovereignty, God used this earthly census as part of his great plan of redemption as it provided the setting for the incarnation and the birth of Immanuel. In a census enforced by imperial power, God launched a kingdom that preached good news to the poor, liberated the oppressed, and declared God's abundant favor (Luke 4:18–19). Despite the absence of direct literary connection between Numbers 1 and Luke 2, the way in which the gospel subverts Caesar's census also reveals the lengths to which God has gone to call people to himself.

Throughout his ministry, Jesus expresses the truth that he knows and names his people. He calls himself the Good Shepherd whose sheep know his voice (John 10:14–15). He is the shepherd who will not permit any of those who belong to him to slip away (Luke 15:4–7). Ultimately, the names and numbers that God preserves in the census of Numbers 1 anticipate the names that are secured eternally through the slain and resurrected Lamb of God (Rev. 13:8).

---

13   Two examples come to mind. The first is from U2's performance at the Super Bowl half-time show in 2002 in which they projected a list of names of those who lost their lives on 9/11 during the finale (https://www.youtube.com/watch?v=pH5tHgXS-2M). The second is the front page of *The New York Times* from May 24, 2020, which was devoted to the names and memories of those killed by the COVID-19 pandemic at that time (https://www.nytimes.com/issue/todayspaper/2020/05/24/todays-new-york-times). These are poignant illustrations of the reality that every life created in God's image has worth, dignity, and deserves to be remembered.

Beyond simply belonging to God's people, the census also reveals how God consecrates them to his service. Its first purpose was to count Israel's fighting force, which recalls God's covenant commitment to make Israel a great nation and to give them the land that he promised to Abraham. In Genesis 15, God put his own reputation on the line in response to Abraham's question, "how am I to know that I shall possess it?" (Gen. 15:8 ESV). He promised through an oath to bring Abraham's descendants back into the land. Israel's growth reflects an anticipatory fulfillment of that promise.

The selection of the Levites also fits this theme. Although all Israel is a kingdom of priests, the Levites are consecrated for special service. In similar fashion, every believer today is part of a holy priesthood that offers acceptable sacrifices to God through Christ (1 Peter 2:5). However, for the edification of the body, some receive callings as pastors, prophets, evangelists, and teachers (Eph. 4:11–14). All of God's people are consecrated to him, and some will serve in specific offices that he has ordained.

PREACHING AND TEACHING STRATEGIES

Exegetical and Theological Significance

God knows the name of every one of his children. Before he called Abram he knew the names of every one of Abram's descendants. He knew that they would go through trials and difficulty. He knew that he would redeem them and liberate them from slavery. He knew he would lead them into the Promised Land. The Good Shepherd has always known the names of his individual sheep. God's love and grace is set on individuals; there is nothing generic in his relationship with anyone. He knows everything about you.

God does not redeem people so that they can live in isolated spirituality, however. The Redeemer is also the creator of a covenant community. Numbers 1:1–54 reveals that God knows every person in his covenant community, but he also organizes them for service. He calls his individual sheep to belong to one flock. What Israel is called to do is not something that can be accomplished by individuals acting as mavericks. God knows how best to arrange his people for service. When individuals are organized into effective groups, they can accomplish far more than they could on their own. The organization is no substitute for the power of God's Spirit and for obedience to his commands (as will be seen with the military "strategy" at Jericho), but Numbers 1 makes it very clear that God is a God of order. God has blessed his people individually and corporately, and he has greater blessings in store for them as they organize and prepare to move forward in faith.

Preaching Idea

God knows every individual, and he redeems, gathers, and organizes people together into his covenant community for worship and service.

Contemporary Connections

What does it mean?
What does it mean that God is creating, redeeming, and organizing a covenant community? Although God is not calling the local church to engage in a census so that they can be prepared militarily and cultically to march into Canaan, this chapter does contain lessons for the church. God is faithful to his covenant people and will fulfill his promises. Those whom God redeems he places in relationship inside of his covenant community.

In 1 Corinthians 12–14 Paul discusses the importance of spiritual gifts and uses the analogy of a body, which is a unity that is made up of diverse parts. When every part works together for the good of the whole, the body is healthy and strong. When the various parts of the body are coordinated, it can accomplish tremendous things. An eye detached from the body cannot do very much! Yet being part of the body does not stamp everyone with uniformity; we are not carbon copies. God knows, loves, and uniquely gifts every member of the church. When the church is organized and all of God's children are prepared to serve in the power of the Spirit, incredible things can be accomplished by God's grace.

God's power is such that he could have let Israel walk into Canaan in a haphazard fashion, or he could have told them to go to sleep while he drove out all of their enemies. Yet God wanted his people to be organized and disciplined. He wanted them to be involved, and to be involved with excellence and planning. Today, churches are called to do things with proper order. Like Israel, we trust God, we thank him that he knows us by name, and we prepare for organized service.

Is it true?
Is it true that organizing God's people into a covenant community really leads to more effective service? Can't we simply follow Christ on our own, being led by the Spirit as opportunities arise? It is important to avoid false dichotomies: we are led by the Spirit as individuals, but we are also part of the body of Christ. In fact, the Spirit leads us to see which part of the body we are and how we fit into the whole.

As mundane as it may sound, God organized Israel and used a census to do so. Earlier in the wilderness Moses appointed judges for smaller groups. Jesus had circles of disciples that he organized to send out on missions trips. Paul commanded spiritual gifts to be used in an orderly way, and he also appointed leaders in churches. From little league baseball to international corporations, organization is important for effectiveness. It is essential not to lose the identity of the individual in the corporate mass (i.e., every Christian is an individual loved and known by God, not merely a cog in the church's ministry machine), but more can be done by God's people when they are organized and equipped for their tasks.

Now what?
Believe it or not, Numbers 1:1–54 is a great passage to call the church to action on three fronts: 1) worshipping God for how he knows and loves us individually; 2) organizing for effective ministry, given the calling and opportunities God has set before us; 3) getting to know our fellow servants in the church. Since God knows and loves people, we ought to as well. Since God calls us to serve with other people, we need to know them as well. We should value and love those whom God values and loves. If God has placed us in a body with others, we need to know who is able to fulfill various functions. We need to appreciate proper diversity in its underlying unity. We need to be organized and set in good order for maximum effectiveness as we are led together by the Spirit.

Creativity in Presentation
The metaphor of a shepherd and sheep is found in numerous places in Scripture, and most people in church are familiar with it. For non-shepherds, sheep may all look the same! Putting a picture up that shows a large flock of sheep may help illustrate the point that to most of us, every sheep has a generic face. Jesus as the Good Shepherd said that he knows all of his sheep by name. Today, his flock throughout history numbers billions. Tell people to look around the church: How many people do they know by name? If there is someone there that they don't know at all—or at least not as well as others—suggest that they get to know them after the service. Churches often do suggest things like this, but without much follow through, so make it an extension of the message—emphasize it. Ask people to send in some stories that week about how they got to know someone better; perhaps some of the stories can be read the following Sunday. It is important to know and love those whom God knows and loves. This shouldn't be something that just happens on one Sunday; it should be part of the atmosphere of the church.

This text also lends itself well to census-taking. A brief survey could be distributed where people can provide their name and contact information, and list gifts they feel they have, their skills, and areas of service they're interested in. This could either be done with paper to be collected or with a number to text the information to. Requesting data is only as good as the follow-up, so the church needs to be ready to process the information and help organize people into effective teams for ministry. There may even be new areas of ministry that develop from people's suggestions and interests. Engaging in such a church census may bring about ministry opportunities and partnerships that help the church minister more effectively. These activities can remind us that God knows every individual, and he redeems, gathers, and organizes people together into his covenant community for worship and service.

One possible outline for this passage is below. It highlights the progression of this text from counting the Israelite fighting men to preparing the nation to worship God:

- God provides the resources to know and name every member of Israel (1:1–15).

- Counting the Israelites reminds them of God's redemption and preservation (1:16–46).

- The Levites reflect the need for special devotion and service in response to what God has done (1:47–54).

DISCUSSION QUESTIONS

1. What do you think the ancient Israelites learned about God in the process of taking the census?

2. Why do you think God commanded Moses and Aaron to take this census?

3. Why do the Levites stand outside of this census? What does this reveal about God and his priorities?

4. What do we learn about God in discovering that he knows and names his people?

5. Can you recall a time when you found comfort or a sense of purpose in finding your name on a list?

Numbers 2:1–34

EXEGETICAL IDEA
God provides specific direction for how the Israelites should encamp around his presence.

THEOLOGICAL FOCUS
God is to be the center of his people's life.

PREACHING IDEA
Both individually and corporately, God is to be the absolute center of our lives.

PREACHING POINTERS
In incredible grace, the holy Creator God of the universe camps in a tent in the middle of the community of his people. He puts his royal presence in the center of his covenant community. The community's whole life was to be organized around him. Everything Israel did had YHWH as the literal center. This physical reality was an object lesson of basic, fundamental moral and spiritual principles. There were to be no competing gods in the camp; there were to be no gods before the Lord God. Only he could be the center of the people's existence.

Even when the people rebelled, God remained enthroned at the center of their camp. He could not be dislodged from his place in the universe, or uprooted from his place in the midst of his people. God remained there because he is holy, just, and good. In covenant grace, he redeemed his people and took them to himself. Human beings were designed and created to flourish only when they build their lives around God in all things. In sin, we try to put other things at the center of our lives and societies, but without God, there is no center that will hold. Unless we acknowledge his reign, we will be lost. It is a high and awesome thing to stand in this relation to a holy God, and it is only by his redeeming grace that we can joyfully live our lives fully for him. Through the work of the triune God, we can love and honor God, submitting to his place at the center of all things. Both individually and corporately, God is to be the absolute center of our lives.

THE ARRANGEMENT OF ISRAEL'S CAMP (2:1–34)

LITERARY STRUCTURE AND THEMES

Following the census, God provides instructions for how the Israelites were to arrange their camp during their sojourn in the wilderness. This chapter is tightly linked to Numbers 1, repeating the names of the tribal leaders and the number of men of fighting age for each tribe.[1] It is also closely connected to Numbers 10:11–33 which details the arrangement of the tribes when they are on the march. It is fitting to focus on Israel's arrangement while encamped here since the nation does not depart Sinai until Numbers 10:11.

This chapter works through the positioning of each tribe. It begins with instructions from God to Moses and Aaron (2:1–2). It then distributes the tribes into four divisions arranged around the Levites and the Tent of Meeting. The first division is situated to the east (2:3–9), while the survey travels clockwise from there, detailing the arrangement of the camps to the south (2:10–16), west (2:18–24), and north (2:25–31). The pattern is briefly interrupted in 2:17 to account for the Levites who encamp between the other tribes and the Tent of Meeting.[2] The discussion of each division is also highly patterned. Each one is assigned a head tribe (Judah, Reuben, Ephraim, and Dan) that lead them in their journey, while the remaining eight tribes are related to one of those four. The chapter then concludes with a summation of the Israelite tribes (2:32–33) and a declaration that they obeyed God's instructions (2:34).

The key theme of this passage is its sense of order. The literary symmetry of the passage matches the physical symmetry of the Israelite tribes finding their place around the central shrine. The orderliness of this arrangement is linked to the order established in creation in Genesis 1. The way in which God shapes and arranges his people reflects the "order, beauty, purpose, and wonder" that is present in the image of a perfect creation (Allen 2012, 93). At its core is the presence of God. As Israel prepares to journey toward the Promised Land, the shape of its encampment reflects the centrality of God to Israel's identity and existence. This further represents God's rightful place in relationship to all of creation. In this chapter, the tribes draw their sense of place from their relationship to the Tent of Meeting, the dwelling place of God.

- *God's Instructions (2:1–2)*
- *The Eastern Tribes (2:3–9)*
- *The Southern Tribes (2:10–16)*
- *The Levites (2:17)*
- *The Western Tribes (2:18–24)*
- *The Northern Tribes (2:25–31)*
- *Conclusion (2:32–34)*

EXPOSITION

As with the census, this preaching unit is laden with repetition. The preacher will want to focus on how the detail and consistency reveals God's provision of specific direction for how the Israelites should encamp around his presence.

---

1 This brings up the same issue of how best to understand these numbers. See the excursus in the previous chapter for further discussion.
2 God gives more specific instructions for how the Levites are to encamp in Numbers 3:21–39.

The Arrangement of Israel's Camp (2:1–34)

God's Instructions (2:1–2)

2:1–2. This passage begins with God providing specific instructions to Moses and Aaron for how the Israelite community should arrange its camp. The key element is that the Tent of Meeting is to be central. The tribes are to encamp "at some distance" (2:2 NET) from it. The necessary distance is indeterminate here, but the Levites provide a buffer zone so that the other tribes do not encroach upon the more sacred space (2:17).

God's instructions begin with a focus on the individual, declaring that "every one" (2:2 NET) should find their appropriate place (Allen 2012, 94). They are to assemble according to their דֶּגֶל, which could refer to either a visible identifying marker or a military unit.

> TRANSLATION ANALYSIS
> During the Persian Period, the term דֶּגֶל had the sense of military unit (Levine 1993, 146–48). However, its meaning at the time of Israel's wilderness sojourn is less certain. A cognate Akkadian verb *dagalu* refers to something visible, such as a flag or banner (Cole 2000, 84). English translations consistently use "standard" for this term, evoking the sense of a visible object that orients the Israelites to where they should assemble.

The individual receives further clarity as they are to camp "with the banners of their fathers' houses" (2:2) (בְּאֹתֹת לְבֵית אֲבֹתָם ESV), which provides a more localized unit of identity. Thus, this arrangement captures a sense of belonging for the individual within the broader corporate structure (Cole 2000, 87). God's desire for Israel is for everyone to know where they belong as they surround the sanctuary.

The Eastern Tribes (2:3–9)

2:3–4. The division of the tribes commences with those who are to camp east of the Tent of Meeting. This is fitting since that is the direction from which the Israelites could enter the tabernacle grounds (Ashley 1993, 71). The pattern of the tribal listings is repeated when discussing the other divisions. Judah is the head tribe of this first division, followed by Issachar and Zebulun. These tribes share Leah as their common matriarch, providing the rationale for this grouping. Numbers 2:3 also declares that Judah possesses the standard (דֶּגֶל) that points to its leadership role. Numbers 2:3b then identifies Judah's tribal leader, while 2:4 provides the total of fighting men. The tribal leader mentioned for Judah along with those from the rest of the tribes is the same as the list found in Numbers 1:5–15. The military nature of the arrangement is expressed through the word צָבָא ("host"), which occurs alongside every number in this chapter.

Judah and its associated tribes (Issachar and Zebulun) move from fourth through sixth in the census list (Num. 1:26–31) to first through third positions here. Whereas the census mostly followed the birth order of Jacob's sons, this arrangement likely reflects the elevation of Judah as the tribe that Jacob prophetically announced would rule over its brothers (Gen. 49:8–10). Reuben, Jacob's firstborn, leads the second division of tribes (Num. 2:10–11) but is no longer given pride of place on account of its patriarch's sin of sleeping with his father's concubine (Gen. 35:22; 49:3–4). This further reflects the biblical theme of God passing over the expected heir to sovereignly choose the one whom he desires (Cole 2000, 88).[3]

2:5–6. Issachar is encamped next to Judah. Numbers 2:5 begins with the expression

---

3   This happens consistently throughout Genesis: Isaac is chosen over Ishmael, Jacob over Esau, and Joseph over the rest of his brothers. Fascinatingly, in Genesis 48:17–20 Joseph objects when Jacob chooses to bless Joseph's younger son (Ephraim) over the elder (Manasseh). Even though Joseph himself had been elevated from his position in the birth order, he struggled when it happened within his own family.

וְהַחֹנִים עָלָיו ("Those to camp next to him," ESV), which is used to mark the second tribe of all four divisions with one minor exception.[4] This is followed by the name of Issachar's tribal leader (2:5b) and its census total (2:6).

2:7–8. The third tribe of this division is Zebulun. It establishes a pattern of the third tribes which receive the briefest introductions. Numbers 2:7 simply begins with "the tribe of Zebulun" (מַטֵּה זְבוּלֻן) before listing the name of the leader (2:7b) and the census total (2:8). English translations frequently insert a phrase like "Next will be" (NET) to provide grammatical clarity.

2:9. The account of this first division concludes with a summation of the fighting men from these three tribes (186,400). The other three divisions will follow this pattern. The final statement is that this division will set out first. This anticipates Israel's departure from Sinai. When it does leave, Numbers 10:14–17 reveals that Judah led the march, in accordance with God's instructions.

The Southern Tribes (2:10–16)

2:10–11. Reuben leads the southern division of tribes. Numbers 2:10 mirrors the description of Judah in 2:3, mentioning Reuben's standard in addition to the name of its tribal leader. The following verse then lists its census total. Although Reuben was Jacob's firstborn, the tribe has been demoted from the first position in the census account. Its position in the south reflects that it is not standing to the east of God's presence, in the "place of pride" that faces the opening of the sanctuary (Allen 2012, 96). Reuben now heads a division of "disgraced sons," joined by Simeon and Gad (Schnittjer 2006, 388).

2:12–13. The introduction of Simeon mirrors that of Issachar. The Simeonites are "those encamped" next to Reuben. The text then lists the leader of the Simeonites (2:12b) and its census total (2:13). Simeon fits this grouping followed Reuben into disgrace on account of its patriarch's actions in slaughtering the city of Shechem in Genesis 34:1–31.[5]

2:14–15. The final tribe of the southern division is Gad. Their introduction mirrors that of Zebulun with its terseness. The text then lists the name of Gad's leader (2:14b) along with its census total (2:15).

> *TRANSLATION ANALYSIS*
> The Gadite leader's name presents a minor issue. Numbers 1:14; 7:42, 47; 10:20 identify him as "Eliasaph son of Deuel." In Numbers 2:14, the text reads "son of Reuel" instead. The Hebrew letters *daleth* and *resh* are very similar in form, so the texts are almost certainly referring to the same individual. Many English versions correct the Hebrew text and read Deuel here (CSB, NASB, NET, NIV), while a few have Reuel instead (CEB, ESV, NRSV).

The patriarch of this tribe was the son of Leah's concubine Zilpah. The Gadites slot into this division along with the Reubenites and Simeonites, who are directly descended from sons of Leah. This is because the Levites, the remaining Leah tribe, are not part of the military census. Gad thus moves up from its second-last position in the first listing of tribal leaders (cf. 1:14).

---

4 See the discussion of Numbers 2:20.
5 It is curious that Genesis 34 does not explicitly condemn Simeon and Levi for slaughtering the Shechemites after the violation of their sister, Dinah. However, Jacob's final address to his sons makes it clear that he does not approve their actions (Gen. 49:5–7). It is also fascinating that the Levites go from the potential disgrace of Jacob's denunciation to the tribe that most closely interacts with God's holiness.

2:16. This verse mirrors 2:9 in providing the summary total of fighting men in the southern division (151,450) and announcing that they shall be second in the marching order. Numbers 10:18–21 confirms this order.

The Levites (2:17)
2:17. After completing two of the four tribal divisions, the text identifies the marching order of Tent of Meeting and the Levites. They set out in the middle of nation, according to their own clans (cf. Num. 3:21–38). The idea is that God's presence is central to the nation as it both camps and marches toward the Promised Land. This arrangement resembles that of the Egyptian war camp under Ramesses II in the thirteenth century B.C., which placed the tent of the supposed god-king at its center (Gane 2004, 302). Instead, the Israelites are oriented around the sanctuary of the true and living God.

The Western Tribes (2:18–24)
2:18–19. After locating the Levites and God's sanctuary at the heart of the camp, the text continues its circuit of the tribal divisions. This group of tribes is associated with Rachel. Its leading tribe is Ephraim, the younger son of Joseph. Its introduction mirrors those of Judah and Reuben, noting that it contains the standard (דֶּגֶל) for this division. These tribes are located west of the sanctuary. The text then lists its leader (2:18b) and census total (2:19).

2:20–21. The second tribe of this division is Manasseh, the elder son of Joseph. This is indicative of Joseph's reception of the status of firstborn which entitled him to a double share of his father's inheritance (cf. Gen. 48:5–20). The expected participle וְהַחֹנִים ("the encamped ones") of the second tribe is missing, but otherwise this mirrors the description of Issachar and Simeon (cf. Num. 2:5, 12). The text lists the tribal leader (2:20b) and the census count (2:21).

2:22–23. The final tribe of this division is Benjamin, the other son of Rachel. Like Zebulun and Gad, its description is very terse, giving just its name, its tribal leader (2:22b), and census total (2:23).

2:24. This verse mirrors 2:9 and 16 by summarizing the division lead by Ephraim, giving its total as 108,100. It also announces that this division is third in the marching order, which is confirmed in 10:22–24.

The Northern Tribes (2:25–31)
2:25–26. The final tribal division is headed by the Danites. It consists of the three remaining sons of the maidservants Bilhah and Zilpah. Dan is the eldest of these which is presumably why it is listed first. The text notes that Dan the standard for this division, before listing its tribal leader (2:25b) and census total (2:26).

2:27–28. The description of the Asherites matches those of the other second tribes. They are beside the Danites, listed along with their leader (2:27b) and census total (2:28).

2:29–30. The final tribe is Naphtali. It mirrors the terseness of the third tribes in every division. Again, its tribal leader (2:29b) and census total (2:30) are listed.

2:31. This verse lists the total of the Danite division (157,600). It also says that it will march under its standards, but unlike the other summary statements, it does not state where in the marching order this division slots. However, contextually it is obvious that this division marches last (cf. 10:25–28).

Conclusion (2:32–34)
2:32–33. The chapter concludes with a declaration that it has enumerated all these Israelites according to their military units (לְצִבְאֹתָם). The total number is identical to that given in 1:46 (603,550). Numbers 2:33 then notes that the Levites are not

counted here, just as God commanded Moses. This again points to the military nature of the census and the arrangement of the camp.

2:34. The final verse announces that the Israelites obeyed the instructions that God gave to Moses. This confirms that what God required in 2:1–2 has been fulfilled. As with the census, the obedience of the Israelites is worth celebrating—given what is to come.

THEOLOGICAL FOCUS

The exegetical idea (God provides specific direction for how the Israelites should encamp around his presence) leads to this theological focus: *God is to be the center of his people's life.* The instructions for Israel's encampment place God's presence at its heart. The Tent of Meeting and its Levitical attendants are at the center of the community, while the military camps spread out around it. This places God's dwelling place in a position of honour where it can be protected and cherished (Sprinkle 2015, 194). The centrality of God's presence is further affirmed by the detail of his instructions. By articulating the proper place for every member of the community, we see that "God cares about the mundane details of communal existence" (Pressler 2017, 20). God fits his people into an arrangement where they surround his holy presence as they encamp and move toward the Promised Land.

The shaping of the Israelite encampment reinforces the beginning of the Decalogue where God declares that he brought Israel out of slavery and in response, they must have no other gods before him (Exod. 20:2–3). God alone is worthy of being at the center of Israel's existence. Their identity is wrapped around his provision. As the Israelites prepare to march to the Promised Land and see the fulfillment of God's covenant promises, their camp physically reflects the spiritual reality of God's preeminence. The prophetic vision of Ezekiel 48 is similar. The prophet envisions an idealized Israel of twelve restored tribes surrounding a central sanctuary (Ezek. 48:9–12). In the land, the hope of Israel's existence after exile and punishment is rooted in the centrality of God.

In the New Testament, God's physical centrality cannot be experienced in the same way, but the theological principle remains. Ephesians 2:20 uses a similar metaphor in describing the church as an edifice built upon Christ Jesus as its cornerstone. As Paul envisions the unity of Jewish and Gentile believers, he pictures a building rising to become a temple to the Lord because of its unshakeable, central foundation (Eph. 2:21). Many other things may draw the attention of God's people, but Scripture reminds us that nothing but Christ and him crucified (1 Cor. 2:2) can stand at the center of the believer's identity.

PREACHING AND TEACHING STRATEGIES

Exegetical and Theological Significance

The fact that YHWH literally encamped in the center of his people was an inescapable object lesson for the community. God's royal, holy presence was not merely camping with them, it was in the middle of their communal existence. This location proclaimed the rule and supremacy of Israel's God, but it was also a remarkable display of divine condescension and grace. Not only is YHWH the one true God who cannot be contained by the highest heavens, but he is perfectly holy and righteous, hating sin and wickedness. In Exodus, God gives instructions for building the tabernacle (Exodus 25–31), but when Moses comes down from Sinai the people are rebelling (Exodus 32). Nevertheless, God reveals his name to Moses and has the tabernacle constructed; then his glory moves in and he takes up residence (Exodus 40). The very fact that God continued to live in the center of his people is an incredible testimony to his forgiveness and grace.

It is on the basis of God's redeeming love and grace that we can live safely with him as the absolute center of our lives. Israel needed to learn that every sphere and area of their lives was related to the holiness of God, and the physical location of the tabernacle was a visible illustration of this life principle. Yahweh, and no other god—whether the gods of Egypt, their man-made idols like the golden calf, or the gods of the Canaanites where Israel was going—was to be given this absolute allegiance as the absolute center of life. Israel was to have no other gods before Yahweh, and as a result they were to have no other gods at the center of their camp and community. In fact, they were to have no other gods *anywhere* in their lives and nation.

Preaching Idea
Both individually and corporately, God is to be the absolute center of our lives.

Contemporary Connections

What does it mean?
What does it mean that God is to be the absolute center of our lives? Unlike Israel, we do not have a glory-cloud or a physical tabernacle in the middle of our church building or neighborhood. Nevertheless, God can truly be the center of our lives. In one sense, the centrality of God for all of life is an objective fact. Not everyone in the Israelite camp honored the Lord, yet he was still the center of the community. Likewise, not every individual acknowledges God, but he is still the center of the universe. As it says in Romans 11:36, "For from him and through him and for him are all things. To him be the glory forever! Amen." In reference to Christ, Paul writes: "For in him all things were created: things in heaven and on earth, visible and invisible, whether thrones or powers or rulers or authorities; all things have been created through him and for him. He is before all things, and in him all things hold together" (Col. 1:16–17). The Triune God is the source, summation, and point of everything. He *is* the center of all things, whether we recognize this truth or not.

Given this reality, we are called to consciously build our lives around God's character and revelation. God is the ultimate metaphysical, ethical, rational, and spiritual reality. There is nothing more important or valuable than he is. No other center can hold an individual or society together. We were created to build our lives around God's holiness, goodness, and truth. No other substitute center—no other gods—can provide us with a point of integration and coherence individually and corporately. All of life is related to the living God.

Is it true?
Is it true that God must be at the center of our lives? If our lives are to have meaning and purpose and be intelligible, God must be at the center of all that we think and do. Since God is transcendent and we were created to find fulfillment and meaning in our relationship with him, nothing less can satisfy. When we look at the world around us, we see all kinds of political, philosophical, social, and ethical "centers" that promise utopia but dissolve into disappointment, chaos, oppression, and even bloodshed. We see secular and spiritual alternatives that promise freedom and significance, but leave people empty and disillusioned. Those who know God through Jesus Christ can testify that his love is better than life. Although there is mystery and there are trials, life makes sense with God at the center. Not only in this the case, but God invites us to organize our entire existence around himself because there is nothing higher, greater, or better than he is. In every area of our lives, God is to be first. In the church, God is our center. Nothing else will do; everything else will fail.

Now what?
How do we organize our lives around God, rejoicing in his centrality in all things? First, we must recognize that in our sin we have *not* wanted God to be our center. In sin, we want to be the center of the universe rather than God. Second, we need to confess this sin and

repent. Third, we need to submit ourselves to God, praising him for his marvelous, forgiving grace. Fourth, we need to pray that God will teach us and show us how to relate every area of our life to him. We all have blind spots where we do not see how we are still living for ourselves. Fifth, we need to study Scripture, both individually and in community fellowship, so that we can learn about the comprehensive plan God has for our lives and for the church. Sixth, we need to make course corrections, always being open to positive reformation as we walk with the Spirit.

Creativity in Presentation

The world provides us with numerous examples of organizing centers in different spheres. Corporate mission statements, political ideologies and platforms, philosophical systems, and endless advertisements push various visions of life that are centered on certain ideals, values, or material goods. Some societies teach citizens to sacrifice themselves for the greater good of the nation; some teach an autonomous individualism where the individual is to live for their own happiness above everything else. Postmodern thinkers deny that there is any coherent organizational center for life, and relativism pits one finite, subjective view against another finite, subjective view, with no court or grounds of appeal. Given the particular strengths of the preacher (e.g., philosophical competence, historical awareness, cultural understanding, knowledge of counseling/psychology, social media savvy), presenting and evaluating alternative centers can help establish our need for God.

In order to know what is necessary and sufficient to hold something together, we need to know what the thing is that is at risk of coming apart. What is required to keep a person from psychological and emotional disintegration? What is necessary to keep the solar system from flying apart? What can keep a nation, society, or community together? What keeps a family whole? What enables a church to experience deep unity rather than division? A broken leg requires a cast (and sometimes pins, plates, and screws); some things require welding, glue, or duct tape. A shared vision, understanding, and goal is required for a functioning society. Sports teams are centered around their superstars. Illustrations of this principle can be multiplied at great length. Given a particular social context and the needs of the local congregation, the preacher should have no trouble addressing the idolatrous pseudo-centers of our world, as well as demonstrating that both individually and corporately, God is to be the absolute center of our lives.

A potential outline that reflects the centrality of God in our lives can be found below:

- The physical layout of Israel's camp reflects the centrality of God to its life (2:1–16, 18–32).

- The presence of the Levites provides a constant reminder of God's holiness (2:17, 33).

- Israel's obedience to God's commands is essential for shaping the community (2:34).

DISCUSSION QUESTIONS

1. How does the physical layout of Israel's camp emphasize that God is to be central to the nation's existence?

2. How does this arrangement give the Israelites a sense of belonging and community?

3. How do believers commit to making God the center of their lives?

4. What other things compete to take center stage in our lives? How can believers resist their temptation?

Numbers 3:1–4:49

EXEGETICAL IDEA
God selected and commissioned the Levites to preserve the holiness of his sanctuary.

THEOLOGICAL FOCUS
God's holiness establishes his authority over his people.

PREACHING IDEA
Through Christ the High Priest, there is now a holy priesthood of all believers.

PREACHING POINTERS
It was an unimaginable privilege for the tribes of Israel to have God dwell in the middle of their community. To know God this way was an awesome thing. But, as in other areas of Israel's religious life, there were spheres of holiness and unique roles accorded to those whom God sovereignly set aside for his purposes. God provided redemption through substitution, and in doing so he freed up the Levites to discharge special responsibilities in his service. As a subset of the Levites, the priests were allowed to minister in the tabernacle itself. Although every Israelite could walk with the Lord, only the priests and Levites could minister in the sacred precincts.

One of the significant—and beautiful—developments from the old covenant to the new covenant is that now the priests of the covenant are not a subset of the covenant community. In the church, the priesthood is coextensive with the covenant membership. In other words, there really is a priesthood of all believers. Gone are the days of setting out the bread of the presence or keeping the lamp burning, but there are still holy tasks to be performed by the people of God. Every believer is a priest, and every believer is to worship God and serve him with all of their heart, mind, soul, and strength. We bring different sacrifices in this era: we bring the sacrifice of praise. Every believer is a holy priest, serving a holy God in the age of new covenant fulfillment in Jesus Christ, through the power of God's Spirit. The church can rejoice that through Christ the High Priest, there is now a holy priesthood of all believers.

THE CENSUS OF THE LEVITES AND THEIR RESPONSIBILITIES (3:1–4:49)

LITERARY STRUCTURE AND THEMES

Numbers 3:1–4:49 engages in a lengthy discussion of the Levites and their responsibilities. It addresses the absence of the Levites in the original census and the discussion of the arrangement of the camp (Numbers 1–2). This passage contains two censuses of the Levites. The first counts every male who is at least a month old (3:14–15). This reflects the status of the Levites as substitutes for the firstborn male of every Israelite family. The second counts those Levite males between thirty and fifty years old who are set aside for sacred service (4:3, 22, 30). These censuses reflect the movement of this passage from the selection of the Levites (Numbers 3) to a detailed presentation of their duties, especially focusing upon the preparations for travel (Numbers 4).[1]

Subunits of the passage include: commissioning the Levites for service at the sanctuary (3:1–13), counting the three major Levite clans and their responsibilities (3:14–40), and expressing how the Levites' service stands in for that of all Israelites (3:41–51). The next chapter then details the responsibilities of each Levitical clan, beginning with Aaron's family and the Kohathites (4:1–20), the Gershonites (4:21–28), and the Merarites (4:29–33). It concludes with a final count of those Levites devoted to God's service at the sanctuary (4:34–49).

The driving theme of this passage is the sacredness of divine service. Living in the presence of God's holiness carries dangers if those who are impure approach him. However, God in his graciousness permits Israel to dwell with him by setting apart the Levites. He calls them to care for the sanctuary where he dwells and the implements used in worshipping him. Although some of their tasks appear mundane, they have incalculable value because they are performed at God's command.

- *The Commissioning of the Levites (3:1–13)*
- *Counting the Levites (3:14–39)*
- *The Redemption of the Firstborn (3:40–51)*
- *Responsibilities of the Levites: Aaron and the Kohathites (4:1–20)*
- *Responsibilities of the Levites: The Gershonites (4:21–28)*
- *Responsibilities of the Levites: The Merarites (4:29–33)*
- *Second Census Results (4:34–49)*

EXPOSITION

This passage presents a daunting challenge for the expositor. However, the detail reflects an essential element of Israel's relationship with God. For Israel to remain in his presence, God selects and commissions the Levites to preserve the holiness of his sanctuary.

---

1 This passage makes for a very long "preaching unit." However, the repetition of the duties of each Levitical clan binds together its overarching theological message. The expositor may wish to highlight particularly salient ideas that emerge from the passage.

The Commissioning of the Levites (3:1–13)

3:1. The unit begins with the declaration "These are the generations of Aaron and Moses at the time when the LORD spoke with Moses on Mount Sinai" (3:1 ESV). The opening formulation recalls the book of Genesis where it divides the book into ten sections, focusing on the progeny of the named patriarch (Gen. 2:4; 5:1; 6:9; 10:1; 11:10; 11:27; 25:12, 19; 36:1; 37:1) Here, it separates the Aaronic priesthood and its Levitical attendants from the account of the other Israelite tribes. However, by placing it after the military census and the arrangement of the camp, it suggests that the work of the priests and Levites is "in service to the larger community of God's people" (Olson 1996, 26).

3:2–4. The text then notes the descendants of Aaron who carry on his priestly responsibilities. It also briefly recounts the tragic episode of Leviticus 10:1–3 where Nadab and Abihu burned incense with unauthorized fire and died as a result. Since they had no descendants, the Aaronic line continues through his remaining sons: Eleazar and Ithamar.

3:5–10. The focus then shifts to the Levites whom God tasks with serving Aaron and the priests.[2] While Aaron and his sons perform the sacrifices at the sanctuary, the Levites care for the furnishings and framework of the Tent of Meeting (3:8). There is resonance here with creation language as the verbal roots used for the Levites' duties (שׁמר; עבד) are the same as those given to the first man in his care for the garden (Gen. 2:15; Hamilton 2022, 66). There is a clear sense of hierarchy as God instructs Moses to give the Levites to Aaron and his sons (3:9). Their responsibilities also involve guarding the sanctuary from unauthorized access (3:10; cf. 1:50–53). Anyone, including non-Aaronic Levites, who entered it would die (Gane 2004, 512).

3:11–13. In these verses God provides the rationale for his selection of the Levites: they are substitutes for the firstborn of all Israelites. Rather than disrupt every family, God commissions one whole tribe for that task (Gane 2004, 513). God lays claim to the firstborn on several occasions in Exodus (Exod. 13:2, 11–16; 22:29–30; 34:19–20). Here, God connects his claim to Israel's firstborn to the death of Egypt's firstborn in the final plague. God's authority over the firstborn thus brought death to a hostile nation but brings life and flourishing to his people. This section concludes with the statement "I am YHWH" (3:13), which is a common concluding assertion that adds "authority, significance, and weight to the text" (Allen 2012, 107).

Counting the Levites (3:14–39)

3:14–16. After commissioning the Levites, God instructs Moses to count them. The criteria are different than the census of Numbers 1 which counted those males twenty years and older, capable of military service. This census counts every male one month and older, likely to ensure that the number of Levites approximated the number of firstborn from the other tribes (Cole 2000, 95). As expected in these early chapters of Numbers, Moses obeyed God's instructions.

3:17–20. The accounting begins by dividing the tribe of Levi into its three constituent branches: the Gershonites, the Kohathites, and the Merarites. It then lists several clans (מִשְׁפָּחָה) for each branch. These provide the sociological groupings for this census.

> **Israel's Sociological Identity**
> Ancient Israel had four levels of sociological identity. At the top was the nation, followed by the tribes. Underneath the tribes were the clan (מִשְׁפָּחָה) and the "house of the father" (בֵּית אָב).

---

2 Although it is not mentioned here, it is worth remembering that Moses and Aaron are also Levites, from a family in the Kohathite clan (Exod. 6:18–20). God sets them apart from the rest of the Kohathites for special priestly service.

> This smallest unit is mentioned in the second Levitical census (Num. 4:2, 22, 29). It was larger than the modern nuclear family, consisting of a male ancestor and his wife (or wives), his sons and their wives, grandsons and their wives, along with their dependent children, unmarried adults, and any servants. Several of these made up a clan, which provided safety and security through duties to protect such as the kinsman-redeemer (Block 2003, 33–37). Marriages often happened within the clan (see Numbers 36).

3:21–26. The census then lists the clans of the Gershonites, setting up a template that will be followed for the other Levitical subgroups. Four elements are covered: 1) the number of males one month old and older; 2) the place where the group should camp; 3) the name of the family leader; and 4) the area of responsibility. First, the Gershonites had 7,500 males of a month and older (3:22). Secondly, although all the Levites camped between the rest of the Israelites and the Tabernacle, each Levitical group had a specified location. The Gershonites camped to the west, between the sanctuary and the tribal group led by Ephraim. Thirdly, the clan head is named: Eliasaph (3:24). Finally, the duties assigned to the Gershonites are given briefly in 3:25–26. The focus is on their duty to guard sacred items. The procedures for transporting them during Israel's travels is given in the next chapter (Ashley 1993, 84–85). The Gershonites are responsible for the curtains and coverings of the Tabernacle and its courtyard, which visually represented gradations of holiness within the space devoted to God.

3:27–32. The focus shifts to the Kohathites. These verses follow the same template as the Gershonites, beginning with a count of the males over a month in age, which totals 8,600 (3:28). Next, the Kohathites were instructed to camp to the south of sanctuary, between it and the tribal grouping headed by Reuben (3:29). The name of the clan leader is Elizaphan (3:30). The Kohathites had the responsibility to protect the most sacred vessels of Israel's worship, including the ark, the table for bread of the presence, the lampstand, and the screen dividing the Holy Place from the Holy of Holies inside the tabernacle sanctuary (3:31–32). Their proximity to these items reflects their favored status, likely because Moses and Aaron came from this clan (Wenham 2008, 80).

3:33–37. Finally, the text addresses the Merarites. They are identified as the smallest Levitical grouping, totaling 6,200 males of the appropriate age (3:34). They camp to the north of the sanctuary, between it and the tribal group headed by Dan (3:35).[3] Their leader is Zuriel (3:35), and their primary responsibility was the tent pegs, ropes, and poles that provided the frames for putting up the enclosures of the sanctuary.

3:38–39. Finally, the text notes that Moses, Aaron, and his sons camp to the east of the sanctuary. This put them between it and the tribal group led by Judah. Since the sanctuary opens toward the east, their placement here reflects a concern to protect its most vulnerable quarter. Two layers of protection are envisioned: protect from rebellious or oblivious Israelites who might encroach upon the sanctity of the tabernacle courtyards and protection for the Israelites from an outpouring of God's wrath that could result from such a violation (cf. Num. 18:1–7; Cole 2000, 98). Again, any violation would result in death.

This section concludes by stating that the total of Levites males of the appropriate age is

---

[3] It is no coincidence that the least populous Levitical group is on the same side of the sanctuary as the tribal grouping consisting of descendants of Jacob's concubines.

22,000. This figure underlies the discussion of the redemption of the firstborn (3:40–51).[4]

The Redemption of the Firstborn (3:40–51)

3:40–43. These verses give the reason for the census of the Levites. God directs Moses to take the Levites and their livestock in place of the firstborn of the rest of Israel and the firstborn of their livestock. This reinforces God's claim in 3:11–13. The total number of Israelite firstborn is 22,273.[5] This is close to the number of Levite males, but not exactly the same.

3:44–48. After again stating his claim to the firstborn (4:44–45), God gives instructions for how to address the discrepancy. It is necessary to address the unredeemed 273 Israelite firstborn for God to receive all that he is due. Since God delivered all Israel through the Passover event, the nation must fully acknowledge his lordship (Allen 2012, 114). This is indicated through the word פְּדוּיֵי ("ransom") in 3:46, 48. This points to a legal transfer of ownership. God has claimed all firstborn; they are his. For them to return to their families, Israel must redeem them from God.

God declares that the redemption of the additional firstborn must be through monetary means. The price is five shekels, which amounts to six months' wages for a day laborer (Cole 2009, 346). It is also the established price for redeeming a male child from one month to five years old (Lev. 27:6) and the price for redeeming all future generations of firstborn (Num. 18:15–16). God's final instruction is for Moses to give this money to Aaron and his sons, devoting it to sacral purposes.

3:49–51. Moses obeys God's instructions. He collects 1,365 shekels (or 273 x 5) and gives the money to the priests. The origins of the money are unknown. It likely reflects a communal donation rather than singling out 273 families and demanding payment from them. The precision of Moses's obedience gives this section a feeling of completion. Israel is established as God's possession and the Levites are a living testimony to his grace in permitting that claim to be redeemed.

Responsibilities of the Levites: Aaron and the Kohathites (4:1–20)

4:1–3. In this second Levitical census, the Kohathites are counted first. This reflects the fact that they were responsible for transporting the most sacred objects, potentially at the risk of their own lives (Num. 4:15–20; Milgrom 1990, 24). This census also uses a different criterion, counting men between the ages of thirty and fifty years old, which is the age of eligibility for service at the sanctuary.[6]

4:4–6. After the initial statement "This is the service of the Kohathites at the Tent of Meeting" (4:4 NET), the Kohathites disappear until 4:17. Instead, the focus is on what Aaron and the other priests must do to prepare the most sacred items of the sanctuary for travel.

---

4   The sum of Levite males from 3:22, 28, and 34 is actually 22,300. The most likely scenario is that the number of Kohathites in 3:28 should be 8,300 rather than 8,600. This reading is preserved in a few manuscripts of the Septuagint. The Hebrew words for six (שֵׁשׁ) and three (שָׁלֹשׁ) are similar enough to produce such a confusion.

5   It is worth noting again that if there are 22,273 firstborn Israelite males, then each Israelite family unit would need to have approximately fifty children to reach the two to three million population figure implied by a literal reading of the census in Numbers 1 (Allen 2012, 113).

6   Numbers 8:24 identifies the age at which the Levites can begin service as twenty-five. It is possible that Levites may have served a five-year apprenticeship (Allen 2012, 119), or that the text introduces different age requirements for carrying the sanctuary and its implements (Numbers 4) and serving there (Numbers 8; Harrison 1990, 156–57).

Since only Aaron and his sons could live in the presence of the holiness of these items, they must properly cover them so that the Kohathites can transport them.

The instructions begin with the curtain separating the Holy Place from the Holy of Holies. They were to take down the curtain and use it to cover the ark of the covenant before placing an additional layer on top of it.

> TRANSLATION ANALYSIS
> The additional covering for the ark is identified as כְּסוּי עוֹר תַּחַשׁ which is also used to cover the sacrificial altar (cf. 4:14). The first two words mean "a covering of skin/leather," but the meaning of תַּחַשׁ is unknown. One suggestion based on a possible Arabic parallel is that it refers to the hide of an aquatic mammal. A number of English translations adopt "porpoise skin" (NASB, NEB) or "hide of sea cows" (NIV). Another suggestion is that it points to the quality of the material: "fine leather" (CSB, NET, NRSV). A final option is "goatskin" (ESV, NLT), which reflects a preference for the material most likely to be at hand. Some scholars suggest that it refers to color: "yellow-orange" (Milgrom 1990, 26).

The preparation of the ark finishes with the third layer: a cloth of blue (תְּכֵלֶת). This is the same color as the tassels that the Israelites were to attach to their garments to remember God's covenant (Num. 15:38). Once the covering is completed, the priests could put in the carrying poles for the Kohathites.

4:7–12. Similar instructions are given for the Table of the Presence, the lampstand, and the golden altar found in the Holy of Holies. The priests are to put a blue cloth between the table, its vessels, and any remaining bread, then put a scarlet (שָׁנִי) cloth overtop before inserting the carrying poles (4:7–8). The procedure for the lampstand and its implements is similar: covered with blue cloth with an additional layer of leather (תַּחַשׁ; but cf. Translation Analysis above) and placed on a frame for the Kohathites to carry (4:9–10). Next, the incense altar is treated in the same way and prepared for transport, along with its accessories (4:11–12). The altar is to be carried on poles while its smaller implements are placed in a carrying frame (Ashley 1993, 105).

4:13–14. The priests' preparations then move to the sacrificial altar in the tabernacle courtyard. God instructs the priests to clear the ashes of previous sacrifices and place a purple (אַרְגָּמָן) cover over the altar. On top of that are the implements used at the altar, which are wrapped in turn with a leather covering. The priests then put the carrying poles in place, preparing it for the Kohathites.

4:15–16. After Aaron and the priests completed their work, the Kohathites could come and carry these things. However, God also gives a clear warning that they must not touch any of the sacred items under the threat of death. God also appoints Eleazar, the son of Aaron, to oversee these procedures along with the oil and incense used in worship.

4:17–20. The final part of this section provides a reminder of the perilous nature of this task (Cole 2000, 105). God instructs Moses and Aaron to closely supervise the Kohathites so that they do not die from unauthorized viewing of the holy items. Aaron and his sons are thus responsible for doing their preparatory work correctly to protect the Kohathites.

Responsibilities of the Levites: The Gershonites (4:21–28)

4:21–23. The account of the Gershonites begins in the same manner as that of the Kohathites. God instructs Moses and Aaron to count the men between the ages of thirty and fifty.

4:24–26. The Gershonites' area of responsibility consists of the curtains in the tabernacle and its courtyard other than the one assigned to the Kohathites (4:5–6). There are six different collections of fabrics for which they are responsible (Cole 2000, 105). Their work is one degree further removed from God's holiness since there is no warning of death and no detailed priestly preparations required. Numbers 7:6–9 reveals that the Gershonites and Merarites could use ox carts to transport their items, again pointing to their lesser degree of sanctity.

4:27–28. As with the Kohathites, the labor of the Gershonites is placed under the guidance of Aaron and his sons. They are responsible for assigning tasks to the Gershonites. Ithamar, Aaron's second eldest remaining son, has direct authority over them. Since Eleazar will be the next high priest (Num. 20:22–29) it makes sense that Ithamar supervises the Levitical clans dealing with the less sacred material.

Responsibilities of the Levites: The Merarites (4:29–33)

4:29–30. The introduction to the work of the Merarites is more terse than the previous two. It lacks the initial command to take a census. However, the rest of this section mirrors the discussion of the Gershonites and Kohathites. The command to enumerate those men between thirty and fifty years old remains (4:30).

4:31–33. The Merarites are responsible for the framework of the tabernacle. Their task follows the removal of the most sacred items by the Kohathites and the sanctuary coverings by the Gershonites. One additional instruction is that each Merarite receives a specific charge for which they are responsible. This presumably aided in reconstructing the sanctuary precinct when Israel was on the march. Their service also fell under the authority of Ithamar.

Second Census Results (4:34–49)

4:34–45. This passage concludes with a summation of Moses's count of those Levites who fit the appropriate age category. It uses the same format to list the number of Kohathites (4:34–37), Gershonites (4:38–41), and Merarites (4:42–45). The number for each clan is similar, totaling 2,750 Kohathites, 2,630 Gershonites, and 3,200 Merarites.

4:46–49. The total number of Levites who could serve at the sanctuary before Israel set out from Sinai is 8,580. The text is also clear to say that this census reflects the obedience of Moses, Aaron, and the other community leaders. The final verse twice notes that this was carried out in response to God's command.

THEOLOGICAL FOCUS

The exegetical idea behind this text (God selects and commissions the Levites to preserve the holiness of his sanctuary) leads to the following theological focus: *God's holiness establishes his authority over his people*. This brings together two intertwined ideas: God's essential nature and his right to direct his people. These chapters first reinforce God's transcendent holiness. It is impossible for humans to stand in its presence except in the ways he permits. This is revealed through the construction of the sanctuary and its items in Exodus 25:1–31:11, and in the sacrificial system and the inauguration of the priesthood in Leviticus 1–9. Numbers 3–4 directs the entire tribe of Levi to participate in the preservation of God's holiness. The Levites, under the leadership of the priests, must perform their assigned tasks for Israel to live in his presence. The details of their responsibilities reflect the precision required to serve a holy God. Every element of God's sanctuary must be properly handled since it reflects God's nature.

Scripture points out the danger of ignoring these stipulations. After the Philistines returned the captured ark of God, David sought to bring it to Jerusalem. On his first attempt, he had it transported on an ox cart, rather than following the instructions established in these chapters. This led to the death of a man named Uzzah, who touched it and was struck down by God (1 Chron. 13:5–14). David then gathered priests and Levites, commanded them to consecrate themselves, and had them carry the ark on poles in accordance with what God required (1 Chron. 15:11–15). This permitted the ark to come to Jerusalem where eventually it took residence in the temple built by Solomon.

The authority embedded in YHWH's holy nature is also revealed through his claim to the firstborn. God cannot be shortchanged; Israel must redeem the additional 273 non-Levitical firstborn with money. The devotion of the firstborn to YHWH reflects "a thankful acknowledgment of God's prior gift of life and ongoing providence as well as God's claim over his creatures as lord and god" (Stubbs 2009, 49). God's holiness requires his people to respond with obedience to his commands and to acknowledge his authority over every aspect of their lives.

In response, God's grace is evident in his choosing of the Levites to substitute for the firstborn of all Israel. This resonates throughout Scripture, culminating in God's substitution of his only son for the judgment that human sin deserves. This makes its own claims on God's people. Paul reminds the church that we do not belong to ourselves because we were bought with the price of Christ's substitutionary death. This compels us to glorify God with our bodies (1 Cor. 6:19b–20). One commentator summarizes, "Because Christ has redeemed us through his death, we owe him our service" (Sprinkle 2015, 202). The substitution of the Levites to bear witness to the holiness of God thus provides God's people with a framework for understanding how Christ could substitute for the sins of all humanity.

PREACHING AND TEACHING STRATEGIES

Exegetical and Theological Significance

Just as in the tabernacle itself, there were spheres of holiness in the camp. The Levites were given special roles to play in the cultic system, but unauthorized worship resulted in death (3:3). In the nation of Israel, only the Levites were chosen to discharge certain special, holy functions and tasks. It was God alone who sovereignly chose them for these positions (Brown 2002, 35). Numbers 3–4 brings together the themes of holy, priestly service, God's electing sovereignty, and the necessity of redemption via substitution. What is true of the old covenant community here is transposed into a much higher key in the new covenant community, where every member is equally redeemed and part of God's royal and holy priesthood, called out of darkness to worship and praise his name (1 Peter 2:9). All of these blessings are mediated through Christ, the great High Priest and the one whose death secures redemption so that we can belong to the people of God and serve him in holiness and joy.

The physical work of the priests and Levites establishes principles for Christian worship today. No subset of believers in the church is tasked with taking care of the structure of the tabernacle or any of its accoutrements, but every believer is called to worship God and help protect his holiness in the covenant community. We are to love God and love our neighbor. There are different spiritual gifts and different roles to play, but every Christian is called to engage in service to the Lord. There are proper ways of dividing up kingdom work, but we are all on the same team; we are all members of the same body, with Christ as our Head.

Preaching Idea

Through Christ the High Priest, there is now a holy priesthood of all believers.

Contemporary Connections

What does it mean?
What does it mean that through Christ there is now a holy priesthood of all believers? Incredibly, this means that no follower of Christ

needs to go to a priest here on earth to have access to the God who is holy, holy, holy (Isa. 6:3). Through union with Christ, even the lowliest Christian receives a holy position that surpasses the roles and tasks assigned to the Levites. As much as it was a solemn and weighty privilege to be in charge of the tabernacle and to guard the holiness of God while protecting the people, the new covenant priesthood is greater. Today, believers worship God and lead others to his holy presence through the gospel of Jesus Christ, who is the fulfillment of the entire old covenant priestly sacrificial system.

The tabernacle was partly designed to bring people to God, but it was mainly set up to keep people *out* of God's holy presence! It was a reminder that God was with them, but that they had been banished from the sanctuary of Eden. Only the Levites could draw near; only the priests could go inside; only the high priest could go into the Holy of Holies once per year, through the shedding of blood. Today, through Christ, the way of access to God is open, and every believer can go in.

Is it true?
Is it really true that every believer is given this special priestly designation? Again, Peter answers this question decisively: "But you are a chosen people, a royal priesthood, a holy nation, God's special possession, that you may declare the praises of him who called you out of darkness into his wonderful light" (1 Peter 2:9). P.eter also declared that every believer is being built into God's house—with Christ as the cornerstone— so that we are all "a holy priesthood" (v. 5). The only mediator we have between ourselves and the Father is Jesus Christ (1 Tim. 2:5). Yes, this is true: there is a priesthood of all believers through the great High Priest, Jesus Christ.

Now what?
How do we live out our God-given identity as a member of a holy priesthood through Jesus Christ? Peter tells us that we are priests in order to declare the praises of our Savior and Redeemer (1 Peter 2:9). We are further exhorted to offer God sacrifices of praise (Heb. 13:15). Without doubt, a major part of our priestly service is acknowledging the holiness of God and calling people to him through the sanctifying blood of Jesus. We are also to pray as or Lord Jesus taught us, asking that God's name be hallowed, which means that his character and nature are seen, recognized, and treated as holy (Matt. 6:9). Sin in the covenant community is also to be dealt with, graciously but firmly.

Creativity in Presentation
Almost everyone can relate to moving from one house to another, or trying to wrap up something fragile for shipping. We know that there is a difference between moving cheap items and moving expensive heirlooms or objects of priceless sentimental value. Imagine being tasked with taking down the *Mona Lisa* and moving it across the ocean, or transporting a Stradivarius violin from one concert venue to another. Now imagine being tasked with moving a container filled with volatile chemicals that will explode if dropped or jostled. Any volunteers?

It can be nerve-wracking dealing with boxes marked *fragile*, but what would we do with a box marked *holy*? The priests and Levites, in handling things that were directly related to God, handled things of incalculable value. They also knew that if they mishandled them, they would die. How would you feel if that was your job? How seriously would you take it, especially if previous workers *had* died in this work (cf. Num. 3:3)?

In Christ, we are covered with righteousness so that we can serve in the presence of the holy God. Our fear of eternal death is removed since Christ died in our place, so now we can handle holy, spiritual realities with awe, wonder, and joy. This does not mean that we take them lightly: on the contrary, we take them with the utmost reverence. But because Christ died for us, there is no condemnation and we are set

The Census of the Levites and Their Responsibilities (3:1–4:49)

free to serve him well. If you had to defuse a bomb, you would be awfully relieved if a bomb squad engineer was able to help you through it. When it comes to handling holy realities in the presence of our holy God, Christ not only guides us; he covers us and protects us with his own perfect holiness. Through Christ the High Priest, there is now a holy priesthood of all believers. Each one of us is equipped to serve God through Jesus Christ who makes us holy so that we can handle holy things.

To emphasize that through Christ there is a priesthood of all believers, this passage can be divided according to the following outline:

- Aaron and his sons serve as priests who mediate between Israel and a holy God (3:1–4).

- God appoints the Levites in place of Israel's firstborn to serve the priests (3:5–39).

- God's holy nature requires an exact redemption of Israel's firstborn (3:40–51).

- Caring for the things that God has ordained as holy is an essential task (4:1–33).

- Preserving God's holiness requires obeying God's commands (4:34–49).

DISCUSSION QUESTIONS

1. What theological significance is there in God's claim to the "firstborn" of the Israelites? Why must the redemption of the firstborn be so precise?

2. What do we learn about God's holiness from the care and precision needed to transport his sanctuary? How do we as sinful people draw near to such a holy God?

3. What comparisons can we make between the different duties of the Levites and the responsibilities of pastors, teachers, elders, and other office holders in the New Testament church?

4. How do the duties performed by the priests and Levites point us to the work of Christ (see Hebrews 9:1–28)?

Numbers 5:1–10

EXEGETICAL IDEA
Living with a holy God requires a commitment to be separate from both physical and moral imperfections.

THEOLOGICAL FOCUS
God provides the means through which his people can dwell in his holiness.

PREACHING IDEA
We are sanctified in Christ, so act like it!

PREACHING POINTERS
God organized his people, established his presence in the middle of the community, and set aside the Levites for special service. However, whether or not someone was a priest or Levite, every member of the community was to be holy and clean. These ten verses establish the principles of being holy in God's presence and faithful toward our neighbor. The physical reality in 5:1–4 points to the spiritual principle of holy moral purity. Those who are unclean cannot remain in the camp of his people. When people sin against each other, justice must be done. In some cases, what is required is not only confession and forgiveness, but also restitution. These verses teach us that we must be holy toward God, and that there are both divine and civil consequences for sin.

In the covenant community, we have responsibilities to both God and our fellow covenant members. Only through the blood of Jesus Christ can we be purified and made clean, and only through his righteousness can we be numbered among his people. Having been redeemed, we must take care not to sin against those who bear his image. When we do, we must make restitution. This is a warning to help keep us from sinning in the first place. Ultimately, the law is fulfilled by Christ, and Paul tells us that love is the fulfillment of the law (Rom. 13:8–10). If we loved God and our neighbor perfectly, we would never sin against them. God reminds us that we are sanctified in Christ, and then tells us to act like it!

MAINTAINING PURITY IN THE CAMP (5:1–10)

LITERARY STRUCTURE AND THEMES

Numbers 5:1–10 marks a significant transition in the first section of the book. Whereas Numbers 2–4 reflects an idealized picture of God's relationship with Israel, the next two chapters consider the procedures necessary to maintain the holiness that God requires. Numbers 5–6 reflects this concern in a few different ways. In 5:1–10, the text addresses how to maintain the holiness of the community in the face of bodily impurity (5:1–4) or sinful activity (5:5–10). These broad categories are followed by an extended discussion of a specific covenantal transgression: marital infidelity (5:11–31). Finally, the Nazirite vow found in 6:1–21 presents the opposite perspective in which an Israelite could seek to show more devotion to God than the law demanded. These three passages thus build upon the administrative arrangements of Numbers 2–4 and explore how the community must respond to God's holiness.

The phrase "the Lord said to Moses" in 5:1, 5, 11, and 6:1 provides the structural cues for these chapters. Numbers 5:1–10 is identified as a preaching unit even though the introductory formula is used twice. A shared concern for the purity of the camp unites 5:1–4 and 5:5–10, which permits the expositor to demonstrate how God's concern for holiness shapes situations of both ceremonial impurity and sinful behavior. Each scenario follows a similar pattern: 1) an introductory statement that God spoke to Moses (5:1, 5), 2) a divine command to tell the people what God requires (5:2a, 6a), and 3) the substance of the command (5:2b–4, 6b–10; Allen 2012, 124). This passage neatly divides into two sections but is shaped by the overarching thematic frame of maintaining holiness in Israel.

- *Preserving the Camp from Physical Impurity (5:1–4)*
- *Preserving the Camp from Moral Impurity (5:5–10)*

EXPOSITION

Living in God's presence is a matter of serious concern. God's essential identity is that he is holy (Lev. 19:2). This motivates his actions and what he requires from his people (Hartley 2003, 420–21). Holiness emanates from him alone which means that people and objects can be sanctified, or considered holy, only through his presence (Alexander 2012, 243–44). Although the specific vocabulary of holiness is rare in this passage (cf. 5:9–10), it provides the necessary conceptual backdrop. Much of Leviticus is devoted to responding to God's holiness through ritual procedure and moral requirement, even including an example of the deadly consequences of violating it (Lev. 10:1–3). That baseline understanding reveals that living with a holy God requires a commitment to be pure from both physical and moral imperfections.

Holiness

At its essence, holiness involves separation from things that are profane or unclean. These are "simply incompatible with the holy Lord God" (Ross 2002, 45). Notably, it is possible to be in a position of uncleanness before God without having committed a moral or ethical transgression. A simple example of that would be contact with a dead body, a common occurrence during Israel's wilderness wandering (Num. 5:2;

> 19:1–22). This type of uncleanness reflects the breakdown of order and systems of life, bringing in the possibility of chaos and death (Stubbs 2009, 54–55). The three forms of uncleanness in Numbers 5:2 all reflect encounters with disorder or death that require a remedy to remain in God's presence. However, uncleanness can also have a moral component. Anyone who breaches a boundary or command established by God has brings iniquity into God's presence and risks spreading it throughout the community (Alexander 2012, 245). This reality reflects the concerns of Numbers 5:5–10. What unifies 5:1–10 is the reality that God cannot coexist with uncleanness, and so the Israelite community must maintain standards of holiness through the procedures that God provides.[1]

It is also important to note that that many of these impurities are impermanent. In Leviticus, purification rituals for restoration accompany the instructions to remove the ceremonially impure from God's presence (Klawans 2000, 25–26).[2] One can see an element of grace at work in this system. Ceremonial impurity is not necessarily a matter of permanent exclusion, but a reflection of God's nature. Restoration back into the community is anticipated and celebrated since "purification is easy, and open to all who wish for it" (Douglas 2004, 158).

Preserving the Camp from Physical Impurity (5:1–4)

5:1–2. The text begins with the formulaic introduction "the LORD said to Moses." Then, 5:2 reveals that the Israelites are to remove from the camp those afflicted with three categories of physical impurity: skin disease (צָרוּעַ), genital discharge (זָב), and uncleanness from a dead body (טָמֵא לָנָפֶשׁ).[3] Many English translations render the first category (צָרוּעַ) as "leper" (NASB, NET) or "leprous" (ESV), which reflects the Septuagint's use of λεπρὸν. While clinical leprosy (known as Hansen's disease) is probably reflected in this passage (Harrison 1990, 101), the term צָרוּעַ almost certainly encompasses other disfiguring skin conditions such as psoriasis and vitiligio (Allen 2012, 125; Gane 2004, 235). Since the focus is on the ritual impurity brought about by any of these conditions, an exact diagnosis is unnecessary. Although not stated here, presumably those afflicted in this way can be restored to the camp following the procedures found in Leviticus 14:1–32. The role of the priests in examining the afflicted individual attests to the sacral nature of the procedure. The presence of these physical impurities reflects disorder that goes against God's perfection. God's priestly representatives determine when an individual can be restored to the community.

The second condition is that of genital discharge (זָב). This word is the participial form of the root זוב, which indicates a flow or an emission. It reflects the regulations found in Leviticus 15 which apply to both men (Lev. 15:2) and women (Lev. 15:19, 25). Although Leviticus 15:19 categorizes the regular menstrual cycle with this root, it seems evident that normal bodily functions are not in view. Instead, it reflects conditions including an excessive secretion of mucus

---

1   To fully comprehend how God's holiness shapes Numbers 5:1–10, we must note that the two scenarios revisit legislation from Leviticus. The first covers situations mentioned at length in Leviticus 13–15, while the second restates the requirements of the reparation offering from Leviticus 6:1–7. Consequently, we can supplement any gaps in the present passage with the more extended requirements found in Leviticus.

2   Klawans notes that the regulations on skin diseases in Leviticus 13 and the purification procedures in Leviticus 14 are roughly the same length.

3   The term נֶפֶשׁ ("person, soul") is typically used for living people; however, on several occasions it points to a dead body. This is made evident in Numbers 19:13 which uses נֶפֶשׁ in conjunction with two words from the root מות ("to die").

on the part of a man, or a chronic vaginal discharge indicating a uterine disorder on the part of a woman (Gane 2004, 258). The persistent loss of these fluids reflects a disordered physical body that spread ceremonial uncleanness to people and items throughout the camp (Lev. 15:4–7, 20–27). People with this condition must leave the camp, though they could be restored to the community following the procedure of waiting for seven days after the cessation of the discharge and offering the proper purification sacrifices (Lev. 15:13–15 for a man, 15:28–30 for a woman).

The final condition in Numbers 5:2 is that of uncleanness brought about by touching a corpse. Since holiness is equated with life and order, a corpse reflects the opposite qualities of death and disorder. Anyone who carries that impurity with them cannot be in God's presence. It is possible that there are hygienic reasons for this restriction, but they pale in comparison to the necessity of keeping death away from God's presence (Cole 2000, 110–11). Leviticus 21:1–3 requires priests to keep themselves free of corpse contamination, but Numbers 5:1–2 along with 19:1–22 expands the requirement to the entire community. Numbers 5:1–4 does not discuss the remedy for corpse contamination, but God provides one in 19:1–22.[4] Fittingly, it is found after Israel's many rebellions against God which have led to the death sentence for the first generation. Although Numbers 5:1–2 is abrupt in calling for Israelites to be removed from the camp because of corpse impurity, the broader context reveals that restitution was possible.

5:3. The next verse articulates the consequence of the impurity: the afflicted man or woman is to be removed from the Israelite camp. The camp represents the space sanctified by God's presence. Within the boundaries of the camp, God manifested his holiness in a graduated fashion, requiring greater and greater sanctification as one approached closer to the divine presence (Jenson 1992, 90). The requirements increased as one moved into the tabernacle courtyard, the outer chamber of the tabernacle itself, and ultimately into the Holy of Holies. This verse strengthens the required response for genital discharge from Leviticus 15 and corpse contamination from Numbers 19. In those passages, the afflicted individual is excluded from the presence of God at the tabernacle, whereas according to Numbers 5:3, all three categories now require the unclean individual to leave the camp (Stubbs 2009, 56). This may reflect an elevation in the sacral status of the camp in the context of the holy war for which God authorized the census in Numbers 1 (Gane 2004, 520).

5:4. This part of the passage concludes with a brief narrative of obedience. There are no specific cases mentioned here, nor is there any discussion of how those affected would be brought back into the community. The thrust of Numbers 5:1–4 thus demonstrates Israel's commitment to be a holy nation. YHWH declares what is necessary to dwell in his holy presence and Israel responds.

Preserving the Camp from Moral Impurity (5:5–10)

5:5–7. The text transitions to the procedure for dealing with failures that incur moral guilt. Numbers 5:6 explicitly indicates that these regulations apply to both men and women, noting that the obligations of repentance apply to every member of the Israelite community (Allen 2012, 129). These verses resemble Leviticus 6:1–7 in terms of the requirement to acknowledge one's sin and to offer the required reparation. The close parallels suggest that similar offenses are in view. Although no specific sins are listed here, the Leviticus passage mentions deceiving a neighbor, stealing lost property, and

---

4   This is known as the "red cow ceremony."

swearing falsely (Lev. 6:1–3). These infractions have a deleterious effect on relationships within the community. God is also a wronged party since violating oaths sworn in his name brings it into disrepute. A possible scenario is that the offender has misappropriated or stolen someone's property and then denied their offense in an oath sworn in YHWH's name. Consequently, "the LORD has been made an accomplice to the defrauding of man" (Milgrom 1998, 337).

> *TRANSLATION ANALYSIS*
> There is some discussion of the expression חַטֹּאת הָאָדָם ("sins of the man") in 5:6. It can be understood as either a subjective genitive ("sins that humans commit") or an objective genitive ("sins toward a fellow human"). Most English translations prefer the subjective genitive:
> - "any sin that people commit" (NET)
> - "the sins that people commit" (ESV)
> - "the sin they have committed" (NIV)
>
> This maintains a broader perspective and permits God to be among the aggrieved parties (Ashley 1993, 112–13).

The concern for the sanctity of the camp comes out again in the declaration that these offenses have the result of "breaking faith with the LORD" (5:6b ESV, NET). The Hebrew term is מָעַל, which involves either improper contact with the holy (Lev. 5:14–19; 14:10–14; Num. 6:12) or the violation of an oath sworn before God (Lev. 6:1–7; Num. 5:6–8; Boda 2009, 54). This confirms that wrongs committed against a fellow Israelite also reflect transgressions against YHWH (Cole 2000, 110).[5]

The last phrase of Numbers 5:6 along with 5:7 moves toward the remedy for the offense. The transgressor must first recognize their guilt. The verbal root אשם in 5:6b–7a reflects an intermediate stage between the sin and the reparation sacrifice in which the offender "realizes his guilt" (5:6b ESV) either through the pangs of conscience or through someone revealing it (Boda 2009, 64). A confession of sin follows the realization, signaling the offender's willingness to make reparations. This means that the infraction can be remediated through the sacrificial system (Milgrom 1990, 35). Following Leviticus 6:5, the offense is given a monetary value, which would be simple to calculate in the case of lost or stolen property but more challenging in other scenarios. The offender must fully restore the value to the aggrieved party and add on a penalty of one-fifth. The one-fifth additional penalty is severe enough to teach a lesson (Harrison 1990, 104), but not excessively punitive, which could discourage confession (Milgrom 1990, 35). The confession and reparation were also necessarily public in nature since the offender must directly repay the aggrieved party before offering a sacrifice that would involve a priest. Public acknowledgement of guilt provides another corrective.

5:8. Numbers 5:8 adds a unique contribution to the process of making reparations. It considers a scenario in which the aggrieved party is no longer living and, beyond that, has no close relative who can receive restitution on their behalf.

> **Kinsman-Redeemer**
> The word referring to the close relative is גֹּאֵל, often translated "kinsman-redeemer." It is a role centered upon protecting the rights and status of an extended kinship group (Allen 2012, 129–30). This took on several very different forms, all of which involved the redemption of some kind of loss for the family (Ashley 1993, 651). The גֹּאֵל was responsible to redeem a kinsman who fell into the hands of a foreigner through debt-slavery (Lev. 25:48–49), to perform levirate marriage (Ruth 3:13), and to redeem the family member's

---

5 In 2 Samuel 12:13, David expresses a similar sentiment in his confession after the murder of Uriah where he acknowledges that he has sinned against YHWH (Allen 2012, 129). See also the poetic acknowledgement of David's sin in Psalm 51.

> property if it became necessary to sell it (Ruth 4:4). The גֹּאֵל also had a responsibility to seek retribution in the case of death. They had the right to take a life for a life in the case of deliberate murder (Num. 35:19–21), but in the case of accidental manslaughter their right would be superseded if the offender fled to a city of refuge (Num. 35:22–25). In the case described in Numbers 5:5–10, the גֹּאֵל represents the deceased family member in receiving the restitution and one-fifth penalty.

Without a גֹּאֵל, the offender who has recognized their guilt has no apparent means to make the necessary amends. YHWH declares that in that scenario, a priest would function as the גֹּאֵל. This makes sense given that all sin is sin against God. In this instance, the offender brings their gift to the sanctuary and devotes it to God (Milgrom 1990, 35).

Numbers 5:8 concludes by noting that the offender will also offer a ram as an atonement offering. This matches the procedure described in Leviticus 6:6–7. In the normal course of affairs, the ram provides expiation for the offense against God, while the monetary penalty provided recompense for the aggrieved party (Gane 2004, 134–35). Of course, in the current scenario, both elements go to God since there is no defrauded party or family representative.

5:9–10. The passage concludes by confirming that the priest has the right to a share of what was provided by the offender. It is one of the perquisites of priestly service. The text essentially says the same thing three times. First, 5:9 refers to the offering as תְּרוּמָה, which elsewhere refers to the priestly portion of cereal offerings (Lev. 7:14), animal sacrifices (Lev. 7:20; Num. 6:20), or required tithes (Num. 18:24–29; Ashley 1993, 116). The offering is also described as "holy donations" (Num. 5:9 ESV), which means that it is devoted to God's purposes and separated from mundane use (Harrison 1990, 106). Numbers 5:9b then notes that when the children of Israel come before the priest, their donations "will be his" (5:9b NET).

The final verse also reinforces this, although the syntax is complicated. The best way to read 5:10a is that the one presenting the offering brings it for the priest (Ashley 1993, 117).[6] The same sentiment is expressed in 5:10b, which explicitly mentions the priest as the recipient of the worshipper's offering. This repetition reinforces that "the offering presented to the priests truly belonged to the priests" (Allen 2012, 129). As God's representatives they could make use of gifts brought to purify the community.

THEOLOGICAL FOCUS

The exegetical idea (Living with a holy God requires a commitment to purity from both physical and moral imperfections) leads to this theological focus: *God provides the means through which his people can dwell in his holiness.*

Numbers 5:1–10 reflects two broad categories of impurities that separate Israel from God. First, God announces that certain types of physical uncleanness cannot exist in his presence, likely because they recall death and disorder. Secondly, transgressions against fellow Israelites and improperly sworn oaths invite moral and ethical impurity into the camp. It is a reminder that all sin is sin against God. This threatens to sever Israel's relationship with God. However,

---

6   Numbers 5:10a in Hebrew reads וְאִישׁ אֶת־קֳדָשָׁיו לוֹ יִהְיוּ. It is easiest to read אִישׁ ("man") as referring to the one who brings the offering, though it could refer to the priest (Milgrom 1990, 36). This does not materially affect the meaning since in that case the priest is the subject of the verb and the referent of the pronominal suffixes on "his holy donations" and "to him." The NIV takes a different approach and suggests that the antecedent of לוֹ is the worshipper himself, reading "Sacred things belong to their owner." This is less likely since the whole intention of offerings to God is that worshippers recognize God's primary claim to their resources.

YHWH desires to maintain communion with his people and provides means of restoration for both physical and moral uncleanness.

As the story of Scripture continues, it points us to the great High Priest who makes lasting atonement through his own blood, rather than through the blood of animals or the ashes of a heifer (Heb. 9:11–14).[7] This inaugurates a new way of cleansing impurity, with Jesus himself paying the penalty to sanctify things that were once unclean. The sacrificial system was a gracious gift of God that provided Israel with the opportunity to be a "holy nation" (Exod. 19:6) whom he had chosen from himself. Israel's commitment to remain physically and morally clean is nothing less than the appropriate response to what God has done. In similar fashion, Peter articulates how the church is called to be a "holy nation" (1 Peter 2:9) in response to the God who chooses us and sanctifies us so that we can offer appropriate spiritual sacrifices (1 Peter 2:5). These include abstaining from sinful desires and moral impurities that wage war against our souls (1 Peter 2:11). Throughout Scripture, God preserves his holiness while graciously providing ways in which his people can come into his presence.

The work of Christ also speaks directly to the issue of physical uncleanness. In the Gospels, Jesus interacts with people afflicted by the same disqualifying ailments mentioned in Numbers 5:1–4: lepers (Mark 1:40–45), genital discharge (Mark 5:25–34), and corpse contamination (Mark 5:35–43). However, this contact does not render Jesus unclean. Rather, Jesus's power overcomes the impurity. It remains true that God is holy, separated from death and disorder, and through the person of Jesus Christ his holiness destroys the uncleanness and restores the afflicted person (Stubbs 2009, 56). Jesus also speaks to the issue of conflating physical disability with moral failure. In John 9:2, the disciples ask, "Rabbi, who sinned, this man or his parents that he was born blind?" (NIV). Jesus declares that neither is true and that this man would display the work of God in his life (John 9:3). While blindness was not a condition that merited removal from the camp, it did disqualify an individual from priestly service (Lev. 21:18). However, Jesus uses his power to heal to show that he can restore those whom he chooses, while also warning the Pharisees of the dangers of their spiritual blindness (John 9:40–41).

The work of Jesus also provides the means of cleansing moral and ethical failings including those described in Numbers 5:5–10. It is through the resurrected Christ that final reparation for sin has been made on our behalf. This reality is why Paul chastises the church in Corinth for its divisions and mistreatment of fellow believers at the Lord's Supper. Such behavior while celebrating our deliverance from sin cannot be countenanced. Paul declares that these sins are not just against brothers and sisters in Christ, but also against the body and blood of Christ (1 Cor. 11:22, 27). The consequence is discipline, aimed at a reformation of character and behavior to avoid final condemnation (1 Cor 11:32).

PREACHING AND TEACHING STRATEGIES

Exegetical and Theological Significance

Numbers 5:1–10 connects with a wide array of biblical and theological themes, each of which have massive implications. Such themes include the character of God, holiness, purity, sin, confession, restitution, forgiveness, obedience, law, maintaining community, and moral responsibility. Verses 1–4 were to be applied literally in Israel, but in the wider context of Scripture they establish spiritual principles through visible, physical realities. Until they are made pure, those who are unclean cannot be

---

7   As mentioned above, Numbers 19 details how the ashes of the heifer provide cleansing for corpse contamination.

inside of the camp with the people of God and in his holy presence. There needs to be a sovereignly provided remedy for our uncleanness. Ultimately, we need a spiritual cleansing and washing: it is our hearts that are unclean. Only through the cleansing blood of Jesus can we be purified from our spiritual and moral contamination. Only through his cleanness can our uncleanness be removed.

Numbers 5:5–10 clearly reveals that there are consequences for our sin, both in terms of our relationship with God and in our relationship with our neighbor and community. Any sin against an image-bearer of God is a sin against God himself. It is important to recognize that this passage is not legitimizing penance or indulgences; on the contrary, it is actually warning us against breaking faith with the Lord and our neighbor in the first place. The penalty for sin isn't given so that we can calculate the risk-reward of sinning—with the fallback of restitution if we're caught—but rather to instruct us not to sin in the first place.

Having been made pure by a holy God and installed as a member of his holy people, we have responsibilities to him and the other members of his community. We are to live out our holy standing before him, loving him supremely and loving our neighbor as ourselves. As Paul says, love is the fulfillment of the law (cf. Rom. 13:8–10). If we truly loved our neighbor, we wouldn't sin against them. In the gospel, we find forgiveness for our sins and purification from them. In Christ, we are made holy, and by the Holy Spirit we are called to walk in holiness.

Preaching Idea
We are sanctified in Christ, so act like it!

Contemporary Connections

What does it mean?
What does it mean that we are sanctified in Christ, and how do we live it out? Even a lifetime of discipleship and a full career of preaching and teaching will not exhaust the depths of this theme. To be holy or sanctified is to be set apart to belong to God, or to be reserved exclusively for his service. God is holy, holy, holy (Isa. 6:3; Rev. 4:8), and his people are called to "be holy, for I am holy" (Lev. 11:44, quoted by Peter in 1 Peter 1:16). Being made holy can only happen through faith in Christ and union with him by the Holy Spirit. Everyone who believes in Jesus is sanctified in this important way: they are transferred into the sphere or realm of the sacred, and they belong to God.

It is from this position of sanctification in Christ that God's people are to think, feel, act, and worship. In systematic theology we talk about *progressive sanctification* as a lifetime process of growing in holiness, in distinction from justification, which is a once-for-all declaration of God. Yet progressive sanctification can only flow from *positional sanctification*: we can only live out holiness if we have been made holy through Christ and the Spirit. We do not make ourselves holy; we live out the holiness that is gifted to us by grace. New ways of behaving flow from our new heart. When it comes to holy living, we are to be what we are; our actions are to reflect our standing before God. Scripture is filled with instructions for worship and moral living, and these reveal the standards for our lives.

Is it true?
Is it true that we are sanctified in Christ, and we are able to live out our holiness? One way of answering this question is to look at the use of the word "saints" in the New Testament. To be a saint simply means to be sanctified, and Paul uses this designation indiscriminately of every believer in the church. Paul further refers to believers as "God's chosen people, holy and dearly loved" (Col. 3:12). Yes, it is true that we are holy in the sight of God, through Jesus Christ.

Since we are holy in Christ, we are empowered to live in a way that is characterized by holiness and purity. Peter tells us that since

God is holy, we are to be holy in all that we do (1 Peter 1:15). The author of Hebrews warns that without holiness no one will see the Lord (Heb. 12:14). Paul tells the Corinthians to separate themselves from evil, and then encourages them by saying: "Therefore, since we have these promises, dear friends, let us purify ourselves from everything that contaminates body and spirit, perfecting holiness out of reverence for God" (1 Cor. 7:1). Having been made perfectly holy in Christ, we can reflect that holiness in all that we do.

Now what?
How do we find sanctification in Christ, and how do we live it out? The former requires belief in Jesus (i.e., accepting the gospel), and the latter requires keeping in step with the Spirit. Motivated by grace and love, Scripture is filled with teaching about how to live in moral and spiritual purity before God and in relationship to our neighbors. The Sermon on the Mount is a good place to start for examples of Jesus's teaching about holy living. Ephesians 4:17–6:20 contains a treasury of moral and practical instructions, rooted in the incredible theology of Ephesians 1–3.

For one memorable illustration, Colossians 3:1–17 grounds our holiness in being raised with Christ, and then tells us to take off our sinful habits and put on new virtues and behaviors, just like we would take off dirty clothes and put on clean ones. Examples could be multiplied across the canon, but the preacher will want to be emphatic that holiness is found only in Christ, and that from this union with him we are to live out our holiness. This calls for action and not just theory!

One particular way that we are to live out our holiness according to Numbers 5:5–10 is to make restitution when we have wronged others. Ask the church if they have any outstanding moral debts to others that they have not repaid. Do we owe people an apology? Do we owe them time, money, or effort? Have we taken advantage of our family, church, neighbor, or employer? Are there things we have done that people don't know about, but which we need to make right? Part of holy living is confession and restitution. Challenge the congregation that if there is anything outstanding, they need to make it right ASAP.

Creativity in Presentation
Positive, healthy transformation is something to celebrate. Whether it's before-and-after pictures of a journey to physical health, the story of an addict who beat their addiction, or simply the tale of an underdog who made good, we can find ourselves inspired to pursue excellence through the successful transformation of others. There is a reason why *A Christmas Carol* by Charles Dickens is a literary treasure, and why it continues to not only be read but also made into both live action and animated movies. (The black-and-white 1951 version with Alastair Sim is still the best movie adaptation![8]) The preacher of this text can tell a story of transformation, show some slides depicting positive change, or show some before-and-after scenes from a depiction of Scrooge. The point is that we were unclean and lost in sin, but through redemption we are transformed to live differently.

If the church has a drama team, having an individual write and perform a short monologue from the perspective of the leper who has healed by Jesus (Matt. 8:1–4) could be very impactful. They were living with the uncleanness that removed them from the community, but Jesus touched them and they were cleansed. Jesus restores the unclean. How would such a person feel? How would their life be different as a result of their encounter with Jesus?

Another perfect story of transformation—also one that can be dramatized well—is found in Luke 19:1–10. There are some humorous

---

8 The Muppets version is a close second in my (Joel's) opinion.

elements in the Zacchaeus pericope, but the text bristles with tension and disdain until Jesus arrives on the scene. Notice that Jesus brings salvation to Zacchaeus, and then Zacchaeus voluntarily and joyfully offers to make restitution to all of those he has taken advantage of. Numbers 5:5–10 gives a law of restitution, but the grace of Jesus motivates us to do more.

In terms of a didactic instruction that illustrates the principle of this passage, Paul told the Ephesians, "Anyone who has been stealing must steal no longer, but must work, doing something useful with their own hands, that they may have something to share with those in need" (Eph. 4:28). Notice the transformation:

1. They used to steal.

2. They are to stop stealing.

3. They are to get an honest job.

4. They are to share with the poor.

That's amazing! The thief used to steal the goods that others earned by their hard work, and now the thief is working hard to freely give what they earn to other people! Paul pleads with his audience to remember that they are sanctified in Christ and now must act like it.

To highlight how our actions must reflect the reality of our sanctification in Christ, one possible outline for this passage is:

- God's holiness cannot tolerate uncleanness (5:1–4).

- Sin is an offense against God (5:5–7).

- God provides means of restitution in cases of sin and uncleanness (5:8–10).

DISCUSSION QUESTIONS

1. Why could uncleanness not exist in God's presence? Does this seem unfair to those suffering from medical maladies? How do the procedures for purification (found in Leviticus) help us read this text?

2. How does Numbers 5:1–4 help us to understand the context of Jesus's interactions with those who had physical impurities?

3. Why is confession of sin necessary to remain in God's presence? How does making restitution help to complete the process of confession?

4. In what ways can we make restitution for our sin, both to those whom we have wronged and to God?

Numbers 5:11–31

EXEGETICAL IDEA
God alone is a suitable judge of cases of suspected adultery.

THEOLOGICAL FOCUS
Marital fidelity among God's people reflects his holiness.

PREACHING IDEA
God designs, creates, sustains, and protects covenant relationships.

PREACHING POINTERS
If we do not understand the divine design and sacredness of the marriage covenant, we will not be able to grasp the significance of this passage. Marriage was created by God, and he alone has the right to set its covenant parameters. Idolatry is often depicted as spiritual adultery, and that analogy helps us understand the significance of both. It is a terrible thing for the people of God to pursue other gods, and since Christ is the bridegroom of the church, it is unthinkable that his bride would engage in illicit relations with others. God is faithful to the covenant, and God's people are called to be faithful in their covenants, too.

This text must be handled with sensitivity and tact. There is a lot of pain in marriages. Some have been divorced, and others are working through confessed adultery. Some people are married to irrationally jealous spouses and face false accusations. In this passage, a guilty spouse is cursed, but an innocent one is exonerated. Nevertheless, in either case, there is no doubt that by the time things had reached the stage of this trial, the damage in the home was already incalculable. Look to Christ for forgiveness and reconciliation, and thank God that he is perfectly faithful to his covenant promises. Given the theological and practical ramifications of marriage dynamics, we need to remember that God designs, creates, sustains, and protects covenant relationships.

THE TEST FOR INFIDELITY (5:11–31)

LITERARY STRUCTURE AND THEMES

Numbers 5:11–31 further addresses the theme of purity in the camp so that Israel can remain in God's holy presence. Whereas 5:1–10 takes a broad view of physical and spiritual uncleanness, 5:11–31 examines a specific issue in great detail: suspected infidelity. One can link the husband's jealousy here with an individual's realization of guilt in 5:6. Both cases reflect situations in which unacknowledged impurity needs to be brought to light (Knierim and Coats 2005, 83). Repetition is a hallmark of the passage as it uses the same expressions related to the nature of the offense, the ritual for determining guilt, and the prescribed penalty throughout.

It needs to be stated upfront that this is a difficult passage to read in a modern context since it only addresses the case where a husband has doubts about his wife's fidelity. However, it should be remembered that the theme of sexual fidelity on the part of both parties is God's creational intention (Gen. 2:24) and Scripture's consistent expectation (Prov. 7:1–27; 1 Cor. 5:1–13; 7:1–5; Eph. 5:25–26).[1] Some of the particularities of this passage will become clearer when it is situated in its context.

- **Introduction to the Case (5:11–14)**
- **The Body of the Case (5:15–28)**
  - *The Initiation of the Proceedings (5:15)*
  - *The Priestly Preparation of the Ritual (5:16–18)*
  - *The Administration of the Oath (5:19–24)*
  - *The Execution of the Ritual (5:25–28)*
- **Recapitulation of the Case (5:29–31)**[2]

EXPOSITION

Marital fidelity is a significant concern for the maintenance of societal cohesion. Apart from reflecting God's creational design, concerns about spousal fidelity have covenantal implications. When the Israelites received their inheritance in the Promised Land, Joshua divided it "clan by clan" (Josh. 13:15, 24, 29, etc.). Thus, knowing who belong to each family reflects the progression of God's promises throughout the generations. Confusion on that score would complicate future inheritance claims (Allen 2012, 133). Further, the spirit of jealousy mentioned in 5:14 is toxic to intimate relationships and disrupts the harmony of the community. Unacknowledged infidelity also means that there is sin among the people that has not been remediated, calling into jeopardy Israel's relationship with God.

This passage addresses a particularly difficult case in which adultery is suspected but not proven.[3] The penalty for proven adultery is the death of both parties (Lev. 20:10), but not all cases are clear-cut. This passage provides much-needed nuance and eliminates potential overreach based solely on a husband's suspicions. It demonstrates that God alone is a suitable judge of cases of suspected adultery.

---

1   This will be developed further in the Theological Focus section.
2   This structure is based upon the work of Frymer-Kensky 1984, 14.
3   Though not explicitly stated, the intended scenario is likely consensual infidelity since a woman did have legal recourse in cases of sexual coercion (Deut. 22:25–29).

The Test for Infidelity (5:11–31)

Introduction to the Case (5:11–14)

5:11–13. This passage is framed as divine instruction in 5:11 through the common expression "The LORD said to Moses." These verses address the consequences if the wife is guilty. This can be seen through declarative statements including "if any man's wife goes astray and behaves unfaithfully toward him" (5:12b NET) and "she has defiled herself" (5:13b ESV, NET).[4] The expression "behaves unfaithfully" is built off of a verb and noun from the root מעל which is also found in 5:6. In that context, it refers to violating an oath against God with resulting judgment on Israel (cf. 2 Chron. 28:19; Ezek. 20:27; 39:26).[5] Further, since the Old Testament uses marriage imagery to describe the relationship between God and Israel (Hos. 2:14–23) unfaithfulness toward a husband may be an analogy for unfaithfulness toward God (Ashley 1993, 126). The phrase "she has defiled herself" (וְהִיא נִטְמָאָה) employs a root (טמא) used in the prophets to cast Israel's idolatry in terms of sexual infidelity. This reinforces the reality that this case in Numbers is also an offense against God (Hos. 5:3; 6:10; Jer. 2:23; Ezek. 20:30, 31, 43).

The other foundational element to this scenario is the lack of certainty. Numbers 5:13 expresses this four times through the expressions "it is hidden from the eyes of her husband," "she is undetected," "there is no witness against her," and "she was not taken in the act" (ESV).[6] If guilt was certain, this case would go to the court, not to God's sanctuary (Sprinkle 2015, 206). Instead, uncertainty requires the husband to avoid precipitous judgment.

5:14. This verse concludes the first scenario and introduces the second in which the wife's innocence is presumed. They are linked by the concept of a "spirit of jealousy" (רוּחַ־קִנְאָה) which can be either justified (5:14a) or unjustified (5:14b). The repetitive nature of this verse emphasizes that a similar course of action is required for both cases. Both halves of the verse use the expression "if a spirit of jealously comes over him and he is jealous of his wife" (ESV), before deviating on the subject of her guilt. She has either "defiled herself" (5:14a) or "not defiled herself" (5:14b). In either scenario, the stability of the marriage covenant is in jeopardy.

The Body of the Case (5:15–28)

Following the description of the scenario, the required course of action follows in 5:15–28. The essential feature is that God takes upon himself the role of judge with the priest acting as his representative. The human parties must submit themselves to the divine verdict since only God can judge a scenario where the truth cannot be proven by purely human means (Gane 2004, 521). This is the only time in Old Testament law in which God requires a ritual that results in a miraculous sign or its absence (Gane 2017, 302). This speaks to the incredibly challenging nature of the problem: God alone is a suitable arbiter.

The Initiation of the Proceedings (5:15)

5:15. The first action is for the husband to bring his wife to the sanctuary along with a grain offering. Some English translations suggest that this is a requirement, saying "he

---

4 The phrase "any man" is actually translating the Hebrew אִישׁ אִישׁ ("man man"). The repetition of a word can have a distributive sense, indicating "each, every, any." This same construction introduces legal material elsewhere, including Leviticus 17:10, 13 (Levine 1993, 192).

5 In fact, Milgrom notes that Numbers 5:12 is the only time that this expression does not point to God as the aggrieved party (Milgrom 1990, 37).

6 The last expression is literally "she was not seized" (וְהִיא לֹא נִתְפָּשָׂה). The context is clearly that the adulterous couple was not apprehended.

must bring his wife" (NET) or "he shall bring his wife" (ESV). Instead, it is more accurate to say that "he *may* bring his wife" if he is unable to move past his suspicions (Ashley 1993, 127). By doing so, the husband surrenders to God the right of deciding this case. The grain offering also reflects God's presence for this occasion. This is an innovation of the regular grain offering described in Leviticus 2. In this case, the man is to bring the grain without oil or incense since those symbolize the joy of the offering (Ps. 104:15; Prov. 27:9; Sprinkle 2015, 206). Further, this is meant to be an accessible judgment since it is the "least expensive sacrifice in the Pentateuch" (Gane 2016, 115). The required grain is the "cheaper and courser barley flour" rather than finely ground wheat flour (Cole 2000, 116).

Numbers 5:15b addresses the function of the offering with three clauses, calling it "a grain offering of jealousy" (מִנְחַת קְנָאֹת), "a grain offering of remembrance" (מִנְחַת זִכָּרוֹן), that is "bringing iniquity to remembrance" (מַזְכֶּרֶת עָוֹן; ESV). These descriptions bring together the husband's suspicions and God's presence. The final clause about iniquity is necessary since all other mentions of "remembrance" (זִכָּרוֹן) before God are positive (Ashley 1993, 127). Instead, the idea of remembrance here suggests that God will bring to light the hidden nature of the act.

The Priestly Preparation of the Ritual (5:16–18)

5:16–17. After initiating the proceedings, the husband fades into the background. The involved parties are now the wife and the priest who guides her through the ritual. The priest is first to bring the woman before God, likely in the courtyard of the tabernacle (5:16). This adds great solemnity to the occasion, indicating that the divine supreme court is in session (Gane 2016, 116). Numbers 5:17 then instructs the priest to take "holy water" (מַיִם קְדֹשִׁים) and mix it with dust from the floor of the tabernacle. The water comes from the basin placed between the tabernacle tent and altar for sacrifices in its courtyard (Exod. 30:17–21). Adding the dust from the sanctuary floor symbolically enhanced the sacredness of the water, further invoking God's presence (Gane 2004, 522).[7] While the dust has no inherently deleterious effects, it is an indication that a holy God is judging this case (Cole 2000, 116).

5:18. The text again calls the priest to bring the woman before God as he concludes his preparations by unbinding her hair, placing the barley offering in her hand, and holding dust and water mixture before her. Unbinding hair can be a sign of mourning (Lev. 10:6; 21:10) or uncleanness (Lev. 13:45), either of which place the individual in a humbled position (Cole 2000, 116). If the woman is guilty, this is preparatory action for her dishonored status following the verdict (Ashley 1993, 129). The grain offering is described with two of the same phrases as 5:15: a grain offering of remembrance (מִנְחַת הַזִּכָּרוֹן), and a grain offering of jealousy (מִנְחַת קְנָאֹת), again combining the husband's suspicion with God's presence. The water and dust mixture is called "the bitter water that brings a curse" (מֵי הַמָּרִים הַמְאָרֲרִים), a phrase also found in 5:19, 24.[8] The bitterness refers to the unappealing taste of the mixture and the ensuing consequences if the curse for infidelity is activated (Feinstein 2012, 303).[9]

---

[7] A modern parallel might be laying a hand on a Bible to swear an oath to be truthful in a courtroom.
[8] 5:23 also refers to the "bitter water" (מֵי הַמָּרִים) without mentioning the curse.
[9] The words "bitter" (הַמָּרִים) and "that bring the curse" (הַמְאָרֲרִים) also sound very similar, perhaps as an aid to remembering the ritual procedure.

> **Bitter Water**
>
> The translation "bitter water" for the Hebrew expression מֵי הַמָּרִים is the subject of much discussion. The Septuagint reads a different Hebrew root and refers to it as "the water of conviction" (τὸ ὕδωρ τοῦ ἐλεγμοῦ), focusing on its legal function. Some appeal to cognate languages to suggest other Hebrew roots which would replace "bitter" with concepts like "contention" (Driver 1956, 73–74) or even "vision/oracle" (Brichto 1975, 59). All of these remain conjectural and require changing the Hebrew text. Another objection is that the mixture of dust and water would be more "brackish" or "gritty" than "bitter." However, Hebrew has few adjectives denoting flavor so there is no reason why הַמָּרִים cannot cover a broad range of objectional tastes. Exodus 15:23–25 exemplifies this as God provides Moses with the means to turn the water from "bitter" (מָרִים) to "become sweet" (וַיִּמְתְּקוּ). It is highly unlikely that the water took on a sugared or honeyed taste. Instead it went from unpalatable to palatable (Feinstein 2012, 303). Consequently, "bitter water" remains the best translation for this phrase.

The Administration of the Oath (5:19–24)

5:19–22. Following the preparations, the priest guides the woman to swear an oath by which YHWH judges her. Numbers 5:19 begins with the presumption of the woman's innocence as the priest declares that if no other man has been with her and if she has not defiled herself (cf. 5:12, 14), then she is acquitted from the curse. Numbers 5:20–22 then describes the scenario in which the woman is guilty. The text here is incredibly complicated as 5:21a interrupts the guilty scenario to again instruct the priest to administer the oath to the woman.[10] However, the gist is reasonably clear: if the woman is guilty of infidelity then she is subject to a curse that will make her an example of oath-breaking among her people (Ashley 1993, 131–32).

Numbers 5:21b–22 details the curse brought about by ingesting the bitter water. Repetition is again key to this section as the priest pronounces the curse in both 5:21b and 5:22a. The curse also reflects a philosophy of the punishment fitting the crime since it involves the woman's reproductive organs. It is rendered in English translations with expressions like God will "make your thigh fall away and your abdomen swell" (5:21b NET). "Your thigh" (יְרֵכֵךְ) is most likely a euphemism for the reproductive organs (cf. Gen 24:2, 9; 46:26) and the idea of "falling away" points to their failure to function (Ashley 1993, 132). Similarly, the swelling of the abdomen (בֶּטֶן) may reflect a prolapsed uterus which would also end a woman's natural fertility (Frymer-Kensky 1984, 20–21). The exact procedure cannot be known but clearly the intention of the curse is to render the unfaithful wife unable to have children.[11] Notably, 5:28 declares that the unfairly accused wife will be able to conceive thereafter, which suggests that the punishment on the unfaithful wife will affect childbearing. The description of the oath concludes in 5:22b with the woman saying "Amen, amen." She surrenders herself to divine judgment and declares her readiness to consume the waters.

5:23–24. These verses introduce an additional element to the oath. The priest is instructed to write the curses he has just described onto a scroll and then wash them into the water and dust mixture. This adds yet another layer of sacredness to the situation since the woman is now required to ingest water from the basin

---

10 The ESV and NASB put 5:21a in parentheses. This is a reasonable solution to the difficulties of the Hebrew text.
11 Some suggest that the punishment is directed more toward miscarriage than sterility (Amzallag and Yonah 2017, 396). This is possible, although it does not address the situation in which the wife's unfaithfulness does not result in pregnancy. It is best to infer that the punishment affects the woman's reproductive abilities without pressing for additional specifics.

before the altar, dust from the floor of the sanctuary, and the words of the curse that will afflict her if she is guilty. She thus takes the curse into her own body and awaits God's verdict (Allen 2012, 136). Ingesting this sacralized mixture while in a state of "irremediable moral impurity" would result "in a prompt, divinely inflicted penalty" (Gane 2016, 118–19).

The Execution of the Ritual (5:25–28)
5:25–26. This section moves from the declaration of oath to the actual performance of the ritual. It begins with the priest taking the grain offering from the woman, presenting it before YHWH and laying it upon the altar. This offering is thus an act of worship before God that permits the case to proceed. Following the grain offering, the woman must drink the mixture (5:26b).

5:27. This verse articulates the consequences for the woman who has been unfaithful. The text reflects on these consequences at greater length than the scenario in which the wife is innocent, mirroring the presentation of the cases in 5:12–14. This verse reiterates the effects on her reproductive system from 5:21–22 and concludes with the declaration that she will be a curse among her people. It clearly connects the setup of the ritual to its execution. The announced consequences are the experienced consequences.

5:28. The passage concludes with the case of the improperly accused woman. Rather than revealing her iniquity, the result of this ritual is that she will be "clean" (וּטְהֹרָה), keeping her in covenantal communion with God (Lev. 11:36; 1 Sam. 20:26). Consequently, she faces no adverse outcomes to her body and status in the community. Rather, her innocence means that she may continue to conceive children. She has been exonerated by the divine Judge, which should alleviate her husband's suspicions.

> **The Ritual**
> This ritual bears some resemblance to the concept of a "trial by ordeal," which the laws of Hammurabi use in cases of suspected infidelity. The idea is that in some manner, the divine realm will adjudicate the case. The parallels are not exact since Hammurabi also considers a situation in which "the finger is pointed" (*ANET*, 171) at the woman by an unspecified third party. Another distinction is that in most ordeals, the onus is placed on the suspected party to perform a task to vindicate themselves.[12] In this case, the suspected woman does not have to participate in an "ordeal of death" (Allen 2012, 132), but simply submit to God's authority. The default outcome of drinking the water and dust mixture is her innocence. God must act in unmistakable power to demonstrate her guilt (Ashley 1993, 123). Further, ancient trials by ordeal could be supplemented by further punishment by human authorities, whereas here the husband submits his wife to YHWH's judgment with no further recourse for himself (Frymer-Kensky 1984, 24). This also eliminates the possibility of death for the woman even if she has been unfaithful. She may be shamed and punished, but she will not lose her life for an offense that cannot be proven by human means.

Further, although reading this passage through a modern frame of reference highlights its one-sided nature, this ritual provides the woman with the guarantee of impartial judgment. She may not receive justice from an all-male legal system, which may find it easier to emphasize with the husband's suspicions than with the wife's denials (Gane 2017, 302). Since a man could initiate divorce

---

12 In the Hammurabic code, this involves casting the individual into the Euphrates River. If they survived onrushing waters, they were presumed innocent.

proceedings (Deut. 24:1–4) or even threaten the life of his betrothed for unfaithfulness (Deut. 22:20–21), a fair means of adjudicating the case is necessary. In some respects the ritual is an "act of mercy," that protected the woman against a cruel or capricious husband (Allen 2012, 131).

Recapitulation of the Case (5:29–31)

5:29–30. The passage concludes with a brief recapitulation. It echoes the introduction in 5:11–14 quite closely, restating that this law is established for cases of a husband's suspicion whether it proves to be warranted. The essence of the case is captured in 5:30b, which states that the man shall set his wife "before the LORD" for the priest to enact this ritual. This reiterates that this case requires a direct judgment from God.

5:31. The passage concludes with contrasting statements about culpability. It notes first that the man who subjects his wife to this examination "will be free from iniquity" (ESV, NET). This means that his suspicions do not fall into the same category as bearing false witness (Deut. 19:16–19) or making improper accusations about a betrothed's virginity (Deut. 22:13–19), both of which carry penalties (Gane 2004, 524). On the other hand, the woman (if found guilty) will "carry her iniquity."

THEOLOGICAL FOCUS

The exegetical idea (God alone is a suitable judge of cases of suspected adultery) leads to this theological focus: *Marital fidelity reflects God's holiness and purity*.[13] Scripture consistently emphasizes human marriage as a metaphor of God's care for his people. Later, Numbers 25:1–3 equates Israel's dalliances with idols with marital unfaithfulness. Many prophetic texts refer to Israel as God's wayward spouse whom he longs to restore (Jer. 2:1–3; 3:1–5; Hos. 2:1–23). Hosea especially reveals the depths of God's passionate commitment to his people, even using the wilderness setting as the backdrop for his renewed pursuit of faithless Israel. Despite Israel's failures catalogued throughout Numbers, God still desires to return to the place in which he established his covenant with the nation. On a more positive note, Paul envisions marriage as an expression of Christ's love for the church. In Ephesians 5:25–30, husbands are to love their wives in the same manner that they love their own bodies and demonstrate to their wives the same sacrificial commitment as Christ. Images of Israel as the unfaithful spouse are thus redeemed by Christ's passionate devotion to his bride (Rev. 21:2). The metaphor of marriage reflects God's unflagging commitment to his people. It should compel his followers to cherish their own marriages in the same way.

Marital fidelity by both parties is also a clear expectation, rooted in God's creational intention for humanity (Gen. 2:23). Jesus reinforces this when he declares that no one should sunder what God has joined together (Matt. 19:4–6). In 1 Corinthians 5:1–5, Paul condemns both the immoral man who is having relations with his father's wife and the church that refuses to address the situation. Similarly, Hebrews 13:4 admonishes its hearers to maintain the purity of marital relationships. Paul further instructs believers in 1 Thessalonians 4:1–8 to be sanctified through the avoidance of sexual immorality. In a study of early Christianity, Larry Hurtado argues that with the expression "holiness and honor" (ESV) used in 1 Thessalonians 4:4, Paul seeks to reframe a double standard in which freeborn men had considerably more sexual license (Hurtado 2016, 157). Honorable wives were expected to be sexually faithful to

---

13 It is important to acknowledge that not all Christians will get married. These theological reflections are in no way meant to exclude those who serve God faithfully without a spouse, but only to illustrate how Scripture uses marriage to reflect God's relationship with his people. Expositors should be careful in their framing of this truth.

their husbands, while men had social latitude to engage in encounters with courtesans and slaves without attendant social dishonor. Applying the criteria of holiness and honor to men (see 1 Thess. 4:6) compels husbands to adhere to the same standards as their wives. Hurtado also discusses Paul's injunction to flee sexual immorality (*porneia*) in 1 Corinthians 6:18. In the immediate context, this term refers to liaisons with prostitutes, which the surrounding cultural norms did not condemn for men of a certain stature. Paul's command thus "reflected an attitude diametrically opposed to the prevailing attitudes of the time" (Hurtado 2016, 163). As Paul seeks to establish a sexual ethic for communities of new believers, he points to fidelity within marriage a distinguishing mark. Through these passages, the gender dynamics of Numbers 5:11–31 come into broader focus, revealing that God's intention for marital fidelity equally applies to both parties.

PREACHING AND TEACHING STRATEGIES

Exegetical and Theological Significance

The ritual and trial of Numbers 5:11–31 is only intelligible given an understanding of the sacred importance of the marriage covenant. Adultery was a sin against God, against the spouse, and against the community (if for no other reason than a community member was required for adultery to occur). Only when marriage is understood in its creational context can we understand the significance of marital unfaithfulness or divorce (cf. Jesus's words in Matthew 5:27–32; 19:1–12). The fact that Israel's idolatry is often depicted as marital unfaithfulness helps reveal the nature of both idolatry and adultery. Proverbs is filled with warnings about avoiding adulterous connections.

Beyond this, the marriage covenant provides a profound spiritual analogue of God's relationship with his people. Israel is God's wife; the church is Christ's bride. Paul points to the mystery that marriage was always designed as an enacted, prophetic declaration of Christ's relationship with the church. In eschatological glory and consummation, there is the great marriage feast of the Lamb (Rev. 19:7–9).

It is precisely because marriage is created by God and touches on so many aspects of religious, personal, and societal realities that it must be protected. Notice that this text reveals that marriage partners are to be protected from being the victim of an adulterous spouse, but also from being falsely condemned as adulterous if they are innocent. Jealousy can poison the mind, cause a spouse to manufacture or interpret evidence in the worst possible way, and turn suspicious thoughts into "reality." An act of adultery can destroy a marriage, but false accusations and judgments can also be incredibly damaging. The negatives, however, point to the positive: marriage is designed by God, and it is good.

Preaching Idea
God designs, creates, sustains, and protects covenant relationships.

Contemporary Connections

What does it mean?
What does it mean that God designs, creates, sustains, and protects covenant relationships? God is triune, so he has a perfectly rich life in his intra-trinitarian relationships. Human beings, however, by our very nature can only relate to those who are other than ourselves. Before God created the world, he envisioned and designed various structures and relationships for human beings to experience. A fundamental relational sphere—as proven by the creation and the bringing together of Adam and Eve—is marriage. Marriage, as with all of God's designs, showcases his glory and allows for human flourishing. However, because of sin, these good purposes have been marred tragically.

With the entry of sin into the world, discord was introduced into the human heart, and this discord spreads infection into every social relationship and obligation. Sin threatens the heart, purpose, and prophetic significance of marriage, so God guarded the sanctity of the marriage covenant with a multitude of instructions and laws. Adultery was so detrimental to Israel—and was such an affront to the holiness of God—that its prohibition was even part of the Decalogue (Exod. 20:14).

Believers are to obey the word of the God and walk in the power of the Spirit. The way that God sustains, upholds, and protects his designs for covenant relationships is by giving grace and power through our union with Christ. This enables us to see the goodness of God's plans and obey his instructions. Marriage is not merely a social contract: it is a God-designed covenant. God is the one who designs, defines, sustains, and protects covenant relationships.

Is it true?
Is it true that God designs, creates, sustains, and protects covenant relationships? According to Scripture the obvious answer is *yes*, but we also need to recognize that Scripture is fully aware that humans can sinfully violate their covenant obligations. God is a perfectly faithful covenant partner, filled with *hesed*, but human beings sin and trespass against God's standards.

The sad reality is that some people *do* commit adultery; in fact, some people are guilty of serial adultery. As a nation, Israel *did* commit idolatry/adultery against her covenant Lord. David *was* guilty of adultery and sexual coercion and then sought to cover it by an egregious abuse of power that shed innocent blood. Jesus recognized the possibility of adultery and extramarital sexual immorality, even expanding it to include lustful thoughts (Matt. 5:27–28). So, as is so often the case, Scripture demands a balance between God's grace and empowerment, and our responsibility to live morally in holiness.

Under the old covenant law, proven adultery resulted in capital punishment. In the new covenant community, adultery is grounds for divorce, but adultery does not necessitate divorce. Although the offended spouse has permission from Jesus himself to secure a divorce in this situation (Matt. 19:9), there is the possibility of forgiveness and reconciliation. *Restoration* is one way that God may protect the covenant relationship. Ultimately, however, the great fulfillment of God's design for marriage awaits the new heaven and new earth, when Christ will wed his bride, the church. There we will see the fulfillment of all of God's plans, and that most special covenant relationship will be so protected in holiness that it will never be broken.

Now what?
Given the fact that God designs, creates, sustains, and protects covenant relationships, how do we fulfill our expected role as faithful covenant partners? Without any doubt, adultery, sexual immorality, pornography, and lust are immediately ruled out. We need to recognize our relational obligations, and that includes the entire community, whether married or not. Love, mutual goodwill, honor, and respect need to be cultivated. By walking with the Spirit, the fruit of the Spirit is produced, resulting in a harvest of righteousness and harmony. Flee from evil and build up and strengthen what is good. Some will need counseling; some will need to repent; some will need to forgive. Our horizontal relationships with others are dependent on the strength of our vertical relationship with God, so maintain the closest possible walk with him. God is marked by covenant faithfulness, so use his strength to be faithful in your relationships.

Creativity in Presentation
One of the oldest and most influential tales in all of Western literature is *The Iliad* by Homer. This story recounts the siege of Troy and is filled with politicking, battles, and the intervention and placation of fickle deities. The root cause

of the war involved the petty jealousies of Hera, Athena, and Aphrodite, but the human catalyst was the adulterous union between Paris of Troy and Helen, who was the wife of the king of Sparta. Tracking out the basic plot of *The Iliad* can show the potential consequences of adultery. From the biblical narrative, the David and Bathsheba narrative demonstrates the real-world potential for adultery to destroy lives and for powerful figures to abuse their authority for the purposes of sexual gratification.

There is another classic tale in English literature that can be set alongside of *The Iliad*. In Shakespeare's *Othello*, a wicked individual named Iago seeks to destroy Othello by causing him to believe that his innocent and pure wife Desdemona has been unfaithful. As Iago builds his case and manipulates the scenes, Othello becomes so convinced of his innocent wife's guilt that he ends up killing her.

Numbers 5:11–31 shows us that the guilt of adultery is very serious, but so is the condemnation of the innocent. Any preacher who handles themes of adultery, sexual immorality, and marital unfaithfulness will have to be extremely sensitive. The fact that adultery—or the suspicion thereof—can figure so prominently in classic stories, shows that it resonates with our deep-seated intuitions, values, and psychological makeup.

One can imagine how terrible things were in the leadup to going before the priest to enact this ritual. If the charge of adultery was proven, the relationship would never be the same. But imagine the consequences if the charge was proven false. The wife has pled her innocence but been disbelieved; she likely feels humiliated, even if vindicated. What was the atmosphere like in their tent when they had to go to sleep that night? What was the conversation like on the trip to the priest, or on the way home? Over the weeks as they waited to see if God would send a curse, how did they feel? May God protect us from adultery, and also from false charges against the innocent. Our only hope is found in the God designs, creates, sustains, and protects covenant relationships.

A possible outline for this passage is:

- Only God can judge questions of suspected marital infidelity (5:11–15).

- The priest is God's representative in addressing these cases (5:16–28).

- The consequences of infidelity affect the body of the guilty party (5:29–31).

DISCUSSION QUESTIONS

1. Why is marital fidelity such an important concern for God?

2. Why do you think this is the only legal scenario in which God directly steps in as a judge?

3. What would be necessary for a marital relationship to be restored after an unwarranted accusation of infidelity?

4. How would you put this passage into a broader biblical framework of marital fidelity?

5. How can couples build trust, honesty, and transparency so that they can avoid such damaging suspicions?

Numbers 6:1–21

EXEGETICAL IDEA
The Nazirite vow permitted any Israelite to mark a period of special devotion to God.

THEOLOGICAL FOCUS
God provides the means for all of his people to express the fullness of their dedication.

PREACHING IDEA
When you dedicate yourself to God, actions speak louder than words.

PREACHING POINTERS
Only a fraction of the Israelites could serve the Lord as priests or Levites, but any Israelite could dedicate themselves to the Lord in a special way by taking the Nazirite vow. A Nazirite had to give up some of the normal pleasures of life, as well as voluntarily place themselves under certain restrictions. People were not forced to make this vow, but if they did, it was binding. Actions speak louder than words, and what counted in God's sight was not a person saying they would uphold a vow, but rather the follow-through and fulfilment of the vow that had been made.

It may sound to us like the restrictions in the Nazirite vow were quite limiting, but what was given up was more than compensated for by the opportunity to live in self-conscious awareness of being specially dedicated to the Lord. The joy and Spirit of the Lord amply repaid the faithful Nazirite. In the new covenant era, we do not have Nazirites, but every follower of Christ has made an even more serious, binding commitment when they put their faith in Jesus. Jesus does not call us to give up grapes, haircuts, and funerals: he calls us to pick up our cross, die to self daily, and follow him. To the world, this looks like a terrible sacrifice, but the ones who love Jesus wouldn't take the entire world in exchange for the riches they have in him. These things are matters of eternal significance, and God holds us accountable for every word we utter, so remember that when you dedicate yourself to God, actions speak louder than words.

THE NAZIRITE VOW (6:1–21)

LITERARY STRUCTURE AND THEMES

Numbers 6:1–21 concludes the series of laws related to ceremonial purity that began in 5:1. As with the previous laws, it begins with the expression "The LORD said to Moses" (6:1). This passage details the requirements and expectations of the Nazirite vow, which offers any Israelite the opportunity to show special devotion to God. It consists of three sections. Numbers 6:1–8 provides the initial requirements of the vow, focusing upon the Nazirite's duty to abstain from wine and other grape products along with instructions not to cut their hair during the period of the vow. Next, 6:9–12 addresses a scenario in which the adherent unintentionally breaches the vow. Finally, 6:13–21 gives instructions for the sacrifices required to mark the fulfillment of the vow and the adherent's release from its requirements.

Thematically, this vow expresses the desire to show "great zeal for God and dedication to God's law" (Stubbs 2009, 65). This wholehearted devotion underlies the specific acts and abstentions required by the vow. Commentators associate it with the requirements of the priesthood, providing a way for Israelites to experience God's promise to make them a kingdom of priests (Exod. 19:6) in an even deeper fashion (Gane 2004, 535; Milgrom 1990, 355).

- *The Requirements of the Vow (6:1–8)*
- *Remediation of the Vow (6:9–12)*
- *The Fulfillment of the Vow (6:13–21)*

EXPOSITION

Although this passage is quite specific in detailing the requirements of the Nazirite vow, there is much that remains opaque. It does not give examples of circumstances that could prompt an individual to become a Nazirite; neither does it specify the length of the vow.[1] Further, this text does not address the situation of those who appear to be lifelong Nazirites such as Samson and Samuel.[2] Instead, this passage takes the existence of Nazirites as a given and focuses upon the guidelines and regulations of this practice (Cole 2000, 119). As the text unfolds, it demonstrates that the Nazirite vow permitted any Israelite to mark a period of special devotion to God.

The Requirements of the Vow (6:1–8)
6:1–2. The first feature of this legislation is that it is available to all Israelites. Numbers 6:2 begins with God's instructions to Moses that "if a man or a woman" desires to make this vow, they

---

[1] Critical scholarship presumes that the Nazirite vow was originally for the duration of the devotee's life, while the time-specific vow came later. This disassociates the vow from its setting as an instruction from God to Moses and is not warranted by the text. See the explanation in Ashley 1993, 138–41.

[2] Samson's parents receive explicit instructions to set him apart as a Nazirite for the purposes of delivering Israel from the Philistines (Judg. 13:2–5, 13–14). His transgression of the restrictions of the vow is a microcosm of the spiritual state of the nation. Samuel is never identified as a Nazirite, but Hannah's promise that she will dedicate her child to God and that no razor will go upon his head (1 Sam. 1:11) implicitly sets him on the Nazirite trajectory. Their careers have a certain parallel as both confront the Philistines, although only Samuel's faithful service results in them being subdued in 1 Samuel 7 (Hahn 2011, 58).

are able. Although the rest of the verbs related to the Nazirite are in the masculine singular form, the initial statement affirms that all Israelites, regardless of gender, may devote themselves to God in this manner. This verse also marks the exceptional nature of this undertaking, calling it a "special vow" (ESV, NET). The underlying verb is an imperfect form of the root פלא, which frequently refers to the extraordinary actions of God. Here it indicates that the Nazirite vow "was an act of unusual devotion to God" (Allen 2012, 138). Numbers 6:2b then consists of wordplay based on the root נזר. The meaning of the noun נָזִיר ("Nazirite") is defined by the following phrase לְהַזִּיר לַיהוה, "to separate oneself to YHWH." The Nazirite thus pursues sanctification before God by abstaining, or separating, from certain acts available to others (Milgrom 1990, 44).

6:3–4. The text then lists three categories of abstention for the duration of the Nazirite vow, beginning with grape products (6:3–4). The requirement to avoid the products of the vineyard goes far beyond what is even required of priests. According to Leviticus 10:9, priests were to avoid wine and other intoxicating drinks when entering the Tent of Meeting (Gane 2004, 533). Numbers 6:3 raises the bar significantly, instructing the Nazirite to abstain from wine and strong drink (מִיַּיִן וְשֵׁכָר), the vinegar (חֹמֶץ) that derives from these drinks, the unfermented juice from the grape (מִשְׁרַת עֲנָבִים), and fresh or dried grapes (וַעֲנָבִים לַחִים וִיבֵשִׁים). Numbers 6:4 encapsulates these instructions by declaring that during the period of the vow, the devotee must not consume *anything* that derives from the vineyard including even the least appealing parts of the fruit: the seeds and skin.[3] The text provides no explicit reason for this requirement, but the suggestion that it reflects a "disavowal of ordinary pleasure" for the duration of the vow is plausible (Allen 2012, 139). It is somewhat akin to Lenten practices where believers willingly abstain from certain foods or practices to demonstrate their devotion to God.

6:5. The second restriction concerns the Nazirite's hair. The connection between Samson's immense strength and his unshaven head is clearly unique, but Numbers 6:5 declares that temporary Nazirites also must refrain from trimming their hair. Again, there is no direct explanation, but rather a statement that this is necessary for the individual to remain holy during this period. One potential explanation for this requirement is that hair symbolizes life force and vitality since it grows even after death (Stubbs 2009, 67). The expression "because his separation to God is his head" (6:7 ESV) provides another clue.

TRANSLATION ANALYSIS
There is a minor issue in this expression regarding the function of the pronominal suffix on 6:7 (נֶזֶר אֱלֹהָיו). In a construct chain, the pronominal suffix can apply to either noun. Many English translations associate it with נֶזֶר, rendering the phrase "his separation to God" (ESV, NASB, NIV). However, it is also possible to associate with the following noun and render the phrase "the separation to his God" (NET). Either reading preserves essentially the same meaning: the symbol of the vow is the unshorn hair on the Nazirite's head.

Even though the immediate context is corpse contamination, this phrase suggests that "the Nazirite's uncut hair is the outward symbol of separation to special holiness to the Lord" (Gane 2004, 534). This is confirmed by the

---

3 The expression מֵחַרְצַנִּים וְעַד־זָג can be rendered "not even the seeds or skins" (ESV, NIV). This is somewhat speculative since the two nouns are found only here. However, context indicates that the likely function of this verse is to make the prohibition as complete as possible: nothing from the vineyard was available to the Nazirite (Allen 2012, 139).

instruction for the Nazirite to offer their hair as an offering to YHWH at the end of their vow (Num. 6:18). Sacrificing the hair reflected the total devotion of the Nazirite's life to God.

6:6–8. The final restriction involves the contamination brought about by contact with dead bodies. This builds upon the idea that holiness "is antagonistic to the impurity caused by death" (Gane 2004, 533). Thus, the Nazirite had to take special care to avoid corpse contamination during the period of the vow. Like the instructions concerning wine, the Nazirite was required to uphold a much higher standard than almost any other Israelite. Even Israel's priests were permitted to be present with the body of a dead immediate relative (Lev. 21:1–3). The high priest alone had the same restrictions as the Nazirite (Lev. 21:11). This prohibition adds even greater weight to the Nazirite office. The devotee's commitment to God was to be so strong that not even the death of a family member was sufficient reason to depart. Numbers 6:8 summarizes all the requirements, declaring, "All the days of his separation, he is holy to the LORD" (ESV, NET).

Remediation of the Vow (6:9–12)

6:9. The following section acknowledges occasions when the ideal cannot be maintained. Life is fragile and the Nazirite could easily encounter a dead body. The Nazirite "does not lead a monastic existence apart but, to the contrary, is an active participant in all his familial and communal affairs" (Milgrom 1990, 355). This verse stresses the unintentional nature of the Nazirite's encounter with a dead body. It creates a hypothetical in which the Nazirite is present with someone who dies "very suddenly" (ESV, NASB, NET).[4] Even though the Nazirite did not intend to be in this situation, the result is that the devotee's "consecrated head" (ESV, NET) is defiled and requires remediation.

While an encounter with a dead body left any Israelite ceremonially unclean, the Nazirite's path to purification was more complicated, befitting the seriousness of the vow. Numbers 6:9b declares that on the day of purification, the seventh day after the encounter with the dead body, the Nazirite must shave their head since it was the sign of their now-breached vow to God (6:7; Gane 2004, 534).[5] Seven days was the standard time for purification for all Israelites, following a ritual sprinkling of water containing the ashes of a red cow on the third and seventh days (cf. Num. 19:11–12).

6:10–11a. Once the hair was removed, the Nazirite had to present themselves at the Tent of Meeting with sacrificial offerings, starting with two pigeons or turtledoves (6:10). Notably, these are the least expensive of the animal offerings set out for purification (Lev. 5:7–11), perhaps reflecting leniency based on the noble intention of a Nazirite vow (Milgrom 1990, 47). One bird made expiation for the Nazirite's transgression while the other was a burnt offering to God. On the need for expiation, Gane notes that "sin is objective: Corpse impurity has simply occurred through adverse circumstances, thereby violating the divine prohibition, without any failure of intention, carefulness, vigilance, or memory on the part of the Nazirite" (Gane 2004, 534).[6] The Nazirite did not intend to break their vow; however, even this inadvertent breach was an offense against God's holiness. Fortunately, God graciously provided means of remediation.

---

4   This is a good translation of the Hebrew idiom בְּפֶתַע פִּתְאֹם. Both words in this construction point to the rapidity with which an action occurs.

5   Allen also notes that this step would take on additional weight if the devotee was a woman (Allen 2012, 142).

6   This is also a good illustration of the popular principle "intent is not magic." That is, just because someone did not *intend* to make an error, or inflict harm, the reality is that it happened and restitution may be required.

6:11b–12. The Nazirite was then required to restart their period of devotion. They had to rededicate their head since that remains the symbol of the vow and add a male lamb as a reparation offering. This was necessary because the corpse contamination technically infringed upon God's rights (Wenham 2008, 99). It could not be reduced to a less costly alternative because YHWH's name or property (the Nazirite's hair) had been desecrated (Milgrom 1990, 48). Further, since YHWH was owed the entire period of the Nazirite's devotion, the offerings permitted the devotee to recommence their period of dedication. This was needed because 6:12b declares that this situation had voided their previous time as a Nazirite. They had to begin from the start with a newly shaved head to mark the breach of the vow and sacrificial offerings to restore their standing before God.[7]

TRANSLATION ANALYSIS
English translations take slightly different approaches to 6:12b. The text reads וְהַיָּמִים הָרִאשֹׁנִים יִפְּלוּ, which could be translated literally as "the former days will fall." The verb יִפְּלוּ clearly does not carry its typical sense of a literal movement from a higher to lower position. English translations render the idiom as "shall be void" (ESV, NASB, NRSV), "will not be counted" (NET), or "do not count" (NIV). These all capture the intention of the text.

The Fulfillment of the Vow (6:13–21)
6:13–14. The final section of this passage provides instruction for the successful completion of the Nazirite vow. The devotee must first present themselves at the Tent of Meeting, again acknowledging God's oversight. Then, they must offer a variety of sacrifices, covering "the four main types of sacrifice: burnt, cereal, peace, and sin" (Wenham 2008, 99). The animal offerings are listed in 6:14: an unblemished male lamb as a burnt offering, an unblemished female lamb as a purification offering, and an unblemished ram as a peace offering. The addition of a peace offering reflects a different tone than the previous section. Rather than making reparation for a broken vow, the peace offering permits the Nazirite to celebrate the fulfillment of their devotion to God (Ashley 1993, 141).

The Purification Offering
The presence of the purification offering in 6:14 merits comment. Requiring it in 6:11 made sense given the unintentional breaking of the Nazirite vow, but here, the devotee is marking its successful completion. Why then, is it necessary for the Nazirite to offer a purification sacrifice? A plausible explanation is that it again reflects the association of the Nazirite with priestly consecration. Gane notes that priests received instruction to offer a similar arrangement of sacrifices when dedicating themselves to divine service (Lev. 8:14–32). He suggests that the function in both cases is for the purification sacrifice to precede consecratory gifts to God (Gane 2004, 535). The situation of the Nazirite differed in that they offered their gifts at the end of their vow, while the priests offered them before beginning their service. Even though there is no explanation in Leviticus 8 of why the priests had to offer a purification sacrifice upon being dedicated, this parallel does suggest this requirement for the Nazirite fit the expected practice of showing devotion to God.

My (Joel's) children frequently struggle to grasp that even though they did not mean to hurt their sibling, they should still apologize when they do!

7   Rabbinic literature suggests that the Nazirite vow was taken seriously throughout the biblical period. Numerous commentators note the example of Queen Helena of Adiabene, a convert to Judaism in the first century A.D. who apparently swore a Nazirite vow for seven years only to accidentally break it near the end of that time. She then rededicated herself for another seven years (Gane 2004, 533; Milgrom 1990, 47; Wenham 2008, 99).

6:15. This verse adds cereal and drink offerings to the animal sacrifices, which reflects procedures explicitly enacted in Numbers 15. Presumably, these requirements were well known in the Israelite community, even if their codification came later in the book (Ashley 1993, 147). The requirement for a drink offering reveals that there is nothing inherently wrong with wine or other grape products. At the end of their period of abstention, the Nazirite was required to include wine poured out on the altar to God (Allen 2012, 143). This further marked the return to normal requirements of sanctity after the vow concluded.

6:16–18. The procedure for ending the vow continues. Since the Nazirite was not a priest, even though their devotion resembled that of a priest, they could not offer their own sacrifices. Instead, a priest brought the offerings before YHWH. Essentially, this law "makes holiness available to the laity even as it subordinates the sanctified laypersons to the priests" (Pressler 2017, 46). All of the offerings from 6:14–15 are repeated here as the priest presents them to God. Numbers 6:18 then requires an additional step: the Nazirite is instructed to shave their hair at the entrance to the Tent of Meeting. The Nazirite then must take it and burn it in the fire underneath the peace offering. This again reflects the worldview of 6:7, which stated that the Nazirite's consecration to God was upon the head. The hair is now another offering to God. Unlike the rest of the Nazirite's body, the hair remains devoted to God for the entirety of its existence (Gane 2004, 535).

6:19–20. These verses provide further instructions for the peace offering and grain offering. According to Levitical instruction, the priest and the worshipper received a portion of these sacrifices (Lev. 2:1–4; 7:12–15, 28–34). Numbers 6:20 describes this meat as "holy for the priest" (קֹדֶשׁ הוּא לַכֹּהֵן). The scenario involving the Nazirite added in another element. Typically, the priest's share was the "breast" (חָזֶה) and "thigh" (שׁוֹק) of the sacrificial animal. To those, 6:19 adds the "boiled shoulder" (הַזְּרֹעַ בְּשֵׁלָה) of the sacrificial ram.[8] Therefore, more of the Nazirite's sacrifice serves a ceremonial purpose. It is yet another reminder that this vow required "an extra degree of consecration to God's service" (Wenham 2008, 100).

The rest of the sacrificial procedure follows the expected course. After the priest took the meat and the cereal offerings, he placed them "on the hands of the Nazirite" (6:19b ESV, NET) who had finished cutting off their hair. This took place to establish a ceremonial transference of the offerings from the worshipper to the priest. The priest then performed a "wave offering" (תְּנוּפָה) and a "contribution offering" (הַתְּרוּמָה) with the meat (6:20).[9] After this, the priest could consume his portion of the meat, presumably as could the Nazirite. However, the discussion of the Nazirite's portion is elided in favor of the declaration that after this, "the Nazirite may drink wine" (6:20b ESV). This focus is understandable since wine and all the products of the grapevine were denied to the Nazirite. The Nazirite's freedom to drink wine, along with their shaved head, visibly marked the end of their period of consecration and their return to the ranks of regular nonpriestly Israelites.

---

8   The priest received his share of the sacrificial meat after it had been boiled, which permitted the fat to burn up and be a pleasing aroma to God. This is why it was so egregious for Hophni and Phinehas, the sons of Eli, to take their portion of the meat before it had boiled (1 Sam. 2:13–17). They were laying claim to a part of God's portion.

9   The exact procedures of these offerings are unknown. One suggestion is that the "wave offering" required a side-to-side motion, while the "contribution offering" involved an upward motion, perhaps ritually presenting the offering to God (Wenham 2008, 100).

6:21. This verse begins with "This the law of the Nazirite" (NET, NIV), forming an inclusio with 6:13. The rest of the syntax is highly convoluted, but the expression מִלְבַד אֲשֶׁר־תַּשִּׂיג יָדוֹ suggests that additional offerings may have been required. The NET translation renders it "as well as whatever else he can provide," which captures the intended sense. Consequently, the restrictions and requirements found in this passage reflected the bare minimum of the Nazirite vow. It would be costly to the devotee, both in terms of behavioral restrictions and outlay of personal wealth. It thus reflected "an act of rugged discipleship" (Allen 2012, 144).

THEOLOGICAL FOCUS

The exegetical idea (The Nazirite vow permitted any Israelite to mark a period of special devotion to God) points to this theological focus: *God provides the means for all of his people to express the fullness of their dedication.* Careful nuance is needed in considering the theological ramifications of this text. It should not be used to justify a framework in which some receive greater status for their public displays of devotion. Such outward displays without accompanying inward transformation are at the heart of Jesus's condemnation of the religious elites (Matt. 23:1–36). It is also antithetical to the promise that all believers have access to God in the manner of priests (Heb. 10:19–22; 1 Peter 2:9–10; Rev. 5:9–10).

In contrast, the theological focus of this text should be upon the openness of the vow to every member of God's community. Although God set aside the Levites for his service, he graciously permitted any Israelite, man or woman alike, to express their devotion. This bridged the gap between the priests and laity in ancient Israel. It perhaps anticipates the even greater unification of Jew and Gentile in the body and work of Christ. While the Nazirite vow permitted any Israelite to approximate the standing of a priest for a time, Christ's death and resurrection provides the means for all to be citizens of God's kingdom and members of his household (Eph. 2:14–19).

Further, while the vow regulates certain external activities, it does not set legalistic guidelines. This special dedication was voluntary. It was never required to be part of God's people and it did not grant superior status (Sprinkle 2015, 213). It is comparable to the relationship between a parent and child who consciously put aside time to be in each other's presence, without distractions (Gane 2004, 538). Carving out that space permits the relationship to deepen and grow. The Nazirite vow thus represents a conscious opportunity for a worshipper to show their devotion to God by establishing parameters on their time and activity.

The restrictions of the Nazirite vow also remind us that nothing is more important than taking advantage of the ways God has given us to show our devotion. As mentioned above, there is nothing inherently wrong with enjoying grapes and wine, trimming one's hair, or helping with the arrangements for dead relatives. However, the Nazirite chose to forgo those things to express the depth of their devotion to God. Jesus likewise calls his followers to put his kingdom above any other commitment. He may even allude to the restriction on corpse contamination when he exhorts his follows to follow and "let the dead bury their own dead" (Matt. 8:22 NIV; Cole 2000, 123). Similarly, Jesus compares the kingdom of God to treasure found in a field and a pearl of immense value. The ones who discover them sell everything to attain them (Matt. 13:44–46). In a world with many pleasures, some more worthwhile than others, biblical wisdom calls Christ-followers to carefully consider what we may need to put aside to focus on things of greater worth.

This passage thus reflects God's desire for his people to be able to fully express their devotion to him. The Nazirite vow "represents the highest ideals of Israel: holy people who voluntarily dedicate themselves, all their strength, vitality, and passion, in the zealous service of

God" (Stubbs 2009, 67). The Nazirites provide a model for Christ-followers who seek to heed his call to deny themselves and take up their cross to follow him (Matt. 6:24).

PREACHING AND TEACHING STRATEGIES

Exegetical and Theological Significance

In the same way that a young child might want to grow up to be a king or queen, in Israel some children almost certainly dreamed about growing up to be the high priest. It must have been very disappointing for some young people from tribes like Naphtali or Zebulun when they learned that only those from Levi were called to be priests. However, for those who loved God and wanted to devote themselves to him fully, the Nazirite vow was open to everyone. God unilaterally set apart the Levites for himself, but the Nazirite vow was an elective option that could be freely chosen by any of God's covenant partners.

Given the strict requirements of the Nazirite vow, the prospective adherent needed to count the cost, in the same way that Jesus soberly instructed would-be disciples (Luke 14:25–33). In the new covenant, the stakes are actually higher than with the Nazirites: we are to pick up our cross daily, die to self, lose our own lives, turn from the world, and follow Jesus to gain eternal life (Luke 9:23–24). This is not optional for disciples of Jesus: it is the requirement at the very beginning of our walk of faith.

Although the Nazirite vow was regulated by legal stipulations, it was not a way of earning legalistic merit before God. Being fully devoted to God is a privilege and delight, not a burden! The small loss of pleasure involved in giving up wine and grapes, for example, was more than offset by the potential joy of drawing nearer and nearer to God. The greatest commandment is to love God with heart, mind, soul, and strength (Deut. 6:5), and the Nazirite vow was one way of living this out with a particular focus. In the new covenant, the forms of the Nazirite vow are obsolete, but the heart and spirit of the vow is to be found in every member of the community.

Preaching Idea

When you dedicate yourself to God, actions speak louder than words.

Contemporary Connections

What does it mean?

What does it mean that when you dedicate yourself to God, actions speak louder than words? In every area of life, we understand that some people talk the talk but do not walk the walk. Whether we think of politicians, business leaders, celebrities, athletes, or even unfortunately pastors and church leaders, we all can call to mind individuals whose actions do not support what they preach. Virtue signaling and social media posts about working to end injustice are not the same as taking concrete action to further justice in the world. Calling people to certain moral and ethical standards while hiding grievous failings destroys the intended message. Positively, we admire people who match their articulate opinions with virtuous actions. Negatively, we are sickened by hypocrisy.

Jesus confronted the religious leaders of his day because of their hypocrisy. He told a parable about two sons who were asked by their father to go and work in the family vineyard (Matt. 21:28–32). One said he would but then didn't go, while the other at first said he wouldn't, then changed his mind and went to work. Jesus's point was that many were saying "yes" to God but not following through, while some who originally said a rebellious "no" repented and actually did the will of the Father. A verbal "yes" without action is really a "no," while an original "no" does not need to be our last word to God if we repent and follow Christ. Either way, our words are meaningless without right responses and actions.

Is it true?
Is it true that when you dedicate yourself to God, actions speak louder than words? As noted in the previous two sections, the teachings of Jesus prove this point beyond any doubt. This is one place where we do not need to spend any time debating the interpretation of the text: we simply need to live it out! Sadly, part of our human condition is that we are masters at excusing and rationalizing our own sin and hypocrisy, while we are quick to despise those we deem as hypocrites. All of us will struggle to see the log in our own eye, while simultaneously imagining we are qualified to spot and then remove the tiny bit of dust in the eye of another. Rather than worrying about the sins of everyone around us, we should check our own hearts, asking the Spirit of Truth to search us and reveal areas of our lives which have not been given over in dedication to God. We judge those whose actions do not match their words, and the same standard is the true measure of our spiritual life and health.

Now what?
Scripture provides our guidance for how to respond to this truth. Paul writes, "Therefore, I urge you, brothers and sisters, in view of God's mercy, to offer your bodies as a living sacrifice, holy and pleasing to God—this is your true and proper worship" (Rom. 12:1 NIV).

The author of Hebrews declares, "Therefore, since we are surrounded by such a great cloud of witnesses, let us throw off everything that hinders and the sin that so easily entangles. And let us run with perseverance the race marked out for us, fixing our eyes on Jesus, the pioneer and perfecter of our faith" (Heb. 12:1–2a NIV).

We are called to dedicate ourselves fully to God. The Nazirite vow set someone apart for God in a special way, as witnessed by their lifestyle. In Christ, we are called to offer all that we are in dedication to God. We ourselves are the living sacrifice offered to the Lord. We need to live out the imperatives: Pick up your cross. Leave everything and follow me. Offer your bodies as a living sacrifice. Throw off sin and everything that entangles. Run your race. Keep in step with the Spirit.

If you are not a follower of Jesus, now is the time to dedicate yourself to him and take the first step of faith. If you are a believer, but you find yourself cold or walking in unrepentant sin, now is the time to confess, repent, and rededicate your life. We do not earn our own righteousness but receive Christ's through faith. If you are walking closely with God, thank him for that empowering grace, and ask for increased love and faithfulness. Every Christian has room to grow, so keep pressing on. As Jewel the unicorn, Farsight the eagle, Tumnus the Faun, and others cry out about Aslan's country, we must go, "Further up, and further in!" We do this at Aslan's own invitation: "Come further up! Come further in!"

Creativity in Presentation
The biblical figure most often connected with the Nazirite vow is Samson. Those who grow up in Sunday school often hear stories of Samson, with an emphasis on his phenomenal strength. For example, his great strength is highlighted when he tears the lion to pieces, when he carries the massive city gates off their hinges and out into the country, and when he fights the Philistines with the jawbone of a donkey. The life of Samson is painted as an adventure story.

Yet the life of Samson shows that he continually disregarded his Nazirite vow. He takes honey from the corpse of the lion, thus defiling himself. (He also gives some to his parents without telling them where it came from, thus making them unclean as well.) To defend himself from the Philistines, he grabs the jawbone from a dead donkey, thus exposing himself to corpse contamination again. Why did he carry the city gates? He was locked inside the city. Why was he in the city? He was sleeping with a prostitute. Although that latter detail needs to be handled delicately with Sunday school children—no flannelgraph characters—Samson carries the gate because he is selfishly using his gift of strength in order to sin and get away with it. He was supposed to be a Nazirite, but his actions spoke louder than the words of the vow.

Our society is filled with covenants and contracts, as well as litigation for broken agreements. A person's word used to be their bond, and a handshake was enough to seal a deal in good faith. How are you doing in fulfilling your vows to God, which you made when you repented of your sins and put your faith in Jesus Christ? Are you like a godly Nazirite walking in faith, or like Samson disregarding the vow and abusing God's gifts? Depending on church environment, the preacher can call people to stand or come to the front for prayers of dedication or rededication to the Lord. People can be encouraged to pray and to go home and write out a commitment to the Lord. They can also be called to setup accountability partnerships. The main point is that if actions speak louder than words, this is more a time for action than for talking.

One potential breakdown of this passage is below:

- Anyone can dedicate themselves more fully to God (6:1–2).

- Abstaining from certain pleasures to focus on God is commendable (6:3–4).

- Devotion to God should be the highest priority (6:5–12).

- Worshippers should follow through on their commitments to God (6:13–21).

DISCUSSION QUESTIONS

1. What do you think might prompt an Israelite to undertake the Nazirite vow?

2. How do the requirements of the vow help worshippers to focus on their commitment to God?

3. Why does even an unintentional breaking of the vow require the worshipper to begin again?

4. How does this vow show that serving God is a joy rather than an obligation?

5. In what ways can believers demonstrate their devotion to God?

6. How do we avoid "spiritual snobbery" when we make commitments to God that fellow believers have not?

Numbers 6:22–27

EXEGETICAL IDEA
God desires to bless and preserve the Israelites.

THEOLOGICAL FOCUS
Pronouncing God's blessing shapes the identity of God's people.

PREACHING IDEA
In Scripture, there is a beautiful spiral between God's benediction and our response in doxology.

PREACHING POINTERS
This benedictory blessing is a gem that has biblical, theological, and literary beauty. It is crafted to be beautiful, and the blessing it conveys is life-giving. To bask in the glowing, holy, and gracious countenance of the Lord, and to feel his love and grace, is an experience that is too definite for words; it is literally inexpressible. For God's representative to stand before the people and pronounce this blessing is a wonder of God's grace and mercy. He truly, truly loves his people.

Throughout Scripture, there are numerous ways that God blesses his people, and numerous ways that his people respond by blessing his name in praise. God pronounces his benediction on his people, and his people break into doxology, worshipping him and extoling all that he is and all that he has done. The more God blesses his people, the more they are drawn into praise. This spiral is beautiful, as benediction leads to doxology, and doxology leads to the outpouring of even greater blessing. It is impossible to be blessed more richly than God's children are blessed in Jesus Christ, and so every believer ought to live a life of praise, thanksgiving, and rejoicing in the Lord. The greater our blessings, the greater our praise ought to be. In Scripture, there is a beautiful spiral between God's benediction and our response in doxology.

THE PRIESTLY BLESSING (6:22–27)

LITERARY STRUCTURE AND THEMES

Numbers 6:22–27 is one of the most well-known passages in the book. Here, God provides a blessing for the priests, beginning with Aaron and his sons, to speak over the Israelites. The blessing itself is succinct and memorable, poetically expressing God's desire for the well-being of his people. It consists of an introduction in which God gives direction for the blessing (6:22–23), the actual blessing (6:24–26), and a conclusion (6:27). The blessing itself contains three parallel couplets, each increasing in length. They expand from three to five to seven words, or fifteen to twenty to twenty-five consonants, or twelve to fourteen to sixteen syllables (Awabdy 2018, 38; Stubbs 2009, 74). Each word in the blessing has been carefully chosen to fit this pattern. Each couplet expresses the intention of God to bless his people, providing a vision of hope for a community awaiting the fulfillment of God's promises.

Thematically, it complements the restrictive nature of the Nazirite vow with an address that is "expansive and gracious, inclusive of the whole community" (Allen 2012, 144). There is no specific circumstance in Numbers that prompts the blessing. Within the flow of the book, this blessing comes after four passages focused on preserving the holiness of the community (5:1–4, 5–10, 11–31; 6:1–21). In this setting, Israel's obedience to God's commands permits "the enjoyment of God's blessing in Israel's midst" (Olson 1996, 43).

EXPOSITION

At the heart of this blessing is the revelation that it is God's blessing. Aaron and his sons are the conduits, but the words and authority behind it belong to God alone. Through it we learn that God desires to bless and preserve the Israelites.

6:22–23. Following the pattern of the other passages in Numbers 5–6, these verses mark the beginning of a new section with "The LORD spoke to Moses" (cf. Num 5:1, 5, 11; 6:1). God then instructs Moses to speak to Aaron and his sons and relate to them the words of God's intended blessing for Israel.

> **Blessing in the Old Testament**
> The concept of blessing in the Old Testament covers quite a broad range. In general it refers to a "pronouncement or bestowal of good" (Sprinkle 2015, 217). God and people can both be the givers and recipients of blessing. When God blesses Israel in the Old Testament, it is a reflection of their covenant relationship since "God bestows blessing on those who are in harmony with him" (McKeown 2003, 84). The evidence of blessing is frequently tangible: the bestowal of fruitful land, good health, children, other signs of prosperity (Gen. 17:16; 22:17–18; Lev. 26:3–13; Deut. 28:2–14; Wenham 2008, 101). Conversely, when a person blesses God it is typically an act of praise (Ps. 115:18; 134:2; Milgrom 1990, 630). Human beings cannot bring about tangible benefits for God, but they can celebrate his character and what he has done.

6:24–26. Each verse of the blessing increases in length but shares the same grammatical structure. They all begin with a verb with the divine name (YHWH) as its subject. A second, related verb then follows, with YHWH as the implied grammatical subject. The verbs all reflect the jussive nuance of the Hebrew imperfect tense, in these instances conferring a benediction as the priests pronounce God's good intentions for the recipients (Arnold and Choi 2018, 75). This is a type of performative speech, in which uttering the words is the means of enacting them (Janzen 2006, 26). Thus, the priests affirm God's intent to bless Israel by speaking the words that he has given them.

The relationship between the verbs can be expressed as *attitude* and *action*. That is, the first verb in each verse expresses a favorable *attitude* for God to have toward his people, while the second verb expresses a related desired *action* for him to undertake (Gane 2004, 539; Miller 1975, 243). Further, each verse also includes the divine name, which is grammatically redundant but emphasizes again that YHWH himself is the author of blessing. Finally, it is noteworthy that the addressees of each verb are singular. Allen views this as "characteristic of covenant language: Yahweh blesses the whole by blessing the individuals; he blesses the individuals by blessing the whole" (Allen 2012, 145–46). Thus, as the priests pronounce blessing on individual Israelites, they reflect a broader perspective in which the entire nation receives divine favor.

The first verse of the blessing (Num. 6:24) is the simplest. It is merely three words in Hebrew (יְבָרֶכְךָ יהוה וְיִשְׁמְרֶךָ), typically translated as "The LORD bless you and keep you" (ESV, NASB, NET, NIV). The priestly blessing thus begins by stating that God's attitude toward his people is to bless them and parallel action is for him to "keep" them. Beginning with God's desire to bless the people also provides a "general summary of everything else in the blessing" (Ashley 1993, 151–52). Next, the verbal root שמר ("to keep") points to God's acts of preservation. No specific circumstance is in view, but rather it expresses a general wish for God to protect the recipient. An image of what it might look like for God to "keep" Israelites can be found in the covenant blessings of Leviticus 26:5–8, which promises God's protection will allow Israel to dwell peacefully in the land. It identifies hostile nations and wild animals as threats from which God will preserve his people (Awabdy 2018, 41). Further, Israel's very existence reflects God's protection. He had already delivered them from slavery in Egypt and preserved them in the wilderness. In the setting of Numbers 6, the expression "the LORD keep you" should remind the people that they "lived under the protective umbrella of his mighty hand and outstretched arm" (Cole 2000, 129–30).

Numbers 6:25 elaborates on what it means for YHWH to "bless" his people while the following verse expands upon the idea of God "keeping" Israel (Stubbs 2009, 74). This provides yet further evidence of the careful arrangement of the blessing. Again, common English translations are close to uniform on 6:25, reading "the LORD make his face shine upon you and be gracious to you" (ESV, NASB, NET, NIV). The metaphor of God's face shining upon his people reflects a positive disposition toward them. It is also found in other texts from the ancient Near East in which the divinity's shining face was linked with the promise of gifts and mercy (Cole 2000, 130). In the biblical context, it recalls God's appearance to Moses on Mount Sinai in which his presence causes Moses's face to shine with reflected glory (Exod. 34:29). Further, Psalm 67:1 parallels God's shining face with the desire for God to bless Israel. Psalm 80 even turns this image into a plea, with a thrice-repeated refrain that calls on God to make his face shine upon his people so that they can be delivered (Ps. 80:3, 7, 19). Thus, God's shining face is an image that reflects God's intention to bless.

The accompanying action in 6:25 is for God to "be gracious" to the recipients. Grace here reflects "the kindly action of a superior party to an inferior one in which the inferior has no claim on the superior" (Ashley 1993, 152). The verbal root translated as "be gracious" (חנן) is theologically resonant as God uses its adjectival form to describe his essential character to Moses (Exod. 34:6). The actions of God's grace are found throughout Scripture, in Numbers perhaps most poignantly in God's refusal to abandon Israel despite its many rebellions.[1] Including grace in this blessing creates space for repentance and renewal when Israel turns away from God. When he shows them grace, their relationship can be restored.

In the third statement (Num. 6:26) God's attitude is described in terms of his face. In this case, the image is of God "lifting up" his face to the recipient of blessing.

| TRANSLATION ANALYSIS
Many English translations use a synonym for "face" in this verse. The ESV and NET translate 6:26a as "the LORD lift up his countenance upon you." However, the word is the same as was translated "his face" in 6:25 (פָּנָיו). This is simply a matter of stylistic variation in English.

This expression only occurs twice where the subject lifts up their own face (Num. 6:26; Deut. 28:50). In context it is synonymous to the desire for God to "make his face shine" from the previous verse. One suggestion for a more idiomatic meaning is for the subject to "smile" upon the recipient (Cole 2000, 131; Gruber 1983, 253–54). This expresses the intended attitude of the blessing. It is noteworthy that the opposite image, God hiding his face, is common in the Old Testament and signifies divine absence or displeasure (Job 13:24; Ps. 13:1; 27:9; 44:24; 88:14; 102:2; 104:29; 143:7). It is "almost always linked with disaster, oppression, and affliction, which in the majority of cases is seen as the result of Israel's sin and unfaithfulness" (Stubbs 2009, 76). Thus, when God lifts up his face, it reflects his deep, abiding covenant love and his faithful presence with Israel.

The corresponding action in this final couplet is for God to provide peace (שָׁלוֹם) to the recipient. This consists of more than an absence of war, but rather a general state of well-being, tranquility, and prosperity (Milgrom 1990, 52). This sense of overriding peace summarizes the entirety of the blessing. God's attitudes of blessing, making his face shine, and lifting his face all point to God's intention to provide peace. This expression of divine intention points to a full restoration of God and his people, and reflects "the goal toward which God moves all of history" (Stubbs 2009, 77). This blessing is thus exquisitely crafted and richly evocative of the much-anticipated promise of God and his people existing in harmony.

6:27. The passage concludes with God's purpose statement for the blessing. In 6:27a, God declares that the priests, as his representatives will "put my name on the Israelites" (NET, NIV). This again emphasizes that the Israelites are his chosen people, claimed by him through the covenant that he had maintained since the time of Abraham. Israel's identity is rooted in the reality that it bears the name of God. This priestly blessing reminds the Israelites that they are known and numbered as the people whom God calls his own (Sprinkle 2015, 218).

THEOLOGICAL REFLECTION
The exegetical idea (God desires to bless and preserve the Israelites), leads to this theological focus: *Pronouncing God's blessing shapes the identity of God's people.* Uttering or receiving this blessing is a powerful reminder that the community exists under God's care and protection. As the people respond to God's presence with obedience, the hope is that he will pour out his peace. The theological resonance of the priestly blessing during this time in Israel's history cannot be understated. Stubbs suggests that "the wilderness experience of Israel can in this way be seen as a deep meditation on what it means to bear the name and presence of God as

---

1 See especially the discussion of Numbers 14, where Moses implores God to remember his gracious character and turn from judgment to restoration.

a people" (Stubbs 2009, 73). If Israel is a people upon whom God has placed his name, then the outpouring of his blessing confirms their essential identity.

Echoes of community formation through the priestly blessing can be found throughout the Old Testament. Psalms 67 and 121 allude to it and set it against the backdrop of God's protection (Wenham 2008, 102). This further reflects the hope of *shalom* for the people of God. This blessing is also linked to worship at the tabernacle through Aaron's blessing in Leviticus 9:22–24. The blessing likely was part of the daily liturgy at the temple and the great pilgrimage feasts (Stubbs 2009, 77–78). Thus, as Israel gathered to worship, the blessing affirmed God's concern for his people and his desire to bring them grace and peace. This blessing also resonated outside of corporate worship contexts. In 1979, archaeologists discovered two inscriptions in silver from a burial complex at Ketef Hinnom, near Jerusalem. The text consists in part of a slight variation of the priestly blessing, suggesting that its written presence was also a means of conferring God's blessing (Barkay et al. 2003, 162–71; Smoak 2017, 1–26). This pronouncement of God's blessing thus gave the Israelites a shared sense of identity rooted in his promises to them.

For Christians, the promise of being a people whom God blesses also shapes our identity. The blessings are not rooted in the covenant blessing and curses of the Old Testament, but in Christ "the source and content of blessing" (Stubbs 2009, 78). Union with Christ shapes the identity of the new covenant people of God as he draws people together to be fellow citizens and members of God's household (Eph. 2:19). As the priestly blessing climaxes with the hope of peace, so Christ is our peace who seeks to reconcile humanity to himself through the cross (Eph. 2:14–16).

The final verse further reveals how God forms his community of faith. This passage concludes with God's statement that through this blessing, the priests will put his name on the children of Israel (Num. 6:27). They are a community that bears the name of the God who delivered them from Egypt and who sustained them in the wilderness. Likewise, the New Testament affirms that the church finds its identity in the name of God. First Peter 4:16 declares, "But if you suffer as a Christian, do not be ashamed, but glorify God that you bear such a name" (NET). This image is connected to Greco-Roman understandings of the household, in which subordinate members gain honor and identity from the family's leader (Howe 2005, 290–91). Thus, followers of Christ bear his name, which gives them their essential identity and provides encouragement even under persecution.

PREACHING AND TEACHING STRATEGIES

Exegetical and Theological Significance

The blessings God gives us are always rooted in his loving-kindness and grace. When we reflect on the wilderness generation and the history of the nation of Israel in the Bible, we can be amazed at the richness of God's mercy and desire to bless. The blessings that God poured out upon his people were for their good, but also for the good of the nations around them. The promises given to Abram stated he would be blessed and that all nations on earth would be blessed through him (Gen. 12:1–3). We can parrot this as a cliché, but there is a deep truth in the saying that we are blessed to be a blessing.

As the canonical revelation unfolds, we can see how the way that God will bless his people with his presence and gifts comes into sharper and sharper focus. There are blessings of fruitfulness, land, and prosperity, but all blessings are pointing to Jesus Christ who is their source and fulfillment. In the end, God's covenant people will live with him in the new heavens and earth, beholding his glory and never being outside of his holy presence. There can be peace and prosperity in a relative sense here on earth, but nothing like the extent that awaits us in the future. In Christ, YHWH blesses us and keeps us. In Christ, his face of favor, grace, mercy, and love shines upon us. In Christ, he gives us peace. In Christ, his name is upon us, and we are blessed.

We are blessed by God for our own good, and also for the good of others. But we are also blessed so that we can respond by blessing his name. Clearly this is asymmetrical; the meaning of *blessing* in this case is analogical and not univocal (i.e., we do not bless God precisely the way that he blesses us). Yet, all through Scripture, God blesses his people so that they will be holy and respond to his love and grace with praise, obedience, and worship. Blessing flows from God, and blessing begets blessing.

Preaching Idea

In Scripture, there is a beautiful spiral between God's benediction and our response in doxology.

Contemporary Connections

What does it mean?
What does it mean that in Scripture, there is a beautiful spiral between God's benediction and our response in doxology? Although this is not a biblical quotation, the spirit of this truth is well-captured in Matt Redmond's song "Blessed Be Your Name." It is vital to recognize that the spiral does not begin with our action, but with God's primary action of pouring out blessings on his people. As redeemed sinners, every believer ought to have a sensitive heart to God's goodness and love and should respond in thankfulness, gratitude, love, adoration, and praise to every blessing we are given. It is always a danger to desire the gifts more than the Giver. Living in responsive praise is one way to remain focused on God over everything else, even our blessings.

Followers of Christ should desire the presence of God—his face, his countenance, his name—above all. If our desire is for God, then we will rejoice when we feel him near. Many know what it is like to have their heart light up when they see someone they love, and when they can talk face to face with an individual they love deeply. In some African cultures and in various other places, men who are good friends often talk while holding hands, exhibiting closeness and trust. It is the presence of God rather than the presents of God that we should desire. If we love him, being near him and having his face shine upon us is what our hearts crave. In Christ, this intimacy is satisfied.

Is it true?
Is it true that God's benediction of blessing rests on believers in Christ? Furthermore, is it in fact true that the recipients of God's benedictory, gracious blessings should respond in doxological praise?

Both of these questions are answered in one statement of the apostle Paul: "Praise be to the God and Father of our Lord Jesus Christ, who has blessed us in the heavenly realms with every spiritual blessing in Christ" (Eph. 1:3 NIV). Notice that those in Christ have *every* spiritual blessing! Also notice that this is a reason to praise the God and Father of our Lord Jesus Christ. God is praised for the blessings he gives us, some of which are enumerated in Ephesians 1:3–14. At one oversimplified level, thanking God for the blessings he gives us is simply basic civility and good manners. How ungrateful would someone be to receive the forgiveness of sins, eternal life, and every spiritual blessing in Christ, and not thank and praise the one who blessed them this way? It is unthinkable. Those who understand the character and work of God through Christ will bless his name.

Now what?
There are times—usually when we are complaining—when we are told to count our blessings. If you want to stir up thankfulness to God, counting your spiritual blessings is a good way to begin. Search the Scriptures for the blessings

and promises of God. For each one, meditate upon its significance, and then reflect on a fitting way to thank and praise God for what he has poured out. Listening to worship music or reciting particular psalms of praise may help guide you in your response of praise. Writing down notes of things may later help you recall that for which you are particularly thankful to God. Resolve not to take without giving: when you are aware of being blessed, make sure you return praise and thanksgiving to the Source of the blessing.

Creativity in Presentation

Although I (Steve) have always been in non-liturgical churches, I close every service by dismissing the congregation with the words, "Go in grace and peace." This represents a benediction taken from the opening of Paul's letters. The order is important: grace comes first, and from grace, peace. Biblical benedictions and words of blessing are powerful in the lives of God's people.

As we receive God's benedictory blessings in Christ, we need to respond in doxological praise. One way to do this is to have either a congregational responsive reading or a team of selected individuals read biblical doxologies in alternating patterns with the benediction in Numbers 6. Here are some examples to consider:

Spiral #1

Benediction Blessing:
The Lord bless you
  and keep you;
the Lord make his face shine on you
  and be gracious to you;
the Lord turn his face toward you
  and give you peace.

Doxological Response:
Blessed be to the God and Father of our Lord Jesus Christ. (2 Cor. 1:3)

To our God and Father be glory forever and ever. Amen. (Phil 4:20)

Spiral #2

Benediction Blessing:
The Lord bless you, etc.

Doxological Response:
Blessed be the Lord God of Israel. (Luke 1:68)

To the King of ages, immortal, invisible, the only God, be honor and glory forever and ever. Amen. (1 Tim. 1:17)

Spiral #3

Benediction Blessing:
The Lord bless you, etc.

Doxological Response:
Praise the Lord, my soul;
  all my inmost being, praise his holy name.
Praise the Lord, my soul,
  and forget not all his benefits—
who forgives all your sins
  and heals all your diseases,
who redeems your life from the pit
  and crowns you with love and compassion,
who satisfies your desires with good things
  so that your youth is renewed like the eagle's.
(Ps. 103:1–5)

Spiral #4

Benediction Blessing:
The Lord bless you, etc.

Doxological Response:
Now to him who is able to keep you from stumbling and to present you blameless before the presence of his glory with great joy, to the only God, our Savior, through Jesus Christ our Lord, be glory, majesty, dominion, and

authority, before all time and now and forever. Amen. (Jude 24–25)

Needless to say, there are different ways of structuring the benediction/doxology spirals, and different verses that could be used, but the emphasis should be on how God's Word moves us from his sovereign benediction to our joyful response in grateful praise. This process reveals that in Scripture, there is a beautiful spiral between God's benediction and our response in doxology.

A useful outline of this passage could be:

- God promises to bless his people through his gracious attitude and his actions of protection and preservation (6:22–26).

- God's blessings reflect God's claim to his people (6:27).

DISCUSSION QUESTIONS

1. Why does God give his priests instructions for how to bless the Israelites?

2. What does it mean for God to keep us, to be gracious to us, and/or to give us peace?

3. How does God's blessing relate to preceding discussions of how to be holy in his presence in Numbers 5–6?

Numbers 7:1–89

EXEGETICAL IDEA
Israel obeyed God's command to bring gifts to mark the dedication of the tabernacle.

THEOLOGICAL FOCUS
God's people should be generous in their gifts to him.

PREACHING IDEA
In Christ, the gifts we bring are not identical, but every believer should have a heart for giving.

PREACHING POINTERS
It is easy for contemporary Christians to miss how much disunity and tribal tension often existed among the tribes of Israel. However, this text gives a welcome example of tribal unity. Each tribe of Israel contributed its share, and its shares in the dedication of the tabernacle were identical. This is more than pedantic record-keeping: it is a witness to the inclusion of all of God's people on equal terms. No tribe owned the ministry, neither was any tribe excluded. The repetition of the gifts, reported in their identical details, ensured that no tribe could claim a greater stake than another. It was a testimony to the unity of the covenant community as it prepared to head for the Promised Land. This was what God desired of his people.

In the new covenant assembly, there is unity but also diversity. At this time, we do not all bring the same gifts when we come into the Lord's holy presence. We are all members of one body, but we are different parts of it and each is to function in their own role, using the special gifts that God has given them. Yet, there is another fundamental unity: every believer is to give God their entire heart through Jesus Christ their Lord. No believer is to hold back or give God less than their best. The gifts in our hands are diverse, but every believer should rejoice in giving to the Lord and working to edify his saints. In Christ, the gifts we bring are not identical, but every believer should have a heart for giving.

GIFTS FOR THE SANCTUARY (7:1–89)

LITERARY STRUCTURE AND THEMES

Numbers 7–8 focuses upon the final preparations for the inauguration of the tabernacle and the whole sanctuary complex. This is part of the community formation that takes place at Sinai. God directs the Israelites to offer rich gifts to the sanctuary (Numbers 7) and orders Moses to consecrate the Levites to its service (8:5–26). This preaching unit focuses upon the gifts of the tribal leaders. Numbers 7 can be divided into three subunits with a final coda: the consecration of the tabernacle (7:1–11), the record of each tribe's gifts (7:12–83), and the summation of the gifts (7:83–88). The final verse (7:89) offers a brief coda concerning Moses speaking with God.

The theme of this unit is that God is worthy of receiving gifts from his people. Free-will donations played a significant role in the construction of the implements of worship (Exod. 25:1–9). This passage builds upon that theme, detailing an additional set of offerings that mark the final stages of constructing the sanctuary for Israel's worship activities as the nation prepares to leave Sinai.

- *The Consecration of the Sanctuary (7:1–11)*
- *The Record of the Gifts for the Sanctuary (7:12–88)*
- *How God Communicated with Moses (7:89)*

EXPOSITION

After the initial account of Moses's activities in dedicating the tabernacle and its precincts, this passage becomes highly repetitive. It records the gifts of the twelve tribes in turn, following the same template. This duplication points to the completeness of the nation's response: Israel obeys God's command to bring gifts to mark the dedication of the tabernacle.

The Consecration of the Sanctuary (7:1–11)

7:1. The actions detailed in this chapter are set "on the day when Moses had finished setting up the tabernacle" (ESV). Based on Exodus 40:16–17, this is actually a month prior to the census in Numbers 1 (Ashley 1993, 160). It is likely that Numbers 7–9 discusses events that occurred during the month between the completion of the tabernacle in Exodus 40 and the taking of the census in Numbers 1 (Wenham 2008, 103). This is another reminder that the organizational principle of Numbers is thematic rather than chronological. The census account details the size and organization of the Israelite community and lists its leaders. These leaders offer the gifts described in this chapter.

This verse also reflects Moses's preparations of the tabernacle and the sanctuary for active worship. The verbs "anoint" (משׁח) and "sanctify" (קדשׁ) occur twice, indicating that both the tabernacle and the sacrificial altar have been made ready for service.

7:2–3. Moses's actions prompt the tribal leaders to approach with their first set of offerings. Further on, this chapter identifies the tribal leaders as those who assisted Moses with the census. The initial gift here serves a very practical purpose: transporting elements of the sanctuary during Israel's travels. The gift consisted of six carts and twelve oxen, which works out to one ox per tribal leader and one cart for every two tribal leaders (7:3). The tribal leaders brought these gifts to the tabernacle, showing that they were intended for sacred service.

7:4–9. God then tells Moses how to assign the gifts of carts and oxen. They are to contribute to the work of the sanctuary, specifically aiding the Levites in their duties. Moses gives two carts and four oxen to the Gershonites, and four carts and eight oxen to the Merarites. These provide the means for transporting the sacred items for which these two Levitical clans bear responsibility (cf. Num. 4:21–33). The text also reiterates that the Gershonites and Merarites served under the authority of Ithamar, the son of Aaron (7:8b). The Kohathites did not receive any carts or oxen. This is because they had charge of the holiest items including the ark and the sacrificial altar (cf. Num. 4:4–12). Their duty was to carry those implements on poles after the priests had prepared them for transport.

7:10–11. Focus shifts to the gifts that the Israelite leaders bring to mark the dedication of the altar. These gifts reflect the altar's readiness for service. This is a moment worth commemorating since the sacrificial system is "now put into practice for the first time, with great fanfare and repetition" (Stubbs 2009, 83). The timing of these gifts coincides with the ordination of Aaron and his sons as priests who minister at the tabernacle (Leviticus 8–9). When they are consecrated to their ministry, the gifts of the Israelites provide them with a supply of necessary items. These gifts are also signs of devotion as they leaders bring them before the altar in response to God's instructions.

> **Dedication**
> The word commonly translated as "dedication" in 7:10–11 is חֲנֻכָּה (so also in 2 Chron. 7:8–9). It reflects setting something aside for sacred use. In the intertestamental period, this word was appropriately used to name the festival of Hannukah, which celebrated the reconsecration of the temple after its desolation by Antiochus IV Epiphanes.

The Record of the Gifts for the Sanctuary (7:12–88)

7:12. The gifts for the sanctuary are enumerated, tribe by tribe. The gifts from the tribe of Judah gifts are listed first, establishing a template that will be followed for the remaining tribes. It consists of: 1) the day of presentation, 2) the name of the tribal leader, 3) offering of sacrificial vessels, 4) offering of animals, and 5) restating the name of the tribal leader (Cole 2000, 140). Judah brings its offerings on the first day, led by Nashon, son of Amminadab. As mentioned above, he and the other leaders helped Moses conduct the census in Numbers 1. He is the only leader not explicitly identified as a "chieftain" (נָשִׂיא). One possibility is that the absence of a title is meant to counterbalance the privilege of presenting the first offering, making sure that Nashon does not stand above his fellow leaders (Milgrom 1990, 54).

7:13–14. The list of the gifts starts with the sacrificial vessels. They begin with implements that would be used in worship: a silver plate (קְעָרָה) and a silver basin (מִזְרָק) filled with the flour and oil of a grain offering. The precious metal and the presence of the grain offering express the suitability of these gifts for God. The exact function of these vessels is unknown, but it is possible that the plate was used with the bread of the presence, while the basins held the blood to be sprinkled on the altar (Allen 2012, 155). The plate and basin are described by weight: 130 and seventy shekels respectively. This works out to roughly three pounds for the plate and two pounds for the basin (Milgrom 1990, 55).

The final vessel is much smaller (4 oz.) and is fashioned from gold rather than silver. It is filled with incense, providing a pleasing aroma that is to accompany sacrifices. Taken together, these vessels reveal that the Israelite tribes gave costly gifts, befitting their purpose of being devoted to service at the tabernacle.

TRANSLATION ANALYSIS
The golden vessel is identified only as a כַּף, which can refer to the palm of the hand. English translations render it several ways, including "dish" (ESV, NIV, NRSV), "pan" (NASB, NET, NKJV), or "bowl" (CSB). Its small size suggests that it might also be understood as a "spoon" or "ladle" (Ashley 1993, 163; Wenham 2008, 105).

7:15–17. The gifts of the tribes also include animals. It is unlikely that these animals were sacrificed on the day that they were offered. Rather, they provided a dedicated herd for the priests and Levites to sacrifice when appropriate (Milgrom 1990, 362–64). The animals listed here are associated with three separate offerings, described in further detail in Leviticus 1–5. First, a bull, a ram, and a year-old male lamb are provided for the burnt offering (עֹלָה), then a male goat is provided for the purification offering (חַטָּאת). Finally, for the peace or fellowship offering (שֶׁלֶם), a number of animals were provided: two oxen, five rams, five male goats, and five male lambs that were one year old. Commentators note that in terms of the order of offering the sacrifices during a festival, the purification offering and burnt offering are inverted from what is listed here. This further demonstrates that the purpose of Numbers 7 is largely administrative (Levine 1993, 263–64).

The list of donated animals reminds the audience of the significance of sacrifice in Israel's worship. The burnt offering (עֹלָה) symbolized "an obedient life given freely to God" (Stubbs 2009, 87).[1] The life of the animal stood in for the worshipper's commitment to live faithfully before God. The purification offering (חַטָּאת), sometimes called the sin offering, used the blood of the sacrificial animal to purge either the individual or the community of contamination that caused separation from God's holiness (Schnittjer 2006, 311).[2] This offering required different animals depending on the identity of the supplicant. The male goat (Num. 4:16) fits the required purification offering for an Israelite nonpriestly leader (Lev. 4:22–26). Finally, several different animals could serve as fellowship offerings (שֶׁלֶם), including those offered to the sanctuary here (Lev. 3:1–17). This sacrifice was never compelled but was offered as an expression of thankfulness (Lev. 7:12) or to mark the fulfillment of a vow (Lev. 7:16). This was the one category of offering where the worshipper received a portion to eat. The list of animals in Numbers 7:15–17 thus reveals the people's commitment to the whole of the sacrificial system.

7:18–83. The pattern established by Judah is then repeated eleven more times with the same gifts for each tribe. The order of the gifts follows the same order as the arrangement of the tribes in Numbers 2:3–32. This makes for monotonous reading but makes it very clear that every tribe fully participated in the dedication of the tabernacle. The fact that each tribe gave equivalent gifts reveals that "No tribe could presume a greater role than any other, and every tribe had a role" (Levine 1993, 247). It also suggests that these verses reflect a tabulated inventory, providing an administrative record of each tribe's contributions. The text becomes slightly terser as it continues, using simple, stock formulae and changing just the name of the leader, the tribe, and the day of the offering (Levine 1993, 261). However, the careful nature of the repetition also suggests a theological purpose—declaring that every tribe was fully committed to the sanctuary and its worship (Wenham 2008, 105–6).

---

1   This is also the category of sacrifice that required the animal to be completed consumed in the fire (Lev. 1:3–9).
2   The term "purification offering" is better than "sin offering" since some actions that require this offering are clearly not sinful. These include unknowingly touching a ceremonially unclean person (Lev. 4:3) or childbirth (Lev. 12:6–8). The purpose of the offering is to remove impurity no matter how it was contracted.

7:84–88. After the twelve tribes brought their gifts, the text summarizes the quantity and weight of the items devoted to the sanctuary. Again, the amount of detail likely reflects a desire for bureaucratic precision. It also indicates that YHWH received exactly the same quantity and quality of gifts from each tribe. In the final accounting, there were twelve silver plates and basins and twelve golden ladles filled with incense (7:84). The text combines the silver vessels in its accounting of the weight, listing a total of 2,400 shekels (7:85).[3] The golden ladles then weighed 120 shekels, representing twelve ladles weighing ten shekels each (7:86). The list of donated animals also reflects the same process of addition. The final count includes twelve bulls, rams, and male lambs for the burnt offering, twelve male goats for the purification offering, along with twenty-four oxen, sixty rams, sixty goats, and sixty male lambs for the fellowship offering. These gifts provide the priests with the necessary items to perform their duties.

How God Communicated with Moses (7:89)

7:89. The chapter ends with a brief coda discussing how Moses communicated with God. It declares that Moses entered the Tent of Meeting that housed the tabernacle and heard the voice of God speaking to him from between the cherubim on top of the ark. This reflects a fulfillment of Exodus 25:22 where God promises to meet with Moses in that location. Previously, the overwhelming presence of God's glory had prevented Moses from entering the Tent of Meeting (Exod. 40:34–25). However, after the dedication of the priests (Leviticus 8–9) and the twelve days of dedicatory gifts, God permits Moses to meet with him in the heart of the community. This anticipates John 1:14, where the Word made flesh tabernacled among his people and revealed his glory (Cole 2000, 144).

The transition from the list of the gifts is abrupt, but it reflects back upon the beginning of the chapter where Moses dedicated the sanctuary and the altar (Gane 2004, 550). This action, along with the donations of the tribal leaders, combine to establish communion between YHWH and his people (Allen 2012, 157). God and his people are in harmony. He speaks to them through Moses, and Israel responds by offering the sacrifices that he requires.

THEOLOGICAL FOCUS

The exegetical idea (Israel obeyed God's command to bring gifts to mark the dedication of the tabernacle) leads to the following theological focus: *God's people should be generous in their gifts to him.* The generosity of Israel's offerings underlies its whole system of worship. As mentioned above, Exodus 25:1–9 shows how Israel's freewill offerings provided the material for the construction of the sanctuary, its implements, and the priestly garments. On this occasion, Israel has yet another opportunity to be generous in its gifts to God. Giving gifts reminds God's people that what they have reflects God's provision. The firstfruit offering commanded in Deuteronomy 26:1–15 frames the worshipper's gifts around God's deliverance and their responsibility to the Levite, foreigner, and widow in the community. Later in Israel's history, the prophet Haggai implores Israel to focus on the house of God, not on the beautification of their own houses. To their credit, the people respond in obedience (Hag. 1:12–15), prompting God to declare "the silver is mine and the gold is mine" (Hag. 2:8 NIV). Similarly in Malachi, God charges Israel with failing to bring him the tithes and offerings that he deserves. He directs the people to bring him what he is due and trust in the bounty of his provision (Mal. 3:8–12).

Being generous with one's offerings to God also reinforces the bonds between the worshipper and God as well as those within the community. This is exemplified in the peace offering where the worshipper, the priest, and the

---

3   This works out to 12 x 130 shekels for the silver plates added to 12 x 70 shekels for the silver basins.

deity all participate and benefit from the worshipper's generosity (Pressler 2017, 61). Further, Deuteronomy 14:26–27 calls for an attitude of rejoicing when bringing tithes and offerings before God. The worshipper celebrates what God has done and shares their bounty with the Levites and those in need in the community.

Of course, it is dangerous to assume a simple correlation between bringing gifts to God and our future material circumstances. Instead, these passages stress that God merits the gifts of his people. This outpouring of generosity at the inauguration of the sanctuary is perhaps paralleled in the response of the early church to the preaching of Christ's resurrection. New believers brought rich gifts to the apostles, culminating with the gift of Joseph the Levite, who sold a field and donated its proceeds to the apostles (Acts 4:36–37). Paul further commends the church in Philippi for its gifts that aided the proclamation of the gospel, comparing them to fragrant offerings and acceptable sacrifices (Phil. 4:18). The generosity of the church in Philippi supported Paul's preaching throughout the ancient Roman world and encouraged him when he was in prison. The gifts of God's people thus reflect their response to his provision and their commitment to the advancement of his kingdom.

PREACHING AND TEACHING STRATEGIES

Exegetical and Theological Significance
The sons of Jacob had a history of division, rivalry, and one-upmanship, but this section ensures their fundamental unity and equality before the Lord. Although this chapter may strike contemporary readers as unduly repetitive and redundant (the reader may wish that Moses used ditto marks or *et cetera*), God wanted the nation of Israel to be fully aware that they were equal participants in his sacred worship and tabernacle system. In Israel, there were no second-class tribes. As Ashley astutely remarks, "The cumulative effect of the repetition is that readers are assured that each tribe had an identical share in the support of the ministry of the tabernacle" (Ashley 1993, 161). At this stage in Israel's history, it was important for there to be a literal and visible equality, as represented by the gifts that were brought from the leaders of each tribe.

Equality among the people of God and accepting one another in unity were vital. Genesis shows division in the patriarchal families. Judges ends with one tribe almost being annihilated by the others. There are significant tensions between various tribes in the time of Saul and David. After Solomon's death, Israel split into two parts, governed by two different sets of kings. Jew, Samaritan, Gentile: ethnic, social, and religious divisions have always abounded. In the church of Jesus Christ, however, familial unity is the norm. When every believer brings God their heart, they do not need the visible equality of identical physical gifts of such things as rams, bowls, or grain.

Preaching Idea
In Christ, the gifts we bring are not identical, but every believer should have a heart for giving.

Contemporary Connections

What does it mean?
What does it mean that in Christ, the gifts we bring are not identical, but every believer should have a heart for giving? In the church of Jesus Christ, there is breathtaking diversity held together in an underlying, foundational unity. Paul's metaphor of the body is well known, and it speaks to the fact that there is only one Head (i.e., Jesus Christ), and only one body, but each and every believer is a member of the body with their own unique function. We need others, and they need us. In Christ, the Spirit distributes a variety of spiritual gifts. When we come to worship God and edify the body, every believer uses the different gifts they have received

from God as the gifts they bring back to him. The gifts are various, but their intended purpose is the same.

As Paul unfolds the metaphor, he notes that some will feel useless compared to other members, while some others will feel superior to everyone else. Both attitudes are inappropriate in the body of Christ. Your gifts are not the same as anyone else's, but they are neither better nor worse. In Christ, we do not need to have identical gifts to know that we are equally acceptable to God or equally a part of Christ's body. Thus, in the church people will bring a variety of gifts in service to God, and they all have an equal share in the Lord and in the body.

Is it true?
Is it true that in Christ, the gifts we bring are not identical, but every believer should have a heart for giving? The truth of this claim is found in both the explicit teaching in Scripture and in our empirical experience in the new covenant community. At one level, the gifts are the same because everyone is to give nothing less than their entire selves. At another level, the Spirit gives us different gifts that we are to bring back to God.

When it comes to financial giving, the New Testament authors do not appeal to laws and regulations about tithing. For example, Paul gives the Corinthians this great principle of giving: "For you know the grace of our Lord Jesus Christ, that though he was rich, yet for your sake he became poor, so that you through his poverty might become rich" (2 Cor. 8:9 NIV). It is this heart of Christ that is to constrain our financial giving. It is also this heart of Christ that is to govern how we spend our time and energy. Everything we are and have belongs to him. Some can give more than others, but the heart dedication of the believer should be identical.

Now what?
Are you honoring God by your attitude and gifts? Do you look at the gifts of others with jealousy or with disdain? Do you accept both the unity and diversity that God has created in the church of Jesus Christ? Is your giving and service actually infected with the desire to be praised by other people, as Jesus warned against? Perhaps a further question is in order: Do you actually give to God at all? If not, you need to repent and revaluate.

Although the questions above may seem negative, unity and giving are extremely positive things. There are other questions to ask: Do you rejoice in giving gifts to God? Do you love seeing the unity of heart and the diversity of gifts in the church? Is your giving done in full recognition that our giving is only possible because of God's superabounding grace lavished out upon us? Prideful giving or work divides—but humble, grateful giving and service unites.

Creativity in Presentation
Imagine how different this text would be if one tribe decided not to participate. What an incredible opportunity would have been missed, and the damage to tribal unity would have been significant. But also imagine what would have happened if every day the next tribe tried to outdo the one before, selfishly and arrogantly attempting to show their superiority or higher importance. Giving a token pittance would have been offensive, but so would ostentatiously trying to trump the offerings of the other tribes.

God judges the heart, and not the amount of money or time given. Do not forget to recall Jesus's assessment of the large financial donations of the Pharisees in comparison with the poor widow's gift of one small coin (Luke 21:1–4).

It is tragic to think that the good gifts of God given to his people, which should be returned in service and gratitude to him, can be a point of pride or division in the church. A dialogue among the parts of the body might help illustrate the folly of such things. Both the receiving and giving of gifts in the church should bring people together, not drive them apart. It would be possible for people to donate larger and larger steeples until the building collapses, or bigger and bigger chandeliers until there is no room for people in the foyer. If you have ever watched little kids playing soccer, they all clump around the ball (or wander around picking dandelions). You get a huge mass of players all in a group, all charging the ball, and that makes the game impossible. Spread out, play your position. Accept your role, for the good of the team.

It is a joy when people work and give together to achieve harmonious and positive ends. If every part of the body performs its intended function, then the whole body will thrive and be healthy. If every believer gives, serves, and blesses according to the grace given them in Christ, the church will flourish. In Christ, the gifts we bring are not identical, but every believer should have a heart for giving.

The basic movements of this passage can be articulated according to this outline:

- The gifts of God's people celebrate his presence among them (7:1–9).

- Gift-giving is marked by obedience, equity, and generosity (7:10–88).

- God graciously speaks to his people through his presence (7:89).

DISCUSSION QUESTIONS

1. Why does God require his people to give gifts to him? How does gift-giving help develop a heart of worship?

2. Why are the gifts of each tribe listed in such precise detail? Why does each tribe give exactly the same gifts?

3. Why do you think that the sacrificial vessels were made out of rich materials like silver and gold?

4. How do we avoid the dangers of making gift-giving into a competition that shows our greater spirituality?

5. What nonfinancial gifts do you feel God is calling you to bring to him?

Numbers 8:1–26

EXEGETICAL IDEA
Setting up the lampstand and dedicating the Levites reflects the holiness of God's presence.

THEOLOGICAL FOCUS
God's holy presence is worthy of reverence by his chosen and holy people

PREACHING IDEA
Come into the light! Be washed, be consecrated, and serve the Lord with reverent awe.

PREACHING POINTERS
Part of the symbolism found in the tabernacle depicts the shining of God's light upon his people, which illustrates the grace of the benediction in Numbers 6:24–26. When the priest blesses the people, it is only because God has already sovereignly determined to make his face shine upon them. No priest or prophet must cajole a reluctant God to bless his people. God is a God of light and life, not darkness and death.

When God's light shines upon his people, they must be purified and cleansed. Having been made holy, they are consecrated to the service of the Lord. In Numbers 7, Israel brought offerings for the tabernacle, but God selects the Levites to be offerings in themselves. When the light dawns, we are called into life, love, and holy service. This chapter is filled with sacred, symbolic details. In God's plan of redemption, it is his Son the Lord Jesus Christ who is the light of the world. It is also the Son who provides the blood needed for washing, purification, and atonement. Levites had to retire, but the Son lives forever and so his priestly office never ends. Hebrews reveals in exquisite detail how the old covenant forms were fulfilled by the new covenant mediator. There were lessons in this text for Israel in their own day, but the fullness and richness are only seen in Jesus Christ. So, since God's light is shining in Jesus, come into the light! Be washed, be consecrated, and serve the Lord with reverent awe.

MINISTERING IN GOD'S HOLY PRESENCE (8:1–26)

LITERARY STRUCTURE AND THEMES

This preaching unit builds upon the gifts given to the sanctuary in the previous chapter. Numbers 7–8 together detail the preparations necessary to prepare the tabernacle and its Levitical attendants (Sprinkle 2015, 228). Numbers 8:1–4 describes the preparation of the lampstand in the Holy Place within the tabernacle. Numbers 8:5–26 then focuses on the dedication of the Levites. Previous chapters have announced God's claim to the Levites, counted them, and assigned duties to them. This chapter narrates the process by which God cleanses them for service. The discussion of the Levites can be further subdivided into the commands to prepare the Levites (Num. 8:5–14), the rationale for the selection of the Levites (8:15–19), Israel's obedient response (8:20–22), and the age range of Levitical service (8:23–26).

The driving theme of this chapter is the need for consecration in serving a holy God. The lampstand must be set up properly to illuminate the place of God's presence. Further, since God had chosen the Levites to serve at the sanctuary, they must be dedicated to that purpose. This chapter again reflects divine transcendence. These elaborate proceedings protect the Israelites from the potential devastation of unauthorized approaches to God's presence (Num. 8:19). However, elements of God's mercy abound as he provides Israel with the means to worship him.

- **The Lampstand (8:1–4)**
- **The Consecration of the Levites (8:5–26)**
  - *Commands to Consecrate the Levites (8:5–14)*
  - *The Rationale for Selecting the Levites (8:15–19)*
  - *Israel's Obedient Response (8:20–22)*
  - *The Age Range of Levitical Service (8:23–26)*

EXPOSITION

To draw near to God is a wonderful and fearful thing. Through his grace, God establishes procedures and consecrates servants so that he can dwell among his people. This chapter reminds its audience of the nature of their God. Setting up the lampstand and dedicating the Levites reflects the holiness of God's presence.

The Lampstand (8:1–4)

8:1–2. God speaks to Moses, building on the coda at the end of the previous chapter (Num. 7:89). The text now shows this form of communication in action. The subject of God's instructions is the lampstand that sat in the Holy Place of the tabernacle, along with the incense altar and the table holding the bread of the presence. The lampstand was briefly mentioned earlier in the book (Num. 3:31; 4:9–10) but only in the context of how it was to be transported. This passage elaborates on its function.

Exodus 25:31–40 details the specifications for the lampstand, noting that it was to be made from pure gold with intricate designs reflecting a blossoming almond tree. This design likely implies a connection between the lampstand and the tree of life (Gen. 2:10; 3:22–24), while its seven lamps reflect the totality or completeness of its illumination. The lampstand thus reflects God's life-giving presence within his sanctuary.

God's specific instruction is for Aaron to make sure that the light cast by the lampstand illuminated the space in front of it (cf. Exod. 25:37). This reflects the arrangement of items within the Holy Place. The lampstand was to be placed on its southern side, while the table with the bread of the presence was on the northern side (Exod. 26:35). The lampstand would cast its light on the table after Aaron followed God's directives. The twelve loaves of bread placed on the table represented the tribes of Israel, so its illumination reflected the promise that Israel would live in the light of God's presence (Wenham 2008, 107).

8:3–4. Aaron did what God commanded. This marked the beginning of the priestly service of the lampstand, which was to be a perpetual duty, making sure that the light of God's presence always shone over his people (Lev. 24:3–4). The inauguration of the lampstand concludes with brief recap of its construction, drawing from Exodus 25:31, 40.[1] It reminds the audience of its priceless nature, fully constructed from hammered gold. The brief discussion of the lampstand thus fleshes out a key symbol of God's holy presence.

The Consecration of the Levites (8:5–26)

Commands to Consecrate the Levites (8:5–14)
8:5–7. In Numbers 3–4, God instructed Moses to set apart the Levites for service at the sanctuary. This passage dedicates them to that service by ritually cleansing them, preparing them to serve a holy God. The absence of temporal markers suggests that this process began at the same time as the gifts for the sanctuary in Numbers 7: the first day of the first month of the second year of their departure from Egypt (Wenham 2008, 103).

God addresses Moses and commands him to take the Levites from among all the Israelites and cleanse them. The selection of the Levites reflects language from Numbers 3–4 where God chose the Levites as replacements for the firstborn of all Israel. For them to do the service God required, Moses must render them ceremonially clean. The verbal root used here (טהר) can reflect individual cleansing from blemishes such as skin diseases (cf. Leviticus 13) but can also point to dedication for sacred duties (Ezra 6:20; Neh. 12:30; 13:22). It is not a statement of moral purity since many things that render a person unclean are not inherently sinful (e.g., menstruation, sexual emissions, contact with a dead body), but it reflects the need to prepare the Levites to enter a sphere of purity where they can interact with the holy objects of the sanctuary (Ashley 1993, 169).

The process begins with God's instructions for Moses to cleanse the Levites with the "water of purification" (8:7 ESV, NET).[2] The word translated "purification" here is חַטָּאת, which can also refer to sin, or offense against God. However, here "there is not the merest hint of sin" (Frevel 2013, 374). Instead, this process removes any potential ritual impurities that could render them unfit for service. God then requires the Levites to shave all the hair on their bodies. This purification process also is found in Egyptian and Mesopotamian practices (Cole 2009, 352) and reflects the totality of their cleansing.[3] It also provides a visually striking signal of the purified status being awarded to the Levites (Allen 2012, 160). Notably, this is a one-time event: future generations of Levites are not compelled to undergo the same procedure. The inauguration of the Levites thus

---

1 It reflects an ancient design, sharing motifs from Mesopotamian iconography in the Late Bronze Age (Cole 2009, 361; Milgrom 1990, 367).
2 The source of this water is unknown. Possibilities include water from the bronze laver which was placed near the altar in the tabernacle courtyard (Exod. 38:8) or the water for cleansing those exposed to the dead (Numbers 19; Cole 2000, 149).
3 See also the cleansing of those stricken with leprosy in Leviticus 14:8–9.

receives a unique symbol of what is needed to serve a holy God. The final element is for the Levites to wash their clothes, a common procedure in preparing to enter God's presence (Exod. 19:10, 14; Lev. 11:25, 28; 13:6, 34; 15:11).

8:8–11. The cleansing process also entails sacrifice and ceremony. The elements of the sacrifice are given: a bull with an accompanying flour and oil mixture (cf. Num. 15:3), along with a second bull for a purification offering (8:8).[4] Then, the whole nation participated in a ceremony in which the Levites assembled before the tabernacle in front of the rest of the Israelites. Then, the people laid hands on the Levites, acknowledging them as God's chosen substitutes for the firstborn (8:9–10; Allen 2012, 161).[5] Then, Aaron presented the Levites before God as a "wave-offering" (8:11; תְּנוּפָה). This must be symbolic since Aaron cannot physically elevate the Levites. With animal sacrifices, Aaron was instructed to literally elevate a portion and present it to God (Lev. 7:30). These verses create a two-step process: the Israelites dedicate the Levites as their replacements for their firstborn, and Aaron presents them to God.

8:12–14. The Levites were then instructed to lay hands on the bulls as part of their purification.[6] This sets up a double substitution in which "the Levites substituted for the people and the bulls substituted for the Levites" (Allen 2012, 161). The purpose of these sacrifices is atonement (I-כפר) for the Levites.[7] Although this can have moral overtones, again in this case the focus is on purification for contact with sacred things rather than expiation from sin. These sacrifices aim "at the inner relationship between YHWH and the Levites, who are singled out as his particular property" (Frevel 2013, 374). YHWH then repeated the instruction to present the Levites as a wave offering, symbolizing their separation from the rest of the Israelites and their dedication to God (8:13–14).

The Rationale for Selecting the Levites (8:15–19)

8:15. YHWH declares that the Levites were to come and serve at the sanctuary. Some of their responsibilities related to transporting the sanctuary and its items are detailed in Numbers 3–4, but their other duties are discussed further in 8:19.

8:16–18. God announces that the Levites are "entirely given to me from among the Israelites" (8:16 NET).[8] These verses reiterate God's claim to the firstborn of both Israel's people and animals from Numbers 3:12–13. The rationale is that God's claim to the firstborn of Israel stems from his destruction of the firstborn of the Egyptians in the final plague (8:17). The Levites are the substitutes that God accepts in place of Israel's firstborn.

8:19. God describes the Levites as gifts to Aaron and the other priests who will do the work of the sanctuary in place of the other Israelites. They support the priests in doing the work assigned to them. The sacrifice of bulls made atonement for the Levites (8:12) and now the Levites are essentially a corporate sacrifice that provides atonement for the whole of Israel. This means that the penalty for unauthorized access to the

---

4 See the exposition of Numbers 7 for why "purification offering" is a superior translation to "sin offering" for this kind of sacrifice.
5 Presumably, representative leaders from the Israelite tribes would perform this dedicatory action.
6 Again, one presumes that leaders of the Levitical clans physically performed this task.
7 This is the same root that lies behind the procedures required on Yom Kippur, or the Day of Atonement (cf. Leviticus 16).
8 This sense of emphasis is achieved through the repetition of the passive participle "being given" (נְתֻנִים נְתֻנִים).

sanctuary (here described as a plague) would fall on the Levites rather than the entire nation (Gane 2004, 556). Their mediatory role provided an additional safeguard for the nation as it interacted with God's holiness.

Israel's Obedient Response (8:20–22)

8:20–22. These verses briefly recount Israel's obedience to God's instructions. As expected in this early part of Numbers, the people and their leaders did exactly what God commanded. The Levites purified themselves (by shaving) and washed their garments (cf. 8:7). Aaron presented them as a symbolic wave offering (cf. 8:13, 15a) and made atonement for them, presumably through the sacrifices that God commanded in 8:12 (Milgrom 1990, 65). Then, the Levites presented themselves to do their required service (cf. 8:15b). The picture is harmonious: God declares what his people must do to live in his holy presence, and the people respond with faithful obedience.

The Age Range of Levitical Service (8:23–26)

8:23–25. God summarizes his instructions by providing an age range for the Levites to perform all the required duties at the sanctuary, including carrying the sacred items and keeping watch to prevent unauthorized access. Numbers 8:24 states that the age range is from twenty-five to fifty years old. Significantly, this is different from the range given in Numbers 4:3 (thirty to fifty years old). No obvious resolution for this discrepancy suggests itself. One possibility was that the census recorded in Numbers 3–4 revealed that there were sufficient Levites in the narrower age range and the lower limit was raised in response (Wenham 2008, 110).[9] This could reflect a desire to prevent immature individuals from taking on this serious role (Cole 2000, 154).[10] The possibility of a five-year apprenticeship before fully taking on all the work of the sanctuary also remains.[11]

Numbers 8:25 then identifies fifty as the age of retirement. Crucially, the elder Levites are not required to withdraw from all elements of sanctuary service. Instead, they are no longer permitted to do the physically onerous tasks of dismantling, transporting, and setting up the elements of the sanctuary (Wenham 2008, 110). This is captured in the phrase צְבָא הָעֲבֹדָה ("duty of service," ESV; "performing the work," NET).

8:26. Levites older than fifty are permitted to continue to minister by serving as guards to prevent encroachment on the sacred precincts. This would free up their younger brethren for the more arduous tasks. In this way, the elder Levites would continue to be a symbol of the presence of God's holiness in the community (Cole 2000, 154).

> **The Role of the Levites**
>
> The role of the Levites developed throughout Israel's history. During the wilderness sojourn, they tended and transported the elements of the sanctuary and guarded against unauthorized access. After the time of wilderness wandering, they were not bound directly to the central sanctuary. Numbers 35:1–5 set aside some towns for the Levites throughout the Promised Land. This suggests that they were to be dispersed throughout the land, serving at the sanctuary in turn. Their purpose was to provide examples of faithfulness to God for the rest of the Israelites to follow.[12] Later, both

---

9   This solution requires the reader to recall that Numbers 7–8 actually precedes Numbers 3–4 chronologically.
10 Ashley suggests that the improper actions of Aaron's sons Nadab and Abihu (Lev. 10:1–3) may have prompted this change (Ashley 1993, 162). This is plausible but highly speculative.
11 See the exposition of Numbers 3–4.
12 It is not surprising that the author of Judges uses Levitical failure as one of the signs of the depraved nature of this period. See the idolatrous Levite in Judges 17–18, and the callous and foolish Levite of Judges 19–20.

> David and Hezekiah assigned the Levites to duties caring for the sanctuary and dropped the age of service to twenty while eliminating the upper age limit (1 Chron. 23:24–27; 2 Chron. 31:16–17). First Chronicles 23:25–26 directly ties this to the fact that the Levites no longer need to carry the sacred items. David also assigned some Levites to be "officials and judges" (1 Chron. 23:4 NIV) while others become temple musicians (1 Chron. 23:5).

THEOLOGICAL FOCUS

The exegetical idea (Setting up the lampstand and dedicating the Levites reflects the holiness of God's presence) leads to the following theological focus: *God's holy presence is worthy of reverence by his chosen and holy people.* The distance between this text and the modern reader is quite wide. The specific duties of the Levites and the ceremony of dedication do not easily resonate. However, the reverence with which this text treats the signs of God's presence merits reflection.

The lampstand of Numbers 8:1–4 signifies God's presence and illuminates his concern for his people. Other images of light throughout Scripture attest to the wonder of God's presence. John conceptualizes the incarnation as the "true light that gives light to everyone" (John 1:9 NIV). This leads into the declaration of Christ's dwelling among his people as the Word became flesh, reflecting the fullness of God's glory (John 1:14). Later, Jesus announced "I am the light of the world" (John 8:12). His light shines on his people perpetually, just as the light of the lampstand illuminated the twelve loaves of bread in the Holy Place. The light of Christ ultimately illuminates churches, which are portrayed as lampstands fueled by Jesus as the eternal Son of Man (Rev. 1:12–20). The appropriate response to this light is reverent worship and an acknowledgement that this light is an imparted gift of God's presence.

The dedication of the Levites similarly calls for reverence in response to God's presence. God claimed the Levites in place of the firstborn of all Israel to set up appropriate channels of access. The Levites were the servants of the priests from the line of Aaron who had the responsibility of entering into God's presence. The author of Hebrews focuses on the priestly work of the old covenant that the Levites supported. He details the layout of the sanctuary and the regulations of the sacrificial system which were necessary to enter God's presence (Heb. 9:1–10). However, Christ, our great High Priest, accomplishes even greater access through his own shed blood, rather than through the blood of animals (Heb. 9:12–13; cf. Numbers 19). This means that there is no longer a need for intermediaries. Christ himself is the only, perfect intermediary who eternally coexists with the Father. Again, the appropriate response is reverent worship. The author of Hebrews exhorts his audience to "draw near to God with a sincere heart and with the full assurance that faith brings" (Heb. 10:22 NIV). They are called to hold onto their professed hope because their intermediary is perfectly faithful (Heb. 10:23).

In a similar vein, Paul calls the Roman church to offer themselves as living sacrifices, being transformed by the renewing of their minds rather than conforming to the world around them (Rom. 12:1–2). This is an act of spiritual worship, reflecting an appropriate response to the reality of God's holy presence dwelling among his people. In order to dwell with his people, God established a hierarchy of those who were permitted access. The Levites were dedicated to God's service, in support of the priestly ministry. These functions are now fully fulfilled by Christ. Just as the Israelites were to celebrate God's presence through sacrifices and obedient response to God's instructions, so God's people ought to be transformed in their thoughts and deeds as they enter his presence through the work of Christ.

PREACHING AND TEACHING STRATEGIES

Exegetical and Theological Significance

The great benediction of Numbers 6:24–26 finds symbolic fulfillment in 8:1–4. God instructed the priests to pronounce these words over the people:

The LORD bless you
 and keep you;
the LORD make his face shine on you
 and be gracious to you;
the LORD turn his face toward you
 and give you peace. (Num. 6:24–26 NIV).

Numbers 8:2 provides an explicit instruction concerning the direction that the light is to shine, but the reason why has to be inferred. Given the location of all of the elements in this sacred space, if the light is shining forward then it is illumining the twelve loaves of the bread of the presence, which represent the twelve tribes of Israel. As a result, "This section therefore expresses symbolically what 6:23–27 affirms verbally" (Wenham 2008, 107). God's face is truly shining upon his people; they are living in his light.

The deeds of darkness are incompatible with living in the light, so the Levites must be cleansed and consecrated before they can serve the Lord. Their bodies and their clothes had to be washed and purified, and atonement had to be made for their impurity resulting from sin or ceremonial uncleanness. They were officially presented to the Lord and dedicated to him. Numbers 7—the second longest chapter in the Bible after Psalm 119—describes the gifts that were brought to the tabernacle. In this chapter, "The Levites did not merely witness the offerings; they *were* the offerings, living sacrifices offered to God for his use" (Brown 2002, 67). When we are called into the light, we are to lay our very selves upon the altar, consecrated wholly and completely to God.

Sacred symbolism and ritual enactments abound in this chapter, all of which point to spiritual principles and find fulfilment in the gospel of Jesus Christ. Ultimately, Christ is the light of God that shines upon the covenant community. He is the priest who perfectly serves the Father in full, holy dedication. It is his blood that washes, purifies, and atones. With an indestructible life, he reigns as king and priest forever: there is no retirement age for Christ in his ministry. According to Hebrews, Christ's work was in the heavenly tabernacle, not the one of earthly shadows (Heb. 9:1–28).

Preaching Idea
Come into the light! Be washed, be consecrated, and serve the Lord with reverent awe.

Contemporary Connections

What does it mean?
What does it mean that we need to come into the light and be washed and consecrated, so that we can serve the Lord with reverent awe? The first thing to note is that God takes the sovereign initiative in shining the rays of his holy light into our lives. God's first verbal command of creation was to speak light into existence, and this holds true for spiritual illumination and life. Peter tells us that God "called you out of the darkness into his wonderful light" (1 Peter 2:9 NIV). Paul has an extended discussion about being called from out of darkness into the light of God, and he says that "you were once darkness, but now you are light in the Lord" (Eph. 5:8). Notice that we were not merely surrounded by darkness, but when we were lost in sin it is *we ourselves* that were darkness. Notice that in Christ, we are light in the Lord.

In grace, God sent his Son into the world, and his Son is the light (John 1:1–14). The light dispels darkness; it triumphs over it. In a similar way, purifying water removes dirt and defilement. Our bodies are cleansed by water, and our souls are cleansed by Christ's atoning blood. It is only after this purification and redemption that we can honor the Lord and offer him our service. The message of light and life in the gospel drives out the darkness, and the purified soul is consecrated for joyful and reverent worship.

Is it true?
Is it true that we are called to come into the light and be washed and consecrated, so that we can serve the Lord with reverent awe? This really is the order of the gospel: the light comes into the world; the light shines in the darkness; people are saved, purified, washed, and cleansed, and then appointed to bear the fruit of light in the name of Jesus.

We can see this truth at work throughout Scripture. Paul writes to Titus, "But when the kindness and love of God our Savior appeared, he saved us, not because of righteous things we had done, but because of his mercy. He saved us through the washing of rebirth and renewal by the Holy Spirit" (Titus 3:4–5). John writes to a church under his care, "This is the message we have heard from him and declare to you: God is light; in him there is no darkness at all. If we claim to have fellowship with him and yet walk in the darkness, we lie and do not live out the truth. But if we walk in the light, as he is in the light, we have fellowship with one another, and the blood of Jesus, his Son, purifies us from all sin" (1 John 1:5–7 NIV). Finally, Paul comments on the need for believers to be cleanse, stating, "Or do you not know that wrongdoers will not inherit the kingdom of God? Do not be deceived: Neither the sexually immoral nor idolaters nor adulterers nor men who have sex with men nor thieves nor the greedy nor drunkards nor slanderers nor swindlers will inherit the kingdom of God. And that is what some of you were. But you were washed, you were sanctified, you were justified in the name of the Lord Jesus Christ and by the Spirit of our God" (1 Cor. 6:9–11 NIV).

Now what?
Our response to these truths should be to repent of our deeds of darkness and receive the light of Jesus Christ that is revealed in the gospel. Having been called and invited into the illuminating splendor of God's light, we need to heed the instructions to "Draw near to God and He will draw near to you. Cleanse your hands, you sinners; and purify your hearts, you double-minded" (James 4:8). In confidence in Christ, "let us draw near with a sincere heart in full assurance of faith, having our hearts sprinkled clean from an evil conscience and our bodies washed with pure water" (Hebrews 10:22 NIV). Like the Psalmist, we should say,

I wash my hands in innocence,
  and go about your altar, LORD,
proclaiming aloud your praise
  and telling of all your wonderful deeds. (Ps. 26:6–7 NIV)

According to Ephesians 5:8–14, the "Now What?" is to:

1. Come out of the darkness.

2. Live as children of the light.

3. Produce the fruit of light.

4. Have nothing to do with the deeds of darkness.

5. Expose the evil fruit of darkness.

6. Wake up.

7. Bask in the glory of the shining light of Christ.

Creativity in Presentation
How dark is your auditorium when the lights are out? If possible, make the auditorium dark

enough that people cannot read their Bibles. This may require covering windows and veiling glowing signs. (Do not cover signs that need to be visible for safety and legal reasons, like those for fire exits.) Then, have workers uncover the windows, and have the lights turned on. Light is absolutely necessary for seeing physically, and God's light in Christ is just as necessary for seeing spiritually.

When the lights are on, a few people can come up on the stage who have had their hands stained with colors that can be easily washed away with soap and water. Have them wash their hands clean in basins, and then move over to an altar where they are presented as a wave offering (perhaps by waving their cleansed hands). This is the order: the light dawns, we are washed, we are consecrated, and we are enlisted to serve. Light signals the dawn of our days, and holy, reverent joy is to burst forth in its wake.

At the end of the service, have the people with clean hands come up and stain them again. Turn the lights down low; make it dark. Why would we want to go back to darkness and defilement, after we are in the light and have been made clean? Consecrate yourself to God and come into the light! Be washed, be consecrated, and serve the Lord with reverent awe.

The expositor may find this outline helpful for considering the movements of this passage:

- God's light shines on his people (8:1–4).

- God dedicates his chosen servants to sacred service on behalf of his people (8:5–22).

- God establishes the parameters of service (8:23–26).

DISCUSSION QUESTIONS

1. Why is light such a powerful image of God's presence?

2. Why do the Levites require such extensive preparations to be suitable for priestly service?

3. How does the preparation of the Levites point us to Christ?

4. How can believers today purify themselves so that they can serve God wholeheartedly?

Numbers 9:1–14

EXEGETICAL IDEA
Everyone who is part of the community of Israel must celebrate the Passover.

THEOLOGICAL FOCUS
The people of God should commemorate God's gracious acts of deliverance.

PREACHING IDEA
Our purpose in the present requires us to remember our origins and look toward our future hope.

PREACHING POINTERS
Without question, the Passover is one of the most important and well-known events in the Bible. Its significance as a redemptive event is paradigmatic. As with its greater fulfillment in the cross of Christ, numerous lines of biblical-theological importance run up to it, intersect within it, and flow out from it. God called Israel to continually look back on the covenant with Abraham and to continue to look back in awe at his mighty work of redemption on that first Passover night in Egypt. Christ is the fulfillment of everything Passover represented: he is the lamb who takes away the sin of the world, and it is his blood that shields his people from the angel of death. Jesus frees us from slavery to Satan, the world, and sin; Jesus redeems us into eternal life.

In order to live well in the present, we need to be able to simultaneously look back and look ahead. Human meaning, purpose, and dignity require meaningful origins, and they also require a significant, future *telos* (i.e., an ultimate goal, purpose, or end). As Christians, our orientation in life comes from being created in the image of God, being redeemed by Christ (in fulfillment of Passover), and looking forward to eternal, eschatological glory in the new heaven and new earth. Our purpose in the present requires us to remember our origins and look toward our future hope.

CELEBRATING THE PASSOVER (9:1–14)

LITERARY STRUCTURE AND THEMES

This passage reiterates the central importance of the Passover. It follows the discussion of gifts to the sanctuary and the appointment of the Levites in chapters 7–8, narrowing the broad perspective on how Israel was to worship to a specific focus. Celebrating this second Passover also anticipates Israel's departure from Sinai in Numbers 10, just as the first Passover marked Israel's escape from Egypt (Milgrom 1990, 67). It is an opportunity to commemorate God's work of deliverance and to remind Israel of its core identity. Remembering the Passover reminds Israel that "its identity is based on a specific and gracious act of redemption by God" (Stubbs 2009, 101). The key theme developed in this passage is that *everyone* associated with Israel must participate in Passover remembrance.

The passage has three sections: 9:1–5 lists the initial instructions from God to Moses, 9:6–8 adds complications by introducing questions from Israelites who were unable to celebrate Passover at the designated time, while 9:9–14 provides God's response to the dilemma. This structure reflects a "dynamic exchange between the Lord and Moses that provides a rare glimpse into how the Lord's instruction for his people could be modified on the basis of new conditions and circumstances" (Allen 2012, 166). This preaching unit reveals a God who interacts with his people and in his grace provides an alternative means for them to participate in this most important feast.

- *Initial Instructions (9:1–5)*
- *Complications Arising from Uncleanness (9:6–8)*
- *God's Response (9:9–14)*

EXPOSITION

This passage reinforces the necessity of Passover commemoration. Remembering God's gracious acts of deliverance prompts obedience to his instructions. Its purpose is mirrored in the common refrain "I am the LORD your God who brought you out of Egypt" (Exod. 6:7; 16:12; 20:2; Lev. 25:38, 55; 26:13; Num. 15:41; Deut. 5:6). The timeframe for this passage is odd at first glance. Numbers 9:1 identifies it as the first month of the second year of their departure from Egypt. This is prior to the census of 1:1, which is set at the beginning of the second month of the second year. This displacement again reminds us that the arrangement of Numbers is "not strictly chronological" (Allen 2012, 166). However, it still fits here since a chief concern of the text is to arrange an alternative time to celebrate Passover. God decrees that the fourteenth day of the second month could be used for that purpose (9:11), thus placing this secondary date two weeks after the command to take the census. The secondary date reinforces the central purpose of the passage: to remind the people that everyone who is part of the community of Israel must celebrate the Passover.

Initial Instructions (9:1–5)

9:1. The first section of the passage provides God's initial directions for commemorating the Passover. It contains few details of what exactly this entails but presumes that the Israelites recall God's directives from Exodus 12:1–28, 43–51. This verse begins with "the LORD spoke to Moses in the Desert of Sinai" (NIV), establishing God as the source of the instructions. The latter half of 9:1 gives the time frame, indicating that God gave these commands in the first month of the second year of their departure from Egypt. Nearly a year has passed since Israel's deliverance from Egypt. They have been at Sinai, learning what it means to be the people of God for most of the ensuing months (cf. Exod. 19:1). Now, just prior to their departure for the Promised Land, God has called them to remember his previous deliverance.

9:2–3. These verses provide God's directives. They begin simply with a statement that the Israelites are to observe the Passover at its appointed time. The root of the initial verb is עשׂה, which in cultic contexts means to offer a sacrifice or to celebrate a festival (Milgrom 1990, 67). The following verse then identifies the appointed time as the fourteenth day of the first month, which lines up with what God commanded in Exodus 12:17–20. Numbers 9:3 also specifies the exact time when this commemoration should occur. The Hebrew phrase בֵּין הָעַרְבַּיִם literally means "between the two evenings," but contextually indicates twilight (cf. Num. 27:3–8). This was the traditional marker of the end of one day and the beginning of the next: a fitting time to begin to observe a sacred occasion (Allen 2012, 167). In the remainder of the verse, God instructs Moses to have the Israelites observe it "with all its statutes and all its customs" (9:3b NET). Israel's knowledge of these is presumed from the guidelines given in Exodus 12, including directions for the preparation and eating of the lamb, unleavened bread, and herbs.

TRANSLATION ANALYSIS
English verses translate the Hebrew phrase כְּכָל־חֻקֹּתָיו וּכְכָל־מִשְׁפָּטָיו as *"with all its statutes and all its customs"* (NET), or *"in accordance with all its rules and regulations"* (NIV), or *"according to all its statutes and all its rules"* (ESV). The underlying nouns חֻקָּה and מִשְׁפָּט form a hendiadys, together conveying "complete compliance to detail, a full respect for and obedience to the regulations that God had established" (Allen 2012, 167).

9:4–5. Moses then relays these instructions to the Israelites. Numbers 9:5 feels almost redundant as it repeats that the Passover was observed on the designated date, commenced at the designated time, and that the children of Israel did all that God had instructed Moses. This repetition concludes the first part of the passage and highlights Israel's compliance with God's commands. It ends with an "obedience formula" found commonly in the Pentateuch (Exod. 39:32, 42; 40:16; Num. 1:54; 2:34; 8:20; Ashley 1993, 178). It also may recall Israel's similar obedience to God's commands for celebrating the first Passover in Exodus 12:28 (Cole 2000, 156).

Complications Arising from Uncleanness (9:6–8)

9:6. The passage then introduces complications. It considers a situation in which some Israelites find themselves ceremonially unclean on account of contact with a dead body. In this instance, the Israelites are faced with two competing requirements: they must celebrate the Passover, but they must remain apart from the community. This new circumstance requires clarification of God's instructions. It is the second of four cases in Leviticus–Numbers where a specific situation prompts Moses to ask God how to apply the underlying law(s) (Gane 2004, 565).[1] The

---

1 The other examples are the man who blasphemes the divine name (Lev. 24:10–16), a man who gathers wood on the Sabbath (Num. 15:32–36), and questions of whether women may inherit property in the absence of a male heir (Num. 27:1–11; 36:1–12).

significance of this kind of impurity can be seen in Numbers 6:1–21 and the discussion of the Nazirite vow. Ordinary Israelites were not under restrictions as severe as the Nazirite, but impurity from a dead body still rendered them unfit to appear before God.[2] Breaking that command and participating in the Passover could bring impurity to the entire nation.

9:7. The men announce their dilemma by first acknowledging their unclean state. They then ask why they are forbidden from presenting the "Lord's offering" (ESV, NET, NIV). On a literal level, the answer is clear: they cannot participate because of their ceremonial uncleanness. However, what they are actually conveying is their desire to observe this momentous occasion and worship God according to what he has commanded.[3] The phrase "the Lord's offering" (קָרְבַּן יהוה) refers to the lamb that would be eaten as a sacrifice to God (Gane 2004, 564). The unclean men are disqualified from bringing their contribution to this sacrificial arrangement.

> **The First Passover**
> Milgrom suggests the idea of bringing this offering at the appointed time helps to mark the transition from the first Passover, which was celebrated in people's homes, to a festival set at the tabernacle, or later, the temple (Milgrom 1990, 372). Key to the first Passover is its hurried nature, anticipating God's actions to release Israel from Egypt. Subsequent Passovers could be anticipated and thus God could command the attendance of the entire community at a designated location.

9:8. This section concludes with Moses asking the men to wait[4] while he asks God what to do in this situation. As with other occasions with a similar dynamic (Lev. 24:10–13; Num. 15:32–36), Moses's response is to be viewed positively. Moses did not have the answer to what is clearly a tricky situation. Rather than presumptuously speak for God, he instead makes himself an intermediary between the people and God (Allen 2012, 169). This also provides confidence in the solution that follows, since it clearly comes from God.

God's Response (9:9–14)

9:9–10. This section begins by presuming that Moses brought this question before God and received God's response. Notably, God answers the specific case from the men who approached Moses while also expanding his response to consider another situation where Israelites may have not properly observed the Passover. In 9:10, God commands Moses to speak again to the Israelites and establish the enduring nature of this ordinance. It is "for you or for your generations" (my translation of לָכֶם אוֹ לְדֹרֹתֵיכֶם). God first addresses the situation of an Israelite becoming unclean due to corpse contamination.[5] He also considers a scenario in which an Israelite cannot attend the Passover celebration for reasons of distance.

> TRANSLATION ANALYSIS בְּדֶרֶךְ רְחֹקָה
> ESV: "on a long journey"
> NASB: "on a distant journey"
> NET: "on a journey far away"
> NIV: "away on a journey"

---

2 The procedure for cleansing from this kind of impurity is found in Numbers 19.
3 In a book where Israelites grumble for many reasons, this is "a refreshing kind of complaint" (Gane 2004, 564).
4 The verb עִמְדוּ literally means "stand!" However, in context, it asks the men to remain where they are while Moses consults God.
5 God's speech begins with אִישׁ אִישׁ ("man man"), an idiom reflecting a hypothetical scenario where a specific individual is not in view. See the discussion of Numbers 5:11–30.

In context, this is an anticipatory consideration, since the entire community is present with Moses and God in the wilderness. It would take effect once the Israelites had claimed the Promised Land. Once they settled and dispersed throughout the land, it is possible that they might not be able to make it to the central sanctuary at the time of Passover. Given the severe consequences of not celebrating Passover, God provides a remedy for these individuals along with those ceremonially unclean. The extent of the distance required for this provision to apply is unknown. Most view it as a reference to those traveling outside the boundaries of the covenant community, linking this scenario with those affected by corpse contamination because in both cases, the Israelite is among those who are unclean (Allen 2012, 170; Ashley 1993, 179–80; Gane 2004, 564). It is also possible that this provision later became available to those whose permanent homes were far away from Jerusalem (Chavel 2009, 19). In any event, the requirement is clear: each Israelite must observe the Passover.

9:11–12. This verse establishes the date of the alternative observance. It is one month after the standard time for Passover: the fourteenth day of the second month. Interestingly, the text provides more specific instructions for this alternative date even though they would fit into the "statutes and customs" mentioned in 9:3. God commands the worshipper to eat the lamb along with unleavened bread and bitter herbs (cf. Exod. 12:8), not to leave any until morning (cf. Exod 12:10), nor to break the bones of the sacrificial animal (cf. Exod. 12:46). Providing the details for the alternative time of celebration confirms that it is equally valid to observe the Passover at this time. The worshipper submits to exactly the same requirements.

> **The Passover and Feast of Unleavened Bread**
> There is one distinction between the primary and alternate dates. Those celebrating the Passover during the first month then immediately observed the Feast of Unleavened Bread, which began on the fifteenth day and lasted for a week (Lev. 23:6; Num. 28:17). This observance was not required for the alternative date as is shown by the departure of the Israelites from Sinai on the twentieth day of the second month (Num. 10:11), which would have been during a hypothetical alternative celebration of the Feast of Unleavened Bread (Milgrom 1990, 371). Later in Israel's history, it appears that the Passover in the second month *could* be combined with a secondary observance of the Feast of Unleavened Bread. This unfolds under Hezekiah in 2 Chronicles 30:1–27 (Cole 2000, 157).

9:13. The passage then articulates the serious consequences of failing to observe the Passover. It directly addresses the first Passover date since it specifically indicts those who are ceremonially clean and not on a journey who fail to attend (Milgrom 1990, 70). However, an Israelite who deliberately disregarded the alternative Passover date would also find themselves outside of God's favor. This verse announces that the person who fails to observe the Passover will be "cut off" (וְנִכְרְתָה) from the congregation and will "bear his sin" (חֶטְאוֹ יִשָּׂא). These phrases are synonymous (Milgrom 1990, 69). Being "cut off" refers to either death or banishment. However, in the wilderness setting, banishment would result in death anyway (Cole 2000, 157). There is no explicit requirement for the community to execute this individual, so ultimately the punishment is left in the hands of God. Along with bearing one's sins, these idioms point to a situation in which the guilty party stands outside of divine protection and grace (Ashley 1993, 181).[6]

This arrangement offers "a certain poetic justice to the penalty; those who refuse to

---

6   See also the discussion of Numbers 15:22–36 for further analysis of the theological implications of being "cut off."

participate in the central identifying ritual of their people will be cut off from those people" (Pressler 2017, 73). God graciously delivered his people from slavery. He calls them to commemorate the occasion and provides an alternative for those who, for valid reasons, cannot participate at first. To spurn such grace and to fail to remember God's deliverance shows that the individual has already separated themselves from the worshipping community.

9:14. The passage ends by anticipating another scenario that the Israelites will face regarding the Passover when they enter the Promised Land: what accommodations to make for the non-Israelites. Numbers 9:14 provides instruction for the "sojourner" (גֵּר). These individuals are not native-born Israelites but have chosen to associate themselves with the Israelite community. They have a greater status than mere foreigners or hired foreign labor (cf. Exod. 12:43; Ashley 1993, 194). In turn, the גֵּר is considered a "protected stranger" (Milgrom 1990, 398). Providing a place for the גֵּר to flourish reminded Israel of its history as oppressed strangers in Egypt (Lev. 19:33–34) and revealed the truth of God's promise to bless the nations through Abraham's descendants (Gen. 12:1–3). This verse reveals that the sojourner was permitted to participate in Passover observance under the same regulations as the native-born Israelite.

> *TRANSLATION ANALYSIS*
> Whether or not the sojourner was required to participate in Passover observance is unclear. In context, the phrase וְעָשָׂה פֶסַח לַיהוה could point to a simple future ("he shall observe the Passover to the LORD") or a contingent future ("he desires to observe the Passover to the LORD"). English translations mostly prefer the contingent future alternative, although the NIV reflects the simple future alternative.
> *CSB*: "wants to observe the Passover to the LORD"
> *ESV*: "would keep the Passover to the LORD"
> *NET*: "wants to keep the Passover to the LORD"
> *NIV*: "is also to celebrate the LORD's Passover"
> *NLT*: "want to celebrate the Passover to the LORD"

Any sojourner who did celebrate the Passover had to meet the requirements for its observance detailed in Exodus 12:43–49. Critically, this would entail circumcision since no uncircumcised man could participate (Exod. 12:48). This regulation points to the extension of God's promise of deliverance. As sojourners participate in commemorating the Passover, they recognize the power of God to bring his people out of slavery and worship him for what he has done.

This preaching unit establishes Passover observance as crucial to the life of the Israelite community. As the Israelites prepare to depart Sinai, they are called to commemorate God's deliverance, which they obediently do. This passage also reveals how God interacts with his people, considering scenarios that depart from the ideal, and providing alternatives for those who seek to fulfill their covenant obligations. Even non-Israelites are given the opportunity to participate in this community-shaping event.

THEOLOGICAL FOCUS

The exegetical idea (Everyone who is part of the community of Israel must celebrate the Passover) point to this theological focus: *The people of God should commemorate God's gracious acts of deliverance*. Celebrating the Passover reminds Israel that it is a people "born in grace and called by God to be his firstborn" (Stubbs 2009, 101). This is true not just for the Exodus generation but throughout Israel's existence. Speaking to the second generation, Deuteronomy 16 declares that "you left Egypt in haste—so that all the days of your life you may remember the time of your departure from Egypt" (Deut. 16:3 NIV). By establishing this commemorative act, God builds into the rhythm of Israel's existence a time for reorientation, a ritual that "incorporates each new generation of Jews in YHWH's great act of deliverance" (Pressler 2017, 73).

In Israel's history, the gracious provision of an alternative date for the Passover shaped one of the nation's brief spiritual renaissances. Second Chronicles 30:1–27 recounts Hezekiah's reestablishment of the Passover after purifying the temple and turning the people away from the idolatrous worship encouraged by Ahaz (2 Chron. 28:22–25). Hezekiah's Passover was celebrated in the second month because of the distance people had to travel and the lack of properly consecrated priests in Jerusalem (2 Chron. 30:1–5). He authorized a lavish celebration on this alternative date which then prompted the people to destroy places of idolatrous worship throughout the land (2 Chron. 30:14; 31:1). God's grace was also evident in his merciful response to Hezekiah's prayer on behalf of those who celebrated the Passover without being ritually pure (2 Chron. 30:18–20). This episode demonstrates how remembering what God had done in Israel's past could prompt obedience and reverence in its present. Celebrating Passover reoriented the people to their essential identity as those who celebrate God's presence and deliverance.

God's command for Israel to remember the Passover also anticipates the coming of the true Passover Lamb: Jesus Christ, the final and perfect sacrifice (John 1:29; 1 Cor. 5:7). The gospel of John alludes to this passage during the crucifixion when it declares that none of Jesus's bones were broken (John 19:36; cf. Num. 9:12). Just as Israel was charged to remember the Passover, so followers of Christ are called to commemorate his sacrifice. Jesus himself used the occasion of Passover to instruct his disciples to take the bread and cup in remembrance of him and in anticipation of his coming kingdom (Luke 22:13–22).

The celebration of the Lord's Supper is essential for Christians to reorient their lives. Paul confronts those who were not celebrating it appropriately and warns of serious consequences (1 Cor. 11:27–30). Although these warnings are not the same as being "cut off" from the community, they call believers to remember Christ's gracious sacrifice as an ordinance he left for us (Wenham 2008, 112). This is not meant to be harsh or legalistic. Christians can also celebrate how God's establishment of an alternative date for the Passover reminds us of his grace. We see that God provides accommodations for those, who by no fault of their own, find themselves unable to follow God's initial instruction. God's holiness demands that his people obey his decrees, but his mercy shows an understanding of human frailty.[7] This Christian ordinance has been celebrated in many ways over the years, but a repentant heart and humble spirit is always integral to the process.[8]

PREACHING AND TEACHING STRATEGIES

Exegetical and Theological Significance

Passover is a paradigm for God's redemptive work. The contours of the story are well known: God's people are oppressed in bondage, he shows his mighty power by means of miracles in Egypt, he provides instructions for the shedding of blood that covers and protects from the angel of death, he leads his people out of slavery, he defeats their enemies, and he ultimately brings them to the land of promise. This story was absolutely foundational for the social and religious life of Israel. Redemption out of Egypt is frequently a key touchstone in the Old Testament.

---

7   The arrangement of the Second Passover may be contrasted with other religious instruction from the ancient Near East. Hittite law instructs temple officials *not* to permit this sort of deviation, and even prescribes penalties for those who accept a bribe instead of compelling attendance at the required festivals (Chavel 2009, 1–2).

8   No doubt there has been a growth of creative means of celebrating it brought about by the COVID-19 pandemic. While forms may change, the function of communal reorientation and celebration of Christ remain.

In the New Testament, Christ is depicted as the one who fulfills the typological significance of the Passover. He is the lamb of God who takes away the sin of the world (John 1:29). Far greater than any amount of human wealth, Peter encourages his readers: "For you know that it was not with perishable things such as silver or gold that you were redeemed from the empty way of life handed down to you from your ancestors, but with the precious blood of Christ, a lamb without blemish or defect" (1 Peter 1:18–19 NIV). Israel's Passover represented an incredible act of God, but it was only a shadow of the redemption that is procured through the life, death, and resurrection of Jesus Christ. The Passover meal in Israel looked back to the historic exodus from Egypt and the original night when the angel of death passed over the homes protected by the blood, but it was also a prophetic act that looked forward to its fulfillment in Christ, God's precious, spotless lamb. Christ's blood saves from eternal death and is sufficient to bring us into the new heaven and new earth, where righteousness dwells.

Preaching Idea

Our purpose in the present requires us to remember our origins and look toward our future hope.

Contemporary Connections

What does it mean?

What does it mean that our purpose in the present requires us to remember our origins and look toward our future hope? Our worldview matters for how we interpret the meaning of life, or how we decide if life even has any meaning. It makes a big difference if the universe came into existence out of nothing and then human beings made an accidental appearance in this cosmic absurdity, or if the universe was intentionally designed by God and human beings were created to bear his image. It makes a big difference if the future holds nothing more for individuals than decay and rotting away, or if everyone will experience an eternity of conscious existence. Where we came from and where we are going make all the difference in the world for how we orient our lives now. This is one of the reasons why so many people feel despair and a sense of purposelessness: their worldview undercuts genuine meaning and purpose at every turn, so they stop trying to find any.

Christians, however, are anchored in the meaningful origin of creation, but also in the accomplished work of Jesus Christ. We not only bear God's image, but we are *redeemed* image-bearers. In the Lord's Supper, we are called to remember Christ our Lord and his finished work of providing atonement. We orient ourselves in our creation and redemption and then look forward to eschatological glory because of what Christ has done. It is these twin poles of past and future that ground our present in God's eternal purposes. Since we are redeemed and have an eternal home and inheritance, we are to live for God fully and completely in the present moment.

Is it true?

Is it true that purpose in the present requires meaningful origins and a significant future? A reading of post-Enlightenment philosophy in the Western world certainly shows that genuine purpose and meaning vanish when God is removed from the equation. Looking at contemporary culture reveals no shortage of existential despair, as well as many attempts to cover up meaninglessness with endless distractions: you do not worry about meaning if you never have time to think. The book of Ecclesiastes clearly teaches that certain perspectives logically lead to the conclusion that everything is meaningless and burdensome.

On the positive side, however, where there are meaningful origins and worthwhile goals for the future, significance and purpose abound. There is a reason why the Bible begins with our origins in creation and ends with a vision of eschatological glory in eternity future. The meaning of life in this world is found between those two anchor points. Remembering the past and envisioning the future is part of the normal human experience. As those created in the image of God, as those who have been redeemed, and as those who are headed to the glorious presence of God, we are enabled to find meanings and purposes in every action and every moment of our lives. Given our past and our future, our present moment bears eternal significance.

Now what?
How do we practically apply the truth that purpose in the present requires meaningful origins and a significant future? First, like Israel with the Passover, we should rehearse, commemorate, and celebrate our origins and redemption. Second, we should be faithful to act in obedience to Jesus's words: "Do this in remembrance of me" (Luke 22:19 NIV). To *remember* is not merely to recall to mind, but to bring to mind for the purposes of proper response. Reflect on Jesus—all he is, all he has done, and all that he calls you to do—when you participate in the Lord's Supper.

The orienting axis of past and future is found in Paul's instructions regarding the Lord's Supper: "For whenever you eat this bread and drink this cup, you proclaim the Lord's death until he comes" (1 Cor 11:26 NIV). Notice that the look to the past (at the Lord's death) is accompanied by an eye to the future (you proclaim his death until his return). At the Lord's Table, the believing community finds grace and strength for the present by looking to Christ's past work and anticipating the glorious consummation.

Creativity in Presentation
I once visited a church where a Christian who had grown up as an Orthodox Jew shared for a few minutes about what it was like to participate in a Passover meal. Near the close of her presentation, she said, "at the end of the meal, all that was left was the lamb's bones, but Christ, the lamb of God, was resurrected and the grave was empty after his completed work." Respectfully walking through the traditional elements of Passover may help enrich people's understanding, but also help them see the greatness of the fulfillment that comes through Christ alone.

Depending on the preacher's expertise and awareness, working through some of the secular and religious perspectives that destroy meaning and purpose can help show the beauty of the Christian worldview and the deep meaning that is embedded in God's story of our lives.

Each individual Christian has a "Passover" night of redemption that is unique. Every testimony has different details, even though every testimony of salvation is grounded in the gospel of Jesus Christ and work of the Holy Spirit. Encourage the congregation to look back on their own day of liberation and redemption. Tell them also to look forward to the eschatological fulfillment of their salvation. Are there current behaviors that need correction on the basis of our past and future? Sharing some testimonies may be an excellent component for a service based on this preaching passage.

This passage also naturally connects itself well to the observance of the Lord's Supper. There is a lot of diversity in the church when it comes to partaking in the Table, but the pastor should have little difficulty in incorporating the Lord's Supper as part of this service. In Christ, the new covenant community has the fulfillment of Passover, and this should be celebrated as a reminder that our purpose in the present requires us to remember our origins and look toward our future hope.

A possible outline for this passage could be:

- Remembering what God has done is crucial to the identity of his people (9:1–5).

- God graciously provides the means to worship him properly to all who seek him (9:6–14).

DISCUSSION QUESTIONS

1. Why is remembering what God has done so crucial to the journey of faith?

2. What encouragement can we draw from seeing how God deals with the complications that arise in his command to celebrate the Passover?

3. What did the Passover lamb signify? How does it point us to the work of Christ?

4. Can you think of a time or situation where you were aware of God working in you or through you? How might regular reflection on it shape your walk of faith?

Numbers 9:15–10:10

EXEGETICAL IDEA
The Israelites were to obey God's instructions as they went where he directed.

THEOLOGICAL FOCUS
The people of God must follow where God leads.

PREACHING IDEA
The call of discipleship has always been, "Come, follow me."

PREACHING POINTERS
After redeeming his people at the first Passover, God led them out of Egypt, across the Sea, and into the desert. This unit shows us that after God redeems his people, he continues to act as their Sovereign Lord, King, and Guide. God does not redeem his people and then let them go off merrily in all directions. He is not a liberator who lets people out of jail and then watches them disappear into the night. God is the covenant Lord of his people, and he redeems them so that they can follow him in holy obedience. He is our Redeemer, but he is also our Master.

There is never a time in Scripture when God is pleased with those who refuse to obey him or follow his law. The importance of following God's decrees is an extremely important theme all through the Bible. Time after time, human characters are challenged to follow God by faith, and the consequences of both obedience and disobedience are clearly revealed. The incarnate Son of God called his disciples to leave everything and follow him. In the gospel, the call for discipleship still goes out, and everyone with ears to hear is to leave their sin and follow Jesus. This passage in Numbers help us see how gracious God is to lead us and guide us, but it also reminds us that he is the holy God, and he rules with infinite authority. Its central theme resonates with the rest of Scripture, where the call of discipleship is always, "Come, follow me."

FOLLOWING WHERE GOD LEADS (9:15–10:10)

LITERARY STRUCTURE AND THEMES

After the command to celebrate the Passover, 9:15–10:10 further develops the theme of following God's instructions. This is the final passage in the first major section of Numbers, set before Israel departs Sinai (10:11). The passage shows Moses and Israel responding obediently to God's commands as has been the case throughout 1:1–10:10 (1:53; 2:34; 3:51; 4:49; 5:4, 8:22; 9:23). Once Israel leaves Sinai, the grumbling spirit quickly takes hold. However, before things devolve, this passage presents an idealized version of Israel's journey, declaring that Israel faithfully moved and rested at God's command.

This preaching unit consists of two sections (9:15–23; 10:1–10) linked by the theme of God's direction of Israel's movements.[1] Numbers 9:15–23 is an almost poetic description of how God guided Israel's travel through his presence in fire and cloud. Verbal repetition marks it as "elevated prose," suitable to the splendor of God's presence (Wenham 2008, 113). Numbers 10:1–10 then details how God ordered the creation of two silver trumpets to further guide Israel's movements. It also anticipates the battles that Israel will fight under God's command.

A key theme of this passage is the wonder of God's presence. This manifests itself through the pillars of fire and cloud that guide Israel's movements. They invite the nation to draw near to God, but in their very nature they are unable to be grasped or controlled. This preserves the transcendence of God, even as he dwells in their presence (Moberly 2020, 57). Further, along with the trumpets that God commands Moses to create, the fire and cloud provide tangible symbols that God is with his people. He has chosen and preserved Israel and he now guides the nation to the place he has promised.

- **The Cloud of Divine Presence (9:15–23)**
  - *God's Presence (9:15–16)*
  - *Israel's Obedience (9:17–23)*
- **The Silver Trumpets (10:1–10)**
  - *Making the Trumpets (10:1–2)*
  - *The Purpose of the Trumpets (10:3–7)*
  - *The Trumpets and Israel's Future (10:8–10)*

EXPOSITION

This passage sits at the end of a foundational era for Israel. They arrived at Sinai in Exodus 19 and remained there for nearly a year, constructing the tabernacle and implements for worship, along with learning more about their God and his character. Despite the unfortunate circumstances of the golden calf episode (Exodus 32–34), the relationship between God and Israel is on solid ground as the nation prepares to follow his lead to the Promised Land. This period of community formation has provided Israel with its identity as the chosen people of a holy and merciful God. As they prepared to depart Sinai, this passage reveals that the Israelites were to

---

[1] It would be possible to derive two sermons from this passage if the expositor wanted to develop the image of God's presence (fiery cloud) and authority (trumpets) in greater detail. However, the shared setting of progression toward the Promised Land also permits the expositor to view 9:15–10:11 as a preaching unit.

obey God's instructions as they went where he directed.

The Cloud of Divine Presence (9:15–23)

God's Presence (9:15–16)
9:15. The first part of this preaching unit returns to symbol of divine presencethat guided Israel. The text reads as an expansion of Exodus 40:36–38, which describes God's guidance of Israel in less stylistic language. The elevated prose in Numbers 9:17–23 in particular creates an atmosphere "of celebration by a community of faith in communion with its incomparable God, by a community following his commands in jubilant obedience" (Cole 2000, 158). This passage develops two themes: God's presence in the tabernacle among the nation (9:15–16) and Israel's obedience to God's direction on the journey (9:17–23; Ashley 1993, 184).

Numbers 9:15 sets this passage "on the day that the tabernacle was set up" (ESV, NET), which Exodus 40:17 identifies as the first day of the first month of the second year of Israel's rescue from Egypt. This is a month prior to the census (Num. 1:1). The passage is placed here since it anticipates Israel's imminent departure from Sinai beginning in 10:11.

The focus of this verse is the divine presence associated with the tabernacle. This was manifested through the presence of cloud during the day and the appearance of fire at night.[2] Exodus 40:38 suggests that this is "cloud-encased fire," in which the cloud was visible in the day while the fire was dimmed by sunlight and became visible after nightfall (Milgrom 1990, 70–71). Cloud and fire have symbolized God's presence with Israel since they first appeared as the nation fled Egypt (Exod. 13:21–22; 14:24). This reflects imagery from the ancient world, where gods and their sanctuaries were portrayed as surrounded by cloud, clothed in fiery garments. One of the cognomens for the Canaanite deity Baal is the "Cloud-Rider," which Scripture appropriates for the true God of Israel in Psalm 68 (Cole 2009, 353). These images convey "a manifestation of elemental power," fitting for a theophany (Pressler 2017, 77).

TRANSLATION ANALYSIS
Numbers 9:15 uses the word "tabernacle" (מִשְׁכָּן) three times. On the second occasion, it is followed by an appositional phrase לְאֹהֶל הָעֵדֻת. This expression is also found in Numbers 17:7–8 and 18:2 (Milgrom 1990, 71). The noun הָעֵדֻת references the tablets containing God's instructions and decrees (Exod. 31:18; 32:15; 34:29). Many English versions translate this phrase "the tent of the testimony" (CSB, ESV, NASB, NET), while the NIV uses "the tent of the covenant law." This expansion of "tabernacle" thus stresses God's covenant relationship with Israel.[3]

9:16. This verse reiterates the presence of the cloud and fire, forming an inclusio with 9:15. Its one addition is to indicate that they were present "continually" (תָּמִיד). This speaks to the constancy of God's presence. It is worthwhile to pause here and reflect on the wonder of having these visible manifestations. For God to make himself known among his people is a tremendous gift. Cloud and fire may further symbolize God's protection: the cloud to provide shade from the harsh wilderness sun, the fire to provide light and warmth in the dark and cold.

---

2   Ashley notes that some texts use the term "pillar" (עַמּוּד) before fire and cloud (Exod. 13:21–22; 14:19, 24; 33:9–10), while others, including this text, do not (Exod. 19:9; 40:34, 38). Both descriptions point to God's majestic presence among the people (Ashley 1993, 184).

3   Milgrom suggests a more prosaic purpose for the phrase לְאֹהֶל הָעֵדֻת. He suggests that it limits the reach of this use of "tabernacle" to the tent itself, excluding the broader courtyard in which the tabernacle was placed (Exod. 38:9–20; Milgrom 1990, 71).

Consequently, "the passage shimmers with awe and delight" (Allen 2012, 173). Unfortunately, as Israel departs from Sinai, Israel acts on many occasions as though God was not present, only to receive stark reminders that he is. God's perpetual presence offers comfort and encouragement. Israel's later rebellions mar this image.

Israel's Obedience (9:17–23)
Numbers 9:17–23 shifts focus from the existence of the fire and cloud to their purpose. They guided the Israelites as to when and where to move as they travelled toward the Promised Land. There is a rhythmic, repetitive quality to these verses as they discuss Israel's movements. Key repetitions include the verbs נָסַע ("to set out") and חָנָה ("to encamp"), which occur nine and six times respectively. These repetitions "give coherence both to the narratives themselves and to the spiritual attitude of the Hebrews that the sources reflected. The people were one in faith, obedience and action, in a recapitulation of the covenant ratification at Sinai (Exod. 24:6–7) that was to become increasingly less frequent" (Harrison 1990, 164).

9:17–18. Numbers 9:17 begins with "And whenever the cloud lifted from over the tent, after that the people of Israel set out, and at the command of the Lord they camped" (ESV).[4] The remaining verses elaborate on that basic truth: Israel moved and rested when God directed. Even without divine speech, the movement of the cloud was a clear signal of God's intentions (Pressler 2017, 78). The latter half of 9:17 notes that the Israelites encamped at the location where the cloud dwelled (יִשְׁכָּן־שָׁם). The verb יִשְׁכָּן is built off the same root as the noun מִשְׁכָּן ("tabernacle"), emphasizing God's presence in both the cloud and in his sanctuary. The next verse stresses the people's obedience, twice employing the phrase "at the command of the Lord" (9:18 ESV) to describe Israel's moving and resting.[5] This same phrase also occurs twice in 9:20 and three times in 9:23, providing a sevenfold refrain to emphasize that Israel followed what God directed.

9:19–22. Israel's obedience to God's command is stressed in this verse, which declares that when the cloud remained in place for many days, the Israelites "kept the charge of the Lord" (ESV) and did not depart. This expression refers to "prohibitions whose violation must be scrupulously guarded against" (Milgrom 1990, 72).[6] Here, the prohibition is against journeying when God has not specifically authorized it. This reinforces the idea that God alone directs Israel's travel: only by mirroring the movements of the cloud and fire may Israel venture forth.[7]

The other key thought is that the Israelites were obedient no matter how long the divine presence signaled them to remain in camp. Various temporal expressions indicate this. According to 9:19, sometimes they remained in place for "many days" (יָמִים רַבִּים), or a "number

---

[4] Exactly what happened when the cloud lifted is unclear. One suggestion is that it remained above the tabernacle, which was carried by the Gershonite and Merarite clans of Levites who followed the section of tribes led by Judah (Num. 10:14–17; Olson 1996, 53). The other possibility is that the cloud went to the head of the column as in Exodus 13:21–22 (Milgrom 1990, 71–72). Given that the cloud's purpose was to direct Israel where to go, this is the more likely option.

[5] The exact phrase is עַל־פִּי יהוה ("by the mouth of the Lord"). Here it is clearly an idiom for God's instructions for when Israel was to journey. This sevenfold repetition of the phrase is "inescapably emphatic" (Allen 2012, 174–75).

[6] Similarly, Ashley notes that this expression ensures "that obedience to Yahweh was exact and complete" (Ashley 1993, 185).

[7] See also Wenham, who states, "The cloud hovering over the tabernacle provided the perfect means of divine guidance: the people had to respond with perfect obedience" (Wenham 2008, 113).

of days" (יָמִים מִסְפָּר) in 9:20,[8] or simply "from evening until morning" (מֵעֶרֶב עַד־בֹּקֶר) in 9:21. Numbers 9:22 summarizes all these, declaring "whether it was for two days, or a month, or a longer time" (ESV) that the cloud of the divine presence remained over the tabernacle, Israel remained encamped. The rest of the verse reinforces this, declaring that the Israelite encamped (יַחֲנוּ) and did not set out (וְלֹא יִסָּעוּ) while the cloud remained stationary. Then, 9:22 concludes by noting that when the cloud did lift, the Israelites would set out.

> TRANSLATION ANALYSIS
> Translating the beginning of 9:22 poses some challenges. The Hebrew reads אוֹ־יָמִים אוֹ־חֹדֶשׁ אוֹ־יֹמַיִם, meaning literally "two days, or a month, or days." Many English versions translate as יָמִים "a year" (NASB, NET, NIV, NKJV). Warrant for this comes from Leviticus 25:29, which puts יָמִים in parallel with שָׁנָה, the word for a literal year (cf. 1 Sam. 27:7). However, absent that cue, it seems best to understand יָמִים in Numbers 9:22 as referring to an indefinite but likely lengthy period.

9:23. This celebration of Israel's obedience ends with more repetition. Again, the text declares that the Israelites encamped and set out according to God's command. Again, it confirms that they kept the Lord's charge. Its only addition is to announce that God's command came "through the hand of Moses" (בְּיַד־מֹשֶׁה). This again reaffirms Moses's mediatorial role in establishing the covenant relationship between Israel and God. He is not the final authority over Israel's travels; he is the intermediary through whom God directs the steps of his people.

Thus, this passage demonstrates that God directly guided Israel's movements in the wilderness. Israel's duty was to respond obediently to God's presence in the fiery cloud. Although Numbers 10:11–25:18 complicates matters, this vision of a people responding faithfully marks a hopeful moment as Israel prepares to journey toward the Promised Land.

The Silver Trumpets (10:1–10)
Along with his presence in the cloud and fire, God also provided direction for Israel through the sounding of horn blasts. This passage anticipates God's presence in battle and in sacral festivals. It looks ahead of Israel's current situation at Sinai, anticipating the travel and settlement to come. Its focus on Israel's obedience renders it "topically appropriate" to follow the discussion of God's presence in the cloud and fire (Allen 2012, 176).[9] Further, since one of the purposes of the trumpets is to signal Israel to break camp, it makes sense to place this passage before Israel departs Sinai (Sakenfeld 1995, 59). One should also envision the trumpets reinforcing the leading of the fiery cloud. They provide an auditory signal to match the visual sign of God's presence. This passage contains a brief introduction (10:1–2) commanding Moses to make the trumpets, followed by explanations of their purpose. Numbers 10:3–7 describes their use in the wilderness setting, while 10:8–10 looks ahead to Israel's presence in the Promised Land (Cole 2000, 160).

Making the Trumpets (10:1–2)
10:1–2. God commands Moses to make two trumpets (חֲצוֹצְרֹת) of hammered silver. This probably involved "rubbing metallic foil over a model" (Milgrom 1990, 73). The trumpets were likely patterned after those found in Egypt from the contemporaneous era. They would likely be around two feet in length with a narrow tube that could produce various tones (Cole 2009, 353).

---

8   Likely a briefer duration than the "many days" of 9:19 (Allen 2012, 174).
9   Wenham notes these instructions "complete and complement the means of divine guidance described in 9:15–23" (Wenham 2008, 114).

> **Horn Instruments**
>
> The Old Testament has a couple of words for horn instruments. The singular form of the term used here is חֲצוֹצְרָה, which is distinguished from the שׁוֹפָר, or "ram's-horn." Both instruments could serve military and cultic functions. In this passage, the חֲצוֹצְרֹת direct Israel on the march and participate in festal celebration. They continue to be employed throughout Israel's history in coronations (2 Kings 11:14), temple dedications and purification (2 Chron. 5:12–13; 15:8–15; 29:27), and consecrating Jerusalem's walls (Neh. 12:35, 41; Milgrom 1990, 73). Likewise, the שׁוֹפָר announced the start of the Day of Atonement (Lev. 25:9) and was blown during Israel's march around Jericho (Josh. 6:2–21). It could also warn of an imminent attack (Joel 2:1–2).

According to 10:2b, the trumpets serve two purposes: assembling the congregation and departing the camp. That is, when the trumpets sound, they either summon Israel to a sacred gathering or to follow God's leading by physically marching where he directs.

The Purpose of the Trumpets (10:3–7)
10:3–4. These verses focus on the functions of the trumpets during Israel's sojourn in the wilderness. These are established based on whether one or both trumpets were blown and on what sound was emitted.

> *TRANSLATION ANALYSIS*
>
> Distinguishing between whether the text calls for one or two trumpets to be blown is simple enough, but the discussion of their sound is trickier. The text describes the sound of the trumpets in several ways: with the verbal root תקע alone (10:3, 4, 7, 8, 10), with תָּקַע followed by the noun תְּרוּעָה as the direct object (10:5, 6), or with a verbal form of the root רוע from which the noun תְּרוּעָה is derived (10:7, 9). Although the exact nature of the distinction between the sounds is unclear, Jewish tradition holds that the root תקע on its own refers to a long blast on the trumpet, while the two other constructions are synonymous and refer to a shorter blast (Milgrom 1990, 74; Pressler 2017, 81).[10] A standard approach for English versions is to translate תָּקַע alone as "blow," while תָּקַע and תְּרוּעָה together or verbs derived from רוע are translated as "blow an alarm" (ESV, NASB, NET). The NIV uses the verb "sound" in the former case and "blast" in the latter case. The choice of "blow an alarm" reflects 10:9, which directly connects this trumpet sound to warfare. I will follow this nomenclature for the rest of the passage.

The first function of the trumpets is to gather Israel. When both trumpets are blown, the entire congregation was to assemble itself at the entrance of the Tent of Meeting. This presumably had a cultic orientation, gathering the nation to worship or to otherwise hear from God. The next verse indicates that if only one trumpet was blown, then only the tribal leaders were required to assemble. They would then disseminate any necessary instructions back to their tribes.

10:5–6. The second function of the trumpets is to guide Israel on the march. This has a military sense since Israel's population was organized according to its fighting men from the census of Numbers 1. These verses delineate the order of march, anticipating the description found in 10:11–28. When the trumpets first blow an alarm, the tribes encamped east of the sanctuary depart led by Judah (cf. Num. 2:3). At the second alarm, the tribes from the south break camp led by Reuben (cf. Num. 2:10). Oddly, the tribes to the north and west are not mentioned, although the summary statement in 10:6b ("an alarm is to be blown whenever they are to set

---

10   Milgrom notes that rabbinic sources put the long blast at three times the length of the short blast.

out" [ESV]) likely encompasses them as well (Ashley 1993, 188).[11]

10:7. This text distinguishes between the two functions again, declaring that to gather Israel, the trumpets should be blown (תִּתְקְעוּ) rather than blow an alarm (וְלֹא תָרִיעוּ). Thus, 10:3–7 establishes the dual functions of the trumpets when Israel was in the wilderness and the signals that announce each one. They instructed Israel when to assemble to hear from God and when to follow his lead on their journey.

The Trumpets and Israel's Future (10:8–10)
10:8. This is a transitional verse between the present situation of Israel and its anticipated future. It details that the priests were responsible for blowing the trumpets. This begins with the wilderness generation with Aaron and his sons, but it is established as an "eternal ordinance" (NET) for ensuing generations. This establishes the cultic nature of these trumpets. They are instruments commissioned by God to convey the instructions of God. This verse also positions the text to look forward to a time when Israel is settled in the Promised Land.

10:9. These verses reverse the order of the two trumpets sounds from 10:1–7: first, 10:9 details when to blow an alarm (וַהֲרֵעֹתֶם), while 10:10 describes the reasons to blow (וּתְקַעְתֶּם) the trumpets.[12] The setting of 10:9 is explicitly militaristic, a logical extension of the commands to march in 10:5–6. Israel's settlement in the land is assumed as the verse envisions a time when the nation will enter battle "in your land" (בְּאַרְצְכֶם). In this instance, blowing an alarm would cause Israel to be remembered before God and to be delivered. Blowing the alarm "is seen to be analogous to prayer, a meaning of participation in activating the will of God" (Allen 2012, 178). It reminds Israel of what God had done for them in the wilderness. In Israel's future in the land, blowing the alarm recalls his deliverance in the wilderness, retrieving Israel's corporate memory and activating the same promise of God's provision and rescue (Leveen 2002, 210).

10:10. The final verse places the idea of assembling before God into a new context. When in the land, the Israelites will no longer be organized around a portable central sanctuary. However, they will share sacred time and places that unite them. This verse identifies joyous celebrations and the beginning of new months as the time to blow the trumpets. The trumpet sounds are also connected to Israel's whole burnt offerings and fellowship offerings as part of proper worship of God. This ordinance was likely observed "during the pilgrimage festivals of Passover, Pentecost, and Tabernacles, and during the monthly New Moon rites" (Cole 2009, 354). This reflects an adaptation of the gathering function of the silver trumpets.

The verse concludes by establishing the trumpets as a memorial (זִכָּרוֹן) for Israel before YHWH. The same word is used of the pile of stones to mark where Israel crossed the Jordan (Josh. 4:7) and the names of the tribes on the high priest's ephod (Exod. 28:12, 29). The trumpets are a physical reminder of God's actions on behalf of the nation, even after the time of their original purpose had passed.

THEOLOGICAL REFLECTION

The exegetical idea (The Israelites were to obey God's instructions as they went where he directed) leads to the following theological reflection: *The people of God must follow where God leads*. Israel's obedience in this text required

---

11 The LXX has additional clauses mentioning the northern and western tribes. This likely reflects an attempt to fill in what is perceived to be lacking in the Masoretic text.

12 There is thus something of a chiastic arrangement as the text progresses from "blow" (10:3–4) to "blow an alarm" (10:5–6 and 10:9), and concludes with blowing the trumpets (10:10; Gane 2004, 571; Knierim and Coats 2005, 131).

physically following God's presence through the wilderness. The fiery cloud marked the divine presence, while the trumpets offered another signal of God's direction. As Israel obeyed God, the fiery cloud reinforced their harmonious connection, although that same cloud could signal God's anger at disobedience and sin (Exod. 16:9–12; Num. 14:10; Gane 2004, 566). As this passage gives an idealized portrayal of Israel's journey and obedience "at the command of the Lord," it offers an aspirational challenge for those who strive to follow where God leads.

God's leading comes to his people in various fashions. He leads through his God-breathed word that is useful for teaching, correcting, and rebuking (2 Tim. 3:14). His people are called not merely to hear it, but also to obey it (James 1:22). Although there is much in Scripture that is challenging to put into context, God's leading in the text is often readily apparent. God's people are to be exemplified by the fruit of the Spirit (Gal. 5:22–23), they are to put off vices and embrace virtue (Eph. 4:20–5:6), and they are to exemplify God's character in showing compassion for "the least of these" (Matt. 25:31–46). Jesus affirms that those who love him will demonstrate it by keeping his commandments (John 14:21). Thus, the people of God demonstrate their identity by following where God leads in Scripture.

God also leads through the indwelling presence of his Spirit (John 14:15–16; Rom. 8:14). Although it is not a visible manifestation of divine presence like the fiery cloud, through the Spirit, God is with every one of his people (Sprinkle 2015, 243). The Spirit leads God's people to discern truth (John 16:13), to flee from the desires of the old self (Rom. 8:5–6), and seek direction for where we should serve (Acts 16:6–10). Just as Israel followed God's direction in the wilderness wherever the cloud led them, or how long it remained, so God's people are to be continually attuned to his call on their lives.

A helpful note from this passage in undertaking this challenge is its focus on memory. After the fiery cloud departed and the trumpets no longer guided Israel's steps, God instructed Israel to blow the trumpets at their feasts as a memorial (Num. 10:10). They remind Israel that God protected and guided them in the wilderness when they responded to him obediently, and they should do the same as they live in the land. The necessity of proper memory will be illustrated throughout Numbers 10:11–25:18 when the Israelites repeatedly conjure up faulty memories of their life in Egypt (Leveen 2002, 214). The people of God continue to remember what he has done, how he has rescued them from darkness and brought them into the light (Eph. 2:1–7). In memory of what God has accomplished, God's people are called to follow his lead.

PREACHING AND TEACHING STRATEGIES

Exegetical and Theological Significance

The God revealed in this preaching unit is both transcendent and immanent. YHWH is the God of Abraham, Isaac, and Jacob; he is the God who is present with his covenant people. Anchored in creation, covenant, and redemption, as well as with the future promise that YHWH would lead them to the Promised Land, Israel could know that the Sovereign Lord was with them and cared for them. Even after their rebellion at Sinai, God did not abandon them. He had redeemed them from Egypt, and he was present with them to lead and to guide in the wilderness.

This picture of God is the opposite of the divine being in deism, who allegedly creates the world and then remains absent from it. Aristotle's "unmoved mover" was not even aware that the world existed. The deities of the ancient world were fickle and could not be relied upon. Israel's covenant God, however, could not only defeat the whole pantheon of Egypt's gods, but would faithfully be present with his people, going before them and bidding them to follow his divine leading.

This section illustrates what theologian John Frame terms "the covenantal triad" of God's "control, authority, and presence" (Frame 2002, 42). God is incorporeal (although visibly manifested in these verses by the representing cloud and fire), so his presence is a consequence of his control and authority (Frame 2002, 94). It is because God is present in his power and authority that he can command his people to follow his lead. Note that this authority is exercised by God whenever he wants, and his people are to follow him anywhere he wants to take them. Since he is their Sovereign Lord and Redeemer, God expects full obedience as he leads his people. Given the character of God and his mighty works on their behalf, the only reasonable response for the people is complete trust and obedience.

Preaching Idea
The call of discipleship has always been, "Come, follow me."

Contemporary Connections

What does it mean?
What does it mean that the call of discipleship has always been, "Come, follow me"? Given who God is, the call to a covenant relationship with him will by necessity be a call to an asymmetrical relationship (i.e., no created being can be an equal partner with the one who sits on the throne of heaven). We are not co-Gods: God will never follow us as our disciples or worship us as his superiors. The distinctions between Creator and creature cannot be erased. God cannot be created, and no created being can be infinite and eternal. Human beings were created in the image of God, but the attributes we were given that correspond to God's are only analogous to the divine ones. The very nature of God and the nature of humanity entail that God alone is the Sovereign Lord, and his covenant people are to recognize who they are and the role they are to play before his holy presence.

The call to discipleship is always a call to obedience. Disciples surrender themselves to the will of their Lord. It is God who sets the parameters and draws the boundary lines. When he wants us to move, we should move; when he wants us to remain, we should remain. Today, the Spirit leads us in obedience to God's Word. We are to conform our thinking and actions to the revealed truth of God. Only one generation was led by a pillar of cloud and a pillar of fire, but God still leads his people today. In order to follow God, the first thing we need to do is respond to the call of Jesus: "Come, follow me" (Matt. 4:19 NIV).

Is it true?
Is it true that the call of discipleship has always been, "Come, follow me"? This was certainly the case with Jesus when he called the first disciples (Matt 4:18–22). Later on, "follow me" was the same message that Jesus gave to Matthew the tax collector (Matt 9:9). In an even stronger way, Jesus also proclaimed, "Whoever wants to be my disciple must deny themselves and take up their cross and follow me" (Matt. 16:24 NIV).

This principle of following Christ has always been the mark of discipleship. Abram—the prototypical person of faith—was called by God to leave his homeland and go to the place that God would show him (Gen. 12:1). Even before sin entered the world, Adam and Eve were given instructions from God about what they ought to do (Gen. 1:28). God also gave them a restriction about eating from the Tree of the Knowledge of Good and Evil, and their disobedience resulted in the fall into sin and the coming of the curse. This is clear proof that, even in Eden, a relationship with God required fidelity and obedience. Following God's ways has always been necessary for maintaining a relationship with him.

Now what?
Without a literal, visible pillar of cloud and fire going before us, and without special trumpet signals being given to guide us, how do we

follow the Lord today? In terms of Christian discipleship, how do we pick up our cross and follow Jesus? Although the question of how to determine the will of God is commonly asked by believers in every generation, at its most basic level the answer is to obey the revealed word of the Lord. God's Spirit illuminates the meaning and significance of holy Scripture and teaches us how to apply it in our lives. God's Word contains everything we need for spiritual life and discipleship.

The real difficulty we have is that we do not want to surrender ourselves fully to God. Sin is powerful and its influence remains, and it tries to draw us away from obedience to the Lord. We need to confess and repent if we are straying, and we need to walk in the pathways that God designs for his people. Jesus is our Lord, our Savior, and also our model: we are to walk and live as Jesus did (1 John 2:3–6).

Creativity in Presentation

Soliloquies with Abram, Peter, or Matthew about leaving everything to follow God, or a dialogue between Israelites in the camp as they reflect on following the pillar of God's presence, could aid in thinking through what it would have been like to be in their position. If there is someone in the church who is gifted in evangelism or discipleship, they could provide a short segment on how the call of Christ for discipleship can be contextualized today.

In terms of illustrations that have wide applicability, the children's games Simon Says and Follow the Leader provide fitting pictures of meticulous obedience. When parents help their young children learn to bake, the child will do well to listen and follow the instructions. It is important to stress, however, that when God asks us to do something, it is not arbitrary or harmful; it is always for our good. God's love for us is demonstrated in the redemptive sacrifice of his Son Jesus Christ, and a call to follow him is a call to follow the one who loves us infinitely and paid the highest price to purchase us for God.

When we follow someone, it matters where we are going. It is one thing to follow the Pirate King off the plank, and another thing to follow the Pirate Queen to the bounty that is marked on the treasure map with a gigantic X. We can follow people to our own destruction, or we can follow Jesus to glory. God is perfectly wise and perfectly loving, and he is leading us to our perfect, eternal home. The call of discipleship in serving this God has always been, "Come, follow me."

One possible outline for this passage could be like:

- God's people stay and move at his command (9:15–23).

- God provides his people with symbols of his authority and presence (10:1–7).

- God directs his people in warfare and sacrifice (10:8–10).

DISCUSSION QUESTIONS

1. How does God continue to make his presence known to his people, now that they no longer see it in fire and cloud?

2. Why are the Israelites commanded to call on God before engaging in battle?

3. Why do you think that Numbers gives us this ideal portrayal of Israel's journey right before the narratives of grumbling start?

4. What obstacles cause you to stumble in your obedience to what God clearly commands?

THE TRAVELS AND TRAVAILS OF THE FIRST GENERATION (10:11–19:22)

This section details Israel's journey through the wilderness. It begins with a presentation of an ideal march done under God's command (10:11–36). Unfortunately, a grumbling spirit quickly takes hold and threatens to destroy Israel's covenant relationship with God. Israel complains about its diet (11:1–35) and Moses's leadership (12:1–16; 16:1–35; 36–50). At the centerpiece of this section is Israel's refusal to enter the Promised Land after receiving a negative report from spies sent out by Moses (13:1–14:4; 14:5–45). God threatens to destroy Israel and begin again with Moses, only to relent after Moses intercedes on behalf of the people. Instead, the penalty is a forty-year death sentence for this first generation. God's mercy and justice are both on display as God cannot leave rebellion unpunished, but also remains faithful to his covenant promises. Interspersed in the grumbling narratives are further regulations that Israel must obey. These include regulations for offerings (15:1–21), sacrifices for the remediation of sins (15:22–36), further instructions for the Levites (18:1–32), and a procedure for cleansing from the impurity brought about by contact with a dead body (19:1–22). Israel's rebellions brings its relationship with God to the precipice; only God's steadfast character permits the relationship to continue.

Numbers 10:11–36

EXEGETICAL IDEA
Israel's journey to the Promised Land begins with obedience to God's commands and evidence of God's presence.

THEOLOGICAL FOCUS
God rewards his obedient people with signs of his presence.

PREACHING IDEA
Obey and be led, or disobey and be scattered.

PREACHING POINTERS
The themes of chapters 9 and 10 continue to build. God redeems his people and then, as their sovereign Lord, he commands them to be obedient to his holy law and follow him wherever he takes them. As we see in this passage, God leading his people is compatible with gifted, knowledgeable human beings helping out along the way. Yet the accent is on the covenant God who has full authority over the movements and direction of his people.

It was an incredible blessing to be led by YHWH. Having been redeemed from bondage, having experienced Sinai, and having lived through numerous manifestations of God's power and holy love, it is hard to believe that any would be so hard-hearted as to not joyfully follow God. Security and peace rested upon those who followed him, but those who persisted in rebellion were scattered. God led his people, scattering their enemies before them. Then God set up camp with his people again, dwelling in the middle of their community. There is no greater safety than the safety found in following God in obedience and faith. Since this safety is available, make sure you are numbered among those who obey and are led, rather than those who disobey and are scattered.

ISRAEL BEGINS ITS JOURNEY TO THE PROMISED LAND (10:11–36)

LITERARY STRUCTURE AND THEMES

Israel had been encamped at Sinai since Exodus 19. This passage details Israel's departure from Sinai as it begins its journey toward the Promised Land. It begins the second major section of the book, in which Israel travels from Sinai to the plains of Moab (10:11–25:18). The prospect of finally moving toward the Promised Land lends this passage an undercurrent of anticipation.

Numbers 10:11–36 consists of one main narrative with a brief sidebar. The main narrative begins with an introduction (10:11–12) and the order of the march (10:13–28). It then contains a sidebar relating a conversation in which Moses tries to convince his brother-in-law to join Israel on its journey (10:29–32). The narrative then concludes with a description of YHWH's presence during the march (10:33–36).

The driving theme is harmony between God and his people. God commanded Israel to march in a certain order (Numbers 2), and here Israel obeys. God promised his presence among this people through the dedication of the sanctuary and its servants (Numbers 7–8), and here he leads Israel on its journey. This passage describes how Israel's journey to the Promised Land should go. Unfortunately, this idyllic picture does not endure.

- *Introduction to the Journey (10:11–12)*
- *The Order of the March (10:13–28)*
- *Moses and Hobab (10:29–32)*
- *God's Presence During the March (10:33–36)*

EXPOSITION

This passage marks the beginning of a new phase of Numbers. Thus far, the book has consisted mostly of cultic and legal regulations that prepare and consecrate Israel for the journey ahead (Lee 2003b, 98–100). In this middle section, narratives of Israel's wilderness travails take center stage, culminating with the sin at Baal Peor in Numbers 25. The geographical movement from Sinai is mirrored by a theological movement away from God (Cole 2000, 164). However, this first passage gives a picture of how matters should have gone if Israel's commitment to YHWH had remained intact. Thus, Israel's journey to the Promised Land begins with obedience to God's commands and evidence of God's presence.

Introduction to the Journey (10:11–12)

10:11. The passage begins by announcing the date of Israel's departure from Sinai: the twentieth day of the second month of the second year since their departure from Egypt. To put it into chronological perspective, this is nineteen days after God's command to take the military census (Num. 1:1–2) and approximately eleven months after Israel's arrival at Sinai (Exod. 19:1). It also falls at the conclusion of the supplementary Passover observance (Num. 9:10–13). Following the community formation that occurred at Sinai, this date signals the next phase of Israel's existence as God's people.

The sign to depart Sinai is the lifting of the cloud from over the tabernacle of the testimony. This appellation (מִשְׁכַּן הָעֵדֻת) defines it as the location housing the tablets of the Law (Levine 1993, 306). The departure of the cloud reveals that God's presence is moving, and that Israel should follow (Num. 10:17–18).

10:12. The initial report on Israel's travel is that they departed from the wilderness of Sinai and followed the cloud until the wilderness of Paran. Numbers 33:16–18 provides a more detailed itinerary, suggesting at least three stops along this phase of the journey: Taberah (Num. 11:3); Kibroth Hattavah (Num. 11:34–35), and Hazeroth (Num. 12:16). This chapter gives an idealized picture of the journey, where Israel obediently follows wherever God's presence leads. The exact location and shape of the wilderness of Paran is unclear. It is most likely a general term encompassing much of the region between Sinai and the southern border of the Promised Land (Milgrom 1990, 76).

The Order of the March (10:13–28)

10:13. Just as Moses has mediated God's decrees throughout 1:1–10:10, so he is also the conduit for God's command to depart Sinai. The magnitude of this occasion is further marked by identifying it as "the first time" (בָּרִאשֹׁנָה) Israel has set out from Sinai. A new era in its history has begun.

10:14–17. Following the instructions given in Numbers 2, Israel marched in four tribal divisions with the priests and the Levites placed strategically between them. The description of each division is very consistent, naming the leading tribe and stating that the division followed its standard.[1] It then lists the head of the leading tribe followed by the heads of the two subordinate tribes. The tribal chieftains are those assigned to help Moses with the census (Numbers 1) and the ones who conveyed their tribes' gifts for the dedication of the sanctuary (Numbers 8). In this first division, the tribe of Judah led the march followed by Issachar and Zebulun, in accordance with Numbers 2:9.

Numbers 10:17 then notes that two clans of Levites (the Gershonites and Merarites) followed this first division. They carried the tabernacle and the items found within its courtyard and transported them on carts donated by the rest of the Israelite tribes (Num. 7:1–8). This provides additional detail to Numbers 2:17, which had all of the Levites and priests departing after the second tribal division. This arrangement permitted the outer boundaries of the sanctuary to be assembled prior to the arrival of the ark and the other implements from the interior of the tabernacle (Num. 10:21).

10:18–21. In accordance with Numbers 2:16, the tribal division led by Reuben set out next, accompanied by its subordinate tribes, Simeon and Gad. Numbers 10:21 then notes that the Kohathites followed this division, carrying the items found within the tabernacle. In accordance with the instructions of Numbers 7:9, these were to be carried on their shoulders. Curiously, the marching position of Aaron and the priests is absent from this passage, but since they were also Kohathites it would be logical for them to be here (Pressler 2017, 85). This positioning affords the greatest degree of protection; these holy items are right in the center of Israel's marching order.

10:22–24. The third tribal division was led by Ephraim, followed by Manasseh and Benjamin (cf. Num. 2:24). There are no additional comments for this grouping, since the text has already given the place of the Levites.

10:25–28. This section concludes with the fourth tribal division led by Dan, also consisting of Asher and Naphtali (cf. Num. 2:31). English translations identify this grouping as the "rear guard" (ESV, NET, NIV), giving an idiomatic translation of the Hebrew מְאַסֵּף ("gathering").

---

1 See the exposition of Numbers 2 for further discussion of what is meant by "standard" (דֶּגֶל).

The order of march has now accounted for all the Israelite tribes and demonstrated that Israel is following God's instructions.

Moses and Hobab (10:29–32)

10:29–32. The text takes a slight pause to recount a conversation between Moses and Hobab, his Midianite brother-in-law. The fit with the presentation of the marching order is awkward, leading to a number of suggestions concerning the combination of putative sources (Olson 1996, 55). However, the content of the conversation fits the context. Israel is heading into unknown territory and Hobab's family had greater familiarity with the region. Moses asks Hobab to be Israel's "eyes" and to tell them where to camp (10:31). This reflects "shared human leadership under the ultimate direction of God" as Moses would be the conduit for God's voice (Cole 2000, 176). Hobab would provide scouting services, while the ark of the covenant would lead the way (Num. 10:33–36).

> **Moses's Extended Family**
>
> The composition of Moses's extended family is complicated. A few things should be noted. First, in 10:29, Hobab is identified as the son of Reuel, Moses's father-in-law. Moses's father-in-law is called Reuel here and in Exodus 2:18. However, he is also identified as Jethro (Exod. 3:1; 4:18; 18:1, 2, 5, 6, 9, 10, 12). Although a number of theories have been suggested, the simplest approach is to read these as alternative names for the same individual (Cole 2000, 176).[2] Secondly, the word translated "father-in-law" is חֹתֵן, which is sometimes ambiguous. It always refers to a relation by marriage, but it is possible that it could encompass other connections besides father-in-law. This affects the interpretation of Judges 4:11, where Hobab is called Moses's חֹתֵן (cf. Judg. 1:16). A possible solution is that Hobab became the head of his clan after the death of his father and the author of Judges is attributing to him a title that his father had possessed (Allen 2012, 182). This is reasonable given that Judges 4:11 is trying to explain the presence of the descendants of Moses's in-laws in Canaan after several generations have passed.

Moses's appeal to Hobab is that Israel will share whatever bounty they receive from YHWH. He informs Hobab that YHWH has declared he will give the land to Israel, meaning that Moses will have resources with which to reward Hobab properly (10:29). Hobab demurs, stating that he wishes to return to his own land and people (10:30). This same expression is found in Genesis 12:1 where God commands Abram to leave his land and people. At first, Hobab is unwilling to take a similar step of faith to maintain an association with YHWH through Moses and the rest of Israel. However, Moses entreats him again, asking him for guidance (10:31) and promising that whatever "good" (הַטּוֹב) Israel receives from YHWH, it will share with him (10:32). Hobab's response to Moses's second exhortation is not recorded, but the presence of his descendants in Judges 1:16 and 4:11 suggests that he assented.

God's Presence During the March (10:33–36)

10:33. The narrative concludes by giving multiple signs of God's presence during the journey. It states that Israel departed from Sinai and went on a "three days' journey" (10:33 ESV, NET). The destination is not mentioned though it could be Taberah, the first location where Israel complained against God. There is a notable parallel between this and Exodus 3:18, which identifies the distance from Egypt to Sinai as a three-day journey (Milgrom 1990, 80). This suggests that a

---

2 A somewhat more complex version of this theory suggests that Reuel was a clan name while Jethro was a personal name (Albright 1963, 1–11). The veracity of this is impossible to ascertain and probably introduces more complications than needed into the text.

journey of this length is sufficient to make a significant break with whatever has come before.

God's presence is central to this journey as the ark of the covenant went before Israel. This suggests that it is separate from the remainder of the holy items carried by the Kohathites in the middle of the order of march. It makes sense for the ark, the most prominent physical symbol of divine presence, to lead Israel on its journey.[3] Its purpose was "to seek out a resting place for them" (10:33b ESV). Thus, God's presence and God's provision are intertwined.

10:34–36. Along with the ark, the cloud of the divine presence also went before Israel (10:34), setting up a pair of poetic prayers that celebrate God's presence (10:35–36). In the Hebrew text, Numbers 10:34–36 is set between special signs (called "inverted *nuns*") which suggests that the Masoretic scribes who preserved the text considered these verses to be out of place, transposed from elsewhere (Cole 2000, 178–79).[4] However, in the present location, these verses offer a ringing affirmation that God leads Israel on its travels.

The narrative concludes with two poetic prayers spoken by Moses. As the ark led Israel, Moses proclaimed, "Arise, O LORD, and let your enemies be scattered, and let those who hate you flee before you" (10:35 ESV). Then, upon its return, Moses said, "Return, O LORD to the ten thousand thousands of Israel" (10:36 ESV). These songs affirm that YHWH is a warrior and a protector for Israel. Psalm 68:1 draws from Numbers 10:35 to begin its celebration of YHWH's supremacy over the nations.

TRANSLATION ANALYSIS
Numbers 10:36 calls YHWH to return to the רִבְבוֹת אַלְפֵי of Israel. The ESV's (and NRSV's) rendering "ten thousand thousands" is a fairly literal rendering of the phrase. Other English translations adopt idiomatic approaches: "many thousands" (NET), "countless thousands" (CSB, NIV), and "myriad thousands" (NASB). The intention here is hyperbolic, conjuring up a sense that Israel is innumerable (Allen 2012, 184).

Taken together, the two invocations imagine YHWH going forth and defeating his enemies before returning to Israel in triumph. This corresponds with the depiction throughout the Old Testament of YHWH providing victory for Israel. Often, the ark is the physical symbol of God's presence. Notably, the ark led Israel to the Jordan River as it entered the Promised Land (Josh. 3:4–6) and preceded Israel's march around Jericho (Josh. 6:6–7). Of course, Israel must be walking with God for the ark to bring them victory; it is not a magic talisman as Israel discovered in a later conflict with the Philistines (1 Samuel 4). However, in this instance, the ark and the cloud signified God's presence while Israel's marching order demonstrated its obedience to God's instructions. Consequently, Moses's prayers celebrate that Israel marches under the protection of its divine covenant partner. Soon enough, Israel's complaints and sin mar this picture. However, harmony between God and his people marks the beginning of their travel toward the Promised Land.

THEOLOGICAL FOCUS

The exegetical idea (Israel's journey to the Promised Land begins with obedience to God's

---

[3] The phrase "three days' journey" is actually found twice in this verse. One possible reading is that the ark was a three days' journey ahead of the rest of Israel. This is implausible. The better reading, adopted by English translations, is that the ark led Israel on that initial journey. See "during the three days' journey" (NET) or "during those three days" (NIV).

[4] One rabbinic suggestion was that these verses originally followed 2:17 and its account of where the Levites and priests were to encamp (Milgrom 1990, 375). The Septuagint places v. 34 after 10:35–36.

commands and evidence of God's presence) leads to the following theological focus: *God rewards his obedient people with signs of his presence.* The biblical presentation of the relationship between God and humanity shows that it is all too frequently broken by the grievous consequences of sin. In the beginning, God was fully present with Adam and Eve, walking intimately with them in the garden (Gen. 2:25; 3:8). However, sin tarnished that perfect picture, leading to a fractured relationship, maintained only by the grace of God. Later, God threatened to depart from his people in the wake of the golden calf incident, only to relent in the face of Moses's pleas (Exod. 33:12–14). As Israel entered the land and became a kingdom, God's presence was symbolized through the temple on Mount Zion. Psalms 46 and 48 envision God dwelling among his people, providing them with peace and security. However, Israel had to obey God's covenant for that situation to endure. The prophets warned of the folly of presuming that God would dwell in Zion when Israel turned from him (Jer. 7:7–28). Ezekiel saw a vision of God's presence leaving the temple because of Israel's continued transgressions (Ezek. 10:1–22).

Fortunately, through God's mercy, his presence was never removed from his people forever. Ezekiel envisions a restored temple illuminated by God's presence (Ezekiel 40–48), while Haggai responds to the people's obedience by promising that God is with them in the rebuilding project (Hag. 1:12–15). Ezra and Nehemiah responded to the trauma of exile by rededicating the returned community to the law of God and acknowledging that their forefathers had transgressed, pleading for God to remember and preserve them (Neh. 9:32–34).

This continues into the New Testament. One of the signs of the resurrected Christ was a miraculous catch of fish, achieved because the disciples obeyed when Jesus spoke, even when they did not recognize him (John 21:4–8). Later, they obeyed God's command to remain in Jerusalem (Acts 1:4–5) and received the indwelling of the Holy Spirit, the undeniable guarantor of God's presence (Acts 2:1–4). From there, the church grew despite all the obstacles placed in its way by religious and governing authorities. The power of the Spirit within God's obedient people pushed the gospel out from Jerusalem into the whole of the Roman world.

The fervent zeal of the early church is a compelling example of obedience leading to evidence of God's presence. It is also a reminder that obedience to what God commands is more than robotic assent to lists of rules and requirements. Instead, his people have the privilege of participating in the divine nature, a matter for rejoicing (2 Peter 1:4). In this way, "Christian obedience is quite different from the lack of will and initiative of slaves who obey the commands of their master. It is rather the outward expression of friendship with and enjoyment of God" (Stubbs 2009, 109). Obeying God is part of a virtuous cycle in which obedience prompts the believer to be more attuned to his presence, providing even greater incentive to walk in the ways that he directs.

PREACHING AND TEACHING STRATEGIES

Exegetical and Theological Significance
The theory of being led by God's manifested presence in the pillar of cloud is now put into practice for the first time. The text makes it clear that it was YHWH who sovereignly decided when the people should leave and where they should go, but the command was also given through Moses (10:13). Later in this passage, Moses entreats Hobab to go with them and help them in the wilderness. Hobab would function as their eyes, helping them see the resources around them. God would bring his people to their camping locations, but once there they would still need all kinds of practical knowledge and skills for survival and being as comfortable as circumstances allowed.

God uses human agency and instrumentality to accomplish certain things in his sovereign plan. In this text, even with the special manifestation of his presence, he uses Moses's leadership, and Moses in turn looks for help from Hobab. When God wanted a message proclaimed, he raised up prophets. Jesus Christ had a large number of disciples, and from that group he appointed twelve apostles to lead in ministry (Luke 6:12–16). In 1 Corinthians 12, Paul makes clear that Christ is the Lord of the church, and that spiritual gifts are distributed according to the divine will, yet people are to use their gifts to edify and build up the body of Christ. God is ultimately in control, but his design includes meaningful human agency.

Those who disobeyed God and persisted in rebellion (i.e., his enemies), would be scattered before him (Num. 10:35), while those who followed him were gathered and protected (10:36). For those who obey, the presence of God is a glorious comfort; for those who rebel with hard hearts, it leads to destruction. Thankfully, God is compassionate and filled with mercy and grace, so the rebellious can turn and be forgiven.

Preaching Idea
Obey and be led, or disobey and be scattered.

Contemporary Connections

What does it mean?
What does it mean to obey and be led, or disobey and be scattered? Although our situation is not the same as the one the Israelites were in, the principle still applies. Today, if we do not walk in the light of God's Word, we will walk in darkness. If we are not found in Christ, then we are lost in sin. If we are not for the Lamb, we are against him. If we are not covered in the righteousness of Christ, we cannot be justified by God. If we are not Christ's sheep, then we are the goats who will be separated from the Good Shepherd.

In the church, the principle of unity centers on Christ as the Head and the bond of peace forged by the Holy Spirit in the gospel. The new covenant community can only be held together by the truth of Christ and by walking in obedience as his disciples. This is one of the reasons why the Epistles take such a negative view of fractures and divisions in the church. God's people are to be united, not divided; they are to be gathered, not scattered. Ultimately, in the new heaven and earth, all of God's people will be united in safety.

Is it true?
Is it true that we will either obey and be led, or disobey and be scattered? The truth of this proposition is illustrated numerous times in the Bible. It can also be discerned in the lives of individuals, societies, and nations throughout history. To take the inspired record of Israel's history in Scripture, track through the times when Israel was blessed and the times when they faced judgment. The book of Judges shows the correlation between Israel's disobedience and judgment, as does the history of the monarchies in both Israel and Judah. The prophets were continually calling the Israelites back to the ways of God, in obedience to the stipulations of the covenant.

Obedience in the new covenant era and faithfully following Christ is necessary for spiritual blessing. The book of Revelation paints vivid pictures of the blessing that attends following the Lord, and the ultimate disintegration and scattering that result from persisting in rebellion against him. Following Christ leads us to eternal life and everlasting glory, while rejecting him and going our own way leads to nihilism and death. If we are his enemies, we will be scattered. If we are his people, he leads us, keeps us together, protects us, and dwells with us.

Now what?
What are we called to do, given the reality that we can either obey and be led, or disobey and be scattered? The answer, quite simply, is we

need to put our faith in Jesus, trusting him completely and doing our best to live our lives by the power of the Spirit, according to his words. We need to be obedient to God's Word, doing what it says. Part of this is a recognition that God will use other people to teach us, advise us, and help guide us in the ways of the Lord. In the end, however, our only absolute authority is God himself.

If you do not know the Lord, you need to turn from your sin and put your trust in him through Jesus Christ. We are all born with a sin nature that makes us enemies of God, but the glory of the gospel is that God would rather save than scatter. Every Christian was at one time an enemy of God, but in Christ there is reconciliation. If you are already a follower of Jesus, strive to follow him more and more closely and with greater dedication. If you are an enemy of Christ, turn to him for salvation: be gathered in his love, rather than scattered in your unrighteousness.

Creativity in Presentation

Many believers are familiar with C. S. Lewis's *The Lion, the Witch, and the Wardrobe*, but not as many have read the entire Chronicles of Narnia. One of the key themes of the penultimate book in that series—*The Silver Chair*—is the vital necessity of following Aslan's words, even when we're confused and a better way of doing things seems to present itself. Reading that book and preparing to share some its contents by way of illustration would fit this passage well. Time and again, the characters learn the wisdom of meticulously following Aslan's instructions as they face dangers and confusing difficulties.

This passage also lends itself well to the metaphor of sheep following their shepherd. As the sheep hear their shepherd's voice and follow along behind, they are led in safety, and the flock is kept together. A good shepherd is a blessing to the sheep but the bane of wolves, predators, and thieves. Remember Jesus's words: "The thief comes only to steal and kill and destroy; I have come that they may have life, and have it to the full" (John 10:10 NIV). Sin steals, kills, and destroys. Sin scatters and divides. Jesus heals, unites, protects, guides, and gives his sheep the gift of eternal life. Christ will protect his people from their enemies, just as God protected Israel. Do not be an enemy of God. Come to Christ in repentance and faith. Obey and be led. Do not disobey and be scattered.

One way of expressing these ideas could be:

- The people of God succeed when they follow the leading of God (10:11–28).

- Being near God allows people to participate in his blessings (10:29–32).

- God's presence provides his people with rest (10:33–36).

DISCUSSION QUESTIONS

1. Why does the text go to such lengths to show that the Israelites did what God commanded them from Numbers 2?

2. How do we maintain the balance between relying on God and making use of human ability and knowledge, as Moses tries to do here?

3. Why do Israel's marches begin and end with poetic appeals to God?

4. What do you think the mood was like as Israel departed Sinai after its sojourn there?

Numbers 11:1–35

EXEGETICAL IDEA
Israel's failure to be satisfied with God's provision brings judgment that is only removed by God's mercy.

THEOLOGICAL FOCUS
The failure to appreciate God's provision reflects a selfish and distorted view of reality that damages our relationship with God.

PREACHING IDEA
Internal grace, not external law, is what makes the heart thankful to God.

PREACHING POINTERS
Those who are familiar with the Pentateuch cannot help but notice parallels between this chapter and Exodus 16, even though the events are not identical. Far from simply being a recast of an old event, Numbers 11 has its own color and nuance. Tragically, it also occurs after the exodus, after Sinai, after the tabernacle was constructed, and after God's glory took up residence in the middle of their camp. Now, they are led forward by the glory cloud. Immediately—as their first recorded act after breaking camp from the base of Sinai—the people grumble and complain against God. After all that they have witnessed and experienced, they continue to repeat their patterns of sin. Greater light, and even the awesome power of Sinai that stands behind the law, does not remove the heart of stone.

At first, this passage leaves the reader utterly discouraged. There are also eerie parallels in our own lives, with how slow we are to learn our lessons and how frequently we fall into the same patterns of sin. Nevertheless, this passage cries out for a greater reality, where we will be moved to obey God's law from the inside out. We need the law written not on tablets of stone, but on the tablets of our heart. Gloriously, in the new covenant, this is exactly what the Spirit does. In Christ, we are given a new heart, and the will and word of the Lord are internalized. Standing under the law will never move us to obey from our heart, but the marvelous, matchless grace of God in Jesus Christ changes our heart and reorients it. The new covenant reality to come is glimpsed in the elders who are filled with the Spirit. This text clearly shows us that internal grace, not external law, is what makes the heart thankful to God.

GRUMBLING AND THE GIVING OF THE SPIRIT (11:1–35)

LITERARY STRUCTURE AND THEMES

This passage initiates the pattern of disobedience and divine judgment found throughout Israel's journey after leaving Sinai. It reframes the idealized depiction of Israel in 9:15–23 and 10:11–36, passages that described Israel marching obediently under Moses's leadership in response to God's direction.

This preaching unit consists of two narratives: a brief story of complaint that results in judgment (11:1–3) and a lengthier account of the people's dissatisfaction with God's provision intertwined with Moses's appeal for help in governing Israel (11:4–35). The first narrative (11:1–3) also establishes a template for other grumbling narratives. Essential elements include: 1) a complaint from the people, 2) God responding with anger and judgment, 3) Moses interceding to alleviate the punishment, and 4) the provision of a placename to memorialize the incident. The second narrative in 11:4–35 expands upon each element of the template. It creates a richer narrative that explores the foolishness of Israel's complaints and the interaction that they prompt between God and Moses. This includes the distribution of God's Spirit to seventy elders after Moses cries out to God for relief.

This passage begins a series of stories in which human weakness and disobedience threaten to derail God's covenant relationship with Israel. The interplay between Israel's grumbling and God's commitment to his covenant is a recurring theme throughout Israel's wilderness wandering.

- *The Initial Grumble (11:1–3)*
- *Manna, Quail, and the Spirit of God (11:4–35)*
  - The Complaint of the Israelites (11:4–9)
  - Moses's Complaint (11:10–15)
  - God's Response (11:16–23)
  - The Prophetic Spirit (11:24–30)
  - The Quail and the Plague (11:31–35)

EXPOSITION

The description of Israel's journey through the wilderness builds upon the tension between human disobedience and divine faithfulness. Both narratives show that the Israelites are dissatisfied with God, suggesting that they no longer appreciate what God has done for them by rescuing them from slavery in Egypt. Israel's ingratitude prompts divine anger, though ultimately God relents and preserves his covenant relationship. Moses's role as intercessor also comes to the forefront. In particular, the second narrative adds complexity to the relationship between God and Moses. Ultimately, both stories reveal that Israel's failure to be satisfied with God's provision brings judgment that is only removed by God's mercy.

The Initial Grumble (11:1–3)

11:1. The first narrative follows the basic template mentioned above: Israel's complaint leads to God's judgment, requiring Moses to intercede on its behalf. This story does not expand beyond the template but rather moves through its elements quickly. It provides a brief introduction to the more complicated grumbling narratives that follow.[1] It begins with the statement that the people complained in the hearing of the Lord. The term "people" (הָעָם) invokes the whole of the community, suggesting general disgruntlement. No specific cause is given for this complaint in the Hebrew text, although some English translations add an explanatory phrase such as "about their misfortunes" (ESV) or "about their hardships" (NIV).

> TRANSLATION ANALYSIS
> The word that the niv and esv translate as "complained" is מִתְאֹנְנִים, from the root אנן which is only found here and in Lamentations 3:37. This translation can be substantiated on the basis of cognate languages and the Septuagint, which translates it with the same verb it uses to translate the more common Hebrew verb for "complaint" (from the root לון; Davies 1995, 99–100).

In the latter half of verse 1, God hears these complaints and responds with anger, which manifests itself in a fiery display. The text does not provide any details about this fire other than identifying that it came from God. The fire falls on the periphery of the camp, serving as a warning of greater judgment to come.

11:2–3. This threat prompts the people to cry out to Moses, who prays to God. His intercession is successful and leads to the end of the fire in 11:2.[2] The last verse provides the final stage of the template, wherein the place receives a name that commemorates the events that unfolded there. In this case, the name is Taberah, which is derived from the verb "to burn" (בָּעַר).

Manna, Quail, and the Spirit of God (11:4–35)

The Complaint of the Israelites (11:4–9)

11:4a. The second narrative expands upon the features of a grumbling narrative. It reveals the identity of the complainants, the grounds of their complaint, and the reality of divine judgment. Perhaps most critically, God's mercy manifests itself in a unique way through the sharing of his Spirit. It begins by stating that "the rabble" (הָאסַפְסֻף) had a strong craving. This word is found only here, and so this translation is speculative. However, it likely refers to the nonethnic Israelites who came with them out of Egypt (cf. Exod. 12:38; Deut. 29:11; Josh. 8:35; Ashley 1993, 208). This prompts the Israelites themselves to join the complaint, making it a widespread expression of discontent.

11:4b–6. These verses reveal the core issue as the community again complains of hunger like they had done previously in Exodus 16. The people's complaint is different since their survival is not at stake: God continues to provide them with manna. Instead, it reflects dissatisfaction with the monotony of God's provision, perhaps providing a reminder of how quickly the miraculous can become commonplace. Rather than appreciating God's continued provision, the Israelites again reflect on their diet while in Egypt, conveniently omitting their status as Pharaoh's slaves. The initial cry of the Israelites is phrased as a rhetorical question in 11:4b: "who will give us meat to eat?" (NASB). This sets the stage for the arrival of the quail in 11:31–33. After the rhetorical question, the Israelites continue to recall their diet in Egypt, adding fish and

---

[1] A similar strategy is at work in the book of Judges, which uses only the basic template to describe Othniel (Judg. 3:7–11). The other narratives in the cycle expand on this template significantly (Milgrom 1990, 82).

[2] Numbers 11:2 provides another parallel with the book of Judges through the verb "cry out" (צָעַק). This is the verb used whenever Israel calls out for deliverance after their sin leads to them falling into the hands of an oppressor. Here, Israel has Moses as an intercessor between themselves and God.

vegetables to the food that they desire. They lament their current state and contrast the manna unfavorably with these other staples.³

> **Complaining in the Wilderness**
> There are important parallels between this passage and Exodus 16:1–35. In that passage, Israel also complains of hunger in the wilderness and remembers with rose-tinted glasses its diet while in slavery in Egypt. However, there are key differences. In Exodus 16:1–35, Israel has not yet received the manna and so it is unaware of what it will eat in the wilderness. Further, God provides quail not because of Israel's dissatisfaction with manna but as a precursor to the manna's first appearance (Exod. 16:13). Divine punishment is also absent from the Exodus episode, even when some of the Israelites attempt to preserve the manna beyond that day's need (Exod. 16:20) or attempt to gather on the Sabbath (Exod. 16:27). The explanation for the different outcome to similar complaints is likely that Israel has affirmed its covenant relationship with YHWH at Mount Sinai and is now being held to a higher standard. Whereas Exodus celebrates Israel as a "liberated community," in Numbers, they are supposed to be a "sacral congregation" who reflect the holiness of God (Knierim and Coats 2005, 17). Grumbling against God carries greater consequences in light of his further self-revelation.

11:7–9. The narrative pauses to describe the manna (cf. Exod. 16:14–21, 31). First, 11:7 briefly describes its appearance as resembling a coriander seed and a substance called bdellium. Neither of these descriptions are especially informative for modern readers. Coriander seed may reflect a kind of condiment (Trever 1962, 681–82), while bdellium is thought to be a gum-like resin (Ashley 1993, 209). The focus remains on the purpose of the manna, which was to provide sustenance miraculously for Israel in the wilderness.

Moses's Complaint (11:10–15)

11:10. After describing the manna, the narrative switches to Moses's perspective and reveals his frustration with Israel's complaints. Moses hears the people weeping at the tents, realizes that God is angry, and views the whole situation with alarm. The final clause of 11:10 declares "in the eyes of Moses it was evil," though English translations nuance it with "troubled" (NIV) or "displeased" (ESV). It is also unclear from this verse whether Moses's displeasure is directed toward the people's complaint (Noth 1968, 86), God's anger (Reis 2005, 212), or the situation as a whole (Ashley 1993, 210). The third option is the most likely, given that Moses's speech in 11:11–15 expresses exasperation with both Israel and God.

11:11–12. Following the template established in 11:1–3, we should expect Moses to intercede between God and Israel. However, Moses's address to God is not a plea for him to relent or cease punishment. Rather, Moses despairs of the challenges in leading Israel. He launches into a lengthy speech in which he challenges God with a series of emotionally fraught questions. He asks why God is treating him poorly. The second question hyperbolically asks why God has punished him by giving him the burden of leadership. In 11:12, Moses attempts to shift responsibility back onto God, asking rhetorically whether he gave birth to Israel and so should be saddled with the duty of bringing them to the Promised Land. Moses asks, "Did *I* conceive all these people?" (NIV). He uses the first-person pronoun אָנֹכִי to emphasize that he did not, and that this is *God's* problem to resolve (Milgrom 1990, 85).

---

3   The ESV translates the phrase נַפְשֵׁנוּ יְבֵשָׁה in 11:6a as "our strength is dried up," whereas the NIV has "we have lost our appetite." The NIV thus focuses more on the monotony of the diet, whereas the ESV introduces a more hyperbolic claim about the loss of strength.

11:13–15. The crux of the issue comes in 11:13, where Moses asks where he is supposed to get meat to feed the people. Clearly, it is beyond human capacity, though Moses should perhaps remember God's provision in Exodus 16:13. The weight of these issues lead Moses to despair in 11:14–15. He expresses his own inadequacy, claiming that the task is too difficult before indulging in further hyperbole, asking God to kill him.

God's Response: (11:16–23)
11:16–17. God responds to both the question of leadership and the absence of meat. His solution to the first issue is to give seventy elders a share of the spirit that is upon Moses. This provides tangible evidence that Moses does not have to lead Israel alone. It is comparable to the incident in Exodus 18:13–26 where Moses's father-in-law persuaded him to share the burden of judging the people. However, that did not involve the transfer of God's Spirit. The arrangement presented here preserves Moses's special status since God declares that he will descend to the Tent of Meeting and use him as the conduit to empower the elders. The nature of this spirit is somewhat ambiguous since it is only described as that which is "upon you" (11:17). However, Moses attributes it to God in 11:29 so the elders now share in the divine Spirit, through Moses (Ashley 1993, 211).

Numbers 11:17 elaborates upon how this action permits the elders to share the leadership burden. Lexical repetition reinforces this since there are three words (two verbs, one noun) derived from the root נשׂא ("to lift, carry, bear"). God declares that the elders will "bear with you (וְנָשְׂאוּ אִתְּךָ) the burden (בְּמַשָּׂא) and you will not bear it alone (וְלֹא־תִשָּׂא אַתָּה לְבַדֶּךָ)." These answers respond to Moses's use of the same root (נשׂא) in 11:11–12 where he complained of having to carry the people (Reis 2005, 218).

11:18–20. God then addresses the issue of meat. He puts Israel's complaints in his own words and emphasizes their ingratitude. He instructs Israel to "consecrate yourself in preparation for tomorrow" (11:18 NIV), an expression that presages a "coming, decisive act of God" (Ashley 1993, 212). The closest parallel is Joshua 7:13, where God calls for consecration before uncovering the sin of Achan. God's negative evaluation is not made explicit just yet, but the way God frames Israel's request is suggestive. In 11:18b, he picks up on the requests for meat and Israel's flawed memories of its diet in Egypt and promises to provide meat. However, this provision comes at a cost. What looks like a generous response to Israel's complaint is actually a sign of displeasure emphasized in the use of repetition for effect in 11:19–20a. God declares that he will provide meat not for one, two, five, ten, or twenty days, but rather for an entire month, until Israel loathes it.[4]

11:21–23. This scene concludes with another exchange between Moses and YHWH. Moses, apparently not catching the warning, focuses on the practicalities of providing meat in the desert. In doing so he questions both his and God's ability to provide (Stubbs 2009, 119). Moses first expresses incredulity that YHWH could provide meat for the whole nation for a month (11:21) before asking rhetorically whether even the slaughter of entire herds or the gathering of all the fish of the sea would suffice (11:22). This prompts God to respond with his own rhetorical question in 11:23, "is the hand of YHWH

---

4 The word translated "loathe" (NIV) or "loathsome" (ESV, NASB) is זָרָא, which only occurs once in the OT. The Septuagint here reads χολέρα ("cholera"), suggesting a disease marked by nausea and vomiting. It is possible that the image of the meat coming out "from your nose" (מֵאַפְּכֶם) that precedes זָרָא is also a reference to vomiting (Davies 1995, 109). While we may not be able to specify the exact nature of God's warning, its general sense is clear. Israel will seriously regret making this demand.

cut short?" (הֲיַד יהוה תִּקְצָר). God's hand is a metonymy for divine power, so with this question God rejects Moses's concerns about the logistics of the situation: God is more than capable of providing an overabundance of meat.

The Prophetic Spirit (11:24–30)
11:24–25. The scene shifts to the fulfillment of God's earlier promise to provide support for Moses. Numbers 11:24–25 is essentially an enactment of the divine pledge found in 11:16–17. Moses's doubts about the provision of meat apparently do not affect his obedience in selecting and gathering the elders as God instructed (Ashley 1993, 213). The elders gather around the Tent of Meeting in the center of the camp and receive a visit from God. Although the elders receive a share of the divine Spirit, Moses maintains a special status. When YHWH descends in a cloud, he speaks with Moses, not the assembled elders, and uses Moses as an intermediary for the provision of the Spirit. The elders then prophesy, confirming that they have received a portion of the divine Spirit. The end of 11:25 reveals that this prophetic activity was a one-time phenomenon, curtly stating that "they did not do so again" (NIV).

> **Elders' Prophetic Activity**
> The nature of the elders' prophetic activity is ambiguous. This verse simply uses the verbal form וַיִּתְנַבְּאוּ without further explanation or expansion. This verb is derived from the noun for "prophet" (נָבִיא) and occurs twenty-nine times in the hithpael stem. Commentators give generic definitions like "to act the prophet" (Ashley 1993, 213) or "exhibit the behavior characteristic of a prophet" (Milgrom 1990, 380), which are not particularly illuminating. The same verbal stem is found several times in narratives of Saul in 1 Samuel 10 and 19. First Samuel 19:18–24 uses this verb in a context that suggests uncontrollable ecstatic experiences and bizarre behavior, including Saul stripping off his royal robes. This experience of prophesying is used to thwart Saul's plans to kill David. However, the setting in Numbers 11:24–25 is dramatically different. Here, God directly authorizes the giving of the Spirit to the elders, and their experience of prophesying legitimates their place in Israel's hierarchy. Consequently, parallels to 1 Samuel may not be of much use in determining the nature of the elders' prophesying. The important point is that the community observes and accepts the elders' activity as a sign of their endowment with the divine Spirit. Its function is to provide support for the established hierarchy, with Moses at the head and the Spirit-endowed elders sharing the burden of leadership (Levison 2003, 512).

11:26–30. These verses introduce a complicating element with important theological ramifications. Two of the selected elders, Eldad and Medad, were not present at the Tent of Meeting when the Spirit of God descended. The text does not explain their absence but instead focuses on the implications of their activity. Whereas the other elders receive their share of the Spirit through Moses, Eldad and Medad do not. This calls into question the orderly nature of the proceedings and Moses's special standing before God. In 11:27–28, Moses learns about the situation from an unnamed young man, which prompts Joshua to implore Moses to stop them. Joshua is here described as Moses's helper from his youth and of course will ultimately become his successor.[5] Joshua's concerns are not stated explicitly, but in 11:29 Moses asks rhetorically if Joshua is "jealous" for Moses's sake. The underlying

---

5 English versions translate the word describing Joshua's position (מְשָׁרֵת) with a number of alliterative synonyms: "aide" (NIV), "assistant" (ESV, HCSB), or "attendant" (NASB).

Hebrew root קנא can indicate both zeal or envy (Harrison 1990, 190). It does not appear that simple jealousy is the issue here. Instead, Joshua views Eldad and Medad's actions as a challenge to Moses's authority.

This incident is unexpected given the way in which 11:16–17, 24–25 describe an organized procedure for the endowment of the Spirit. However, Moses's response in 11:29 does not reflect any concern. Instead, he expresses a desire that the entire nation would receive the empowerment of God's Spirit. While the narratives of Numbers preserve a special significance for Moses, this incident suggests that the forthcoming description of his humility in 12:3 is accurate. Moses does not desire to limit access to God to himself. Instead, he willingly shares it with the appointed elders, including Eldad and Medad. This section concludes with Moses and the other elders leaving the Tent of Meeting and reentering the broader encampment, presumably ready to take up their duties now that their positions have been validated.

The Quail and the Plague (11:31–35)

11:31–32. Moses's response ends the concerns about the burden of leadership and the process of Spirit-endowment, but the issue that initiated Moses's complaint remains unresolved. Israel's craving for meat still awaits resolution. YHWH promised to simultaneously demonstrate his power and to punish Israel in 11:18–20, and now that promise comes to fruition. This verse declares that a wind went out from YHWH which drove quail to their deaths around Israel's camp. The Hebrew word רוּחַ can be translated as both "wind" and "spirit," setting up a play on words: the רוּחַ of YHWH first solved the leadership problem and now another רוּחַ from YHWH resolves the meat crisis. It is not necessary to search for a meteorological process to explain the arrival of the quail.[6] It is sufficient to attribute it to God's design. Numbers 11:31b–32 continues by describing the overwhelming amount of meat that God provides. Essentially the quail surround the camp for about a day's walk and are piled about three feet high. The people gathered them nonstop for two days and through the intervening night, collecting what is clearly intended to be understood as a large amount.[7] This answers Moses's concerns in 11:21–23. YHWH reveals that his arm is *not* too short for this task.

11:33. The gift of meat also carried the seeds of God's anger. A plague struck Israel while the meat was still "between their teeth" (בֵּין שִׁנֵּיהֶם). Exactly how long it took this plague to arrive is debated. The next clause is טֶרֶם יִכָּרֵת ("before it is cut off") The sense of the verb יִכָּרֵת is unclear. Its meaning is "to cut," frequently as in to cut animals for a covenant in passages like Genesis 15:10, 18; 21:27. By figurative extension, one possibility is that the cutting refers to cutting with teeth (i.e., chewing), indicating that the Israelites never even ate the meat before the plague arrived (HCSB, KJV, NASB). Another option is that the verb refers to the ending or exhaustion of the thing in question (cf. Josh. 1:5–6; 3:13; Ruth 4:10; Joel 1:5), suggesting that the plague struck before the abundant supply of quail was completely eaten. This latter perspective seems more reasonable. YHWH permits the Israelites to sate their hunger before expressing the full measure of his displeasure.

11:34–35. The text concludes by naming this location Kibroth Hattaavah. Hattaavah is derived

---

6   Many sources note that migratory quail sometimes fall into the Sinai wilderness, especially if the winds shift against them. However, the fact that these quail fall when they do and in the described quantity indicates that God is the cause of this event.

7   Numbers 11:32 says that the people collected "ten homers" (עֲשָׂרָה חֳמָרִים). This is apparently a dry measure equivalent to about five bushels or more than two hundred liters (Milgrom 1990, 92).

from the root אוה also found in 11:4 and points Israel's craving for other food. The place name thus reflects the events that transpired there. This section concludes with Israel's departure from this location and its arrival at Hazeroth, the next stage of its journey.

THEOLOGICAL FOCUS

The exegetical idea (Israel's failure to be satisfied with God's provision brings judgment that is only removed by God's mercy) leads to this theological focus: *The failure to appreciate God's provision reflects a selfish and distorted view of reality that damages our relationship with God.* Israel's unwillingness to be satisfied with the food that God provided in the middle of the wilderness led to a deeply erroneous perspective on its past. Israel's memories of captivity in Egypt recede behind the desire for a varied diet. Israel forgets that it cried out to God from harsh captivity and was rescued by a mighty display of his power. God is angered, and Moses's frustrations even boil to the surface. Although the sharing of the divine Spirit is a welcome outcome, it is set alongside God's judgment. Being in covenant relationship with God should inspire gratitude and praise, rather than complaint and grumbling.

Scripture provides frequent encouragement toward gratitude for what God has done. This is captured throughout the Psalter. Psalm 95:1–7 calls Israel to worship the Lord because he stands at the pinnacle of creation and has made Israel his people. Tellingly, the second half of the psalm (Ps. 95:8–11) reflects on a different experience of Israel's grumbling (cf. Exodus 17) and warns the people not to harden their hearts. The community that grumbled against God failed to enter his rest (Ps. 95:11). On a more positive note, Psalm 100 encourages all creation to shout for joy because YHWH is good, and his love endures forever. Psalm 136 expands on this using "his love endures forever" as its refrain while it rehearses God's creative acts (Ps. 136:1–9) and his preservation of Israel throughout its time in the wilderness (Ps. 136:10–22). The Psalms thus consistently give expression to the voice of praise for God's provision: an antidote to the attitude expressed in Numbers 11.

New Testament worshippers are also called to remember God's provision. Paul reminds the believers in Colossae that they are God's chosen people (Col. 3:12) and that this should lead them to be thankful (Col. 3:15). Paul charges believers to meditate on the message of Christ, while using psalms and hymns in "singing to God with gratitude in your hearts" (Col. 3:16).

This does not diminish the presence of pain and heartache. The voice of lament is also part of the expression of faith. However, the grumbling expressed by the Israelites shows a willful ignorance of what God had accomplished on their behalf. Scripture calls the people of God to remember his provision and to respond in gratitude and obedience.

PREACHING AND TEACHING STRATEGIES

Exegetical and Theological Significance

As pointed out in the sidebar on page 173, there are similarities and differences between the events here and the ones described in Exodus 16. Nevertheless, the parallels are too exact not to recall the previous incident. If the events in Exodus—right after their redemption from Egypt—seem inexcusable, what happens in Numbers 11 is worse, partly because they have already experienced God's provision in Exodus 16. Beyond this, Exodus 16 occurred before the revelation of God on Sinai. It took place before the rebellion with the golden calf, Moses's intercession, God's judgment, and God's mercy. This first incident of grumbling took place before the construction of the tabernacle and the moving-in of God's glory when he took up residence.

The accounts of grumbling in Numbers 11 are *the first thing* we are told about Israel after they depart from Sinai, where they have been encamped for one year. Right before Sinai, they are grumbling about food (Exodus 16). Right after Sinai, they are grumbling about food (Numbers 11). Tragically, one year at Sinai has not changed the hearts of the people. They are not any more trusting or thankful now than they were before God's self-revelation at Sinai and the descent of his glory into the tabernacle.

Living under the Law does not change the heart. The Decalogue, the Book of the Covenant, and the rest of God's revelation to Moses did not turn hearts of stone into hearts of flesh. Faced with the problems in the camp, the solution was not more law but more of the Spirit. The elders needed the work of the Spirit in their hearts, not more commandments on tablets of stone. Only by the Spirit and grace can sinners be led to honor God and obey his word as they ought.

One of the promises of the new covenant is that the law will be internalized, written on the heart (Jer. 31:33; Heb. 8:10). This new covenant work is done by the power of the Spirit (Ezek. 36:24–28). Although the grumbling of Israel does show us that God hates ingratitude, there is a larger lesson in this text: only grace—not law—can change the human heart. Grumbling about food bookends Israel's time at Sinai, forming an inclusio that encompasses Exodus 16 through Numbers 11.

Preaching Idea
Internal grace, not external law, is what makes the heart grateful to God.

Contemporary Connections

What does it mean?
What does it mean that internal grace, not external law, is what makes the heart grateful to God? Given the propensity of the human heart to grumble against God, changing external factors does not guarantee a change in attitude. One of the reasons that the reader judges the grumbling of the Israelites so negatively is that their attitudes seem totally incompatible with their liberation from slavery. Not only that, but then they had their needs met in a miraculous way by YHWH in the wilderness. Many contemporary readers believe that if they had seen the theophany on Sinai, or the pillar of cloud going before the people, they would never have grumbled. However, this story demonstrates that even God's providential arrangements and God's revealed law are not sufficient to change the human heart. For inner change, there needs to be a work of grace through the ministry of the Holy Spirit.

Far from saving us, it is through the law that we become conscious of sin (Rom. 3:20). Take the time to engage in a careful reading of Romans 1–4, Galatians, and Acts 15. Law can only condemn since we do not meet its standards. In fact, law on its own stirs up our desire to defy God (Rom. 7:7–12). Grace, however, changes our hearts and causes us to love God's word.

Is it true?
Is it true that internal grace, not external law, is what makes the heart grateful to God? According to Scripture, there really is no doubt about the veracity of this proposition. Anecdotally, we have likely all known people who are spoiled and ungrateful, even though they are surrounded by comforts and material goods. Likewise, we have all known people who live in extremely difficult situations, but they are filled with joy and thanksgiving. It is grace in the heart rather than law or creature comforts that leads to gratitude toward God.

The real connection to thanksgiving in God's grace comes through our salvation in Jesus Christ. In Christ, our redemption represents the fulfillment of Passover and Israel's liberation from their bondage in slavery. Their liberation was physical, whereas every member of the new covenant community has experienced spiritual redemption. Some also have seen changes in their material and physical circumstances that they can only attribute to the work of the Spirit in their lives. There is no higher motivation for praise and thanksgiving in the universe than that which flows from union with Christ. If we cannot be content with God, eternal life, and the new heaven and new earth, will we really become spiritually content with a pay raise or a gourmet meal?

Now what?
In response, believers ought to heed Paul's words: "Be very careful, then, how you live—not as unwise but as wise, making the most of every opportunity, because the days are evil. Therefore do not be foolish, but understand what the Lord's will is. Do not get drunk on wine, which leads to debauchery. Instead, be filled with the Spirit, speaking to one another with psalms, hymns, and songs from the Spirit. Sing and make music from your heart to the Lord, always giving thanks to God the Father for everything, in the name of our Lord Jesus Christ" (Eph. 5:15–20).

Notice the connections between being filled with the Spirit, the state of your heart, and being thankful to God for everything. We need to pray to God for grace that is greater than our sin; we need to pray for the grace that makes us thankful. We have all seen what happens when an ungrateful child is told that they should be thankful: the result is sulking, not gratitude. Demands of the law do not change the heart. We need to pray for a full measure of the Spirit, the grace of Christ, and a God-given perspective so that we can evaluate our lives accurately.

Creativity in Presentation
Giving people the command, "Be patient" does not change the heart. Patience is part of the fruit of the Spirit. It is not hard to offer illustrations that show that our impatience and grumbling are often the result of incredible privilege. For example, in Numbers 11, Israel was grumbling about manna, which was a *miraculously provided food*, which was sustaining them *after they were miraculously liberated from slavery, and spared from genocide*! Today, Christians can complain about a long line at the drive-thru, but that presupposes the affluence to own a car, pay for gas, and line up for food or coffee that someone else has made for you. Being in the drive-thru automatically makes you one of the wealthiest people in the history of the world, yet we complain if it takes a few extra minutes. We complain if the internet is slow, yet having a device that connects to the internet means that you are among the most technologically privileged people in the history of the world. In a world where two billion people live on a few dollars or less a day, Christians should not be guilty of complaining about First World problems which only exist because of our affluence and luxury.[8]

The first time I (Steve) was in Africa, I was teaching in Uganda and I met an indigenous evangelical Anglican minister. This was in the early 2000s, and his parish was in a remote location where the guerrilla-terrorist group known as the LRA (Lord's Resistance Army) had been active. One night he was stopped at gunpoint and pulled over onto the side of road. He was roughed up, stripped naked, and sent off into the jungle. Later, he decided to stay and continue to serve in that area, and he wrote a letter to a friend where he described the incident. He then added, "They can take everything from me, but they can't take my Jesus." If we are dependent on external things, our thankfulness

---

8 In using examples of First World problems, the expositor should also be aware that some congregants may be experiencing challenges that go beyond mere inconvenience. Some may have lost employment, or have had rising costs threaten their ability to pay bills, rent, and feed their families. Some may be facing tremendous personal or family trauma. When speaking to our own propensity for complaint, the expositor should be careful to differentiate between complaints stemming from a disgruntled heart and those that threaten a family's life and well-being.

will ebb and flow. If we are dependent on the grace that the Spirit gives through Jesus Christ, we will be able to be thankful to God in everything. This minister is a living example that internal grace, not external law, is what makes the heart grateful to God.

One possible arrangement of this passage could be:

- Unwarranted complaint arouses God's anger (11:1–3).

- People are prone to forget God's mercy (11:4–9).

- God provides the help needed to lead his people (11:10–17).

- God can meet needs through his miraculous power (11:18–23).

- God's Spirit empowers those whom God has chosen to lead (11:24–30).

- Provision does not preclude punishment if people do not repent (11:31–35).

DISCUSSION QUESTIONS

1. Why did the Israelites fail to remember what life was actually like in Egypt when this crisis arose?

2. What can we learn about spiritual gifts and authority from Moses's response to the report about Eldad and Medad?

3. Why are we tempted to believe that God's arm is "too short" (Num. 11:23) to address the situations that we encounter? What should our response be instead?

4. Why did God use the quail as both a means of meeting Israel's needs and of demonstrating his displeasure?

5. What do we learn about human nature from the fact that the first recorded events of Israel's journey from Sinai are grumbling narratives? How can we turn from grumbling to gratitude?

Numbers 12:1–16

EXEGETICAL IDEA
God rejects Miriam and Aaron's challenge to Moses's leadership.

THEOLOGICAL FOCUS
Humility is an essential quality for those whom God chooses to lead his people.

PREACHING IDEA
Leaders are not perfect and sometimes sin against each other, but there can be intercession, reconciliation, and renewed partnership.

PREACHING POINTERS
Anyone who has long experience in pastoral or other kinds of Christian ministry knows that many, many times there are terrible tensions and divisions among leaders. Sometimes there is open animosity in the office. This passage shows us that such problems are not new. Here, there is a collocation of personal, prejudicial, and professional antagonism. Even today, the pain in the text comes through. The events described here are both very sad and very sinful. Unfortunately, many Christian leaders can identify with the general scene. But if we are honest, we must also remember that we have sometimes been the attackers as well as the target.

There are consequences for this arrogant attack on Moses, but there is also an incredible note of grace and forgiveness. This is a bitter squabble that brings personal family and social issues into the wider sphere of public ministry among the people of God. It challenges God's own decisions about leadership. Nevertheless, there is mercy and restoration. They remain brother and sister, and they are all still to fulfill their roles in the covenant community. Sadly, leaders can fight against each other, and there may be consequences for doing so, but in God's grace there can be forgiveness, reconciliation, and restoration. We need to recognize that leaders are not perfect and sometimes sin against each other, but there can be intercession, reconciliation, and renewed partnership.

MIRIAM AND AARON'S COMPLAINT (12:1–16)

LITERARY STRUCTURE AND THEMES

This narrative introduces another challenge to Moses's leadership. On this occasion, it comes not from the people (11:1) or from the "rabble" (11:4), but from his own brother and sister. It contains most of the expected elements of the grumbling narrative template, even though it does not actually use the Hebrew root for "grumble" (לוּן). It begins with an initial complaint (12:1–3), an expression of divine displeasure (12:4–9), and Moses's intercession (12:10–16). Unlike the previous grumbling narratives, it does not conclude by naming the location. This is likely because the rest of Israel is not involved. Instead, the conflict is contained within Moses's own family.

The overarching themes of this unit are authority and leadership. It explores the question of who has the authority to establish leadership over Israel, and to determine its scope. Human grasping for greater power usurps God's authority and merits judgment.

- *Miriam and Aaron's Complaint (12:1–3)*
- *God's Displeasure with Miriam and Aaron (12:4–9)*
- *Moses's Intercession (12:10–16)*

EXPOSITION

In Numbers 11, Moses complained about carrying the burden of leadership himself, and God shared the divine Spirit with the seventy elders. However, God preserved Moses's special position by awarding the Spirit to the elders *through* Moses. Perhaps in response to the extension of the Spirit to the elders, Miriam and Aaron express their desire have the same status as Moses. It is true that God has spoken to them as well as to Moses, but their access to God is not the same. The narrative then demonstrates how God rejects Miriam and Aaron's challenge to Moses's leadership.[1]

Miriam and Aaron's Complaint (12:1–3)

12:1. Miriam and Aaron's challenge to Moses's leadership shifts even with the first two verses. Their initial complaint concerns Moses's foreign wife. Numbers 12:1 stresses this through repetition, noting that they spoke[2] against Moses "on account of the Cushite wife whom he had taken, for he had taken a Cushite wife." Nothing in the text thus far has suggested that this should be a matter of concern. Further, the stakes are on a different order of magnitude than other complaints, which often focus on the necessities of life (e.g., food, water, deliverance from enemies).

> **Moses's Cushite Wife**
> The identity of the Cushite wife is unclear. We know that Moses married Zipporah, daughter of the priest of Midian (Exod. 2:21). No other wives are named in the text. However, it is not easy to identify Zipporah as the "Cushite wife" since Cush is usually identified with an area south of Egypt, such as Ethiopia, while the Midianites are

---

1. The same issue of using feigned piety to cloak a desire for greater power will arise on a larger scale during Korah's rebellion (16:1–3).
2. The verb here is actually in the feminine singular form (וַתְּדַבֵּר), which does not agree grammatically with the compound subject "Miriam and Aaron." However, in these cases the verb often agrees with the first element of the subject. See van der Merwe, Naudé, and Kroeze 2017, 289.

based in northwest Arabia (Graf 2016, 432–34). The Septuagint adopts this reading, identifying her as an Ethiopian (Αἰθιόπισσαν).³ Further, it would be strange for Aaron and Miriam to object to Zipporah now, given that she was reunited with Moses prior to Israel's arrival at Sinai (Exod. 18:5–6). In this reading, the text is referring to a second wife for Moses, either after Zipporah's death or in a polygamous arrangement. On the other hand, the complete absence of other references to this woman pushes some to harmonize this description with what we know of Zipporah. One suggestion is that the term translated "Cushite" here actually refers to a region called Cushan, which is placed in parallel with Midian in Habakkuk 3:7 (Harrison 1990, 195; Noth 1968, 94). In this case, the woman is identified with a subset of the Midianites. Another possibility is that "Cushite" here is being used as an adjective meaning beautiful (Milgrom 1990, 93). In the opposite direction, there is a suggestion that "Cushite" is an ethnic slur, referencing Zipporah's potentially darker skin (Gane 2004, 590). Ultimately, this question is irresolvable and should not derail exposition of the passage since it is not raised again after 12:1.

12:2. Although the identity of the Cushite wife cannot be determined, Miriam and Aaron's complaint appears to have initial justification since Moses has married outside the community of Israel.⁴ However, the remainder of the story suggests that their complaint was a pretext to get at their real issue. There is no further mention of the Cushite wife. Instead, when Miriam and Aaron speak, they pose two linked rhetorical questions: "Has God spoken only through Moses? Has he not also [spoken] through us?" Rhetorical questions like these are not actually requests for information, but instead are assertions that intend to persuade the hearer to accept their underlying premises. They work on the principle of "negative polarity" so that the expected answer is opposite to the framing of the question (Moshavi 2009, 33). Here, the expected answer to the first question is "no, God has not only spoken through Moses," while the second expects the answer "yes, God has also spoken through us." This suggests that the problem is one of status and authority. Aaron and Miriam are jealous of Moses's special prerogatives and use the Cushite wife as an oblique means of challenging him (Adamo 2018, 8).

Numbers 12:2 ends with the two-word clause "YHWH heard." Presumably, Miriam and Aaron intended for their grumbling to garner support among the Israelite community, but God does not permit this challenge to proceed unanswered.

12:3. An editorial comment interrupts the narrative. It declares, "Now the man Moses was very humble, more so than all who were on the face of the earth." Many of those who presuppose Mosaic authorship view this as parenthetical aside since Moses would not be trumpeting his own humility (Cole 2000, 202). Its function is to explain why God steps in: a humble Moses would not defend his own prerogatives, but God sees a need to affirm Moses's authority (Ashley 1993, 224).

God's Displeasure with Miriam and Aaron (12:4–9)

12:4–5. God speaks "suddenly" (פִּתְאֹם) in response to Miriam and Aaron's complaint.

---

3   There even arose a legend mentioned by the Jewish historian Josephus that Moses traveled to Cush/Ethiopia and became a successful general, earning the love of an Ethiopian princess (Schneider 2019, 113–19).

4   The modern concept of racism based on skin color is probably not the primary issue here. The fact that this woman is not an ethnic Israelite provides the opening needed for Aaron and Miriam's objection, no matter her place of origin (Milgrom 1990, 93).

This word is typically found in contexts of invasions or disasters, suggesting that serious repercussions are forthcoming (cf. Josh. 10:9; 11:7; Isa. 47:11; 48:3; Jer. 4:20). His intervention reveals that Miriam and Aaron are not simply challenging Moses but also God's ordained structure of leadership. God summons the three siblings to the Tent of Meeting in 12:4b. He descends in a pillar of cloud, a key sign of divine presence (cf. Num. 9:15–23), and summons them. There is a certain irony here, since their assertion in 12:2 was that God has spoken through them as well. Now, it will become undeniable that God speaks to them, but not in a manner that they desire.

12:6–8. These verses contain God's response to Miriam and Aaron. Some translations (NASB, NIV) break it into poetic lines, while others (ESV) format it as prose address. The message itself is clear either way, but the poetic formatting brings out the elements of parallelism in the text. It may also reflect a chiastic arrangement, hinging on the contrast between Moses and other prophets in 12:7 (Milgrom 1990, 95). At the core of God's address is the contrast developed between Moses and other recipients of the divine word. After an initial command to hear God's word, 12:6 consists of three clauses that establish how God speaks to individuals other than Moses. The first sets up the scenario of the non-Mosaic prophet among Israel ("if there is a prophet of YHWH among you"[5]), while the second and third reveal the means of God's communication. God declares that he makes himself known "in a vision" (בַּמַּרְאָה) and speaks to these figures "in a dream" (בַּחֲלוֹם). Visions and dreams are common signs of the prophetic office, but they remove the recipient from their source. This is not the case with Moses. In 12:7 God calls him "my servant" and declares that "he is faithful in all my house (ESV, NIV)/household (HCSB, NASB)." This could refer either to Moses as the most faithful of God's servants (Harrison 1990, 196) or that God has entrusted Moses with his house (Wenham 2008, 127). In either case, God gives Moses a special status that the prophets who rely on dreams and visions cannot attain.

The crux of Moses's special status is found in 12:8. God declares he speaks with him "face to face, clearly, and not in riddles." The word translated "clearly" (מַרְאֶה) is very similar to the word for vision in 12:6, while "riddle" (חִידֹת) parallels the word for dream (Ashley 1993, 226). This again reinforces the contrast between Moses and other prophetic figures.

Communicating with God face to face reflects the intimacy of the relationship. In the next clause, God declares that Moses "beholds the form of YHWH." The word "form" (תְּמֻנַת) is found ten times in the Old Testament and refers to the visible presence of God.[6] Moses's special access to God's presence is found throughout Israel's sojourn at Sinai and in the wilderness, most vividly when he is permitted to glimpse God's back (Exod. 33:18–23). This part of God's speech confirms without a doubt that Moses has a unique status, rooted in his direct and unmediated access to the divine presence. This again reinforces his authority since others, including Miriam and Aaron, receive revelation from God through indirect means (Pressler 2017, 104).

The final clause of 12:8 is a rhetorical question posed by God that effectively counters

---

5. The Hebrew of this clause reads יהוה אִם־יִהְיֶה נְבִיאֲכֶם. The difficulty is with the last two words since a noun with a pronominal suffix (נְבִיאֲכֶם) usually isn't in a construct relationship with the following noun. Wenham suggests that this is an example of a "broken construct chain," noting Leviticus 26:42 as another example. This approach preserves the Hebrew text without emendation (Wenham 2008, 112).
6. Five of the ten occurrences are found in Deuteronomy 4, in which God forbids Israel from trying to capture his form in any kind of image or idol.

Miriam and Aaron's previous queries. YHWH asks, "Why then were you not afraid to speak against my servant Moses?" (12:8b NIV). The implied answer is that they should have trembled to take this step.

12:9. God then does not even provide Miriam and Aaron with an opportunity to respond. His anger burns against them and he departs. Miriam and Aaron are thoroughly rebuked for what they have done and face the weight of divine displeasure.

Moses's Intercession (12:10–16)

12:10. God's response to Miriam and Aaron does not end with a verbal rebuke. When the divine presence leaves the Tent of Meeting, it is revealed that Miriam has been struck with a disfiguring skin ailment. The text again uses repetition to drive home the shock of this development. The word for the ailment (מְצֹרַעַת) is found two times in the verse, once as a general description, and once as Aaron perceives what has happened to her. This verse also expands upon Miriam's condition, describing her as being "like snow" (כַּשָּׁלֶג). This stands in ironic contrast to 12:1 wherein the initial complaint was about Moses's foreign wife, who may well have had darker skin (Ashley 1993, 227). Numerous commentators note that the word מְצֹרַעַת in Scripture covers a range of skin diseases and may not be restricted to Hansen's disease, the clinical name for leprosy (Ashley 1993, 110; Pressler 2017, 39; Wenham 2008, 77). Leviticus 13–14 provides the fullest discussion of the term, including signs, symptoms, and treatment. This passage likely has a range of conditions in mind, especially given the procedure for welcoming a cleansed person back into the community (Lev. 14:1–31). In this passage, it is unnecessary to determine the exact nature of Miriam's affliction. God's punishment has rendered her unclean and facing the prospect of death and disfigurement.

> **Miriam's Punishment**
> One lingering question is why only Miriam is punished visibly when both she and Aaron spoke against Moses. One suggestion is that on the basis of the feminine singular verb וַתְּדַבֵּר in 12:1, Miriam instigated the complaint about Moses's wife (Milgrom 1990, 93). Another element to consider is Aaron's role as high priest. If he were to be rendered ceremonially unclean (perhaps permanently), the entire sacrificial system would be thrown into chaos. In this reading, Aaron's punishment is having to subordinate himself to Moses and recognize that Moses alone can intercede with God in this situation.

12:11–12. Miriam's condition prompts a cry from Aaron. Aaron recognizes the folly of his challenge and humbles himself before Moses, calling on him to intercede. In doing so, Aaron is forced to reckon with the impropriety of the assertion in 12:2 that he and Miriam were Moses's equals in receiving divine revelation. Now, in 12:11 Aaron appeals to Moses, calling him "my lord," and twice uses the Hebrew root for "sin" to acknowledge their misdeeds.[7] Aaron must acknowledge Moses's superior position and hope that Moses's intercession can turn aside God's anger. Aaron's speech continues in 12:12 where he paints a graphic picture of Miriam's condition. He pleads with Moses not to leave her "as a dead person who comes from the womb of their mother and their flesh is half-eaten." In effect, Aaron compared Miriam's affliction to the decomposition of a stillborn fetus, an image clearly

---

7 English translations obscure this double use of the root "sin" (חטא). The NIV has "I ask you not to hold against us the sin we have so foolishly committed." The ESV reads "do not punish us because have done foolishly and have sinned." A very literal rendering would be "do not hold against us the sin in which we acted foolishly and in which we sinned."

intended to evoke maximum revulsion (Pressler 2017, 105). God may well speak through Miriam and Aaron as they claim in 12:2, but he has ordained special prerogatives for Moses, which Aaron must now acknowledge.

12:13. Moses responds with a heartfelt cry, appealing to God for restoration. The particle נָא ("please") appears twice in the five words of Moses's plea, stressing Moses's posture of supplication. In spite of Miriam and Aaron's attempt to undermine him, Moses demonstrates his character by appealing to God on behalf of his stricken sister.

12:14–15. Moses's plea prompts a response from YHWH. In keeping with the pattern of the grumbling narratives, elements of punishment remain as a reminder of disobedience, even as restoration occurs. God uses yet another rhetorical question to drive home the point. He constructs a hypothetical scenario in which Miriam's father spit in her face, an act conveying disgrace and shame (Deut. 25:9; Job 30:10; Isa. 50:6), and asks "should she not be shamed seven days?" Again, the implied answer is "yes," so God establishes a seven-day period for Miriam to remain outside the camp, symbolically reflecting her removal from fellowship with God and the Israelite community. God's presence in the camp is incompatible with her unclean state and so she must be removed. The geographical locations that Miriam occupies in this narrative reflect the gravity of the misconduct. Within this narrative, Miriam has gone from the center to beyond the periphery, as her location has shifted from the Tent of Meeting (12:4–9) to outside the boundaries of the camp (12:14–15).

This narrative ends with Miriam's restoration. Notably, Israel does not move while Miriam is temporarily unclean, which reflects her stature. She is not abandoned, but the nation's progress is delayed. There is no comment on her position in the community when she returns, which makes it impossible to speculate about any ongoing consequences to her actions. However, Miriam is not mentioned again before her death in 20:1, meaning that her final activity in the text has this negative connotation.

12:16. Upon Miriam's return, Israel departs from Hazeroth and travels to the wilderness of Paran where it receives firsthand reports about the Promised Land.

THEOLOGICAL FOCUS

The exegetical idea (God has the authority to establish the leadership structure for his people) leads to this theological focus: *Humility is an essential quality for those whom God chooses to lead his people*. This narrative turns on humility and its absence. We read that Moses does not defend his own prerogatives even when confronted by his brother and sister. This confirms the description of his character in 12:3. On the other hand, Miriam and Aaron are not content with their roles as leaders in Israel and seek to undermine Moses by attacking his wife. Their desire for greater influence undercuts the true statement they make in 12:2 ("Has [God] also not spoken through us?"). Yes, he has, but it remains within God's purview to apportion leadership of his people.

Miriam and Aaron's improper use of a correct statement calls to mind the temptation of Jesus in the wilderness. There, the devil quotes Scripture in an effort to persuade Jesus to act against the Father's will and to seek his own power and dominion (Matt. 4:6). Jesus rebukes Satan with Scripture, rightly contextualized, and remains God's humble chosen servant all the way to the Cross.

The kingdom that Jesus proclaimed also has its share of struggles with the virtue of humility. Jesus rebuked his disciples for seeking to be greatest (Matt. 18:1–5), while Paul boasts about his suffering and humiliation (2 Cor. 11:24–30) while challenging those who called themselves super-apostles (2 Cor. 11:5; 12:11). Yet in spite of this, it is true that the desire to "use one's chosen status, authority, and religious connections in order to secure power and position is a constant temptation for the people of God and their leaders" (Stubbs 2009, 125). Those who serve the kingdom of God are not immune from the temptations of using their power and authority for personal advancement. The virtue of humility must be the mark of every Christian leader if they wish to emulate the example of Moses and avoid the cautionary tale of Miriam and Aaron.

PREACHING AND TEACHING STRATEGIES

Exegetical and Theological Significance
It is rather unexpected to find Moses being vehemently opposed by his sister and brother, especially since they were established leaders in the community. Aaron, of course, was the first high priest of Israel. He was with Moses when Moses encountered Pharoah before the exodus. Miriam led the people in worship after God's deliverance at the Red Sea (Exod. 15:21). Even though God blessed Miriam and Aaron with incredibly high positions, they wanted one level more. They didn't want anyone to have what seemed to be an advantage in position over them. Rather than being thankful to God for his grace in gifting them with their roles in the community, they focused on what they didn't have and grumbled. Then they attacked. In attacking Moses, however, they were really attacking God. It was God who had set apart Moses for his unique and special role. God has the right to choose his servants and to install them in the positions he wants them to fulfill. Miriam and Aaron should have used their energy to discharge their own duties and to support Moses in his God-given responsibilities.

Despite their discontent and rebellion, God did not cast Miriam and Aaron away. He affirmed the special role that Moses played in the covenant community and unfolding drama of redemptive history, but he also graciously forgave both Miriam and Aaron for their sin. Leaders fail and sin against each other and the Lord, but God can reconcile leaders when there is heartfelt contrition, repentance, intercession, and forgiveness. Grumbling and slander did not uproot Moses from his position in God's economy, and neither did it lead to a promotion for Miriam or Aaron. The way to move forward is to trust God, be thankful for the roles God has given us, and support those in positions of leadership authority above us. There is no place for ego in the ministry. God is very displeased with discord and faction among those he entrusts with positions of leadership in his covenant community. In the church, we need to walk by the Spirit and avoid critical, arrogant, and jealous attitudes.

Preaching Idea
Leaders are not perfect and sometimes sin against each other, but there can be intercession, reconciliation, and renewed partnership.

Contemporary Connections

What does it mean?
In business, there is a phenomenon known as the Peter Principle. This principle states that some people who are competent at one level of management will continue to be promoted until they arrive at a level of leadership that is beyond their ability to manage effectively. In athletics, numerous first-round draft picks come out of college and then have disappointing careers in the pros. The world recognizes that skills and aptitudes align with certain levels of leadership, and that not everyone excels at the highest levels. That's okay, though, because groups and teams require all kinds of work, skills, and personnel to be successful. Sometimes reaching for more influence or power ends up leading to frustration and hurting yourself and others. Success requires cooperation at every level.

Is it true?
Spiritual gifts are required to lead God's people, but we must never overlook the role of spiritual virtues. Numerous churches can attest to the catastrophe that results when egos assert themselves and leaders jockey for position or engage in turf wars. Pastors, elders, deacons, and boards with agendas and lack of humility have caused many churches to split. Even when leaders disagree on certain issues, they need to be united in virtue and humility. People in the church need to know that their leaders are modeling positive spiritual attitudes. Leaders need to ask themselves not only if they are competent, but if they are spiritually mature enough to assume levels of responsibility. It is very dangerous when we start comparing ourselves to others, measuring our giftedness, and believing God should give us more—or as much—as someone else. Miriam and Aaron had amazing roles to play in the covenant community! We need to learn to serve God in contentment and allow him to place his people in leadership and use them as he sees fit.

Now what?
This is a time for leaders in the church to affirm their unity—not for optics or perception, but in reality. Depending on the situation, this may be done either publicly or privately. Has there been gossip or slander among the staff? Is the board split into leadership factions? Is the atmosphere one of respect and good will, or are people undercutting each other? Are younger or junior leaders jealous of those with more responsibility? Are senior leaders egotistical and aggressively assertive of their power? This text acknowledges the reality of sin, but it also acknowledges the reality of forgiveness and reconciliation. Notice that Moses was the one who was spoken against, and yet he was the one who interceded in prayer for the guilty! Hopefully your church has not experienced anything negative in terms of the relationship between leaders. Hopefully your church knows the beauty of a united leadership operating with mutual good will and respect. If there have been problems, though, they need to be addressed.

Creativity in Presentation
A variety of illustrations can show the folly and impossibility of trying to accomplish anything worthwhile when leadership is going in opposite directions. Two people in a canoe facing and paddling in opposite directions can illustrate this; a pilot and copilot fighting for control, trying to make the jet go up or down, north or south; basketball players who all run five different plays, ignoring what was called by the coach; a general signalling "attack" while another signals "retreat"; a string quartet where everyone plays whatever song they feel like performing. It is often said, "It takes more grace than I can tell to play the second fiddle well." It doesn't take much grace to be the first chair violinist; it takes grace to play the supporting role.

In the church, it is not merely about skills and gifts; it also about humility, submission, and supporting one another. This should start with the leadership. It could be very powerful to invite church leaders up to the front for a time of prayer at the end of the message. They could join hands in a circle or kneel down together. Then they could pray for unity and virtue. If there needs to be confession and forgiveness, this can be done either in front of the church or privately (depending on the situation). People should be invited to pray for their leaders throughout the week. Unfortunately, the kind of leadership struggle that we see in Numbers 12 is exactly the sort of tragedy that unfolds in many of our churches today. Leaders are sinners, and leaders sin against the Lord, their people, and each other. Leaders should not pretend that they are without fault, nor should they demand submission to their authority—that's the opposite of humility! Instead, leaders confirm their aptitude for their positions by exemplifying virtues like wisdom, grace, humility, and forgiveness. When a church sees that their leaders acknowledge their failures and that they still love and respect each other, this can help unify the entire congregation. It reminds them that leaders are not perfect and they sometimes sin against each other, but there can be intercession, reconciliation, and renewed partnership. In this chapter, Israel's leadership fractured, but through confession, humility, and prayer there was forgiveness and restoration.

A suggested outline for the progression of this text is:

- Unwarranted jealously undermines godly leadership (12:1–3).

- God supports the leaders whom he has chosen (12:4–9).

- Repentance leads to restoration, although punishment may still occur (12:10–16).

DISCUSSION QUESTIONS

1. Why do you think that Miriam and Aaron used the ethnicity of Moses's wife to cloak their actual complaint?

2. How is Moses's humble character confirmed throughout this story?

3. Why is humility such a hard virtue to attain? What can we do when we feel jealous of the spiritual gifts or position of others?

4. What signs of God's grace do we find in this narrative, even after Miriam and Aaron's sinful actions?

Numbers 13:1–14:4

EXEGETICAL IDEA
The spies' fearmongering triumphs over the call to faithfully trust God when the time comes to enter the Promised Land.

THEOLOGICAL FOCUS
God's people are called to respond in faith and obedience rather than succumb to fear.

PREACHING IDEA
We are to respond in faith to God's promises, trusting his word more than those who incite fear and disbelief.

PREACHING POINTERS
This is a familiar story, and one that connects well with our experiences. It is a pivotal moment in the Pentateuch and is used as a warning lesson throughout the canon. Israel's failure in that particular historical moment cannot be repeated (since nobody else will ever stand in that epoch facing that exact decision), but the underlying reason for their failure to enter the Promised Land is one that people face day after day. When we stand on the brink of momentous, life-changing decisions, or as we make our countless daily choices, we will either choose to put our faith in God's promises, or we will give way to fear and abandon our trust in God.

There are many frightening realities in this world, and our strength indeed is small. Yet, the Lord is our covenant God, and we are called to trust in him. In the Gospels, this dichotomy between fear and faith recurs over and over again. If we trust Jesus, we will not give way to fear. If we give way to fear, we are not exercising proper faith in Jesus. God's Word must be taken over every lie, piece of propaganda, and alternative opinion. We must not look to our own wisdom, strength, and goodness, but to God's. Only by faith can we be saved and enter the Promised Land. We are to respond in faith to God's promises, trusting his word more than those who incite fear and disbelief.

FEAR AND FAITH AT THE BORDERS OF THE PROMISED LAND (13:1–14:4)

LITERARY STRUCTURE AND THEMES

Numbers 13–14 is an extended narrative that focuses on the conflict between God's provision and Israel's failure to trust. Numbers 13 establishes the basis of the conflict, while the following chapter works out the consequences of Israel's rejection of God's promises. Numbers 13 provides greater detail than many biblical narratives, preserving the names of otherwise unmentioned characters and working slowly through dialogue. This preaching unit breaks into four sections: assembling the spies (13:1–16), sending the spies (13:17–25), the report of the spies (13:26–33), and Israel's fearful response (14:1–4).

The driving theme of this preaching unit is the conflict between fear and faith. Trusting in God's promises and provision is set against fear of the inhabitants of Canaan. The narrative reveals that the land is fruitful and rich, but that strong opponents inhabit its cities. The question is whether the Israelites will listen to the voice of fear as exemplified by the ten spies, or will demonstrate the faith in God's protection shown by Caleb (and later, Joshua [Num. 14:6–9]). Unfortunately, fear triumphs over faith, leading to devastating consequences.

- **Assembling the Spies (13:1–16)**
  - *God's Command to Send the Spies (13:1–3)*
  - *The Names of the Spies (13:4–16)*
- **Sending the Spies (13:17–25)**
  - *Moses's Instructions (13:17–20)*
  - *The Spies' Journey (13:21–25)*
- **The Spies' Report (13:26–33)**
- **Israel's Fearful Response (14:1–4)**

EXPOSITION

Numbers 13:1–14:4 introduces one of the most tragic narratives in the Old Testament. After generations of servitude in Egypt and a miraculous rescue, Israel is on the verge of seeing the fulfillment of God's promises. They are about to enter Canaan and celebrate the faithfulness of God to the assurances he gave to Abraham, Isaac, and Jacob (Gen. 15:13–16; 26:3–5; 28:13–15). After the rebellions of Numbers 11–12, Israel appears to be back on track as God gives Moses instructions to pass on to Israel, who appear at first to respond obediently (Pressler 2017, 114). However, fear and faithlessness still lurk. This narrative is an "historical watershed," elevated above other grumbling narratives (Wenham 2008, 116). It demonstrates how the spies' fearmongering triumphs over the call to faithfully trust God when the time comes to enter the Promised Land.

Assembling the Spies (13:1–16)

God's Command to Send the Spies (13:1–3)
13:1–2. The narrative begins with God instructing Moses to send men to explore the land. Two features are noteworthy. First, God identifies Canaan as "the land which I am giving to the Israelites" (13:2 NIV). This provides the theological orientation for the narrative; it is God's gift to his covenant people. The purpose of the spies is to confirm the land's goodness and reassure the community of God's faithfulness (Stubbs 2009, 128). Secondly, the spies represent each of Israel's ancestral tribes. This symbolically communicates that land is for all of God's people, as each tribe participates in entering it for the first time. It also links to the

enduring nature of the divine promise as past generations are invoked.

13:3. This first subsection concludes with the report that Moses sent them from the Wilderness of Paran and reconfirms that they were all leaders within Israel. The initial contours of the drama have been established: Israel is on the border of the land that God has promised. The community awaits the report of those selected to survey the land.

> **Sending of the Spies**
>
> This account of the sending of the spies differs slightly from how Moses recounts it in Deuteronomy 1:22–25. In that passage the focus remains squarely on Israel's unbelief so that the request to send the spies originates with Israel itself, rather than God. Some attempt to harmonize the texts in favor of Deuteronomy, noting that the initial command in Numbers 13:2 could be read reflexively as "send for yourself" (שְׁלַח־לְךָ). In this reading, God does not authorize the sending of spies, but rather states that if Moses feels it necessary to send them on Israel's behalf, there should be one from each tribe (Milgrom 1990, 100; Stubbs 2009, 127). This approach is hard to substantiate given the absence of other examples of the imperative form of שלח being used this way. Further, the two narratives are not incompatible, but emphasize what is important for their own context. Numbers 13–14 focuses on the contrast between God's provision and Israel's fear, with God as an active character. Conversely, God does not speak directly in the historical retelling in Deuteronomy 1:6–3:29, as his voice is mediated through Moses. All parties involved (God, Moses, Israel) were in favor of sending out spies. Numbers and Deuteronomy simply approach the event from different perspectives.

The Names of the Spies (13:4–16)
13:4–16. The narrative flow is interrupted by a list naming the spies. These individuals are not identical to the list of tribal leaders found in 1:5–15 and 7:12–83, which suggests that the spies are younger men, better suited for the rigors of the journey (Olson 1996, 77; Stubbs 2009, 127). There is no representative from the tribe of Levi, which is understandable given that God himself is their inheritance (3:11–13; Josh. 13:33). Since only Caleb and Joshua have any significance beyond Numbers 13–14, the expositor should not devote much time or energy here, but two details stand out. First, the name of one spy again reinforces Joseph's status as the firstborn who receives a double share of the inheritance. It reads "from the tribe of Joseph (that is, from the tribe of Manasseh)" (13:11 ESV). Although the same identification with Joseph is not found for Ephraim in 13:8, its presence with Manasseh reminds the reader of Joseph's status (Gen. 48:5). Secondly, 13:16b reveals that Moses has changed the name of Ephraim's representative from Hoshea to Joshua. This simply requires the addition of a single consonant in Hebrew (הוֹשֵׁעַ→יְהוֹשֻׁעַ). It gives the name an explicitly Yahwistic sense, changing it from "he saves" to "YHWH saves" (Ashley 1993, 233).[1]

Sending the Spies (13:17–25)
Following this list, the spies depart for the Promised Land. This section neatly divides in two, beginning with Moses's instructions (13:17–20), followed by the spies' compliance (13:21–25).

Moses's Instructions (13:17–20)
13:17. Moses directs the spies to go through the Negev wilderness and up into the hill country that makes up the central spine of the land. These rather imprecise instructions indicate that Moses is unfamiliar with Canaan and can

---

1 This character has had the name Joshua in his previous appearances in Exodus 17:8 and Numbers 11:28 as well as throughout the book of Joshua. This is likely an editorial comment making sure that the audience identifies the figure in the list with Israel's next great leader (Harrison 1990, 203).

13:18–20. Moses instructs the spies are to see the land and determine whether its inhabitants are "strong or weak, whether they are few, or many?" (13:18 ESV). The dichotomies continue in 13:19–20a, as Moses asks the spies to evaluate if the land is good or bad, likely a reference to its fertility, and whether its cities are open or fortified. Moses then turns back to the land itself and again asks if it is rich or poor and whether it has flourishing plant life. Moses's final instruction in 13:20b is for the spies to bring back proof of the land's bounty. Given Israel's complaints about food throughout the wilderness wandering, some tangible evidence of Canaan's fruit could prove useful. Essentially, Moses has given the spies parameters to consider the feasibility of a military invasion. They are to determine if the land can support Israel and if it will be difficult to conquer. Moses's instructions are about evenly weighted between the two concerns, which provides a sharp contrast to the spies' report.

The Spies' Journey (13:21–25)

13:21–22. The text then gives the account of the journey. Now that Moses is no longer speaking, the narrator can provide more geographical detail, tracing the journey of the spies from the Wilderness of Zin, which represents the extreme south of the land (Num. 34:3–4; Josh. 15:1–3) to Lebo-Hamath, which is found in the extreme north (cf. 1 Kings 8:65; 2 Kings 14:24). This indicates that the spies have conducted a thorough survey. Numbers 13:22 moves away from general comment toward some of the spies' significant discoveries. It notes that the spies encountered descendants of Anak in Hebron, which will eventually become part of Judah's tribal allotment (Josh. 15:13–19). Ahiman, Sheshai, and Talmai probably represent clans of Anakites whom Israel will need to dispossess (Ashley 1993, 238; Budd 1984, 145). The Hebrew word עֲנָק also refers to the neck, so this is probably also a reference to their towering height (Wenham 2008, 118).[2] Hebron has biblical connections stretching back to Abraham. It was near Hebron that Abraham received the promise that his descendants would inherit the land (Gen. 13:14–18). Now, Hebron is cast as the seat of strong opposition to the fulfillment of God's promise.

13:23–25. The final element of the spies' journey shifts back toward the fertility of the land. The spies come to the Valley of Eshcol and cut down a cluster of grapes as well as other fruit.[3] Its exact location is unknown, but the fact that it is within the Promised Land is all that Israel should need. Laden with tangible proof, the spies return to Moses after forty days.

The Spies' Report (13:26–33)

13:26–27. The narrative now takes a sharp downward turn as the conflict between fear and faith comes to the forefront. The spies return to the Wilderness of Paran and address the community. Their report begins with the positive: they display the fruit of the land (13:26b) and verbally confirm that it does "flow with milk and honey" (13:27 NIV). However, these comments are cursory in comparison to the lengthy, fear-filled description of the inhabitants of the land that follow. There may even be a brief hint of the spies' perspective in 13:27 when they describe Canaan as the "land to which *you* sent us." Wenham notes that when the land is qualified by a relative clause in other places it is usually

---

2 This narrative provides the first mention of the Anakites in Scripture (Num. 13:22, 28, 33). They also are found in Moses's historical summation (Deut. 1:28; 2:10, 11, 21) as well as accounts of Joshua's conquest (Josh. 11:21, 22; 14:12, 15). Most of these references stress their height and portray them as frightening opponents. This perspective shapes the spies' report in 13:26–33, so the Anakites will be discussed in more detail there.

3 Eshcol (אֶשְׁכּוֹל) means "grape-cluster." The location is named for what the spies found there.

something like "the land *YHWH* has promised to give them" (13:2; 14:16, 23, 30, 40; Wenham 2008, 119). God is thus absent from the spies' assessment and the community's initial reaction, leaving Moses and the rest of Israel to consider the situation only from a human perspective.

> **Flowing with Milk and Honey**
>
> The expression "flowing with milk and honey" (זָבַת חָלָב וּדְבָשׁ) is a shorthand for the overall fertility of the land. It builds off of the foundation of the land as suitable for grazing animals that produce milk and providing habitats for bees (Stubbs 2009, 129). This expression is often intertwined with the concept of the land being a refuge that God provides Israel after slavery (Exod. 3:8, 17; Ezek. 20:6) and an expression of his faithfulness to Israel through all its generations (cf. Exod. 13:5; Deut. 6:3; 11:9; 26:9, 15; 27:3; 31:20; Jer. 11:5; 32:22).

13:28–29. In contrast to Moses's balanced instructions, the spies dwell heavily on the question of opposition and downplay the fruitfulness of the land. Their negative assessment looms over the rest of the narrative. A strong disjunctive (אֶפֶס כִּי) marks the beginning of 13:28, making an abrupt transition from the fruit of the land. The spies then classify the inhabitants of the land as strong, the cities as fortified, and very large. All of these are questions that Moses asked to them to examine, but the negative assessment does not end there. In 13:28b–29, the spies report the inhabitants of the land, beginning with the Anakites in the Negev, with Hittites, Jebusites, Amorites, and Canaanites rounding out the summary. This list is undoubtedly accurate but is intended to instill doubt.

13:30. This report causes a disturbance that requires Caleb to first silence the crowd before giving his minority opinion. He urges Israel to go up and take possession of the land, and although he does not mention God in his brief speech, several cues alert us to his underlying faith. First, the verbs Caleb uses are "go up" (עלה) and "possess" (ירשׁ), which are associated with God's promises about the land in other passages, including Exodus 3:8, 17; 33:3; and Leviticus 20:24 (Wenham 2008, 120). Secondly, in his short address Caleb twice uses a Hebrew grammatical construction that intensifies the conviction of his words.[4] The ESV captures this with "We should by all means go up and take possession of it, for we will surely overcome it." Thirdly, this speech anticipates his next address in which he and Joshua urge Israel to trust that he can bring them into the land (14:6–9).

Caleb provides a countervailing voice of faith to the fear evoked by the rest of the spies. He alone seems to remember that promise that Israel's enemies would scatter before YHWH (Num. 10:35). As long as Israel obeyed YHWH and remained in his presence, then surely he could fulfill his promise to give them the land (Condie 2001, 129).

13:31. The immediate effect of Caleb's testimony is to cause the other spies to elevate their rhetoric until it verges on hyperbolic. It is notable that even though we have the names of the fearful spies from 13:4–16, they are treated as a nameless collective in the rest of this narrative. This perhaps anticipates the ignominious fate that awaits them in 14:36–37.[5] In 13:31, they directly counter Caleb's appeal by stating, "We are not able to go up against the people for they

---

4 The grammatical feature in question is the repetition of the verbal root. When the root is given in its infinitive absolute form followed by a perfect or imperfect form, it "affirms and intensifies the authenticity and conviction of the verbal action" (Arnold and Choi 2018, 87). The two examples in 13:30 are עָלֹה נַעֲלֶה ("let us surely go up") and יָכוֹל נוּכַל ("we are surely able").

5 Joshua is not mentioned here, but given God's positive affirmation of him in 14:30, 38, he should not be lumped in with the rest of the unnamed spies.

are too strong for us" (ESV). They use the same verbs as Caleb (עלה "to go up" and יכל "to be able") in order to communicate the opposite message.

13:32–33. The faithless spies then detail their reasoning in what English translations call a "bad report."[6] They first refer to the land as one that "devours those living in it" (13:32 NIV). This could refer to the unforgiving and hostile nature of the land itself (Milgrom 1990, 106), though this seems unlikely given that the spies themselves acknowledge its fruitfulness in their first address. More likely is the possibility that it refers to the inhabitants of the land, suggesting that they are so violent and warlike that Israel would surely be devoured if it sought to challenge them (Pressler 2017, 117). This is in keeping with the spies' focus on the military unfeasibility of entering Canaan.

The spies continue in 13:32b–33 by referring to the stature of the inhabitants. They are "men of great height" (13:32b ESV), whom the spies then identify as Nephilim who are linked to the Anakites mentioned in 13:28. The reference to Nephilim draws on the fascinating and challenging passage of the intermixing of the "sons of God" and "daughters of men" in Genesis 6:1–4. Given all of the references to height here, it seems likely that the spies are using the Nephilim in the sense of mythological giants (Olson 1996, 79). This may be sheer hyperbole on the part of the spies, since there is no mention of the Nephilim in the narrator's report of their mission in 13:21–25. In any event, the mention of the Nephilim, along with the spies declaring that they were "like grasshoppers" before them, is meant to evoke maximum fear. The spies portray the land that God has promised as terrifying. Giant-sized fears overwhelm the prospect of faith and obedience—even on the brink of seeing God's promises fulfilled.

> **Nephilim**
>
> The mention of the Nephilim is tantalizingly elusive, especially given the interpretive challenges posed by Genesis 6:1–4 and the references to Anakites and other apparent giants in the Pentateuch and conquest narratives (Deuteronomy 2–3; Josh. 11:21–23). In popular imagination, the Nephilim provide plenty of fodder for bizarre speculation.[7] While the expositor of Numbers 13 should not get sidetracked for too long, it is inevitable that questions will arise. It is impossible to resolve what Scripture leaves ambiguous, but a few observations can be made. First, as mentioned above, the spies' mention of the Nephilim comes in response to Caleb's attempt to persuade Israel to trust God. They are not mentioned in narrated accounts of the spies' travels, although the Anakites are (13:22). Consequently, many commentators suggest that the spies' words are unreliable; they intentionally exaggerate the threat in order to dissuade their audience from listening to Caleb (Olson 1996, 79; Routledge 2015, 40; Wenham 2008, 120). Secondly, based on the parallel to Genesis 6:1–4, the spies are probably trying to portray the Nephilim as the product of union between the divine ("sons of God") and human ("daughters of men") realms. Questions then arise as to how such figures would have survived the Noahic flood, which are not addressed in Scripture (Routledge 2015, 40). However, if the spies are untrustworthy narrators, then the logical challenges are not as important. Thirdly, it is important to note that in recent years there have been serious attempts to wrestle honestly with the

---

6 The word translated "bad report" is דִּבָּה. In most of its uses it conveys negativity (Num. 14:36; Prov. 12:22), which is emphasized in some cases by qualifying it with the adjective רָעָה, meaning "evil" (Gen. 37:2; Num. 14.37; Ashley 1993, 242; Milgrom 1990, 106).

7 Once, when I (Joel) was checking into a hotel at a conference for the Evangelical Theological Society, the desk clerk quite earnestly informed me that the Nephilim were signs of alien activity on the earth. Routledge has compiled a list of popular investigations into the Nephilim (Routledge 2015, 20).

> supernatural in Scripture, including this passage. In particular, Heiser considers the possibility that the spies *did* see Nephilim in Canaan and ties that into an explanation for God's mandate to clear the land of its inhabitants (Heiser 2015, 192–214).

The question of the Nephilim cannot be fully resolved, but it seems likely that the faithless spies expected Israel to see them as frightening giants, perhaps resulting from the blending of heavenly and earthly realms. In Numbers 13, the spies use the threat of the Nephilim as the ultimate trump card that causes Israel to break faith with God.

Israel's Fearful Response (14:1–4)

14:1–2a. This preaching unit concludes with the response of the community to the report of the spies. The spies' fear-filled words have wormed their way into the hearts of the Israelites, whose uncritical acceptance of the potential exaggerations about the Nephilim may point to Israel's apparent gullibility (Stubbs 2009, 129), or at least its willingness to use any possible reason to complain. This short selection also contains four synonymous verbs, reflecting the passionate fury of Israel's complaint (Wenham 2008, 120). The Israelites "lift up" (וַתִּשָּׂא) and "give" (וַיִּתְּנוּ) their voice, they "weep" (וַיִּבְכּוּ), and finally they "grumble" (וַיִּלֹּנוּ). The root לון is crucial to this passage, as it recurs in 14:27, 29, and 36 when YHWH announces his judgment. It also echoes Israel's earlier complaints about food and water on the way to Sinai in Exodus 15–17. Israel's penchant for grumbling now provokes divine judgment.

14:2b–4. Israel expresses a wish to have either died in Egypt or in the wilderness (14:2b). Their despair leads them even to question God's motives, asking why God has brought them here to be slaughtered while their wives and children are enslaved (14:3a). This attitude reflects a failure to trust God's good intentions and to remember God's sustaining presence among them (Stubbs 2009, 130). Israel quickly forgets that God has already defeated powerful enemies and provided for them through the escape from Egypt and in the wilderness. Every time they face a new challenge, it is as though they cannot remember the events that have led them to this place. This failure of memory leads to the rhetorical question "wouldn't it be better for us to go back to Egypt?" (14:3b NIV). Numbers 14:4 turns this from a question into a plan of action, stating "let us choose a leader and go back to Egypt" (ESV). The Israelites declare that they would rather settle for slavery than trust in God's power. The God who saved them by casting Pharaoh's chariots into the heart of sea (Exod. 15:1–2) apparently is incapable of defeating these new foes. This reflects the triumph of fear over faith at the borders of the Promised Land.

THEOLOGICAL FOCUS

The exegetical idea (The spies' fearmongering triumphs over the call to faithfully trust God when the time comes to enter the Promised Land) leads to this theological focus: *God's people are called to respond in faith and obedience rather than succumb to fear.* Israel stands on the borders of the Promised Land. Their God has brought them through wilderness to this point. He has promised his presence will remain. He has rescued them from slavery, hunger, thirst, and foreign oppression. Against this reality stands the testimony of ten faithless spies who see only giants. Their inability to orient their perspective around God prompts them to give a message of fear that has disastrous consequences.

The struggle between faith and fear resonates throughout Scripture. When Israel finally enters the Promised Land after its period of wandering, YHWH repeatedly exhorts Joshua to be strong and courageous (Josh. 1:6, 7, 9) because YHWH will be with him whether he goes. In another confrontation with a giant, David alone demonstrates faith while Saul and the rest of Israel cower in fear. David chooses not to trust in Saul's armor (1 Sam. 17:38–39) but instead faces Goliath armed with the knowledge that YHWH gives the victory. David's address to Goliath in 1 Samuel 17:45–47 is the mirror opposite of the spies' speech to Israel. He declares that he comes against the giant in the name of the YHWH Almighty. Physical strength and weaponry are irrelevant because YHWH alone determines victory.

In nonmilitary contexts, Paul encourages Timothy with the reminder that God does not give his followers a spirit of timidity, but instead calls them to bold proclamation of his name, in spite of the possibility of suffering, imprisonment, or even death (2 Tim. 1:7–8). In a similar vein, the author of Hebrews quotes Psalm 118, declaring, "So we say with confidence, the Lord is my helper; I will not be afraid. What can mere mortals do to me?" (Heb. 13:6 NIV). For the author of Hebrews, likely addressing a church facing some form of persecution, "mere mortals" could persecute, imprison, and even execute those who claimed loyalty to Jesus and the gospel. However, trust that God has secured the eternal hope of believers through the cross of Christ provides courage to cling to faith even when fear would be understandable.

The theological focus on this preaching unit can be summarized as, "Faith is courage that conquers. Disbelief is cowardice that correctly assesses the impossibility of the situation but fails to take God into account, thereby snatching defeat out of the jaws of victory" (Gane 2004, 602). Numbers 13 provides a stark example of how easy it is to lower one's gaze and see only the earthly obstacles, failing to respond in trust and obedience to what God has commanded.

PREACHING AND TEACHING STRATEGIES

Exegetical and Theological Significance

This passage provides a paradigmatic example of a major biblical theme: Will people respond to God's promises in fear or in faith? The necessity of a proper response to God is set before both the nation as a corporate whole and individuals within the community. Even when the majority doubt the promises of God, those with faith can master fear and live with courage. Aristotle argued that courage was the golden mean between cowardice and rashness, and there is some insight in his analysis. Yet for the child of God, it is never rash to trust in God's promises—trusting God is the most reasonable, rational, and secure thing to do in any situation. Regardless of the seeming odds or obstacles, nothing is too difficult for the Lord.

This passage also provides an excellent opportunity to move beyond the immediate context to a wider, biblical-theological treatment of the themes of fear and faith. There are numerous links along the way (even including more giants: think of David and Goliath), but one very rich section is found in the gospel of Mark. When Jesus calms the storm, he asks his disciples, "Why are you so afraid? Where is your faith?" (Mark 4:40). These two statements put fear and faith together in an antithetical relationship. The next few pericopes in Mark work with this same oscillation between fear and faith. Mark 5:1–20 tells the story of the man with the Legion of demons, and when the demons are cast out there is either a response of fear or faith. Mark 5:21–43 contains two interwoven stories. The woman subject to bleeding touches Jesus's cloak and is healed. She stands before Jesus "trembling with fear" and then is told "your faith has healed you" (vv. 33–34). Immediately Jesus is told that Jairus's daughter has died, and he says, "Don't be afraid, just believe" (v. 36).

Whether we face storms, an army of demons, chronic illness, or death itself, we are told not to fear but to trust in God by faith. God always fulfills his promises, and our Lord Jesus Christ is able to conquer any enemy. He even defeats death. Climactically, when Jesus has been resurrected, he says to the women at the empty tomb, "Do not be afraid" (Matt. 28:10).

Fear and Faith at the Borders of the Promised Land (13:1–14:4)

Preaching Idea
We are to respond in faith to God's promises, trusting his word more than those who incite fear and disbelief.

Contemporary Connections

What does it mean?
What does it mean that we are to respond in faith to God's promises, trusting his word more than those who incite fear and disbelief? This means that we are to have confidence in God and trust him that he will fulfill his promises. Courage does not mean that we have perfect emotional tranquility, but it does mean that we act in accordance with what we know. Feeling nervous or even scared is not wrong, but letting those emotions overwhelm our trust in God so that we fail to act in line with his Word is a sign that we need to exercise stronger faith. God is very gracious and he knows our weaknesses, but he also expects us to walk beside him in childlike trust. Rejecting God's instructions in fear is sin, and it can have lasting consequences.

We must also make very, very certain that we are not fomenting and inciting fear and lack of faith in the community of believers. Our words and actions have the potential to help or hurt those around us. The spies were responsible for the reports they gave and for their own attitudes and actions, but their reports also persuaded the community to turn away from a faith-filled response to God. Church leaders who employ the tactics of fear turn their people away from faithfully trusting that their eternal hope is in Christ. This can have devasting consequences, such as persuading people that when they encounter hostility and resistance they should abandon virtues like the fruit of the Spirit: "love, joy, peace, forbearance, kindness, goodness, faithfulness, gentleness, and self-control" (Gal. 5:22–23 NIV). Instead, they should put their trust in their own strength or in supposedly strong human leaders who use whatever tactics are necessary to preserve power. In this way, the church rejects the victory of slain but risen Lamb and chases after the illusory strength of the dragon (Revelation 12).

In the church we can either encourage people to follow God wholly, or we can discourage them and hinder their walk with God. In our own strength, we cannot take the Promised Land, nor make our way to the new heavens and the new earth. However, that is not what we are called to do. Instead, through faith in Jesus Christ we see how God's promises find their ultimate fulfillment. Our eternal hope is secured through faith in Christ's sacrificial submission to the will of the Father.

Is it true?
Is it true that we are to respond in faith to God's promises, trusting his Word more than those who incite fear and disbelief? Scripture gives us multiple examples of faith triumphing over fear. Sadly, it also gives us multiple examples of fear triumphing over faith. In our own lives we can see times when we walked by faith and experienced great victories, and also times when we gave into fear, did not trust God as we ought, and experienced defeat. One very important principle that we need to understand is that God always fulfills his promises, but not every desire or dream we have is a promise from God. There are some people who are extremely disappointed with God and they struggle to trust him, but their disappointment is not because he has failed to uphold his *promises*. Whatever God promises he will fulfill. We need to make sure that we distinguish our own ideas, opinions, wants, and desires from the actual promises of God in Scripture.

Trusting God does not mean we decide what God should do and then we convince ourselves that he will do it. On the contrary, trusting God takes him at his word and allows him to set the agenda. We trust his promises, and he is the one who tells us what his promises are. In this life there are disappointments, heartaches, and tragedies, and God has never promised to exempt us from all of them. We need to carefully study the Word of God so that we know what his promises actually are. Then we need to trust him enough to walk by faith.

Now what?
So how do we respond in faith to God's promises? How do we trust him more than those who incite fear and disbelief? As individuals and churches, we need to evaluate honestly whether we are walking by faith or living in fear. Church leaders can look at the situations they are facing in the church and prayerfully inquire as to whether they are truly meeting them by faith. Individuals can take an honest look at their own walks with God and look for areas in their lives where they are not trusting God as they should. If there are areas in our lives where we are not honouring or obeying God, that is proof of a lack of faith. Now is the time to confess our fears, to renew our commitment to walk with God by faith, and to ask him to strengthen our trust in him.

Creativity in Presentation
This passage lends itself well to drama. During the service—perhaps right before the message—the group of spies could be recounting their experiences, debating whether to go into the land by faith or to turn back. They don't think that they're too cowardly; they think they are being pragmatic and reasonable. Yes, they are afraid, but in their eyes they are afraid with good reason! Going into the land against such occupants would be reckless and not worth the risk.

Given the pervasive nature of the fear-or-faith theme in Scripture, this would also be a great opportunity to present other dramatic vignettes from Scripture. Depending on the size and style of the congregation, this could be done with small drama groups or dramatic readings. Although there are numerous passages that could be used to illustrate the theme, the ones mentioned above in the Exegetical and Theological Significance section would work well. The major point is that we need to look to God rather than our external circumstances. If we look at the giants, or the storm, or the demons, or the disease, or death itself, we can be afraid. However, when we look at the promises of God and the person of Jesus Christ, we can have a faith that masters fear. At the end of the message the pastor can point people to the ultimate reason why we do not have to be afraid, and the last vignette can be with the women at the empty tomb. Jesus speaks to them and tells them not to be afraid. This is our ultimate hope and the strongest foundation for faith rather than fear. Jesus has been raised from the dead, and we have eternal life by faith in him. All of God's promises will be fulfilled because of Christ. Let us walk by faith.

One possible outline could be:

- God allows his people to confirm the truth of his promises (13:1–16).

- God seeks to bring his people to good places (13:17–25).

- Fear can triumph over faith when God is forgotten (13:26–14:4).

DISCUSSION QUESTIONS

1. How do the faithless spies distort Moses's instructions to serve their agenda?

2. What could they have said in their report that would have both acknowledged the challenges ahead and shown faith in God?

3. Why can the allure of fear be stronger than the call to have faith in God in difficult circumstances?

4. How can believers avoid succumbing to fear and instead turn to God in faith when challenging situations arise?

Numbers 14:5–45

EXEGETICAL IDEA
Israel's failure to trust God yields fatal consequences as God decrees that the generation rescued from slavery in Egypt will die in the wilderness. However, evidence of God's grace and mercy is found in his continued presence among his sinful people.

THEOLOGICAL FOCUS
God's great mercy redeems human sinfulness but does not eliminate all of the consequences of sin.

PREACHING IDEA
Although there can be enormous consequences for sin, God is forgiving and merciful to fulfill his redemptive promises.

PREACHING POINTERS
This chapter reveals the consequences of walking in fear rather than in faith. Having come so far and having experienced so much of God's redeeming grace and power, the Israelites now turn away from him. On the brink of having one of God's significant promises fulfilled, their faith fails. Instead of going into the Promised Land, they talk about going back to slavery in Egypt. In saying this, they are literally contemplating a total rejection of God's redemption and covenant promises. Given their response, God threatens to destroy the people totally and start a new nation with Moses. However, Moses intercedes on the basis of God's glory and name.

After numerous examples of hard-hearted stubbornness and high-handed rebellion, the amazing thing about this passage is that God decides to bear patiently with his people. Yes, this generation will die in the wilderness, but the next generation will enter the land. God will not swerve from his covenant loyalty, and he will not cast aside his people or his plan. There are real consequences for those who rebel, but God is filled with covenant mercy, grace, and kindness. God has a plan, and he is going to bring it to fruition. If we put our faith in him, we will be blessed and enter into salvation. If we turn from him in lack of faith, we will be lost. Although there can be enormous consequences for sin, God is forgiving and merciful to fulfill his redemptive promises.

ISRAEL'S REBELLION AND ITS CONSEQUENCES (14:5–45)

LITERARY STRUCTURE AND THEMES

Numbers 14:5–45 continues the story of the spies by detailing the fallout of their negative report. It continues the pattern of Israel succumbing to its tendency to grumble and disobey whenever it encounters adversity. This preaching unit contains three sections: Caleb and Joshua's failed appeal (14:5–10a), God's announcement of judgment and Moses's intercession (14:10b–35), and the initial consequences of God's judgment (14:36–45). In the first section, Caleb and Joshua plead with Israel once again to trust the God who brought them out of Egypt and to enter the Promised Land. The second section recounts the consequences of their rebellion through divine speech. Numbers 14:10b–25 establishes the weight of Israel's sin and its attendant consequences, although Moses's intercession in 14:13–19 averts Israel's total destruction. God then expands on his judgment in an address to Moses and Aaron in 14:26–35. The third section reveals the individual and national consequences of disobedience. It ends with Israel defeated, driven back into the wilderness, about to begin its forty-year period of wandering.

The themes of this preaching unit are the devastating consequences of sin and the depths of God's grace. Israel's rejection of his commands sees God withhold the fulfillment of his promises. However, he also demonstrates his essential character by combining his capacity to judge with his desire to show mercy. These attributes are held in tension as God punishes faithless Israel but leaves open the hope of a future fulfillment of his covenant promises.

- *Caleb and Joshua's Failed Appeal (14:5–10a)*
- *God's Judgment and Moses's Intercession (14:10b–35)*
  - God Pronounces Judgment (14:10b–12)
  - Moses Intercedes (14:13–19)
  - God Responds (14:20–25)
  - God Reiterates His Judgment (14:26–35)
- *The Consequences of Rebellion (14:36–45)*
  - Individual Consequences of Rebellion (14:36–38)
  - National Consequences of Rebellion (14:39–45)

EXPOSITION

Numbers 14:5–45 explores the interrelationship between Israel's failure to obey, Moses's role as intercessor, and God's character. It is a story of blessing deferred as God declares that the generation counted in the military census of Numbers 1 will not enter the Promised Land (14:22–23, 29). This necessitates a new census in Numbers 26 to tally the fighting force of the generation that will experience God's promises (Olson 1996, 75). Ultimately, Israel's failure to trust God yields fatal consequences as God decrees that the generation rescued from slavery in Egypt will die in wilderness. However, evidence of God's grace and mercy is found in his continued presence among his sinful people.

Caleb and Joshua's Failed Appeal (14:5–10a)

14:5. In response to the people's announced intention to return to Egypt and slavery,

Moses and Aaron fall on their faces. This idiom occurs twenty-five times in the OT and is an expression of deference or subservience (Ashley 1993, 247).[1] Here, one can imagine Moses and Aaron anticipating the appearance of God and engaging in a preemptive call for clemency. However, God delays his appearance, permitting one final attempt to reorient Israel through Caleb and Joshua. As two of the twelve spies from the previous chapter who have seen the land and its inhabitants, they have standing to speak. Caleb previously offered a succinct appeal for Israel to obey God's commands (Num. 13:30), but here, he and Joshua provide a theologically rich response to the faithless words of the people.

14:6–8. Similar to Moses and Aaron, Caleb and Joshua display emotional distress by tearing their clothes (14:6) as a precursor to their address. They attempt a systematic reorientation of the people's perspective by emphasizing the virtues of the land and the frailty of its inhabitants in comparison to the sovereign power of God (Olson 1996, 80). Caleb and Joshua first counter the argument of the other spies about the nature of the land. It is not a land that devours its inhabitants (13:32) but an "exceedingly good land" (14:7 ESV, NET) that "flows with milk and honey" (14:8b ESV).[2] Caleb and Joshua then reframe what is necessary to enter the land. The key is a conditional clause in 14:8 that reads "If YHWH delights in us, then he will bring us into this land and give it to us." In other words, the size and ferocity of Canaan's inhabitants is irrelevant: if God acts for Israel, then they will take possession of the land.

14:9. Caleb and Joshua here exhort the people not to rebel against YHWH. This again provides the proper theological framing. In succumbing to fear the people are rejecting the commands of God. Caleb and Joshua then urge the people not to fear the inhabitants of the land because they are "our bread" (לַחְמֵנוּ), which here suggests that Israel will devour the nations (Milgrom 1990, 109). They then declare that the nations have lost their "shade" (צֵל), which metaphorically suggests that they are no longer protected.[3] In contrast, YHWH is "with us," which means that there is no reason to fear. Caleb and Joshua thus provide theologically astute encouragement. The faithless spies have Israel thinking in purely human terms. Caleb and Joshua reintroduce Israel's God back into the equation and remind the people that God's provision is all that is required.

14:10a. Unsurprisingly, given the trajectory of the narratives in Numbers, Caleb and Joshua's speech fails to persuade. Instead, the people threaten to stone them.[4] They are so committed to their faithless understanding of the situation that they will not even tolerate the presence of dissenting voices.

---

1   Among these occurrences are several more in Numbers: 16:4, 22, 45 [17:10 in Hebrew]; 20:6. The context is similar in all of these cases. After Israel rebels, Moses (and sometimes Aaron) falls on his face as God appears to provide judgment.

2   The superlative quality of the land is expressed through the repetition of מְאֹד מְאֹד ("very very") at the end of 14:7. On the idea of the land "flowing with milk and honey," see the sidebar in the discussion of Numbers 13.

3   This word is used to describe protection whether from the sun (Isa. 25:4; Ps. 121:5) or from human enemies (Isa. 30:2–3; 32:2; 49:2; Jer. 48:25; Ashley 1993, 250).

4   Some commentators suggest instead that the congregation intended to stone Moses and Aaron (Levine 1993, 364; Milgrom 1990, 109) noting that the Israelites had previously threatened them in this way in Exodus 17:4. This is less likely because Moses and Aaron have not been mentioned since 14:5. Caleb and Joshua are perfectly reasonable antecedents of the pronoun "them" in 14:10a. Of course, all four would need to be eliminated if Israel were to act on its intentions to return to Egypt (Gane 2004, 608).

Israel's Rebellion and Its Consequences (14:5–45)

God's Judgment and Moses's Intercession (14:10b–35)

God Pronounces Judgment (14:10b–12)

14:10b. In the wake of the people's failure to listen to Caleb and Joshua, YHWH's presence appears at the Tent of Meeting. Israel's public rejection prompts a visible response.

14:11. God does not address the entire nation, instead addressing Moses. He begins with two cries of anguish prefaced with the exclamation עַד־אָנָה ("How long!") reminiscent of lament language (cf. Pss. 13:1–2; 62:3; Job 19:2). God asks for how long Israel will despise him and for how long they will refuse to believe despite all the signs that they have seen. The word "signs" (הָאֹתוֹת) recalls God's acts of deliverance in Egypt (Exod. 4:8, 9; 7:3; 8:23; 10:1, 2).

14:12. YHWH then turns to a pronouncement of judgment: he resolves to strike Israel with pestilence, dispossess them, and replace them with a new nation initiated through Moses.[5] Previously, YHWH brought pestilence against Egypt (Exod. 9:15) to deliver Israel. If Israel desires to return *to* Egypt, then they are subject to the same treatment *as* Egypt (Olson 1996, 80). The final declaration in 14:12b is the most stark. Israel's total rejection of God's leadership introduces the possibility that God may reject them and restart his covenant promises through Moses. This recalls Exodus 32:10 where God makes the same threat in the wake of the golden calf incident. God's initial speech emphasizes the gravity of the situation: Israel's continued existence hangs in the balance.

Moses Intercedes (14:13–19)

14:13–14. Although Moses did not lend his voice to support Caleb and Joshua, he now pleads for the entire nation. As in Exodus 32, when Israel's existence is at stake, Moses takes on the role of prophetic intercessor. This all happens under divine sovereignty, since "YHWH addresses Moses *before* inflicting punishment on Israel, providing Moses with an opportunity—and perhaps even an invitation—to intercede" (Pressler 2017, 120). Moses's intercession has two foci: divine reputation (14:13–16) and divine character (14:17–19).

Moses begins with God's reputation. He suggests that if God destroys Israel, it will become known among hostile nations. Numbers 14:13–14a envisions the Egyptians learning of Israel's demise and informing the Canaanites. Israel's destruction would raise questions about God's power even though he delivered them from Egypt (14:13b). Further, God's continued presence in Israel is known throughout the nations as he goes before them (14:14). Thus, Israel's fate has ramifications for how the nations view God.

> **TRANSLATION ANALYSIS**
> The Hebrew syntax of 14:13–14a is difficult even though the general meaning is relatively clear. Moses's speech begins unexpectedly with a *waw*-consecutive + perfect verb וְשָׁמְעוּ מִצְרַיִם ("Egypt will hear") before using a כִּי clause to describe what God did for Israel in Egypt. Verse 14a begins by revealing that Egypt will recount Israel's fate to the nations of "this land" (Canaan). The verb שָׁמְעוּ ("they heard") then occurs without an explicit subject. It probably refers to the Canaanite nations who have now heard that God is "in the midst of this people"

---

5 The first person verbs אַכֶּנּוּ and אוֹרִשֶׁנּוּ in 14:12 are frequently translated "I will smite them," and "I will dispossess them" (ESV, NASB). It is also possible grammatically to view these verbs as cohortatives, "let me smite them" and "let me dispossess them." This nuance may suggest that God is "cuing Moses in his role as intercessor and intermediary" (Milgrom 1990, 109).

(בְּקֶרֶב הָעָם הַזֶּה). The NET translation best captures these difficulties: "When the Egyptians hear it—for you brought up this people by your power from among them—then they will tell it to the inhabitants of this land. They have heard that you, LORD, are among this people."

14:15–16. Moses expands on these thoughts through a conditional clause. He suggests that if God destroys Israel, then the nations who know God's name (or reputation) will declare that God lacked the power to bring his people into the land. This would diminish God among the nations and validate the perspective of the faithless spies. Consequently, Moses argues that the preservation of God's reputation requires him not to destroy Israel.

14:17–18a. The heart of Moses's intercession is rooted in character of God. Moses urges God to display the greatness of his power, not for destruction but for forgiveness. He then uses a shortened version of God's self-declaration of his character from Exodus 34:6–7 in the wake of the golden calf incident. This is a "shrewd debater's move" as Moses recalls a precedent in which God turned from his initial pronouncement of total destruction (Pressler 2017, 122). The words that Moses cites in 14:18 are part of a key theological creed repeated throughout the Old Testament to reveal the nature of God (cf. 2 Chron. 30:9; Neh. 9:17, 31; Pss. 86:5, 15; 103:8; 111:4; 112:4; 116:5; 145:8; Joel 2:14; Jonah 4:2; Nah. 1:3). This quotation captures the tension between God's mercy and God's judgment. It begins by declaring that God is "slow to anger," an idiomatic translation of the Hebrew אֶרֶךְ אַפַּיִם, which literally means "long of nose." God is also "abounding in steadfast love" (ESV), which prompts him to forgive iniquity and transgression.

> **Steadfast Love**
> The ESV appropriately uses "steadfast love" to translate the Hebrew word חֶסֶד, which is one of most theologically resonant terms in Scripture. While humans can show חֶסֶד to each other such exemplified by David and Jonathan (1 Sam. 20:8, 14) or Ruth, Naomi, and Boaz (Ruth 2:20; 3:10), only God is described as being רַב־חֶסֶד, or "great in steadfast love" (Sakenfeld 1995, 90). Recent research into this term emphasizes its dimension of covenant loyalty or faithfulness, while earlier discussions focused on the concepts of mercy and graciousness (Boda 2017, 39). A translation like "steadfast love" that seeks to express both domains is best. They are at work in Exodus 34:6–7 as God maintains his covenant commitments to Israel while demonstrating grace in not destroying them for their rebellion (Boda 2017, 40). The same combination of covenant faithfulness and graciousness apply to Moses's quotation of the divine character here in Numbers 14:18.

14:18b. Moses acknowledges that God's demonstration of חֶסֶד and his forgiveness of sin do not eliminate sin's consequences.[6] The latter half of his citation of Exodus 34:6–7 acknowledges that God will still bring punishment on the guilty with effects that could stretch to the third and fourth generation.[7] The key idea is mitigated punishment. Israel's rebellion demands serious consequences, but they are "mitigated as an act of mercy by a holy God" (Boda 2017, 41). Moses thus recites God's own declaration of his character and brings to the forefront God's covenant loyalty and grace, as well as acknowledging God's right to punish sin.

---

6   This idea will be explored further in the discussion of Theological Focus.
7   Exodus 34:6–7 contrasts the punishment to the third and fourth generation with God's demonstration of חֶסֶד "to thousands," thus tilting the balance of God's character toward graciousness rather than punishment. Moses's quotation of these verses lacks "to thousands" in Num. 14:18, but the hearing audience would likely be aware of this fuller context.

14:19. After reiterating the attributes of God, Moses implores God to put them into practice. He pleads with God, addressing him with an imperative verb, urging him to forgive the people according to his steadfast love in the same way he has done throughout Israel's sojourn in the wilderness.[8] Moses thus stands in between God and sinful Israel, interceding through an appeal to God's reputation and to God's character in way evocative of Israel's other great rebellion at Mount Sinai.

God Responds (14:20–25)
14:20–23. God's response to Moses's intercession reveals the tension of the elements of the divine character. He declares in 14:20 that he has forgiven according to Moses's request, using the same verb (סָלַח) found in 14:19. However, God's forgiveness does not eliminate the consequences of Israel's rebellion. Instead, in 14:21–23 God swears a lengthy oath according to his life and his world-spanning glory that none of those who have rejected God will see the Promised Land. God's relationship with Israel will endure, but the fulfillment of God's promises will be delayed. Numbers 14:22 captures the depth of the transgression: the current generation has seen God's glory and his miraculous acts but has put God to the test continuously.[9] Consequently, this generation will not see the fulfilment of God's promises.

> **Testing God**
> The idiom of humans "testing" (נסה) God is also found in Israel's demand for water in Exodus 17:2, 7 and in poetic memory of that event (Pss. 78:18, 41, 56; 95:8–9). While God can test individuals (Gen. 22:1) or Israel to see if they will be obedient (Exod. 15:25; 16:4), Israel testing God is uniformly negative.

14:24–25. These verses provide two brief codas. The first is that Caleb is exempt from this judgment.[10] Consequently, God promises, "I will bring him into the land to which he went." This is in keeping with Caleb's speeches in which he urges Israel to remember that God is with them. God declares that Caleb's faithfulness will be rewarded. The second coda sets up Israel's route of travel: they must return to the wilderness by way of the Red Sea. There is a deep tragedy at work here since this body of water marked Israel's deliverance from Egypt in Exodus 14–15. Now, it marks a return to square one (Pressler 2017, 124).

God Reiterates His Judgment (14:26–35)
14:26–27. God's next speech to Moses and Aaron expands upon his decreed judgment. The key verbal root לון ("to grumble") is found three times in 14:27 and again in 14:29, highlighting the heart of Israel's transgression. God also refers to Israel as the "wicked congregation" (הָעֵדָה הָרָעָה) in 14:27 and 35. As in 14:11, God's judgment is prefaced by the cry of "how long?" before he declares that he has heard Israel's complaints.

14:28–30. An element of this speech is the idea of reciprocity, in which the complaints of the Israelites will be used as the means of their punishment (Olson 1996, 84). In 14:2, the Israelites expressed a wish to die in the wilderness rather than confront the

---

8   Imperative verbs take on the nuance of entreaty or request when used by an inferior toward a superior (Arnold and Choi 2018, 76).

9   The idiom is that Israel tested God "these ten times" (זֶה עֶשֶׂר פְּעָמִים). The Talmud identifies ten times that Israel has tested God via rebellion since the escape from Egypt began (Ashley 1993, 260–61). However, it is more likely that ten is not intended to be literal here. Rather, it conveys the sense of "too many times." See Jacob's accusation that Laban has cheated him out his wages "ten times" in Genesis 31:7 (Gane 2004, 609).

10 Joshua joins Caleb in escaping the fate of this first generation in 14:30.

inhabitants of the land. In 14:29, YHWH declares that their wish is granted. YHWH's judgment also connects back to the beginning of Numbers as those who are sentenced to death in the wilderness are those who were listed in the first census except Caleb and Joshua (14:29–30). Gane here turns a good phrase, noting that "to be counted is to be accountable" (Gane 2004, 610).

14:31–35. The symmetry continues in these verses. In 14:3, the Israelites use fear for the fate of their wives and children as a pretext for rejecting God's commands. Now, in 14:31, God declares that those children will enter the Promised Land. Finally, since the spies spent forty days surveying the land (13:25), God declares that Israel will spend forty years in wilderness wandering (14:34). This is emphasized through repetition as 14:34 reads "a day to a year, a day to a year" (יוֹם לַשָּׁנָה יוֹם לַשָּׁנָה).

The Consequences of Rebellion (14:36–45)

Individual Consequences of Rebellion (14:36–38)

14:36–38. The consequences of Israel's rebellion begin quickly and persist throughout the rest of the Pentateuch. Israel goes from being on the border of the Promised Land to experiencing a generation of nomadic wandering. The hammer falls first on the spies who brought the bad report. While the whole of the rebellious generation must die, God sets apart these ten spies for immediate death through a plague. Further, the faithless spies are lumped into a single nameless group. Their names are recorded in 13:3–15 before they embarked on their mission but now that they have caused Israel to rebel against God, they are unnamed. In contrast, both Caleb and Joshua are named and given their full patronymics in 14:38.

National Consequences of Rebellion (14:39–45)

14:39–43. This chapter concludes with a brief narrative demonstrating that God will fulfill his oath. When Moses recounts YHWH's declarations, the people mourn greatly (14:39) and then attempt belated obedience. They arise, march toward the land, and declare "Here we are! We will go up to the place that the LORD commanded, for we have sinned" (14:40 NET).[11] The acknowledgement of sin is rather cursory and not marked by signs of contrition. This verse also reflects Israel's continued failure to heed God: "Before they were unwilling to go where he led. Now they want to go where he is no longer leading" (Gane 2004, 611). Moses attempts to correct Israel's perspective in 14:41–43, describing their actions as "transgressing the commandment of the LORD" (ESV, NET) in 14:41. He then shifts to a warning, calling Israel not to go up because "the LORD is not among you" (ESV, NASB, NET), an expression strengthened by the presence of the Hebrew particle of negation אֵין. This cuts to the heart of the situation, since "the critical issue is not human strength or even human resolve or determination. The key is the presence of God in their midst" (Olson 1996, 86).

14:44–45. The Israelites again fail to heed Moses and proceed with their march. The revelation that neither the ark of the covenant nor Moses left the camp foretells the futility of the endeavor. Israel was supposed to move according to God's direction symbolized in the pillar of cloud and pillar of fire (Num. 9:15–23). Now, the Israelites, who previously were too fearful to attempt to conquer the Promised Land *with* God's help,

---

11 The expression "Here we are" is a translation of the Hebrew exclamatory particle הִנֵּה with an attached first-person plural suffix (הִנֶּנּוּ). Its use can be described as "presentative," in which the speakers present themselves "as available to participate in an event" (van der Merwe, Naudé, and Kroeze 2017, 415).

attempt to seize it *without* God. The result is predictable, as the Amalakites and Canaanites defeat Israel.[12] They are driven to a place called Hormah, which is derived from the Hebrew root I-חרם ("to devote to destruction").[13] This conveys the idea that Israel was completely and utterly defeated (Gane 2004, 611). The extended narrative of Numbers 13–14, which began with the hope of God's promises being fulfilled, now ends with Israel disobedient, defeated, and in total disarray.

THEOLOGICAL FOCUS

The theological focus of this chapter builds off the exegetical idea (Israel's failure to trust God yields fatal consequences as God decrees that the generation rescued from slavery in Egypt will die in the wilderness. However, evidence of God's grace and mercy is found in his continued presence among his sinful people.). It is rooted in the interaction between human sinfulness and the attributes of God. It can be summarized as: *God's great mercy redeems human sinfulness but does not eliminate all of the consequences of sin*. Israel rejects God outright in this chapter, which opens the possibility of God abandoning them to their fate. It is possible to imagine him fulfilling his covenant promises to the patriarchs through Moses after enacting judgment on sinful Israel. However, as Moses recalls God's steadfast love (חֶסֶד) and his willingness to forgive iniquity and sin in 14:18a, we see that Israel will not be destroyed. Nevertheless, there are still ramifications for sin, as 14:18b reveals that God will certainly not leave the guilty unpunished and points to generational consequences of sin. Here, the punishment is that the rebellious generation will not see God's promises to Israel come to fruition.

One may ask whether or not there is a contradiction in forgiving transgression but not remitting punishment (Pressler 2017, 123). However, it is better to say that forgiveness maintains the relationship while punishment serves as a corrective to urge the guilty party toward greater holiness. It can be said that "Forgiveness in Num. 13–14 means at least the willingness of God to remain with Israel, even in its sin. Ultimately, however, sin itself must be cleansed, blotted out, made white; the sanctification of Israel must eventually be complete" (Stubbs 2009, 133). This perspective is strengthened by considering the nature of corporate solidarity in the ancient world. Israel as a people endures because God has demonstrated his covenant faithfulness and willingness to forgive. Future generations have the hope of experiencing the bounty and blessing of God's promises, even if the current generation is subject to God's judgment.

The interplay of God's forgiveness and the consequences of sin is found throughout Scripture. Israel continues to rebel throughout Numbers and receives God's judgment, but God ultimately preserves his loyalty to his covenant and bring his people to the Promised Land. Elsewhere, God forgives David for the murder of Uriah and his taking of Bathsheba by sparing his life (2 Sam. 12:13), but the consequences of his sin reverberate throughout the rest of 2 Samuel. God's declaration that the sword will not depart from David's house (2 Sam. 12:10) is proven true repeatedly through the narratives of Amnon and Tamar (2 Sam. 13:1–22), Absalom's murder of Amnon (2 Sam. 13:23–39), and Absalom's rebellion (2 Sam. 15–18). Contemporary

---

12 The inclusion of the Amalakites recalls Exodus 17:8–17 where the Israelites defeated them as Moses raised his arms in the air to symbolize God's presence. Now that God is absent, Israel cannot defeat Amalek.

13 The explanation for this name is found in Numbers 21:3 when the Israelites enact חֵרֶם on a Canaanite king named Arad. In Numbers 14:45, we can see Israel symbolically on the receiving end of what God commands it to do to the Canaanite nations.

believers can reflect on the consequences of sin upon their communities, even as they trust in the cleansing death and resurrection of Christ. One might imagine a scenario in which a church treasurer who embezzled may be forgiven and restored to fellowship, but not restored to their previous position. Pastors and elders who abuse their position may repent, but should face lengthy and humbling roads to restoration in ministry. Israel's behavior in Numbers 14 intertwines with God's character to reveal both the vastness of God's mercy and the severe, though mitigated, consequences of sin.

PREACHING AND TEACHING STRATEGIES

Exegetical and Theological Significance

Not for the first time since their redemption and liberation from Egypt, Israel provokes God to the point where he threatens to destroy the nation and start afresh with Moses. When the people say that they want to go back to Egypt, they are not merely complaining but fundamentally rejecting God's redemptive plan. They stand on the cusp of the fulfillment of God's promise, but pull back in fear and failing faith. God offers them redemptive blessings and they refuse them. In doing so, they are rejecting God. In the New Testament, Hebrews contains severe warnings for those who may look back and be tempted to reject the redemption that comes exclusively through Jesus Christ (Heb. 10:38–39).

What is astounding about this text is not that God allows the people to suffer the consequences of their sinful choice, it is that he holds unswervingly to his covenantal intention to bless the world through Abraham's seed. God does not destroy the nation and start again with Moses. God continues to work with these people, patiently waiting for the next generation and preparing them to receive the land he has marked as theirs. Human sin cannot destroy God's patience and plan. There are real and lasting consequences for our sin, but God's goals will be accomplished. Forgiveness is real, yet the ramifications of sin are not always obliterated. There are consequences—some of which may be severe—when we do not live by faith in God.

Preaching Idea

Although there can be enormous consequences for sin, God is forgiving and merciful to fulfill his redemptive promises.

Contemporary Connections

What does it mean?

What does it mean that although there can be enormous consequences for sin, God is forgiving and merciful to fulfill his redemptive promises? It is easy to look at Israel's lack of faith and wonder how they could possibly doubt God at this time. They had experienced God's awesome power and grace in the exodus. They had known the protection of the blood of the Passover lambs that had turned aside the angel of death. They had seen the parting of the Red Sea, the theophany at Sinai, and they had experienced both the displeasure and forgiveness of God after the incident of the golden calf. Now, after all of these experiences and proofs of God's character, they still doubt his goodness and power. We may find ourselves almost speechless in disbelief at their attitudes: *How* can they act this way? Surely if we had experienced these things, we would have been heroes of faith!

Yet we also fail sometimes to walk by faith, and God has given us even more convincing proofs of his kindness, goodness, mercy, forgiveness, love, and power than anything that Israel had experienced at that time. *How* can we act the way we do when we live this side of the incarnation, atonement, resurrection, and Pentecost? What more can God do to show us his love and the goodness of his plans for us? When we sin against him in fear and lack of faith, his love does not erase all of the consequences of our behavior. Christ died to pay the penalty for our sins, so that we can live forever in the new heavens and new earth, the home of righteousness. Nevertheless, our actions still have consequences in this lifetime, for good or for ill.

Is it true?
Is it true that although there can be enormous consequences for sin, God is forgiving and merciful to fulfill his redemptive promises? The Bible teaches in numerous places that we reap what we sow. If we walk by the flesh we reap destruction, but if we walk by the Spirit we can produce a harvest of righteousness. Discipleship entails acknowledging that Jesus is Lord and following him. We are to walk with God by faith, not by our own finite and fallen sight. Sin is forgiven in Christ, but the effects of sin can continue to impact ourselves and others. Sexual promiscuity may lead to AIDS and death. One person driving under the influence of narcotics or alcohol may result in the injury or death of innocent people. Eating too much unhealthy food may negatively affect quality of life and shorten one's lifespan. Estranged relationships can cause psychological pain for a lifetime. Children are not immune from suffering for the sins of their parents. Of course, it is possible that a criminal may commit a crime and be sentenced to jail, where a chaplain leads them to Jesus. Finding Jesus, however, does not terminate their jail sentence, nor does it undo the damage caused to the victim of their crime.

Now what?
How do we respond to the truth that although there can be enormous consequences for sin, God is forgiving and merciful to fulfill his redemptive promises? Those who were numbered in the first census failed to go into the Promised Land because of their sinful rebellion against the plan of God. The generation that died in the wilderness had to accept the consequences of their disbelief, but they also had an opportunity to teach their children about the importance of making good decisions and walking by faith.

In life, we also get the opportunity to teach people to avoid the mistakes that we have made. This is a time for people to check their own hearts and lives to see if there is any area in which they are refusing to trust in God. It is also a time to seek reconciliation and forgiveness with God and with others. Most importantly, this is an opportunity to make sure they have entrusted their life to Jesus Christ and that they know him as Lord and Savior. Ask God if there is someone who can benefit from the wisdom you have gained through your mistakes. Pray that even the sin in your life can be redeemed, so that others can be spared the consequences you have experienced. Our humble contrition and regret—joined to faith and thankfulness in God's goodness and forgiveness—can provide a powerful testimony.

Creativity in Presentation
In the 2009 championship game of the Canadian Football League, the team from Montreal was losing by two points. There was no time left on the clock as they lined up for one attempt at a field goal. If the kicker was successful, they would win the game by one point; if he missed, they would lose. The ball was snapped and placed, the kick went up, and it sailed wide of the goalposts. It was a clear miss. The other team started celebrating. Penalty flags, however, were tossed on the field by the referees. Montreal's opponents had had an extra man on the field during the field goal attempt. As a result, the ball was moved ten yards closer, and Montreal was given another chance. This time, the kicker made good, and Montreal won the game 28–27.[14]

---

14 Expositors with congregations who are not familiar with the Canadian Football League can probably think of a similar anecdote from their local contexts.

Imagine what it was like to be in the locker room of the losing team. Imagine the shock and disappointment. Perhaps there was blaming and shaming. The majority of players were not on the field when the penalty was called, but they suffered just the same. Perhaps there was understanding and forgiveness. No matter how they responded, however, their mistake had incurred a penalty, and that one penalty cost them a championship. All of their work that season—and all of the training of their lifetime—resulted in nothing but disappointment as they stood on the brink of a championship and saw it slip away. They may have bonded and grown closer together as a result of their heartache, but the consequences would last a lifetime. No matter what they did, that championship game was lost forever. Showing this clip (or one from an athletic competition better known to the expositor's congregation) and inviting the congregation to imagine the aftermath of the penalty may help illustrate the fact that personal forgiveness does not always erase painful consequences. We can forgive one another, and God can forgive us, but consequences for mistakes and sin can remain in this world. However, we have hope in that although there can be enormous consequences for sin, God is forgiving and merciful to fulfill his redemptive promises.

One possible outline for this passage could be:

- A faithful appeal cannot overcome the power of fear (14:5–10a).

- God's gracious character permits the forgiveness of sins, but consequences remain (14:10b–35).

- Failing to listen to God brings devasting consequences (14:36–45).

DISCUSSION QUESTIONS

1. How does Israel's lack of faith "show contempt" (14:11) for God?

2. What do we learn about God's essential character from Moses's intercession and God's response to it?

3. Why do you think that the Israelites attempted to enter Canaan after being told that God was not with them in this effort?

4. What scenarios can you think of when people might repent of their sin, be forgiven, but still face lasting consequences from their actions?

Numbers 15:1–21

EXEGETICAL IDEA
The sacrificial system requires both obedience to God's commands and generosity on the part of the worshippers.

THEOLOGICAL FOCUS
Offerings remind God's people to show gratitude for what he has done for them.

PREACHING IDEA
God's rich, infinite grace is the best motive for joyful giving.

PREACHING POINTERS
Coming out of the previous chapter, Numbers 15:1–2 should stop you in your tracks. God says, "After you enter the land I am giving you as a home . . .". What just happened? Despite the continued grumbling about food, despite the infighting, and despite the colossal failure of faith and the rejection of God in the previous two chapters, God still promises that one day he will give them the land. It would be difficult to find a text that showcases the covenant faithfulness and love of God more clearly than this. After all of this provocation—and in his eternal omniscience God knows that more is coming, even in this book—the Lord God is still operating to bless the children of Abraham.

The details of the offerings and sacrifices that will be offered in the land may not strike the contemporary Christian as having immediate interest or value, but the underlying principle is incredible: God will not only bring his people into the Promised Land, but he also will bless them abundantly. He has redeemed them and will bless them with superabounding grace.

God's grace is necessary for us every step of the way. Without his grace and power, we would not be redeemed, and without it we would not be able to worship him as he deserves. He is so good to us that he gives to us so that we have something to return to him. It is in Jesus Christ where we see how richly we are blessed, and it is God's rich, infinite grace that is the best motive for joyful giving.

REGULATIONS FOR SACRIFICIAL OFFERINGS (15:1–21)

LITERARY STRUCTURE AND THEMES

Numbers 15 makes an abrupt departure from the grumbling stories of the previous chapters. The literary genre of this chapter changes from narrative to legal instruction. It resembles the "eye of the hurricane" as it provides the reader with some space to breathe before examples of Israel's rebellion resume (Gane 2004, 619). There is no simple way for an expositor to divide this chapter. The phrase "The LORD said to Moses" found in 15:1, 17, and 37 provides some guideposts for a structural outline. However, it is possible to discern "five distinct sections" found in 15:1–16, 17–21, 22–31, 32–36, and 37–41 (Baden 2013, 352). Similarities between these sections permits the suggestion of three preaching units. The first focuses upon first two sections (15:1–16, 17–21), which are united by their provision of instructions concerning different offerings to God. The third and fourth sections (15:22–31, 32–36) address the question of remediation for sin, while the fifth (15:37–41) considers the law requiring Israelites to wear tassels on their garments. A possible mnemonic for this arrangement is: regulations (15:1–21), remediation (15:22–36), and remembering (15:37–41; Bailey 2005, 474).

Thematically, this chapter reinforces the hope that God will fulfill his promise to bring the children of the rebellious generation into the Promised Land. The instructions in 15:1–21 are established for the time "when you enter the land . . . which I am giving to you" (15:2 NET), which implies that Israel *will* arrive at their destination after their refusal in Numbers 13–14. Further, Numbers 15:38 imparts the instruction to attach tassels to garments "throughout their generations" (ESV, NET), which indicates that there will be future generations who enter into covenant relationship with God.

- ***Regulations for Fellowship Offerings (15:1–16)***
- ***Regulations for Firstfruit Offerings (15:17–21)***

EXPOSITION

This passage provides instructions for how to perform offerings to God. Its guiding idea is that the sacrificial system requires both obedience to God's commands and generosity on the part of the worshippers.

Regulations for Fellowship Offerings (15:1–16)

15:1–3. This unit begins with the declaration "The LORD spoke to Moses," which occurs frequently throughout Exodus–Numbers to introduce regulations and instructions. These instructions are connected to the offerings discussed in Leviticus 1; 3; 7:11–37. The Leviticus passages provide step-by-step directions for the sacrifices that are absent here. This passage instead reveals that animal sacrifices are to be accompanied by grain, oil, and drink offerings, thus symbolically presenting a full meal to God (Stubbs 2009, 138). The term אִשֶּׁה ("offering by fire" NASB, NET; or "food offering" ESV, NIV) is used as a catchall at the beginning of 15:3 before being subdivided into different classes of offerings in the rest of the verse. These subcategories include the עֹלָה ("whole burnt offering"), which represents giving the sacrificial animal fully to God (Stubbs 2009, 138), and the זֶבַח offering, which is an abbreviation of the term זֶבַח הַשְּׁלָמִים ("peace offering").[1] Offerings of this variety were partially burned on the altar to give God his portion (the fat and blood, cf. Lev. 7:22–27), with some of the meat then being shared by the priest and the one offering the sacrifice (Cole 2000, 245).

The rest of 15:3 discusses occasions on which one would make such offerings such as the fulfillment of a vow, a freewill offering, or a required festival offering.[2] These are celebratory offerings, reflecting the desire of the community to express worship and devotion to God either voluntarily or in response to one of the decreed festivals (Milgrom 1990, 118).[3] The purpose of these offerings is to make "an aroma pleasing to the LORD" (15:3 NIV), a refrain repeated throughout this section (Num. 15:3, 7, 10, 13, 14). This refers to the suitability of the offerings to God. It does not, as was thought in other ancient Near Eastern contexts, indicate that God was hungry or had need of this offering (Ashley 1993, 279).[4]

15:4–10. These verses provide specific regulations for the amount of grain, oil, and wine to accompany each sacrifice. Although grain and wine offerings have been mentioned in other contexts, this is the first time that it is indicated that they accompany every votive, fellowship, or festal animal sacrifice (Wenham 2008, 143). The grain and oil were to be mixed and presented alongside the wine. There is no specific procedure given for how to bring these offerings before God, but it is likely that in keeping with instructions found in Leviticus 2:1–3 and 6:14–18 that a portion of the grain offering would be burned on the altar to be dedicated to God while the rest would eaten by the priests (Ashley 1993, 280; Wenham 2008, 143). The wine offering, or libation, was likely poured out in front of the altar.

These verses are highly repetitive as they address the requirements for each sacrificial animal in turn. Two principles emerge. The first is that the quality of the offering was to match the requirements that God had given. The worshipper was to use a substance called סֹלֶת, translated as "finely ground flour" (NET), which commentators identify as semolina, the finest grade of flour (Gane 2004, 620; Milgrom 1990, 119). This recalls the regulations in Leviticus 1 and 3 for the sacrificial animals to be without defect. The second principle is that the offerings were to be generous (Pressler 2017, 132). Further, greater offerings were required as the size and value of the sacrificial animal increased. Precision with ancient units of measure is impossible, but a reasonable suggestion is that an *ephah* of flour or grain equals about 11.75 liters, while a *hin* of oil or wine equals about 1.2 liters (Gane 2004, 620).[5] Numbers 15:4–5 reveals that the offering of a sheep or goat required one tenth of an ephah of flour mixed with a quarter of a hin of oil to provide the grain offering, while the drink

---

1 See Ashley 1993, 278, for a discussion of Leviticus 7, in which זֶבַח הַשְּׁלָמִים is abbreviated to זֶבַח several times throughout the chapter.
2 Further information about offerings for the fulfillment of vows and freewill offerings is found in Leviticus 7:16–18.
3 Notably, the regulations here do not apply to the purification offering (sometimes called the sin offering) from Leviticus 4:1–5:13 or the reparation offering (sometimes called the guilt offering) in Leviticus 5:14–6:7 (Gane 2004, 620). See the exposition of Numbers 7 for why purification offering is a superior term.
4 It also stands in contrast with other ancient Near Eastern stories in which the smell of sacrifice secured the attention of the god (Pressler 2017, 132). Notably, in the flood story in the Epic of Atrahasis, the gods descend in a swarm to "eat" Atrahasis's sacrifice, because with the destruction of other humans they are not being fed.
5 The word *ephah* itself does not occur in Numbers 15 but it is the most likely unit of measure (Milgrom 1990, 119).

offering was also a quarter of a hin of wine. For a ram, 15:6–7 increases the amounts to two tenths of an ephah of grain mixed with one third of a hin of oil, alongside one third of a hin of wine. In 15:8–10, these amounts increase to three tenths of an ephah of grain mixed with half of a hin of oil, plus half of a hin of wine. According to these regulations, a sacrifice to God recalled multiple avenues of God's gracious gift of the land: animals from the flocks or herd along with produce from the grain, olive, and grape harvests.

15:11–12. These verses offer a brief summary, recounting the animals in reverse order by beginning with the largest (bull) and ending with the smallest (sheep or goat). Numbers 15:12 is arranged according to a simple A B::B A chiasm. It can be translated "According to the number you perform, thus you shall perform each according to their number" (Cole 2000, 247). This brings closure to the discussion of the amounts required for acceptable grain and wine offerings that accompany animal sacrifices.

15:13–14. These verses declare that everyone who is part of the Israelite community must follow these regulations. Notably, this not only includes Israelites but also foreigners who are residing with them. The noun אֶזְרָח ("native-born") in 15:13 points to this, since it occurs almost exclusively in legal contexts that articulate equal responsibilities for Israelites and non-Israelites (Exod. 12:19, 48, 49; Lev. 16:29; 17:15; 18:26; 23:42; 24:16, 22; Num. 9:4). This sentiment continues in Numbers 15:14, which pairs native Israelites with the גֵּר ("sojourner") as well as those who dwell among the Israelites without a formal status. As noted in Numbers 9:14, the class of גֵּר ("sojourner") refers to those who live in the Israelite community and choose to be bound by its laws and customs. They can be compared to the modern concept of landed immigrants or resident aliens (Ashley 1993, 181).

> **Sojourner**
> The term גֵּר ("sojourner") is theologically resonant given Israel's experience of captivity and rescue from Egypt. It is frequently paired with "widow" and "fatherless" to make up a trio of people to whom Israel was to show special care and consideration (Exod. 22:21–24; Deut. 10:18; 14:29; 16:11, 14; 24:19–21; 25:12–13). However, the context of Numbers 15:14 is not charity but belonging. Requiring "sojourners" to fulfill the same responsibilities as Israelites indicates that they are members of God's people.

These non-Israelites are commanded in 15:14b to do exactly what the Israelites do when it comes to bringing sacrifices and offerings before God. The regulations in this chapter are thus another example of how legal instruction equates these groups.

15:15–16. The text declares that there is to be "one statute" (15:15), "one law," and "one rule" (15:16) for both groups.[6] The combination of these three terms covers the breadth of legal obligations, giving the same requirements to everyone who is part of the community (Levine 1993, 393). The rationale for this is rooted in passages such as Leviticus 19:34 that recall that the Israelites were sojourners themselves in Egypt (Cole 2000, 247). They are to remember what it was like to be treated as inferiors and they are not to carry that attitude into the Promised Land. Consequently, part of their witness of being a light to the nations is to reveal that those who choose to follow Israel's God are fully welcomed into the worship rhythms of the community.

---

6   Levine differentiates between these terms, suggesting that "one law" (תּוֹרָה אַחַת) points to what God has shown or instructed, "one statute" (חֻקָּה אַחַת) points to what is inscribed as a requirement, and "one rule" (וּמִשְׁפָּט אֶחָד) refers to following what has been determined to be just (Levine 1993, 393).

Regulations for Firstfruit Offerings (15:17–21)

15:17–19. The second section begins with the announcement "The LORD said to Moses," mirroring 15:1. Again, Israel's future presence in the land is presumed since these arrangements are set up for the time "when you enter the land to which I am bringing you and you eat some of the food of the land" (15:18–19a NET). The temporality of these arrangements is indicated through two infinitive construct verbs preceded by the preposition *beit* (בְּבֹאֲכֶם; "when you enter"; בַּאֲכָלְכֶם "when you eat"). This construction points to action simultaneous with the main verb of the sentence, which in this case is to "present a contribution to the LORD" in 15:19b (Arnold and Choi 2018, 82). The topic is still regulations for offerings, but the category has changed. These regulations are extensions of the requirement to offer the firstfruits of the harvest (Lev. 23:9–14) and the grain (Deut. 26:1–15) to God. These verses reveal that the "end products of the human endeavor of baking bread" are to be offered to God as well (Olson 1996, 94). This reflects a situation when Israel has entered the land and has residents who are not agriculturalists with crops, flocks, and herds from which to tithe. The nonagriculturalist is still to make an offering of their food products to God (Milgrom 1990, 121).

15:20. This verse reveals the exact nature of the regulation. The Israelites are to give from "the first of your dough" (ESV) or "the first of your finely ground flour" (NET). This instruction likely also applies to every time the baking activity took place. Whenever they prepared this food, the Israelites were to remember that it reflects God's provision and bounty (Ashley 1993, 283).[7]

This section is further marked by the fourfold repetition of the תְּרוּמָה ("contribution") and the threefold repetition of the similar sounding verb תָּרִימוּ ("you shall present") in 15:19–21. The linguistic repetition creates a "resounding staccato effect" that would likely aid in remembering these requirements (Cole 2000, 248). This is most evidenced in 15:20, where both words occur twice.[8]

The latter half of 15:20 identifies this dough offering as equivalent to a contribution from the threshing floor, which equates it to an offering that the priest would share as God's representatives. Numbers 18:12 declares that the priests are entitled to the firstfruits of the grain produced on a threshing floor (Milgrom 1990, 122). Further, the term תְּרוּמָה ("contribution") itself is commonly used to indicate the priests' share of Israel's offerings (Lev. 7:14; Num. 18:8, 29–30; Deut. 12:6–11, 17; Levine 1993, 191). There is a symbiotic process at work as God graciously gives Israel the land and its bounty, while Israel acknowledges that by offering the first of the dough back to God. The priests, as God's representatives, are nourished by these offerings even as God provides sustenance for the whole of Israel.

15:21. The final element to note for these regulations is their enduring nature. This verse summarizes the requirement to give the first of the dough before concluding with the declaration that this instruction is "for your generations" (לְדֹרֹתֵיכֶם). This provides an extensive temporal horizon for Israel to enjoy God's continued gift of the land and its bounty.

THEOLOGICAL FOCUS

The exegetical idea of this passage (Offerings to God require both obedience to God's

---

7   This instruction endured past the fall of the second temple, wherein pious Jews would throw a portion of dough into the fire to devote it to God (Wenham 2008, 145).

8   A fairly literal rendering of this verse would be, "the first of your dough you shall present a loaf as a contribution, as a contribution of the threshing floor, thus you shall present it."

commands and generosity on the part of the worshippers) leads to this theological focus: *Offerings remind God's people to show gratitude for what he has done for them.* The regulations surrounding the sacrifices in Numbers 15:1–21 direct the worshipper to give back to God out of what he has supplied them. Although the immediate context of this chapter is the wilderness, it casts its gaze into a future in which God has graciously brought his people into the land. When they are in a situation in which they have animals as well as agricultural produce to offer, the Israelites are instructed to devote portions of these good gifts back to God. This is a necessary reminder because it is very easy to forget the source of blessing. In Deuteronomy 8:10–14, Moses cautions the Israelites against a scenario in which, after savoring the bounty of the Promised Land, they become proud and believe that they have acquired all of these things through their own strength and merits. The requirement to add grain, oil, and wine to an animal sacrifice in 15:1–16 and offering the firstfruits of the dough in 15:17–21 reminds Israel that God has provided generously for them and that they should respond in the same way.

This perspective can be carried into the New Testament. Although the laws of sacrifice are fulfilled through Jesus, the perfect sacrificial lamb, the offerings of God's people come as a response to what God has done. The paradigm passage of Acts 2:42–47 envisions a community so inspired by the miraculous work of the Holy Spirit in concert with the proclamation of the gospel that people joyously devoted all that they had back to God and his people so that they could continue to praise God. In the context of asking for offerings for the suffering church in Jerusalem, Paul encourages the Corinthian believers to trust that God will make his grace abound to them. This will result in an increase of "seed," which the believers can use to be generous to those who have need. All of this will redound to the praise of God (2 Cor. 9:6–15).

Another way in which these offerings call God's people to gratitude is in their connection to the Lord's Supper. The Passover lamb is a זֶבַח sacrifice, which means that it requires the grain and wine accompaniments instituted in Numbers 15:1–16. Christians celebrate the Lord's Supper by remembering Jesus as the Passover lamb and consuming the bread and wine as the accompanying elements (Gane 2004, 624). In participating in our version of these offerings, we are called again to deep gratitude for the sacrifice that Christ made on our behalf. Whatever we can offer him in return pales in comparison with what he has provided for us.

PREACHING AND TEACHING STRATEGIES

Exegetical and Theological Significance

It is a major mistake for contemporary readers to gloss over the significance of this section of Numbers. For some people, moving from narrative back into old ceremonial laws may seem like an unwelcome development. Yet this section is a marvelous example of God's patience, mercy, loving-kindness, and grace. It also shows us how to respond to God's faithfulness, by prescribing both obedience and offerings.

The context of this chapter is vitally important. Israel has had an opportunity to go into the Promised Land, but they have pulled back in rebellion as their trust in Yahweh failed. Then they attempted to take the land in their own strength and were soundly defeated. God told them that the whole generation would die in the wilderness.

In this chapter, however, God reaffirms his plan and promises concerning Israel's future. Although one generation will die outside of the Promised Land, the next generation will go in and live in it. They would be blessed abundantly as they obeyed the word of the Lord. They would have sufficient agricultural resources and possessions to make generous offerings to God. These offerings are only made possible because

God is more generous to them than they can ever be in return.

By the grace of God, the Israelites will occupy the land that he gives them. By this same grace, they will be blessed with bounty. God's grace will so overflow to them in blessing that sacrifices and offerings will be made by both native Israelites and the people of foreign ethnicity who join them. The worshippers of YHWH would worship and honor him, joyfully giving back to him out of the abundance of what he first gave them.

If God acted toward Israel on the basis of their sin, they would never have survived the incident of the golden calf. If God blessed Israel in proportion to their holiness, he never would have moved his glory into the tabernacle. If God rewarded Israel according to their merit and faithfulness, they never would have received the Promised Land. Yet not only did Israel survive, they were blessed with abundance so that future generations in the land could worship the Lord. God's people have always been blessed by the overflow of his grace, rather than being treated exactly as their sins deserve.

Preaching Idea
God's rich, infinite grace is the best motive for joyful giving.

Contemporary Connections

What does it mean?
What does it mean that God's rich, infinite grace is the best motive for joyful giving? As noted above, the location of Numbers 15 is highly significant. These instructions about sacrifice are contextually grounded in God's promises to graciously fulfill his plan, despite Israel's rebellion. As Israel took stock of the consequences of their sin, God spoke "for the purpose of reviving the hopes of the new generation," pointing them to his promises for the future in recognition that currently they were experiencing a "mournful and barren time" (Keil and Delitzsch 1983, 1.3

100). As they sat in their tents and contemplated their defeat and their future, they would have known that the Promised Land could only be theirs by the grace of God.

It was this grace, therefore, that provided the highest motivation for their offerings. Far from being a dry, boring recipe book for acceptable sacrifices, this section declares the glory of God's abundant grace and calls the people to remember it and celebrate it. For the generations that would live in the land, literally *everything* they had was theirs on the basis of grace. The very fact that they could offer a sacrifice in the land was dependent on God's unmerited favor. As a result, every single sacrifice and offering was a reminder of divine grace, and therefore was a reason for thanksgiving and joy.

Is it true?
Is it true that God's rich, infinite grace is the best motive for joyful giving? The most extended discussion in the New Testament about Christian giving is 2 Corinthians 8–9. In instructing the Corinthians about giving, Paul identifies *giving* as a grace (2 Cor. 8:6–7). The great principle for giving is not law, and it is not tithing. The principle and motivation for Christian giving is Christ himself: "For you know the grace of our Lord Jesus Christ, that though he was rich, yet for your sake he became poor, so that you through his poverty might become rich" (2 Cor. 8:9 NIV). As Christians, we are to look at how much Christ has given us, and we are to bless others in that same spirit and in accordance with the resources with which we have been entrusted.

All of this giving is to take place in the atmosphere of joy and grace, not legalism. It should not be done grudgingly, since "God loves a cheerful giver" (2 Cor. 9:7 NIV). God generously blesses us so that we can generously bless others, which results in increased thanksgiving to God (2 Cor. 9:11–15).

It is good to help the poor and engage in humanitarian projects, but the highest motivation is not alleviating temporal hardship—it is joyfully giving back to God by using the gifts of his grace to bless other people in his name. Again, Christ is both our Lord and our exemplar. Having benefited so richly from his grace, we are to be generous with what he gives us.

Now what?

In 2 Corinthians 8–9, Paul is not merely providing a theoretical theology; he is motivating the Corinthians to follow through with a plan for generous giving. Listening to Moses in Numbers 15 was not the same as actually presenting offerings to the Lord when they were finally in the land. Doctrinal truth must be applied; theology must be lived.

Money and possessions are undoubtedly idols in many societies today. As believers, do we spend our money just like everyone else? Do we give God the minimum or the leftovers? When we give, do we begrudge it, or do we give generously with open hearts, rejoicing in God's grace and thanking him for blessing us so richly? Some people will need to repent of their failure to give to the Lord, and others will need to repent of their sinful attitude toward their offerings.

The message of this chapter, however, is not negative but incredibly positive! Even after his people flagrantly rebel against him, God is giving them a hope and a future. In the gospel of Jesus Christ, we see even more of the grace of God than Israel could have imagined. If the Israelites in the Promised Land had reason to be grateful and give joyfully, we have much, much more. So prepare to give, and give generously. Give joyfully to God because of his grace given to you in Christ Jesus.

Creativity in Presentation

To get everyone's attention, the preacher might want to consider saying something like: "Numbers 15 should not exist. This book should have ended at the end of the fourteenth chapter. Actually, the book should have ended after the eleventh chapter. Actually, the story should have ended in Exodus 32 with the golden calf. Now that I think about it, the story of the human race could easily have ended all the way back in the garden of Eden in Genesis 3, when Adam and Eve sinned against God."

The only reason the human race exists is because of God's grace. This text is a good one for tracing out a biblical theology of the grace of God that makes humanity's survival possible. The Numbers account makes this crystal clear, and it is in keeping with the general themes of human sin and God's grace that are found throughout the Scriptures.

The specific point here, however, is that this incredible grace of God serves as the grounds and motive for our giving. The preacher can walk the people through the specific scene in Numbers, expand the horizon line to take in more of the canonical theme, and focus in the end on Christ himself. The greatest display of God's grace is found in the work of Jesus, and it is the gospel of Jesus Christ that supplies us with the highest possible motive for giving generously and joyfully. Having given us Jesus and the gift of eternal life, our hearts should be open and thankful to God. This heart attitude will be reflected in how we give and the offerings we make.

Although some churches talk far too much about giving money, there are times when it is appropriate to do so. There are also times when it is appropriate to take up a special offering, or to ask people to really prepare themselves for giving to the Lord. To give people time to reflect and respond, it may be fitting to tell the congregation that the following Sunday the offering will be received as a special act of worship. Ask people to spend time praying and meditating during the week, and then come prepared to give in response to God's grace to them in the gift of Jesus Christ. In this way, they will be prepared to acknowledge the truth that God's rich, infinite grace is the best motive for joyful giving.

One way to approach this passage could be:

Regulations for Sacrificial Offerings (15:1–21)

- God ordains the ways in which his people should offer sacrifices (15:1–12).

- Everyone who lives in the land is under God's authority (15:13–16).

- Offering God a portion of the land's bounty reminds Israel that God has graciously given it to them (15:17–21).

DISCUSSION QUESTIONS

1. What comfort can this passage provide in the aftermath of the rebellion stories of Numbers 13–14?

2. Why does God command his people to give offerings to him?

3. Why does the text explicitly mention foreigners and sojourners, and subject them to the same instructions as native-born Israelites?

4. How does being generous in our offerings to God strengthen our faith?

Numbers 15:22–36

EXEGETICAL IDEA
The sacrificial system can remediate sin classified as unintentional; however, defiant or high-handed sin stands outside of this process.

THEOLOGICAL FOCUS
Remediation of sin requires a repentant heart.

PREACHING IDEA
Our new covenant mediator can forgive all of our sins, but if we reject Christ no forgiveness is possible.

PREACHING POINTERS
There can be no doubt about the kindness, mercy, and grace of God, but there must also not be any doubt about his holiness and justice. Everyone falls short and everyone sins, but where there is sin there needs to be confession and repentance. There are also sins that constitute a fundamental, total rejection of God and his ways. In this passage, we find that people who sin that way against God were to be put to death. The man violating the Sabbath command was symbolically rejecting the entire covenant, and as a result he died. There is no life outside of a saving relationship with the God of Abraham.

The author of Hebrews is at pains to show his readers that there is no salvation outside of Jesus Christ. If Christ is rejected, there can be no salvation. The Son of God is the covenant mediator of the new covenant, and it is only in this mediator that we can find forgiveness for sins, and the gift of eternal life. Like the man in this text who died for rejecting the covenant, if we reject the new covenant in Christ we will experience the second death. There is no atonement and forgiveness outside of Jesus Christ. Do not reject him. Come to him and be saved. Take seriously the truth that our new covenant mediator can forgive all of our sins, but if we reject Christ no forgiveness is possible.

REMEDIATION FOR SIN (15:22–36)

LITERARY STRUCTURE AND THEMES

Following the regulations on different offerings, Numbers 15:22–36 discusses sacrifice as a remedy for sin along with a scenario in which sacrificial remediation is not possible. There are two sections to this passage: further instructions in 15:22–31 and an illustrative narrative in 15:32–36. First, 15:22–31 consists of instructions for the proper sacrifice to bring when the community (15:22–26) or an individual has gone astray (15:27–29). The most notable feature of this section is the introduction of the "high-handed" (יָד רָמָה) sin in 15:30–31. It is distinct because it does not provide a means of restoration but results in the offender being "cut off" (כרת) from the congregation. The narrative found in 15:32–36 illustrates the principle of the high-handed or defiant sin.

The unifying theme is what is required to maintain communion with a holy God. The sacrificial system permits Israel to remain in fellowship with God, but this passage reveals that it has limits. High-handed sin, such as a willful violation of the Sabbath, requires further instructions from God. This recalls other examples of narratives that illustrate legal or cultic principles (see Exod. 16:27–30; Lev. 10:1–3; Num. 9:6–14). The text communicates both by *telling* its audience the instructions and regulations and *showing* the audience what they look like in action.

- ***Remediation for Unintentional Sins (15:22–29)***
- ***The High-Handed Sin (15:30–31)***
- ***High-Handed Sin: A Case Study (15:32–36)***

EXPOSITION

This passage contains several interpretive pitfalls. Differentiating sin into categories may obscure the reality that any sin is an offense against a holy God. Further, the discussion of sin that cannot be remediated through sacrifice needs to be approached carefully. However, exploration of this passage along with reflections on its biblical-theological context will illuminate the nature of God and the provision he offers for those who fall short of his holiness. This passage demonstrates that the sacrificial system can remediate sin classified as unintentional; however, defiant or high-handed sin stands outside of this process.

Remediation for Unintentional Sins (15:22–29)

15:22–23. These verses introduce the instructions for remediating sin. The language is repetitive as the phrase "all these commandments that the LORD has spoken to Moses" (ESV, NET) in 15:22b is immediately followed by "all that the LORD has commanded you through the authority of Moses" (NET) in 15:23a.[1] The temporal designation "from today . . . and onward through your generations" then follows in 15:23b. Numbers 15:22 on its own might only be thought to refer to the previous set of instructions, but the repetition and expansion in 15:23 makes it very clear that these verses apply to all divine legislation (Ashley 1993, 286). The scope of what is addressed in these verses is thus

---

1 The NET translates the phrase בְּיַד־מֹשֶׁה as "by the authority of Moses." The expression בְּיַד literally means "by the hand of," but it can be used metonymically to indicate authority or power.

exceptionally broad. Any act that goes against any of God's requirements for Israel fits here.

> **Unintentional**
>
> Most English translations use the word "unintentional" or "unintentionally" to describe the sin being addressed in 15:22–29. This begins with the second word of 15:22, which is a second-person plural verb תִּשְׁגּוּ from the root שׁגה. The following verses then employ words from the synonymous root שׁגג: a noun (שְׁגָגָה) seven times in 15:24–29 and a participial form (הַשֹּׁגֶגֶת) in 15:28. The rationale for understanding inadvertent or unintentional sin from these words does not come from this passage but from other contexts. Leviticus 4:22 and 27 reveal that sins committed in this manner must be made known to the offender. Further, Numbers 35:11, 15 uses שְׁגָגָה to refer to inadvertent killing in its instructions on the cities of refuge (Sklar 2012, 469). Although "unintentional" does not capture every nuance of this category, it is a reasonable translation.

15:24. The context of this verse is communal sin, building upon second-person plural forms in 15:22 (לֹא תַעֲשׂוּ; "You [pl.] do not do") and 15:23 (לְדֹרֹתֵיכֶם; "for your [pl.] generations"). It is unclear whether this refers to a group within the broader community (Cole 2000, 251), to the actions of the community as a whole (Ashley 1993, 287), or both. It is hard to see how the whole community could err "without the knowledge of the congregation" (15:24a ESV).[2] However, a possible analogy is Leviticus 4:13, which refers to communal inadvertent transgressions, wherein the entire congregation does not recognize its fault until it is revealed (Milgrom 1990, 123). In any event, the communal nature of the transgression establishes the types of sacrifice that are required.

In discussing remediation for communal sins, it is important to note that these instructions differ from those found in Leviticus 4:1–5:19. In Leviticus 4:14, a bull was required as a purification offering (חַטָּאת) for the entire community.[3] That sacrifice was the sole requirement. Numbers 15:24 now states that before the purification offering takes place, a bull was to be offered as a whole burnt offering (עֹלָה) to make a pleasing aroma to God along with the grain and wine accompaniments prescribed in 15:1–16. This addition helps to link the seemingly disconnected sections of this chapter. Following the burnt offering, a priest offered a male goat as a purification offering (15:24b). Previously, sacrificing a male goat was the remedy for a leader's inadvertent sin (Lev. 4:23). Thus, for communal transgression this passage requires the sacrifice of two animals as well as the additional offerings.

> **Amendment to the Purification Offerings**
>
> It is not entirely clear what function is served by this amendment to the purification offerings. Some ancient rabbinic commentators tried to make a distinction between sins of commission in Leviticus 4 (transgressing God's commands) and sins of omission in Numbers 15:22–29 (failing to follow divinely-authorized procedures). However, modern commentators reject that distinction as artificial (Gane 2004, 521; Milgrom 1990, 402–3). One suggestion is that Numbers differentiates the community's required purification offering from that of the high priest which required the sacrifice of a bull in Leviticus 4:1–12. This distinction may reflect the reality that many of the complaint narratives in Numbers (chs. 14, 16–17) involve conflict between the community and high priesthood (Gane 2004, 621). Another suggestion is that this modification anticipates

---

2   This is an idiomatic translation of אִם מֵעֵינֵי הָעֵדָה, which could be rendered more literally as "away from the eyes of the congregation."
3   See the discussion of Numbers 7 for why it is preferable to translate חַטָּאת as "purification offering" rather than "sin offering," even if the context in 15:22–29 is clearly sin.

> Israel's eventual presence within the Promised Land and the celebration of festivals in which sacrifices for cultic worship and for purification were to be offered together (Num. 28:16–31; Levine 1993, 396).

15:25–26. These sacrifices were to be performed by a priest and accomplished atonement for the whole of the community.[4] The verb וְכִפֶּר here summarizes the "priestly sacrificial manipulation" of the animals and their blood (Ashley 1993, 287). This is the same verb that underlies the procedures of Yom Kippur in Leviticus 16, which yields annual atonement for the nation. The text then simply states "they will be forgiven" (NASB, NET, NIV) as a result of these sacrifices. The second half of 15:25 twice mentions the inadvertent nature of the error through the noun שְׁגָגָה, while also repeating that the congregation has brought both its burnt offering and purification offering to God. The discussion of communal sin concludes in 15:26 with a declaration reminiscent of 15:13–14. This verse explicitly notes that this atonement covers the whole congregation of Israel along with the sojourner who dwells among them. Again, the sojourner receives the same divine grace as native-born Israelites.

15:27–29. The text then gives instructions for individual transgressions. In this instance the requirements are nearly the same as the equivalent passage in Leviticus 4:27–31: the offender must bring a female goat for a purification offering and the priest will perform the sacrifice, presumably following the instructions laid out in Leviticus.[5] The ministry of the priest will bring atonement and forgiveness for the individual's offense. In addition, Numbers 15:27 specifies that the goat is to be in its first year, a detail not mentioned in Leviticus (Cole 2000, 252). Unlike the procedure for communal transgression, there is no whole burnt offering to accompany the purification offering. Numbers 15:29 again puts the native-born Israelite (הָאֶזְרָח) and sojourner (גֵּר) on the same footing, declaring that "one and the same law" (15:29 NIV) applies to both groups.

The High-Handed Sin (15:30–31)

15:30–31. The text addresses a category of sin that the previously listed sacrifices do not cover. As with the transgressions mentioned previously, this type of sin carries the same penalty for both the Israelite and the sojourner. The Hebrew idiom for this sin is "with a high hand" (בְּיָד רָמָה) which the ESV translates literally, though other English versions translate it idiomatically as "defiantly" (NASB, NET, NIV). The underlying image is that of ancient Near Eastern deities portrayed with raised right hands holding weapons ready to strike (Milgrom 1990, 125). It is important to note that despite the militaristic imagery, "high-handed" sin can be done in secret since it expresses defiance against God even if the rest of the community is unaware. The example of Achan in Joshua 7 is illustrative: his sin was secret to everyone except for God, but he was punished as a high-handed sinner.

When an inferior acts with a "high hand" toward their superior, they express a brazen rejection of the established order (Stubbs 2009, 140).[6] First Kings 11:26–27 uses this expression in the context of Jeroboam's rebellion against Solomon (Sklar 2012, 473). Acting

---

[4] The specifics of how the priests were to perform purification offerings for the community can be found in Leviticus 4:13–21.
[5] Leviticus 4:32–35 also permits the use of a female lamb, which is not mentioned in Numbers 15.
[6] Notably, the same phrase is used to describe Israel's defiance of the Egyptians during the Exodus (Exod. 14:8; Num. 33:3). However, in that instance God is acting on Israel's behalf and has already asserted his superiority over pharaoh.

with a "high hand" against God thus indicates sin committed that deliberately challenges God's sovereignty. It is sin committed without remorse, regret, or guilt.

> **High-Handed Sin**
> Although it is not identified as "high-handed sin," a good argument can be made that Israel's refusal to enter the Promised Land in Numbers 13–14 fits this category. Israel brazenly defies God's commands, and the offending generation is barred from entering Canaan. Later, in Numbers 20, Moses raises his hand to strike a rock, using similar terminology to that of "high-handed sin." He receives the same punishment. Based on the shared fate, Moses's raised hand is a microcosm of the nation's utter rejection of God's instructions (Noonan 2020, 79–92).

The negative evaluations continue by declaring that the one who acts this way is guilty of "reviling the LORD" (ESV). This is the sole occurrence of the verbal root נדף in the Pentateuch, though it is used elsewhere to describe foreign foes or idolatrous Israelites who blaspheme against God (2 Kings 19:6, 22; Isa. 37:6, 23; Ezek. 20:27). Numbers 15:31 uses synonymous descriptions of the offense, declaring that the guilty party has "despised the word of the LORD" (ESV, NET) and "broken his commandment" (ESV, NET).[7] The accumulation of these negative descriptions in two short verses bears witness to the serious nature of the offense.

That fate is described in 15:30b, which declares that those guilty of high-handed sin will be "cut off" (וְנִכְרְתָה) from among their people. The same penalty is reinforced in stronger terms in 15:31, announcing that the offender will be "utterly cut off" (הִכָּרֵת תִּכָּרֵת).[8] This punishment is reserved for grievous offenses against God such as the violation of sacred time (neglecting God's appointed holy days), the violation of sacred substances (consuming parts of the sacrifice devoted to God), neglecting purification rituals such as circumcision and cleansing after corpse contamination, illicit worship of idols or improper sacrifice, and illicit sexual behavior such as incest or bestiality (Milgrom 1990, 406). The punishment of being cut off is also enacted by God, though human intermediaries may carry out parallel judgment (cf. Lev. 20:1–3; Num. 15:32–36).

The nature of the punishment merits discussion. It appears to be a penalty that goes even beyond death and results in the offender's name and lineage being removed from Israel (Gane 2017, 96).[9] This is incredibly harsh, since the perseverance of one's name and lineage is essential to how ancient Israelites formulated their identity. One may note how the patriarchs were "gathered to their people" in their death accounts to get a sense of the importance of posterity (Gen. 25:8, 17; 35:29; 49:33; Num. 20:24). In contrast, to be "cut off" is to be removed from Israel's story, with no one "to recollect or serve as a reminder" of the offender's name (Gane 2017, 96). Alongside the enduring consequences there are also immediate repercussions, since the offender continues to bear the weight of their iniquity (Stubbs 2009, 140). Consequently, their uncleanness

---

7   The expression "broken his commandment" is also found in Ezra's confession of the people's intermarriages with foreigners (Ezra 9:7). The penalty that Ezra anticipates for this offense is utter destruction (Sklar 2012, 475).

8   The grammatical structure here is the infinitive absolute followed by a finite form of the same root (כרת). This "affirms and intensifies the authenticity or conviction of the verbal root" and "may stress the thoroughness of the verbal action" (Arnold and Choi 2018, 87).

9   Gane notes this by looking at the penalty for offering a child to Molech in Leviticus 20. The offender is to be stoned to death by the community (Lev. 20:2), and then God will cut him off from his people (Lev. 20:3). Thus, the penalty must go beyond death, since the execution of the offender is apparently not the final word.

persists; they cannot be permitted to remain in God's holy presence. This appears to necessitate their death (Ashley 1993, 289).

> **Sin and Punishment**
>
> The severity of this penalty prompts some broader reflection on the categories of sin established in 15:22–31. At first glance it appears that there are two: inadvertent sins that can be remedied according to 15:22–29 and defiant/high-handed ones that result in the offender being "cut off." However, this is an oversimplification. There are certainly offenses that are deliberate or intentional but do not fall into the category of described in 15:30–31 because they are listed along with the sacrifices required for restoration. These include failing to testify about a legal matter (Lev. 5:1–3), deceiving and perhaps stealing from a neighbor (Lev. 6:1–7), or sleeping with a slave woman promised to another man (Lev. 19:20–22; Schnittjer 2006, 312–13). It thus appears that deliberate sins can be further subdivided into those that are expiable through sacrifice and those that are not. How are they to be distinguished? Scripture suggests that one means of differentiation is whether or not the offender displays a repentant heart and makes restitution (Lev. 5:5; 6:4–5; Num. 5:7; Gane 2005, 211). Thus, discussions of the sacrificial system are aware of human propensity to sin against God and leave room for a penitent heart. The offender may acknowledge their guilt and offer the prescribed remedy. It is likely that 15:22–31 does not address this intermediate category in order to cast the defiant sinner into sharper relief (Gane 2005, 212–13; Sklar 2012, 484). Inadvertent transgression of cultic regulations may occur, but 15:30–31 strongly encourages the audience to avoid even the hint of defiant sin.

High-Handed Sin: A Case Study (15:32–36)

15:32. Immediately after introducing the category of high-handed sin, 15:32–36 provides an illustrative narrative. Although the language of "high-handed" or the punishment of being "cut off" is not mentioned explicitly in these verses, the placement of this narrative after the previous instructions suggests that they should be linked. Further, the offender is guilty of Sabbath-breaking, which according to Exodus 31:14 was to result in death and in being cut off from Israel.

The story is given a general temporal setting: "When the people of Israel were in the wilderness" (15:32a ESV, NET). Consequently, this event may not have occurred immediately after receiving the instructions on the high-handed sin but was placed here to exemplify the principle (Sprinkle 2015, 277). The offense is described succinctly in 15:32b. The Israelites discover one of their number gathering wood, presumably for kindling a cooking fire, on the Sabbath (Stubbs 2009, 140). The text provides no rationale or defense for this action. On the contrary, the general warmth of the wilderness climate and God's daily provision of manna indicates that there was likely no urgency. It is cast as deliberate defiance against God's Sabbath requirements (Gane 2004, 622).

15:33–34. The Israelites bring the man before Moses, Aaron, and the entire congregation. Although the end result appears obvious, YHWH did not require the deaths of those who went to gather manna in Exodus 16:27–30, so it is fitting to permit him to judge this case. Further, there may have been some doubt as to whether the act of gathering sticks counted as a high-handed offense if the man had been apprehended before actually lighting the cooking fire (Stubbs 2009, 140).

15:35–36. The punishment is then announced and enacted. God commands Moses to take the man outside of the precincts of the camp, which is consecrated as holy space, and execute him by stoning. The whole congregation obeys God's command, thus disassociating themselves from the anonymous offender (Gane 2017, 331).[10] Capital punishment for this offense seems quite harsh, but violating the Sabbath commandment shows defiant disregard for God's establishment of sacred time. The Sabbath reflects the memory of God's creative acts in Genesis 1:1–2:4 and invites Israel to rest as a sign of trust in his sustaining power. Further, for Israel the Sabbath served as a memorial of their deliverance from Egypt (Deut. 5:15). Violating it demonstrates a lack of regard for what God has done on their behalf.

THEOLOGICAL FOCUS

The exegetical idea (The sacrificial system can remediate sin classified as unintentional; however, defiant or high-handed sin stands outside of this process) leads to this theological focus: *Remediation of sin requires a repentant heart.*

This passage is uncomfortable for Christian readers. The notion of animal sacrifice is foreign to us, thanks to the redemptive work of the true Passover Lamb. Further, the idea of irredeemable "high-handed" sin is frightening. In light of this, a few observations should be made to place this passage in its proper theological framework. First, it is important to note that any means of atonement, sacrificial or otherwise, is a mark of the graciousness of God. As the offended party, God has the right to establish whatever ramification he chooses for sin. He commands Israel to "be holy, for I am holy" (Lev. 11:44), a standard that it never attained. However, it is a sign of his desire to remain in relationship with sinful humanity that he permitted animal sacrifices to serve as a response to sin, even providing for yearly cleansing of the community via the Day of Atonement (Sklar 2012, 471). Thus, remediation for sin has always been and continues to be an expression of God's great mercy.

Secondly, characterizing this category of sin as "defiant" has important ramifications. Gane defines it as "personal disloyalty and an affront against the LORD" (Gane 2004, 625) to which it is possible to add the idea that *sustained* defiance and failure to acknowledge guilt are dangerous for those who claim to be God's people. Heart attitudes in response to sin are deeply significant as Jesus illustrates in the Sermon on the Mount when he declares that hatred and lust already evoke murder and adultery (Matt. 6:21–27). The remediation offered through the sacrificial system on its own is not sufficient to counteract the effects of hearts and attitudes bent on defying God. The Old Testament prophets consistently attest to this (cf. Mic. 6:1–8).

Thirdly, this passage reminds us that it is easy to become hard-hearted toward our own sinfulness. The journey from sin for which we experience guilt and penitence to defiantly expressed deliberate sin is "deceptively short and very quick and easy to take" (Sklar 2012, 484). It is for this reason that Jesus hyperbolically calls for the loss of an eye or a limb rather than permitting sin to continue in one's life (Matt. 5:29–30). If left unchecked, a person may find themselves in the situation described in Hebrews 6:4–6 and 10:26–27, passages which are thought to draw from Numbers 15:30–31 (McAffee 2014, 545–48). Ultimately, clinging to one's own defiant sin may lead the offender to renounce Christ and his work on their behalf. This is a dark and dangerous road (Heb. 10:26).

Finally, however, it is crucial to remember God's mercy and the work of repentance can redeem the stain of defiance. It was always possible for God to go beyond the strictures of the sacrificial system and forgive even the worst kinds of sin. This happens through the work of mediatorial figures whose intercession could bring about mitigated punishment (Boda 2009, 95). We can see this at work in Moses's appeals for God to forgive Israel's rebellion in the preceding chapter. Though Israel explicitly rejected God's command, in response to Moses's appeal to God's own character, he chose to forgive

---

10 See also the execution of the one who blasphemes the name of the Lord in Leviticus 24:10–17.

rather than destroy (Num. 14:20). Although Israel faced severe consequences, their punishment was not total and their covenant relationship with God remained.

Another parallel comes from the story of Manasseh in 2 Chronicles 33. He acknowledged YHWH while in captivity (2 Chron. 33:14–20) after profaning the temple in Jerusalem with an Asherah (Gane 2004, 626–27). It is hard to imagine a more defiant and high-handed sin! Yet God, who is rich in mercy, chose to hear Manasseh's cry and rescued him, even preserving his place in the Davidic lineage that leads to Jesus (Matt. 1:10). There were no purification or reparation offerings prescribed for these situations. Only the graciousness of God and his commitment to his covenant people could preserve them. Through these and other examples we see that the witness of Scripture attests that if God delays his judgment, he will not reject a repentant heart.

PREACHING AND TEACHING STRATEGIES

Exegetical and Theological Significance

Contextually, Numbers 15 stands as a witness to God's grace and faithfulness, despite the previous sin and rebellion of his people in Numbers 14. Mercy and forgiveness do not erase all the consequences for sin, and neither does God's grace provide a license for sin or a guarantee of cheap forgiveness. It is a glorious truth that God forgives repentant sinners, but this truth is mirrored by the reality that God does not forgive those who harden their hearts and defy him, refusing to repent or follow his covenant stipulations.

The man who violated the Sabbath command was guilty of despising a law that symbolized God's covenant with Israel and his authority over all creation. He rejected and repudiated the offer to enter God's rest, and he spurned the significance of his redemption from Egypt. This was not a minor matter of picking up a few sticks; it was a rejection of God's redemptive work in the life of Israel. The lesson is clear: if you reject God and his covenant terms, you cannot live.

Given the fulfillment of the law that comes through Christ Jesus, no one today should be executed for picking up sticks, no matter the day of the week. Yet anyone who rejects the Sabbath-rest offered in Christ will be excluded from God's people and will die outside of God's rest (Heb. 3:7–4:13). There is forgiveness for all of our sins, but that forgiveness is found only through faith in Christ Jesus. You cannot despise the covenant grace of God and be saved. Mercy and grace are precious, and eternal life is given to all who believe, but those who never turn from their rebellion against God will experience the second death.

Preaching Idea
Our new covenant mediator can forgive all of our sins, but if we reject Christ, no forgiveness is possible.

Contemporary Connections

What does it mean?
What does it mean that our new covenant mediator can forgive all of our sins, but if we reject Christ, no forgiveness is possible? This is only possible because our mediator is both the perfect high priest and the perfect sacrifice that makes atonement for our sins. The mercy of God is mediated to us through Jesus—he is the avenue through which it flows. Apart from Christ, there is no forgiveness for sins. In Christ, however, all of our sins can be washed away.

To reject Christ is to reject the only mediator of the new covenant, and that means a rejection of the covenant itself. Rejecting Jesus Christ and dying in unbelief is thus the highest example of continuing to sin against God with a high hand. When the gospel is held out to people, and sinners are urged to repent and believe, the corresponding truth is that if they do not come to Christ, they will be lost. With Christ, the stakes are eternal.

As a follower of Christ and a member of the new covenant community, perseverance in our faith is not incompatible with continuing to fall short in sin. In this life, no Christian will be morally and spiritually perfect. Our sins require ongoing confession and repentance, but believers remain in the new covenant even though they sin over and over again. Being weak and falling into sin is not the same as repudiating Christ and rejecting the gospel with a hard heart. However, where there is true faith, there should also be evidence of love for Christ and spiritual fruit.

Is it true?
Is it true that our new covenant mediator can forgive all of our sins, but if we reject Christ, no forgiveness is possible? Famously, John 3:16 proclaims that *whoever* believes in Christ will have eternal life; this is not contingent on previous lifestyle or the types of sins committed. First Corinthians 6:9–11 and Romans 1–3 also show that God forgives all kinds of sinners through Jesus the Savior.

On a personal level, Paul never stopped marveling at the saving grace that was given to him. Paul firmly believed that if he could be saved, then anyone could be saved, no matter their past. Meditate on his words in 1 Timothy 1:12–17 (NIV):

> I thank Christ Jesus our Lord, who has given me strength, that he considered me trustworthy, appointing me to his service. Even though I was once a blasphemer and a persecutor and a violent man, I was shown mercy because I acted in ignorance and unbelief. The grace of our Lord was poured out on me abundantly, along with the faith and love that are in Christ Jesus.
>
> Here is a trustworthy saying that deserves full acceptance: Christ Jesus came into the world to save sinners—of whom I am the worst. But for that very reason I was shown mercy so that in me, the worst of sinners, Christ Jesus might display his immense patience as an example for those who would believe in him and receive eternal life. Now to the King eternal, immortal, invisible, the only God, be honor and glory for ever and ever. Amen.

Now what?
What do we do in response to the truth that our new covenant mediator can forgive all of our sins, but if we reject Christ, no forgiveness is possible? When Peter preached on Pentecost, the people were cut to the heart and cried out asking what they should do in response to the message. Peter replied, "Repent and be baptized, every one of you, in the name of Jesus Christ for the forgiveness of your sins" (Acts 2:38a NIV). Since we need Christ as our Savior, we should lose no time in turning from our sin, going to God, and clinging to Christ by faith. For those who are already safe in Christ, continue to exercise your faith and grow in grace.

Creativity in Presentation
The principle of forgiveness for sin is found in these instructions in Numbers 15, in Peter's sermon on Pentecost, and in Paul's statements in 1 Timothy 1:12–17. This is a passage on which the preacher can easily center everything around the gospel of Jesus Christ. Creativity in presentation should not eclipse the simplicity, urgency, and necessity of the gospel. (This should go without saying, but creativity in presentation should *never* eclipse the truth of any part of God's Word. Nothing that draws attention to itself rather than the Word should ever be done.)

This message should call people to respond in repentance and faith. Depending on a church's tradition, this may involve asking people to pray where they are, or to come up to the front of the auditorium to pray with others. Pastorally, I have sometimes found that the most effective way of ministering to sincere people is to have some of the elders sit up near the front after the service, and then those who want guidance or prayer can come up unobtrusively. There are numerous ways of configuring the logistics, and different congregations can have equally effective ways of organizing for the time of response. It is vital that people hear the gospel, and that they are told to respond in faith to the work of Christ in his life, death, and resurrection.

It may seem that Numbers 15:22–31 is an unlikely evangelistic text, but it works remarkably well since it runs on the themes of sin, repentance, sacrifice, mercy, and forgiveness for the people of faith. From a wider perspective, this section establishes biblical-theological connections to Christ and the fulfillment of his covenantal work. On the level of the local, immediate context the principles of the text are clear, but this text moves the message organically and with ease to the larger framework of canonical fulfillment. This passage represents a real opportunity for the preacher to show the congregation how Numbers and antecedent revelation lead us to Jesus. This text reminds us that our new covenant mediator can forgive all of our sins, but if we reject Christ, no forgiveness is possible.

One means of approaching this passage could be:

- Corporate and individual sin should be remediated as soon as it is acknowledged (15:22–29).

- Defiant, unrepentant sin has severe consequences (15:30–36).

DISCUSSION QUESTIONS

1. In this passage, animal sacrifices were part of the process of remediation for sin. Why were such sacrifices required? What did they symbolize? How are our sins remediated now?

2. How does the "high-handed sin" of this passage relate to the warning to those who deliberately continue to sin in Hebrews 10:26–31?

3. Is there any sin that cannot be covered by confession, repentance, and the grace of God shown through Jesus Christ?

Numbers 15:37–41

EXEGETICAL IDEA
The requirement of placing tassels on garments provides Israel with a tangible reminder to obey God and to not follow their own desires.

THEOLOGICAL FOCUS
Remembering what God has commanded is crucial to the life of faith.

PREACHING IDEA
"Thy word have I hid in mine heart, that I might not sin against thee" (Ps. 119:11 KJV).

PREACHING POINTERS
Most Christians today do not put tassels on their garments to remind themselves of the words of God. We do, however, live in a society filled with reminders, alarms, notifications, calendars, day planners, and memory aids. Consequently, the principle of jogging our memories is one that resonates with people in our contemporary society. Everyone knows that when you get a notification reminding you of a meeting in fifteen minutes, the point isn't the notification—it's *the meeting*. Similarly, the point in this passage wasn't a fashion accessory; it was remembering and obeying *the commands of God*.

More importantly, the notification to go to the meeting is of no help unless you actually go to the meeting. Knowing there's a meeting and attending the meeting are not the same thing. Likewise, knowing the commands of God is not the same as obeying the commands of God. Memorization and knowledge have their place, but God wants us to put his words into practice. We are to be doers of the word, not hearers only. We must be able to say with the psalmist, "Thy word have I hid in mine heart, that I might not sin against thee" (Ps 119:11 KJV).

REMEMBERING GOD'S COMMANDS (15:37–41)

LITERARY STRUCTURE AND THEMES

The final preaching unit of Numbers 15 focuses on the necessity of Israel remembering God's commands. The tassels that they must affix to their garments provide tangible reminders of what God has called them to do. This instruction is fitting in the wake of the discussion of cultic regulations in 15:1–21 and remediation for transgression in 15:22–36. Israel has received important commands from God. Now it is incumbent upon them to uphold them. This expository unit also reminds Israel of their rescue from Egypt by their divine covenant partner. Israel should remember that God's instructions are not abstract legal principles but are rooted in a story of mercy and redemption. The structure of these verses is straightforward. The section begins with the introductory phrase "The LORD said to Moses" in 15:37 before giving the instruction in 15:38. The purpose of the instruction follows in 15:39–40, before the section ends with God twice declaring "I am the LORD your God" in 15:41.

EXPOSITION

This passage is a fitting conclusion to the commands given throughout Numbers 15. Instructions on how to offer sacrifices and warnings of high-handed sins now culminate in the creation of tangible reminders to obey God. The requirement of placing tassels on garments provides Israel with a tangible reminder to obey God and to not follow their own desires.

15:37–38. Following an introductory phrase, God gives instructions to Moses. He commands Moses to speak to the people of Israel and tell them to make tassels (צִיצָה) and affix them to the corners of their garments along with a blue thread (פְּתִיל תְּכֵלֶת) for each corner. Several features here require further explanation. First, the word for "tassels" (צִיצָה) is found only in this passage and once in Ezekiel 8:3 where it refers to the prophet's hair. The noun צִיצָה is a grammatically feminine variation of the noun צִיץ, which is used to refer to the ornamented front plate worn by the high priest (Exod. 28:36; 39:30; Lev. 8:9; Levine 1993, 400). Garments with tassels were found in other contexts in the ancient Near East and may have served religious functions (Wenham 2008, 148–49). Garments with tassels were also a sign of royalty or nobility, so requiring the whole of the community to wear them attributes to each Israelite the symbolic status of a priest or noble.[1] The tassel likely consisted of material added to the hem of the outer garment rather than being part of the garment itself (Ashely 1993, 294; Milgrom 1990, 411).[2] Even if the exact appearance is difficult to reconstruct, the function of the צִיצָה is clear. They are as visible symbols like the מְזוּזוֹת ("doorposts") on which the Israelites were to inscribe God's commands (Deut. 6:9; 11:20). Wherever the Israelites went, they were to carry symbolic

---

1   The royal connotation of tassels also helps to explain the story in which David secretly cuts Saul's robe in 1 Samuel 24. By removing the edge of the garment, David is symbolically removing Saul's royal authority.

2   Moses gives a parallel instruction in Deuteronomy 22:12 that uses a different word for "tassel" (גְּדִלִים), but the terms appear to be synonymous.

reminders of God's commandments on their bodies.

Secondly, this command was to be "for their generations" (לְדֹרֹתָם) and thus orient Israel's memory throughout its existence. As Israel anticipates its new life in the Promised Land, God instructs them to remember his provision for them in the wilderness and the instructions and commandments he has given them to follow. The resonance of this section extends down through the centuries and even into modern Jewish practice. Prayer shawls (called *tallith*) have tassels (the *tzitzit*, mentioned above) on their corners which are composed of four white threads each and serve as a reminder of all of the instructions in the Torah (Milgrom 1990, 127). This passage, along with Deuteronomy 6:4–9 and 11:13–21, is part of the recitations that call Jews to continually remember God and his commands (Stubbs 2009, 141).

Thirdly, the "blue thread" (פְּתִיל תְּכֵלֶת) that goes along with the tassels carries deep symbolic meaning. The dye used to create this color came from the gland of snails found off the coast of Israel and Lebanon (Bailey 2005, 476; Levine 1993, 400–401; Milgrom 1990, 127). It is noted for its durability and its scarcity, which means that it was typically reserved for royal or priestly clothing.[3] Indeed, many of the priestly garments described in Exodus 28 have this color. By instructing all Israelites to wear a thread of this color, God is putting into practice his promise that Israel would be a kingdom of priests, consecrated and dedicated to himself (Gane 2004, 622–23). Milgrom helpfully refers to the tassels and thread as "the uniform of all Israel" and as equality "not through levelling by through elevation" (Milgrom 1990, 414). Affixing tassels and the blue thread to garments declares that every Israelite belongs to God's holy community and is called to serve him in a manner befitting a priest.

15:39. The text then articulates the purpose of the command to affix tassels, describing both what they should cause Israel to do (15:39a) and what they should cause Israel to *not* do (15:39b). The positive functions of the tassels are given in three closely related verbs. Through Moses, God instructs the Israelites that "you shall look" (רְאִיתֶם) upon the tassels, which leads to the expectation that "you shall remember" (זְכַרְתֶּם) all of God's commandments, with the result that "you shall do" (עֲשִׂיתֶם) them. Consequently, the visual reminder provided by the tassels and blue thread should prompt Israel to remember what God requires and live in obedience. The tassels and blue thread are thus symbols that are to reflect a greater reality: Israel is a royal and priestly people consecrated to God's service. They are to demonstrate that reality by how they live.

Numbers 15:39b flips the picture around and articulates what pitfalls Israel will avoid by adhering to the prompting provided by the tassels. Essentially, if Israel remembers the commandments of God and does them, they will not go after their own inclinations. This warning draws from vocabulary used in the episode of the spies in Numbers 13–14, which again recalls the magnitude of that transgression (Gane 2004, 622; Olson 1996, 98; Stubbs 2009, 141). Wearing the tassels should prompt Israel not to "follow after your own heart" (ESV, NASB, NET). The verb translated "follow" is from the root תור which occurs in 13:2, 16, 17, and 14:34 to describe the mission of the spies. English translations obscure this connection, using "spy out" (ESV, NASB), "investigate (NET), or "explore" (NIV) to translate this root in Numbers 13–14. Noticing this connection helps the reader to contrast how Israel disastrously followed its own desires with the call to remember God's commandments. Further, 15:39b concludes with the statement that in following their own desires, the Israelites were "prostituting themselves."

---

3   The color may have been closer to blue-purple or violet. Its scarcity was such that apparently it took twelve thousand snails to produce 1.4 grams of the dye (Milgrom 1990, 127).

Remembering God's Commands (15:37–41)

The Hebrew root here is זנה which is also found in 14:33 in reference to Israel's unfaithfulness in not obeying God's commands. The implication is that if the tassels on their garments prompt Israel to remember what they should, they will not commit the same infidelity.

15:40. This verse summarizes the function of the tassels by reusing the verbs "you shall remember" (תִּזְכְּרוּ) and "you shall do" (וַעֲשִׂיתֶם) from 15:39a. God declares that using the tassels as a guide means that Israel will remember and enact his commandments. The result of this is that Israel will be "holy to your God" (קְדֹשִׁים לֵאלֹהֵיכֶם). This recalls the inscription on the plate affixed to the high priest's turban which read "Holy to the Lord" (Exod. 28:36–37; 39:30–31). Although not all Israelites were ordained to priestly ministry, this call to be holy along with the tassels and blue thread again reinforces that the whole nation was to be a "kingdom of priests" (Exod. 19:6).

15:41. Finally, this section concludes with a divine self-declaration. The verse begins and ends with "I am the Lord your God," recalling Exodus 6:2–8 in which God declared his intention to rescue Israel (Cole 2000, 258). In between these declarations, God reminds them that as "your God" he brought Israel up from Egypt so that he would be "your God." This refrain is found throughout the Pentateuch. It reminds Israel that God's regulations are not arbitrary but rather spring from his salvific actions on their behalf (Deut. 6:20–24). Whenever the tassels and blue thread prompt Israel to remember God's commandments, they should also recall their liberation from slavery and obey out of deep gratitude for his deliverance.

THEOLOGICAL FOCUS

The exegetical idea (The requirement of placing tassels on garments provides Israel with a tangible reminder to obey God and to not follow their own desires) leads to this theological focus: *Remembering what God has commanded is crucial to the life of faith*. Physical symbols of some higher purpose are ubiquitous in the human experience. We often need "physical reminders of matters of spiritual importance" (Cole 2000, 255). On a secular level, one may think of a country's flag or coat of arms. In more explicitly religious contexts, a crucifix or an *ichthys* affixed to a car bumper can serve as means of recalling one's essential identity. Of course symbols can lose their significance and become mere ornamentation, but when properly used they can prompt reflection and reorientation (Sprinkle 2015, 281). Memory of God and his acts should prompt a humble response of obedience from those who claim to be his people.

The theme of memory and the danger of forgetfulness is crucial to Moses's instructions to Israel in Deuteronomy 6–11. Moses anticipates a coming time in which Israel will live in a fruitful land, have peace from their enemies, and begin to think that they deserve all of this based on their own works and merits. The antidote to this self-interested amnesia is memory (Schnittjer 2006, 486). It begins with the instructions in Deuteronomy 6:7–12 to teach the children the Lord's commandments and to never forget that he rescued them from slavery and oppression. Israel is to remember that they defeated their enemies not through their own strength but because God was faithful to his covenant promises that he made with their forefathers (Deut. 7:7–8). Similarly, the prosperity of the Promised Land should prompt Israel to remember that God provided for them in the wilderness. They would eat from the bounty of the land only because God had humbled them in the wilderness, showed them his care through the provision of manna, and demonstrated that life comes from obeying every word that comes from his mouth (Deut. 8:2–3). Finally, Israel is to remember they were reliant on God's grace to restore his relationship with them because they were a "stiff-necked people" (Deut. 9:4–6). Even with the prompting of the tassels and blue thread, Israel's future experiences in the wilderness reveal the gap between what a holy God requires and sinful Israel's behavior.

In the New Testament, we can view the institution of the Lord's Supper as a symbol that prompts memory and obedience. As Jesus's interpretation of the Passover meal, it already contains resonances that stretch back through the entire story of Scripture. Paul gives his instructions for celebrating it in 1 Corinthians 11 in the context of a church that was not living out the reality of what the symbols intended to proclaim. Instead, factions and class distinctions created divisions, even when partaking in the symbol that announced Christ's salvific death for all people. Paul seeks to reorient their perspective by reminding them that the bread and wine reflect the body and blood of Christ. In partaking, believers announce, or recall, his death until he returns (1 Cor. 11:26). This act of remembering should encourage reorientation as the celebrant becomes freshly aware of what is accomplished through the death and resurrection of Christ: forgiveness of sin, bridging barriers between God and humanity, and the restoration of all who call upon the name of Christ. Participation in that symbol prompts believers to remember the new life they have in Christ. Even if the elements of the Lord's Supper are humble cracker squares and juice, the reality that they evoke should inspire awe, reverence, and a commitment to act in a way that shows remembrance of Jesus's sacrificial death and resurrection.

PREACHING AND TEACHING STRATEGIES

Exegetical and Theological Significance

Fresh from the consequences and judgment at the end of Numbers 14, the people have now had God's promises renewed for the future. They have also just been told about forgiveness and unforgiveness for unintentional and intentional sins, respectively. Given that there is mercy for sins that are not committed with a high hand, how seriously do the Israelites need to take the commands of God? This passage provides the answer to this question: obeying God's commands and being holy is a matter of life and death. Given the stakes, their lives depended on remembering God's commands so that they could obey them.

The significance of the tassels was not intrinsic (although they were designed with symbolic elements). In fact, the point of the tassels was two steps removed from the core intention of God. The tassels were visible reminders of God's commandments. They were not an end in themselves, but a means to remembering the words of the Lord. Thus, it was the commandments—not the tassels—that were truly important. Furthermore, it was not even the bare memory of the commandments that sufficed—it was *putting them into practice*.

Israel did not fulfill the intention of the tassels simply by putting them on their garments, but neither did they fulfill God's design by merely memorizing the words of his commandments. God's intention was only fulfilled when the people saw the tassels, were reminded of God's word, and then obeyed the Holy One of Israel. God's law gave them instructions for what they ought to do and what they ought not to do, and both positive prescriptions and negative proscriptions were to be obeyed by his people.

Preaching Idea
"Thy word have I hid in mine heart, that I might not sin against thee" (Ps. 119:11 KJV).

Contemporary Connections

What does it mean?
What does it mean that, "Thy word have I hid in mine heart, that I might not sin against thee"? Psalm 119:11 represents the internalized fulfillment of Numbers 15:37–41. The tassel-reminders were only as good as one's knowledge

of God's commandments, and this knowledge was only as good as one's willingness to obey. The point was never the clothing, but rather the action of remembering, heeding, and doing God's will.

"Hiding" God's Word in our heart does not mean that it cannot be found. It means that God's Word is treasured in our hearts; it is kept safe and protected. The tassels were like the X that marked the spot, pointing beyond themselves to the priceless bounty.

In talking about the importance of his commandments, God instructed the Israelites to "Tie them as symbols on your hands and bind them on your foreheads. Write them on the doorframes of your houses and on your gates" (Deut. 6:8–9). Once again, these symbols were useless and ineffective without heartfelt obedience. Jesus excoriated some religious leaders because "Everything they do is done for people to see: They make their phylacteries wide and the tassels on their garments long" (Matt. 23:5). It is always a danger that we will take good things with real spiritual value and twist them into lifeless rituals or means for enflaming our own vanity. The tassels should engender humility, gratitude, love, and holy obedience.

Is it true?
Is it true that we can hide God's Word in our hearts, and that treasuring his Word can keep us from sinning against him? Two verses before Psalm 119:11, the psalmist writes: "How can a young person stay on the path of purity? By living according to your word" (Ps. 119:9 NIV). Even the young and inexperienced can live a life of holy purity if they live according to the Word of the Lord. Some religious leaders could abuse and pervert the intention of the tassels and phylacteries, but that does not mean that they were not given for good purposes or that they cannot be used well. Knowing the Word of the Lord is essential for obedience, and reminders of God's commandments point us back to his truth.

Now what?
What does it look like today to hide God's Word in our heart so that we do not sin against him? Christians do not have to sew tassels on to their garments, but they do need to remember God's Word. It may be worthwhile to experiment with things that remind us of the things we ought to be doing to honor the Lord. Some people get tattoos of Bible verses. Years ago, one trend in many evangelical churches was for people to wear "What Would Jesus Do?" bracelets. Tattoos and bracelets—like tassels and phylacteries—are utterly useless, however, unless they help spark a proper response to God's truth.

In generations past, Scripture memorization seems to have been a more frequent part of Christian practice. Even with digital copies of the Bible with easy access and search capabilities, you have to know what you're looking for; there is no replacement for actually knowing the Word of God. The goal is obediently walking with the Lord, but Scripture is a means of teaching us what pleases God. We need to learn the Scriptures.

One of the most frightening rebukes given by Jesus is directed toward experts in the Scriptures. Jesus said to them, "You study the Scriptures diligently because you think that in them you have eternal life. These are the very Scriptures that testify about me, yet you refuse to come to me to have life" (John 5:39–40 NIV). Although there are not too many people of whom we can truly say, "You study the Scriptures diligently," we should notice that studying the Bible and knowing Jesus are not the same thing.

Perhaps the clearest and most succinct answer to the "Now what?" question is found in the book of James. This is what we need to do: "Do not merely listen to the word, and so deceive yourselves. Do what it says" (James 1:22 NIV).

Creativity in Presentation
From tying strings to fingers, to writing reminder notes on our hands, to setting alarms on our devices, we all recognize the importance of

remembering. In oral cultures, stories and information are usually organized with verbal tricks that help link one detail to the next. Memory devices are essential. Giving examples of such aids can be instructive but showing a prayer shawl or real garment tassels can help provide context for this passage.

On my desk, I (Steve) have a thimble that I bought in Dubai when I was a guest lecturer at Gulf Theological Seminary. It reminds me of many things, but one purpose is that it is supposed to serve as a reminder to pray. Even ordinary things can be invested with significance as memory aids: for example, the thimble could be a button, but serve the same purpose. We can set a special time of the day to turn our memories. Seeing the moon in the night sky can bring certain things to mind. The possibilities are endless.

The danger, however, is that we become like the religious authorities whom Jesus castigated, where we have the symbol but not the heart and soul of what is symbolized. I remember a game show years ago, where in one segment contestants were asked to describe things in various rooms in their house. For example, the host may have asked something like, "How many plants are on top of your fridge?" or "What is the saying on the poster in the basement?" In the evangelical community, there may be lots of people who have Bible verses in their homes on plaques, posters, cards, calendars, or cross-stitched pictures. Some have chalk boards where they chalk Bible verses and then change them every so often. Ask the congregation: "How many of you remember the verses that you have displayed around your home?" It is important to not only display the verses or have memory-aiding symbols, but to know God's Word and pay attention to it. Then, we are to do what it says.

Depending on space, congregation size, and other factors, the preacher could possibly ask people to bring in some of the Bible verses they have displayed around their home. This could either be done the week before—without telling people the point of the message—or the week after, when people have been encouraged to make sure the words are not merely displayed on the artistic medium but are rooted deeply in their hearts.

A helpful thought for approaching this passage is:

- Visible reminders help God's people remember what he has done and what he calls them to do (15:37–41).

DISCUSSION QUESTIONS

1. Why do people need memory aids to help them to recall God's instructions? What are some that could work for believers today?

2. How can believers combat the possibility that such memory aids will lose their significance as they fade into the background of our routines?

Numbers 16:1–35

EXEGETICAL IDEA
Dissatisfaction with their allotted roles fuels some of Israel's leaders to rebel against God by attempting to undermine Moses and Aaron.

THEOLOGICAL FOCUS
Jealousy and envy at what God has given others can motivate rebellion against God.

PREACHING IDEA
Pastors are not Moses, and Christians must not act like Korah, Dathan, and Abiram.

PREACHING POINTERS
Even this far removed from the events described in this passage, it is difficult to read this account without feeling the stress of the situation. These accusations against Moses are incredibly unfair. Those who rise up against Moses slander him, make false accusations, and rebel against God. The very ones who refused Moses's pleading and God's commands are now blaming Moses for the outcome of their own sinful failure. It is rare to find so much hypocrisy and intransigence.

Faced with this onslaught, Moses placed himself in the hands of the Lord, and the Lord defended and vindicated him. The rebellion was crushed by a supernatural act of God (for which Moses is also blamed in the next section). Today, no pastor or Christian leader has the role or authority of Moses, but this passage does serve as a strong warning against rebelling against the authorities that have been instituted by God. Every one of us needs to guard our attitudes and hearts. It is easy to be willfully blind to our own sin, as well as willfully blind to the plan of God in appointing certain people to the offices that they hold. Pastors need to remember that they are not in the position of Moses, and Christians who are members of a church must not act like Korah, Dathan, and Abiram.

REBELLIONS IN THE WILDERNESS (16:1–35)

LITERARY STRUCTURE AND THEMES

Numbers 16:1–35 makes a sharp transition away from legal material and back into dramatic narrative. After a brief pause to discuss issues of sacrifice, sin, and remembrance (15:1–41), this passage thrusts the reader back into the maelstrom of Israel's rebellion and God's response.[1] Although there is no temporal marker in 16:1–35, its placement suggests that these events took place following Israel's disobedience and refusal to go up to the Promised Land in chapters 13–14 (Allen 2012, 243). This sets it during an indeterminate time of Israel's period of wandering in the wilderness. One can easily imagine how the difficulties of this generation-long period of punishment could prompt even more grumbling.

Moses deals with complaints from multiple directions throughout 16:1–35, which makes it difficult to determine a structural breakdown.[2] The different confrontations present Moses with a game of rebellion-whack-a-mole. The simplest approach is to break this narrative into its constituent scenes: First, 16:1–11 details the initial complaints from Korah, Dathan, Abiram, and other rebels, along with Moses's first response to Korah. Next, 16:12–15 provides the interaction between Moses and the Reubenites led by Dathan and Abiram. Then, 16:16–19 initiates Korah's challenge to Moses and Aaron's authority. Finally, 16:20–35 reveals God's judgment upon the rebels.

The overarching theme is again dissatisfaction with Moses and Aaron's leadership, and by extension with God himself. Underneath that, two lines of complaint stick out, generated by different antagonists. The first is the argument that Aaron and Moses are inappropriately elevating themselves above the rest of the Israelite community (16:3). In fact, this is the first of three consecutive passages (16:1–35, 36–50; 17:1–13) that address Aaron's standing within the community. This complaint echoes Aaron and Miriam's earlier grumbling against Moses in Numbers 12. The second complaint is that Moses has not fulfilled his promise to bring Israel into its new homeland (16:13–14). Reubenites named Dathan and Abiram spearhead this critique.

- *The Initial Complaints (16:1–11)*
- *Moses's Address to Dathan and Abiram (16:12–15)*
- *Korah's Trial by Censer (16:16–19)*
- *God's Judgment on the Rebels (16:20–35)*

---

[1] If Numbers 15 is a pause in the storm, in this chapter "the 'hurricane' of rebellion slams back with climactic force" (Gane 2004, 633).

[2] Unsurprisingly, critical scholarship views this as a composite text, weaving together multiple stages of redaction throughout a complex history of transmission. A standard view is that this chapter combines three different rebellion stories: 1) Dathan and Abiram, 2) the 250 chieftains, and 3) the Levites personified by Korah. The blending then reflects issues related to the status of the priests from a much later era in Israel's history (Jeon 2015, 381–83). It is interesting that some biblical texts refer to the fate of Dathan and Abiram without mentioning Korah (Deut. 11:6; Ps. 106:17). However, it is possible to view these variations as part of the narrative's intent (Cole 2000, 259 note 253). In its present form, the text offers a reasonably coherent narrative in which Moses and Aaron are simultaneously challenged on multiple fronts. The difficulties in the text mirror the confusion of the situation.

EXPOSITION

This passage reveals that Israel's grumbling spirit was not quenched by the punishment handed down in Numbers 14. Israel refuses to be chastened and spurred on by various leaders finds new avenues of complaint. This text traces how dissatisfaction with their allotted roles fuels some of Israel's leaders to rebel against God by attempting to undermine Moses and Aaron.

The Initial Complaints (16:1–11)

16:1. The narrative begins with the list of complainants. The first is Korah, whose lineage is given for three generations, confirming his Levitical heritage. He is identified as a Kohathite, the clan given the responsibility to carry the Tabernacle furnishings (Num. 4:1–20). This sacred responsibility was not sufficient for Korah's sense of self-worth. The other conspirators are Reubenites: Dathan, Abiram, and On.[3] It is possible that the Reubenites sought to restore their status as the firstborn tribe, which Reuben's actions caused his descendants to forfeit (cf. Gen 49:3–4; Ashley 1993, 303; Cole 2000, 262). However, the text is silent on their motivation.

TRANSLATION ANALYSIS

Numbers 16:1 begins with the verb וַיִּקַּח, with Korah and the coconspirators as the subject. This looks like the typical form of the root לקח "to take." The difficulty is that there is no direct object. Some English versions supply one from context. The ESV and NET say that Korah and the others "took men," while the NASB has "took action." The NIV takes another approach and reads an otherwise unattested root יקח, which it vocalizes differently than the form in MT and translates "became insolent" by comparison to an Arabic root. Either solution is appropriate.

16:2. In addition to Korah and the rest, 250 men of significant status join the rebellion. They are first identified as "chiefs of the congregation" (ESV). The term נְשִׂיאֵי ("chiefs") is also used to describe those assigned to help Moses with the census in 1:16. The final phrase of 16:2 confirms their stature, calling them "famous men" (NET).[4] Taken together, 16:1–2 establishes the seriousness of the situation. Moses's authority has been challenged before by the general grumbling of the community and by the specific complaint of his brother and sister. However, on this occasion, figures of repute are challenging him, with the support of other unnamed leaders. As a collective, these men are "humanly speaking, qualified to run the nation," laying the groundwork for a potentially effective coup (Gane 2004, 634).

16:3. The complainants now present their initial grievance. They accuse Moses and Aaron of having gone "too far" (רַב־לָכֶם) and exalting themselves over the rest of the Israelites.[5] They justify their attack by declaring "all in the congregation are holy, every one of them" (ESV) and that God is among them. As in Numbers 12, this line of attack is especially pernicious since it contains kernels of truth distorted to serve the conspirators' ends. It comes right after the law of tassels on garments in 15:37–41, which were to be a reminder of the holiness God required from all Israelites. Further, in Exodus 19:6, God declares that all Israel will be a "holy nation" if they follow God's commandments and decrees. Also, the Levites as a group are set aside for service at the tabernacle (Num. 8:5–22). Given this context, Korah and his co-conspirators wonder:

---

3   On is not mentioned again, so his fate is unknown.
4   The underlying Hebrew is אַנְשֵׁי־שֵׁם, literally translated as "men of name." As in English, this can refer to one's reputation or status.
5   The expression רַב־לָכֶם is literally "much for you." In context it clearly refers to exceeding the scope of one's allotted authority.

Why should Moses and Aaron stand apart from the rest of the community?

In response, at least two answers present themselves. The first is simply that God chose Moses and Aaron and sanctified them for the roles that they play (Stubbs 2009, 144). Moses has been set apart since the burning bush in Exodus 3, and his special status was confirmed in Numbers 12:8 when God declares that he speaks with him face to face. Further, no Levites other than Aaron and his sons went through the ordination rites of Leviticus 8, which set them apart for divine service. God alone determines the degrees of holiness necessary to approach him.

Secondly, the motivations of Korah and the others are questionable. It is unlikely Korah really intended to accord the same level of holiness to each Israelite and abolish the prerogatives of the Levites. Rather, he found an argument that could garner support for his campaign to supplant Aaron. Moses later attributes Korah's complaint to envy and a desire to claim the priesthood (16:9–10). Korah is an "archetypal heretic," who speaks just enough theological truth to serve his own ends (Wenham 2008, 150). He resembles a dishonest populist who claims to act on behalf of the community while looking to enhance his own position.

16:4–7. Following Korah's charge, Moses responds with two speeches. In the first, Moses proposes a challenge to see who is holy enough to approach God. He begins by falling on his face (16:4), a gesture of intercession where he places himself between the congregation and God's wrath (Olson 1996, 103). In this way, Moses recognizes that Korah's rebellion is first and foremost against God. He then addresses Korah and his followers, declaring that on the following day God will adjudicate their dispute (16:5). He instructs Korah and his followers to take censers and burn incense to YHWH. He declares that whichever offering God accepts will reveal who is holy before YHWH (16:6–7). This specific test is fitting since it is a priestly responsibility, the status that the rebels appear to desire (Cole 2000, 263). It should also remind them of the deadly fate of Aaron's sons Nadab and Abihu who offered incense with unauthorized fire in Leviticus 10:1–2 (Gane 2004, 634).[6] Moses ends this first speech with a poetic flourish, accusing the Levites (led by Korah) of going "too far." He inverts Korah's initial accusation in 16:3 and applies it to the rebels.

16:8–10. In his second response, Moses reframes Korah's challenge to expose its underlying motivations. He asks rhetorically if the Levitical status of being set apart from the congregation of Israel, being brought near the divine presence by God, and helping their fellow Israelites worship is "too small a thing for you" (ESV). The same rhetorical question continues into 16:10, in which Moses highlights that Korah shares this elevated status with "all your brothers, the sons of Levi" (16:10). That is, are the status and responsibilities that God has already given Korah and the rest of his compatriots not sufficient? The target of Korah's ambition is expressed in 16:10b in another rhetorical question: "Do you now seek the priesthood also?" (NET). Serving Israel in the manner God decreed for his Levitical clan is apparently insufficient and he seeks to supplant Aaron. Like the situation in Numbers 12, Korah and his followers focus more on what they lack compared to Moses and Aaron than on what God has graciously given them.

16:11. This scene concludes as Moses declares that "You and all of your company have

---

[6] That passage along with Leviticus 16:12 are the only other places where the word translated "censer" (מַחְתָּה) refers to an instrument used to offer incense. It appears that these implements belonged to the individuals in question, since it is hard to imagine the wilderness sanctuary having 250 censers for priestly use (Ashley 1993, 307).

assembled together against the LORD" (NET). This gets at the heart of the issue. By themselves, Aaron and Moses are of no great import. However, since God has clearly and visibly given them their roles, Korah's rebellion challenges the "theocratic leadership of the community" (Gane 2004, 634). Framing it this way also rejects Korah's claim in 16:3 that Moses and Aaron have gone "too far" in elevating themselves over the rest of Israel. Instead, Korah and his followers reject God's intentions.

Moses's Address to Dathan and Abiram (16:12–15)

16:12. Moses now moves to address the Reubenites led by Dathan and Abiram. In a gesture of immense disrespect, Dathan and Abiram declare that they will not come up to meet with Moses, presumably referring to the location where he is dealing with Korah's complaint (Wenham 2008, 152).[7] Their refusal to "go up" is ironic, given their eventual fate (Magonet 1982, 18).

16:13–14. Dathan and Abiram launch into their rendition of Israel's typical complaints. They steal the format of Moses's response in 16:8–11 and frame their objections as a rhetorical question. They ask Moses if it is such "a small thing" (16:13a ESV, NET) to take Israel out of a land "flowing with milk and honey" (Egypt!) and lead it to its doom in the wilderness—and that he must also exalt himself as a tyrant. In other words, Dathan and Abiram level at Moses the same charge—that he seeks power and privilege—that he brought against Korah. Dathan and Abiram then declare that Moses has not brought Israel into a new land "flowing with milk and honey" nor given Israel its promised inheritance (16:14). There is just enough surface truth here mixed with bad faith interpretation to be maximally infuriating. As slaves, the Israelites did not enjoy the "milk and honey" of Egypt but rather endured grueling labor. Further, the reason why Israel is not currently living in the "milk and honey" of the Promised Land is that they rejected the opportunity to trust God and enter Canaan in the preceding narrative! Dathan and Abiram also accuse Moses of deliberate deception via another rhetorical question, asking "will you gouge out the eyes of these men?" (16:14b). This is roughly equivalent to the modern idiom "pull the wool over their eyes."[8]

16:15. Unsurprisingly, Moses is furious. He becomes an "anti-intercessor" for Dathan and Abiram (Gane 2004, 635). Whereas he frequently stands between sinful Israel and God's wrath, this personal accusation prompts him to ask God to reject their offerings (מִנְחָתָם). This word typically refers to cereal/grain offerings but here appears to have a more general meaning, requesting that God not find favor with any of their sacrificial gifts (Milgrom 1990, 134). Moses defends himself against this slander in 16:15b by declaring that he has not taken a single donkey from them, nor done any harm to any one of them. Since Moses has not abused his authority, YHWH should look upon this request favorably.

Korah's Trial by Censer (16:16–19)

16:16–17. Following Dathan and Abiram's rejection, the text returns to the challenge from

---

7   It is possible that Dathan and Abiram are trying to keep some physical and metaphorical distance between themselves and Korah. Perhaps they are happy enough to latch onto his complaint but have their own agenda in mind (Wenham 2008, 152). Their shared fate suggests that God does not accept such pretexts.

8   It bears noting that gouging out eyes is attested as a punishment for one's enemies (Judg. 16:21; 1 Sam. 11:2; 2 Kings 25:7) so it is possible to read this verse as an expression of fear of Moses's retribution (Gane 2004, 635). However, in this specific context, Dathan and Abiram's focus is on Moses's apparent failure to deliver on what he had promised which fits best with an idiomatic reading of the expression.

Korah and the other leaders of Israel. This section enacts Moses's proposed challenge from 16:6–7, summoning Korah and his followers to appear before YHWH on the next day. The syntax of 16:17 is convoluted and repetitive but the basic idea is clear. Moses instructs Korah and his companions, including the 250 unnamed leaders, to prepare to offer incense to God with their censers. In 16:17b, Moses explicitly calls Korah and Aaron to prepare their censers as well. Aaron thus stands alone against a challenger from the Levitical ranks, along with 250 other aggrieved leaders.

16:18–19. Moses and Aaron confront their opposition at "the entrance of the Tent of Meeting" (פֶּתַח אֹהֶל מוֹעֵד). This is the place where Aaron and his sons received their divine investiture (Lev. 8:33, 35; 10:7) and where Moses summoned Israel to attend Aaron's ordination (Lev. 8:3–4). By conducting the challenge here, "Moses asserts the legitimacy of his power, and Aaron his right to the priesthood" (Mirguet 2008, 320). In response, Korah assembles the "whole congregation" (כָּל־הָעֵדָה) against them, perhaps seeking to demonstrate that all Israel is holy enough to be in this space (cf. Num. 16:3).[9] The loyalties of the Israelites outside of the known rebels are undetermined, but this suggests that Korah's appeals have found a receptive audience. As the players take their places, 16:19b announces that the glory of YHWH appeared to the whole community. This dramatically raises the stakes of the confrontation.

God's Judgment on the Rebels (16:20–35)
16:20–21. When God appears, he speaks directly to Moses and Aaron, commanding them to "separate yourselves from among this congregation that I may consume them in a moment" (16:21 ESV). This places Korah's rebellion on par with the idolatry of the golden calf (Exodus 32) and Israel's refusal to go up to the Promised Land (Numbers 14). On these occasions, Israel's behavior provokes God to announce devastating judgment.

16:22. Moses and Aaron take up the intercessory role and fall on their faces before pleading with God to relent. They address YHWH as "the God of the spirits of all flesh" (ESV), which emphasizes his authority over all living creatures, "especially the humanity whose lives were suspended over the fulcrum of life and death" (Cole 2000, 266). Moses and Aaron recognize that Israel's very existence hangs in the balance. Their response must begin by recognizing God's supremacy over his people. They then try to isolate Korah from the rest of the Israelite community, asking, "shall one man sin, and will you be angry with all the congregation?" (ESV). This somewhat underplays the situation since clearly Korah is not the only one at fault. However, by focusing on Korah, Moses and Aaron ask God to spare the rest of the congregation, appealing to his mercy and grace (cf. Num. 14:17–20).

16:23–24. God's response indicates that he accepts Moses and Aaron's intercession. Dealing with such changes of divine intention is challenging, but it is reasonable to think that God foreknew that Moses and Aaron would intercede once his initial declaration afforded them that opportunity (Allen 2012, 251). YHWH does not destroy the entire congregation but separates out the ringleaders. To that end, he instructs Moses to tell the Israelites to move away from the dwellings of Korah, Dathan, and Abiram. Fascinatingly, the verbal root used for

---

9 The Hebrew word עֵדָה ("congregation") serves two different functions in this passage. In 16:5–6, 11, 16, it refers to Korah and his associates, usually marked with a possessive pronominal suffix (i.e. "your congregation"). When it appears without that pronominal suffix, it refers to the whole community of Israel (16:2–3, 9, 19, 21, 24, 26, 33; Ashley 1993, 313).

this instruction (*niphal* of עלה) is the same one found in 16:12, 14 for Dathan and Abiram's refusal to meet with Moses. This nuance cannot be brought into English, but it reflects a wordplay in which Dathan and Abiram's refusal to "go up" now prompts Moses's command for Israel to "go away" from them.

TRANSLATION ANALYSIS
English translations obscure an issue in 16:24. The word מִשְׁכָּן is used to refer to the place where the conspirators live. It is strange that it is singular given all three of the ringleaders are mentioned. Many English translations simply pluralize it: "tents" (NIV), "dwellings" (NASB), "homes" (NET). One suggestion is that מִשְׁכָּן refers to the general area in which these individuals lived (Magonet 1982, 21). It is also possible that it serves a narrative function to relink Korah with Dathan and Abiram, viewing their complaints as part of the same rebellion (Ashley 1993, 317). Another issue is that מִשְׁכָּן in the singular usually refers to the tabernacle of God. One suggestion is that מִשְׁכָּן is being used sarcastically to suggest that the rebels have set up their own rival place of worship (Allen 2012, 251). Another is that this word can be used for private dwellings, though that is rare (cf. Num. 24:5; Levine 1993, 416).

16:25–26. For judgment to unfold, there is a shift in location. Moses, along with an unspecified group of elders (presumably those still loyal to him), leave the Tent of the Meeting and go to the geographical heart of the rebellion. This puts an end to Dathan and Abiram's attempted separation. Once there, Moses repeats God's command for the rest of the Israelites to leave the vicinity. He supplements it in 16:26 with an instruction not to touch anything belonging to the rebels. Their wickedness carries a degree of contagion that could render the other Israelites impure and subject them to the same fate (Cole 2000, 267).

16:27–30. As the rest of the Israelites back away from the scene, Dathan and Abiram along with their families come out to face Moses. Presumably Korah is there as well (cf. 16:32). Moses then announces a test to confirm the legitimacy of his position. Moses does this to prove that he has not acted "of my own will" (16:28b NET). He seeks to prove that "God had directed him and given him words to speak" (Cole 2000, 268). The test is simple in conception but stunning in effect. If nothing happens and the rebels simply die of natural causes at a future time, then Moses does not speak for God (16:29). However, if God creates "something totally new" (16:30a NIV), and the earth opens up and drags the rebels down to Sheol, that proves that Moses speaks for God. The verb for create is בָּרָא, the same as in Genesis 1:1, and it is the province of God alone. This rebellion is so egregious that it prompts the Creator to use his creative powers for destruction (Gane 2004, 635).

> **Sheol**
> Sheol in the Old Testament represents the realm of the dead. It is a place where people experience "some sort of shadowy existence in the afterlife" (Sprinkle 2015, 284). It is not always a place of judgment, but Isaiah 14:11–15 conceives of it as a fitting destiny for an unnamed tyrant. Being drawn down there while still living reflects an unimaginably horrific fate. Also pertinent to this passage are places where Sheol is personified as an insatiable monster that opens its mouth to devour (Prov. 1:12; 27:20; 30:16; Isa. 5:14; Hab. 2:5). The fate of Korah and the other rebels fits this image-world.

16:31–33. The text then enacts the judgment that Moses announced. The ground splits open and everyone and everything associated with Korah falls to its doom. Dathan and Abiram are not mentioned by name, but biblical tradition confirms that they suffer the same fate (Deut. 11:6; Ps. 106:17). The imagery here is terrifying. There is something cinematic in the picture of the earth opening up and dragging people down to destruction.[10] The swift and horrifying nature of the judgment confirms the seriousness of the offense. The judgment levied upon the whole of the first generation in Numbers 14 was heavy enough, but at least those condemned could live out their allotted lifespans. Here, Korah's attempt to seize higher office and Dathan and Abiram's conniving attempts to denigrate Moses's leadership lead to swift and unmistakable judgment. The ones who led Israel against God's consecrated leaders face the reality of divine wrath.

Household Punishment

The revelation that the ringleaders' households suffer the same fate is difficult to reconcile with modern notions of individual responsibility. However, in ancient Israel, the extended family (or "house of the father") was an essential unit of collective identity (Bendor 1996, 47). On multiple occasions, we see that this group experiences the fate brought upon it by one of its constituent members. The fate of Achan and his family in Joshua 7 is representative. Further, as a counterpart to his mercy, YHWH declares that he visits the iniquity of the father to the third and fourth generation (Exod. 34:7). This is likely a reference to the multigenerational family unit, rather than a sign that God will curse successive generations in turn (Bendor 1996, 50). Although this realization may not still all the qualms that this passage evokes, it does help us to make sense of it in context. The tragedy of rebellion against a holy God is that its consequences can engulf everyone associated with it. Interestingly, Numbers 26:11 declares that the sons of Korah did not die and that his name continued.[11] No explanation is given. Perhaps they separated themselves enough from his rebellion to be spared (Harrison 1990, 319–20), but we cannot say for certain.

16:34–35. The main rebellion concludes with two additional notes. First, appropriately enough, the rest of the Israelite community is terrified. Perhaps this reflects the pangs of guilty consciences, although it could simply be a natural response to the judgment that God has unleashed (Olson 1996, 105). Unfortunately, it will not take long for this fear to turn once again to grumbling (16:41). Secondly, God sends forth fire that consumes the unnamed 250 leaders who supported Korah. This is the same fate that befell Nadab and Abihu but on a much grander scale. Burning unauthorized incense before God results in a form of poetic justice for the offenders.

The Punishment of Korah and the Stoning of Moses and Aaron by Sandro Botticcelli. Public domain.

THEOLOGICAL REFLECTION

The exegetical idea (Dissatisfaction with their allotted role fuels a series of rebellions against God and his anointed leaders) leads to this theological focus: *Jealousy and envy at what God has given others can motivate rebellion against God.*

The theological significance of this passage resembles Numbers 12 and the experience of Aaron and Miriam. Those to whom much has

---

10 I (Joel) have in mind a scene near the end of cinematic version of *The Return of the King* following the destruction of the One Ring when Mordor crumbles and casts Sauron's army down to its doom.
11 Note the attribution of many of the Psalms to the "sons of Korah."

been given envy those who have more. Korah and his followers have significant responsibilities. Only Korah and his clan were responsible for carrying the furniture and utensils of the sanctuary. Meanwhile Dathan, Abiram, and the 250 leaders had status and influence in the community. However, they wanted more. In order to achieve what they perceived to be their rightful position, they were willing to do whatever was necessary, even if that meant distorting God's words. Yes, all the people are holy, and yes, leaders should bring their people to a place where they can flourish, but the rebels use these truths for suspect purposes. The narrative reveals that they have rejected God's clear ordination of Aaron and Moses and substituted a view of leadership based on "power, position, and envious desire for them" (Stubbs 2009, 146).[12]

In her excellent work on deadly vices, Rebecca Konyndyk DeYoung subtitles her chapter on envy as "feeling bitter when others have it better" (Konyndyk DeYoung 2009, 41). This gets at the way in which this sin distorts our thinking so that we are unable to appreciate what we have. Instead, we engage in destructive comparisons that yield only dissatisfaction. In order to "win" at such comparisons, any action can be justified, which has a corrosive effect on all of our relationships, including those with the people of God. In 1 Corinthians 12:12–19, Paul uses the metaphor of the body to discuss spiritual giftedness. He emphasizes that all parts are needed and have significant roles to play, even those that do not receive as much public acclaim as others. Attempting to elevate oneself over the rest of the body means that it fails to function as God intended.

James 3:13–18 shows the contrast between actions rooted in humility versus those rooted in envy. The humble person acts "in the meekness of wisdom" (James 3:13 ESV), which reveals a character "full of mercy and good fruits" (James 3:17 ESV). On the other hand, he warns those with jealousy and ambition in their hearts not to boast and distort the truth (James 3:14). Jealousy and selfishness lead to "disorder and every vile practice" (James 3:16 ESV), which encapsulates the rebellion against God in Numbers 16:1–35 quite well. Korah and his coconspirators were willing to falsely accuse Moses and Aaron of acting out of arrogance and a desire for power, when those motivations more aptly characterize the rebels (Sprinkle 2015, 286). Their actions caused great pain and suffering for themselves and those closest to them.

PREACHING AND TEACHING STRATEGIES

Exegetical and Theological Significance

The tension and frustration in this section is palpable. The opposition that Moses is facing in this scene is simply so incredibly *unfair*. Even from the time of the theophany at the burning bush, Moses did not want the mantle of leadership. When the Spirit filled the seventy elders so that they prophesied, Joshua worried that Moses's unique role may be threatened, but Moses rejoiced to see others filled and empowered by God's Spirit. In fact, Moses longed to see all of God's people in the grip of the Spirit of God. At no point did Moses exalt himself over the people or engage in political strategies to ensure that he was at the top of the hierarchy.

It was God, not Moses, who appointed Aaron to the priesthood. Furthermore, it was God, not Moses, who redeemed the people and brought them out of Egypt. It was Moses who had to intercede for the people when God said he would destroy them for their sin and start again with Moses as the head of a new

---

12   There is a danger here for a congregation to hear a text like this as an attempt to shut down criticism of a church's leadership. Expositors should take great care here not to identify themselves too closely with Moses and Aaron. The spirit of envy lurks within all of us.

nation. Moses supported going into the Promised Land, while others—who likely would have included Korah, Dathan, and Abiram—were against it. Yet, in what must have been one of the most bitter and jaw-dropping "you can't be serious" moments of his life, Moses was accused of failing to bring them into the Promised Land! The total inversion of reality exhibited by the complainants can only be the result of willful blindness. What no doubt added to the pain is that these were leaders in the community, not merely members of the rabble.

Faced with such a completely unfair and wicked rebellion, God defended his appointed leaders. Since God had selected and installed Moses and Aaron into the positions that they occupied, God took care of them through special divine protection and publicly vindicated them. The rebellion against God's specially appointed leaders was actually rebellion against God himself; rejecting Moses and Aaron constituted a rejection of God.

Preaching Idea
Pastors are not Moses, and Christians must not act like Korah, Dathan, and Abiram.

Contemporary Connections

What does it mean?
What does it mean that pastors are not Moses, and that Christians must not act like Korah, Dathan, and Abiram? This preaching idea builds on the continuities and discontinuities between what we find in this passage and what we find in the local church. Pastors do not have the theocratic authority of Moses; they are not the leaders of a nation. They have not ascended to Sinai to receive special covenantal revelation, nor does God speak to them "face to face, as a man speaks to his friend" (Exod. 33:11 ESV). There is a special redemptive-historical context with Moses and Aaron that must be recognized.

Moses and Aaron were also innocent in this affair. However, modern pastors are not always humble and holy. Some pastors are arrogant and authoritarian. They bully their people and try to dominate. Unlike Moses and Aaron, there are pastors who should be removed from office. Not every challenge is illegitimate or rebellious. Sometimes leaders are unfairly attacked, but other times the church has every right to remove a pastor. Pastors must not always believe that they are unfairly persecuted. Sometimes they are, but sometimes they are the ones who are in the wrong.

Members of the church, however, are not always in the right every time they are upset with a church leader. There is likely no pastor with any years of experience who does not know what it is like to be unfairly criticized. As much as Korah, Dathan, and Abiram were grotesquely wrong in their interpretation of reality, they were convinced of the justice of their cause. They likely believed that they were experiencing righteous indignation and anger. The truth, of course, was the opposite, as conclusively proven by the actions of God.

Is it true?
Is it true that pastors are not Moses, and Christians must not act like Korah, Dathan, and Abiram? Even a pastor who happens to be named Moses does not wear the same leadership mantle that was put on this Moses's shoulders. Church leaders do have a proper, God-given sphere of authority, but it is not identical to the domain of authority given to Moses and Aaron.

Believers—including pastors and church leaders—must not have the same attitude as Korah, Dathan, and Abiram. They were grumbling, haughty, bitter, dissatisfied, grasping, malcontented, jealous, and power-hungry. No believer should exemplify such attitudes, nor be motivated to act out of such a spiritual-emotional state.

Unfortunately, this attitude of self-love is not restricted to the time of the wilderness wandering. John had to write about Diotrophes, who loved to be first and would not listen to apostolic authority (3 John 9–10). Paul knew of some who preached Christ out of envy and pride (Phil. 1:15), and he knew the pain of being slandered by those who exalted themselves as super-apostles (2 Cor. 11:1–15). Jesus rebuked the Pharisees for loving honor and power, engaging in religion to be seen by men, and for delighting in their titles and prestige (Matt. 23:5–12).

Now what?
How do we ensure that our attitudes in the new covenant community are pleasing and honoring to the Lord? How can pastors remain humble, and the church be supportive? Wherever attitudes like the ones exhibited by Korah and the others exist, there needs to be repentance, and if actions have been taken which have been damaging, there needs to be confession, reconciliation, and restitution. A solution is to cultivate a habit of gratitude, rooted in the reality that "we are loved already and unconditionally—not because of our moral worthiness, our attractiveness, our worldly achievements—but simply because we are God's children" (Konyndyk DeYoung 2009, 53). Every member of the church is equally a child of God, made in his image. Fulfilling certain roles does not reflect superior standing before God.

When conflicts do arise, these issues are best dealt with in the individual's heart and in smaller settings. Pastors need to remind themselves of their fallibility and dependence on God. Members of the congregation also need to remind themselves of their own fallibility. A humble heart is not going to be found in an oppressive leader, and neither is it going to be found in a rebellious congregant.

Where people have issues with leadership, rather than nurturing bitterness, wallowing in self-pity, puffing oneself up with pride, or gossiping with others, the right thing to do is pray, and then talk with the person with the smallest group possible. Korah should have talked with Moses long before he had slandered Moses to hundreds of community leaders and got them to join his rebellion. A humble person with legitimate concerns is circumspect: a rebellious heart is often loud and public right from the beginning.[13] Search your heart by the light of God's Word and through the power of the Spirit, and humbly address things according to God's revealed wisdom.

Creativity in Presentation
Since most auditorium platforms are not equipped with a large trapdoor, having "Korah" and his followers disappear in judgment is not likely going to be a dramatic possibility. As mentioned in the expositional section above, however, a good cinematic depiction of this type of scene is found in the movie version of *The Return of the King*.

This is a time for being careful in the tone, content, and delivery of the message. Pastors can sometimes be self-righteous and self-vindicating, and the text is not a club to use in ongoing disputes. At the same time, this passage does serve as a strong warning against people who are like Korah and his followers, and in order to be faithful to the text the preacher must set forth the theological principles that are embedded in the narrative. There are pitfalls on the left and right, and wisdom is required to navigate this section in a particular church setting.

Virtually every preacher has a stock of stories they can tell about their experiences with unruly and rebellious congregants. These stories need to be used judiciously and with the utmost care. It is a danger for preachers to present themselves as the heroes of their own

---

13 This is reminiscent of the counsel given for dealing with conflict in Matthew 18. An important challenge for pastors is to cultivate such personal humility and openness that congregants feel comfortable expressing their legitimate concerns privately, rather than fearing that they will be labeled as troublemakers who refuse to submit to authority.

stories. Sharing true stories about the trials that colleagues in other churches have faced may be a safer way of communicating the truths and principles we learn in this passage.

Without being ostentatious or fake, this may also be a time for a church that is experiencing harmonious union to celebrate the grace of God in their midst. The elders and leaders could be brought up after the message, and they can re-affirm their commitment to work together and give each other mutual support. They can ask people in the congregation to please bring issues to their attention, before any gossip or rumors of discontent poison the church. Then, have the church stand in a sign of solidarity and join in prayer for humility for all, as well as love, unity, good will, and a willingness to serve in whatever area God has assigned. Given the disaster with Korah's rebellion, this is a time to foster a spirit of unity that pleases the Lord. Such a display can serve as a stark reminder that pastors are not Moses, and Christians must not act like Korah, Dathan, and Abiram.

A helpful outline for this passage could be:

- Those leading God's people may face unfair challenges and conflict (16:1–15).

- True leaders intercede for their people (16:16–22).

- Rebelling against God's authority yields serious consequences (16:23–35).

DISCUSSION QUESTIONS

1. What parts of the complaints from Korah, Dathan, and Abiram are legitimate? What parts are not?

2. Why do these complaints prompt such a harsh response from Moses?

3. What does the fate of the rebels' families teach us about the unintended consequences of rebellion against God?

4. Where might jealousy be doing its corrosive work in your churches or communities of faith? How can jealousy be turned into humility?

Numbers 16:36–50

EXEGETICAL IDEA
God uses Korah's rebellion to further instruct Israel about his holiness. However, Israel's refusal to learn necessitates intercession to avert God's wrath.

THEOLOGICAL FOCUS
Sinful humanity requires an intercessor to dwell with a holy God.

PREACHING IDEA
Ultimately, there is only one priestly mediator and intercessor, but he is sufficient for all of our needs.

PREACHING POINTERS
Immediately following God's supernatural vindication of Moses and his swallowing up of the rebellion, the people are accusing Moses of murder. Rather than learn their lesson, they actually want to imitate and follow the example of Korah. God is angry and strikes the people with a plague. Ironically, the only way for the people to be saved is for Aaron as high priest to intercede for them. The people rebelled against Moses and Aaron—and in so doing rebelled against the Lord God—and now it is Aaron who will save their lives through priestly intercession.

In this passage we see the incredible blindness and folly of sin, but we also see the grace of God in providing a means for forgiveness. One of the major lessons to learn in this text is that sinners need a priestly mediator and intercessor or they will die. This is not merely an Old Testament principle; it is a typological one that is fulfilled in the high priestly ministry of the Lord Jesus Christ. In Christ, God provides the high priest, covenant mediator, and intercessor that we so desperately need. Those who trust him will be saved and forgiven, but those who refuse him will be irrevocably lost. Ultimately, there is only one priestly mediator and intercessor, but he is sufficient for all of our needs.

A FAILURE TO LEARN: THE AFTERMATH OF KORAH'S REBELLION (16:36–50)

LITERARY STRUCTURE AND THEMES

Numbers 16:36–50[1] comprises the aftermath of the rebellion. It is marked as a separate preaching unit because of the length and complexity of the previous passage. It is also an instructive portrait of the depth of the grumbling spirit within Israel. The structural outline of this passage is straightforward. Numbers 16:36–40 details God's instructions to Eleazar that require him to make the censers of the 250 elders into an object lesson for the rest of the nation. Then, 16:41–50 demonstrates that the grumbling spirit is going to prevent the Israelites from learning it. The second half of the story can be further subdivided to Israel's complaint (16:41–43) and Moses and Aaron's intercession (16:44–50).

Following the stunning display of divine judgment, God takes the opportunity to teach Israel about his holiness. Unfortunately, in keeping with the trajectory of the narratives in Numbers, Israel is unwilling to learn. There is a thematic conflict between the obedience of Eleazar (Aaron's son) to God's command and the behavior of the rest of the congregation. The complaints of the Israelites reveal more sympathy for Korah and his conspirators than recognition of their egregious sin. This requires Moses and Aaron to intercede again and stand between a holy God and sinful Israel. As with 16:1–35, the actions undertaken by Aaron confirm that God has appointed him as high priest.

- *God Teaches a Lesson (16:36–40)*
- *Israel Refuses to Learn (16:41–50)*
  - Israel's Complaint (16:41–43)
  - Moses and Aaron's Intercession (16:44–50)

EXPOSITION

This passage provides a window into the mindset of the rest of the congregation. Although they may have been frightened by the judgment that fell on Korah and the rest, and although God may try to instruct them in the ways of his holiness, the Israelites do not turn toward repentance. Instead, they receive further divine judgment averted only by dramatic intercession from Moses and Aaron. In this text, God uses Korah's rebellion to further instruct Israel about his holiness. However, Israel's refusal to learn necessitates intercession to avert God's wrath.

God Teaches a Lesson (16:36–40)

16:36–37. Through Moses, God commands Eleazar, the son of Aaron, to deal with the censers of those consumed by fiery judgment. Eleazar likely received this job instead of Aaron because of the higher standards of holiness required for the high priest. Along with the censers, Eleazar no doubt encountered the remains of the 250 leaders, invoking the prospect of corpse contamination. It also marks the beginning of the transition from Aaron to Eleazar as the leading priestly figure in Israel, since he inherits his father's position in Numbers 20:28 (Cole 2000, 270). In 16:37, God instructs Eleazar

---

1   Numbers 16:36–50 in English translations corresponds to Numbers 17:1–15 in the Hebrew text. I will use the English versification.

to take the censers from where they had fallen and to scatter the remains of the fire.² There are multiple explanations for why the fire had to be scattered, including it was necessary to prevent the fire from being used for some common purpose because it had been offered to God (Ashley 1993, 324); it had come in contact with the remnants of the dead, raising the probably of corpse contamination for anyone who handled it (Cole 2000, 271); or, like the "strange fire" offered by Nadab and Abihu (Lev. 10:1–2), it was a fire that brought judgment on whoever offered it (Allen 2012, 254). The first explanation agrees best with the declaration that the censers "have become holy" (16:37 NIV).

16:38–39. The holiness of these objects seems strange given that God rejected the offering of the 250 leaders. It is possible that God's fiery judgment purified the censers (Cole 2000, 270). Others posit that the mere act of offering them to God renders them God's property (Levine 1993, 419; Pressler 2017, 150). In any event, their holy nature means that they are only suitable for sanctified use. Through Moses, God instructs Eleazar to take the censers of the "men who sinned at the cost of their lives" (16:38 ESV) and hammer them into a bronze plating to cover the altar in the courtyard of the tabernacle. Eleazar did exactly as God commanded (16:39). His work memorializes the "utter folly" of the rebels (Allen 2012, 254), while also preserving the implements that God now declares holy. The text does not discuss how this bronze plating would fit with the original bronze covering mentioned in Exodus 27:2 and 38:2. The simplest explanation is that it was added on top via an unspecified procedure (Ashley 1993, 325–36; Cole 2000, 270; Milgrom 1990, 140).

16:40. The plating is a reminder to the children of Israel that no one outside the Aaronic priesthood is to offer incense before God. The word used to identify the non-Aaronic Israelites is זָר, which is often applied to non-Israelite foreigners. As mentioned previously, in legal material it refers to Israelites who are unauthorized for elements of divine service (cf. Num. 1:51; 3:10, 38). The fact that זָר is further clarified as "not of the descendants of Aaron" (ESV) points to its very restrictive sense in this case (Milgrom 1990, 140). The plating on the altar is thus a tangible symbol of the dangers of transgressing God's arrangements. It is an object lesson like the tassels on garments (15:37–41), Aaron's staff (17:10), or the bronze serpent (21:4–9).

Israel Refuses to Learn (16:41–50)

Israel's Complaint (16:41–43)
16:41. Unsurprisingly, Israel's first response is not to heed the lesson. Instead, on the next day they grumble against Moses and Aaron. This verse begins with the verbal root I-לון ("to grumble") which is almost exclusively reserved for the Israelite congregation in the wilderness (cf. Exod. 15:24; 16:2, 17:3; Num. 14:2, 29, 36; 16:11). Their specific complaint is about as valid as Dathan and Abiram blaming Moses for not leading Israel into a land of milk and honey. They are upset, declaring, "You killed the people of the LORD" (ESV).³ Fear over the fate of Korah and his associates has swiftly turned to ill-advised complaint. It is perhaps easier to blame Moses and Aaron than to acknowledge the depths of the conspirators' sin. Referring to them as "the people of the LORD" is somewhat ironic, since YHWH himself pronounced the final verdict.

---

2   This probably refers to the coals used to light the incense in the censers (Milgrom 1990, 139).
3   The Hebrew includes the redundant personal pronoun אַתֶּם ("you"). This is a marker of emphasis, demonstrating that the Israelites hold Aaron and Moses responsible for what transpired on the previous day.

A Failure to Learn: The Aftermath of Korah's Rebellion (16:36–50)

16:42–43. As the congregation gathered against Moses and Aaron, possibly looking to put actions behind their grumbling words, their gaze turned to the Tent of Meeting where again God was coming to address the situation.[4] God's presence is invoked through the cloud that rested on top of the sanctuary when Israel was at rest (9:15–23). The appearance of the "glory of the Lord" could be the pillar of fire within the cloud intensifying so that it could be seen in the daylight (Milgrom 1990, 141). Its usual purpose was to signal that God wanted an audience with Moses. Here, it is prominent enough to stop the grumbling of the Israelites while Moses and Aaron approach the entrance to the Tent of Meeting (16:43).

Moses and Aaron's Intercession (16:44–50)

16:44–45. Israel's grumbling spirit prompts yet another threat to its very existence. YHWH addresses Moses and instructs him, "Get away from the midst of this congregation, that I may consume them in a moment" (16:45a ESV). This is almost identical to his command in 16:21 in the middle of Korah's rebellion, changing only the initial imperative.[5] Moses's response in that incident was to preserve the community by isolating Korah, asking God not to destroy the people on account of one man. Here, YHWH's response indicates that the rest of the Israelites are aligned with Korah in God's eyes and are subject to the same judgment. Although the first generation is under a lingering death sentence because of their failure in Numbers 13–14, God threatens immediate destruction that would require him to fulfill his promises to the patriarchs through Moses alone (cf. 14:12). In response, Moses and Aaron fall on their faces (16:45b) as they did in 16:22. Even though the Israelites blamed Moses and Aaron for the fate of the rebels, these leaders still took on their intercessory roles. Consequently, there is hope that God's judgment may be mitigated.

16:46. The manner of Moses and Aaron's intercession is closely connected to Korah's rebellion. Moses instructs Aaron to take his censer, light it with fire from the altar, and burn incense to make atonement for the congregation (16:46a). This is a logical progression from the situation involving Korah and the 250 community leaders. God rejected the offering from their censers since he had set apart Aaron and his sons to be Israel's priests. Now, Aaron properly fulfills the priestly role and uses the implement that had brought wrath upon the rebels to bring mercy upon the rest of the congregation (Allen 2012, 256).

Aaron's intercessory work confirms his position. His censer was not among those turned into a covering for the altar and he is able to access its fire to burn the incense. Again, this contrasts the actions of Korah and his followers who likely tried to burn incense from unauthorized fire (Milgrom 1990, 139). Aaron's actions "make atonement" (כִּפֶּר) for the Israelites. The Hebrew root is the same as that found in the instructions for the Day of Atonement in Leviticus 16. On that day, Aaron performed multiple rituals to cleanse Israel from its accumulated sins. The key purgation activities involved animal sacrifices, but incense was to be burned in the Holy of Holies to permit him to be present with "YHWH's lethal glory" (Gane 2005, 237). Here, the incense itself was sufficient to make intercession for the people and appease God's

---

[4] There is a bit of ambiguity in this verse. Numbers 16:42b begins with "they turned to the Tent of Meeting." The antecedent of the pronoun could be the congregation of Israel, or it could be Moses and Aaron. It is not that important to resolve the issue since the results of the divine theophany are far more significant.

[5] The imperative in 16:45 is הֵרֹמּוּ ("Get away"; ESV, NET) while 16:21 has הִבָּדְלוּ ("Separate yourselves"; ESV, NET). Context indicates that the two are synonymous (Allen 2012, 257).

wrath.⁶ This is unusual, since typically animal sacrifice was required. A plausible suggestion is that Aaron's properly offered incense counteracted the improper incense of Korah and his followers (Ashley 1993, 328). Their attempts to claim the prerogatives of the priesthood led to their deaths, while Aaron's performance of them preserved life.

16:47–48. Another component of Aaron's actions is haste. Aaron "ran" (16:47) into the midst of the congregation. The reason for this is evident. God's judgment in the form of an unspecified but lethal plague had already begun. The word for plague (נֶגֶף) is also found in Exodus 12:13 in the context of God striking down the firstborn of Egypt. Whereas the blood of Passover lambs protected the Israelites from that plague, their own rebellion renders them vulnerable to this one. Only Aaron's quick response to Moses's command averted total destruction. Numbers 16:48 confirms this with the declaration that Aaron "stood between the dead and the living" (ESV). This required him to come in contact with death, which as high priest he was supposed to avoid (Lev. 21:11). However, in these unique circumstances, Aaron disregarded his ritual purity and put himself in between the Israelites and God's wrath (Cole 2000, 272). This urgent priestly intercession put an end to the plague.

16:49–50. The story ends about where it began, with Aaron and Moses at the entrance of the Tent of Meeting. This was the place where all Israel had gathered against them. Now, Aaron returns, having fulfilled the intercessory role of his office. However, things are not the same as they were before. Israel has paid a heavy penalty for its rebellion. Numbers 16:49 lists the death toll from the plague as 14,700, on top of those who died in Korah's rebellion. This story thus follows a similar pattern to other grumbling narratives in Numbers. Israel's sin leads to devastating judgment that is only mitigated by the intercession of a mediating figure (Boda 2009, 95). Israel's failure to learn the lesson about God's holiness comes at a heavy cost, but a measure of mercy is found as God permits his chosen servant to make atonement.

THEOLOGICAL REFLECTION

The exegetical idea (God uses Korah's rebellion to further instruct Israel about his holiness. However, Israel's refusal to learn requires intercession to avert God's wrath) leads to this theological focus: *Sinful humanity requires an intercessor to dwell with a holy God.*

Although Israel had every chance to learn from the errors of Korah and his followers, their propensity to grumble prevailed. They could not get beyond their own fears and instead chose to blame the ones who carried out the will of God. This failure of the Israelites in the wilderness is hardly unique. Throughout the centuries, the people of God have continued to receive lessons about what God requires, yet fail to live them out. Paul captures this tension in Romans 7:14–25 when he describes the war within himself between the desire to delight in God's law and the law of sin. Even though he knows the good he ought to do, he finds himself doing evil instead (7:18–19). The war rages inside of himself with victory accomplished only through Jesus Christ who rescues him from the body of death (7:24). Paul's inner turmoil should encourage believers not to elevate themselves over the Israelites in the wilderness. Just as God's attempt to instruct Israel concerning his holiness fell upon hostile ears, so our own deeply embedded sinful natures can keep us from hearing and following his will.

---

6   Incense burning performs similar functions in other ancient Near Eastern religious contexts. It appeased divine wrath by enhancing the aroma of burning sacrifices that symbolically entered into the nostrils of the deities (Cole 2000, 272; Milgrom 1990, 142).

Given this reality, the example of the rejected intercessor carries great theological weight. The Israelites again rejected Moses and Aaron when the plague broke out so suddenly that there was not even time for them to plead for deliverance. Moses, whom Israel has rejected again and again, still called upon Aaron to intercede for the people. This image of a rejected priestly intercessor recalls the work of Christ, a priest in the order of Melchizedek, whose perfect sacrifice accomplished what even Aaron's could not (Cole 2000, 272). Even though he was God's consecrated representative, Aaron's sinful nature meant that his intercession could not provide lasting cleansing. Instead, Jesus offered himself as a once-for-all sacrifice that made perfect intermediation between God and humanity (Heb. 7:27). Those who acknowledge Christ as Lord have an intercessor who is worthy to stand in the throne room of God and whose blood has purchased people from every nation (Rev. 5:9–10). This is the ultimate hope for those who cannot fully learn and respond to the evidence of God's holiness. Christ our advocate enters a plea on our behalf when we acknowledge that his sacrifice brings us mercy and hope (Gane 2004, 647). Aaron's intercession stopped a plague. Christ's intercession leads to the promise of an existence with no tears, death, crying, or pain (Rev. 21:4).

PREACHING AND TEACHING STRATEGIES

Exegetical and Theological Significance
After the distressing events in 16:1–35, Moses and Aaron would have been exhausted. The amount of discouragement they would have experienced by waking up to face another rebellion is unimaginable. Once again, they are faced with the most outrageously unfair lies: it was God's supernatural, miraculous judgment that had been exhibited, yet the people accuse Moses and Aaron of being the murderers of God's chosen people. Ironically, these "murderers" spare the lives of the Israelites by interceding with God. Mercy, the exodus, and blessings did not change the people's hearts. Sinai, theophany, law, tabernacle, and glory did not change the people's hearts. Even a terrifying divine judgment did not change the people's hearts. How could the people possibly be spared by a holy God?

In an irony of grace, the only reason the people are saved is because the person they are rejecting is actually their God-appointed intercessor, and intercession is efficaciously made on their behalf. Sinners can only be saved through the intercession of God's covenant mediator.

What would have happened to the people if there was not a real high priest who made intercession for them? Without the priest's intercession, the plague could have raged unchecked, and death would have been inescapable. This theological principle is developed across the canon: without a mediator who intercedes, there can be no salvation. Aaron typologically foreshadows the one who will fulfill the role of high priest, mediator, and intercessor. In rich and multifaceted ways, the canonical text prepares us for Christ, and then shows us the glory of his intercessory work as our high priest and covenant mediator. Without the intercession of Christ, there can be no salvation.

Preaching Idea
Ultimately, there is only one priestly mediator and intercessor, but he is sufficient for all of our needs.

Contemporary Connections

What does it mean?
What does it mean that ultimately there is only one priestly mediator and intercessor, but he is sufficient for all of our needs? When Aaron interceded by standing between the Holy One of Israel and this sinful, rebellious people, God checked the outpouring of his wrath and the plague stopped. Aaron's act of priestly mediation saved people from death in this one particular

event. This entire generation, however, was still going to die outside of the Promised Land as a penalty for their sin.

As much as the text witnesses to the goodness, efficacy, and necessity of Aaron's act of intercession, it cries out for a more ultimate and lasting solution. Just like the sacrifices offered on the Day of Atonement could never ultimately atone for sin, the priestly mediation of Aaron was never going to be sufficient for the deepest needs of the people before God. For all of our sin, we need a perfect sacrifice of atonement, a perfect high priest, and perfect intercession.

Christ Jesus is the ultimate priestly mediator and intercessor for God's covenant people. Everything that was pointed forward to by Aaron was fulfilled in the person and work of the incarnate Son of God. It is Christ who stands between the holy God and the sinful people, and it is only through his intercession that we are spared.

Is it true?
Is it true that ultimately there is only one priestly mediator and intercessor, but he is sufficient for all of our needs? This question was answered definitively nearly two thousand years ago by the author of Hebrews: "because Jesus lives forever, he has a permanent priesthood. Therefore he is able to save completely those who come to God through him, because he always lives to intercede for them. Such a high priest truly meets our need—one who is holy, blameless, pure, set apart from sinners, exalted above the heavens" (Heb. 7:24–26 niv).

The point of the phrase "he always lives to intercede for them" is not that Jesus is never doing anything other than interceding: it is that having been resurrected into glorified, eternal life, he will never die, and therefore his intercessory ministry is eternal. Where there is a perfect high priest who lives forever, we never need to worry that one day we will be left without an intercessor before God.

Now what?
Not having taken part in the events in Numbers 16, how do we learn from the principles of this passage? First, make sure you do not have a rebellious, sinful, complaining heart. Second, confess, repent, and humbly look to God for mercy if you are guilty of such sins. Third, recognize the God-ordained system where approaching his throne requires us to have a perfect covenant mediator who intercedes for us. Fourth, thank God for the provision of his Son Jesus Christ, who is the perfect intercessor and high priest. Fifth, since we have such a great high priest, "Let us then approach God's throne of grace with confidence, so that we may receive mercy and find grace to help us in our time of need" (Heb. 4:16). Sixth, let us tell others the good news that there is an atoning sacrifice for sins, a perfect high priest, and one who can bring us to God. There is only *one* mediator and intercessor, but he is the only one we need.

Creativity in Presentation
No one is unaware that there is a great deal of diversity in the musical style and songs that are sung in different churches. Recommending particular songs can only be done in recognition that not every title will suit every local congregation. The themes of this passage in Numbers 16 are themes that songwriters have often drawn on. By engaging in a short exposition of a song's lyrics, the minister can illustrate the meaning of the biblical text, call people to respond in worship, and prepare people to sing the song with the full engagement of their heart, mind, and soul. Although other songs could be used, two that might be reasonably familiar are "Arise, My Soul, Arise" and "Before the Throne of God Above."

Note just these two verses from Charles Wesley's "Arise, My Soul, Arise":

> Arise, my soul, arise;
> Shake off thy guilty fears;
> The bleeding Sacrifice

In thy behalf appears.
Before the throne my Surety stands,
Before the throne my Surety stands;
My name is written on his hands,
My name is written on his hands.

He ever lives above,
For me to intercede,
His all-redeeming love,
His precious blood to plead.
His blood atoned for ev'ry race,
His blood atoned for ev'ry race,
And sprinkles now the throne of grace,
And sprinkles now the throne of grace.[7]

That is a powerful hymnic presentation of the truth that we need Christ as our sacrifice and priestly intercessor. But since Christ is enough, we can arise before God without guilt, shame, or fear.

"Before the Throne of God Above" begins this way:

Before the throne of God above
I have a strong and perfect plea;
a great High Priest whose name is Love,
who ever lives and pleads for me.[8]

The remainder of the song develops and expands on this theme of Christ's great intercessory work on behalf of his people. It rightly applies the glory of these truths on the personal level: Christ pleads *for me*. He is all that I need. He is only one priestly mediator and intercessor, but he is sufficient for all of our needs.

A message on this passage could be divided into these sections:

- God instructs his people as to how they are to worship him (16:36–40).

- A chosen intercessor stands between God's anger and sinful people (16:41–50).

DISCUSSION QUESTIONS

1. Why did the censers of the rebellious leaders have to be collected and made into an overlay for the altar?

2. Why did this rebellion provoke such a harsh response from God?

3. How does Aaron's work of intercession point us forward to Christ?

---

7 Charles Wesley. "Arise, my Soul, Arise." Public Domain, 1742, https://hymnary.org/text/arise_my_soul_arise_shake_off_thy_guilty.
8 Charitie Less Bancroft. "Before the Throne of God Above," Public Domain, 1863, https://hymnary.org/text/before_the_throne_of_god_above_i_have_a_.

Numbers 17:1–13

EXEGETICAL IDEA
God provides a miraculous sign to confirm Aaron's consecrated status and to quell Israel's spirit of rebellion.

THEOLOGICAL FOCUS
Only the one whom God has chosen can mediate between humanity and God.

PREACHING IDEA
The great High Priest is chosen by God, bears spiritual fruit, and makes his followers fruitful in the Spirit.

PREACHING POINTERS
Although the context for this passage is God's response to the unspeakable wickedness of the previous chapter, it is somewhat refreshing. Here, God takes the initiative to settle the matter once and for all. He will not wait for the next wave of rebellious grumbling before he vindicates his chosen priest. This chapter proves that it is God who selects the high priest and it is God who makes him bear spiritual fruit. The miracle of the staff that blossoms and bears almonds points beyond the physical miracle to these spiritual principles. God elects, and then God makes his chosen ones bear fruit.

This principle finds its highest fulfillment in Jesus Christ. He is the great high priest, and the only high priest the church will need both now and through eternity. Not only is Christ maximally fruitful in the spiritual realm—he is so powerful that he makes his followers fruitful too. By the Spirit of God, and in union with Christ, God's children are able to see spiritual fruit grow in their lives. In the same way that Aaron was identified through the fruitfulness of the staff, now Christ's disciples are known by the fruit of their lives. Incredibly, the great high priest is not only chosen by God and bears spiritual fruit, but he is powerful enough to make his followers fruitful in the Spirit.

AARON'S STAFF BLOSSOMS (17:1–13)

LITERARY STRUCTURE AND THEMES

Following Korah's rebellion and the plague that struck the grumbling Israelites, this passage confirms Aaron's status as high priest by peaceful means.[1] Its structure is relatively simple. Numbers 17:1–7 comprises the first scene where God instructs Moses concerning the staffs of each tribe. Moses and the Israelite leaders respond in obedience. The second scene covers 17:8–11 and takes place on the following day, revealing the results of placing the staffs before God. Finally, there is a brief coda in 17:12–13 revealing that this object lesson has not resolved all of Israel's concerns.

This is the third consecutive passage to focus on Aaron's role but the first one in which he and Moses are not facing outright hostility. Instead, God uses the tribal leaders' staffs of office as object lessons. Previous preaching units demonstrated that Aaron was authorized to burn incense before God (16:1–35) and that this gave him the standing to intercede for the whole nation (16:37–50). Now, God performs a miracle that provides visual evidence of Aaron's standing in the community. The express purpose is to stop the grumbling against Moses and Aaron's leadership (17:5, 10). Unfortunately, the grumbling spirit resurfaces when Israel again encounters hardship, although on that occasion the Israelites do not attempt to replace Moses and Aaron (cf. 20:1–13).

- *The Preparation of the Sign (17:1–7)*
- *The Results of the Test (17:8–11)*
- *A Final Coda: The People's Fear (17:12–13)*

EXPOSITION

Throughout biblical narratives, God uses miraculous signs to convey messages or to confirm his authority. The most notable examples are the plagues that gave God's response to Pharaoh's question "Who is the LORD?" (Exod. 5:2). As God multiplied his signs, the arrogant ruler learned the answer to his question (Exod. 7:2–5). In this passage, God again responds to human stubbornness with a sign (Num. 17:10). The sign displays God's power over the natural world and confirms his selection of Aaron, and by extension the entire tribe of Levi, for divine service. It provides yet another rebuttal to Korah's half-truth that all Israel is holy and should have the same rights and prerogatives as Moses and Aaron (Num. 16:3). This preaching unit shows that God provides a miraculous sign to confirm Aaron's consecrated status and to quell Israel's spirit of rebellion.

The Preparation of the Sign (17:1–7)

17:1–3. The passage begins with God addressing Moses and commanding him to take the staffs of office from the leaders of the Israelite tribes. The word staff (מַטֶּה) is found four times in 17:2, making it the focus of the verse. God's instructions increase in specificity through four clauses in 17:2a. Moses is commanded to take staffs, which come from each tribe, from the leaders of those tribes, yielding twelve staffs in all. Presumably Aaron's own staff (17:3) is the thirteenth, so the two Joseph tribes (Ephraim and Manasseh) are represented with their own staffs.

There are a couple of important literary and linguistic features. First, the word for

---

[1] This passage is 17:16–28 in the Hebrew text. I will use the English versification.

"staff" (מַטֶּה) can refer to a physical object as it does here, but it can also be a metonymy for an entire tribe. It means "tribe" eighty-nine times in Numbers alone (Ashley 1993, 331). The test of bringing the staffs before God and seeing which one miraculously blossoms also confirms which tribe God has blessed (Milgrom 1990, 142). Secondly, the expression "each fathers' house" (בֵּית אָב) found in 17:2 (ESV) here carries an atypical meaning. Usually, it refers to individual family groupings of a man, his wife (or wives), children, and servants. However, the context of this verse indicates that it refers to the entire tribe.[2] The presence of the term "leaders" (נָשִׂיא) confirms this. The same word was used to indicate tribal leaders earlier in the book (1:5–15; 2:3–31; 7:12–83; 10:14–27; Ashley 1993, 331). This rare use of "father's house" is necessary because the usual term for a tribe (מַטֶּה) has already been used to refer to the physical staffs. The sign that God is going to perform thus works on the individual level (Aaron and the other tribal leaders) and the corporate level (Levi and the other tribes).

God then commands Moses to write the names of the tribal leaders on their staffs, mentioning Aaron by name as the representative for the tribe of Levi (17:2b–3). This foreshadows the outcome of the sign.

17:4. Moses must then bring the staffs into the Tent of Meeting and place them before the "Testimony" (הָעֵדוּת). This is shorthand for "the Ark of the Testimony" (4:5; 7:84), which houses the tablets of the Decalogue. The staffs are to be placed in the Holy of Holies, in the place most consecrated to God's presence. This imagery suggests placing the staffs in the "lap" of God (Allen 2012, 259).[3]

17:5. God reveals that the proximity to the divine presence will cause one of the staffs to sprout. For the dead wood of the staffs to produce vegetation, God must act miraculously. This will be a sign that God has chosen the individual whose staff blooms. YHWH declares that in this way he will "make to cease from me the grumblings of the people of Israel" (ESV). He also acknowledges that the people grumble against Moses as well, again acknowledging Moses as his appointed spokesman. Although the Israelites have not complained about Moses's leadership in this passage, the memories of Korah's rebellion and the subsequent grumbling of the Israelites are fresh at hand (Milgrom 1990, 144). Perhaps a peaceable demonstration of God's power will be more persuasive than the preceding terrifying acts of judgment. This act is intended to quash further doubt or dissent. The flowering of a long dead piece of wood must surely reflect God's power (Allen 2012, 259).

17:6–7. Moses and the Israelite leaders comply with God's instructions. The repetition of much of the vocabulary in 17:2 in 17:6 makes this clear. The word "staff" (מַטֶּה) is found three times along with the mention of "leaders" (נָשִׂיא) and "fathers' house" (בֵּית אָב). The obedience of the Israelite tribal leaders is worth noting given the recent actions of many of Israel's other leaders, including the 250 who aligned themselves with Korah. The nature of the proposed test may help to reopen the lines of communication. Rather than a competition of incense burning which proved perilous, the tribal leaders simply must surrender their staffs of office for a single night. All of the tribes are thus represented in the most holy presence of God, but God will choose one that bears a special blessing (W'Ehusha 2010, 130).

---

2 The NET and NIV make this explicit in their translation, using "tribe" (NET) or "ancestral tribe" (NIV) in 17:2.
3 This also suggests that Moses has access to the Holy of Holies, which after his death will be restricted to the High Priest on the Day of Atonement. This is in keeping with Moses's special relationship with God, as one with whom God speaks face to face (12:8).

The Results of the Test (17:8–11)

17:8. Moses returns the next day and retrieves the staffs. This verse focuses upon Aaron's staff with four verbs that refer to it sprouting, putting out buds, blossoming, and bearing almonds (Cole 2000, 275). Only the verb "sprout" occurs in 17:5 in the initial announcement of the test. The sequence of verbs slows down the report of God's miracle to emphasize that Aaron's staff is visibly set apart from the others. There is no clear reason why almonds are the vegetation of choice here for Aaron's staff, although some possibilities have been put forward. Almonds mature early in the land's agricultural cycle and are used in Jeremiah 1:11–12 as a metaphor for a watchman (Ashley 1993, 335). Their blossoms are also white, which symbolizes purity before God. Holiness can be connected to life and fruitfulness and so the fruitfulness of Aaron's staff confirms the bestowal of God's holiness (Gane 2004, 644). This miracle may also speak to the function of Aaron and the Levites for the Israelite community. They reflect God's holiness more than any other tribe, and they watched over the community by instructing them in the Torah (Wenham 2008, 157). It may also reflect God's eternal watchfulness over his people from the presence of his sanctuary (Gane 2004, 645). The potential implications of the almonds remain speculative and should not detract from the main point, which is that God has performed a miracle and Aaron's budded staff confirms his calling.

17:9–10. After the other tribal leaders take back their unblossomed staffs, God speaks to Moses again and commands him to return Aaron's staff back to "the Testimony." There, it remains in the Holy of Holies along with the ark containing the stone tablets and a sample of the manna.[4] Moses and Aaron placed the manna there as a reminder of God's provision in the wilderness (Exod. 16:32–35). A shared context of grumbling also links these physical symbols (Cole 2000, 276). Numbers 17:10 declares that Aarons' staff is "to be kept as a sign" (ESV) for those who rebelled against God. The Hebrew actually consists of two nouns and is more literally rendered "for safekeeping, as a sign" (Milgrom 1990, 144). The word for "safekeeping" (מִשְׁמֶרֶת) is also applied to the manna sample (Exod. 16:32–34) and the ashes of the red cow that provide cleansing for corpse contamination (Num. 19:9). These objects illustrate some part of God's holiness and thus merit preservation as a reminder to the Israelites.

The staff is also a sign for the "children of rebellion" (בְּנֵי־מֶרִי) that they have no cause to complain about how God has arranged the Israelite community. The phrase "children of rebellion" is unique to this verse and it is likely a "degrading rhetorical metonym" for the common expression "children of Israel" (Cole 2000, 276). In a way, they lose their status as Israel when they engage in this kind of rebellion. Their allegiance is no longer to God, but to their own spirit of complaint. Preserving Aaron's staff as a memorial should stop the grumbling by reminding the Israelites of the deadly consequences of rebellion. Like those who challenged Moses in Numbers 11 and 14, or Moses and Aaron in Numbers 16, they would be under a sentence of death.

It is fascinating to consider that this sign wound up in a place where it would be visible only to the high priest. Future generations of Israelites would hear the story but never see the sign. It would become an element of faithful devotion to God to accept that Aaron's staff had budded, confirming YHWH's selection of the Aaronic priesthood. Anyone who challenged their position would be contradicting a symbol placed at the heart of Israel's sacred space (Allen 2012, 261).

---

4 Hebrews 9:4 suggests that Aaron's staff was placed inside the ark. Numbers 17 does not specific its exact resting place in the Holy of Holies.

17:11. Moses obeyed these instructions just as he had the first set (17:7). This is seemingly unremarkable given the presentation of Moses throughout the book; however, this is the final time Moses's obedience is mentioned before he joins the Israelites in rebellion in 20:2–13 (Cole 2000, 277). The dual mentions of Moses's obedience along with the compliance of the tribal leaders in this passage is noteworthy, given the rarity of such actions in the narrative sections of Numbers along with the proximity to Korah's rebellion. However, it turns out that neither divine judgment nor the sign of Aaron's staff is fully sufficient to end Israel's propensity for complaint. When Moses does rebel against YHWH in 20:2–13, his penalty is an eventual death, sharing the fate of the rest of the rebellious generation.

A Final Coda: The People's Fear (17:12–13)

17:12–13. God's demonstration with Aaron's staff perhaps teaches the lesson too well. The complaints of the Israelites go from challenging Moses and Aaron's authority to fearing for their lives (Olson 1996, 111). It is unclear why the sprouting of a staff causes this reaction, but perhaps in conjunction with God's previous displays of destructive power including the earth swallowing up Korah and the other rebels (16:34), one more sign of divine authority is more than the congregation can handle. The intensity of the people's response is conveyed through repetition: "we perish, we all perish!" (17:12 NET). The hyperbole continues into 17:13, where the congregation declares "anyone who even comes close to the tabernacle of the LORD will die! Are we all to die?" (NET). Even though God's only miracle in this passage has been creative rather than destructive, the memory of previous judgments is still fresh.

The fear of the Israelites here is more appropriate than their blatant disregard for God's right to determine how he is to be approached. However, their fear also reflects a deficient understanding of what God has been trying to teach. Yes, those who come before God in an unauthorized manner risk losing their lives, but God's intention is not to obliterate the entire community. Instead, if the Israelites submit to the structure that God has ordained under the leadership of Moses and Aaron, then the community will not die. At this moment, the rebellious spirit has been replaced with fear. The next two chapters (Numbers 18–19) provide further instructions for the Aaronic priesthood for how they can stand between God and the Israelites, preserving them so that they will not be destroyed.

THEOLOGICAL FOCUS

The exegetical idea (God provides a miraculous sign to confirm Aaron's consecrated status and to quell the spirit of rebellion among the Israelites) leads to the following theological focus: *Only the one whom God has chosen can mediate between humanity and God.* This is very similar to the theological focus of the preceding passage since both address Aaron's status within the Israelite community. The focus of this passage is less the sinfulness of the Israelites and more God's creative act to confirm Aaron's status. The mediatory role is necessary to remain in communion with a holy God. In the very next passage, God declares that Aaron and his family must bear responsibility for offenses committed against the sanctuary and the priesthood (18:1). God has selected Aaron and the Levites to perform divine service. Any others who approach the center of God's holiness will perish (18:6–7).

Only God can determine who can fulfill that mediatorial role. In the Old Testament, it is the Aaronic priesthood who can stand between God and Israel. Others, like foolish King Uzziah, face death when they take priestly prerogatives upon themselves (2 Chron. 26:19–21). As the story of redemption continues, God provides the perfect mediator in the person of Jesus Christ. One commentator rightly notes, "It is difficult to overestimate the importance of

Aaron and his sons in the worship system of Israel. It is *impossible* to overestimate the role of the Priest who replaced Aaron, the Lord Jesus Christ" (Allen 2012, 261). On multiple occasions, including Jesus's baptism (Matt. 3:13–17) and the transfiguration (Matt. 17:1–5), God displays his power to confirm Christ's status.

The author of Hebrews provides further evidence of God's confirming work. Hebrews 5:1 begins by describing the priestly role as offering gifts to God and sacrifices to make expiation for sin. Particularly relevant to this passage is the declaration that no one can take this honor upon themselves. Instead, they must be called by God as Aaron was (Heb. 5:4). Hebrews 5:5–6 then provides evidence that God has called Christ to this role by appealing to his royal stature and his priestly lineage through Melchizedek. The next few chapters of Hebrews expound upon Christ's superiority over the Aaronic priesthood, including the reality that as a sinless High Priest, Christ does not have to make atonement for his own sins (Heb. 4:15; 7:26–28). Like Aaron, Christ was chosen for his intercessory role. Unlike Aaron, Christ's intercession is eternal through his once-for-all sacrifice of himself.

This is a fitting example of the attitude that followers of Jesus Christ should emulate, especially those called to leadership. Stubbs notes that "The besetting sin of many leaders is seeking or using authority for their own benefit or prestige" (Stubbs 2009, 151). Aaron himself fell prey to this instinct when he saw that Moses's prestige outstripped his own (12:1–2). Here, the example of Aaron's budding staff provides a symbol of authority that reflects the flourishing of life. This is the goal of Christian leaders: to use their place and position to guide their people along the paths of life and obedience to the calling of Christ. Although leadership in modern Protestant contexts does not have the same signs of confirmation as Aaron or Christ, it is possible to see a validation of calling in an attitude and character that emulates Christ.

PREACHING AND TEACHING STRATEGIES

Exegetical and Theological Significance

After being confronted on two consecutive days with groups of rebellious, defiant Israelites, God takes the initiative to settle the matter of who he wants to serve as his divinely appointed priests. Given that he had already chosen Aaron and his sons, and that he had already confirmed this calling at several times, Numbers 17 is a climactic act of ratification. It should have been completely unnecessary, but God is protecting his anointed priests and rejecting those who are self-important, self-righteous, and self-nominated.

The theological themes of God's election and divinely generated fruitfulness are found together in this text. God could identify his servants through direct verbal identification, by fire, or by any number of other signs. Here, after having vindicated them by miraculous judgments and answering fire in chapter 16, God identifies his chosen priest through a miraculous harvest. Without engaging in allegorical exegesis, it is not difficult to see that this sign is charged with symbolic significance. God's anointed priest will bear fruit.

The staff that blossomed served to identify and vindicate Aaron, and it also served as a memorial witness to the people so that they would not die. After all of the grumbling against God, enough was enough. Today, in an analogous way, God identifies his servants by the spiritual fruitfulness of their lives. This fruit is produced by the Spirit in virtue of a believer's union with Christ. Once again, the ultimate fulfillment is found in Jesus Christ himself. He bears maximal spiritual fruit, is vindicated by God in the resurrection, and empowers his disciples with the Spirit so that they can be fruitful, too.

Preaching Idea

The great High Priest is chosen by God, bears spiritual fruit, and makes his followers fruitful in the Spirit.

Contemporary Connections

What does it mean?
What does it mean that the great high priest is chosen by God, bears spiritual fruit, and makes his followers fruitful in the Spirit? The author of Hebrews makes it crystal clear that priests must be chosen by God, and that God chose Aaron (Heb. 5:1–4). In an even greater way, God set apart and appointed his Son to be the great High Priest (5:5–10). Whereas Aaron was vindicated by the budding staff, Christ was vindicated by his resurrection from the dead.

One key difference between Aaron and Christ is that God had to make Aaron fruitful, but Christ himself makes people fruitful. Aaron was entirely dependent on God, and we are entirely dependent on Christ. As Jesus said, "Remain in me, as I also remain in you. No branch can bear fruit by itself; it must remain in the vine. Neither can you bear fruit unless you remain in me" (John 15:4). We are familiar with the fruit of the Spirit (Gal. 5:22–23a), and this list represents the fruit that the Spirit produces in the lives of believers. The Spirit is sent by the Son, however, and they work cooperatively. As the Spirit works in us and unites us to Christ, we can bear fruit that will last (John 15:16). False teachers are known by their kind of fruit, and the true disciples of Christ are known by the fruit of righteousness (Matt. 7:15–20; John 15:8).

Is it true?
Is it true that Christ is the great High Priest chosen by God? Is it also true that those who are united with him will bear spiritual fruit through the power of the Spirit? Even if this is one means for being spiritually fruitful, in a pluralistic, multicultural world, are there no others? Furthermore, can't anyone experience positive changes in their behavior through following psychological practices or social conditioning?

Although those questions deserve thoughtful, nuanced answers, the short response is that apart from Christ, we cannot bear spiritual fruit that lasts. The type of fruit that the Spirit produces is qualitatively distinct, and it can only have its source and origin in him. Spiritual virtue is not the result of self-help, psychological therapy, or religious works. Only in Christ is there salvation, and only when they are connected to the vine can the branches bear fruit that honors God.

Now what?
If we are totally dependent on Christ and the Spirit for spiritual fruit, what do we do? One of the complex realities that Scripture frames out for us is the relationship between God's full sovereignty and our moral agency and responsibility. Even as he tells his disciples that apart from him they can do nothing, Christ commands them to remain in him, and he also commands them to love one another (which can only come through the power of the Spirit, whose first fruit is love). In progressive sanctification, we are to work with energy and zeal, while simultaneously recognizing our utter dependence on the Spirit and grace of God. We need to look to Christ, pray, and work. We are not to be passive, but active, even though on our own we can do nothing.

Creativity in Presentation

To impress upon people the miraculous nature of the staff budding, hold up a walking stick or wooden cane, and let them see a physical object that will clearly never bear fruit. Get the people to imagine how they would react if the next day the staff or cane had produced a harvest of almonds. We are not always as impressed as we ought to be by these miraculous events in the Bible!

Depending on climate, season, and availability, it would also be possible to have a fruitful vine or small tree brought into the auditorium, so that the horticultural analogy can be easily developed. The symbolism in Numbers 17 and the metaphor in John 15 are intuitive, so there does not need to be a large amount of time spent on helping people understand the referent.

We are also not as impressed as we ought to be by the miraculous production of fruit in the lives of a believer. It is just as much a divine work of God to produce love, joy, peace, etc., in our lives, as it was for him to make the staff bloom. There are a host of children's songs about the fruit of the Spirit, and this may be a good opportunity to have the children involved in the service. After they sing, the preacher can make the proper textual connections between Numbers 17, Christ's priesthood, and spiritual fruitfulness.

Coming out of Numbers 16–17, it is also appropriate to call people to self-examination. Are we bearing fruit? Is the work of the Spirit and our union with Christ evident? Are we growing in holiness and in our witness for the truth of the gospel? Encourage the people to pray and meditate on these things, and to test themselves to ensure that they are rooted and healthy in union with Christ. As they follow the great High Priest chosen by God, they will remember that bears spiritual fruit, and makes his followers fruitful in the Spirit.

One possible outline for this text is:

- God confirms his choice of intercessory leadership (17:1–9).

- God's people should remember the lessons that God teaches (17:10–11).

- Fear and disbelief can undercut God's lessons (17:12–13).

DISCUSSION QUESTIONS

1. Why does God choose the budding of a staff as the sign of Aaron's status?

2. Why does this sign prompt fear among the Israelites, even though it was not intended as judgment?

3. How is Aaron's intercessory role ultimately fulfilled in Christ?

Numbers 18:1–32

EXEGETICAL IDEA
God confirms the calling of Aaron and the Levites and directs the whole community to support them.

THEOLOGICAL FOCUS
Faithful ministers merit the support of God's people.

PREACHING IDEA
There is a relationship between spiritual responsibility, true prosperity, financial support, and generous giving.

PREACHING POINTERS
The staggering importance of the roles of the priests and Levites in the wider Israelite community runs through Numbers. Here, coming out of Numbers 16–17, God provides detailed, clear instructions so that there will not be any confusion about proper role delineation in the community. Each group has their own responsibilities and obligations. The special privileges and service to which the Levites are called brings with it an accompanying responsibility and high stakes; how they perform their service is literally a matter of life and death. Their lives are on the line in the holy spheres in which they minister.

In the nation of Israel, the non-Levites had the responsibility of providing the Levites with food and the essentials of life. God arranged the nation's economy so that the tribes were blessed so abundantly that they not only had all that they needed but had more than enough to share. As a result, the Levites could be fully supported out of the bounty given to the other tribes. This arrangement set up a virtuous spiral. Those with spiritual responsibility ministered for the glory of God and the good of the people, and the people were blessed. The people responded by joyfully giving back to God and the Levites. Material blessings, spiritual responsibilities, financial support, and generous giving all intersected and fed into one another. This text helps illustrate the wider biblical principle that there is a relationship between spiritual responsibility, true prosperity, financial support, and generous giving.

DUTIES AND BENEFITS OF THE PRIESTS AND LEVITES (18:1–32)

LITERARY STRUCTURE AND THEMES

This preaching unit builds upon the confirmation of Aaron's office in the previous chapter. Like Numbers 15, it interrupts the sequence of grumbling narratives to address issues related to proper worship. It details the priestly duties and responsibilities of Aaron and his household before widening its scope to the whole tribe of Levi. It also lists the recompense that the priests and Levites are to receive for the service to God. While they will not receive portions of the Promised Land, God himself promises to be their inheritance (18:20). It begins with the responsibilities of the priests and Levites (18:1–7), before detailing the shares of Israel's offerings that belonged to the priests (18:8–20) and the Levites (18:21–24). It concludes with the related responsibility of the Levites to tithe from the share of what they have received (18:25–32).

Thematically, this unit adds further detail to prior discussions of priestly and Levitical duties (Num. 1:47–54; 3:1–39; 4:1–49; 8:5–26). It confirms that they have been set apart for God's service and that their task is to preserve the sanctity of the place where God dwells. Violations of this duty results in death. This preaching unit also expresses the theme of God's provision for those who serve him. Although the priests and Levites do not produce their own food, they fit into a God-ordained system in which they trust him to provide for their needs.

- *Priestly and Levitical Responsibilities (18:1–7)*
- *The Priestly Share of the Offerings (18:8–19)*
- *The Levites' Share of the Offerings (18:20–24)*
- *The Levitical Tithe (18:25–32)*

EXPOSITION

This unit responds to the frightened cry of the Israelites in 17:12–13. The fate of Korah and the miracle of Aaron's staff have the community fearing death if it approaches the divine presence (Gane 2004, 652). This unit alleviates those concerns by making Aaron and his family responsible for the holiness of the sanctuary (18:1). The references to Aaron's family remind the reader that this system is meant to endure after Israel's sojourn in the wilderness, so a clear understanding of the role and recompense of the priesthood is appropriate (Allen 2012, 262). The overarching purpose of this unit is to demonstrate how God confirms the calling of Aaron and the Levites and directs the whole community to support them.

Priestly and Levitical Responsibilities (18:1–7)

18:1. This unit begins with the rare expression "YHWH said to Aaron." Outside of Numbers 18, only in Leviticus 10:8 does God address Aaron alone. Even when focusing on priestly duties, typically God speaks to Moses and Aaron together. This direct address further reinforces Aaron's status confirmed by the budding of his staff. It marks the end of the "rebellious contention for the priesthood" (Milgrom 1990, 146).

This verse also details the key responsibility of the priests: to "bear iniquity connected with the sanctuary" (ESV). Aaron, his sons, and the whole of his "father's house" stand in for the whole nation.

> **Bearers of Iniquity**
>
> The extent of the group that bears iniquity is unclear. The Hebrew expression is וּבֵית־אָבִיךָ ("the house of your father") which typically refers to an extended family unit. Some commentators broaden its meaning here to the whole tribe of Levi (Gane 2004, 652; Wenham 2008, 160) while others suggest restricting it to the Kohathite clan to which Aaron belongs (Ashley 1993, 339; Cole 2000, 281; Milgrom 1990, 146). The latter option is preferable since 18:2 refers to the whole tribe of Levi as a different entity than that mentioned in this verse.

Essentially, they serve as lightning rods that take on divine wrath on behalf of the nation. Israel was to be a holy and undefiled people, and this arrangement provides a layer of protection in case of a breach of that sanctity (Cole 2009, 365). Further, Aaron and his sons are responsible for iniquity related to priestly duties such as approaching the sanctuary or offering sacrifices while unclean (Exod. 30:20–21; Lev. 21:16–23) or inebriated (Lev. 10:8–9; Pressler 2017, 160).

18:2–5. While Aaron and his family perform the priestly duties, the remainder of the Levites also have roles to play. They are to minister to Aaron and the priests before the sanctuary and keep watch over its sanctity. However, 18:3 expresses a clear delineation of roles in which these non-Aaronide Levites must not touch or approach the sacred vessels or the sacrificial altar while they are in operation.[1] The penalty for violation is the death of the Levites and Aaronide priests, following 18:1. This is harsh, but less so than the destruction of the entire nation.

The Levites were also to maintain the purity of the tabernacle-complex by standing watch over its outer boundaries, while Aaron and the priests preserve the sanctity of its inner space (Ashley 1993, 340). Numbers 18:4 establishes a further limit, declaring that no outsiders may approach. This commonly refers to non-Israelites but, in this context, it bars any Israelite who is not a priest or Levite from trespassing the sacred space. The reward for this duty is the absence of divine wrath upon the nation (18:5).

18:6–7. The duties of the Levites and the priests are reiterated. In 18:6, God reminds Aaron that he has taken the Levites from the midst of Israel as a gift for Aaron in performing divine service. God thus ordains both the means of approaching him and the people who are sanctified for that task. The Levites provide the necessary support so that Aaron and priests can fulfill their roles. In 18:7, God gives the priests the responsibility "for everything at the altar and within the curtain" (NET). This is a merism, delineating the whole area of priestly service from the veil covering the Holy of Holies to the sacrificial altar in the tabernacle courtyard (Gane 2004, 653).

The Priestly Share of the Offerings (18:8–19)

18:8. The grave responsibilities undertaken by the priests and Levites require a discussion of appropriate recompense. God again speaks to Aaron and declares that he has awarded "all the consecrated things of the people of Israel" (ESV) to the priests. This is an overview of the rest of this section which delineates the priestly share of different kinds of offerings.

---

[1] Numbers 4 reveals that the Levites were tasked with carrying some of the sacred implements and tabernacle furnishings, but they could only do that after Aaron and his sons had covered them (Num. 4:15).

18:9–10. The first classification is the "most holy offerings" (NET), which refers to cereal offerings along with purification (sin) or reparation (guilt) offerings (Lev. 4:1–35; 5:14–19; 7:1–20; Cole 2009, 366). The priests receive the portion "from the fire" (מִן־הָאֵשׁ), which probably refers to what remained after the portion devoted to God had been burned on the altar (Ashley 1993, 348). These offerings of meat and grain are only to be eaten by Aaron and his sons, those actively engaged in priestly service. The priests' consumption of it is thus a perquisite of their service and a signal of its innate holiness.

18:11. The next category is the "wave offering" (תְּנוּפָה). This refers to the process of elevating a portion of the offering to reflect its dedication to God (Cole 2009, 366). It is associated with the fellowship offerings found in Leviticus 7:28–36 (Sprinkle 2015, 295). These offerings have a lesser degree of sanctity associated with them, which means that the priests' entire families may consume them. The only requirement is that the family members must be ceremonially clean. These offerings thus extend the support for the priests by providing sustenance for their wives and children as well.

18:12–13. The share due to the priests and their families also includes offerings of grain, wine, and oil. They are to receive the "best" (חֵלֶב) of these offerings (18:12a). This word literally means "fat," but contextually has the sense of "choicest part." These regulations anticipate a time when Israel will have possession of the land and be able to harvest agricultural bounty. The principle here is that the best and the first is to be brought to God's sanctuary, where it is part of the recompense allotted to God's priestly servants.

18:14. The idea of God awarding the first part of offerings continues. Everything "devoted" (ESV, NET, NIV) to YHWH is assigned to the priests.

> **Devoted**
> The word for "devoted" here is חֵרֶם. In the conquest of Canaan it refers to the people and treasure "devoted" to God, probably indicating their death or destruction (Deut. 7:28; 13:18; Joshua 6–7). However, the clarity for its use here comes from Leviticus 27:21, 28, in which fields and animals could also be devoted to God (Meyer 2017, 137). The idea is that they were set apart for divine use and could no longer serve mundane purposes. Thus, it appears that whatever flocks and fields were considered חֵרֶם were set aside for priestly use (Cole 2009, 367).

18:15–16. God also awards to the priests the "first of the womb" (פֶּטֶר רֶחֶם) of both humans and animals. This recalls Numbers 3:41–48, where God claims the Levites in place of the firstborn sons of all Israel. Now, God reveals that what belongs to him also belongs to the priests as recompense for their service. Firstborn human males[2] must be redeemed for a sum of five shekels (18:16; cf. 3:47–48) and the money would be given to the priests. This reminds Israel that God had redeemed them from Egypt and that they are his people (Cole 2009, 368).[3] The firstborn of unclean animals could also be redeemed for a monetary amount.

---

2 The gender of the firstborn is not specified here, but related passages consistently assume that is male (Exod. 13:12–13; 34:19–20; Num. 3:40–41; Ashley 1993, 350).

3 Jewish tradition suggests that this was a small amount (Milgrom 1990, 153). However, Wenham calculates the price as approximately six months' wages (Wenham 2008, 161). The principle of God's claim over the Israelites holds true no matter the value of this amount.

> **Redemption Price**
> It is possible to read the suffix on the expression וּפְדוּיָו or "redemption price" (18:16a ESV) as referring to the firstborn of both the humans and unclean animals. This would mean that the unclean animals should be redeemed for the same price. However, many suggest that it only refers to the firstborn human male (Ashley 1993, 351; Meyer 2017, 139; Milgrom 1990, 152; Wenham 2008, 161). This leaves unstated the price of redeeming unclean animals. Leviticus 27:27 also discusses the redemption of unclean animals but does not provide a specific price, instead referring to the animal's "set value" (NIV), to which a fifth must be added.

18:17–18. After discussing things that could be redeemed for money, God declares that the firstborn of clean animals (cows, sheep, and goats) cannot be redeemed because they are holy. They must be sacrificed to God. The ritual of sacrifice resembles that of a fellowship offering (Lev. 3:1–17) with the exception that the priests have claim to the whole of the meat after God's portion has been burned off, rather than sharing the meat with the worshipper (Ashley 1993, 352). This offering provides both a pleasing aroma to God (18:17b) along with sustenance for the priests (18:18).

18:19. YHWH announces that the priestly allotments are a "perpetual ordinance" (NET) or "perpetual due" (ESV) for the priestly line. Although instituted in the wilderness, these regulations provide for the support of the priests when Israel lays claim to the Promised Land. YHWH declares that this is a "covenant of salt forever" (בְּרִית מֶלַח עוֹלָם). This is a rare expression that most likely attests to the permanence of the arrangement.[4] Salt's preservative value points to the enduring nature of this arrangement, guaranteed by God's covenant fidelity (Cole 2009, 367; Garlington 2011, 719).

The Levites' Share of the Offerings (18:20–24)

18:20. The discussion of compensation shifts with God's declaration to Aaron that he will not have an inheritance in the Promised Land.[5] Milgrom suggests that God is speaking to Aaron here as the head of the Levites, since the lack of physical inheritance applies to the entire tribe (Milgrom 1990, 154). Instead, God is their portion and inheritance. In light of previous verses, it is clear that God intends for his ministers to have their needs met as they serve him.

18:21. This verse establishes the details of the relationship between the Levites' duties and their compensation. God grants the Levites "every tithe" (כָּל־מַעֲשֵׂר) in exchange for their service at the Tent of Meeting. The tithe here appears to involve agricultural products (cf. Num 18:27) but in Leviticus it also included animals (Lev. 27:30–33). In Leviticus, the Israelites gave their tithe to God. This reveals that part of the purpose of the tithe was to support those engaged in cultic service.

> **Tithing**
> Tithing in the Bible dates back to Abraham's tithe to Melchizedek (Gen. 14:19–24) and Jacob's vow to tithe if God returns him safely back to the land (Gen. 28:20–22). Those were one-time voluntary occasions. The Pentateuch actually institutes two systems of tithing: the tithe for the support of the sanctuary and the Levites described here and in Leviticus 27:30–33, and a celebratory tithe in the land that was to be converted into a joyful meal that the worshipper and their family would eat

---

4 Second Chronicles 13:5 also identifies the Davidic kingship as a "covenant of salt."
5 This verse can be read as either the conclusion of this subunit or the beginning of the next. Numbers 18:21 explicitly mentions the Levites, marking a shift from the regulations involving the priests. However, 18:20 begins with the expression "YHWH said to X" (here, Aaron) which typically marks the commencement of a new unit.

before God (Deut. 14:22–27).[6] Every third year, this tithe was to be used to support the disadvantaged or landless, which could include foreigners, widows, and Levites (Deut. 14:28–29). Both tithing systems benefited the Levites. The difference is that the Leviticus–Numbers tithe supported those Levites engaged in cultic service at God's sanctuary, while the Deuteronomy tithe supported the Levites living throughout the Promised Land once Israel took possession (Gane 2017, 349).

18:22–23. The Levitical service is to preserve the sanctity of the divine presence. The rest of the Israelites are not to approach the Tent of Meeting under the threat of death. The Levites will "bear their iniquity" (18:23a ESV), likely referring to their responsibility to prevent other Israelites from encroaching on this sacred space (Ashley 1993, 357). A violation of this would result in divine judgment falling on the Levites rather than the whole nation.

18:24. The subunit concludes by reframing 18:21. It announces that the Levites' reward for this service is the tithe and that this is their inheritance among the people of Israel. In a future time when Israel dwells in the Promised Land, the Levites were to be sustained by tangible contributions from the rest of the nation, in response to God's blessings.

The Levitical Tithe (18:25–32)

18:25–28. The final set of instructions direct the Levites to give to YHWH a portion of what they have received from the other Israelites. This means that only the priests are exempt from tithing, by virtue of their greater responsibilities. Numbers 18:25 begins with God speaking to Moses rather than Aaron. This is appropriate since the Levites present their tithe to Aaron and his sons (Num. 18:28). It would be self-serving for Aaron to issue this command (Olson 1996, 116). God specifies the amount of their offering in 18:26b as "a tithe from the tithe" (מַעֲשֵׂר מִן־הַמַּעֲשֵׂר), or presumably 10 percent of the 10 percent that the other Israelites provided. This contribution counts for the Levites "as though it were the grain of the threshing flood, and as the fullness of the winepress" (18:27 ESV). These were staple offerings, part of daily worship of God (Cole 2009, 369). Since the Levites do not have their own grainfields and vineyards, they receive credit for devoting to God a portion of what the other Israelites have presented to them (18:28a).

18:29–30. God also instructs the Levites about the quality of their offerings, stating that they must present "the best and holiest part of everything given to you" (18:29 NIV). This matches the instructions to the other Israelites in 18:12–13. It further emphasizes that God merits only the best of the best. His worshippers must not keep back from him what he is due. After they have offered an appropriate tithe, the rest is credited to the Levites as grain and drink offerings (cf. 18:27).

18:31–32. This set of instructions ends by permitting the Levites and their households to eat their portion after tithing to God. It is their "wages" (NET, NIV) or "reward" (ESV). They have a right to this portion from the tithes of the rest of the Israelites as compensation for their service at God's sanctuary (Ajah 2010, 118). This refers to their obligation to stand watch over its outer areas and preserve the sanctity of the sacrificial implements (18:4–6).

---

[6] There is a discussion over whether Deuteronomy 14 institutes one or two tithes. I (Joel) follow Gane in reading it as a single tithe that served two different purposes: two years out of three it was to be eaten at the sanctuary as a thanksgiving celebration, while in the third year it was to remain in the local communities for the benefit of the disadvantaged (Gane 2017, 347–48).

There is a further warning in 18:32a for the Levites in God's statement that they will bear no sin for eating their portion *if* they have devoted the best of the tithes to God. If they keep for themselves what God is due, the consequences will be severe. The final instruction in 18:32b is for the Levites not to "profane" (תְחַלְּלוּ) the sacred offerings of the Israelites. This is a summary statement covering the potential offenses described throughout this unit (Cole 2000, 296–97). Again, the penalty for violation is death.

THEOLOGICAL FOCUS

The exegetical idea (God confirms the calling of Aaron and the Levites and directs the whole community to support them) leads to the following theological focus: *Faithful ministers merit the support of God's people.* This chapter establishes a reciprocal relationship between responsibility and compensation. The priests and the Levites took on the weight of approaching God's holy presence on behalf of the nation. In light of Israel's propensity toward sin and rebellion, the fact "that there was a legitimate priesthood was an act of God's mercy" (Allen 2012, 264). Since this duty was all-encompassing, God awards them a share of the offerings given to him.

Providing the proper recompense for the priests and Levites remained important throughout biblical literature. In response to the ravages of a locust invasion, Joel calls upon priests to lament the cessation of grain and drink offerings because it affects the nation's relationship with God and their own ability to sustain themselves (Joel 1:13–14). In the Persian Period, Nehemiah claims to have enforced the collection of the priestly share (Neh. 12:44–47). As the priests collaborated in the effort to reshape the postexilic community around the Torah (cf. Nehemiah 8), it was important for them to receive appropriate compensation for their work. Nehemiah dedicates the storehouse of the temple to this purpose (Neh. 10:38–39; 12:44; 13:5, 12), confirming that providing this portion was a worshipful act (Ajah 2010, 118–19). Part of Ezekiel's vision of a rebuilt temple is a restored priesthood who minister faithfully and receive the wages described here (Ezek. 44:28–30).

This principle continues into the New Testament. In 1 Corinthians 9:13–14, Paul states, "Do you not know that those who are employed in temple service get their food from the temple, and those who serve at the altar share in the sacrificial offerings? In the same way, the LORD commanded that those who proclaim the gospel should get their living by the gospel" (ESV). In the same discourse, he cites the regulation in Deuteronomy 25:4 about not muzzling an ox while it is treading grain (1 Cor. 9:9–10). This suggests that those who are faithfully committed to declaring and announcing the gospel merit support from God's people.

This must be balanced with Paul's declaration here that he did not take advantage of these rights (1 Cor. 9:15–18) and his claims elsewhere that he did not intend to be a burden upon the believers (1 Thess. 2:9). Further, Peter calls upon elders not to exalt themselves over their congregation or seek dishonest gain (1 Peter 5:3–4). Instead, just as God is the true inheritance of the priests (Num. 18:20), a minister's bequest is "the deposit of the gospel that has been entrusted into their care" (Sprinkle 2015, 298). Faithful service merits support for further gospel proclamation, not personal enrichment.

PREACHING AND TEACHING STRATEGIES

Exegetical and Theological Significance

Numbers continues to build on the conflict between the priests, Levites, and wider community. Having dramatically ended Korah's rebellion, sent down a plague, and caused Aaron's staff to bud, God now gives specific instructions to lay the conflicts to rest once and for all. Clear delineation is made between the people, the Levites, and the priests. Each group is equally part of the nation of Israel, but they do not have the same responsibilities or spheres of service. Each group has unique responsibilities toward God, and these responsibilities are partly expressed as responsibilities to one another.

Over and over, human jealousy and the desire for power and privilege sparks conflict. This is exactly what we see in Numbers 16. Yet what is often missed is that privileged service before God also carries massive responsibilities. Numbers 18 makes it clear that the priests and Levites have special spheres of service, but those spheres involve a responsibility that is literally a matter of life and death. Many want what they perceive as prestigious appointments, but far fewer are willing to voluntarily take on a responsibility that may cost them their life.

In light of different spheres of responsibility and service, there are different obligations laid upon the various groups. The non-Levites are to give the best of what they have to the Levites, and the Levites in turn are to share the best of their goods with the priests. Those who do not have the weighty responsibility of the Levites are to share with them, and the Levites in turn are to share with the priests (whose responsibility is even greater).

From a theological perspective, the most important point in the text is that the priests and Levites do not receive land; they are given YHWH as their portion. Nothing is greater than this. Nothing can be greater than having God himself as one's own. In the new covenant community, where there is a priesthood of all believers, every priest has God as their share and inheritance.

Preaching Idea

There is a relationship between spiritual responsibility, true prosperity, financial support, and generous giving.

Contemporary Connections

What does it mean?
What does it mean that there is a relationship between spiritual responsibility, true prosperity, financial support, and generous giving? As this text indicates, God set up a moral-spiritual-practical economy in Israel on the basis of their spheres of responsibility. Those who exercised spiritual responsibility (i.e., the priests and Levites) had the right to expect support from those they served. Those who benefited from their service were commanded by God to share the best of the blessings and wealth that God gave them. This system of mutual support in Israel was created by God himself, and it established links between spiritual responsibility and material giving.

There are a few things that this idea does not mean, however. It does not mean that those who exercise spiritual authority and responsibility will be rich; you cannot tell if someone is godly by the amount of money they have. It also does not mean that ministers should live high above their congregations. The Israelites supported the priests and Levites, but God set the limits on what they had to give. Selfishness, covetousness, and the worship of money is not limited to either ministers or congregants; sadly, both can be affected equally. The great antidote to the love of money is a greater love for God and our neighbor. In the end, how we discharge our responsibilities—including our financial ones—is one way of showing what our hearts truly value.

Is it true?
Is it true that there is a relationship between spiritual responsibility, true prosperity, financial support, and generous giving? Although we do not live in the era of the tabernacle and the Levites, the New Testament is clear that this matrix still exists, albeit in a revised configuration. First Corinthians 9:14 alone makes this principle explicit. In the new covenant community, there

are some who give their full time to the ministry of the Word, and their work is hampered if they must divide their time in order to earn an income. In every field we understand that a full-time worker is able to be more productive and hone their skills and craft more readily than someone who works only part-time. The same is true in Christian ministry. In order to be full time in ministry, however, one either needs to be independently wealthy, or one needs financial support. This support is to come from the generous hearts of the people of God.

Why will people pay large amounts of money for taking lessons in gymnastics, figure skating, or art? Why will people pay for swimming lessons or horseback riding? The truth is, we pay for what we value. There should be nothing that people value higher than knowing the truth of God. If we pay those who teach us in other areas of life, we should be generous to those who give us the most important knowledge of all (cf. Gal. 6:6; 1 Tim. 5:17–18).

Regardless of material goods, however, the greatest blessing of all is having God as one's inheritance. This is what allows us to be generous with others and to not be obsessed with material things. Simply put, God is greater than anything in creation. In fact, he is greater than everything in creation put together!

Now what?
The right response is to give what you ought to give. Ministers should give their very best in service to their people, and the congregation should bless them so that they do not have financial worries. One important caveat, however, is that many churches are poor, struggling, and small. There are times when ministers simply have to be bivocational. We are to serve where we are called, and everyone needs to do their best in every situation. A great deal of ministry and church life revolves around attitudes and intentions. There is no one "right" number to set for a minister's salary, but where goodwill and a desire to bless prevails all around, and where both pastor and congregation are endeavoring to serve the Lord in humility and truth, even the act of giving can be an act of love and worship.

Creativity in Presentation
During the message the preacher can poll the congregation and ask them to call out things that people in the world are living for. Without almost any doubt, answers will include power, sex/pleasure, and money. Although sex is not mentioned in Numbers 18, notice the connections in Hebrews 13:4–5: "Marriage should be honored by all, and the marriage bed kept pure, for God will judge the adulterer and all the sexually immoral. Keep your lives free from the love of money and be content with what you have, because God has said, 'Never will I leave you; never will I forsake you'" (NIV).

The point the author of Hebrews is making is that sexual gratification needs to take place in a context of covenant holiness, but our attitude toward money and God is likewise to be covenantal. Do not live for sex, and do not live for money and possessions. Why? What do we have that is better than all that the world can provide? What we have is God. *We have God.* And God will never leave us nor forsake us. This is extremely powerful, and it connects well with Numbers 18:20. In the new covenant community, we can all be generous with one another, and we can all have the absolute confidence that comes from having the Lord himself as our eternal possession.

One principle of investment is to diversify your portfolio. But God calls us to put everything we are and have into his kingdom—no hedging our bets. As people call out various things the world is living for, the preacher can write them down and place the strips of paper in a jar. There can be one other jar where he puts the word "God." Which jar is more valuable? Which one would you rather have? Which one will matter in eternity? If you live for the world, you won't have God, but if you live for God, he gives you himself and also material

Duties and Benefits of the Priests and Levites (18:1–32)

blessings throughout your life. In other words, if you choose God you get the world and eternal life; but if you choose the world, you lose it, your soul, and a covenant relationship with God himself. Choosing the Lord is what allows you to be generous with material goods; it is what allows you to make right valuations and to get your priorities straight. This demonstrates that there is a relationship between spiritual responsibility, true prosperity, financial support, and generous giving.

One possible outline for this text is:

- Priestly service preserves the holiness of God (18:1–7).

- Those devoted to God's service deserve the generosity of God's people (18:8–19, 25–32).

- God himself is the truest inheritance (18:20–24).

DISCUSSION QUESTIONS

1. Why do the rest of the Israelites need to faithfully support the priests and Levites? What benefits accrue to both the people and the priest/Levites from this arrangement?

2. What does it mean for God to be the priests' inheritance (18:20)?

3. Why do the Levites need to tithe in turn to the priests?

4. Does this passage have any relevance for how ministers in the church should be compensated? What principles from the New Testament can we compare to it?

Numbers 19:1–22

EXEGETICAL IDEA
Impurity from contact with a dead body can be remedied through the ritual of the red cow.

THEOLOGICAL FOCUS
God provides the means for his holy presence to remain among his people.

PREACHING IDEA
God gives us rituals to increase our appreciation of the realities found in Christ.

PREACHING POINTERS
The details of this text are very foreign to the contemporary reader. In our churches, we do not use this water of cleansing, and we do not go through with these rituals. Even at the level of rationality, it seems doubtful that anyone could ever have thought that the ashes of a dead bovine mixed with water could make someone clean. Since God's instructions are not absurd, the obvious explanation is that there is a deeper, abiding principle that is being illustrated by the production and application of the water of purification.

Christian readers should know that these types of symbolic acts point forward to Jesus Christ. It is by his shed blood and sacrificial death that we are made clean; it is by being washed in the water and the blood that we are made pure. Christ's death brings about the ultimate purification that this text in Numbers can only hint at. The water of purification in this text is the shadow, but Christ is the substance and fulfillment. Today in the church, we still enact religious rites when we follow the ordinances of our Lord. Baptism and the Lord's Supper are divinely appointed rituals of worship for the new covenant community. It is important for us to understand that God gives us rituals to increase our appreciation of the realities found in Christ.

CLEANSING FROM CORPSE IMPURITY (19:1–22)

LITERARY STRUCTURE AND THEMES

Numbers 19 continues the discussion of maintaining the purity of Israelite community. The previous chapter charged the priests and Levites with the responsibility of preventing impurity from sundering the relationship between God and Israel (Num. 18:1–7). Now, this chapter addresses the very serious need to address the impurity brought about by contact with a dead body. It introduces a new ritual in which the ashes of a red cow were combined with water and other substances. A number of structural arrangements are possible for this chapter, but the presence of the phrases "this is the statute of the law" (Num. 19:2a ESV) and "this is the law" (Num. 19:14a ESV) suggests that it can be divided into two panels (Cole 2000, 303; Milgrom 1990, 437). Numbers 19:1–13 details the procedure for purification and warns of the danger of not following it. Numbers 19:14–22 addresses the scope of the impurity brought about by contact with a dead body, detailing which members of the community require cleansing.

The theme of this passage is again the need for holiness in God's chosen community. Divine holiness "is characterized by life" and opposed by the "birth-death cycle of human beings" (Gane 2004, 659). Or, stated differently, life is sacred to the Creator of life, and death is a breach of that sanctity. This chapter also resonates with the Nazirite vow in Numbers 6, where that special degree of devotion to God required a reset if there was contact with a dead body. Numbers 19 demonstrates that this kind of impurity affects all Israelites and requires a remedy for Israel to remain in relationship with God.

- *The Procedure for Purification (19:1–13)*
- *The Scope of Impurity (19:14–22)*

EXPOSITION

It is somewhat surprising that the instructions to address contact with a dead body are found this late in the Pentateuch. Leviticus 11–15 discusses several situations that cause impurity (skin diseases, bodily discharges, childbirth) and where the physical effects may somewhat mirror death, but the regulations in those chapters do not include corpse contamination. Locating the instructions here is appropriate, since Israel has been sentenced to a period of wandering that endures until an entire generation dies (Num. 14:30). Further, Israel's rebellions have prompted divine judgment, leading to large numbers of dead.[1] God's instructions address these situations. This preaching unit teaches that impurity from contact with a dead body can be remedied through the ritual of the red cow.

The Procedure for Purification (19:1–13)

19:1–2. The passage begins with YHWH addressing Moses and Aaron, giving them a "statute of the law" (חֻקַּת הַתּוֹרָה). This exact phrase is only found elsewhere in Numbers 31:21, again addressing impurity from a dead body. The use of two Hebrew words for this instruction "emphasizes the definitive nature of the law" (Ashley 1993, 363).

---

1 For example, Numbers 16:49 lists 14,700 as the number of those who died from a plague in the aftermath of Korah's rebellion. Although the numbers in Numbers may be hyperbolic (see the discussion of Numbers 1), this kind of mass casualty event would create a great deal of impurity.

God commands the Israelites to bring to Moses and Aaron a red cow with no physical deformities that has not been used as a work animal. Redness here likely reflects the color of blood. A cow, as the largest available sacrificial animal, would produce the greatest quantity of ashes to use for purification (Gane 2004, 660).

> **Animal Sacrifice**
> Bulls were the required purification sacrifice for priests and the whole of the community, while male goats were offered for Israelite leaders, and female goats and lambs for individual Israelites. This means that female bovines are only used in this purification offering (MacDonald 2012, 359).

There is a double statement of the requirement for physical purity ("without blemish, which has no defect," 19:2 NET). Rabbinic interpretation extrapolated from this to mean that the cow had no hairs of any other color (Cole 2000, 306). This goes beyond the likely intention of the phrase.

> *TRANSLATION ANALYSIS: HEIFER VS. COW*
> The vast majority of English translations identify the animal as a "red heifer." However, commentators note that the word used here (פָּרָה) is a more generic term for female bovine and that there is another word (עֶגְלָה) that more directly corresponds to a heifer (Ashley 1993, 364; MacDonald 2012, 358–59; cf. Gen. 15:9).[2] The requirement that the animal must not have been used for work does suggest that it is young. On balance, it is more reflective of the Hebrew to identify this animal as "red cow," but "heifer" is probably still appropriate.

Both the absence of physical deformities and lack of a yoke on the neck point to the suitability of the cow for sacrifice (Lev. 22:20; Deut. 17:1; 21:2). Unblemished sacrificial animals reflect giving one's best to God, while the absence of prior labor suggests that the animal's value is given to God alone.[3] The all-too-human temptation is to designate for sacrifice only animals that could not improve one's own flock. This regulation requires the worshipper to have sufficient faith to place obedience to God ahead of self-interest (Allen 2012, 272).

19:3–5. The cow is to be given to Eleazar, son of Aaron (19:3). This is probably so that Aaron, the high priest, can avoid any possible impurity that may come from going outside of the camp (Cole 2000, 306; Milgrom 1990, 158). The slaughter of the cow took place beyond the Israelite encampment. This resembles the disposal of the remains of purification sacrifices (cf. Lev. 4:1–21) but differs in that the actual killing of those animals took place on the altar in the tabernacle courtyard. Next, Eleazar is to dip his finger in the blood and sprinkle it seven times toward the entrance of the Tent of Meeting (19:4). This establishes "a symbolic interaction with the sanctuary in order to make the procedure a sacrificial one" (Gane 2004, 660). This ritual will be called a "purification offering" (חַטָּאת) in 19:9, so the blood manipulation here establishes a link between it and other sacrifices of that nature.

The slain cow is then to be burned in its entirety, including "its skin, its flesh, its blood, with its dung" (19:5 ESV). In a typical purification offering, the blood was poured out on the altar and would not be available to be burned. The reason for burning the animal with its blood is evident. Since the purpose of slaughtering the cow is to produce ashes that will remedy impurity from corpse contamination and since blood is the agent of cleansing, the blood must be involved in the creation of the ashes (Ashley 1993, 365).

---

2 For the uninitiated, a heifer is a female bovine that has never given birth to a calf. My (Joel's) farm-raised parents will be disappointed to learn that I did not know that until working on this chapter.

3 See Malachi 3:7–9 for condemnation of Israel for failing to offer unblemished animals in its sacrifices.

19:6. The priest then adds cedar wood, hyssop, and scarlet thread to the fire (19:6).[4] No explanation for these is given, but notably the same three elements appear in Leviticus 14:5–7, 51–52 in the ritual for cleansing from scaly skin disease. The combination of material thus adds to the cleansing effect (Frick 2002, 228). The color of the scarlet thread and possibly the cedar wood is reminiscent of blood (Cole 2009, 369). Hyssop (אֵזוֹב) is likely to be majoram, "a small, aromatic, bushy plant" (Sprinkle 2015, 302). It is sufficiently absorbent to be used to sprinkle blood (Exod. 12:22; Lev. 14:6–7) and is used symbolically to express David's desire for cleansing after his sin with Bathsheba (Ps. 51:7). These additional elements thus heighten the cleansing properties of the sacrificial red cow.

19:7–8. At the conclusion of the burning, both the priest (9:7) and the man who burned the cow (19:8) are required to wash their clothes and bathe. They are both declared ritually unclean until that evening, though the process of washing will restore them to the community after the elapsed time. This points to a paradox in the red cow ritual: it cleanses those defiled by contact with a dead body but renders unclean those who prepare the cleansing ashes. There is some parallel in the washings required on the Day of Atonement (Lev. 16:26, 28), where the one who handles the scapegoat and the one who burns the remnants of the goat and bull used in purification offerings are considered unclean until they bathe. The idea is that interacting with elements used in a purification sacrifice transfers some of the absorbed impurity to the handler (Milgrom 1990, 439). However, the uncleanness of the priest and the lay individual here is much less serious than that of those affected by corpse contamination. Ritual washing and simply waiting until evening is sufficient (Lev. 11:24–25, 27–28, 31–32; 14:16–18; 17:15).

19:9–10. A third individual is then tasked with gathering up the ashes produced by burning the cow and the accompanying elements. This individual must be ceremonially clean (19:9) and then must undergo the same cleansing required from the priest and the one who burned the cow (19:10). Notably, the ashes are to be kept outside the Israelite encampment but placed in a clean vessel and kept in a clean place. The term "keep" (מִשְׁמֶרֶת) more likely implies "safeguarding" in order to prevent the ashes from becoming contaminated themselves (Milgrom 1990, 159). The ashes are "for use in the water of purification" (19:9b NET). The procedure is explained in more detail in 19:17–19, but essentially the ashes were mixed with water to produce a purifying substance.

Numbers 19:9 also directly states the purpose of this ritual, identifying it as a חַטָּאת which is best translated as a "purification offering." As mentioned throughout this commentary, this is often a better translation than "sin offering" (ESV) or "purification from sin" (NASB, NET, NIV). Although the חַטָּאת sacrifice can denote cleansing from sinful activity (Leviticus 4), it also addresses situations where sin is not implied (Lev. 12:6–8; 16:15–16). Coming into contact with a dead body renders a person ritually impure and in need of cleansing, but it does not indicate a moral failing.

Numbers 19:10b declares that this is a lasting ordinance for both Israelites and the foreigners who dwell among them. This ritual will thus endure past Israel's time in the wilderness and become part of how they live in the presence of a holy God. Specifically identifying foreigners demonstrates the inclusive nature of the community. Anyone who chooses to dwell with Israel must be purified in the same manner as full Israelites.

---

4   The generic title "priest" is used in place of Eleazar in 19:6–7. This reflects the reality that this ritual will be needed beyond the time of the present generation.

19:11–12. The text transitions from the preparation of the red cow to the use of its ashes. It first declares that contact with a dead body renders a person unclean for seven days (19:11), which stands in stark contrast to the impurity that befalls the priest and those involved in creating the ashes. The unclean individual must purify themselves on both the third and seventh days to be cleansed. English translations rightly stress that the water-and-ash mixture must be applied twice (e.g., "He shall cleanse himself with water on the third day and on the seventh day, and so be clean," 19:12 ESV).[5] This double application likely indicates the seriousness of the impurity brought about by contact with a dead body (Ashley 1993, 371). Afterward, Numbers 19:12b draws the next logical conclusion: failure to follow this procedure means that a person is not cleansed.

> **Corpse Contamination**
>
> Although there are no exact ancient Near Eastern parallels for impurity brought about by corpse contamination, one Babylonian text prescribes a seven-day period of isolation for anyone who comes in contact with "dust from a place of mourning" (Cole 2009, 370). The individual also had to recite a prayer, bathe, and change their clothes. This points to a broader concern to make sure that the dead did not bring deleterious effects upon the living.

19:13. This section concludes by detailing the severe implications of failing to cleanse oneself. That individual "defiles the tabernacle of the LORD" (19:13 ESV). This suggests that unaddressed impurity from contact with a dead body could have consequences for the entire nation. Further, failure to follow God's clearly articulated commands adds an element of defiance and rebellion, especially since "the ashes are available at no charge and the procedure is quick and easy, so there is no excuse for noncompliance" (Gane 2004, 661). The offender must be "cut off" (וְנִכְרְתָה) from Israel. This is an incredibly serious penalty, removing the offender's name and posterity from Israel and possibly necessitating their death.[6] Their failure to cleanse themselves means that they cannot remain in God's holy presence.

The Scope of Impurity (19:14–22)

19:14–15. The text articulates which situations this ritual addresses. The first is where the dead body is found in a tent. This can be extrapolated for any indoor dwellings once Israel is living in the land. Anyone who enters the dwelling or who was in it at the time of death is considered unclean for seven days. Notably, this differs from the kinds of impurity addressed in Leviticus 11–15 where touch is required to transmit (MacDonald 2012, 368–69). Impurity brought about by a dead body is so virulent that simply sharing the same dwelling is sufficient to pass it on. Further, the uncleanliness pervades any container without a fastened lid (19:15). Numbers 31:23 suggests that they must undergo cleansing through the application of this water-ash mixture.

19:16. The second scenario involves encountering a dead body while outside. This corpse could have died by violence or of natural causes. Further, touching a human bone or a grave is similarly defiling. Possible situations include caring for an injured warrior who succumbs to their wounds, transporting a body for burial, or a random stumbling upon a dead body (Cole 2000, 312). The primary distinction between this scenario and the previous one is the means

---

5   The Hebrew text could be read as requiring only one application of the water-ash mixture: on the third day. However, commentators strongly assert that two applications are intended (Ashley 1993, 370–71; Milgrom 1990, 161; Gane 2004, 661).

6   See the exposition of Numbers 15:22–36 for a more detailed discussion of being "cut off."

of transmission of the impurity. When outside, impurity is only transmitted by having physical contact with the dead body or gravesite. The absence of shared walls permits the contagion to dissipate so that only direct contact renders a person unclean.[7]

19:17–19. The text then provides a step-by-step set of instructions for this cleansing. The ashes of the purification offering consisting of the red cow, cedar wood, hyssop, and scarlet thread are to be mixed with "living water" (מַיִם חַיִּים), which English translations take as a metaphor for fresh water (ESV, NIV) or flowing water (NASB, NET). The adjective "living" (חַיִּים) is appropriate here in a ritual combatting the impurifying effects of death (Gane 2004, 662). Then, a ceremonially clean person (19:18) is to take some hyssop,[8] dip it in the mixture, and sprinkle it on the walls and furnishings of the dwelling along with all the people who have been in the house. This same requirement applies for those who have had direct contact with a dead body while outside (19:18b). Numbers 19:19 then repeats the instruction that this cleansing must take place on the third and seventh days (19:12), adding in the detail that the ceremonially clean person performs the ritual of sprinkling the unclean with the water-ash mixture.

The ceremony concludes with bathing and washing clothes, recalling the requirements found in 19:7, 8, 10. Unfortunately the syntax of 19:19b is ambiguous as to who must undergo these ablutions: the unclean person or the clean one. On one hand, it seems reasonable that the unclean person should complete their restoration with a full washing, similar to cleansing from skin diseases (Lev. 14:9). On the other hand, in this chapter the ceremonially clean people (the priest, the one burning the red cow, and the other gathering the ashes) have been required to bathe and have been cleansed by that evening. Further, the clean person (הַטָּהֹר) is the subject of the first two verbs in 19:19: "he will sprinkle" (וְהִזָּה) and "he will purify him" (וְחִטְּאוֹ). There is no clear indication that the subject should change for the next verbs: "he will wash" (וְכִבֶּס) and "he will bathe" (וְרָחַץ). On balance, it is more likely that the requirement to wash clothes and bathe applies to the clean person (Cole 2000, 314; Milgrom 1981, 63; Pressler 2017, 172). The unclean are restored by receiving the sprinkling of the water-ash mixture.

TRANSLATION ANALYSIS
English translations either leave the subject of the verbs "bathe" and "wash" ambiguous or assign them to the unclean person. Versions maintaining the ambiguity include the ESV and NASB, "he shall wash his clothes and bathe himself in water," and the NET, "he must wash his clothes and bathe in water." Versions assuming that the unclean person is the subject include the NIV, "those who are being cleansed must wash their clothes and bathe in water," and the CSB, "the one being purified must wash his clothes and bathe in water." Given the lack of clarity in the Hebrew syntax and the parallels to the clean person's washing and bathing earlier in the chapter, an ambiguous translation is preferable.

19:20. This verse reiterates the warning of 19:13. Those who fail to complete the cleansing

---

[7] This scenario also recalls how God commands Israel to address an unsolved murder in Deuteronomy 21:1–9 (MacDonald 2012, 356). In that situation, no one touches the dead body, but the elders are required to bring a heifer that has never had a yoke place on it and break its neck by flowing water. After washing their hands, the elders declare their innocence from causing this death and entreat God to consider this atonement for the bloodshed. This situation reveals another facet of how death violates the holiness of God's presence. It must be atoned for, even when the guilty party is unknown.

[8] Again, probably the plant known as majoram (Cole 2000, 312).

procedure must be cut off from the community because their uncleanness defiles the sanctuary of YHWH. This may also suggest that, unlike skin diseases, the unclean person does not have to remain outside the camp during their period of cleansing (Milgrom 1990, 442–43). Their uncleanness defiles the sanctuary presumably only if they enter its courtyards.

19:21–22. The text concludes with a summation of previously elaborated principles: the one who performed the cleansing must bathe and wash their garments while items touched by an unclean person become unclean and can transmit that uncleanliness to anyone else who touches it.[9] These items would remain in a "state of virtual isolation" to prevent contamination (Cole 2000, 315).

The Perfect Red Heifer

This chapter has also given rise to a vein of interpretation that occasionally makes waves in mainstream media. In brief, the idea is that the appearance of a perfect red heifer would set in motion a chain of events leading to the construction of a third temple, and in the course of time, the end of history through the onset of the apocalypse. A crowdfunding project to breed such an animal was even launched in 2015.[10] An alternative version suggests that a set of ashes was hidden prior to the destruction of the second temple and awaits discovery (Browning 1996, 74–75). This interpretation is fraught with all manner of pitfalls. First, as discussed above, it is unlikely that the cow used in creating the ashes had to be perfectly red. Its perfection relates to its absence of disqualifying flaws for acceptance as a sacrificial animal, not the color of all of its hairs. Secondly, claims to know what must happen to spark the end of this world run counter to Jesus's claim that no one knows the day or the hour (Matt. 24:36). Thirdly, attempting to engineer the end suggests a rather large degree of hubris. History and the final judgment of this world rest in the hands of God; he cannot be compelled to act by genetic experimentation that produces a certain color of cow.

THEOLOGICAL FOCUS

The exegetical idea (Impurity from contact with a dead body can be remedied through the ritual of the red cow) leads to the following theological focus: *God provides the means for his holy presence to remain among his people.* It is worth noting that this passage is among the strangest in Numbers. The idea of being separated from the community on account of something as common as the death of a family member is quite foreign to a modern audience. Similarly, the efficacy of the procedure is not immediately apparent. How does the symbolic sprinkling of water and ashes bring about a restoration of purity? Part of the answer lies in the power of ritual. Essentially, rituals are able to create reality for their communities as they shape "the conceptual, symbolic world . . . not bound by mundane material constraints" (Gane 2004, 663). The symbols and actions of the red cow ritual provided part of the means by which "a holy God could remain present among a sinful people" (Olson 1996, 123).

This passage also provides a reminder of the importance of communal action in response to what God has done. Those who were ceremonially clean had the opportunity to restore their

---

9 The fact that 19:21 explicitly requires the clean individual to bathe and wash may lend some weight to arguments that 19:19b addresses the unclean individual. However, it is equally possible that the purpose of 19:21 is to clarify previous ambiguity and that the clean individual is addressed in both verses.

10 Peter Beaumont, "Jewish Activists Launch Crowdfinding Appeal to Breed Perfect Red Heifer," *The Guardian*, August 10, 2015, https://www.theguardian.com/world/2015/aug/10/jewish-activists-crowd-funding-breed-red-heifer-third-temple-cow.

brethren by participating in the preparation of the ashes and the sprinkling of the impure individuals. In other parts of the Pentateuch, Israelites are commanded to look out for each other by looking for lost animals (Exod. 23:4–5), building safety features into their dwellings (Deut. 22:1–4), and providing for the needs of the weakest in their midst (Exod. 23:10–11; Lev. 25:8–17). The text communicates a "strong sense of responsibility each member has to help other members of the community" (Graves 2021, 31). Paul calls on believers to encourage their brethren toward greater holiness by avoiding unwholesome speech and speaking to each other with psalms, hymns, and spiritual songs (Eph. 5:18–19). Perfection in this matter is of course unattainable this side of the grave, but exhortations toward confession and repentance remind God's people of the means he has provided for their sanctification (1 John 1:9).

On the other side, this text also provides a reminder of the deleterious effects of impurity on the broader community. The person who fails to undergo this cleansing procedure is banished from the community lest they contaminate God's sanctuary. In Joshua 7, Israel learns that Achan's hidden sin brings defeat on the entire nation. In 2 Samuel 24, David's census-taking sparks a devastating plague throughout Israel. In the New Testament, Paul calls on the Corinthian believers to expel one of their number engaging in flagrant, unrepentant sinful behavior (1 Corinthians 5). In David's case, repentance mitigated the punishment, but the situation still provides a reminder of the consequences of falling short of God's holiness.

No theological reflection on Numbers 19 is complete without considering Hebrews 9. The author of Hebrews suggests that the red cow ritual and other legal observances are shadows or copies of the ultimate cleansing brought about by Christ (Heb. 9:23). He describes the cleansing effect of the red cow ritual before declaring that the blood of Christ is even more efficacious since it will "cleanse our consciences from acts that lead to death, so that we may serve the living God" (Heb. 9:14 NIV). As we are all theologically dead in our transgressions (Eph. 2:1), the blood of Christ cleanses more than contamination brought about by a dead body. Instead, it undoes the consequences of every sin that separates us from the living and holy God. Just as God graciously instructed Israel how to remedy the effects of corpse contamination, so he offers the means to dwell in his holy presence through the sacrifice not of a red cow, but of his only begotten son.

PREACHING AND TEACHING STRATEGIES

Exegetical and Theological Significance

The instructions in this passage for using the water of purification to cleanse from corpse contamination can be taken as a standalone unit, but they are deepened by remembering the historical context of the multiple deaths in Numbers 16. Without a professional caste of undertakers, funeral directors, hospice nurses, and hospital physicians, the average Israelite would be confronted with death far more often than the average North American today. In many ways, our societies have tried to sanitize and hide death, but death still bears witness to the effects of sin. Death also epitomizes the power of sin, since it is the antithesis of life; death stands in contrast to the eternal, immortal God.

At one level, the ritual with the water of purification—like all the pageantry in the sacrificial system—was incoherent if taken as the ultimate reality. How did this mixture of water and ashes actually decontaminate a person who was unclean? How did the scapegoat actually bear the sins of the people? No matter how many animals were sacrificed, how did the death of an animal pay for my sins? Imagine a judge who found a person guilty of a crime, but then punished a sheep in their place. How is that justice?

Clearly, these rituals were literally *sign*-ificant: they were signs that were meaningful because they pointed beyond themselves to a deeper, richer reality. Sacrificial blood needed to be shed in order for the people to be washed clean. Paradoxically, the uncleanness brought through death could only be overcome by the cleanness which came through another death. The water of purification symbolized something that it could not bring about by itself: it symbolized the cleansing that can only come through God's provision in Christ.

Preaching Idea

God gives us rituals to increase our appreciation of the realities found in Christ.

Contemporary Connections

What does it mean?

What does it mean that God gives us rituals to increase our appreciation of the realities found in Christ? In the Old Testament, God builds theological, spiritual categories through physical object lessons. The Spirit inspires verbal prophecy about the coming Messiah, but God also provides persons, events, and institutions that have prophetic value as typologies. Most readers of this commentary are familiar with the idea that Christ is the fulfillment of the sacrificial system, and thus they understand that the old covenant ceremonies and rituals involving sacrifice are pointing forward to Christ. The instructions God provides for the water of purification and the ashes of the red cow are no exception: they point forward to the "water of purification" that Christ provides, which cleanses us from defilement, sin, and death.

In the new covenant, there are also symbolic rituals and enacted portraits of Christ. The old covenant rituals looked forward to Christ, but now we look back on what Christ accomplished in his life, death, and resurrection. We also look at his ongoing work through the Spirit, and cast our gaze forward to his future return. The Lord's Supper is filled with symbolic meaning, as we remember our Lord. Baptism is the sign of the new covenant, signifying belonging in the new covenant community by virtue of union with Christ. These physical acts allow believers to participate in Christ-ordained, new covenant rituals. They are not magical, but rather point beyond the elements of the ritual enactment to the reality that is found in Christ.

Is it true?

Is it true that God gives us rituals to increase our appreciation of the realities found in Christ? There can be no doubt that God prescribes numerous rituals in Scripture, so the real question is whether or not they are given to show us Christ. In the New Testament, baptism and the Lord's Supper are clearly connected to Jesus and find their significance in him. Beyond this, there can be no doubt that Jesus and the apostles were united in the belief that he fulfilled the Old Testament law. Even a cursory glance at the book of Hebrews proves this point beyond a shadow of a doubt.

It is also worth saying that ritual enactments and participating in ordinances can deepen our practices of faith. Christ was well aware of the power of the Lord's Supper to draw the church into reflection and worship. We are physical-spiritual beings, and what we do with our bodies matters. The tangible, corporeal nature of baptism and the Lord's Supper are a tremendous advantage to us. We know that the cup symbolizes the blood of Christ, but that symbol makes the reality that it symbolizes easier to grasp; it increases our wonder and appreciation. We ought not to be more "spiritual" than God: he has given us rituals to increase our appreciation of the realities found in Christ.

Now what?

How do we engage in rituals so that they actually increase our appreciation of Christ and his work, rather than become the dry, lifeless forms of traditionalism? It is certainly possible to eat and drink the elements of the Lord's Supper without any spiritual engagement whatsoever. How do we overcome this?

First, we need to know the Lord. In order to increase in our appreciation for Christ, we need to know Christ in the first place. The new covenant ordinances are not religious rituals that confer saving grace upon those who participate, regardless of their heart and faith. Second, we need to prepare for participating. Prayer and meditation on the significance of the symbols is vital. Third, by the power of the Spirit, we need to concentrate and self-consciously thank God for the realities that the rituals symbolize. The physical act is a connection point to a greater reality, and by God's grace it can enrich our love and worship, leading us into thanksgiving.

Creativity in Presentation

This text lends itself well to a service where the new covenant ordinances will be practiced. The preacher can develop the meaning of the passage in Numbers 19 and then lay down the typological principles that move the contemporary reader to Christ. It is important to recognize that this passage does not merely "remind us of Christ" or "kind of look like Christ," but rather is typologically prophetic and *fulfilled* by Christ. The connection is intentional, rather than invented.

If there are people in the church who are going to be baptized, the preacher may want to consider this text as a way of establishing the significance of symbolic rituals in Scripture, starting here and moving forward to establish a biblical-theological framing of the ordinance. The same approach is compatible with participating in the Lord's Supper. We are not building bridges between old and new: God has built the bridge, and we are simply walking over it.

Although nothing we do will ever have the significance of the ordinances given by Christ, there are other physical acts we can engage in, if they help us reflect more deeply upon Christ. For example, basins of water could be placed around the auditorium and in the foyer, and people could be invited to dip their hands in the water, reminding themselves of the water of purification and the need of cleansing. They can say a simple prayer of repentance and faith as they wash their hands, remembering the fulfillment of the water of purification which is Jesus Christ himself. (Alternatively, given our age of disinfectants, there may be a parallel that can be pointed out with hand sanitizer. Water is a better image, but the principle of the analogy should be clear.) There are many ways to demonstrate that God gives us rituals to increase our appreciation of the realities found in Christ.

A possible breakdown for considering this text could be:

- God provides symbolic means of cleansing from impurity (19:1–13).

- The uncleanness of death must be remedied to be in the presence of the God of life (19:14–22).

DISCUSSION QUESTIONS

1. Why does being in the presence of dead bodies bring about ritual impurity? Why is a return to purity necessary to be in God's presence?

2. How does the ritual for cleansing impurity point us to Christ (see Heb. 9:23–28)?

3. Think of other symbolic actions or rituals that we practice today.[11] What purposes do they serve?

4. What rituals or routines are helpful in reorienting our thoughts to focus on God's presence?

---

11 Examples might include a bride wearing white or playing an anthem before a sporting event. Reflecting on modern ritual actions should help in comprehending the function of biblical rituals.

SIN AND REDEMPTION FOR THE SECOND GENERATION (20:1–25:18)

As the forty years of wandering draw to a close, a new generation of Israel comes to the forefront. Unfortunately, it soon becomes evident that this generation is prone to some of the same flaws as its predecessors. Although this generation does not flagrantly refuse to go where God leads, it does complain about physical hardships, causing even Moses to respond in a way that does not honor God (20:1–13). Israel's faithfulness culminates with a descent into idolatry that requires a shocking remedy (25:1–18). This section also begins the process of transferring leadership to the next generation (20:14–21:3). Despite these challenges, evidence of God's mercy abounds as he guides them through the wilderness and defeats foreign enemies (21:4–35) and turns the efforts of Balaam to curse Israel into promises of blessing (22:1–41; 23:1–26; 23:27–24:25). At the end of this section, the second generation of Israelites are on the Plains of Moab, close to seeing God's covenant promises fulfilled. This generation maintains a propensity to grumble and complain, but through God's grace, the covenant endures, and God's promises are on the brink of fulfillment.

Numbers 20:1–13

EXEGETICAL IDEA
Moses and Aaron's failure to show God as holy disqualifies them from leading Israel into the Promised Land.

THEOLOGICAL FOCUS
God's servants must reflect God's character.

PREACHING IDEA
Moses was an imperfect servant, but Christ is the perfect Son of God.

PREACHING POINTERS
According to the divine verdict, we know that Moses and Aaron sinned in what they did in this pericope. Most Christian leaders, however, can probably look at times in their lives when they have said and done things that seem worse in the face of much less provocation. It's natural that our hearts go out to Moses: he was human, just like us, and this was the straw that broke his back. Nevertheless, God's holy standards are not lowered for any of his servants, and there were real consequences for his and Aaron's sin.

One of the marks of the honesty and trustworthiness of the biblical witness is that it is unflinching when it comes to reporting both the successes and failures of its main characters. This deep honesty is all the more remarkable when it comes to the presentation of Jesus Christ. In a book that depicts the sins of the heroes of the faith, Jesus alone is depicted as sinlessly perfect. No sin is reported of him, because there was no sin to report. Moses and Aaron were servants of God, and they were imperfect—like all of us—but Jesus is the Son of God, and he is infinitely perfect and matchless in every way. Moses's sin prevented him from going into the Promised Land, but Jesus leads his redeemed people into eternal glory in the new heaven and earth. Moses was an imperfect servant, but Christ is the perfect Son of God.

WATER FROM THE ROCK (20:1–13)

LITERARY STRUCTURE AND THEMES

This unit returns to narrative, following two chapters of religious legislation (Numbers 18–19). It revisits Israel's propensity toward grumbling but is unique in its condemnation of Moses for his response. It begins with a brief statement about the death of Miriam (20:1), followed by the people's complaint (20:2–5). God appears and gives instructions to Moses (20:6–8). However, Moses does not follow them, leading to serious consequences (20:9–12). The unit concludes with a brief declaration, naming the place of the encounter (20:13).

Key themes of this unit include Israel's ongoing failures to trust God to meet their needs and the absolute necessity of bearing witness to God's holiness. Moses's departure from God's instructions is not a minor matter; it undermines God's presentation of himself to his people.

- *The Death of Miriam (20:1)*
- *The People's Complaint (20:2–5)*
- *God's Appearance (20:6–8)*
- *Moses's Response and Its Consequences (20:9–12)*
- *Summary Declaration (20:13)*

EXPOSITION

Israel's grumbling spirit has not been quenched despite the consequences of previous rebellions and ample evidence of God's ability to meet their needs. They again complain about their food and the absence of water. The provision of water from a rock recalls Exodus 17:1–7, prior to their arrival at Sinai. However, Moses's flawed response causes the stories to diverge. Instead, this unit reveals that Moses's failure to show God as holy disqualifies him from leading Israel into the Promised Land.

The Death of Miriam (20:1)

20:1. This verse contains a brief announcement of Miriam's death. She has been absent from Numbers since she and Aaron challenged Moses's leadership (Num. 12:1–16). The brevity of the commentary reflects her fall from grace. She once led the whole nation in joyful song (Exod. 15:21–22), but her death merits only a passion mention.

The timing of her death and the rest of the narrative is uncertain. This verse identifies it as "in the first month" (בַּחֹדֶשׁ הָרִאשׁוֹן) but does not specify the year. Further on, Numbers 20:22–29 recounts the death of Aaron, which the wilderness itinerary places in the fortieth year (Num. 33:38–39). This suggests that Miriam's death is in the same year (Ashley 1993, 380; Cole 2000, 323–24). Her death is thus a sign of the end of the condemned generation and may prefigure the imminent downfall of Moses and Aaron.

Miriam's Death

The timing of this narrative emphasizes the selectivity of the biblical narrator. The forty-year period of wandering is announced in Numbers 14:33. If this narrative occurs at the tail end of that period, then Korah's rebellion and its aftermath are the only stories drawn from the intervening thirty-eight years (Schnittjer 2006, 410). Whatever else happened during that period is not deemed necessary for the biblical audience to know. Gane turns alliterative here, referring to this interval as "dull decades of death in the desert" (Gane 2004, 672).

Miriam's death and the subsequent narrative are set at Kadesh, in the Wilderness of Zin.[1] Kadesh was the place from which the spies entered the land, prompting Israel's great rebellion and its forty years of wandering. This location thus hangs "an ominous cloud" over the rest of the narrative (Allen 2012, 281).

The People's Complaint (20:2–5)

20:2. Again, the people face a shortage of water and as on previous occasions, "they assembled themselves against Moses and Aaron" (ESV). The absence of water provides the first echo of Exodus 17:1–7.

20:3–5. The people's complaints are prefaced with the expression "[they] contended with Moses" (NET). This comes from the Hebrew root ריב which typically has legal connotations but can reference other types of disputes. Notably, it is also found in the parallel story of Exodus 17:2 (cf. Gen. 13:7; 20:26). The Israelites then launch into series of familiar invectives. They express that it would have been better to die with their fellow Israelites (cf. Num. 14:2), likely referring to the consequences of Korah's rebellion (Ashley 1993, 381). They accuse Moses and Aaron of bringing Israel into the wilderness to kill them (cf. Num. 16:12–14) and complain about the lack of variety in their diet (cf. Num. 11:5). The capstone complaint is in 20:5b, where they declare that there is no water to drink.

The Israelites' complaint is justifiable on one level; a lack of water was a serious threat. However, the accusation that Moses and Aaron deliberately sought to destroy the nation and the protests about the absence of certain food are unfounded. Further, these complaints suggest a failure to remember God's many acts of provision and the consequences of previous complaints. There is a crisis at hand, but the Israelites' hyperbolic claims threaten to obscure it.

God's Appearance (20:6–8)

20:6. Moses and Aaron do not respond to the complaints of the Israelites. Instead, they approach the entrance of the Tent of Meeting and fall on their faces, recalling the response to the report of the spies (Num. 14:5), Korah's challenge (Num. 16:4), and the people's grumbling after Korah's judgment (Num. 16:45). It is a "position of entreaty and intercession," meant to avert the expected wrath of God (Cole 2000, 325). YHWH's glory then appears, presumably in the form of a fire-encased cloud (Num. 9:15; Milgrom 1990, 165). The only other complaint narrative where this occurs is Israel's refusal to enter the Promised Land, which also took place at Kadesh (Num. 14:10). This parallel may prefigure the outcome of this narrative (Ashley 1993, 382).

20:7–8. God commissions Moses to redress the situation and provide water. Noticeably absent from the divine speech are signs of anger or threats of judgment (Allen 2012, 283). Indeed, "no evidence of God's displeasure is reported" (Lee 2003b, 229). God issues seemingly straightforward instructions, directing Moses to take the staff, gather the congregation along with Aaron, and speak to the rock.[2] This is of course different from the instruction to strike the rock in Exodus 17:5. However, the result is to be the same. God declares to Moses that in doing this, "you shall bring water out of the rock" (20:8b ESV). God thus promises to meet the most immediate concern, without

---

1 Numbers 13:26 locates Kadesh in the Wilderness of Paran. It is likely that Zin is a subsection of the larger Paran region (Cole 2000, 323).

2 The command to "speak" is plural, referring to both Moses and Aaron (וְדִבַּרְתֶּם) while the commands to "take" (קַח) and "gather" (וְהַקְהֵל) are singular. Notably, Aaron does not speak at all in this narrative. His silence and Moses's unauthorized speech are both implicitly condemned (Num. 20:12).

comment on Israel's additional complaints. This is "surprisingly merciful" (Pressler 2017, 178).

Moses's Response and Its Consequences (20:9–12)

20:9. At this point the narrative takes a unique turn, as Moses fails to follow all of God's instructions. It starts off promisingly as Moses takes the staff just as God commanded him. The identity of this staff is unclear, but presumably it is intended to mark Moses's position and authority.[3] The staff also lacks an obvious function on this occasion since Moses was instructed to speak to, not strike, the rock (cf. Exod. 17:6). However, its presence provides a means to demonstrate Moses's departure from God's instructions.

20:10. Once Moses and Aaron assemble the nation as instructed, the situation quickly derails. In contrast to YHWH's neutral speech, Moses begins by addressing the community as "rebels" (הַמֹּרִים), an appellation that in the Pentateuch refers to defiance against God (Budd 1984, 218–19). It is clearly true that Israel has rebelled against God in the past (and will in the future), but Moses goes beyond what God himself has stated about this situation.

After heightening the hostility of the situation, Moses then asks, "shall we bring water for you out of this rock?" (20:10b ESV). The nuance of this question is hard to ascertain as the verb (נוֹצִיא) can be read in several different ways. The most likely possibilities are that Moses is warning the people to "be careful what you wish for," similar to the provision of quail in Numbers 11, or he may be expressing his reluctance to give the Israelites what they want (Emmrich 2003, 55; Olson 1996, 127).[4] Regardless of what exactly Moses meant, the fact that he phrases it as "must *we* bring forth" (referring to himself and Aaron) is noteworthy. Moses appears to be upstaging God, making himself the arbiter of whether the Israelites deserve water (Lioy 2020, 42). Moses thus presents himself and Aaron as Israel's providers, rather than God (Burnside 2017, 129). Even though YHWH has already given him instructions to meet Israel's needs, Moses inserts an unnecessary question that eliminates YHWH from the equation and sounds a discordant note.

Moses Draws Water from the Rock by Francois Perrier. Public domain.

---

3   There are two main possibilities for the identity of the staff that Moses takes. It could refer to his own staff which he raised to part the Red Sea (Exod. 14:16), elevated to secure Israel's victory over the Amalekites (Exod. 17:8–16), and struck the rock to provide water (Exod. 17:5; Allen 2012, 283; Gane 2004, 674; Milgrom 1990, 165). The other option is that it is Aaron's staff that budded to confirm his office in Numbers 17:8. Moses then placed it in the Holy of Holies (Num. 17:10) to remind the Israelites not to rebel against Aaron (Cole 2000, 326; Harrison 1990, 264; Wenham 2008, 168). The Hebrew supports either reading, given the lack of possessive suffix on the noun for staff (הַמַּטֶּה). Alternatively, Sprinkle suggests that actually Exodus only identifies one staff and that both Moses and Aaron used it for miraculous purposes (Sprinkle 2015, 308). The precise identity of the staff is not nearly as significant as what Moses does with it.

4   For a discussion of other possible meanings, see Olson 1996, 126–27.

20:11. The divergence between God's instructions and Moses's actions continues as Moses takes the staff and strikes the rock twice. On one hand, he is successful in providing water, but on the other, he has clearly not followed God's commands. The verse begins with a statement that "Moses raised his hand" (NET). Notably, this collocation (from the verbal root רוּם "to raise" with יָד "hand" as its object) resembles the description of the "high-handed" (בְּיָד רָמָה) sin which uses an adjective from the same root in Numbers 15:30.[5] Further, God's command to speak to the rock carries an implicit corollary: do *not* strike it, even though that has worked before (Burnside 2017, 133). The physical action of raising a hand to strike thus also points toward direct defiance of God.

Moses then strikes the rock twice. This is a further difference from Exodus 17:6 where it appears that he only struck it once. This is presumably a reflection of his exasperation with the repeated complaints of the Israelites; a physical outlet for his frustration no doubt felt appropriate. However, the primary note about this action is not the number of blows, but the fact that he struck the rock *at all*. The rock represented the means by which God would show his benevolence; physically striking it reflects lashing out at God (Cole 2000, 328–29).[6]

Even though Moses did not follow God's commands, God graciously permitted this action to provide water for the community and its animals. Just as God preserved his relationship with the Israelites when they rebelled against Moses and Aaron, God now preserves the life of the community when its leaders fail.

20:12. God's grace does not preclude judgment on disobedience. God addresses Aaron and Moses and states that they will not lead the community into the Promised Land "[b]ecause you did not trust me enough to show me as holy" (NET). The verb "trust" (הֶאֱמַנְתֶּם) reflects a willingness to rely on God which is absent here; Moses instead substitutes his own strength and judgment. This constitutes a failure to "show me (God) as holy" (לְהַקְדִּישֵׁנִי), a serious transgression. God's holiness sets him apart from flawed, sinful creatures; when Moses acts out of a fit of pique, it poorly reflects the divine nature. As God's representative, he here makes God appear "as emotionally flawed as human beings" (Lioy 2020, 43).

There is a certain symmetry to the judgment passed down on Moses and Aaron. It was at Kadesh in Numbers 14 that the first generation disqualified itself from entering the Promised Land because of its stubborn defiance of God's will. Now, nearly a generation later at Kadesh, Moses sets himself against God's will and, along with Aaron, receives a similar fate (Noonan 2020, 85).

> **What Is Moses's Sin?**
> Those studying this text have wrestled throughout the centuries with the relationship between Moses's transgression and its consequences. After a lifetime of faithful service, does Moses's behavior warrant the penalty he receives? It is also noteworthy that in later references to this incident, Moses places the blame on the Israelites (Deut. 1:37–40; 3:32–29; 4:21–24). However, whenever the text has God speak, he places the blame

---

5   Noonan points out that this collocation almost always expresses "an attitude of determination to triumph over another individual" (Noonan 2020, 85). In this case, Moses seeks to put his will ahead of God's. He also notes that another verb (נָשָׂא) is used when describing the basic physical act of lifting one's hand.

6   It is also possible that striking the rock reflected an attempt to seek a more human solution to the problem. Some have noted that in this region, there are occasionally stores of water trapped in limestone by a mineral cap. A sharp blow could dislodge the cap and bring out the water (Beck 2003, 140). Whether Moses's motivations are to go with what worked before (Exodus 17) or to take advantage of physical geography, his refusal to obey God is central.

on Moses (Num. 20:13; 27:12–14; Deut. 32:48–52). The historical reflection on this event preserved in Psalm 106:32–33 castigates both parties, charging Israel with rebellion and Moses with speaking rashly. Thus, the balance of biblical tradition does ascribe blame to Moses.

The exact nature of Moses's transgression is also a point of contention. Milgrom lists ten different options, broken into three broader categories: Moses's action of striking the rock, Moses's character, and Moses's speech (Milgrom 1990, 448). These reflect a desire to specify one element of the story as the tipping point that doomed Moses. The wide range of possibilities has even led some to conclude that the exact nature of the transgression is deliberately ambiguous, giving its readers the opportunity to "wrestle with and converse regarding the story itself" (Schnittjer 2006, 414).

In contrast, a close reading of the text reveals problems with nearly everything Moses says or does. He receives direct instructions from God and does not obey them. Further, he evinces more anger and frustration than God at the complaints of the Israelites, perhaps taking upon himself the role of enacting judgment (Allen 2012, 283). Finally, he inserts himself (and Aaron) into the provision of water, asking "shall *we* bring forth?" when his appointed role is to enact God's declared will (Burnside 2017, 139). This may suggest that he is acting like a pagan miracle workers (Milgrom 1990, 454). Taken together, Moses's words and actions reflect flagrant defiance of God which understandably incurs divine judgment.

The fates of Moses and Aaron reflect those of the first generation of Israelites in Numbers 14. Both defied God's instructions and both ultimately failed to reach the Promised Land. However, in both cases God mitigated the punishment (Boda 2009, 94–95). God did not destroy Israel but permitted the children of the rebels to experience his covenant promises. God also does not remove Moses and Aaron from leadership or immediately demand their lives. Aaron is memorialized by the community (Num. 20:22–29) while Moses leads Israel until it is right on the border of the Promised Land. God even grants him a glimpse of the land right before his death (Deut. 34:1–4).

Summary Declaration (20:13)
20:13. This unit concludes by calling the place where this occurred "the waters of Meribah." This is a pun on the verbal root ריב ("to strive/contend"). The name reflects the conflict that occurred (cf. Num. 11:3, 34). The same name was given to the site of the previous conflict over water (Exod. 17:7). Other passages refer to this location as "Meribah-Kadesh" to distinguish it (Num. 21:14; Deut. 32:51; Ezek. 48:28). It is perfectly understandable that a similar course of events would occasion a reuse of this name.

The final clause announces that God "showed himself holy" (ESV) in these events.[7] This of course is a direct challenge to Moses and Aaron who failed to demonstrate God's holiness. God demonstrates his essential nature through both his gracious provision of water and his judgment against those who misrepresented him (Cole 2000, 330).

THEOLOGICAL FOCUS
The exegetical idea of this passage (Moses and Aaron's failure to show God as holy disqualifies them from leading Israel into the Promised Land) leads to the following theological focus: *God's servants must reflect God's character.* Although the errors of Moses and Aaron in this passage may not seem as extreme as those of the other Israelites, they had a deleterious effect on

---

[7] The full clause is וַיִּקָּדֵשׁ בָּם "he showed himself holy among them." The referent of the pronoun is probably the Israelites, which is reflected in the major translations (CSB, ESV, NET, NIV, NKJV). It could also refer to the waters themselves, suggesting that God revealed himself through the provision of water.

how God was presented to his people. Moses and Aaron were "to show forth God's holiness, to represent his power, providence, care, and concern for the people in and through their words and actions" (Stubbs 2009, 161). Instead, Moses's anger and Aaron's silence misrepresented God's evaluation of the situation.

The gravity of a distorted witness to God's character is even stronger for those in positions of authority. When "God's man" (or woman) performs a harmful act, it casts doubt on the nature of God whom they claim to serve. The sons of Eli commit crimes far worse than that of Aaron in this text, indulging their desires for sensual pleasure and even claiming a portion of God's share of the offerings (1 Sam. 2:12–25). In this way, they suggest that God is not concerned with his own holiness and that his servants can lay claim to whatever they desire. Likewise, David's encounter with Bathsheba was devastating on multiple levels, but if the "man after God's own heart" (1 Sam. 13:14) can violate his subjects in this way, what does that say about God's heart? David at least acknowledges his grievous offense against God, crying out hyperbolically, "Against you, you only have I sinned" (Ps. 51:4 NIV).

This theme continues in the New Testament. Jesus's harshest words are reserved for Pharisees and other spiritual authorities who profess to completely follow God's instructions and yet neglect its essential qualities of justice, mercy, and faithfulness (Matt. 23:23–26). Authority figures in the church can also misrepresent God with their words and deeds. Paul challenged Peter for his refusal to eat with Gentile Christians, thus denying the essential equality that all believers have in Christ (Gal. 2:11–18; Sprinkle 2015, 309). James declares that not many should seek to become teachers because weightier judgment may fall on them (James 3:1). An authority figure or teacher has an even more pressing obligation to properly reflect the essential character and nature of a perfectly holy God.

Ultimately, all of God's servants depend on God's mercy and grace for redemption when, inevitably, they fall short of God's standards. However, the distortion that Moses introduces into this story misrepresents God's character and fails to show his holiness (Num. 20:12). This leads to devastating consequences.

PREACHING AND TEACHING STRATEGIES

Exegetical and Theological Significance

The long-suffering Moses is finally overcome by the persistent grumbling of the Israelites. Although he is fully responsible for what he does in disobeying the Lord's instructions, the fact that he made it this far before breaking is a sign of his incredible faithfulness over the years. Nevertheless, Moses is a person who sins like any other human being, and his record of service is imperfect and marred by this event.

Oliver Cromwell was the Lord Protector of England in the 1650s, and he is reported to have said to his portrait painter that he wanted to be painted "warts and all." This could be considered the guiding philosophy behind Scripture's depictions of God's people. Scripture is unfailingly clear about the imperfections, failures, and sins of the human characters. Despite the great good that Moses did, he fell short of God's glory, failed to uphold God's holiness, succumbed to anger and pride, and as a result could not enter the Promised Land. Since he himself could not enter the land, he could not lead the people into it either.

Just as the figure of David causes the reader to cry out for a greater King, so the figure of Moses causes the reader to long for a perfect leader who never fails. Thankfully, we are not dependent on an imperfect servant; on the contrary, we are dependent on God's perfect Son. The author of Hebrews lays out the contrast between the imperfect Moses and the perfect son of God:

Therefore, holy brothers and sisters, who share in the heavenly calling, fix your thoughts on Jesus, whom we acknowledge as our apostle and high priest. He was faithful to the one who appointed him, just as Moses was faithful in all God's house. Jesus has been found worthy of greater honor than Moses, just as the builder of a house has greater honor than the house itself. For every house is built by someone, but God is the builder of everything. "Moses was faithful as a servant in all God's house," bearing witness to what would be spoken by God in the future. But Christ is faithful as the Son over God's house. And we are his house, if indeed we hold firmly to our confidence and the hope in which we glory. (Heb. 3:1–6 NIV)

Preaching Idea

Moses was an imperfect servant, but Christ is the perfect Son of God.

Contemporary Connections

What does it mean?

What does it mean that Moses was an imperfect servant, but Christ is the perfect Son of God? As mentioned above, Scripture presents its human characters "warts and all." This tradition of reporting even the unflattering mistakes and egregious sins of God's servants is what makes the presentation of Christ so absolutely breathtaking: If people sin, the Bible says so, but Christ *was literally perfect.*

While the human agents in Scripture are shown warts and all, the sacrificial animals had to have an observable lack of imperfection. The sacrificial animals—including the red cow of the previous chapter—were all to be without blemish or defect. No person in Scripture is perfect, except Jesus Christ the Son of God. Jesus is not simply better than everyone else; he is in a category all of his own.

It is also likely significant that Moses, who represents the Law, is not the one who takes God's people into the Promised Land. That job is given to Joshua. As is well known, the Hebrew name *Joshua* is brought over into Greek as *Jesus*. It is Jesus, not Moses, who fulfills the plan of redemption by bringing God's people into the ultimate land of promise. As John writes, "For the law was given through Moses; grace and truth came through Jesus Christ" (John 1:17). In every way, Jesus is greater than Moses.

Is it true?

Is it true that Moses was an imperfect servant, but Christ is the perfect Son of God? The failure and sin of Moses—as well as his death outside of the Promised Land—prove that he was an imperfect servant. Jesus, however, could challenge his enemies to point out even one sin that he had committed (John 8:36), knowing that they could not do so successfully.

The manifold perfection of Jesus as the Son of God is revealed in place after place in the New Testament. One particularly helpful verse, however, is 2 Corinthians 5:21: "God made him who had no sin to be sin for us, so that in him we might become the righteousness of God" (NIV). This verse explicitly affirms the sinlessness of Jesus. He was able to be the sin-bearer and function as the morally spotless substitutionary sacrifice because he himself had no sins that defiled him and rendered him unclean. If Jesus had been a sinner, he would have had to die for his own sins, and his death on the cross would be of no avail to others.

Now what?

What do we do in response to the fact that Moses was an imperfect servant, but Christ is the perfect Son of God? Immediately after contrasting Moses as the servant with Christ who is the Son, the author of Hebrews calls his readers to repentance and faith in Jesus (Heb. 3:7–4:13). He warns them not to harden their hearts, which is what the wilderness generation did and what resulted in their being barred from the Promised Land. The author points people to the fulfillment of Sabbath rest, which is found not in a day of the week, nor in a geographical location, but only in Jesus Christ himself, since he gives his people redemptive rest from their sins. It is through the Son that we can enter into the eschatological rest of the Seventh Day.

It is easy to look at Numbers 20 and draw out moral lessons about persevering in faithfulness and how one sin can disqualify us from glory. It is permissible to point out the necessity of strict obedience to every word of God and to warn against sinning in the face of unending provocation. There are certainly lessons here for both leaders and followers. Yet, more than anything else, placing this passage in the broader framework of Scripture should move us from the historical event involving Moses to the time of the Savior, Jesus Christ. Let the people see the failure of Moses, but as a springboard to the perfection of Jesus. Then, as the author of Hebrews does, urge people not to harden their hearts but rather to put their faith and trust in Jesus Christ, God's one and only Son.

Creativity in Presentation

The preacher could place a rock on the platform and demonstrate the futility of trying to get water to flow from it, whether it is spoken to or struck. This will highlight the fact that, even though Moses sinned, what happened was still a miraculous display of God's mercy, grace, and power.

Next, the preacher should be careful in explaining that although it may not seem consequential whether the rock is struck or spoken to, once God has told us how to do something, we must obey with the greatest of care. When God tells us to do something, we are to do it exactly as he has specified.

The punishment and consequence given to Moses for his failure may strike us as disproportionate. It is God, however, who determines the penalty that fits the crime. What is even more important is the fact that Moses is a symbolic leader of God's people, and that God's people actually need a perfect leader if they are going to experience the fullness of redemption and blessing. Any blemish disqualifies someone from the Promised Land, and the ultimate Promised Land of the new heaven and new earth can only be opened up by a perfect leader who never sins.

It may be helpful to put up a simple slide that contrasts Christ and Moses. There are numerous important similarities and dissimilarities between the two, although you can come up with your own list. By way of example:

1. Both are special sons who are saved from death as infants.
2. Both are prophets.
3. Both lead God's people.
4. Moses sins; Jesus doesn't.
5. Moses dies for his sins; Jesus dies for the sins of others.
6. Law comes through Moses; grace and truth come through Jesus Christ.
7. Moses is the servant in God's house; Christ is the Son over the house.
8. Moses cannot enter the Promised Land; Jesus does, and brings in the people of God.
9. Moses is insufficient; Jesus is the all-sufficient Savior.
10. Moses deals with shadows and promise; Jesus with the substance and fulfillment.

Altogether, this comparison demonstrates that Moses was an imperfect servant, but Christ is the perfect Son of God.

One approach to the exposition of the this text could be:

- Sin leads to a diminishment of legacy (20:1).

- The grumbling spirit is hard to shake (20:2–5).

- Disobedience to God's commands fails to reflect his holiness (20:6–13).

DISCUSSION QUESTIONS

1. Why do the Israelites continually return to the same complaints, even when they have witnessed both God's provision and God's judgment in the past?

2. Why do you think that this incident is the one that made Moses disobey God's instructions?

3. In what ways does Moses fail to show God as holy in this text? Does he deserve the punishment that he receives?

4. What lessons can pastors, teachers, and other Christian leaders draw from the requirement to reflect God's holiness in this passage?

Numbers 20:14–21:3

EXEGETICAL IDEA
Israel's progression toward the Promised Land is marked by hostility from foreign enemies and a transition in leadership.

THEOLOGICAL FOCUS
God remains sovereign over both the nations and his people.

PREACHING IDEA
God is sovereign over every nation and every person, and he is sovereign over *you*.

PREACHING POINTERS
God is sovereign over all things. He rules the macro-level and the micro-level. He is sovereign over the nations and sovereign over every individual. This passage draws the past into the present and then looks into the future. Israel was a relatively small and weak nation, but God has already shown that he is faithful to his covenant people and more powerful than superpowers like Egypt. No gods can oppose him, and no human armies can defeat him. These lessons of the past are essential for Israel to take to heart as they move toward the Promised Land.

Yet even though God is moving in the large events of world history, and he is sovereign over the nations, he is intimately aware of every detail in the lives of every one of his children. He knows each one of us by name. The King of the Universe is also a personal God who delights in relationship with each individual in his family. Nations are composed of individuals, and God does not lose the individual in the crowd or the mass. His track record is one of holy, steadfast faithfulness, and no power can resist him. Nations should call on him, and every person on earth should trust in him. If he is your heavenly Father, trust his sovereign will and know that he cares for you as he directs the affairs of the world. God is sovereign over every nation and every person, but he is also sovereign over *you*.

ISRAEL IN TRANSITION (20:14–21:3)

LITERARY STRUCTURE AND THEMES

Numbers 20:14–21:35 consists of six vignettes mostly focused on Israel's interactions with hostile foreign powers, although two episodes have an internal focus: Aaron's death (20:22–29) and a final grumbling narrative (21:4–9). These vignettes bring Israel from its camp at Kadesh to a position just across the border from the Promised Land (cf. Num. 22:1). They are divided into two preaching units on account of the impracticality of covering six separate stories in one sermon.

The first three episodes consist of Edom's rejection of Israel's request to pass through their territory (20:14–21), the account of Aaron's death (20:22–29), and Israel's defeat of a Canaanite king (21:1–3). Two externally focused episodes thus flank the internal focus on Aaron's passing.

These stories bring the theme of foreign hostility to Israel's presence into Numbers. God delivered Israel from Egypt and there was a battle against nomadic Amalekites in Exodus 17:8–16, but since then the focus of the text has been upon God's relationship with Israel. The Canaanites, including the Anakites, briefly appear in Numbers 13–14 as a reason for Israel's refusal to obey God but they are minor players. Here, foreign powers return to the stage, and their interactions with Israel prefigure the conquest accounts.

The other theme is that of Israel's leadership in transition. As the nation prepares to approach the Promised Land, Aaron's passing is one further marker of the end of the first generation. His son Eleazar succeeds him, establishing continuity in the priestly office.

- *Hostility from Edom (20:14–21)*
- *Aaron's Death (20:22–29)*
- *Israel Defeats a Canaanite King (21:1–3)*

EXPOSITION

As Israel nears the end of its forty-year sojourn, its circumstances change. New challenges arise, and old leadership is replaced. These three episodes demonstrate that Israel's progression toward the Promised Land is marked by hostility from foreign enemies and a transition in leadership.

Hostility from Edom (20:14–21)

20:14a. Israel's preferred route to the Promised Land led it around the Dead Sea, through the territory of Edom. In an effort at diplomacy, Moses sent messengers to Edom's king. At the time of the Exodus, it was unlikely that Edom was actually a nation with a centralized monarchy in the manner of Israel under David or Solomon (Cole 2000, 332). However, the term "king" (מֶלֶךְ) could refer to lesser rulers of more localized regions (Ashley 1993, 389). No matter the exact political arrangement, the issue at stake is that this entity could impede Israel's journey.

20:14b–16. Moses's request follows the pattern of ancient Near Eastern diplomatic correspondence (Cole 2009, 373). In these verses, he identifies their past relationship and provides the background for his request. He sends the messengers in the name of "your brother Israel" (אָחִיךָ יִשְׂרָאֵל), pointing to their shared heritage. Genesis 36 identifies the Edomites as descendants of Esau. Later, in Deuteronomy 2:4–6, Moses recounts that God has awarded this territory to the Edomites. The Jacob and Esau narratives ended with reconciliation (Gen. 33:1–11), providing hope that the request of a brother might be accepted.

Moses then provides a historical summary of Israel's situation, intended to elicit sympathy. In 20:14b, he talks about the "hardship" (הַתְּלָאָה) Israel has endured, using a rare word found in both descriptions of the exodus and the exile (cf. Exod. 18:8; Lam. 3:5). He further specifies this as their mistreatment by the Egyptians for generations (20:15) and acknowledges that Israel has been rescued by YHWH who brought them out of Egypt (20:16).[1] Now, YHWH has led them to Kadesh, "a city on the edge of your territory" (20:16 ESV). This background frames the request that Moses is about to make.

20:17. Moses then issues his formal request along with certain stipulations by which Israel promises to abide. He asks to cross through their country by means of an ancient thoroughfare known as the King's Highway (דֶּרֶךְ הַמֶּלֶךְ). This is a well-known road that runs north-south to the east of the Jordan River and connects Egypt and the Arabian peninsula with major trade centers such as Damascus (Cole 2009, 373). The idea is that Israel will take the quickest and most direct route through the territory of the Edomites.

Moses adds further stipulations to his request, attempting to forestall anticipated objections. He declares that Israel will leave Edom's crops and wells untouched. Further, it will not "turn aside to the right hand or to the left until we have passed through your territory" (ESV). Given that a common image of an army is a horde of ravenous locusts, Moses's preemptive assurances are understandable.

20:18. Edom refuses without providing a further explanation. The king's response is given in the first-person singular, making him a metonym for the entire nation. Although, Israel's request may have been "eminently reasonable" (Pressler 2017, 182), especially after the reminder of their shared origins, it is unsurprising that Edom does not accede. Its ruler threatens to respond violently to any territorial incursions.

20:19. The people of Israel respond with greater assurances. It is possible that this refers to the diplomatic envoys sent by Moses who may have had some latitude to negotiate (Ashley 1993, 392). Essentially, Israel promises to take the least disruptive path through Edom's territory and offers financial remuneration for any water that they or their animals would consume. This reflects an acceptance of Edomite control over the region, as governing powers could impose tolls on trade caravans going through their territory (Cole 2009, 373). Of course, the migration of an entire people group is a much more threatening prospect.

> *TRANSLATION ANALYSIS*
> This verse contains a unique collocation: אֵין־דָּבָר. Its purpose seems to be to minimize further the effect of Israel's passage as they ask to pass through Edom's territory on foot. It cannot be translated literally so English translations adopt a variety of approaches:
> *ESV*: "Nothing more"
> *NET*: "without doing anything else"
> *NASB, NIV*: "nothing else"
> *CSB*: "there will be no problem"

20:20–21. These protestations continue to fall on deaf ears. Edom repeats its denial from 20:18 and marshals a strong force to march against Israel. Israel avoids a confrontation and turns away from its desired course. This sends the nation further east in its journey to eventually wind up on the Plains of Moab (cf. 22:1).

---

1   Moses's summation here is similar to other brief accounts of Israel's origins. See Deuteronomy 26:5–9 and Micah 6:4–5 (Pressler 2017, 182).

God's silence in this episode makes it hard to evaluate Israel's course of action. However, given Israel's historical connection through Esau and God's provision of this region to Edom (Deut. 2:5–6), it does not appear that armed conflict is warranted. It is possible that Israel's rebuff reflects the position of this story between the episode of Moses and Aaron's rebellion (20:1–13) and the account of Aaron's death (20:22–29; Cole 2000, 337).

Aaron's Death (20:22–29)

20:22–23. Rather than proceeding on the King's Highway, Israel journeys from Kadesh and comes to Mount Hor. Its precise location is unknown, but it is identified as being "on the border of the land of Edom" (20:23b ESV).[2] Israel is thus following the detour forced upon it from the previous passage. It is also fitting that this event is set on a mountain, given the significance of mountains such as Sinai for encountering God.

20:24. At Mount Hor, God instructs Moses to prepare for the death of Aaron and the transition to the next generation of priestly leadership. God declares, "Let Aaron be gathered to his people" (ESV), an expression with resonance throughout the Pentateuch. It occurs in conjunction with the deaths of Abraham (Gen. 25:8), Ishmael (Gen. 25:17), Isaac (Gen. 35:29), Jacob (Gen. 49:29), and Moses (Num. 27:13; Deut. 32:50; Milgrom 1990, 169). It implies a reunification "with one's ancestors who had entered the realm of Sheol previously" (Cole 2000, 340). It is a means of describing a dignified death, where the individual's passing does not remove them from their broader kinship and familial associations. The latter half of the verse declares this is happening now because he and Moses rebelled against YHWH. However, his death is framed with honor rather than disgrace.

20:25–27. God's instructions continue as he commands Moses to bring Aaron and his son Eleazar up onto the mountain. He then directs Moses to remove (וְהַפְשֵׁט) Aaron's garments and place them upon Eleazar (20:26a).[3] Contextually, this refers to the high priest's regalia, marking the transition in priestly leadership. Moving from Aaron to Eleazar is an expression of continuity and divine grace. The office granted to Aaron and his sons in Leviticus 8–9 remains within his family after his death despite his failure at Meribah.

Moses did just as God commanded (in contrast to his actions at Meribah) and the three men ascended the mountain. The ceremonial aspect of this event is evident in the statement that this happened "in the sight of the whole community" (20:27 NET). Public witness provides additional solemnity to the situation.

20:28. Once on the mountain, events proceeded as God had directed. Moses takes the priestly vestments from Aaron and places them upon Eleazar. Aaron dies and the remaining two men descend from the mountain. Numbers 33:38–39 places Aaron's death in the fortieth year in the wilderness. His death, like Miriam's, is another marker of the nearly complete transition to the next generation of Israel. It also prefigures the forthcoming death of Moses, which will also take place on the top of a mountain outside the boundaries of the Promised Land.

---

2 See Cole 2009, 374, for an evaluation of possibilities. The most likely is a location known as Jebel Madurah which is approximately fifteen miles from where Kadesh has been located.

3 Usually, the hiphil of the root פשט has negative connotations as seen in Joseph's brothers removing his garment (Gen. 37:23) or the Philistines despoiling Saul's corpse (1 Sam. 31:9). However, in this context, the idea of being gathered to one's people and the ceremonial transference of office to Aaron's son argues for a more positive framing.

20:29. This episode concludes with communal mourning for Aaron that lasts for thirty days. Moses receives the same mourning period in Deuteronomy 34:8. An ordinary mourning period was seven days (Gen. 50:10; 1 Sam. 31:13), so this reflects the stature accorded to Aaron (Ashley 1993, 397). His disobedience brought about his death, but his legacy within Israel endures as his son takes over his office.

Israel Defeats a Canaanite King (21:1–3)

21:1. Israel moved on from Mount Hor, and their route took them in proximity to a Canaanite ruler whose realm stretched into the Negev. He is identified only as the king of Arad. Locating this place is challenging, but it presumably was somewhere along Israel's route around Edom.[4] The ethnicity of this ruler is significant. As a Canaanite, he represents those peoples whom God had promised to drive out so that Israel could take possession of the land. Israel's previous encounter with the Canaanites had resulted in defeat (Num. 14:45). This king initiated military hostilities by attacking and capturing some of the Israelites.

21:2–3. This initial setback did not prompt grumbling or fear as might be expected, but an appeal to God. Israel vowed that if God granted them victory, they would devote the cities of their enemies to him. The first mention of a vow in this book is the Nazirite vow in Numbers 5. Although the context is quite different, in both cases, making a vow reflects a wholehearted commitment to what God requires (Stubbs 2009, 164). The key to this vow is the verb וְהַחֲרַמְתִּי. The verbal root חרם and its related noun (חֵרֶם) describe what Israel was to do to the Canaanite population and its possessions during the conquest (Deut. 20:16–17; Josh. 6:18; 7:1). If they are devoted to God, then they cannot be put to mundane use. Treasures like silver and gold can be devoted to God's sanctuary, but devoting people and cities to God necessitates their destruction. Israel's vow thus reflects a transactional arrangement in which it will forgo the bounty of its conquest in exchange for God's strength in providing the victory.

Both parties fulfilled their part of the arrangement, and YHWH granted Israel victory over these Canaanites (21:3). Verbal forms of חרם appear in relation to Israel's actions, pointing to the destruction of the king, his army, and his territory. The final act is to assign the name Hormah to the places Israel destroyed. This is also derived from the root חרם. Significantly, this name recalls Israel's defeat at the hands of the Canaanites in Numbers 14:41–45. The name Hormah is thus somewhat redeemed by its association with an Israelite victory rather than a defeat.

This brief episode demonstrates what should happen when Israel encounters hostile enemies. The first battle was fought contrary to God's expressed command by the generation that had just refused to enter the Promised Land. This battle was fought after a direct appeal to God for strength. The brevity of the account corresponds to the lack of drama involved. Simple obedience and trust in God's strength is sufficient to secure victory.

THEOLOGICAL FOCUS

The exegetical idea (Israel's progression toward the Promised Land is marked by hostility from foreign enemies and a transition in leadership) points toward the following theological focus: *God remains sovereign over both the nations and his people.* God is silent in the encounter with Edom, but in the retelling of this event in Deuteronomy 2:2–6, he directs Israel not to attack Edom because he has granted Edom its territory. This is reminiscent of the Table of Nations in Genesis 10 in which God allots territory

---

4 See the discussion in Cole 2009, 374.

to many nations. Similarly, in Amos 9:7 God declares that he is responsible for giving the Philistines and Arameans their current homelands. Consequently, this interaction with Edom reflects God's authority over the nations. Since Edom is Israel's "brother," God does not permit open warfare at this point. Israel's actions implicitly affirm that God has allowed Edom to claim this region.

God's sovereignty over the nations is demonstrated in another way in Numbers 21:1–3. This text provides a brief preview of God's authority to award possession of the Promised Land to Israel by driving out the Canaanites. It reflects an initial fulfillment of God's covenant promises to Abraham in Genesis 15:13–16, that his descendants will take possession of the land after the sin of its current inhabitants reached its full measure. Deuteronomy 7:1–9 calls Israel to destroy all the elements of the Canaanites' idolatrous presence in the land because Israel is to be a holy people. The same passage affirms that this is not because of any inherent moral superiority in Israel, but rather a demonstration of God's faithfulness to his covenant promises. This brief interaction with the Canaanites further confirms that God reigns over these nations and can decree their destiny. As the biblical story progresses, these texts remind us that eventually every tribe, tongue, and nation will bow and acknowledge the absolute sovereignty of God revealed in Christ (Phil. 2:10–11).

Aaron's death further reflects the sovereignty of God over Israel. God appointed Aaron and his family to the priesthood and now decrees when the time has come to transition priestly duties to the next generation. Further on in the biblical story, God took the priesthood away from the house of Eli and awarded it to Samuel. Eli's response was simply, "He is the LORD; let him do what is good in his eyes" (1 Sam. 3:18 NIV). God's rule thus encompasses those whom he appoints to lead his own people along with his authority over other nations.

PREACHING AND TEACHING STRATEGIES

Exegetical and Theological Significance

In Roman mythology, Janus was a god depicted with two faces, each pointing in opposite directions. The association was that he was the god of time and transitions, bringing the past through the present and into the future. Numbers 20–21 has the qualities of a literary Janus. The chapters look back on previous themes, bring those themes up to date in the present, and cast an eye forward to the future.

Numbers 21 begins with the death of Miriam, and it concludes with the death of Aaron. Although they had sinfully challenged Moses in 12:1–15, they were still his family and significant leaders in Israel. Now, in accord with God's judgment on the wilderness generation, they died outside of the Promised Land. The death of Aaron was particularly significant, given his role with Moses in the court of Pharaoh, and because he occupied the office of high priest. Eleazar is appointed in his place. The old guard is passing, and the new is being appointed for the future.

Conflict with the nations also pulls forward events from the past and connects them to the present and a foreshadowed future. Israel's first misguided attempt to enter Canaan without God's help ended in disaster (14:44–45). However, when Israel was being oppressed by the superpower Egypt, YHWH systematically showed his power over the gods of Egypt and led his people out of the land of bondage. The exodus proves that God is the Lord of the nations, but Numbers 14 proved that Israel would be defeated if they did not rely on his power by faith. God can conquer Egypt, and yet the Canaanites can conquer Israel unless they go forward in the power of the Lord. Past these chapters, the oracles with Balaam also point to the present and future, establishing God's absolute sovereignty over the nations.

Has Israel established a track record of faith, trust, and confident belief throughout the narratives of Numbers? Far from it. The reader is now to wonder about what will happen as they progress toward the land. Readers who are familiar with how the story ends may not notice how fraught the text is with tension and uncertainties. The promises of God will be fulfilled, but the promises are not incompatible with judgments and the multiple failures of his people.

There is one great principle to cling to: God is sovereign. In the death of Aaron and the transition to Eleazar, God is in control. When confronted with giants, God is in control. Over the events of our lives, over our enemies, and even over our deaths, God is in control.

Preaching Idea
God is sovereign over every nation and every person, and he is sovereign over *you*.

Contemporary Connections

What does it mean?
What does it mean that God is sovereign over every nation and every person, and that he is sovereign over *you*? This theological principle means that no individual or collection of individuals acts autonomously in the world. People and nations are morally responsible for what they do, but they do not act outside of God's sovereign plan. There has never been a nation or individual that surprised God or placed his divine purposes in jeopardy.

God not only has power and authority over societies and nations, but he is also sovereign over every individual. As we see with the saga of Job, even Satan himself is limited by God's sovereignty. Nothing befalls us that puts God in a position of powerlessness.

From the global scale to the details of every individual life, God is sovereign. This doctrine has been of great comfort to believers all through the history of the church. That God is in sovereign control; that he is omnipotent; and that he is wise, compassionate, loving, gracious, and good provides a strong foundation for trust and assurance. We are not at the mercy of random forces; we are not even at the mercy of capricious foes. In the end, our lives are in the hands of a sovereign, holy God. Our lives are in the hands of a sovereign God who loves us so much that he sent his Son to redeem us and die in our place.

Is it true?
Is it true that God is sovereign over every nation and every person, and that he is sovereign over *you*? To cite Bible verses about God's sovereignty, let alone to make comments on them, would fill a book. Common passages to note include Genesis 45:5–7; 50:19–20; nearly the entire book of Job; Proverbs 21:1; Isaiah 10:5–19; 45:7–9; Matthew 10:29–31; Romans 8:28; 11:33–36; Ephesians 1:11; and James 4:13–17. This is a miniscule sampling of the biblical texts that address God's sovereignty. In fact, God's sovereignty is so woven through the entire Bible that it is impossible to make sense of the Scriptures without the doctrine of God's comprehensively good authority, power, and rule.

The foundation for the exodus out of Egypt and the conquest of Canaan is that God is sovereign over the nations of the earth. To see the truth of these things, read the long section of Isaiah 10–39 and see God's comprehensive lordship over every nation on earth. Then read Revelation and see God's sovereign power over the world and over all of his enemies and the powers of darkness. Read the gospel of John and Paul's epistles to the Romans and Ephesians. These books leave no doubt that God is sovereign over all things, from the cosmos, to the nations, to individuals.

Now what?
How do we respond to the truth that God is sovereign over every nation and every person, and that he is sovereign over us personally? The truth of this doctrine is not up for debate; it is not a matter for theological quibbling. In Scripture, when people think about the sovereignty of God, they praise him (e.g., Eph. 1:3–14). This doctrine is a revealed truth about God, and revelation is to lead us to praise.

God's sovereignty is also a reason to trust him and commit ourselves to him through Jesus Christ. It is a comfort in weariness and a foundation in storms. Turn to the sovereign God and rest in his perfect wisdom and power. This doctrine is not an abstract point of theology, but as practical as can be. God is in control of the past, present, and future.

On the personal level, this doctrine should drive us to Christ. Only by grace can we come to him, and only by grace can we be saved. Since God is sovereign, he is the lawful king over all nations and every individual. To persist in sin is to live in treason and rebellion. Because of Christ's perfect work, "Therefore God exalted him to the highest place and gave him the name that is above every name, that at the name of Jesus every knee should bow, in heaven and on earth and under the earth, and every tongue acknowledge that Jesus Christ is Lord, to the glory of God the Father" (Phil. 2:9–11).

In the end, every person will bow their knee before Jesus and acknowledge that he is king. This will either be done in joyful submission or in grudging defeat. Because God is sovereign, bow the knee now, repent of your sins, and put your trust in him. If you already know him, rejoice! Your God is the Sovereign Lord of heaven who rules over all things—including you.

Creativity in Presentation
This passage lends itself well to connecting biblical-theological dots. Like the Roman Janus, the preacher can situate the text in its relationship to themes that are antecedent and future in the unfolding of God's progressive revelation. Placing this passage in its textual flow will make it more comprehensible and richer for the congregation.

Taking the tremendously important biblical theme that God is sovereign over nations and individuals, the text can be applied to tumultuous political times (with prayers for peace, and thanks if peace obtains). It should also be pressed upon people in terms of individual reflection, appropriation, and response. What does God's sovereignty mean for their lives? Are they living as those with a robust and joyful acceptance of God's control over all things?

In the wider service, it may be worthwhile to provide a time for a testimony about God's sovereign work in someone's life. Given the enormous amount of important biblical data concerning God's sovereignty, having a team of readers read selected verses and short passages of Scripture may help build up a cumulative effect. God's sovereignty is not a matter for abstract philosophy, but rather for concrete theology.

Songs of praise should also be selected that highlight these truths. The song leader should point out the doctrinal contours of the songs and draw attention to the way that they declare these truths. Taken as a whole, every element of the worship service can be thematically related.

One note of caution: there are analogies between God's sovereignty and those of human authorities, but God is sovereign in a way that no one else is. It is not just that he has more power, more control, or more authority—it is that he alone has *absolute* power, control, and authority. He alone has intrinsic sovereignty; every other power is derivative and dependent on him. God alone is sovereign over the human heart. Analogies and illustrations can help, but it is vital that people understand that God's sovereignty is categorically unique. He is sovereign over every nation and every person: He is sovereign over *you*.

One possible outline for expositing this text is:

- God's people continue to face hostility when they go where he leads (20:14–21).

- God provides leadership for his people throughout their generations (20:22–29).

- God can overcome any foe when his people rely upon him (21:1–3).

DISCUSSION QUESTIONS

1. Why is God silent during Israel's interactions with Edom? How should we evaluate Edom's response to Israel's request?

2. What legacy has Aaron left behind at the end of his tenure as Israel's high priest? How does the text convey that this is an honorable transfer of authority?

3. How can churches and other Christian ministries make successful transitions at the end of a leader's tenure?

4. How does the account of the battle with the king of Arad prefigure what will happen in the book of Joshua?

Numbers 21:4–35

EXEGETICAL IDEA
Israel's journey to the Promised Land is marked by God's discipline and God's provision.

THEOLOGICAL FOCUS
God sustains his people in the face of their own failings and external challenges.

PREACHING IDEA
Our victory is secure through God's provision of atonement and Christ's victory over every evil power.

PREACHING POINTERS
Jesus refers to this passage in John 3, and in doing so ensures that it will be one of the best-known events in Numbers. The incarnate Christ himself tells us the prophetic significance of this event: the bronze serpent lifted up on the pole symbolizes his own atoning death when he is lifted up on the cross. People cannot control what their external enemies do, but even more frighteningly, apart from grace they also cannot control their internal, deadly enemy (i.e., their sin nature). Human beings stand in absolute need of forgiveness and atonement for sin, but we also need a conquering champion to win a victory over enemies we cannot defeat. Biblically speaking, we need a Savior to save us from ourselves.

Numbers 21 shows us that God provides atonement for his people, and then he leads them on in victory over their enemies. Christ's substitutionary atonement is multifaceted, and one vital element of it is that in his death and resurrection he is the victor over sin, death, hell, and all the powers of darkness (*Christus victor*). Only in Christ can we find atonement for our sins, and only in Christ can we be led forth in victory. In order to defeat our spiritual enemies, we must first bow our knee and look to Christ as he is lifted up on the cross. Thanks be to God, our victory is secure through God's provision of atonement and Christ's victory over every evil power.

INTERNAL AND EXTERNAL CHALLENGES (21:4–35)

LITERARY STRUCTURE AND THEMES

This preaching unit comprises the final three episodes in Israel's journey from Meribah to the Plains of Moab (Num. 22:1). The death of Aaron signifies that Israel is mostly composed of the second generation. The first episode (21:4–9) shows that this new generation still has the complaining spirit as it reprises Israel's previous grumbling but is unique through God's command to construct a bronze serpent. The second traces Israel's journey toward Moab and offers further evidence of God's provision (21:10–20). The third and final episode returns to Israel's interaction with hostile nations and details its defeat of Sihon and Og, two imposing Amorite rulers (21:21–35). The overall tone of this unit is positive, with even the grumbling narrative reaching quick resolution. At its conclusion, Israel has progressed to the border of the Promised Land and learned that God can defeat its enemies.

The driving theme of this unit is the necessity of relying on God. Israel must look to God for restoration when it sins, trust God for provision on its journey, and defeat its enemies through God's strength. As Israel moves closer to the Promised Land, God demonstrates his covenant faithfulness yet again.

- **The Copper Serpent (21:4–9)**
- **Provision on the Road to Moab (21:10–20)**
- **Conflict with Sihon and Og (21:21–35)**

EXPOSITION

The first episode in this unit is much better known than the latter two. It also marks the end of grumbling narratives in the Pentateuch. In a few chapters, Israel will face divine judgment again, but not because of its complaints against Moses or God (Num. 25:1–9). The resolution of Israel's grumbling sets up the transition to the following two narratives which point to God's care for his people. Thus, Israel's journey to the Promised Land is marked by God's discipline and God's provision.

The Copper Serpent (21:4–9)

21:4–5. The narrative begins with Israel leaving Mount Hor after the death of Aaron. They travel via "the road to the Red Sea" (21:4a NET), which here must represent the route they took to avoid crossing through the territory of Edom (Cole 2000, 346). It most likely refers to a route toward the eastern arm of that body of water, not the western arm which they crossed in their escape from Egypt (Allen 2012, 294–95). This would necessitate backtracking from Mount Hor and adding a substantial distance to the journey through a barren landscape (Beitzel 2009, 114). Consequently, the people "became impatient" (21:4b NET, NIV), which is an idiomatic translation of וַתִּקְצַר נֶפֶשׁ־הָעָם (Milgrom 1990, 173).[1] This detour provides yet another opportunity for Israel to complain.

The people speak against both God and Moses. Directly targeting God intensifies the previous complaint which was directed against Moses and Aaron (20:2). The people's

---

1 Literally, "the soul of the people became short." This verb with either "soul" (נֶפֶשׁ) or "spirit" (רוּחַ) as its subject typically points to a loss of patience. See especially Proverbs 14:29, where this expression is set in contrast with another (אֶרֶךְ אַפַּיִם) that means "slow to anger" (Stubbs 2009, 167).

grievance again is a microcosm of previous grumbling narratives. Once more, they accuse Moses of bringing them up from Egypt to die and further complain about the absence of food and water. The final complaint contradicts the previous one as the Israelites state that they despise "this worthless food" (21:5b NET).[2] Their claim that there is no food actually is a hyperbolic exaggeration leading into their disgust with manna. This also echoes the complaint of the previous generation in 11:6–7.

21:6. This narrative proceeds quickly to God's response. On this occasion, God does not speak to Moses, nor does Moses immediately intercede. Instead, God moves directly to punishment. He sends "fiery serpents" (הַנְּחָשִׁים הַשְּׂרָפִים) whose bites kill an unspecified number of Israelites.[3] Although the adjective הַשְּׂרָפִים can refer to heavenly beings (see the "seraphim" in Isa. 6:2, 6), in this context it refers to the sting of their bite. A number of venomous snakes are attested in the region, including carpet vipers, sand vipers, and puff adders (Cole 2009, 375).

21:7. In response to serpents, the people approach Moses and acknowledge their sin and ask him to intercede. This is rare, since prior admissions of guilt are found only with Aaron, who confesses that he and Miriam sinned in speaking against Moses (12:11–12) and with Israel's belated confession after refusing to enter the Promised Land (14:39–40). This occasion closely mirrors Aaron's admission of guilt. In both cases the guilty parties appeal to Moses who mediates on their behalf (Boda 2009, 95). Although the initial complaint is unwarranted, the people's confession and Moses's prayer reflect appropriate responses to transgression.

21:8–9. God's response to Moses's intercession is quite strange. He instructs Moses to make a serpent and set it on a pole so that those who have been bitten can look on it and live. Moses obeys and constructs a copper (or bronze) serpent (נְחַשׁ נְחֹשֶׁת).[4] This resembles an apotropaic approach taken in Mesopotamian religions in which the image of a thing (such as a demon) can ward off the real thing (Sprinkle 2015, 320). Further, some Egyptians wore serpent amulets to prevent snake bites (Cole 2009, 375). However, the purpose of the serpent here reflects its specific context; looking at it reminds Israel of its transgressions and their consequences. It is "the spiritual equivalent of looking in a mirror" (Gane 2004, 680). Gazing upon the copper serpent reminded the people of their transgression along with acknowledging God as the source of their deliverance (Stubbs 2009, 169). The image of the serpent itself did not have any power, a fact apparently Israel's long history of idolatry caused it to forget. Later, Josiah had to destroy it during his reforms because it was being worshipped (2 Kings 18:4).[5]

---

2   The phrase "worthless food" is בַּלֶּחֶם הַקְּלֹקֵל. The expected word for manna (מָן) is not found here, even though that must be what they are complaining about.
3   The expression עַם רָב often refers to a nation or fighting force, but here has a more generic sense of a multitude (Levine 2000, 87–88). Numbers is occasionally specific with the death toll from Israel's rebellions (Num. 16:49; 25:9).
4   The word נְחֹשֶׁת can be translated as either copper or bronze. Archaeologists have uncovered copper snakes in several places in the ancient Near East, suggesting that it is the more likely metal that Moses used (Cole 2000, 349–50).
5   Some have argued that this incident had an aetiological purpose: "to explain the origins of the snake cult in Hezekiah's time" (Levine 2000, 90). This presumes a much later date of composition for Numbers. It is also noteworthy that the serpents in these stories have opposite effects. In Numbers it is an agent of healing, while in 2 Kings it is an idol that pointed to coming divine judgment (Cole 2000, 347–48).

Internal and External Challenges (21:4–35)

> **The Serpent**
> There is an aural element to this story as well. The phrase "copper serpent" comes from two words that sound very similar (נָחָשׁ נְחֹשֶׁת). The shared consonants (נחש) are found seven times in Numbers 21:6–9, suggesting an element of completeness. The third shared consonant is *shin* which has a sibilant sound. Its repetition here in an oral retelling of this narrative could be reminiscent of a snake hissing (Hurowitz 2004, 278–87).

Provision on the Road to Moab (21:10–20)

21:10–12. The next episode consists mostly of a travelogue that records the names of several places that Israel passed on its journey. This is a small part of the fuller account given in Numbers 33. Matching the locations with specific geographical sites is exceedingly difficult, but it is possible to follow the basic contours.[6]

The Israelites first camp at Oboth (21:10) before moving onto Iye Abarim (20:11). This second location is clarified with the description that it is "in the desert that faces Moab toward the sunrise" (20:11b ESV). This suggests that the Israelites stayed well to the east after marching around the territory of Edom. They then marched north to the Zered Valley (21:12), which runs toward the southern end of the Dead Sea (Ashley 1993, 410).

21:13. The Israelites then proceeded to the Arnon, a river that enters the Dead Sea a little ways north of its midpoint (Ashley 1993, 410–11). It also marks the northern border of Moabite territory, separating it from the region of the Amorites. The battles with Sihon and Og recorded in 21:21–35 probably fit here chronologically, but Numbers instead focuses on the travel itinerary before discussing Israel's encounters with those rulers.

21:14–15. The travelogue briefly breaks into poetry, citing a brief snippet from a source called *The Book of the Wars of YHWH*. This is the

The Brass Serpent by Palma il Giovane. Public domain.

---

6   See Miller 1989, 577–95, for a presentation of the challenges.

only mention of this source, leaving its contents highly speculative. One plausible suggestion is that it consisted of songs celebrating YHWH's victories over his enemies (Ashley 1993, 411).

This selection consists of a series of place names, leading one commentator to call it "The Song of Places" (Allen 2012, 297). Waheb in Suphah (21:14b) is otherwise unattested, but its association with Arnon places it somewhere within the region associated with Moab (Cole 2009, 376). Also mentioned is Ar (21:15), which is connected to the borders of Moab. It is plausible that the mention of these names was supposed to prompt memory of Israel's journey through these places and recall God's provision in bringing the people through them.

21:16–18a. Israel then moves on to Beer (21:16), a word that simply means "well." It is presumably in the same vicinity, but Cole rightly notes that this word is used so frequently that any attempts to be more specific are impossible (Cole 2000, 354). This place derives its name from what YHWH does there. He instructs Moses to assemble the people and provides water.

Israel responds by breaking into joyful song, a welcome and rare change from its predilection for complaint. This "Song of the Well" follows the "Song of the Places" (Allen 2012, 298). The initial lyric is "Spring up, o well" (21:17b ESV, NET, NIV), which reflects the people's confidence in God's promise. They accept that the water is there and anticipate its imminent appearance (Gane 2004, 680). The song then goes on to describe how the "princes" (שָׂרִים) and "leaders of the people" (נְדִיבֵי הָעָם) employ their staffs of office in the digging of the well. These would not make good digging implements so this probably reflects that the leaders used their authority to commission and supervise the construction of the well (Milgrom 1990, 178). Thus, as the community approaches the Promised Land, it faces one of its recurrent issues. However, on this occasion, it is resolved through divine initiative and human obedience.

21:18b–20. This subsection ends with another series of place names, beginning with Mattanah (21:18b). This can mean "gift" and may reflect another acknowledgment of what YHWH has done (Cole 2009, 376). Israel then proceeds to Nahaliel and Bamoth, before ending its peregrination in a valley in the region of Moab, near a mountainous region known as Pisgah. It offered an excellent vantage point from which to view Israel's encampment and to survey the Promised Land (Cole 2009, 376).[7]

In summary, this subsection sees Israel complete its detour around Edom and arrive at a location bridging Moabite and Amorite territory. Although the place names cannot be conclusively identified, the spirit of celebration and the evidence of God's provision give this passage an encouraging tone.

Conflict with Sihon and Og (21:21–35)

21:21–22. The longest episode of this passage details Israel's conflicts with two Amorite rulers: Sihon and Og. These encounters have similarities to previous conflicts, including Edom's denial of passage (20:14–21) and the defeat of Arad (21:1–3). As mentioned above, they likely took place during Israel's travels in 21:10–20 (Milgrom 1990, 175; Pressler 2017, 188).

The conflict with Sihon begins just like Israel's encounter with Edom. Israel sends heralds asking for safe passage. They promise that Israel will remain on the main highway and refrain from pillaging the land. Sihon's kingdom stretched north of the Dead Sea, so the Israelites needed to traverse it to reach a place where they could cross the Jordan River (Cole 2009, 377). Sihon is identified as an Amorite, a people group that originated in Mesopotamia and expanded westward. On occasion, this

---

7 One of Balaam's attempts to curse Israel is set at the top of Pisgah (Num. 23:14).

term is used to refer to all the inhabitants of Canaan (Gen. 15:16; 48:22; Amos 2:9–10). Of critical importance is the absence of kinship between the Israelites and Amorites (unlike the Moabites and Edomites).

21:23–24. Like the Edomites, Sihon refuses passage for the Israelites. However, unlike the Edomites, God does not direct the Israelites to avoid the conflict. Sihon's forces march out to meet Israel in the wilderness and fight a battle at Jahaz. Again, this location is uncertain. However, the outcome of the conflict is clear: Israel defeats him and takes possession of his land (21:24a). His territory extended from the Arnon River in the south to the Jabbok River in the north (cf. Gen. 32:22–31). Its eastern border ran up against the Ammonites, whom Israel did not displace (21:24b). The reason given here for not displacing the Ammonites is that "the border of the Ammonites was strong" (21:24b ESV).

> **The Ammonites**
> Biblical tradition has the Ammonites as descendants of Lot (Gen. 19:38). In Moses's later recounting of these events, he affirms that God had given the Ammonites the territory they possessed; Israel was forbidden to attack them (Deut. 2:16–19). Later, Jephthah addresses a territorial dispute over the Ammonites' claim to the former kingdom of Sihon (Judg. 11:21–22).

21:25–26. Israel's defeat of Sihon is the first conquest account when it states that Israel settled the region that it conquered. This marked the beginning of its presence in the Transjordan region, which Reuben, Gad, and half of the tribe of Manasseh claimed as their allotment (Numbers 32).[8] The key conquest was the city of Heshbon, which later became a city for the Levites (Josh. 21:39). The text then provides further historical context by stating that Sihon had previously fought and defeated the Moabites, extending his territory to the Arnon at their expense. This begins to shift the focus from Israel's conquest to its implications since Israel remained in the vicinity of the Moabites.

21:27–29. The episode with Sihon concludes with another fragment of poetry. It calls for the reestablishment of Heshbon (21:27b) and the defeat of Moab and its god Chemosh (21:28–29). The reference to rebuilding Heshbon probably refers to its fate after the Israelite conquest (Ashley 1993, 424). The underlying context shifts in 21:28–29. It suggests that prior to Israel's appearance, Sihon had defeated the Moabites and commemorated that victory in song. This culminates with Sihon taking the defeated Moabites into captivity. The Moabites are called the "people of Chemosh," a reference to their national deity. Ancient warfare often depicted battles as conflicts between gods (cf. 2 Kings 18:32–35). Moab's defeat is also a defeat for Chemosh and a tacit acknowledgement of the superiority of Sihon's gods.

The interjection of a victory song of Sihon in the text is unexpected, but it has a certain logic. If Sihon defeated Moab, but Israel defeated Sihon, the remaining Moabites would have even more reason to fear when they saw Israel encamped near their borders.[9]

21:30. This verse reverts to Israel's point of view through the first-person verbs וַנִּירָם and וַנַּשִּׁים. The first comes from the root I-ירה, commonly translated "to shoot." Contextually, English translations expand its meaning to more generic verbs of conquest ("overthrow" in the ESV, NET, NIV; "threw them down" in the CSB; "shot

---

8   See the discussion of Numbers 32 for the complications that this claim creates.
9   Previous generations of scholarship have tried to resolve this oddity by changing the text so that the whole of it reads as a celebration of either Israel's defeat of Sihon or its conquest of Moab in 2 Kings 3. Both of these approaches required substantial, unneeded changes to the text (Wenham 2008, 181).

at them" in the NKJV and RSV). This verse uses more place names to establish the boundaries of the conquest. Israel took Heshbon to Dibon and desolated the region from Nophah to Medeba. The location of Nophah is unknown but must be within Sihon's territory.

21:31–32. The text then reasserts Israel's lasting claim to its conquests, noting that it dwelled in the land of the Amorites (21:31). Israel even expanded its holdings by spying out a place called Jazer and defeating its Amorite inhabitants (21:32).

21:33–35. This sets up a final confrontation with another ruler: Og, king of Bashan. Deuteronomy 1:4 locates his capital at Ashtaroth, which is located on the Yarmuk River, a tributary of the Jordan (Cole 2009, 378). It is north of Sihon's territory, extending to the eastern side of the Sea of Galilee. As Israel marched toward Bashan, Og assembled an army in response.

In contrast to the battle with Sihon, YHWH took a direct hand. He informed Moses that he had already given Og into Israel's hand and that Israel should treat him the same as Sihon. This establishes that the conflict here is holy war; Israel received divine commands and must obey them (Allen 2012, 303). This leads to total victory as Israel defeated Og, his sons, and his entire force (21:35). Israel then added his lands to its conquests. Edrei, the place of the battle, is found in the list of territorial allotments for Manasseh in Joshua 13:31.

> **Sihon and Og**
>
> The Old Testament looks back upon these victories over Sihon and Og on several occasions. Moses retells the story in Deuteronomy 3:1–11, adding in the fascinating detail that Og was a Rephaite. The Rephaites are connected to the Anakites (Deut. 2:11) whom the spies considered to be descendants of the terrifying Nephilim (Num. 13:33). Deuteronomy 3:11 portrays Og as a giant, pointing to his thirteen-foot "iron bed" (עֶרֶשׂ בַּרְזֶל) that Israel has put on display, presumably as a war trophy (Lindquist 2011, 487–91). God's speech to Moses in Numbers 21:34 can be viewed as needed assurance of divine support before engaging in battle with such an imposing foe.
>
> Later, Rahab looks back on the defeat of Sihon and Og as reasons why Jericho fears Israel's arrival (Josh. 2:10), while the Gibeonites reference it in their submission to Israel (Josh. 9:10). These victories are also celebrated in a rehearsal of Israel's history (Neh. 9:22) and preserved in song (Pss. 135:11; 136:19–20). Although the accounts are brief in Numbers, the recurrence of Sihon and Og throughout the text suggests that these victories had an outsized impact on Israel's understanding of God's power.

THEOLOGICAL FOCUS

The exegetical idea (Israel's journey to the Promised Land is marked by God's discipline and God's provision) leads to the following theological focus: *God sustains his people in the face of their own failings and external challenges.* The overriding theme of this chapter is that God is present with his people. In the episode with the copper serpent, Israel's grumbling prompts discipline but not abandonment. God even provided a means of restoration. Notably, Jesus appeals to this story in his conversation with Nicodemus: "Just as Moses lifted up the snake in the wilderness, so the Son of Man must be lifted up" (John 3:14 NIV). In the same way that God sustained sinful Israel through this image, so the crucifixion of Christ brings full restoration to all those who acknowledge him as Lord and Savior.

The other episodes in this unit offer further examples of God's sustaining presence. As Israel takes its detour around Edom, God provides water to meet the people's needs. This gives yet another reminder of Israel's dependence on God for its needs. When teaching his disciples how to pray, Jesus encourages them to ask their heavenly Father for their daily bread

(Matt. 6:11). In the same address, he urges them to rely on God's sustaining power to provide what they need to eat, drink, and wear (Matt. 6:25–34). This trust is to be matched with diligence in God's service and productive labor for those who are able (2 Thess. 3:6–10). However, this episode reminds the people of God that he is the ultimate source of what they need. His provision should prompt rejoicing.

God's provision is also essential to Israel's victory over formidable enemies. Although the people of God are no longer identified with any single geopolitical entity, the episodes with Sihon and Og are further proof of God's authority over any hostile powers. This offers continued encouragement for the people of God, who recognize that our struggles are not with flesh and blood but against cosmic powers and authorities (Eph. 6:12). God has equipped his people for such struggles through his armor, including the shield of faith that protects against the attacks of hostile powers (Eph. 6:16). As the people of God reflect on his protection, they can add their voices to the author of Hebrews, declaring, "So we say with confidence, the LORD is my helper; I will not be afraid. What can mere mortals do to me?" (Heb. 13:6 NIV).

PREACHING AND TEACHING STRATEGIES

Exegetical and Theological Significance

In this passage, the nation of Israel faces a plethora of challenges, both internal and external. They have just experienced a disappointing setback in 20:14–21, Aaron has died (20:22–29), and they have also suffered a minor defeat (21:1–3). Now, they are once again faced with issues concerning the provision of their food and water. They encounter poisonous snakes as a result of their grumbling and then face their largest battles to date. These external struggles and enemies serve as catalysts for their internal foes: discontent and a lack of faith.

This entire section shows that the Israelites are completely dependent on God. They are dependent on him for priests and leaders. They are dependent on him for food and water. They are dependent on him for healing when they sin. They are dependent on him for victory over their enemies. They are dependent on him for victory over their own hearts.

As this passage unfolds, it reveals different aspects of God's multifaceted, victorious work. Because of the sin of the people, God needs to provide a means for healing and forgiveness. The bronze serpent that is lifted up foreshadows the lifting up of Christ who provides full atonement for sin (John 3:14). Christ's atonement is also multifaceted. It is substitutionary and penal. It provides our greatest example and model of love and our highest ethical principle. It is a ransom price. It is also the means through which Christ conquers the powers of darkness (*Christus victor*).

Preaching Idea

Our victory is secure through God's provision of atonement and Christ's victory over every evil power.

Contemporary Connections

What does it mean?

What does it mean that our victory is secure through God's provision of atonement and Christ's victory over every evil power? In this text in Numbers, we see how God provides a symbol of redemption and then leads his people to victory over their enemies. In the work of Christ, the redemption and victory are both accomplished simultaneously in his death and resurrection. As we are united with Christ, our sins are forgiven, and then God leads us forward in the triumph of Jesus. It is because Christ has triumphed that we triumph; it is because we are justified in Christ that we can be led forward in progressive sanctification.

Israel did not provide their own plan of redemption, and neither did they defeat their enemies in their own strength. Today, we do not atone for our own sin, and neither do we grow in holiness apart from the power of God's Holy Spirit. The road to our Promised Land starts at the cross, and then moves forward into dangers, trials, and enemy-occupied territory. Only by being forgiven at Calvary can we move forward with confidence, knowing that the enemies of Christ cannot match his power. We know that they will be defeated because they are already defeated! They continue to fight, but they fight in desperation, trying to hurt and maim, even while knowing that Christ has conquered.

Is it true?
Is it true that our victory is secure through God's provision of atonement and Christ's victory over every evil power? The first thing to note is that Christ has conquered every evil power. As Paul states, "And having disarmed the powers and authorities, he made a public spectacle of them, triumphing over them by the cross" (Col. 2:15 NIV; cf. Eph. 1:20–22).

It is in this triumph that we walk as we follow our Lord. Speaking of the dragon, the ancient serpent, our archenemy Satan, we are told that God's people: "triumphed over him by the blood of the Lamb" (Rev. 12:11 NIV). We have victory, not because of our superior strength, goodness, and wisdom, but because "You, dear children, are from God and have overcome them, because the one who is in you is greater than the one who is in the world" (1 John 4:4 NIV).

God provided atonement and led Israel on to victory over their enemies. In Christ, the victory comes through the atonement and the application of his righteousness to our account by the Spirit of God. The bronze snake had no power over sin, and Israel had no power to defeat Sihon and Og. Christ Jesus our Savior, however, has power to pay the penalty of our sin and to lead us forward in victory over every spiritual foe we can ever face.

Now what?
What do we do with this principle that our victory is secure through God's provision of atonement, and that Christ's has gloriously triumphed over every evil power? Without a doubt—and without hesitation—we need to make sure that we have looked to Christ who was lifted up on the cross. We are guilty and we will die if we do not appropriate by faith the provision of God in Christ Jesus.

Next, we need to walk in the power of the risen Christ. Paul was in anguish that the Galatians seemed to want to exchange the power of the Spirit for their own works, righteousness, and ability (Gal. 3:3). Do not attempt to outsmart or defeat the devil on your own. He is greater than we are, but the one who is in us is greater than he.

This progression of starting with repentance and faith then walking in victory over the powers of darkness is succinctly captured by James when he writes: "Submit yourselves, then, to God. Resist the devil, and he will flee from you" (James 4:7 NIV). To do this, put on the full armor of God (Eph. 6:10–17).

Creativity in Presentation

One pitfall of preaching the Old Testament is that we can mistake our own imaginative allegorizing with the meaning of the text itself. We need to remember that what is happening in Numbers is not a fable, and that there are historical realities and contexts that need to be taken seriously. It is also vital that when we establish connections (as was done above with Christ), we show that the principles are *actually grounded in the texts*, rather than wild leaps of unrestrained fancy. These theological principles are fulfilled in Christ through intracanonical connections,[10] and the congregation should be able to see the organic links as the message is developed.

One successful example of the genre of allegory is John Bunyan's *Pilgrim's Progress*. Christians in previous generations used to be far more familiar with this book, but it is still well worth reading, and it may be helpful to expose people to it. If there is time in the service, a dramatic reading of Christian's confrontation with Apollyon may help impress these biblical themes upon the people.

It may also be helpful to show people how God achieves victory over his enemies in the very end. Revelation 20:7–9a depicts Satan gathering a countless host that surrounds the people of God. Cinematographers would not miss the buildup of suspense, and then have a climactic battle scene. But in Revelation, when the people of God are besieged and surrounded, fire falls from heaven and their enemies are destroyed. The battle is literally over before it begins. God's victory is absolute and guaranteed. When the orcs are arrayed against Helm's Deep, or when the armies of Mordor are lined up against Gondor, the vision is terrifying. But when the enemies of God—led by Satan himself—surround the camp of God's people, there is no cause for alarm. The Lamb has conquered, and all of his enemies will be put under his feet.

Although not every church sings old hymns, "A Mighty Fortress Is Our God" by Martin Luther is one of the best known. A short exposition of its lyrics (as well as historical setting), followed by singing it as a response to the message, may tie the elements of the service together and remind the congregation that our victory is secure through God's provision of atonement and Christ's victory over every evil power.

The key movements of this passage could be articulate like this:

- God reminds people of the gravity of rebellion (21:4–9).

- God provides for his people in their times of need (21:10–20).

- God is able to defeat every hostile power (21:21–35).

DISCUSSION QUESTIONS

1. How is this final grumbling narrative similar to previous ones? How is it unique?

2. How does the copper serpent point us to Christ (see John 3)?

3. How is God's provision of water in this passage different from the other times Israel has asked for water in its wanderings?

4. How is God's sovereignty over the nations expressed in the time of the church, where believers are found in nearly every geopolitical entity?

---

10 The first time I (Steve) heard the lovely phrase "intracanonical connections" was in a lecture given by D. A. Carson at a conference for pastors. He went on to say something like, "These kinds of terms are useful shorthand for ourselves, but if I ever hear that you used the phrase 'intracanonical connections' with your people, I will personally drive up to your church and throttle you myself."

Numbers 22:1–41

EXEGETICAL IDEA
Balaam cannot curse Israel because God alone controls the spiritual realm.

THEOLOGICAL FOCUS
God is sovereign over all creation: material and spiritual.

PREACHING IDEA
The more we see, the more we see that our God reigns.

PREACHING POINTERS
Everyone enjoys the story of Balaam's donkey, but just as with Jonah and the big fish, it is vitally important to see beyond the surface details and understand what God is doing and communicating in these texts. If all people remember about Balaam is the story with the donkey, they simply did not understand these chapters. As a preacher, do not major on the minor details: bring out the point of the text. What we have in the Balaam narrative is an attempt to destroy Israel and control the Lord God through occultic means. Human military power alone will not avail, so Balak looks to magic and spiritual manipulation.

This is a test of the power of God, as well as a test of his faithfulness. Will God change his mind about Israel, or will he fulfill all of his covenant promises to Abraham? Does divination work? Does God truly reign over both the heavens and earth, and all that is within them? Westerners may only have a vague, general sense of this, but for many people in history and for many people in various cultures around the world today, the power of God over evil spirits is a vital truth they cling to. The witchdoctor, shaman, or magician cannot control the Lord God, and this provides incredible comfort and security. In this passage, we see that God cannot be manipulated, challenged, or thwarted. He remains absolutely faithful, and his will *will* be done. No one can make him change his mind or his plan, and none can coerce him. The more we see, the more we see that God is sovereign and immutable. Pray that God will open the eyes of our hearts—because the more we see, the more we see that our God reigns.

BALAK SUMMONS BALAAM (22:1–41)

LITERARY STRUCTURE AND THEMES

Numbers 22:1–24:25 comprises a discrete unit within the larger book. It focuses upon the words and deeds of Balaam: a foreign spiritualist who encounters the God of Israel. The Balaam section comes after the account of Israel's journey to the Plains of Moab across from Jericho (22:1). These chapters begin with the two episodes of narrative: Balak's embassies to Balaam (22:1–20) and Balaam's journey to Balak (22:21–41). Once Balaam arrives, he utters prophetic oracles with elements of narrative interspersed to provide additional context (23:1–24:25). This preaching unit combines the two narrative episodes.[1] The first episode chronicles Balak's initial response to the fears of his people (22:2–6) and the first failed embassy to Balaam (22:7–14), followed by the second successful embassy (22:15–20). The second episode consists of Balaam's journey to Balak, highlighted by the humorous and theologically significant story of the talking donkey (22:21–35), concluding with Balaam's initial interactions with Balak (22:36–41).

Thematically, the Balaam material is both "very funny and deadly serious" (Wenham 2008, 185). It blends the comedic tone of the episode with the talking donkey with the absolute certainty of God's intention to bless his people. These chapters also shift the perspective away from Moses and the Israelites. Instead, they provide an outside perspective on God's authority and Israel's status as his people. The focus is on how God has chosen and preserved Israel, with no mention of its grumbling and disobedience. While Israel may test God and merit divine judgment, these chapters offer "a remarkable picture of God working on behalf of his people in spite of their almost complete failure to follow him faithfully" (Cole 2000, 364). In conjunction with the forthcoming oracles, these narratives emphasize that God has indeed chosen to bless Israel, and that no outside force can disrupt his plans.[2]

- ***Introduction (22:1)***
- ***Balak Summons Balaam (22:2–20)***
    - *Balak's Response to the Fears of His People (22:2–6)*
    - *The First Embassy (22:7–14)*
    - *The Second Embassy (22:15–20)*
- ***Balaam's Journey to Balak (22:21–41)***
    - *Balaam and the Donkey (22:21–30)*
    - *Balaam and God (22:31–35)*
    - *Balaam and Balak (22:36–41)*

---

1   A less-than-scientific sampling of preachers to whom I (Joel) am connected on social media showed a strong preference for dealing with the whole chapter as one preaching unit.

2   The presence and organization of the Balaam chapters has been one of the crucial questions for critical interpreters. Most see them as later additions to the stories of Israel in the wilderness. Further debates arise over the compilation of the chapters themselves. Some argue that the poetry is tightly linked to the narratives (Milgrom 1990, 467), while others propose that the poems predate the narratives, which were composed to give context to the poems (Levine 2000, 209–38). This commentary is committed to reading the text in its final form and thus will not address the question of the putative origins of the Balaam material. A good discussion of the theological linkages between this material and the rest of Numbers can be found in Cole 2000, 373–77.

EXPOSITION

The Balaam chapters commence with Balak's initial recruitment of the seer and the story of Balaam's journey. This narrative reveals something of Balaam's stature as a man who has access into the spiritual realm and suggests that he may be willing to use this for his own benefit. Repetition further characterizes the story as 1) Balak sends multiple embassies to Balaam before he agrees to come, 2) Balaam has three separate encounters with God, 3) the donkey avoids the angel of the LORD on three occasions, and 4) three times it is revealed that Balaam can only speak what God permits (Wenham 2008, 185–86). On the whole, this narrative is crafted to demonstrate that Balaam cannot curse Israel because God alone controls the spiritual realm.

Introduction (22:1)

22:1. The text begins with a note of geographical orientation. Israel has reached the Plains of Moab and encamps across the Jordan River from Jericho. They are on the verge of the Promised Land. This is the only verse that reports anything about Israel's actions in the entire Balaam collection (Lee 2003b, 168). The Israelites now occupy liminal space, preparing to leave the wilderness behind but not yet in the land that God has promised. However, they have achieved a major milestone: the nation is no longer wandering (Pressler 2017, 205).

In trying to fit this passage with the conquest accounts of the previous chapter, Numbers 21:26 suggests that the Moabites had been under the dominion of Sihon the Amorite king and were now looking to drive out this new entity (Ashley 1993, 444; Cole 2000, 377). Israel's presence on the Plains of Moab thus provides the setting for confrontations with external forces (Numbers 22–24), along with one further example of Israel's rebellious and idolatrous nature (Numbers 25).[3]

Balak Summons Balaam (22:2–20)

Balak's Response to the Fears of His People (22:2–6)

22:2–3. The perspective now shifts to Balak and the Moabites. They witnessed what Israel did to the Amorites in the preceding chapter and fear suffering the same fate. Numbers 22:3 employs two synonymous verbs for "fear" (וַיָּגָר; וַיָּקָץ), perhaps prefiguring the text's transition into poetic oracles ahead (Milgrom 1990, 185). This verse also focuses on their fear of Israel's great size, stating that "they were so numerous" (22:3 NET). Although no exact figure is given, this speaks to God's preservation of the people throughout the forty years of wilderness wandering. Many have died on account of Israel's rebellions, but it remains a nation whose size prompts dread.

22:4a. This half-verse envisions Moab speaking as a collective with another nation. The Midianites were a loose arrangement of seminomadic tribes who typically were hostile to Israel (Judg. 6:1–6).[4] This group of Midianites, led by their elders, join with the Moabites in seeing Israel as a threat (Cole 2009, 378). The text conveys the Israelite menace through an agricultural simile: the Israelites will strip the land of its resources in the way that an ox devours grass.

---

3   Numbers 25:1 locates Israel at a placed called Shittim. This should be seen as a more specific place within the larger area of the Plains of Moab since it too is found close to Jericho (Num. 33:49–50; Josh. 2:1; 3:1; Knierim and Coats 2005, 252).

4   The fact that Moses's wife Zipporah is Midianite complicates this picture. Further, Numbers 10:29–31 suggests that Midianites led by Moses's brother-in-law accompanied Israel. Clearly, they stand apart from the Midianites in this passage.

TRANSLATION ANALYSIS
The Israelites are identified as a קָהָל in this verse. Often, this is a neutral or positive term, translated with words like "assembly" or "congregation." In this instance, many English versions translate it as "horde" (CSB, ESV, NASB, NET, NIV). This is reasonable, given the hostile context of this verse.

22:4b–5a. These verses focus on the actions of Balak, the Moabite ruler. His solution is to send messengers to Balaam, who resides at a place identified as Pethor. This is commonly identified as a city named Pitru, located well north of Israel on a tributary of the Euphrates River (Cole 2009, 379). Abraham sojourned in the same general region for awhile prior to his entry into Canaan (Gen. 11:31–32).

TRANSLATION ANALYSIS
The description of Balaam's location in 22:5a ends with the phrase אֶרֶץ בְּנֵי־עַמּוֹ. Some English versions translate this as "the land of the sons of his people" (CSB, NASB, NKJV), which the NIV renders colloquially as "his native land." Other versions take the final Hebrew word עַמּוֹ as a place name itself, rendering it "the land of the people of Amaw" (ESV) or "in the land of Amaw (NET, NRSV). Both readings are challenging, but possible. Since Balaam's point of origin is not significant to the flow of the narrative, it is not necessary to resolve this issue.

22:5b–6. The messengers convey Balak's words for Balaam. Balak again emphasizes Israel's size, claiming that they "cover the face of the earth" (ESV, NET). Balak urges Balaam to come and curse the Israelites because he cannot fight them directly. However, if Balaam can curse them, then Balak hopes to be able to drive them from the land. He ends with a note of flattery, declaring that whomever Balaam blesses is blessed, whomever he curses is cursed.

Balak assumes that Balaam has some special ability to both see and manipulate the spiritual realm. This is in keeping with ancient perceptions of the spiritual world, in which practitioners could employ sacrifice, augury, or pronouncements to claim insight into the will and ways of the gods, and even perhaps to wield that power for various ends (Cole 2000, 381).[5] If Balaam accepts Balak's commission, it sets up a potential challenge to God's claim to be Israel's protector.

> **Balaam**
> Numbers 22 does not explain Balaam's origins or the source of his power. It simply presents him as a spiritualist of international renown. Fascinatingly, there is extrabiblical attestation of a "Balaam, son of Beor" who received dreams from the gods. Archaeologists have recovered fragmentary texts from a place called Deir 'Alla in the Transjordan region, dating from the eighth or seventh centuries B.C. (Cole 2009, 380). Although there are many gaps, the text seems to recount a figure called Balaam receiving a vision of devastation coming from the divine realm before he confronts the hostile deities and somehow averts the threat (Cole 2009, 381). Balaam thus acts as both observer and manipulator of the spiritual realm. Both Scripture and the Deir 'Alla text declare that Balaam received visions at night, which he recounted in the morning (Ashley 1993, 440). The relationship between this Balaam material and that found in Scripture is hard to determine but suggests that Balaam traditions had an enduring legacy beyond what is found in Numbers 22–24 (Pressler 2017, 206).

---

5   Some have devoted a great deal of attention to Balaam's actual relationship to the spiritual realm. Milgrom, for example, finds the tension of the story in whether Balaam is a seer who can merely receive messages from the spirit world, or a sorcerer who can manipulate it (Milgrom 1990, 471–73). The text is not concerned with this question, instead portraying Balaam as capable of fulfilling multiple roles, including seer, magician, and even truthful prophet of God (Stubbs 2009, 177–78).

The First Embassy (22:7–14)

22:7. Balak's emissaries arrive and present Balak's message. They also bring to Balaam what most English versions call the "fees for divination" (CSB, ESV, NASB, NET, NIV). This translates the Hebrew word קְסָמִים, which on its own simply means "divination(s)" (Deut. 18:10; 1 Sam. 15:23; 2 Kings 17:17). This reflects the tradition of Balaam as a diviner-for-hire and anticipates Balak's explicit offer of payment (Num. 22:17). Scholars suggest instead that this word could indicate that the emissaries themselves were diviners (Milgrom 1990, 187), or that they brought "tools of divination," perhaps to support Balaam in his work (Moberly 1999, 4). Another suggestion is that they brought evidence of unfavorable divination against Moab that they hoped Balaam could use his power to reverse (Cole 2009, 379). Thus, the common English translation of "fees for divination" is not secure. The question of payment is significant as the story unfolds but it is likely not the point here.

22:8. Balaam responds by encouraging the emissaries to remain overnight so that he can consult with the divine realm. Interestingly, he uses the proper name of the God of Israel, stating that he will bring back the word of YHWH. This does not necessitate that Balaam is a follower of YHWH. A reasonable suggestion is that since Balaam has "encountered" many deities throughout his career, he perceives Israel's God as yet one more for him to consult (Cole 2000, 383). The difference between YHWH and the so-called gods of the nations will soon become apparent.

22:9–12. YHWH visits Balaam, presumably during the night, and engages him in conversation. God of course knows who these men are and their purpose with Balaam. The question in 22:9 is simply a means of beginning divine-human communication (cf. Gen. 3:9; 4:9). Balaam answers with a near-exact citation of Balak's entreaty from 22:5b–6a, again raising the spectre of a curse from the spiritual realm falling upon Israel. However, in 22:12, God provides a clear and direct denial. Balaam cannot go with the men and curse Israel because Israel is blessed. This places Balaam "between the demands of Balak and the commands of God. It is this conflict that sustains the whole drama that follows" (Wenham 2008, 191). In upcoming scenes, the story will also provide some insight into Balaam's own preferences.

22:13–14. The first embassy concludes with Balaam conveying YHWH's message to Balak's men. At this stage, the text has shown that YHWH speaks through Balaam and that Balaam is willing to listen to his directions.

The Second Embassy (22:15–20)

22:15. Balak refuses to accept Balaam's answer. He may view Balaam's initial refusal as a negotiating ploy, or may feel increasingly desperate, but he quickly sends a second embassy. Whereas the first one was comprised of "messengers" (22:5) identified as elders from Moab and Midian (22:7), this one consists of "princes, more numerous and more distinguished than the first" (NET). This is the first indication that Balak is upping the ante. The quality of his emissaries reflects the honor that he accords to Balaam.

22:16–17. These new messengers convey a new message. Notably, it focuses on the material rewards available to Balaam. Balak's promise to Balaam is "I will surely do you great honor" (22:17 ESV). Balaam's understanding of this "honor" is revealed in the next verse, where he talks about silver and gold (Cole 2000, 385). Balak's message ends with a renewed entreaty for Balaam to come and curse Israel.

22:18–19. Balaam's response to these emissaries operates on at least two levels. He begins with what reads as another explicit rejection of Balak's plea. Balaam correctly notes that even if Balak were to give him all the silver and gold of his palace, he could not go against God's word. Fascinatingly, he speaks of Israel's deity as "YHWH my God" (22:18). The implications of this are unclear. It is unlikely that the text intends to present Balaam, a non-Israelite, as a monotheistic worshipper of YHWH. A good suggestion is that his claim echoes "the reality that he had indeed had an encounter with the God of Israel" (Cole 2000, 386). In this part of his response, Balaam presents himself as a faithful conveyer of YHWH's words.

Balaam's response does not end with his statement of refusal. Instead, he encourages Balak's emissaries to remain for the night with the reasoning "that I may know what more the LORD might say to me" (22:19 NET). This introduces dissonance into the presentation of Balaam. YHWH spoke clearly to him in 22:12, so why does he require an additional message? Given what transpires on Balaam's journey, a plausible assumption is that Balaam's desire to hear more from YHWH reflects his yearning to go to Balak and receive the promised remuneration. Balaam speaks in pious language, but shapes it into "a tool of self-interested financial negotiation" (Moberly 1999, 7).

22:20. God permits Balaam to go, but limits his freedom. He instructs Balaam to only do what he permits. In the flow of the story, it is possible to wonder if this means that YHWH will permit a foreigner to curse Israel, perhaps for its continued unfaithfulness (Ashley 1993, 451). However, these words also prefigure the failure of Balak's scheme as Balaam acknowledges that he cannot speak anything other than what YHWH permits (22:38; 23:12, 36; 24:13).

Balaam's Journey to Balak (22:21–41)

Balaam and the Donkey (22:21–30)
22:21–22a. Balaam begins his journey along with the Moabite emissaries who disappear from the narrative only to briefly resurface in 22:35 after the drama has concluded.[6] The key development is that God becomes angry and sends his own emissary, the angel of YHWH, to stand in Balaam's way. The angel of YHWH acts as a שָׂטָן, a term that later becomes personified as "Satan." In this instance, the term does not have those theological connotations, but rather reflects the angel's function of being an adversary to Balaam (cf. 1 Sam. 29:4; 2 Sam. 19:22; 1 Kings 5:4; 11:14, 23, 25).

The reason for YHWH's anger is not immediately evident. He had just given Balaam permission to go with Balak's men, so this turn of events is unexpected. Critical scholarship views it as evidence that 22:21–35 is from a different source and was added later into the Balaam narrative.[7] However, in its present context, it builds upon the potential of Balaam's self-serving nature. Although YHWH gave him permission to go, his commission to curse Israel goes directly against YHWH's initial response in 22:12. If Balaam truly had spiritual insight, then he would not have been tempted by the allure of remuneration (Moberly 1999, 8). Stubbs suggests that the angel's purpose is not to stop Balaam but to communicate God's displeasure, once Balaam is permitted to perceive it (Stubbs 2009, 185). The presence of the angel also communicates to Balaam that he is not in control. He will speak what God permits him to speak (Gane 2004, 693–94). Regardless of the exact reason for divine displeasure, this episode makes it clear that God will use Balaam for his own purposes.

---

6   It is left to the realm of speculation whether or not the Moabite officials and Balaam's servants (22:22) perceived the angel, or if they were as blind as Balaam.
7   See the discussion in Ashley 1993, 434–35.

22:22b–23. This selection is the first of three times that the donkey sees the threat from the angel that Balaam does not.[8] The angel's drawn sword reflects Balaam's peril. Even with this image, the scene is clearly intended to be comedic. Balaam receives the commission from Balak because he can see into the spiritual realm and potentially manipulate it. Meanwhile, he is blind to an obvious sign of divine presence. Even in the ancient world, donkeys were renowned for stubbornness and stupidity. To have the donkey have the vision of a seer, while Balaam acts like a donkey, is an exquisite twist (Way 2011, 184–85). Balaam's response to his spiritual blindness is to inflict harm on the beast, further displaying his ignorance.

22:24–25. The threat is heightened as the angel appears again. The path is narrower on this occasion, giving the alert donkey less room to maneuver. The process of clearing land for vineyards created walls of piled stones that could also be used to set boundaries (Cole 2000, 391). When the donkey went to dodge the angel, she crushed Balaam's foot against one of these walls, resulting in the oblivious seer striking the donkey yet again.

22:26–27. The scene repeats for a third time, again raising the stakes. Now, the angel stands in a narrow place where the donkey cannot slip by. The donkey thus comes to a halt and lies down. This enrages Balaam, who responds by beating the donkey again, this time with his staff. The same expression (וַיִּחַר־אַף) describes both God's anger in 22:22 and Balaam's anger in 22:27.[9] This is yet another example of irony in the story. YHWH's anger stands in contrast to Balaam, who compounds ignorance with cruelty. These scenes have made it obvious that the supposed seer is more blinded to spiritual realities than his unfortunate animal (Ashley 1993, 457).

22:28–30. In one of the most shocking developments in Scripture, YHWH opens the mouth of the donkey and permits her to address her tormentor. While some have tried to explain this as Balaam's perception of the donkey's natural braying (Harrison 1990, 300) or as a prophetic vision (Milgrom 1990, 191), the most natural reading of the text is that God granted this animal human speech, likely as a way to help pierce Balaam's veil of ignorance

Balaam and His Ass by Rembrandt. Public domain.

---

8   The word used for "donkey" here is אָתוֹן. It always refers to a female donkey, also known as a "jenny" (Way 2011, 162–63). The verbs referring to the actions of the donkey are all feminine in the Hebrew text.

9   A good English translation of this expression would be, "and the anger of X was kindled." Note also Balak's anger in 24:10, which rivals Balaam's for its impotence and misguided nature.

(Allen 2012, 312–13). The plausibility of the event is not a concern of the text.

Balaam's conversation with the donkey is also laden with irony. The donkey, quite naturally from her perspective, asks why he has beaten her three times. Balaam responds from wounded pride, claiming "you have made a fool of me" (2:29 ESV, NIV).[10] He then wishes that he had a sword to kill the donkey. Of course, by seeing and avoiding the danger to Balaam's life, the donkey *has* made a fool of the ignorant seer (Pressler 2017, 210). Balaam's wish for a sword is also ironic, given the presence of the sword-wielding angel.

The conversation concludes with the donkey defending her record as Balaam's mount. She asks rhetorically if she has habitually gone astray like this, to which Balaam can only reply in the negative. This reflects a lack of discernment. He should be familiar with the donkey's reliability, and her deviations from the round should have caused him to take notice. Instead, the audience of the story is left wondering, how can a man "who cannot interpret the obvious actions of his ass interpret the more difficult actions of God?" (Moberly 1999, 11).

Balaam and God (22:31–35)
22:31. Just as YHWH opened the donkey's mouth; he now opens Balaam's eyes. The angel is described exactly in the same manner as 22:23, equating Balaam's vision with that of the donkey. All Balaam can do is take a pose of reverent devotion this representative of YHWH.

22:32–33. The angel first echoes the donkey's question before declaring that he is opposing Balaam because his actions "are perverse" (יָרַט).

TRANSLATION ANALYSIS
The verbal root ירט occurs elsewhere only at Job 16:11, rendering the translation speculative. Many English versions go with "perverse" (ESV, NET, NKJV, NRSV), while the NIV chooses "reckless." Context suggests that the key point is that Balaam's actions are contrary to God's will.

The angel then informs Balaam that without the donkey's clear sight, the angel would have killed him and spared the donkey. Of course, YHWH presumably also arranged for the donkey to perceive the angel, so the purpose of this declaration is to show Balaam that there is much he cannot see and that his insights are based on what YHWH chooses to reveal.

22:34–35. This encounter concludes with Balaam's confession. He acknowledges that he did not know that the angel was in his path. The sincerity of Balaam's repentance is unknown. Hey may have simply been lamenting his failure to perceive the angel (Cole 2000, 393), or he could be reflecting a deeper sense of conviction (Moberly 1999, 13). Although he does offer to return home, his subsequent participation in luring Israel into idolatry and immorality (Num. 31:8, 16) does not indicate a thoroughly reformed character. Further, his offer to return home is based on a conditional "if" God is displeased. The whole preceding encounter should have made it clear that God is very definitely displeased (Gane 2004, 694)! However, YHWH permits him to continue his journey, reiterating that Balaam is only to speak what he permits.

Balaam and Balak (22:36–41)
22:36–37. The story concludes with direct interaction between Balaam and Balak. There is dramatic irony at work here as the text emphasizes Balak's eagerness. He goes to meet Balaam

---

10 It is also amusing that Balaam seems to have no difficulty engaging in conversation with an erstwhile speech-free animal. I (Joel) consider it the storyteller's prerogative to omit any cries of confusion or alarm from Balaam and simply focus on the conversation.

at the edge of his territory, presumably out of impatience to begin the cursing process (Allen 2012, 313). He addresses Balaam with three rapid-fire questions, the last of which conveys his understanding of Balaam's character. Balak asks "Am I not able to honor you?" (22:37 ESV, NET), where again "honor" clearly has the subtext of "financially reward" (Cole 2000, 395). Balak presumes that this should be a simple transaction: he has hired a spiritualist to curse Israel and he is eager to receive the return on his investment.

22:38. Balaam's answer sounds a discordant note. For the third time in the chapter, either YHWH or Balaam announces that Balaam can only speak what God permits. Using the generic term for God (אֱלֹהִים) rather than the covenant name YHWH also permits Balaam to hedge his bets. He conceals exactly who will authorize his speech while also setting the stage for his failure to curse Israel. Readers and hearers of the text can detect the implications, but Balak is oblivious.

22:39–41. The narrative concludes by setting the stage for the oracles to follow. Balak escorts Balaam to Kiriath-huzoth, an unknown location, perhaps near the Moabite capital (Harrison 1990, 304). There, he sacrifices animals and hosts Balaam and the princes who had been his emissaries. It is possible that these sacrifices were preparatory for a divination process where Balaam would use their organs as a means of cursing Israel (Allen 2012, 313). They could also simply reflect Balak's hospitality and a ceremonial meal (Cole 2000, 397). This latter perspective is more likely since Balaam himself oversees further sacrifices prior to beginning his oracles (23:1–2). The narrative concludes with Balak leading Balaam up to a high place where he can see a portion of Israel (22:41).[11] The conflict between what Balak expects and what God has enjoined Balaam to speak now awaits resolution.

THEOLOGICAL FOCUS

The exegetical idea (Balaam cannot curse Israel because God alone controls the spiritual realm) leads to the following theological focus: *God is sovereign over all creation: material and spiritual*. At the heart of this passage is the question of whether Balaam has the authority to curse Israel. Balak is banking on Balaam's reputation as one who can effectively bless or curse. The question of Balaam's motivations, financial or otherwise, and the comedic tone of the passage are secondary to the issue of Balaam's ability to manipulate the spiritual realm.

Balak's initial summons poses a challenge to God's promises to Abraham in Genesis 12:1–3. Balak's claim that whatever Balaam blesses or curses is blessed or cursed comes up against God's promise that he will make Abraham into a great nation and bless him and his descendants. Other nations will be cursed or blessed based on their response to Abraham and his descendants. Is Balaam's ability to curse and bless greater than God's? These opening narratives reveal that it is not. Balaam cannot curse and bless according to his own whim. Instead, he can only speak what God commands. Balaam must acknowledge God's sovereign control over the spiritual realm.

The New Testament looks back at Balaam as a paradigmatic false teacher. Second Peter 2:15–16, Jude 11, and Revelation 2:14 use him as an epithet for those seeking to lead faithful believers astray. These writers emphasize the ephemeral nature of this false teaching in contrast to the sure and certain cleansing judgment of God. Thus, those who follow in the way of Balaam will eventually be confronted with undeniable proof of God's sovereignty.

God's absolute sovereignty over creation is further articulated in the visions of his heavenly throne room throughout Scripture. In 1 Kings 22, the prophet Micaiah sees God holding court over the spiritual powers and

---

11 Bamoth-baal literally means "high place of Baal."

authorizing a lying spirit to deceive wicked King Ahab. Despite the counterprophecy of the five hundred court prophets, God's intentions are accomplished through Ahab's inglorious death. What God ordained in the spiritual realm is accomplished on the earth. God's majesty is articulated as Isaiah sees the seraphim crying out continuing praise (Isa. 6:1–4), and in Ezekiel's vision of an enthroned figure whose radiance he can barely articulate. All these prophets can do is submit themselves to God (Isa. 6:5–8; Ezek. 1:24–28). Finally, John witnesses the risen Christ as the slain lamb and conquering lion who purchased people from every tribe, tongue, and nation for God (Rev. 5:6–10). As John's visions unfold, he learns that the hostile fury of the devil and his followers cannot threaten God's preservation of his people.

Scripture's presentation of God's sovereignty provides tremendous comfort for his people, even when immediate circumstances are bleak. Paul asks, "if God is for us, who can be against us?" (Rom. 8:31 NIV). In that same passage he affirms that no other power or authority can separate us from the love of God through Christ Jesus our Lord (Rom. 8:38–39). Now, God's sovereignty does not preclude suffering, either resulting from our own sin, or as a consequence of living in a broken world. However, there is tremendous encouragement in trusting that God works out all things in his time, and that those who put their trust in him are guaranteed eternal blessing.

PREACHING AND TEACHING STRATEGIES

Exegetical and Theological Significance

As the reader moves into the Balaam narratives and oracles, there is continuity and development with the previous two chapters. Israel's free movement has been blocked by Edom, and they have fought their first battle against Arad. They have also been attacked by the fearsome figures Sihon and Og. In each instance, God either has given his people victory or preserved them as they avoided conflict.

Balak is aware of Israel's victories (22:2), and he is worried about Israel's might. As he reflects on the potential problem facing him, "His disturbed mind hit on a bright idea: he would seek supernatural help rather than rely solely on military strength" (Brown 2002, 204). Balak's desire is to oppose Israel with the combined power of his own armies and the enlisted power of the supernatural realm. In his attempt to forge this alliance, Balak looks to Balaam to be a mercenary, bought to manipulate and control the spirit world.

Although the Balaam material plays out in fascinating ways, the thoughtful reader will already know that the most powerful alliance between the supernatural and natural has been tried before against Israel's God, and it has already failed. Egypt was a great power in the ancient world, and Egypt's gods—represented by Pharaoh—seemed to be the greatest in the cosmos. Pharaoh had no end of soothsayers, priests, and court magicians. Yet all of Egypt's gods, occultic magic, soldiers, and chariots could not stop the God of Abraham, Isaac, and Jacob from leading his people out of their bondage and slavery.

Numbers 22:6 is also a direct challenge to God's promise to Abram in Genesis 12:3. When he confronts Balaam, God immediately reiterates the principle of this promise (Num. 22:12). God cannot be strong-armed into reversing his promises and plan. As Balaam finds out with the incidents involving the angel and his donkey, spirit beings do interact in the physical world, but the ultimate power lies with God himself.

Preaching Idea

The more we see, the more we see that our God reigns.

Contemporary Connections

What does it mean?

What does it mean that the more we see, the more we see that our God reigns? The ironies of Balaam's spiritual blindness and the perception of his donkey are rich fodder for sermons and Sunday school lessons. Yet the narrative contains a principle that applies widely to our lives: there is a spiritual vision that sees beyond the material realm. We are to pray that God will open the eyes of our hearts (Eph. 1:18) and open our eyes to see the wonders of his Word (Ps. 119:18). Yes, we are to "walk by faith and not by sight" (2 Cor. 5:7), but faith provides spiritual vision. Scripture frequently calls us to walk in the light, seeing clearly according to God's Word.

In the previous preaching unit, we saw that as God provided atonement for Israel's sins and then led her on to victory, Christ fulfills those motifs in his atoning death and victory over all of the powers of darkness. God reigns in the spiritual realm. Numbers 22 provides another layer of understanding, allowing us to see that God's sovereign rule is not up for purchase or manipulation. No one can gain power over God or turn God to their own purposes. God cannot be overpowered; he cannot be bribed; he cannot be tricked. We are to pray that the Holy Spirit will allow us to see these truths, and trust in the Lord.

Is it true?

Is it true that the more we see, the more we see that our God reigns? This is certainly true for those who walk closely with the Lord. Over time, they grow in their spiritual perception and repose with more and more confidence in God's sovereign control.

The concept of reigning is tied to might and authority, both of which are ubiquitously ascribed to God in Scripture. He is the Great King. Christ is termed the "King of kings and Lord of lords" (Rev. 19:16).

Although one could look at any number of passages in Scripture for support of these claims, two may be particularly helpful. In the book of Job, an enormous part of the tension is that Job is trying to understand what he sees happening all around him without having seen what has happened in God's heavenly throne room in Job 1. At the end of the book, the resolution only comes when Job sees the Lord (Job 42:5). The second passage is in Revelation 4. In that passage, John is in the Spirit and is shown a drama that is unfolding in heaven. It is highly instructive that the very first thing he sees is God's throne, symbolizing God's sovereign rule and reign. Taken together, these passages elaborate on the theme in Numbers 22, providing further proof that the more we see, the more we see that our God reigns.

Now what?

What does a proper response look like to the truth that God reigns? Psalm 97:1 leaves no doubt: "The Lord reigns, let the earth be glad; let the distant shores rejoice" (NIV). God's sovereign rule and reign over all things is a reason to be glad and rejoice. As with everything about God, this truth should lead us into reverent worship.

Knowing that God reigns, we should also make sure that we can say *"our* God reigns." Individualizing it, every one of us needs to be able to say *"my* God reigns." This does not mean that we get to create our own personal god, but rather that the living God is the one that every believer can call upon. Make sure that you are trusting in the one true God, through faith in his Son.

We also need to be careful that we humbly and prayerfully walk with him, looking to the Spirit for greater vision and insight. We may not be as crass as Balak, but there is a myriad of ways that we can continue to try to manipulate God. Almost every religious practice—fasting, prayer, going to church, almsgiving, good works, Scripture reading, etc.—can be used by us to try to gain leverage over God. There is a reason why Jesus warned his followers not to pray like pagans who think that God will have to answer them (Matt. 6:7). Praying for long periods of time, with intensity and fervor, does not mean that God will have to do whatever we want him to. God reigns, and religion is not a way to manipulate him or bend him to our will.

Creativity in Presentation

Some professors excel at leading PhD seminars, while others are far better at teaching "101" courses to first-year undergraduates. Some teachers are excellent with Grade 12 students, while others work best with preschoolers. If the preacher is gifted at teaching children, this familiar text can provide opportunities in the message to speak directly to them. If there is someone else in the congregation who is a gifted teacher for children, or if the children are normally taken out of the service for their own time of learning, it may be worthwhile to keep the children in the service for a few extra minutes while the teacher makes the Balaam story come to life. This narrative also provides good material for some children to be involved in putting on a short skit.

In the congregation, there may be people with many different experiences with the occult and spiritual warfare. Around the world, people have extremely different perspectives and engagements in these spheres. Reading sections of Letter #7 in C. S. Lewis's *Screwtape Letters* may help provide some connection with how demons operate in our context. Without being naively credulous, and without trying to be exotic, if there is a credible testimony in the church about demonic activity—either here or on the mission field—it may be worth sharing. In the Western world, many people struggle to see beyond the material/physical, and trying to move their perception to the reality of these things may help them enter into the world of the Balaam narrative.

Since God reigns over the material and spiritual realm, we should praise his name! Those who are attempting to manipulate God need to repent, as do those who are trusting in other things. For those who know God and can say with the assembly of his people, "our God reigns," there should be prayer, praise, and rejoicing. God can grant a donkey eyes to see, and he can grant us spiritual vision too. The more God enables us to see, the more we see that our God reigns.

A possible outline for expositing this text could be:

- God's presence makes his opponents afraid (22:1–4).

- God's people are blessed and not cursed (22:5–12).

- Spiritual authorities still must submit to God's will (22:13–20).

- Spiritual authorities only have the insight that God permits (22:21–35).

- Spiritual opposition to God is doomed to fail (22:36–41).

DISCUSSION QUESTIONS

1. What is the logic behind Balak's plan? Why does he think he needs Balaam's services?

2. What are we supposed to make of the character of Balaam? Is he a pious prophet? A selfish opportunist? Something in the middle?

3. In what ways might we be blinded to messages that God is trying to communicate to us?

4. How does this story remind us of God's sovereignty and power over the spiritual realm? How does that speak to modern Christians?

Numbers 23:1–26

EXEGETICAL IDEA
Israel is a nation that God has chosen to bless.

THEOLOGICAL FOCUS
God's blessing provides protection for his people.

PREACHING IDEA
The people of God are blessed both in life and in death.

PREACHING POINTERS
The first message delivered by Balaam immediately proves that God, not Balak, is going to prevail. Far from having power over God, Balak's chosen prophet is helpless to say anything outside of what the Lord allows him to say. Balak wants to turn the gods against Israel, but the living God has determined to fulfill his covenant promises to Abraham, and he will not change his mind. God will not only *not* allow his people to be cursed; he is going to ensure that they are blessed superabundantly. God's word of promise and blessing cannot be defeated, no matter what people try to do to oppose him.

In this message, God emphatically shows Balak and Balaam that he will fulfill his previous promises. He is steadfast in his resolve and infinite in his power, so what he said he would do will be accomplished. Balaam knows this is true, and Balaam extols the blessed nature of belonging to God's covenant people. God's people are so deeply and richly blessed that Balaam confesses that in the end, nothing could be better than dying as a righteous member of God's covenant community. Because of the infinite grace and goodness of God, nothing can be better than living and dying in his loving care. As Christians, living in union with Christ, we are prepared for both life, death, and the life to come. It is a profound and solemn truth, yielding to joy, that the people of God are blessed both in life and in death.

BALAAM'S FIRST TWO ORACLES (23:1–26)

LITERARY STRUCTURE AND THEMES

Dividing Balaam's oracles into preaching units is challenging. The first three (23:1–24:14) follow a similar pattern of preparations-oracle-conclusion. The latter four (24:15–25) eliminate the narrative setup and aftermath. This preaching unit consists of the first two oracles based on shared themes and structure. The third through seventh oracles will be examined together since they address the fate of both Israel and the nations. The structure of this unit is quite repetitive, with each oracle receiving a similar setup and conclusion. In both, Balak takes Balaam to observe Israel, they offer preparatory sacrifices, Balaam receives a divine revelation from God, Balaam proclaims of the oracle, and Balak reacts with dismay.[1]

As the oracles begin, Balaam tries to undertake his commission from Balak. It goes poorly. The overriding theme is that God has blessed Israel. No hint of curse emerges from Balaam's lips as he speaks what God commands. These oracles also link Israel's blessing to God's presence. They cannot be cursed because God is with them as protector and deliverer.

- **The First Oracle (23:1–12)**
  - The Preparations (23:1–6)
  - Balaam's First Oracle (23:7–10)
  - Conclusion (23:11–12)
- **The Second Oracle (23:13–26)**
  - The Preparations (23:13–17)
  - Balaam's Second Oracle (23:18–24)
  - Conclusion (23:25–26)

EXPOSITION

These first two oracles establish God's complete control over the situation. Despite the lavish preparations and contrary to Balak's expectations, Balaam cannot curse Israel. Balaam's motivations throughout this process are opaque. On some level he seems to recognize the futility of the exercise, but his willingness to go along with Balak's increasing desperation may reveal a desire for his promised remuneration (Gane 2004, 703). As the oracles unfold, it becomes abundantly clear that Balak's desires will be thwarted. Balaam is not capable of cursing Israel, because Israel is a nation that God has chosen to bless.

The First Oracle (23:1–12)

The Preparations (23:1–6)
23:1–2. Balaam and Balak begin by building seven altars and sacrificing a bull and a ram on each one. The number seven of course has theological significance for an Israelite audience since it reflects the creation event, the sanctity of the Sabbath, and the cleansing of the sacrificial altar on the Day of Atonement (Cole 2009, 382). Whether the number seven would have the same significance for Balaam and Balak is unknown, but it likely reflects a general sense of fullness or completion, even in pagan contexts (Cole 2000, 399).

Bulls and rams were incredibly valuable animals, so devoting seven of them to this sacrifice reflects the importance of the situation.[2] It is possible that Balaam would use the organs of the animals to perform divination, though

---

1 See Cole 2000, 398, for a more detailed discussion of the shared format of the first three oracles.
2 God required Job's friends to sacrifice seven bulls and rams, likely reflecting the depths of their error in speaking about him (Job 42:8).

the text makes no mention of such an attempt (Allen 2012, 314). The more likely function of the sacrifices is to secure the divine presence: if a supplicant goes to such effort, then surely the divine realm will respond favorably (Levine 2000, 361–62; Pressler 2017, 212). There are no other biblical examples of multiple altars being erected in a singular setting, although there is a Babylonian text in which the supplicant is instructed to erect seven altars to different deities and perform sacrifices. If the rituals were performed properly, then the deities were expected to give that individual what they desired (Cole 2000, 399). God of course is not compelled by such rituals, and Old Testament prophets did not sacrifice before receiving God's messages. However, since God is going to use Balaam for his own purposes, he meets with him anyway (Gane 2004, 700).

The text announces that Balak did what Balaam instructed, using the same terminology it used to describe Moses and Israel's obedience to God in chapters 1–17 (Cole 2000, 400). Even though Balak hired Balaam, he has no control over the situation. He is only able to follow directions. Further, once he assists with the sacrifices, he is relegated to the role of bystander.

23:3. Balaam directs Balak to remain with the sacrifices while he goes off to meet with God. Balaam refers to the sacrifices as עֹלָתֶךָ ("your whole burnt offering"). This refers to a specific type of sacrifice that is entirely devoted to God, with no share for the priest or worshipper (Lev. 1:3–17; 6:8–13). The Moabites may have had a similar kind of sacrifice, or the author may be framing the sacrifices in a way that an Israelite audience would understand (Ashley 1993, 465). Balak remains with the sacrifice, performing a priestly function, while Balaam goes in search of a divine message (Cole 2009, 383).

Balaam's words to Balak are interesting: "perhaps the LORD will come to meet me" (WSV). The particle אוּלַי ("perhaps") denotes a wise degree of restraint. By now Balaam should be aware that he cannot compel God. He cannot guarantee that he will bring back a curse, but neither is it apparent that he will pronounce blessing. Balaam can only report what God permits (Knierim and Coats 2005, 256). He moves off to "a bare height" (שֶׁפִי). The exact meaning of this is uncertain, but it likely reflects an ancient understanding that gods lived in elevated locales (Ashley 1993, 466).

23:4–5. The text simply states that "God met with Balaam" (ESV, NET) without further explanation. There is no statement of fear or falling on one's face as often happens in a theophany. Balaam then announces to God that he had set up the altars and offered sacrifices. This likely reflects a ritual statement, in which Balaam declares that he has done his part (Cole 2000, 401). God responds by putting a word in Balaam's mouth, recalling his commission of Jeremiah (Jer. 1:9). He instructs Balaam to return and speak it. The simplicity of this interaction reinforces the declarations in the preceding chapter that Balaam will only be able to speak what God permits.

23:6. This verse sets the stage for Balaam's first oracle. He returns to Balak, who is waiting with the princes of Moab. The mood is anticipatory, conveyed through the Hebrew particle וְהִנֵּה (commonly translated "and behold"). It invites the audience to put themselves in the place of Balak, who is undoubtedly waiting with ill-concealed eagerness (van der Merwe, Naudé, and Kroeze 2017, 412).

Balaam's First Oracle (23:7–10)

23:7a. The beginning of this verse introduces Balaam's speech. It is called a מָשָׁל, which Gane identifies as a species of discourse that uses parallelism and figurative language (Gane 2004, 700). Multiple commentators note that it is never used for the orations of biblical prophets (Allen 2012, 316; Cole 2000, 403; Milgrom 1990, 196).

23:7b. Balaam's speech begins with the first of seven parallel couplets. Parallelism is a key feature of biblical poetry. Essentially, it consists of paired clauses that are connected on one or multiple levels including semantics, grammar, phonology, and word choice (Berlin 2008, 31–126). The paired clauses reinforce each other, with the second extending, reinforcing, or clarifying the meaning of the first (Kugel 1981, 8–11). In the first couplet, Balaam recounts how Balak summoned him from his homeland.[3] In the second couplet, he recalls Balak's commission to "come, curse Jacob for me; come denounce Israel" (NIV). Jacob is a metonymy for Israel as a nation, and there are two synonymous verbs for "curse." These parallel phrases clearly communicate Balak's desires.

23:8. In the third couplet Balaam asks two rhetorical questions, indicating that he cannot do what Balak desires. He asks how he can curse those whom God has not cursed or denounce those whom the Lord has not denounced.[4]

TRANSLATION ANALYSIS
As is typical of Hebrew poetry, these questions are posed in a terse manner. In both parts of the couplet, there is no actual direct object for the verbs "curse" and "denounce." In poetic style, the direct objects are unnecessary here since the referent is clearly Israel. English translations supply words or phrases like "those whom" (NIV, NLT), "whom" (ESV, NASB, NKJV), "one" (NET), or "someone" (CSB) to fill in the gap.

This couplet poignantly expresses Balaam's problem. He has received his commission from Balak, but God has authorized his speech. He cannot explicitly contradict the authority whom he represents (Gane 2004, 700–701). He is God's mouthpiece, unable to speak what would materially benefit him.

23:9–10a. The next three couplets express Israel's elevated status among the nations. Balaam looks down from the heights and sees Israel spread out before him. He identifies Israel as a people that dwells alone, not counting itself among the nations (23:9b). This reflects on Israel's election by God to be his people. Israel lives "apart from the other nations in safety and security as recipients of Yahweh's blessing" (Cole 2000, 405). Of course, Israel's unique status does not derive from what it has done, but from God's sovereign choice to make it his holy nation and kingdom of priests to testify to his purposes on the earth (Exod. 19:3–6; Deut. 7:7–9). Balaam then points out Israel's current blessed state through further rhetorical questions. He asks, "who can count the dust of Jacob, or number the fourth part of Israel?" (23:10a ESV, NET). This probably refers to Balaam's ability to see one of the four camps into which Israel was divided according to the instructions in Numbers 2 (Ashley 1993, 471).[5] Israel's current blessed state is exemplified in Balaam's inability to fully view it or count all of it.

23:10b. The first oracle concludes with Balaam's desire to be associated with Israel. He proclaims, "let me die the death of the upright, and let my end be like his!" (ESV). This does not reflect an immediate desire for death, but rather his hope for posterity. Essentially, "Balaam's wish illustrates the blessing that every nation and person will desire to receive from God—to share the fate of Israel" (Milgrom

---

3 Balaam identifies his homeland as Aram, which is probably a shortened form of Aram-Naharaim (cf. Deut. 23:4). This is a broad region in which Pethor (22:5) was located (Ashley 1993, 470).

4 The typical root for "curse" is ארר, found in 23:7. This verse uses the root קבב which seems to be functionally equivalent.

5 There is also some textual uncertainty here, suggesting that the phrase for "fourth" (אֶת־רֹבַע) could be read instead as a synonym for "dust" in the first half of the couplet. The NRSV and HCSB follow this reading. Lexicons

1990, 197). This again recalls God's promise to Abraham in Genesis 12:3 that all nations will find blessing in Abraham and his descendants (Wenham 2008, 196).

Conclusion (23:11–12)

23:11. There is a brief exchange between Balak and Balaam at the conclusion of the oracle. Balak first expresses incredulity at what Balaam has just said. One can hear Balak's dismay as he asks, "what have you done to me?" He then reminds Balaam "to curse my enemy, I summoned you, but look, you have instead blessed!" Hebrew word order here fronts the verb "to curse" putting it in greater prominence in the sentence and highlighting the contrast with what Balaam has actually done.

23:12. For his part, Balaam simply reasserts that he can only speak what God directs. He is caught between Balak's expectations and what God permits. However, he does not try to shut down the whole pointless exercise.

The Second Oracle (23:13–26)

The Preparations (23:13–17)

23:13. Balak decides that what is needed is a change of scenery. Perhaps another location will permit Balaam to tap into the spiritual power needed to curse Israel. Balak's primary justification for this place is that Balaam will not be able to see as many Israelites, presumably strengthening his chances of enacting a successful curse. This reflects a serious misunderstanding of God's authority, which does not weaken on account of distance.

> *TRANSLATION ANALYSIS*
> The phrase תִּרְאֶנּוּ אֶפֶס קָצֵהוּ תִרְאֶה is challenging. A very literal rendering would be "you shall see it from there, only its end you will see," referring to Israel's camp. English translations employ a variety of idioms: "only a fraction of them" (ESV), "only the outskirts of their camp" (NIV), "only a part of them" (NET), "only the extreme end of them" (NASB).

23:14. Balaam and Balak perform the same offerings as before. Their new location is the field of Zophim, upon the top of Pisgah. This is a mountain peak within Moabite territory. It was also possibly a known place for observing the movements of heavenly bodies or other potential omens (Cole 2009, 383; Milgrom 1990, 198). It thus seems like an auspicious location for Balaam to do his work. However, Balak's preparations merely lay the foundation for God to give Balaam another message of blessing.

23:15–17. These verses are a truncated version of 23:3–6. Again, Balaam tells Balak to wait with the sacrifices. Again, God gives Balaam a message to speak. Again, Balaam returns to a presumably anxious and eager Balak. There is a slight variation in that Balak asks Balaam what YHWH has said. This may suggest that Balak now recognized the name of the deity who was opposing him, but did not understand God's full nature (Ashley 1993, 476). Here, Balak's question prompts Balaam to launch into his second oracle.

Balaam's Second Oracle (23:18–24)

23:18. This oracle expands upon the themes of the first: Israel's blessed nature and the reality of God's presence. It consists of eleven parallel couplets, again laden with vivid imagery. It begins by calling upon Balak to arise and hear. This oracle thus directly confronts Balak and his intention of cursing Israel.

23:19. Balaam gives Balak a crash course in the difference between God and men. God is not a

---

list both "fourth" and "dust" as option for רֹבַע (e.g., CHALOT, 331) Another option is a proposed textual emendation to תַּרְבָּעֹת (Milgrom 1990, 197). In either case, the meaning is relatively unchanged. Through God's preservation, Israel is a vast nation.

man who lies or deceives, nor does he change his mind. The focus here is on God's constancy and the inability for him to be manipulated by sacrifices and rituals. His promises are trustworthy, including those that he made to bless Abraham and his descendants with offspring, land, and an enduring covenant relationship (Pressler 2017, 214). The latter half of the verse confirms this via rhetorical questions. It asks "does he speak and not act? Does he promise and not fulfill?" (NIV). These questions have a positive answer. When God speaks, he acts. When he promises, he fulfills.[6]

> **Does God Change His Mind?**
> The question of whether God changes his mind is theologically fraught. There are times in Scripture where God is said to regret something (Gen. 6:6; 1 Sam. 15:11, 35) or to change his mind (Exod. 32:14; Jer. 18:8). Even within Numbers, God has pronounced what looks like final judgment against Israel, only to relent when Moses intercedes (Num. 14:20). It is helpful to note that "all such language about God is anthropopathic and thus only an analogy" (Ashley 1993, 478). God may appear to change his mind from a human perspective, but his divine character is unchanged. The focus in this oracle is on God's constancy as Israel's covenant partner. He cannot be swayed by sacrifices or by ritual to curse a people whom he has promised to bless. Elsewhere in Scripture, when God appears to change course, it is in keeping with his essential character. Unlike the gods of the nations, he is never capricious or untrustworthy.

This verse also portrays Balaam as a foil for God as the seer shifts between declarations that he can only say what God commands and efforts to angle for his own advantage (Allen 2012,

321). Behind this changeable mouthpiece lies the reality of a stalwart and faithful God.

23:20. The next verse presents the implications of YHWH's nature. Because YHWH is faithful, Balaam is unable to revoke his command to bless. "Since Yahweh is unlike fickle people, the command to bless is not subject to change" (Allen 2012, 321).

23:21. In this verse, the oracle transitions the effects of God's blessing upon Israel. The key theme is divine protection through God's presence. The verse begins "he has not beheld misfortune in Jacob, nor has he seen trouble in Israel" (ESV). That is, God's gaze over Israel prevents them from experiencing turmoil and pain. The latter half of the verse reinforces God's protection. He dwells among his people as their king. Consequently, they were "invincible from outside attack" (Allen 2012, 321).

TRANSLATION ANALYSIS
There is some discussion over whether this refers to Israel's sinful behavior in the wilderness. The word אָוֶן ("misfortune") can be used to denote wrongdoing (Isa. 1:13; Jer. 4:14; Hos. 6:8), though the parallel term עָמָל ("trouble") typically does not. The NET and NKJV translate "iniquity" for the first term, suggesting that God overlooks Israel's sin. However, in the context of a foreign seer pronouncing blessing, Israel's internal rebellions against God are probably not in view. Instead, this verse celebrates God's preservation of his people in the wilderness (Cole 2000, 412).

23:22–23. The oracle then focuses on the implications of God's presence. It recounts the fact that he delivered Israel from Egypt before shifting to an image of the horns of an ox. This is likely a

---

6 Numbers 23:18–19 is an example of the literary device of inclusio, where an element from the beginning of the selection reoccurs at the end to mark completion. Here, the initial command to Balak ("Arise") is a qal form of the root קוּם. The final phrase of 23:19 ("and not fulfill") is based on a hiphil form of the same root. English versions cannot easily capture this feature.

symbol of the animal's strength and power (Deut. 33:17; 2 Sam. 22:3; Ashley 1993, 480). The terseness of the poetic line makes it unclear whether the image is pointing to God or Israel. It could reflect God's strength through which he delivered Israel (CSB, ESV, NASB, NKJV, NLT), or Israel may be strong as an ox now that God has delivered them (NET, NIV).[7] The former option is more likely, since it keeps God's actions at the forefront (Allen 2012, 322; Ashley 1993, 480–81; Cole 2000, 413; Wenham 2008, 197).

God's protective presence is further emphasized in 23:23, which celebrates his authority over spiritual powers. This verse announces that there is no divination or evil omen against Israel.[8] With this, Balaam effectively concedes the futile nature of his current enterprise. No one can bring malevolent spiritual power against a nation that God has chosen to bless. The verse ends with a final ringing declaration: "Look at what God has done" (NET).[9] He has delivered them from captivity, and continues to protect them against all dangers as they move through the wilderness.

23:24. The oracle concludes with more animal images, this time with Israel as the clear referent. They are compared to ravenous lions that do not rest until they have devoured their prey. Balak sought to weaken Israel through curses so that he could defeat them, but this second oracle concludes with Israel as the predator.

Conclusion (23:25–26)
23:25–26. The aftermath of the second oracle resembles the first (cf. 23:11–12). Balak expresses dismay, while Balaam again declares that he can only speak what God permits. Balak implores Balaam to neither curse nor bless Israel, since all of his attempts to curse have resulted in blessing. Whereas Balak's response to the first oracle was "what are you doing?", his reaction to the second essentially is to say, "just stop talking!" (Allen 2012, 323). Unfortunately for Balak, his desire to curse Israel has not actually abated.

THEOLOGICAL FOCUS

The exegetical idea (Israel is a nation that God has chosen to bless) leads to this theological focus: *God's blessing provides protection for his people.* In these oracles we see the extensive preparations made by Balak and Balaam for cursing Israel. And yet, whenever Balaam goes off to meet with God, he receives a message of blessing that he must pronounce. Balaam's inability to curse reflects the constancy of God's presence with Israel, providing protection from the schemes of a hostile king.

These oracles reflect God's covenant promises to Israel. Leviticus 26:1–13 and Deuteronomy 28:1–14 recount the blessings that the Israelites will receive when they are faithful. They include abundant fruitfulness in the land, victory over enemies, and acknowledgment by the nations that they are God's people. Throughout the subsequent history of Israel, God blesses his people with protection when they are faithful to him, and sometimes when he is moved by their suffering even absent repentance. Israel's exile and captivity come about only after repeated rebellion and flagrant rejection of God as their

---

7   The KJV, somewhat amusingly, reads "unicorn" instead of "ox," likely following the Septuagint's use of μονοκέρωτος. This is "one of the most misguided guesses in translation history" (Sprinkle 2015, 345).
8   It is also possible that this verse means that there is no divination or evil omens in Israel. That is, Israel does not participate in forbidden spiritual practices to discern God's will. This depends on whether the Hebrew preposition should be translated with a spatial sense ("in" or "among") or an adversative sense ("against") (Arnold and Choi 2018, 117–18). The spatial sense is more common, but the context of Balaam's attempt to curse Israel suggests that the adversative sense is more fitting. English translations overwhelmingly go with the adversative sense.
9   There is no Hebrew word in the text for "look at," but adding it is helpful for finding a parallel English idiom.

only God (2 Kings 21:10–15). However, God faithfully preserves a remnant of the people and again promises to provide protection through his presence from a rebuilt sanctuary (Hag. 2:1–9; Zech. 2:1–13). Israel is encouraged to trust God and celebrate his presence as a means of deliverance from the nations (Isa. 12:1–6).

In the New Testament, this promise manifests itself differently. The people of God are no longer a nation but rather a multiethnic, multinational body created and preserved by the work of Christ (Eph. 2:11–22). However, they still enjoy the promise of God's protection through his blessing. Paul warns believers that their struggle is not with flesh-and-blood enemies but with the rulers and spiritual authorities of a broken and sinful world (Eph. 6:12). God equips believers through the provision of his armor and the presence of the Holy Spirit (Eph. 6:13–20).

The culmination of God's blessing comes in his ability to secure his people's eternal fate. Revelation celebrates the triumph of the Lamb over hostile spiritual forces, proclaiming that the slain Lamb has purchased for God people from every tribe, tongue, and nation (Rev. 5:9–10). Their eternal hope is secure, even as they face the wrath of the defeated dragon. As God's people remain faithful to their testimony, they rest securely knowing that they have the hope of his eternal presence (Rev. 12:13–17; 21:1–4).

Again, this theological focus does not deny the reality of pain and suffering in the lives of believers. However, it does remind us that just as Balak and Balaam could not contravene God's intentions for his people, no hostile spiritual powers have the authority to affect the eternal security of those who trust in God.

PREACHING AND TEACHING STRATEGIES

Exegetical and Theological Significance
Having finished the prelude and stage-setting, Balaam now speaks the first message that God has given him. The desires of Balak are immediately contrasted with the intentions of God (23:7–8), and there is no doubt who will have their way in the end. Right before entering the Promised Land, as they travel in the wilderness as their father Abraham did before them, Israel must trust in the promises given to Abraham. In both Numbers 22 and 23, the language of blessing and cursing echoes Genesis 12:3. Like Abraham, this is the promise that Israel must cling to. Can a shamanic prophet curse them? Can a skilled diviner offer the right sacrifices to God and bend God to a human will? Will God change his mind and alter his plan to bless?

The answers to these questions are an emphatically "no!" in Balaam's first two oracles. The entire first oracle provides the central response: God is going to bless Israel abundantly. No matter what Balak wants, Israel literally cannot be cursed. Moreso, Israel will be blessed beyond measure. Despite armies and enemies, Israel will be more numerous than the grains of sand. This statement affirms God's promise to Abram in Genesis 13:16, "I will make your offspring like the dust of the earth, so that if anyone could count the dust, then your offspring could be counted." In context, 13:15 and 17 surround verse 16 with promises that Abram's offspring will possess the land—the land that Israel is marching toward in Balaam's time.

Israel's assured success is highlighted in the second oracle, and is anchored in the fact that God has promised and will not change his mind. When God speaks, he acts and fulfills his word. Since nothing can overpower him and he never has cause to alter his perfectly wise plans, once he has said something it is as good as done. What a great confidence boost for Israel at that juncture! Their God had the power to bring them into the Promised Land, and he was never going to change his mind or annul his promises.

Preaching Idea
The people of God are blessed both in life and in death.

Contemporary Connections

What does it mean?
What does it mean that the people of God are blessed both in life and in death? In Israel's context in Numbers, God was promising to bless the nation in multiple ways. Not only were they to be blessed with the land and fruitfulness, but they were also to grow in their knowledge of the Lord. What God revealed to Balaam caused Balaam to proclaim that God's people could not be cursed. Then, as he reflected on the vision he saw and the revealed will of the Lord for his people, Balaam could only exclaim, "Let me die the death of the righteous, and may my final end be like theirs!" (23:10b).

Scholars debate how much understanding there was at that time concerning the details of the afterlife, but at least one thing is clear: Balaam saw the goodness of living and dying as part of the righteous people of God. This represents complete and comprehensive blessing. God showed Balaam that the people of his chosen nation were going to be blessed in both life and in death. What more could someone desire in this world than to live and die under God's hand of blessing, love, and care? Even Balaam could not deny the superiority of this relationship with God.

Today, the historical and theological situation is not identical with what we find in Numbers, but this principle still abides: God's people are blessed in both life and death. Now, in union with Christ, death is defeated. Now, in union with Christ, we have eternal life. In Christ, God's people are blessed *eternally*. May our final end indeed be the end of the righteous.

Is it true?
Is it true that the people of God are blessed both in life and in death? Many Christians often speak the truth of Psalm 116:15, "Precious in the sight of the Lord is the death of his faithful servants." Another familiar verse is Revelation 14:13a, "Then I heard a voice from heaven say, 'Write this: Blessed are the dead who die in the Lord from now on.'" For the believer, death is the gateway into the presence of our Lord. As Paul wrote, "I eagerly expect and hope that I will in no way be ashamed, but will have sufficient courage so that now as always Christ will be exalted in my body, whether by life or by death. For to me, to live is Christ and to die is gain. If I am to go on living in the body, this will mean fruitful labor for me. Yet what shall I choose? I do not know! I am torn between the two: I desire to depart and be with Christ, which is better by far; but it is more necessary for you that I remain in the body" (Phil. 1:20–24). For the people of God, the divine blessings will be experienced more, not less, after death.

Now what?
Given the fact that the people of God are blessed both in life and in death, what do we do? Among other things, take warning from the example of Balaam: he knew all of these truths, yet in the end rejected God and tried to lead God's people astray. Wanting to go to heaven—or being afraid of hell—is not the same as trusting in Jesus. Many want the benefits of the righteous without being righteous. You cannot have eternal glory except by way of the cross.

Use these great truths to shape your perspective and priorities. As we see in Philippians 1, Paul's attitude to life and to death was entirely controlled by the reality of Christ. We do not live as the world, and we do not die as the world. If we have confidence and hope in life and death, it is because of God's promises in Christ Jesus. Cling to him in faith and praise his name. What more could we want than blessing in this life and even greater blessing after death?

Creativity in Presentation
Different local churches have very different levels of engagement with liturgies, creeds, confessions of faith, and catechisms. For those who regularly incorporate the reciting of creeds or readings from confessions or catechisms into

their worship services, such an experience will be familiar. Nonetheless, when it is specially tied to the biblical text and message (i.e., when it is just the right fit), it can be special. For those who attend services where these resources play little to no part on a regular basis, engaging with a well-selected passage for such a resource can be deeply enriching.

Likely the most famous question and answer for a Protestant catechism is the Westminster Shorter Catechism Q & A #1:

> Q. What is the chief end of man?
> A. Man's chief end is to glorify God and to enjoy him forever.

Although that may be the most well known, to me personally the most beautiful is found in the Heidelberg Catechism question-and-answer:

LORD'S DAY 1, HEIDELBERG CATECHISM

What is your only comfort in life and in death?
That I am not my own, but belong—body and soul, in life and in death—
to my faithful Savior, Jesus Christ.
He has fully paid for all my sins with his precious blood,
and has set me free from the tyranny of the devil.
He also watches over me in such a way
that not a hair can fall from my head without the will of my Father in heaven;
in fact, all things must work together for my salvation.
Because I belong to him, Christ, by his Holy Spirit, assures me of eternal life
and makes me wholeheartedly willing and ready from now on to live for him.

What must you know to live and die in the joy of this comfort?
Three things:
First, how great my sin and misery are;
Second, how I am set free from all my sins and misery;
Third, how I am to thank God for such deliverance.

Take a moment and savor those words. It would be difficult to find a more helpful quotation for the preaching point in this unit than those words in the Heidelberg Catechism. What is our comfort in life and in death? What is our hope and joy? What is our confidence, strength, and assurance? God has blessed his people in Christ, and they are blessed both in life and death.

A possible outline for this passage is the following:

- No spiritual manipulation can change God's intention to bless his people (23:1–12).

- God's steadfast love preserves and protects his people (23:13–26).

DISCUSSION QUESTIONS

1. Why does the text list such extensive preparations for these oracles when they do not succeed in permitting Balaam to curse Israel?

2. How does God's commitment to bless his people play out for contemporary believers?

3. How is the steadfast character of God presented in these oracles?

4. What lessons should we draw from the fact that Balak and Balaam have no control over what Balaam can say about Israel?

Numbers 23:27–24:25

EXEGETICAL IDEA
God's blessing of Israel means that it will triumph over hostile foreign nations.

THEOLOGICAL FOCUS
God reigns over the nations.

PREACHING IDEA
There is no greater kingdom than the kingdom of God, and no greater king than King Jesus.

PREACHING POINTERS
Throughout these oracles and messages, the themes of God's sovereignty and authority and his faithfulness to his covenant promises are often repeated. Vibrant language is used to describe the rich blessings that are going to rest upon Israel. As a nation, they will prosper under God's hand, but all of their enemies will be destroyed. These messages speak comfort to Israel but warning to Balak and all those nations which will oppose God's chosen people or try to interfere with God's plans to bless.

This section contains the famous prophecy in 24:17. Scholars debate its exact significance, question how much Balaam could know or understand of it, and look for figures who may be possible fulfillments of it. Living this side of Christ, however, this prophecy is connected with the Messiah, king, and conqueror, and even if there is a typological stop along the way, the ultimate fulfillment is found in Jesus Christ. It is through Jesus that God's enemies are destroyed, and it is through Jesus that God's people are blessed. Christ the Lord is prophet, priest, and king, and his reign will never cease. Of the increase of his government there be no end. The oracles of Balaam had direct application in his original context, but they also point forward to an era and figure of greater fulfillment. There is no greater kingdom than the kingdom of God, and no greater king than King Jesus.

BALAAM'S REMAINING ORACLES (23:27–24:25)

LITERARY STRUCTURE AND THEMES

This preaching unit consists of Balaam's third through seventh oracles. The third oracle has a similar structure to the first two, beginning with a shift in geographical locale and the offering of sacrifices. However, it shifts how Balaam receives God's message. Further, its concluding exchange between Balaam and Balak is more detailed and ends with Balaam preparing to give further prophecy without Balak's prompting. The fourth through seventh oracles are simply prophetic declarations from Balaam without any narrative introduction or conclusion. The fourth oracle is similar in length to the preceding ones, while the fifth through seventh are extremely brief.

The overall theme of Israel's blessing continues throughout these oracles as Balaam remains unable to curse it. As these oracles unfold, they shift toward the implications of God's blessing for both Israel and the other nations. As God protects and preserves Israel, hostile nations find themselves the recipients of divine judgment. Balaam is God's mouthpiece throughout this passage, eventually even abandoning the pretense of trying to curse Israel.

- **The Third Oracle (23:27–24:14)**
  - *The Preparations (23:27–24:3a)*
  - *Balaam's Third Oracle (24:3b–9)*
  - *Aftermath (24:10–14)*
- **The Fourth Oracle (24:15–19)**
- **The Final Oracles (24:20–25)**

EXPOSITION

By now, it is clear to everyone except Balak that his plan will not succeed. However, that does not deter him from making one last attempt to have Balaam curse Israel. Balak receives more than he bargained for as Balaam not only blesses Israel again, but also offers four further unprompted oracles. The relationship between Israel and foreign nations comes into view as the oracles progress. Israel's flourishing is contrasted with the fate of the nations who face defeat and destruction. These oracles reveal that God's blessing of Israel means that it will triumph over hostile foreign nations.

The Third Oracle (23:27–24:14)

The Preparations (23:27–24:3a)
23:27–28. Balak again hopes that another change of location will permit Balaam to curse Israel. He seems less confident this time, hoping that "perhaps" (אוּלַי) God will let it happen. Moving to three different locations recalls how Balaam beat his donkey three times when he could not perceive the angel. Balaam at least has equivalent insight to his donkey while Balak now plays the fool (Pressler 2017, 215). The text refers to this location as the "top of Peor" (רֹאשׁ הַפְּעוֹר). Its exact location is unknown, though it is likely in the same vicinity as Pisgah. Subsequent narratives identify it as the place from which the Moabites seduced Israel (literally and metaphorically) into idolatrous worship of Baal (Num. 25:18; 31:16; Josh. 22:17). At this point, Balak probably hopes that proximity to a place linked to Baal will permit Balaam to break through Israel's divine protection (Cole 2000, 415).

23:29–30. The preparations resemble those of 23:1, 14. Again, Balaam instructs Balak to build seven altars and sacrifice a bull and a ram on each one. Again, Balak complies.

24:1–3a. At this point, the differences between this oracle and its predecessors begin. Balaam does not depart from Balak to go and meet God. Neither does he engage in any divinatory activity, which was at least implied in the preceding oracles (Ashley 1993, 486). In Balak's eyes at least, Balaam's departures were for him to try to manipulate the spiritual realm to curse Israel. In this oracle, Balaam dispenses with that pretense. He simply turns his face toward the wilderness, where he could see Israel encamped in its tribal arrangements.[1] There is likely a double meaning of "sight" here, with Balaam both observing Israel and receiving clarity of perception of God's purposes for the nation (Cole 2000, 416). Balaam also receives God's message in a new way. Rather than God "putting a word in his mouth" (23:5, 16), the Spirit of God (רוּחַ אֱלֹהִים) comes upon him. It indicates that as Balaam receives the divine spirit, he speaks as a God-inspired prophet (Milgrom 1990, 202).

Balaam's motives continue to be opaque. It is not evident whether he is still angling for his reward or is resigned to speaking only what God permits. The ambiguity even allows him to pursue both courses of action at the same time. He tells Balak to prepare sacrifices, suggesting the potential of enacting a curse, while also omitting other divinatory practices, perhaps reflecting his submission to God's intention to bless (Oswalt 2011, 211–12).

Balaam's Third Oracle (24:3b–9)
24:3b–4. Balaam's speech clearly indicates that he is communicating God's words. The word נְאֻם ("oracle, declaration") occurs three times in this selection. It almost always marks divine speech and is very common in the prophetic books (Isa. 14:22; Jer. 23:21; Ezek. 13:6–7; Jonah 2:12; Mic. 4:6; Zech. 8:17; 10:12; 11:6; Ashley 1993, 487). Although this is "an oracle of Balaam," its divine source is not in dispute.

The other key theme is perception. Balaam identifies himself as "the man whose eye is opened" (24:3b ESV).[2] Further, he hears the words of God, perceives the vision of the Almighty, and falls prostrate with uncovered eyes (24:4). These images of sight and sound reveal Balaam's qualifications to pronounce the message that he has received. He proclaims that his eyes and ears are attuned to God's purposes (Oswalt 2011, 214).

> **El Shaddai**
> Numbers 24:4 refers to God with the terms אֵל and שַׁדַּי. The former is a generic term for divinity and can also refer to the head of the Canaanite pantheon. The latter is the name that God says that he gave to the patriarchs (Exod. 6:4, cf. Gen. 49:25). The two terms occasionally form a single title: אֵל שַׁדַּי ("El Shaddai," often rendered "God Almighty," cf. Gen. 17:1; 28:3; 35:11; 43:14; 48:3). The term שַׁדַּי also recalls the *shaddayin* (the council of ancient Near Eastern deities) with whom Balaam interacts in the Deir 'Alla inscription (Cole 2000, 419). In this verse, the covenant God of Israel is clearly in view, though it is likely intentional that these other titles resonate with nonbiblical Balaam traditions (Ashley 1993, 489).

As Balaam sees and hears God's message, he also describes himself as "falling." This may refer to an ecstatic prophetic trance, although

---

1. A different interpretation is that Balaam looked *away* from Israel to try to be able to announce a curse without God blocking it (Gane 2004, 709). This seems unlikely given that he sees Israel in the very next clause (Oswalt 2011, 211).
2. A more idiomatic rendering is the man "whose eye sees clearly" (NIV). There is some discussion about whether the word שְׁתֻם means "open" or "closed." Closed eyes here would indicate that Balaam had been unable to perceive what God was doing, but is now able to. English versions universally prefer the "open" eyes interpretation. This also fits with the image of Balaam's eyes being uncovered in 24:4b (Milgrom 1990, 203).

it could equally refer to falling prostrate in submission to God (Cole 2000, 419; Milgrom 1990, 203; Oswalt 2011, 217). By the end of 24:4, Balaam has established his credentials to pronounce the blessing that follows: he perceives God's intentions through the presence of the divine spirit, and he adopts an appropriate posture for a human spokesperson of God's words.

24:5–7a. Balaam now transitions into his blessing of Israel. It begins with two parallel declarations of the beauty of Israel's encampment. This does not refer to the actual aesthetic qualities of Israel's tents, but because God has blessed Israel, even its temporary shelters are worthy of praise (Sprinkle 2015, 346). The image is strengthened by four similes in 24:6, drawing from the natural world. Israel is compared to multiple types of flourishing vegetation that receive life-giving water. The specifics of what kind of plant life is in view here are unimportant compared to its stunning juxtaposition with Israel's forty-year wandering in the barren wilderness.

> *TRANSLATION ANALYSIS*
> The first agricultural simile merits brief discussion. It describes Israel's dwelling as נְחָלִים, which usually refers to wadis, or river valleys. However, it may also have a secondary gloss of "palm tree." This would match more closely with the following images (Allen 2012, 326). English versions adopt both readings. River valleys or an equivalent is found in the CSB, NASB, NET, NIV, and NKJV. Palms or palm groves is found in the ESV, NLT, and NRSV.

These images of fruitfulness culminate in 24:7a. It begins by picturing someone carrying water in overflowing buckets. This again is a vivid image of nourishing life for a people dwelling in the wilderness. This is paralleled with the expression "his seed shall be in many waters" (ESV). This refers to Israel's own fruitfulness and recalls God's promises to Abraham that his "seed" (or "offspring") would become a great nation (Gen. 12:7; 13:16; 15:5; 24:7). The pictures of fertility in the natural world point to Israel continuing to grow in numbers and prosperity under the blessing of God (Ashley 1993, 492).

24:7b. This half-verse marks the shift from Israel's prosperity to Israel's strength. Under the influence of God's Spirit, Balaam envisions a time when Israel will be an exalted kingdom with a powerful king, a promise that God also gave to the patriarchs (Gen. 17:6, 15; 35:11). Balaam announces that Israel's king will be "greater than Agag." This is the name of an Amalekite king whom Saul defeated (1 Sam. 15:7–9) but also could reflect a generic ruling name for that nation (Allen 2012, 327).[3] It fits with the celebration of Israel's triumph over hostile nations in the rest of this oracle and in the ones that follow.

24:8–9a. The oracle continues to extol Israel's power by drawing upon images of formidable animals. The image in 24:8a is identical to that in 23:22, comparing God's strength in delivering Israel from Egypt to the horns of a wild ox.[4] The next image is that of hostile nations being devoured, having their bones broken, and being pierced with arrows. English versions are divided as to whether God (ESV, NASB, NKJV, NRSV) or Israel (NET, NIV) is the conqueror. Grammatically, both are possible implied subjects of the three verbs in 24:8b. Cole sees these images as echoing the portrayal of Israel's king in 24:7b in his chiastic structure of this oracle

---

[3] The Septuagint reads "Gog" here in place of "Agag." This would give the passage "an eschatological thrust" as it referenced this legendary future enemy of Israel from Ezekiel 38–39 (Milgrom 1990, 204).

[4] See the exposition of 23:22 for a discussion of whether this image refers to God or Israel as the wild ox. English versions are divided here as they were in the preceding chapter.

(Cole 2000, 417–18). Regardless, even if Israel is the one who crushes its enemies in this verse, they only do so because God has delivered them and is their source of strength.

The ambiguity continues with the lion imagery in 24:9a. The text uses two synonyms: אֲרִי and לָבִיא. English versions typically translate "lion" and "lioness" respectively. Notably, this expression closely resembles the blessing that Jacob gave to Judah in Genesis 49:9, making it preferable to understand Israel as the one being compared to a lion (Milgrom 1990, 205). The pictures of a lion crouching and lying down reflect satiation after devouring its prey. Balaam thus portrays Israel as a fearsome predator whom all the nations will fear to awaken.

24:9b. The oracle concludes with language reminiscent of Genesis 12:3 and 27:29. Those who bless Israel are blessed, while those who curse it are cursed. Hostile nations will be like a lion's prey when they resist God and the people whom he has chosen to bless.

Aftermath (24:10–14)

24:10–11. Balak and Balaam have their most detailed exchange after the third oracle. It begins with Balak's anger with Balaam. This is the third mention of anger in the Balaam cycle. Previously, God was angry with Balaam (22:22), and Balaam was angry with his donkey (22:27). Balak's anger resembles the latter in terms of its impotence and misperception. In both cases Balaam and Balak were, in actuality, futilely opposing God. Balak strikes his hands and notes that although he called Balaam to curse, he instead blessed Israel three times. The Hebrew term וְהִנֵּה reflects Balak's incredulity as he reacts to a situation that he did not expect (van der Merwe, Naudé, and Kroeze 2017, 410). Balak attempts to dismiss Balaam, telling him to flee back home and reflect on the payment he will not receive. Balak names YHWH as the reason why Balaam will not receive his reward. This is unintentionally accurate on his part. In the tug-of-war between Balak and YHWH, Balaam had no choice as to whom he must serve.

24:12–14. Balaam answers by reminding Balak that he had already told Balak's messengers that he could not go beyond what God permitted, no matter the reward. However, this is not Balaam's final word. Balak has dismissed him, but God is not finished with him. Therefore, before Balaam return to his people, he prepares to foretell what Israel ("this people") will do to Moab ("your people") in the coming days. This sets up the fourth and following oracles, which announce Israel's triumph over foreign nations.

The Fourth Oracle (24:15–19)

The fourth through seventh oracles consist of only prophetic speech. There is no narrative framing. This emphasizes Balak's complete lack of control over the scenario he tried to orchestrate. Not only can Balak's hired seer not curse Israel, but Balak must now also stand there and hear unsolicited prophetic declarations of Israel's supremacy over the nations.

24:15–16. The fourth oracle has nearly the same beginning as the third, with references to Balaam's clarity of vision and falling prostrate. There is one additional line in the middle of 24:16, stating that Balaam "knows the knowledge of the Most High" (ESV). Balaam's insight now goes beyond the sense of sight and hearing; he now expresses an intimate knowledge of God's intentions (Cole 2000, 425).

24:17. This verse is among the most discussed in the entire book. It begins with God permitting Balaam to glimpse the future and see a figure who is "not now" and "not close." This figure is identified as a "star" (כּוֹכָב) that comes forward from Jacob and a "scepter" (שֵׁבֶט) that arises from Israel. A star is a reasonably common image of a royal figure in the ancient Near East, though not used frequently in Scripture (Isa. 14:12; Ezek. 32:7). Revelation

22:16 does identify Jesus as the descendant of David and bright morning star, capturing the royal implications. Another touchpoint for this image is Joseph's vision of a solar system (sun, moon, stars) bowing down to him in Genesis 37. Balaam's star could be seen as similar to the eleven stars that represented the brothers who were also "out of Jacob." In combination with the scepter imagery, this star will reign over fellow Israelites and enact God's will upon the nations (Gane 2004, 712). The word translated "scepter" (שֵׁבֶט) can also refer to an Israelite tribe or a ruler, but the parallelism with "star" suggests that another symbol of royal costume is intended (Stubbs 2009, 195).

The intended referent of the star and scepter imagery is not immediately evident. In context, this figure is a conqueror who "crushes the skulls of Moab" (NET) and defeats the Edomites (24:18).[5]

TRANSLATION ANALYSIS
The word that the net renders as "skulls" is פַּאֲתֵי. Its literal meaning is "corner" or "edge." However, it is used to refer to a part of the head in other contexts (Lev. 13:41; Jer. 48:45). English versions render it with "skulls" (NET) or synonyms like "forehead" (CSB, ESV, NASB, NIV) or "brow" (NKJV).

This is certainly suggestive of David and his conquests (2 Sam. 8:1–12; 2 Kings 11:15–16). It is also possible to look even further forward and see the beginning of messianic hope in a figure empowered by God to reign and to defeat those arrayed against God's people. It is doubtful that the first audiences understood this text as messianic. However, when read with the whole of the biblical canon, its celebration of a future victory of God foreshadows Christ's triumph over hostile powers (Ashley 1993, 503).

> **Messianic Prophecy**
> Numbers 24:17 has been read messianically in both Jewish and Christian traditions. The *Targum Onqelos* (an Aramaic translation and paraphrase of the Old Testament) comments on this verse, "When a mighty king of Jacob's house will reign, and the Messiah will be magnified." The Hasmonean ruler Alexander Jannaeus, who ruled from 103–76 B.C., had a star imprinted on some royal coins, implicitly connecting himself with this verse (Cole 2000, 426). The *Damascus Document* (CD) of the Dead Sea Scrolls community uses the reference to star and scepter to foretell the appearance of two messianic figures: one priestly, one royal (CD-A 7:18–21). Later, a leading rabbi granted the Jewish revolutionary Simon bar Kosiba the title "Bar Kokhba" ("Son of the Star") during a doomed revolt against Rome in 132–136 A.D. (Collins 1995, 202). Church fathers including Justin Martyr and Athanasius identified Christ as the ultimate referent of this verse (Allen 2012, 332).

24:18. Balaam further announces that Edom will share the fate of Moab, since it is the enemy of the star-scepter figure. Seir is another title for Edom, so its presence here simply marks the parallelism of this verse. The final phrase of this verse contrasts Israel's fate with that of these other nations. While they will experience destruction, Israel will be strong.

24:19. This oracle concludes with a terse summation of its message. It begins with an

---

5   The phrase following the reference to Moab is incredibly challenging. On the basis of the Samaritan Pentateuch and Jeremiah 48:45, many suggest reading קַרְקַר as קׇדְקֹד, which is a synonym for "skull" (Cole 2000, 327). This involves a simple and common confusion between two very similar Hebrew letters. It then equates the fate of Moab with that of the "sons of Sheth." There is no obvious referent for this group, but the most likely scenario is that it is a "parallel ethnic term for Moab" (Allen 2012, 333). This matches the paralleling of Edom and Seir in the next verse.

imperfect form of the verb רָדָה ("to rule over, have dominion") that lacks an explicit subject. English versions and modern commentators nearly uniformly identify the implied subject as the star-scepter ruling figure.[6] As he exercises his authority, he will bring about the destruction of "the survivors of the cities" (24:19b ESV). In this context, it refers to the Moabites and Edomites whose downfall Balaam is announcing.[7]

The Final Oracles (24:20–25)

Balaam's oracles conclude with three short denunciations of additional foreign nations. They do not have any evident connection to the preceding material. However, it is possible that these curse oracles resembled what Balak intended for Balaam to pronounce against Israel, providing one additional ironic element to the saga (Allen 2012, 334). Further, these oracles bring the final total up to seven, representing totality or completeness. Although the specifics are unclear, these oracles continue the theme of destruction for nations hostile to God's people.

24:20. The fifth oracle consists of a single verse. It employs wordplay to suggest that although Amalek was "first" among the nations, its "end" will be destruction. The Amalekites were never a major power, but they were the first enemy that Israel encountered after leaving Egypt (Exod. 17:8–16). They also defeated the Israelites when the people tried to enter the land after being rebuked for listening to the ten cowardly spies (Num. 14:43–45). Later, Israel did defeat the Amalekites decisively under Saul (1 Sam. 15) and David (2 Sam. 8:12).

24:21–22. The sixth oracle targets the Kenites, who are probably a subset of the Midianites. At the time of the wilderness wandering they were not actively hostile against Israel, since Moses's in-laws are identified as Kenites (Judg. 1:16; 4:11). However, this one instance of harmony is not necessarily indicative of the entire relationship, nor is there any sense that the Kenites ever submitted to the lordship of Israel's God. This oracle portrays the Kenites as having a secure dwelling place ("your nest is in the rocks" 24:22 ESV), yet still facing destruction. The instrument of devastation is identified as "Asshur" (אַשּׁוּר), which usually refers to Assyria. However, this seems historically incongruous since Assyria was not a presence in the region until much later. Many commentators suggest that here it refers to a tribal group called "Ashurites," linked in Scripture to a descendant of Abraham's wife Keturah (Gen. 25:3, 18; Ps. 83:9; Ashley 1993, 509; Cole 2000, 430; Sprinkle 2015, 352; Wenham 2008, 204). Although there is no stated reason for the Kenites to be targeted here, they represent another nation whose destiny is determined by the declarations of Israel's God.

24:23–24. The seventh and final oracle is also the most obscure. It begins with an exclamatory cry "Alas, who shall live when God does this?" (24:23 ESV). This reflects the futility of the nations' ability to resist God's plans. The final vision foretells an invader arriving on ships and

---

[6] See the insertion of "a ruler" (NET, NIV, NLT), or "one from Jacob" (ESV, NASB), or "one who comes from Jacob" (CSB).

[7] The challenging nature of the last two verses prompts some commentators to suggest emendations to the Hebrew Masoretic text. Milgrom and Wenham argue that "his enemies" from verse 18 should be shifted to verse 19 and that an incorrect word division means that the first letter should be removed from מִיַּעֲקֹב ("from Jacob") and placed on the end of the verb וְיֵרְדְּ ("and he will have dominion"). This would make Jacob the subject of the verb, leading to a translation of "Jacob shall rule his enemies, and destroy the survivors" (Milgrom 1990, 208; Wenham 2008, 202). This is a reasonable attempt to clarify a very difficult verse, but the translation found in standard English versions is sufficient for the purposes of expositing the text.

afflicting Ashur and Eber. It is probably best to take Ashur as the same Levantine tribe as in the previous verse, with Eber being a related group (Sprinkle 2015, 352). The invader is identified as the Kittim (כִּתִּים) whom the Table of Nations in Genesis 10:4 associate with the sons of Javan who settle in the Aegean and eastern Mediterranean regions. It may derive from an ancient city on Cyprus called Kition (Cole 2000, 431). English versions either keep Kittim (CSB, ESV, HCSB, NASB, NET, NRSV), or render it as Cyprus (NIV, NLT) to make the region identifiable to contemporary readers.[8] Interestingly, the oracle ends with the Kittim facing destruction themselves. In this context, the most likely referent is the Sea Peoples' invasions that upended the political order in the region through the thirteenth and twelfth centuries (Milgrom 1990, 210). This final oracle thus portrays an unceasing cycle of nations rising and falling who fail to acknowledge the sovereignty of Israel's God.

24:25. The chapter ends with the parting of Balaam and Balak. No further words are exchanged as each one returns to his home. No doubt Balaam has said far too much already for Balak's liking.

THEOLOGICAL FOCUS

The exegetical idea (God's blessing of Israel means that it will triumph over hostile foreign nations) leads to the following theological focus: *God reigns over the nations*. As Balaam pronounces his third and following oracles, the fate of the nations comes into closer view. Just as the Egyptians under Pharaoh could not keep God from freeing his people, a Moabite king cannot compel his hired seer to curse a people whom God has blessed; likewise, other nations including Edomites, Amalekites, and more will face divine judgment. God chose to put these messages into the mouth of a pagan seer, demonstrating that he can use whomever he wishes to accomplish his purposes.

Pictures of God's universal reign continue throughout Scripture. Psalm 2 envisions rulers futilely plotting against God's reign as he establishes Israel's king on Mount Zion and gives him the nations as an inheritance (Ps. 2:1–8). These kings are encouraged to show their wisdom by serving God with fear and submitting to Israel's king (Ps. 2:9–11). Psalm 99 begins with a ringing crescendo, "The LORD reigns, let the nations tremble" (Ps. 99:1 NIV). It then exemplifies his character and his preservation of his people (Ps. 99:2–9). The New Testament is set against the backdrop of the might of Caesar, yet it declares that a child born to woman of no special status will establish an even greater kingdom characterized by humility, love, and self-sacrifice (Luke 1:52; Phil. 2:5–8). Paul notes the paradox of the God's triumph over hostile powers through the humiliation of the cross (Col. 2:14–15). This established a kingdom to which all powers and all rulers must bow and confess the lordship of Jesus Christ (Phil. 2:9–11).

The reference to Jesus as the morning star and son of David in Revelation 22:16 is, at the very least, evocative of the star and scepter imagery of Balaam's fourth oracle. While David is a more obvious historical referent, ultimately his kingship finds its culmination in Christ who will reign eternally not just over Edom and Moab but over the whole of creation. At Christ's return, "all of the enemies of God and his people, including war, famine, pestilence, and death, will be finally conquered" (Stubbs 2009, 196). In this way, the Amalekites, Kenites, and other nations mentioned here point to God's ultimate sovereignty over all human powers. Nations rise

---

8 The Kittim continue to be a way of referencing hostile powers even after the time of the Old Testament. First Maccabees 1:1, 8; 8:5 associate it with the Macedonian powers, while various Qumran documents expands its use to include the Romans (Milgrom 1990, 210).

and fall, while the God who controls their destiny preserves his people for a coming day when his glorious reign will be established forever.

PREACHING AND TEACHING STRATEGIES

Exegetical and Theological Significance

As we have seen in earlier sections in Numbers, the theme of God's sovereignty and power over the nations is pervasive. Whether present in explicit statements or as a tacit presupposition, the fact that God rules and reigns over every nation and people group is a central, controlling motif. This doctrine, combined with God's covenant promises to Abraham and his plan to bless Israel and give them the Promised Land, gave encouragement to the Israelites and strengthened their hearts.

In the biblical material for this preaching unit, we see again that since God is determined to bless them, Israel is literally uncurseable. Despite the machinations of Balak and Balaam—just like despite Pharaoh, Sihon, and Og—God is going to bless his people with redemption and rest. At the end of the third oracle (24:9b), Balaam himself now speaks in affirmation of the language of Genesis 12:3, "May those who bless you be blessed and those who curse you be cursed" (NIV).

Israel is going to be beautiful and flourish (24:5–7a), and be strong and victorious (24:8–9). They are going to have a greater king and greater kingdom that surpasses the mighty kings and kingdoms of their day (24:7), and one day in the future a figure will arise who will crush their enemies for good (24:17–19). At first read, the last three short oracles may seem to diverge from the general theme of the previous messages, but they illustrate the principle that those who curse Israel will be cursed, and that Israel can take heart knowing that her enemies will be defeated (Wenham 2008, 203).

As expected, there are all manner of academic discussions concerning the meaning of 24:17–19, as well as other referents in these oracles. As a Christian teacher, it is of course vital to understand the text in its original context. We do not want to overinterpret the text or read back into Balaam's mind a fully orbed Christian theology. However, we *do* have the completed canon, and we *do* live this side of the advent of the Messiah. What was often opaque to the Old Testament prophets is clearer to us (cf. 1 Peter 1:10–12)—not because we are godlier or wiser, but because we live in the era when so many of the prophecies have been fulfilled. This means that it is entirely legitimate—in fact, mandatory—to show people how Christ Jesus is the fulfillment of the prophetic word.

There may be links and intermediate steps along the way to Christ. For example, David may be a referent in 24:17–19, but Scripture is clear that David is a type of Christ and points forward to him. Thus, even if some of the Balaam material moves you to David, the rest of Scripture moves you past David to Jesus. As a Christian preacher, you have the tremendous privilege of pointing people to prophetic words that have been fulfilled in Christ.

Preaching Idea

There is no greater kingdom than the kingdom of God, and no greater king than King Jesus.

Contemporary Connections

What does it mean?

What does it mean that there is no greater kingdom than the kingdom of God, and no greater king than King Jesus? The superlative is important: King Jesus is the greatest, and so is the kingdom of God. They can never be surpassed by anyone or anything. The theocratic nation of Israel was indeed blessed by God, and Israel did have some good kings (although relatively very, very few). Yet, if you read the Old Testament in its entirety, you cannot help but see the constant failure—and grotesque wickedness—of Israel's leaders and the nation itself.

Clearly, Israel did not constitute the greatest kingdom imaginable, and Israel's kings were often the embodiment of ungodliness.

Even in the New Testament, most of the religious and political leaders of Israel opposed the gospel of Jesus Christ, supported the crucifixion, and tried to stamp out the fledgling church. Nevertheless, the Messiah had come, and he arose from the grave after providing atonement for sins. Empowered by the Spirit of the living God, the apostles preached the good news, and the kingdom of darkness was driven back as the kingdom of light advanced.

Today, the people of God are blessed by virtue of their union with Christ, and by joyfully submitting to his rule and authority over every aspect of their lives. Christ is the great king, the fulfillment of God's prophetic word. The progressively unfolding revelation of God through the canonical Scriptures makes this indisputably clear.

Is it true?
Is it true that there is no greater kingdom than the kingdom of God, and no greater king than King Jesus? Reading the text with an eye to fulfillment, Psalm 2 answers this question with a resounding *yes*! In terms of living under the blessing of God, Psalms 1 and 2 are to be taken together, with 1:1 and 2:12 forming an inclusio that tells the reader what they need to do to be blessed. First, they must not be numbered among the wicked; second, they must submit to God's anointed king and take refuge in him. Between those poles, they must walk by faith in meditation on the law of the Lord. Psalm 2 as a whole depicts all of the kings of the earth rising up in opposition to the Lord's anointed king, who is installed by God himself on Mount Zion. Far from being threatened, the messianic King completely and utterly defeats his enemies.

The book of Daniel also underscores these truths. Daniel 2 contains the interpretation of a dream that is given to reveal that God will set up a kingdom that will never be destroyed but that endures forever (v. 44). Daniel 4 proclaims that the Most High God's kingdom is eternal and enduring (v. 3), and that God does whatever he wants with the nations of the earth (vv. 34–35; cf. 6:26). In Daniel 7, one like a son of man comes into the presence of the Ancient of Days and, "He was given authority, glory and sovereign power; all nations and peoples of every language worshiped him. His dominion is an everlasting dominion that will not pass away, and his kingdom is one that will never be destroyed" (7:14 NIV).

When the Son of God incarnate was on earth, he proclaimed that the kingdom of heaven was near. The reason it was at hand was because Christ the king was present. The book of Revelation shows the ultimate fulfillment and consummation of the themes of Christ's kingly reign, the overthrow of all of his enemies, and the establishment of the eternal kingdom. All through Scripture, these truths are taught and proclaimed. We are not to question whether they are true; we are to hear them and say, "Amen."

Now what?
Since there is no greater king than Jesus, and since his kingdom will endure forever (while all of those who oppose him will be destroyed), the right response should be apparent. The last strophe of Psalm 2 gives us the necessary directions:

> Therefore, you kings, be wise;
>   be warned, you rulers of the earth.
> Serve the Lord with fear
>   and celebrate his rule with trembling.
> Kiss his son, or he will be angry
>   and your way will lead to your destruction,
> for his wrath can flare up in a moment.
>   Blessed are all who take refuge in him. (Ps. 2:10–12 NIV)

Thankfully, the one who rules over all things and who will defeat all of his enemies is the one who died to reconcile his enemies to God. Through King Jesus, there is forgiveness, salvation, and eternal life. Kiss the son (i.e., an act of royal homage, like kneeling before him to kiss the ring on his hand), and own him as your Lord and King. His kingdom will endure forever, and we are invited to be citizens of the heavenly kingdom, through the merit and grace of the king.

Creativity in Presentation

On its own, this text is dramatic. If there were people in the church who could memorize the lines of Balak and Balaam and then present them verbatim from the text, it could be very powerful. These oracles were originally delivered orally, to be heard. Hearing them pronounced and articulated in character may help establish the framework for the message.

Depending on time and the way that the worship service is organized, it may also be possible to intersperse thematic readings. This would likely be best done near the end, after faithful biblical exposition has connected the dots and made the prophecy-fulfillment development clear. For example, Numbers 24:7b could be read, or 24:17, and then verses from Psalm 2, or Daniel, or Revelation. The goal would be to build up a layered intertextuality, moving from seed to blossom to fruit.

Another related idea would be to present either dramatic (enacted) vignettes, or the reading of texts as in the paragraph above. For example, Abraham could be seen hearing the words of Genesis 12:1–3 (or the text could simply be read), and then the echoing verses in the Balaam material could be read by a reader or recited by a role player. Another vignette could involve Nebuchadnezzar in Daniel 4, or the apostle John speaking some of the words of his vision in Revelation. There are a variety of ways that this could be done, and a variety of suitable biblical passages from which to choose.

Something to remember is that God is already very creative in the way that he presents his revelation in Scripture. Whatever we do must be done to shine a spotlight on the truth of his Word, rather than distract people from it by focusing the attention on ourselves or a nice presentation by a member of the drama team. The power is in the Word of God, and everything we do needs to be done in service of the Word. It must emphasize that there is no greater kingdom than the kingdom of God, and no greater king than King Jesus.

The glory of God's kingdom in this text may be expressed in this outline:

- God's presence makes his people secure from the nations (23:27–24:9).

- God uses Balaam to demonstrate that he reigns over the spiritual realm (24:10–14).

- A foretold ruler will come and reign over the nations (24:15–19).

- Hostile nations cannot stand against God (24:20–25).

DISCUSSION QUESTIONS

1. Why does Balak persist in having Balaam attempt to curse Israel, even when the project seems futile?

2. What do these oracles teach us about the status of God's people in the eyes of outsiders and those hostile to his kingdom?

3. How does the picture of a star from Jacob ultimately lead us to Christ?

4. What encouragement can these oracles give the people of God when they face hostile governments or authorities?

Numbers 25:1–18

EXEGETICAL IDEA
Israel succumbs to the temptations of idolatry, and God's wrath is averted only by the zealous actions of Phinehas.

THEOLOGICAL FOCUS
Appropriate worship of God requires zealous commitment.

PREACHING IDEA
Zeal is important in living for God, but sincerity and passion are not enough on their own.

PREACHING POINTERS
Having failed to gain control over Israel by controlling Israel's God, a new plan for Israel's destruction is hatched. Since they cannot manipulate the spiritual realm, they will attempt to manipulate Israel through physical seduction. There is a great meal provided (very tempting, given the complaints of the Israelites about their food supply), and an opportunity for unbridled sexual indulgence in pagan revelry. Many Israelites fall into this trap, and as a result many are killed in a plague of judgment. Phinehas's action may shock modern sensibilities, but God approves of it and calls it righteous (Ps. 106:30–31). Moab and the Midianites were engaged in a subtle war against Israel, and Phinehas's act was an act of war.

Phinehas's zeal is commendable, and his action was righteous given the circumstances, but zeal and sincerity alone are not enough to please God. In our contemporary society, many people insist that as long as a person is sincere, they are justified in almost anything they think or do. Scripture, however, takes a very different view. We ought to be filled with zeal for the Lord, but zeal is only as good as the end it is directed toward. Jesus was filled with zeal for his Father's house, but Paul was filled with zeal to destroy the church, until he met the risen Lord and was converted. Zeal is important in living for God, but sincerity and passion are not enough on their own.

IDOLATRY AND ZEALOTRY AT BAAL PEOR
(25:1–18)

LITERARY STRUCTURE AND THEMES

This passage makes an abrupt transition from the Balaam material in Numbers 22–24. Israel's conduct and Moses's leadership are again at the heart of the narrative. The presence of Moabites in this chapter provides a link to what has just transpired, but the tone is quite different. Whereas the Balaam chapters show YHWH's ability to preserve his people, this passage reveals Israel's continued propensity to turn away. This juxtaposition underscores Israel's unfaithfulness, even after experiencing "dramatic demonstrations of God's love and power" (Cole 2000, 433).

This chapter consists of two major episodes: Israel's immorality with the Moabites (25:1–5) and Phinehas's zealous response (25:6–18). This second episode can be further divided into Phinehas's actions (25:6–9) and YHWH's evaluation (25:10–18). As the final passage prior to the second census, this narrative leaves the reader with the disconcerting realization that Israel's inclination to turn away from God has not abated.

Key themes of the passage include the allure of idolatry and the necessity of rooting it out. Although Israel has seen the mighty work of God on its behalf and knows what he requires, the nation far too easily turns aside to other deities. In this case, a shocking response is necessary to mitigate the damage.

- **Israel's Immorality with the Moabites (25:1–5)**
- **Phinehas's Zealous Response (25:6–18)**
  ◦ *Phinehas's Actions (25:6–9)*
  ◦ *YHWH's Evaluation (25:10–18)*

EXPOSITION

This passage concludes the second major section of the book (Num. 10:11–25:18). Israel has left Sinai, and its journey through the wilderness has brought it to the edge of the Promised Land. Throughout its travels, Israel's rebellions and complaints have had serious consequences but God's mercy has preserved his covenant promises. In this final episode prior to the second census (Numbers 26), Israel turns from God one more time. Although it is not explicitly stated, the fact this incident is set after the death of Aaron and in the final year of wandering suggests that the second generation of Israelites is guilty (Schnittjer 2006, 435). They are not of superior moral character to their forefathers, although they have avoided refusing to enter the land (cf. Numbers 13–14). Unlike the grumbling narratives, there is no specific circumstance or hardship that prompts these actions. Instead, Israel succumbs to the temptations of idolatry, and God's wrath is averted only by the zealous actions of Phinehas.

Israel's Immorality with the Moabites (25:1–5)

25:1–2. Numbers 22:1 locates Israel on the plains of Moab, across the Jordan River from Jericho. Here, that same region is called Shittim (25:1a), which Joshua 2:1 and 3:1 identify as the staging ground for Israel's invasion. Israel's presence here confirms that Balak and Balaam's efforts have failed to dislodge Israel. God has preserved his people against the Moabite king's attempts to bring hostile spiritual powers against them.

Unfortunately, although God protects Israel from outside threats, the people are still capable of turning from him of their own volition. The text declares that they "began to commit sexual immorality" (Num. 25:1 NET) with Moabite women. The term for their behavior is לִזְנוֹת, whose root (זנה) typically implies prostitution. The term is not used in a technical sense here, but rather as a derogatory evaluation of Israel's actions (Olson 1996, 154).[1] It also fits the common linkage of prostitution with worshipping other gods (Exod. 34:16; 2 Chron. 21:11, 13; Ezek. 16:15–43; Hos. 4:10, 18; 5:3). The text does not state how these liaisons began, although Numbers 31:15–16 attributes them to a previously unmentioned scheme of Balaam. Israel's presence in Moabite territory provides the necessary opportunity for fraternization.

The Moabite women invite the Israelites to sacrificial feasts. To participate in these feasts is to honor the deity to whom the feast is dedicated (Gane 2004, 717). The text drives this home, declaring that the Israelites "bowed down to their gods" (Num. 25:2b ESV). There is a long history of trying to find "sacred prostitution" behind these verses, suggesting that the sexual liaisons themselves had a cultic purpose. Evidence for this is lacking, and the combination of illicit sexual encounters with outsiders and participating in feasts devoted to other deities is more than sufficient to condemn Israel (Pressler 2017, 226).

25:3. Through these actions, Israel tied itself to the Baal of Peor. Peor is one of the locations from which Balaam attempted to curse Israel (Num. 23:28) and was likely seen as a place of spiritual power. Baal is the name of a significant Canaanite deity who has numerous local manifestations mentioned throughout the Old Testament. By linking themselves to this deity, the Israelites kindle the anger of YHWH to whom they should be exclusively devoted.

This incident also recalls the golden calf episode in Exodus 32. These are the only stories in the Pentateuch that explicitly mention Israel worshipping another god (Olson 1996, 153).[2] Israel may complain about physical hardship or about Moses's leadership, but joining itself to another deity is a transgression of a different magnitude.

> **Baal**
>
> This is the first mention of Baal in the Old Testament. He soon becomes "the primary antagonist to Yahweh for the hearts of the Israelites" (Cole 2009, 385). Baal is one of the major Canaanite deities. He defeats the forces of chaos and disorder represented by the gods Yam (Sea) and Mot (Death). A roughly contemporaneous Egyptian text from the Hyksos period (c. 1720–1570 B.C.) shows Egyptians lamenting that a group of foreigners worships a deity named Baal-Hazor rather than Amon-Re (Cole 2009, 386). From this point onward in the biblical text, Baal is the key representative of Israel's idolatry (Judg. 2:11–13; 10:6; 1 Sam. 7:3–4; 12:10; Jer. 7:9; 11:13; Zeph. 1:4). King Omri (Ahab's father) of Israel even erected a temple to Baal in Samaria (1 Kings 16:31–32). Baal was thought to ritually die and return every year as a reflection of his struggle with Mot (Death), which is probably what Elijah is alluding to when he taunts Baal's prophets (1 Kings 18:27). Baal also has influence over natural forces and is called the "Cloud-Rider." Psalm 104:3 then attributes that title to YHWH.

---

1 This is only location in the Old Testament where "this verb in its literal sense takes a masculine subject" (Milgrom 1990, 212).

2 Olson views Exodus 32 and Numbers 25 as bookends of the experience of the first generation's journey from Sinai to the borders of the Promised Land (Olson 1996, 152–54). If, as argued above, Numbers 25 involves the second generation, then instead of bookends, these chapters are mirrors. They reveal that the new generation is prone to the same failures as their predecessors.

25:4. YHWH's anger manifests itself in a command to kill the "leaders of the people" (רָאשֵׁי הָעָם). The term for "leader" (רֹאשׁ) is not precisely defined, but elsewhere in Numbers it refers to heads of the tribal units (Num. 1:4, 16; 10:4; 13:3; 14:4; Ashley 1993, 247).[3] Presumably, these leaders have failed in their duty to maintain Israel's exclusive devotion to YHWH. God places the responsibility for this apostasy onto them. Their punishment is representative of the judgment on the entire community. God commands Moses to execute them by means of a rare verb (וְהוֹקַע) only used elsewhere to describe the vengeance of the Gibeonites against the house of Saul (2 Sam. 21:6, 9). Translations vary, but since the bodies are then to be put on public display "before the sun" (נֶגֶד הַשָּׁמֶשׁ), impalement is likely intended. Their exposed corpses would be a serious object lesson of the consequences of sin. This action would then turn aside God's wrath.[4] Although this command is harsh, it is reflective of the responsibility given to the leaders of the tribes. They may fail in other ways, but permitting idolatry to take root cannot be tolerated.

25:5. Moses responds by instructing Israel's judges (שֹׁפְטֵי יִשְׂרָאֵל) to kill the individuals who had "yoked themselves to Baal of Peor" (25:5 ESV). These figures probably reflect the office initiated by Moses to help him in judging disputes between the Israelites in Exodus 18:13–26 (Cole 2000, 440). This focuses the response on those specifically guilty of apostasy.

The connection between Moses's command and God's instructions from the previous verse is ambiguous. Do the terms "leaders of the people" and "judges" refer to the same group? Are leaders who have not apostatized put to death? A few approaches can be found. First, if "leaders of the people" and "Israel's judges" refer to the same group, then the command in 25:4 is *not* directed at the leaders themselves. Instead, when God says, "kill them," the antecedent is the guilty Israelites from 25:1–3, not the leaders (Sprinkle 2015, 359). This is possible, although it runs contrary to the most obvious syntax of the sentence. Secondly, Moses may be interpreting God's command by providing more specific instructions, telling the judges to execute only the guilty, not every tribal leader (Cole 2000, 439; Gane 2004, 717). Thirdly, Moses may be interpreting God's command by ordering the judges to execute *any* idolatrous Israelite. This would protect the leaders who had not committed idolatry from suffering God's judgment (Milgrom 1990, 477). This suggests that Moses does not mediate God's word exactly as it was presented to him. He has done that previously when striking the rock rather than speaking to it (Num. 20:1–12), which had serious consequences (Briggs 2018, 200–201).

Resolution of this matter is difficult. The third possibility provides the most natural reading of the Hebrew syntax and is probably to be preferred, even if it further clouds the character of Moses. Adding to the ambiguity is the absence of a statement that either God or Moses's command was carried out. The text leaves both instructions hanging and transfers its attention to a single, most striking incident.

Phinehas's Zealous Response (25:6–18)

Phinehas's Actions (25:6–9)
25:6. As the situation unfolds, another complication arises. An Israelite man with some authority in the tribal hierarchy brings a

---

3   The word for "leader" (רֹאשׁ) frequently begins a construction like "leader of his father's house" (רֹאשׁ לְבֵית־אֲבֹתָיו) or "leader of the children of Israel" (רָאשֵׁי בְנֵי־יִשְׂרָאֵל).

4   Notably, the occasioning incident for the parallel action in 2 Samuel 21 was an ongoing drought, attributed to God's displeasure (2 Sam. 21:1–3). After the executions, God "answered prayer in behalf of the land" (2 Sam. 21:14b NIV). Presumably this marked the end of the famine.

Midianite woman into the congregation while it was weeping at the opening of the Tent of Meeting.[5] Although this woman is not Moabite, the narrative suggests that her presence brings a similar threat to the community. Further, Numbers 22 links the Midianites and Moabites as co-conspirators in the scheme to bring Balaam to curse Israel (Blenkinsopp 2012, 90–91). The text portrays this action as particularly brazen since it occurs simultaneously with Israel's laments, which are presumably attempts to avert divine judgment. This action also took place "in plain view of Moses" (NET).

25:7–8a. Moses does not respond, leaving an opportunity for Phinehas, the son of Eleazar. Phinehas has likely inherited his father's role as chief supervisor of the Levites and the tabernacle-sanctuary with the elevation of Eleazar to the high priesthood (Gane 2004, 718).

> **Moses's Inactivity**
>
> Moses's inactivity is unexplained. Rabbinic tradition suggests that Moses either did not want to draw attention away from the mourning or that he was compromised by his own marriage to a Midianite woman (Milgrom 1990, 214). This line of reasoning continues into the present day, with some suggesting that part of this story's purpose is to critique Moses's marriage to Zipporah (Pettit 2018, 468). However, when Miriam and Aaron attempted to use the ethnicity of Moses's wife against him in Numbers 12, God rebuked them sharply. Zipporah likely fits into a similar category as Rahab and Ruth: foreign women who willingly identified themselves with YHWH and his people. Further, as seen in Numbers 10:29–32, Moses had positive relations with his wife's family, suggesting that they can be separated

> out from other Midianites. Midianites are also thought to have been "nomadic caravanners and raiders," permitting further differentiation between their branches (Monroe 2012, 230).

Phinehas arms himself with a spear, leaves the rest of the assembly, and follows the couple into a tent (הַקֻּבָּה). This is not the usual word for "tent" and in fact it is found only here. It likely refers to a separate chamber within a tent or a special kind of tent fit for a member of the tribal leadership (Gane 2004, 718).[6] In a shocking act of violence, Phinehas drives the spear through the man and through the belly (קֳבָתָהּ) of the woman. There is a pun here, as Phinehas first penetrates the tent (קֻבָּה) and then part of the woman's anatomy (קֵבָה). The implication is that Phinehas kills them while they are engaged in sexual activity (Pressler 2017, 229). Their actions could be seen as a prelude to further idolatry following the pattern of 25:1–3 (Cole 2000, 441).

25:8b–9. This action causes the end of a plague that presumably resulted from the events of 25:1–3 and possibly from the failure to act as God commanded in 25:4. The death toll is 24,000, a total only exceeded in divine punishment in God's response to David's census in 2 Samuel 25:13 (Gane 2004, 719). Phinehas's actions, although not exactly following God's instructions, fall into a similar category. Phinehas makes an example of an Israelite man with authority (along with his Midianite partner), and God permits this symbolic repudiation of apostasy and illicit sexual activity to turn aside his outpouring of anger against Israel.

YHWH's Evaluation (25:10–18)

25:10–11. God confirms his approval of Phinehas's actions by speaking directly to Moses. His

---

5   See the discussion of Numbers 25:14 for the individual's name and position.
6   Another possibility is that it refers to a shrine-tent set up in opposition to the Tent of Meeting to make appeals to the Midianite deities (Organ 2001, 2008). However, the absence of divinatory activity renders this highly speculative.

speech involves an emphatic repetition of the verbal root קנא ("to be zealous"), which occurs three times in 25:11. A literal rendering would read, "Phinehas, son of Eleazar, son of Aaron the priest turned back my wrath from the children of Israel in being *zealous* with my *zeal* in their midst, so I did not destroy the children of Israel through my *zeal*."[7] Zeal here reflects the passionate commitment to the covenant between God and Israel. God thus evaluates Phinehas's actions as reflective of his own attitude toward Israel's betrayal of the covenant.[8]

25:12–13. God then declares that he is establishing a covenant of peace with Phinehas and granting him a lasting priesthood. This parallels God's selection of the entire tribe of Levi for special service after it responded to the idolatry of the golden calf incident by rallying to Moses to punish the guilty Israelites (Exod. 32:25–29; Gane 2004, 719). Being descended from Aaron and Eleazar, Phinehas was deeply embedded within Israel's priestly hierarchy. God's judgment determines that he is the "rightful priest by his interest in divine righteousness" (Allen 2012, 346).

The final statement of Numbers 25:13 is that Phinehas "made atonement" (וַיְכַפֵּר) for the Israelites. This typically refers to reparation and purification sacrifices listed in Leviticus 4:1–6:7 that were essential to priestly intermediation between God and his people. Here, God accepts Phinehas's action as "a representative intentional act that covers over, atones for, the sins of Israel and Israelites" (Stubbs 2009, 201).

25:14–15. There is a brief interlude in God's evaluation to provide the names of parties whom Phinehas killed. The man is called Zimri, who was a Simeonite chieftain (נָשִׂיא) near the top of the tribal hierarchy (Milgrom 1990, 7). The woman is named Cozbi, and she came from a high-ranking Midianite family. This background suggests that the liaison might also reflect an unauthorized alliance with a part of a foreign nation. God warned Israel against such arrangements, noting that they would lead the people into idolatry and kindle his anger (Exod. 34:15–16; Deut. 7:3–4; Pettit 2018, 460–61).

25:16–18. The passage concludes with a further command from God to treat the Midianites as enemies (צָרוֹר) in 25:17.[9] This is viewed as a reciprocal arrangement, since the Midianites treated the Israelites as enemies (צֹרְרִים) through their deception (25:18a) and then through seeking retribution for the fate of Cozbi (25:18b). Again, the text does not draw a clear distinction between the Moabite women of 25:1–3 and the Midianite Cozbi of 25:6–9. It conflates these foreign influences and focuses on the threat they pose to Israel's devotion to YHWH. This incident at Baal Peor thus shapes the Israelites' understanding of the allure of idolatry and the threat posed by joining themselves to foreign nations.

THEOLOGICAL FOCUS

The exegetical idea (Israel succumbs to the temptations of idolatry, and God's wrath is averted only by the zealous actions of Phinehas) leads to the following theological focus: *Appropriate worship of God requires zealous commitment*. This incident and the

---

7   This rendering builds upon that given in Briggs 2018, 204.
8   This same root occurs in Numbers 5:14, 29, reflecting a husband's concern for his wife's fidelity. This parallel offers some perspective on the sense of deep betrayal evoked by Israel's dalliances with other gods.
9   Numbers 31 later describes a detailed military campaign against the Midianites. As mentioned earlier, given the fractured identity of the Midianites, it is probable that this would not include the family of Moses's wife.

legitimation of Phinehas's actions make for uncomfortable reading. Rabbinic tradition proposed that Phinehas would have been excommunicated if God had not spoken in his defense (Milgrom 1990, 477). Modern commentators are rightly uneasy with the ramifications of making Phinehas an exemplar of commitment to God (Briggs 2018, 207–11; Collins 2003, 3–21). However, this narrative offers a stark reminder that God's people are to be solely, passionately devoted to him.

This theme is woven throughout Scripture. In Deuteronomy 6:4–5, Moses declares "Hear, O Israel: The LORD our God, the LORD is one. Love the LORD your God with all your heart and with all your soul and with all your strength" (NIV). In the same chapter, he implores the Israelites to "Fear the LORD your God and serve him only" (Deut. 6:13 NIV). Jesus then cites this verse when tempted by Satan with the prospect of ruling over the kingdoms of the world (Luke 4:8). Moses's appeals continue in Deuteronomy 8:19–20 where he warns the Israelites on the brink of the Promised Land that if they should abandon YHWH for other gods, they will be destroyed. Similarly, Joshua urges the people not to turn aside after foreign gods and hears their commitment to serve YHWH alone (Josh. 24:19–24).

Unfortunately, the biblical story bears witness to the inability of God's people to live up to their commitments. Judges 2:11–12 announces that Israel served Baal and forsook YHWH its covenant partner, a pattern attested through the rest of its history. Even Elijah's demonstration of YHWH's sovereignty over Baal and the ensuing destruction of Baal's prophets in 1 Kings 18:16–46 could not avert Israel's tendency to succumb to the allure of the idols. Eventually this led to the exile and captivity. Through God's grace, the covenant endured, and figures like Ezra and Nehemiah are celebrated for their zealous commitment to avoid the dangers of God's people linking themselves with foreigners (Neh. 14:25–27).

In the New Testament, Jesus makes shocking claims about the necessity of zealous commitment, declaring that his disciples must "hate father and mother, wife and children, brothers and sister—yes, even their own life" (Luke 14:26 NIV). Although this statement is undoubtedly hyperbolic, it points to the need to place following Jesus at the pinnacle of our priorities. In his preaching in Athens, Paul declared that idols could not represent the divine image and that all people are called to worship the true and living God (Acts 16:29–31). John ends his first epistle with a plea: "Dear children, keep yourselves from idols" (1 John 5:21 NIV).

The need for zealous commitment to God goes beyond the danger of the physical idols themselves. In Colossians, Paul emphasizes the supremacy of Christ before urging that church not to be taken captive by other thought systems including "hollow and deceptive philosophy" (Col. 2:8 NIV), the worship of angels (Col. 2:18), and arbitrary ascetic regulations (Col. 2:20–23). John attributes Jesus's actions in clearing the temple courtyard to his zeal for his father's house (John 2:17). The presence of moneylenders and vendors diminished the sacred purpose of the place where God dwelled among his people and provoked a notable, if non-lethal, response from Jesus.

God's passionate zeal and commitment to his people is finally and fully demonstrated through selfless sacrifice of Christ on the cross to make atonement for all humanity. His people are called to a reciprocal commitment, where they acknowledge that he alone is God and that nothing else merits our reverence.

PREACHING AND TEACHING STRATEGIES

Exegetical and Theological Significance
Immediately before the Balaam material, Edom opposed Israel while the Aradites and

later Sihon and Og attacked Israel. Balak hired Balaam to curse Israel, hoping that Israel would be made weak so that the nation could be destroyed. None of these confrontations were successful. God's power preserved his people. Now, Moab tries a new strategy to bring about the destruction of Israel. Make no mistake: Numbers 25 reveals a battleplan to conquer Israel, and Israel will be annihilated unless they defeat their foes. In this context, Phinehas's act occurs in a war for Israel's survival: he realizes that Israel is being led to the slaughter by their foes. Just as Egypt attempted to kill all of the male Hebrew infants, now Moab is trying to lure the Hebrews to their spiritual deaths.

The divine evaluation of Phinehas's actions is found in Psalm 106:30–31, "But Phinehas stood up and intervened, and the plague was checked. This was credited to him as righteousness for endless generations to come." Living this side of the Reformation, it may be hard to understand how any actions or works can be credited to us as righteousness. After all, isn't righteousness imputed to us, and doesn't it come through faith rather than works? The language of righteousness and justification can take on complex nuances, but fundamentally *to be righteous* is simply to be on the right side of a proper standard. Phinehas is not perfectly, spotlessly righteous in every way, and neither does this action wash away his sins and make him perfectly righteous before God. Rather, the text means that when Phinehas acted this way, what he did was fundamentally right in the sight of God. In other words, he did the right thing; it was the righteous thing to do.

Numbers 25 rounds off the Balaam narrative but also provides a signpost for future danger. Israel is protected by God and cannot be cursed by its enemies, but Israel can bring curses and plagues upon itself through rebellion, idolatry, and immorality. The greatest danger facing Israel is not external enemies but internal sin. In the words of the famous *Pogo* comic, "We have met the enemy, and he is us."

This is one of the reasons why it is so important to be filled with the zeal of the Lord. The Israelites were undoubtedly eager for pagan revelry; they were zealous for their sin. Zeal, desire, and energy can all be misguided and channeled in the wrong directions. Zeal is a necessary, but not sufficient, condition for living a life that is pleasing to God.

Preaching Idea
Zeal is important in living for God, but sincerity and passion are not enough on their own.

Contemporary Connections

What does it mean?
What does it mean that zeal is important in living for God, but sincerity and passion are not enough on their own? Whereas Phinehas exemplifies righteous, courageous zeal, the apostle Paul—prior to his conversion—was an exemplar of exactly the wrong kind of zeal. In Philippians, Paul wrote that in his zeal he had persecuted the church (Phil. 3:6). He lamented that Israel had many people who were zealous for God, but "their zeal is not based on knowledge" (Rom. 10:2). Paul's misguided, dangerous, and destructive zeal was something he was saved out of: "For you have heard of my former life in Judaism, how I persecuted the church of God violently and tried to destroy it. And I was advancing in Judaism beyond many of my own age among my people, so extremely zealous was I for the traditions of my fathers" (Gal. 1:13–14 NIV).

One critical difference between Phinehas and the pre-conversion Paul was that the former's zeal opposed God's enemies, whereas Paul—although he thought he was zealously opposing God's enemies—learned in his conversion that he had actually been opposing God and God's people. Sincerity and passion are good, but they can be destructive. Sincerely believing something does not make it true: our beliefs need to correspond to God's reality.

God does not want apathetic, unemotional worship. But neither does he want someone who is on fire for false gods or ideologies. Zealous people can create a tremendous amount of damage. Provided the cause is good, zeal is good; zeal does not *make* something good. No amount of sincerity can transform evil into good; no amount of zeal can make the work of the devil pleasing to God.

Is it true?
Is it true that zeal is important in living for God, but sincerity and passion are not enough on their own? Given our relativistic society and the progression of the subjective turn, how can anyone hold that their religious or philosophical views are actually *true*, rather than merely opinions or preferences? Since we do not have objective knowledge, and since pluralism in religion is observed all around us, isn't it someone's emotional commitment and sincerity of belief that really matters? This is the way many in the world think, but they cannot live it out consistently. Furthermore, that way of thinking is diametrically opposed to God's.

According to Scripture, zeal, passion, and sincerity are marvelous things, but only if they are channeled in the right direction. Religious extremists are often sincere in their zeal, even killing themselves and others in accordance with their religious convictions. Zealous commitments to political parties or other cultural institutions can lead to dangerous results. Paul himself recognized that his earlier zeal had been destructive and actually led to actions that opposed God. Zeal is a wonderful thing, but it needs to be directed to the right means and ends.

Now what?
What do we do with the fact that zeal is important in living for God, but sincerity and passion are not enough on their own? This is an extremely important question for today, since it seems like all kinds of Christians are filled with "righteous anger" a great deal of the time. The culture wars are continuing, and COVID-19 responses varied tremendously from church to church and believer to believer. We need to be very careful that our zeal does not lead to sin and to hurting others. We also may want to consider whether our zeal and passion are directed more to nonbiblical issues, or more to secondary doctrinal issues than to the fundamental doctrines of the faith. Even if we are following Christ and worshipping God, we can waste our time and dissipate our energy in areas of little importance. Worse yet, we may hurt the witness of the church and wound Christ's bride by an angry zeal that is based on our self-righteousness, pride, and lack of knowledge.

Returning to the Scriptures and seeking God's priorities and perspectives is necessary. Self-aggrandizement and our own political agendas need to be put away; it is the glory of God that we are to seek and promote. If we burn with zeal, let it be for Christ. And may God's holiness refine us, so that our zeal burns as a pure flame before him. Pray that God will allow us to see if we are acting out of our own wisdom and passion, or if we are acting with Spirit-fueled, righteous zeal.

Creativity in Presentation
When I was in university, I was given the privilege of working with a church youth group. One day I saw a book entitled *Jewish Historiography and Iconography in Early and Medieval Christianity*, which was part of the

Compendia Rerum Iudaicarum ad Novum Testamentum. At that time I'm not entirely sure that I understood the meaning of the title, but I noticed that it was co-authored by Heinz Schreckenberg and Kurt Schubert. This was interesting to me because one of the teens in the youth group was named Kurt Schubert. I ordered the book because of that, and then tried to convince the youth group that I had been mentoring Kurt and guided him in authoring it.[10]

In that book, there is a reproduction of a fourth-century artistic depiction of the event with Phinehas, Zimri, and Cozbi, as well as quotations from various texts that comment on the account in Numbers (Schreckenberg and Schubert 1991, 206–9). Although few pastors are art critics or art historians, the scene in Numbers 25 has been depicted by a variety of artists, and showing some representations of the event may be enriching. (I'm [Steve] not an art critic, but my administrator Stephanie Ferris earned a university degree in fine arts. Pastors, make sure you know the gifts and areas of expertise that your people have; they can help you understand all kinds of things if you take the time to ask and listen.) It may also be helpful to quote some extrabiblical rabbinic material—not because it is inspired, but because it helps provide perspective on how Phinehas was viewed in subsequent times (https://www.jewishencyclopedia.com/articles/12117-phinehas is a good place to find information in this regard).

Moving from visual to literary art, William Butler Yeats has several famous lines in his poem "The Second Coming," one of which is, "The best lack all conviction, while the worst are full of passionate intensity." Stirring up zeal for the Lord is a noble goal, and it should be twinned with smothering the passionate intensity of the worst. The preacher should fan the flame of proper, God-honoring zeal, while leading to repentance those whose "zeal is not based on knowledge" and are opposing Christ. Believers should exemplify zeal in their walk with the Lord, but sincerity and passion are not enough on their own.

One possible outline for working through this passage is:

- Idolatry yokes God's people to false gods (25:1–3).

- Combatting idolatry may require drastic actions (25:4–10).

- Zealous devotion to God is worthy of remembrance (25:11–19).

---

10 Kurt's parents Garry and Rosemary let me (Steve) stay in their house on weekends (the church was located about a thirty-to-forty-minute drive from the city where I went to university), and their son Kyle would faithfully drive out to pick me up on Fridays and drive me back on Sunday evenings. The blessing that a kind and generous family can be to a young person in university, or a young person going into ministry, cannot be exaggerated. I'll never forget their care.

DISCUSSION QUESTIONS

1. What is the effect of having this story right after Balaam's poetic presentation of how YHWH has blessed Israel?

2. What are some modern-day "gods" to which believers could be tempted to yoke themselves?

3. Why are Phinehas's actions celebrated here? What considerations need to be kept in mind when thinking about how to bring this text into our day?

4. What does zealous commitment to God look like today? Who should we look at as examples of the zeal that God requires?

SHAPING THE COMMUNITY ON THE PLAINS OF MOAB (26:1–36:13)

Numbers concludes with Israel encamped on the Plains of Moab. This section focuses upon the preparations for the community to enter the Promised Land. The nation is recounted (26:1–65) and given the guarantee of faithful leadership after the death of Moses (27:12–23). God also gives instructions for how to properly worship him through sacrifices (28:1–29:40) and provides cautions related to the swearing of vows (30:1–16). Israel's inheritance is also a major theme, addressed through the case of the daughters of Zelophehad (27:1–12; 36:1–13), the addition of Transjordanian territory (32:1–42), and the description of the borders of the land (33:50–34:29). Further, the Israelites are commanded to give cities to the Levites, some of which will provide refuge for other Israelites in cases of accidental killing (35:1–34). God's faithful sustaining presence is also evident in Israel's battle with the Midianites (31:1–54) and the itinerary of Israel's journey (33:1–49). At the end of Numbers, Israel stands at the borders of the Promised Land thanks to God's grace and mercy, and looks to the fulfillment of his covenant promises.

Numbers 26:1–65

EXEGETICAL IDEA
Israel's second generation inherits God's covenant promises.

THEOLOGICAL FOCUS
God's faithfulness endures despite human frailty.

PREACHING IDEA
God blesses his people through covenant grace, but we all need to take warning.

PREACHING POINTERS
The second census is important both historically and theologically. After all that Israel had done, it was a testimony to grace that the nation still existed. The generation that refused to enter the Promised Land has died off, and the new generation was being prepared to go in. As a result, even the historical context is charged with both grace and judgment. Then, throughout the chapter, there are multiple reminders of the danger of rebelling against the Lord. God has proven that he will remain faithful to his covenant, and he has proven that no power in the physical or spiritual realm can challenge him. He has also proven that he will punish whole generations for their sin. He is a great and good God, but he is also holy, righteous, and just. No one in any generation can trifle with him.

As the people prepare to approach the Promised Land, they are given necessary reminders of God's covenant grace and his covenant wrath. The new generation needed hope, but they also needed warning. None may presume on God's grace. He is a God of love, but he is also holy, holy, holy. It was an awesome privilege for the Israelites to have God encamped at the center of their community, and he was with them to guide and to bless. He would not, however, tolerate rebellion, idolatry, and wickedness. Every generation needs to know of God's grace, love, mercy, kindness, faithfulness, and covenant promises, but every generation also needs to know the fear of the Lord. Every generation needs to know that God blesses his people through covenant grace, but we all still need to take warning.

THE CENSUS OF THE SECOND GENERATION (26:1–65)

LITERARY STRUCTURE AND THEMES

This preaching unit begins the final segment of Numbers (chs. 26–36). After its forty years of wandering, Israel has arrived on the Plains of Moab (Num. 26:3) and remains there until it crosses the Jordan River (Joshua 3–4). The previous generation who refused to enter the land has passed away, except for Moses, Caleb, and Joshua. A new generation has come to the forefront. As the events of the previous chapter suggest, this generation is not necessarily any more holy than its forebears, but through God's grace, the covenant endures.

Numbers 26 marks a new beginning by recording a second census, again counting all the men capable of military service. Towards its end, this chapter also identifies the Levites according to their clan divisions. It essentially combines the material from Numbers 1 (the military census) with that of Numbers 3–4 (the census of the Levites). It can be divided into an introduction (26:1–4), the military census (26:5–56), the Levitical census (26:57–62), and a conclusion (26:63–65).

The driving theme of this chapter is continuity. It affirms that despite Israel's rebellions and idolatry, the family that went down to Egypt with seventy people (Gen. 46:26–27) is still a nation in covenant with the God that delivered it from slavery.[1] Future chapters anticipate life in the Promised Land, a destiny only made possible through God's covenant grace.

- *Introduction (26:1–4)*
- *The Military Census (26:5–56)*
- *The Levitical Census (26:57–62)*
- *Conclusion (26:63–65)*

EXPOSITION

The military census is arranged slightly differently than Numbers 1, even though they both count the number of fighting men. It counts the tribes in almost exactly the same order as the first census, only flipping Manasseh and Ephraim. There is no mention of tribal leaders who assist Moses. Instead, this census provides clan divisions for each tribe, tracing their lineage in greater detail. This reinforces "the sense that another new generation has been added" to Israel (Olson 1996, 161). The military and Levitical censuses also insert significant historical events (26:9–11, 19, 61–62) or anticipate an issue to come (26:33). Some tribes increase in population while others decrease, but the final tally is remarkably consistent with the first census.[2] Altogether, this chapter affirms that Israel's second generation inherits God's covenant promises.

---

1. If the daughters of Zelophehad (26:33) and the clans of the Levites (26:57–61) are included, then there are seventy clans in total (Milgrom 1990, 219). This elegantly reflects Israel's growth and God's provision.
2. The first census had a total of 603,550 while the second totals 601,730. See the excursus in Numbers 1 for a discussion of ways to understand these numbers.

Census Results Compared

Tribe	Census of Numbers 1	Census of Numbers 26	Change
Reuben	46,500	43,730	-2,770
Simeon	59,300	22,200	-37,100
Gad	45,650	40,500	-5,150
Judah	74,600	76,500	+1,900
Issachar	54,400	64,300	+9,900
Zebulun	57,400	60,500	+3,100
Ephraim	40,500	32,500	-8,000
Manasseh	32,200	52,700	+20,500
Benjamin	35,400	45,600	+10,200
Dan	62,700	64,400	+1,700
Asher	41,500	53,400	+11,900
Naphtali	53,400	45,400	-8,000
Total	603,550	601,730	-1,820

Introduction (26:1–4)

26:1–2. God commands this census to be taken following the plague that resulted from the sin of Baal Peor. Hebrew versification identifies "after the plague" (וַיְהִי אַחֲרֵי הַמַּגֵּפָה) as Numbers 25:19, but English translations understandably attach it to 26:1. God's command is spoken to both Moses and Eleazar, the son of Aaron. His presence further reflects the transition to the next generation. The command to take the census resembles that found in Numbers 1:2–3. The focus is on counting those able to participate in the conquest of the Promised Land.

26:3–4. Moses and Eleazar transmit God's request to the people. There are no tribal leaders identified to help them, though presumably Moses and Eleazar commissioned aid. Numbers 26:3 also identifies the location of this census as the Plains of Moab, across the Jordan from Jericho. The first census took place at Sinai. Now that the Israelites have reached the border of Canaan, they again obey God's command to count their forces.

The Military Census (26:5–56)

26:5–7. This second military census begins with the Reubenites. It establishes a pattern of four elements repeated for each of the twelve tribes: 1) a heading (usually, "the descendants of X by their clans"), 2) the accounting of the clans for the tribe, 3) a summary statement (usually, "these are the clans of X"), and 4) the sum total of fighting men (Kislev 2013, 237). The names of the clans build off the list of Jacob's family members found in Genesis 46, establishing further continuity between that family and this nation. Here, all of Reuben's sons from Genesis 46:9 are listed as heads of their associated clans.

26:8–11. An occasional digression intrudes upon the census. Here, it notes that the clan of Pallu produced Dathan and Abiram, who participated in Korah's rebellion against Moses in Numbers 16. It recalls the horrific fate of those rebels and declares that they became a warning sign for the nation. Their inclusion here should prompt the second generation not to follow their example (Allen 2012, 354). This may also provide the rationale for why the tribe of Reuben decreased in the second census. The final note is that the family of Korah was not totally destroyed, which can only be viewed as an act of divine grace (Sprinkle 2015, 365).

26:12–14. The Simeonites come next and are counted according to their clans. It is noteworthy that they suffer the largest decrease by a significant margin (-37,100). They have fewer than half of the fighting men they had in the first census. This may indicate that they bore the brunt of God's wrath in the Baal Peor incident, especially since one of the Israelite ringleaders (Zimri) was from the tribe of Simeon.

26:15–18. The clans of Gad are then presented without elaboration. There are some differences in the spelling of the names between here and Genesis 46:16, but both lists likely intend to refer to the same individuals (Allen 2012, 356).

26:19–22. There is a brief digression before the text enumerates the clans of Judah. Numbers 26:19 recalls that Judah's first two sons (Er and Onan) died in Canaan. This recalls the sordid tale of Genesis 38 where Er and Onan's misdeeds led to their death, and Tamar's ingenuity preserved her place in Judah's family. Tamar's twins Perez and Zerah are listed among the clans of Judah. A further oddity is that the text further celebrates Perez by listing two clans descended from his sons (Hezron and Hamul), going down one generation further than expected. This anticipates Perez's place as the forefather of David (Ruth 4:18–21) and ultimately points to Christ as the greatest son of David (Cole 2000, 455).

26:23–27. The tribes of Issachar and Zebulun follow without any divergence from the established pattern.

26:28–34. The text then lists the tribes descended from Joseph, beginning with Manasseh. This is an inversion of Numbers 1, where Ephraim preceded Manasseh in keeping with Jacob's blessing in Genesis 48:12–20. Manasseh may be listed first in Numbers 26 because it had the largest growth of fighting men of any tribe (+20,500). This tribe is unique in that it does not divide into subclans until the great-grandchildren of Manasseh. No reason for this is attested. The line of descent goes from Manasseh to Makir, then to Gilead, and then to the six sons of Gilead. The region east of the Jordan where the partial tribe of Manasseh settled (Num. 32:39–42; Josh. 13:31) bears the name Gilead on account of this grandson of Manasseh.

An additional oddity occurs in Numbers 26:33, which mentions Zelophehad, a grandson of Gilead who had no sons but had five daughters instead. The absence of women from this census is understandable given its military purpose, so their presence is worthy of notice. No further information about them is given here, but Numbers 27:1–11 and 36:1–12 further elaborate on the story of these women and how they fit into Israel's land and lineage. Their appearance in this census foreshadows their upcoming role.

26:35–37. The Ephraimite clans follow those of Manasseh. They are listed accorded to the established pattern. Numbers 26:37b forms an inclusion with 26:28, bracketing off these tribes as the descendants of Joseph.

26:38–41. The tribe of Benjamin is next. The main challenge it poses is the lack of correspondence between the names listed here and those found in Genesis 46:21. Numbers 26:40 lists Ard and Naaman as grandsons of Benjamin (through Bela), while Genesis 46:21 lists them as sons. Further, Genesis 46:21 lists several sons not found in this census. There are also further discrepancies when comparing this text to the listing of Benjaminites in 1 Chronicles 7–8. It is impossible to determine what is happening, though Cole suggests that there may be a combination of imprecision in differentiating between sons and grandsons, orthographical variations and potential scribal errors, and variations brought about through the history of transmission (Cole 2000, 458).

26:42–50. The enumeration of the remaining tribes (Dan, Asher, and Naphtali) essentially follows the template with minimal deviation. Numbers 26:46 mentions a daughter of Asher named Serah, but unlike the daughters of Zelophehad she has no further bearing on the rest of the book.

26:51. The military census concludes with a summation of the fighting men: 601,730. The similarity between this total and that of the first census (603,550) attests to God's provision through Israel's wilderness wandering. It also suggests that this second generation is heir to the same promises squandered by the first.

26:52–56. God provides an additional purpose for the second census. It shapes the tribal allotments of the Promised Land, as "each is to receive its inheritance according to the number of those listed" (Num. 26:54 NIV). God also decrees that this apportionment should happen by lot (Num. 26:55–56). This suggests a concern for fairness, with God himself presumably overseeing the outcome of casting lots (Cole 2000, 461). It may also provide a safeguard against the larger tribes trying to claim the more desirable territory (cf. Josh. 17:14–18).

The Levitical Census (26:57–62)

26:57–58a. A brief census of the Levites comes after the enumeration of the fighting men. It follows the military census in listing the clans of the tribe of Levi. These begin with the Gershonites, the Kohathites, and the Merarites. Unlike Numbers 3–4, there is no discussion of their duties and responsibilities to the tabernacle and its furnishings. Presumably, those obligations continue. Numbers 26:58 then lists subclans descended from Gershon, Kohath, and Merari without assigning each one to its forebearer, which the text did in Numbers 3:17–20. The subclans identified here are Libnites, Hebronites, Mahlites, Mushites, and Korahites. Several of the subclans listed in the first Levitical census (the Shimeites, Uzzielites, and possibly the Izharites[3]) are absent. It is possible that they ceased to be operational subclans by the time of this census (Ashley 1993, 539).

26:58b–59. The enumeration of the Levites then focuses on the lineage of Moses and Aaron, separating them out from other Levites. They are descended from Kohath through the subclan of Amram. Their mother Jochebed is also identified as a Levite who was born during the Egyptian captivity. Her origins further validate Moses and Aaron's suitability for the roles that God gives them. The text identifies Jochebed as the mother of Moses, Aaron, and Miriam.

> **From Kohath to Moses and Aaron**
> The line of descent from Kohath down to Moses and Aaron is hard to determine. Numbers 26:58b reads that Kohath fathered (הוֹלִד) Amram, which is reflected in many English translations (ESV,

---

3   The Izharites (Num. 3:19) may be identified with the Korahites (Num. 26:58), since Korah is listed as a son of Izhar in Numbers 16:1.

NASB, NET, NKJV). However, if this Amram is married to Jochebed and the father of Moses, Aaron, and Miriam, then the length of Israel's captivity in Egypt could not be as long as the 430 years suggested in Exodus 12:40–41. One suggestion is that Kohath fathered Amram, but that 26:59 refers to a later descendant with the same name. On account of the shared name, the text elides the intervening generations (Ashley 1993, 539). The other possibility is that Kohath fathering Amram does not refer to an actual son, but rather identifies Kohath as the forefather of the Amram who fathered Moses, Aaron, and Miriam. Some English translations adopt this approach (CSB, NIV, NLT).

26:60–61. The text then traces the descendants of Aaron, listing his four sons. It recalls the account of Leviticus 10:1–3 where Aaron's first two sons, Nadab and Abihu, offered unauthorized incense before God and were struck dead. This reminds the audience why Eleazar is currently the high priest and reinforces the message that the priests and Levites have an important responsibility to follow God's directions fully and precisely.

26:62. The numbers of Levites listed is 23,000. As in Numbers 3–4, this census counts those male Levites who were one month old and up. This reflects the nonmilitary purpose of the Levites as God's substitute for all of Israel's firstborn (Num. 3:12–13). Also, the enumeration of the Levites happens here because the Levites will not have an inheritance in the land, so they are not part of the instructions given in 26:52–56. Finally, this verse shows an increase of one thousand from the first census.

Conclusion (26:63–65)
26:63–65. The census concludes by restating that Moses and Eleazar performed the census when Israel was on the Plains of Moab, just across the Jordan River from the Promised Land. Crucially, it declares that none of the ones counted were part of the first census conducted at Sinai. This recalls God's judgment on the first generation for their failure to enter Canaan. Numbers 26:65 identifies Caleb and Joshua as exceptions to this fate, confirming God's declaration from 14:30 and also marking an end to that promised period of judgment (Stubbs 2009, 206).

THEOLOGICAL FOCUS
The exegetical idea (Israel's second generation inherits God's covenant promises) leads to this theological focus: *God's faithfulness endures despite human frailty*. Numbers 26 essentially resets Israel's relationship with God. The book of Numbers begins with a census preparing Israel to march to Canaan before further deepening its understanding of how to serve and worship YHWH. Its sojourn through the wilderness is marked with rebellion, culminating with the idolatry at Baal Peor. However, Israel now stands on the border of the Promised Land, and God again directs Moses to enumerate Israel's fighters and religious functionaries. Israel's failures have had dramatic consequences and delay the fulfillment of God's promises, but through divine mercy Israel remains his covenant people. This census attests to the endurance of God's faithfulness, even when his covenant partners fall short.

This theme is central to the unfolding of the biblical story. Israel's entry into Canaan quickly goes from the victories of Joshua to the cautionary tales of Judges. In 1 Samuel 8, Israel even rejects YHWH as their king, preferring to have a "king like the nations" (1 Sam. 8:5). Dalliances with idolatry become too many to count. And yet, God continues to uphold his covenant with Israel. Even the covenant curses of exile and captivity did not sever God's relationship with his people. Through his covenant faithfulness, the promise YHWH made to Abraham that all nations on earth would be blessed through him and his descendants endures (Gen. 12:1–3).

God's faithfulness ultimately manifests itself in Christ, God-made-flesh, who incarnated and dwelled among sinful people. Human frailty and sinfulness could not help but continue to mar the relationship between God and his creation, and so "God made him who had to sin to be sin for us, so that in him we might become the righteousness of God" (2 Cor. 5:21 NIV). Consequently there is no condemnation, or broken relationship with God, for those who are in Christ (Rom. 8:1). Instead, through repentance and confession, sinful and broken human beings have the promise of restored communion with God. This should lead God's people to a posture that is "confident in the faithfulness of God and deeply grateful for God's forgiveness" (Stubbs 2009, 206). God's people continue to have the opportunity to look back on the failures of their forebearers and take on the urgent cry of Psalm 95 (echoed in Hebrews 3:7–11) not to harden their hearts and turn away from him as they have done before.

PREACHING AND TEACHING STRATEGIES

Exegetical and Theological Significance

Although censuses and genealogies are not favorite biblical passages for most believers, in Numbers they are theologically significant and contribute to our understanding of the biblical story. In terms of the history of redemption, Israel has competed its punitive time of wilderness exile, and God is now going to bring them into the Promised Land. When the first and second census of Numbers are compared, the gracious providence and care of God over those decades is made apparent.

Theologically, the second census speaks volumes about God's providence, grace, mercy, wrath, judgment, faithfulness, covenant love, patience, and sovereign plan. It also speaks a strong message of warning against faithlessness, rebellion, and sin. Interspersed throughout the census are examples of sin and judgment, which are to serve as warnings for the generation being numbered. Examples include:

26:1 The first verse locates this sentence "after the plague," which fell as a judgment after the sin at Baal Peor.

26:8–10 Korah's rebellion is remembered, and those who died are "a warning sign."

26:19 Long before Israel was enslaved in Egypt, Judah's wicked sons were put to death for their sins.

26:61 Before the nation refused to enter the Promised Land, Nadab and Abihu died because they offered unauthorized fire before the Lord, violating their priestly calling and God's holiness.

26:63–65 The entire generation of adults who listened to the rebellious spies were condemned to live and die in the desert, banned from the Promised Land.

As they stood on the brink of the Promised Land, this new generation needed two things: they needed hope, and they needed warning. Their hope came in the power of God's covenant grace and promises, and the warning came through the historical examples of failure, sin, and judgment. The God of Abraham, Isaac, and Jacob was faithful to his covenant, but faithless covenant-breakers could not presume his forgiveness. It was a solemn, awesome, and holy thing to have the living God dwell in the camp of his people. As the new generation prepared to follow God's lead into Canaan, they also needed to know the fear of the Lord.

Preaching Idea

God blesses his people through covenant grace, but we all need to take warning.

Contemporary Connections

What does it mean?
What does it mean that God blesses his people through covenant grace, but we all need to take warning? Many Christians today might not turn to Numbers very often, but Paul applied the lessons of Numbers to the church in Corinth:

> Now these things occurred as examples to keep us from setting our hearts on evil things as they did. Do not be idolaters, as some of them were; as it is written: "The people sat down to eat and drink and got up to indulge in revelry." We should not commit sexual immorality, as some of them did—and in one day twenty-three thousand of them died. We should not test Christ, as some of them did—and were killed by snakes. And do not grumble, as some of them did—and were killed by the destroying angel. (1 Cor. 10:6–10 NIV)

In Paul's mind, the material in Numbers spoke to the New Testament church. The author of Hebrews also dedicated a long chapter to the examples of the past, so that the contemporary church could learn about faith through their spiritual ancestors (Heb. 11:1–40). Great lessons of faith, grace, and judgment can be learned through studying Numbers, as well as the rest of Scripture. In Scripture—and in life as we are given eyes to see—we learn by both precept and example.

Is it true?
Is it true that God blesses his people through covenant grace, but we all need to take warning? Psychologists, sociologists, and educators are well aware that human beings are hardwired to learn through imitating others. Little children learn virtually everything through example and modeling. "Individuals" in cultures and subcultures tend to look, act, and speak just like the members of their inner circles. Trends run on imitation; this is why our contemporary online culture is chock full of supposed "influencers."

Since imitation is such a huge part of our development, having good models is essential. However, it can also be impactful to see the disastrous consequences of certain behaviors in the lives of others. When we see someone paralyzed because they were driving while texting, or hear the guilt that someone lives with because they killed someone while driving intoxicated, we have an opportunity to take warning.

God knows that sobering, negative examples can help people learn. He also knows that positive, godly examples can inspire people to faithful living and zealous worship. There is a real place for historical awareness and biography in the Christian life. The best thing we can do, however, is learn to imitate Jesus (1 Cor. 11:1).

Now what?
Bringing together the truth that there is both grace and judgment, with the fact that we learn by example, it is vital that we choose the right people to imitate. Being influenced is an inescapable part of life, so we need to make sure that we are being influenced by the right sources and examples. Seeing the outcome of the lives of the wicked can help keep us safe from a similar end, but our sinful hearts are also easily and foolishly allured by the deceptions of the world and the traps of the devil.

Spending time with mature, godly mentors is one excellent way to learn and grow in the faith. Look to those who are more seasoned and who have learned life lessons as followers of Jesus. As the author of Hebrews wrote, "Remember your leaders, who spoke the word of God to you. Consider the outcome of their way of life and imitate their faith. Jesus Christ is the same yesterday and today and forever" (Heb. 13:7–8 NIV).

The Census of the Second Generation (26:1–65)

Creativity in Presentation

The book of Proverbs is given to reveal all kinds of wisdom and instruction. One teaching device found throughout is the use of positive and negative examples in everyday life. The voice of a wise father points his son to the fool and considers how their life turns out. He further discusses the blessings that attend being godly, and the ruinous consequences that come to the wicked. He notes the circle of the wise and the company of fools, and he helps his son draw the proper conclusion about good life choices. Wisdom can come from imitating the wise, but it can also come from seeing the outcome of evil and fleeing from that path. Given the importance of example in Numbers 26, the preacher may want to give some readings from Proverbs, 1 Corinthians 10, or Hebrews 11 to help emphasize the biblical importance of learning lessons from those around us. See the incredible nature of God's covenant grace, but also see the fearful possibility of wrath for unrepentant sin.

Many children have learned the following song:

O be careful little eyes what you see
O be careful little eyes what you see
For the Father up above
Is looking down in love
So, be careful little eyes what you see

O be careful little ears what you hear
O be careful little ears what you hear
For the Father up above
Is looking down in love
So, be careful little ears what you hear

O be careful little tongue what you say . . .
O be careful little hands what you do . . .
O be careful little feet where you go . . .
O be careful little heart whom you trust . . .
O be careful little mind what you think . . .

The second census list in Numbers may not seem like the most obvious time to have a children's choir, but it might be perfect![4] If the children sing that well-known song, the preacher can spend a few minutes talking to them about the importance of their choices, and how important it is to be influenced by the right people. Who we spend time with and imitate will affect what we see, hear, say, do, and think. Who we spend time with and imitate will affect where we go and who we trust. The people numbered in the second census were young when their parents' generation rebelled against God. From the earliest age, it is essential to learn about God's covenant grace, and also to take warning so that we walk in the fear of the Lord.

One possible outline for expositing this text is:

- The second generation is counted just like the first (26:1–4).

- The second generation is almost as numerous as the first and should learn from its mistakes (26:5–51).

- God will fulfill his promise to give his people an inheritance in the land (26:52–56).

- God continues to set aside Levites and priests to minister to Israel (26:57–62).

- God's judgment on the first generation is fulfilled (26:63–65).

---

4   It also offers the preacher the opportunity for a gentle joke contrasting the "old generation" in the pews with the "new generation" of children singing this warning song.

The Census of the Second Generation (26:1–65)

DISCUSSION QUESTIONS

1. How does this second census demonstrate that God is still with Israel, in spite of its many failures?

2. What should be learned from the fact that the census of the second generation has nearly the same total as the first census?

3. Why does this census make reference to Korah's rebellion and its aftermath?

4. Why does this census divide the tribes into clans, whereas the first one did not?

5. How does this census contribute to Israel's future hope in the Promised Land?

Numbers 27:1–23

EXEGETICAL IDEA
The daughters of Zelophehad preserve their father's name, and Joshua inherits Moses's legacy.

THEOLOGICAL FOCUS
God responds graciously to the concerns of his people.

PREACHING IDEA
God takes care of his flock and gives them a good shepherd.

PREACHING POINTERS
There can be no doubt that a modern interpreter needs to exercise due tact and sensitivity in a text like this one. Given that the problem is generated on the basis of sex and gender, contemporary hearers may be prone to miss what the text is actually saying, as well as anachronistically read back into it all kinds of modern debates and concerns. Of the utmost importance to see is that God considers the needs of each one of his children, and he ensures that justice will be done.

From the level of concern for individuals to the level of concern for the entire nation, this chapter moves from Zelophehad's daughters to the need of a shepherd over all of God's people. Moses will die outside of the Promised Land, and Joshua is appointed to take over as leader of the people. In terms of biblical theology, this shepherding motif carries forward in all kinds of ways and then is fulfilled in Jesus the Good Shepherd. It is only because of Christ that God's flock is not left scattered like sheep without a shepherd. Psalm 23, Psalm 100, and John 10 give us a beautiful picture of what it means to have the Lord as our shepherd. In the end, we are able to live and have a name because our shepherd laid down his life for the sheep, only to take it up again in resurrection power and glory. As a loving heavenly Father, God takes care of his flock and gives them the ultimate Good Shepherd.

THE PROMISE OF A LEGACY (27:1–23)

LITERARY STRUCTURE AND THEMES

Following the second census, Numbers casts its gaze forward toward Israel's anticipated entry into the Promised Land. This perspective is found repeatedly throughout Numbers 27–36. Numbers 27 consists of two episodes linked by a shared concern for what will happen after Israel leaves the Plains of Moab. The first episode (Numbers 27:1–11) features the daughters of Zelophehad. It addresses a question of inheritance rights once God gives Israel the land. It also prominently features the voices of women. These women return in the final episode of the book (Numbers 36:1–13), which provides further parameters regarding the family's place in the Promised Land. The second episode (Numbers 27:12–23) discusses who will lead Israel after Moses's death. Since Moses cannot lead the nation into Canaan (Num. 20:12–13), a suitable replacement must be found.

A theme found in both episodes is the responsiveness of God to his people's concerns. In both scenarios, God hears the appeals directed to him and addresses them. Another theme is the idea of legacy. The daughters of Zelophehad do not want their father's name to be lost from Israel's story, and their advocacy successfully preserves it. Similarly, Moses does not want his work leading Israel to be undone after his death.

- *The Daughters of Zelophehad (27:1–11)*
- *Joshua Succeeds Moses (27:12–23)*

EXPOSITION

God's faithfulness brought the people through the wilderness to the Plains of Moab. As the Israelites prepare for the next phase, questions arise concerning who will lead them and how they will be remembered. Addressing these questions preemptively, while still across the Jordan, is an expression of faith that God will fulfill his promises and bring Israel into the land (Gane 2004, 740). This passage affirms that the daughters of Zelophehad preserve their father's name and that Joshua inherits Moses's legacy.

The Daughters of Zelophehad (27:1–11)

27:1–2. This episode begins with a lengthy recitation of lineage. It gives much of the same information found in Numbers 26:29–33 but in reverse order, starting with Zelophehad and moving back through his father Hepher and his forefathers Gilead, Makir, Manasseh, and ultimately Joseph. This presentation is crucial to the story, since the absence of sons for Zelophehad foretells the end of his family name. Zelophehad himself was part of the first generation that died in the wilderness, and now that the next generation is preparing to enter the land the question of his legacy needs to be addressed.

Zelophehad's five daughters come forward to advocate on his behalf. The narrative names them: Mahlah, Noah, Hoglah, Milkah, and Tirzah. This gives them an identity beyond their family lineage and preserves their memory in Israel's recollection of its history. These women approach Moses, Eleazar, and the whole assembly. The collocation "stand before" (וַתַּעֲמֹדְנָה לִפְנֵי) suggests that they are appearing before God to await his judgment (Levine 2000, 344). This is confirmed by placing this interaction at the entry of the Tent of Meeting. This is where the community gathered for worship, for intercession, and for God to render a legal verdict (Pressler 2017, 243–44). The daughters plead their case in the place where God is present.

27:3–4. The essence of the daughters' appeal is that their father did not participate in Korah's rebellion but rather died "for his own sins" (בְּחֶטְאוֹ). This places him on the same footing as the rest of the Israelites who died in the wilderness (27:3). However, since he has no sons, as matters currently stand his name will disappear from his clan within Manasseh. The daughters imply that this is unwarranted, since their father had not been cut off from the covenant community. Consequently "the God of the covenant was still the God of his family" (Ulrich 1998, 535). Since dying without leaving a lineage suggests "divine judgment leading to societal abandonment" (Cole 2009, 387), the situation needed to be remedied. The daughters plead with Moses to award them property within the allotment given to their father's clan. In this way, they can pass down their father's name to future generations.

The connection between land and identity is deeply woven into ancient Israel. It builds off the premise found in Leviticus 25:23 that the land belongs to YHWH who has given it to the Israelites for them to flourish. Every family was to have a place and a name within Israel. Joshua 13–19 largely consists of dividing the land into tribal allotments to achieve this goal. Later, Isaiah calls down woe on those who add "field to field and house to house till no space is left and you live alone in the land" (Isa. 6:8 NIV; cf. Mic. 2:1–5). It also explains why Naboth is vehemently opposed to selling his vineyard to King Ahab (1 Kings 21:1–16). The daughters of Zelophehad are thus asking for the inheritance promised to all Israel. They question the justice of denying it to their family because it lacks a male heir.

27:5–7. Moses then brings the daughters' case before God, who issues a verdict in their favor. This is the fourth time in the Pentateuch where a specific case stands outside of the established law and requires consultation with God.[1] These incidents reveal that God and his law take into consideration the concern of the Israelites when difficult situations arise. God decrees that Moses "must certainly give them possession of an inheritance among their father's relatives" (27:7 NIV).[2] The final clause of the verse declares that Moses must transfer over their father's inheritance to these women. This suggests that the women received a bequest that they could pass down to their own children, again preserving their father's name as though he had sons (Allen 2012, 371). Joshua 17:3–6 confirms that this took place as the women go before Joshua and again ask for what God promised them. The daughters have made a request of God in keeping with their understanding of his covenant with Israel, and in his response God vindicates them.

27:8–11. This specific scenario then leads into a larger amendment of Israel's inheritance laws.

> ### Israel's Inheritance Laws
> The standard expectation was for a man's patrimony to pass down through his sons, with the firstborn receiving a double share (Deut. 21:15–17). In Genesis 25:29–34, Esau foolishly gives away this birthright for a bowl of stew. Daughters received dowries, which would bring them some status and support as they joined their husband's family.[3] Without sons, a man's patrimony would be subsumed within the larger clan structure, leading to the loss of the his name within Israel.

---

1. The others are the case of a man who blasphemes God's name (Lev. 24:10–22), those who cannot celebrate the Passover when commanded (Num. 9:6–14), and the Sabbath violator (Num. 15:32–36).
2. God's words (נָתֹן תִּתֵּן) are stated forcefully. The combination of an infinitive absolute with an imperfect verb from the same root conveys the necessity of Moses following God's instructions.
3. A dowry could include land, though that was rare. In another story where women boldly assert their rights, Caleb's daughter Achsah directly asks her father for springs of water (Judg. 1:13–15).

God directs Moses to award a man's inheritance to the closest surviving relative following a given pattern. If the man has no sons, then the daughters have a claim to the inheritance as in this case. If the man has no children at all, then the inheritance is to go to his brothers (27:9). If he has no brothers, then it is awarded to his uncles (27:10). If the man is even bereft of that level of kinsmen, then the property goes to the nearest living relative in his clan (27:11). These regulations supplement the laws of property redemption in the Year of Jubilee in Leviticus 25:23–28 (Cole 2000, 466). Relatives had the duty to redeem land sold for debt repayment and now they are also awarded the right to inherit the land if unfortunate circumstances occur.

The rights of daughters to inherit will require further modifications once the daughters of Zelophehad contemplate marriage (Num. 36:1–12). However, this episode celebrates their courage in speaking up to preserve their father's name.

Joshua Succeeds Moses (27:12–23)

27:12. The second episode also deals with the transition to the next generation. God instructs Moses to go up a mountain in the Abarim range and survey the land. Deuteronomy 34:1 further specifies it as Mount Nebo. This range extends through the Transjordan region, permitting Moses to see the Promised Land although he will not cross into it (Cole 2009, 388).

27:13–14. After viewing the land, God confirms to Moses that he will die just as his brother Aaron did because of their failure to show God as holy at Meribah Kadesh (Num. 20:1–13). Again, this punishment appears harsh, but the failure of Israel's leader to properly convey God's holiness distorts God's testimony to his people.

27:15–17. For his part, Moses does not protest God's judgment but shows concern for the fate of the people whom he has led through the wilderness for the past forty years. Moses's appeal begins with an uncommon expression: "the LORD, the God of the spirits of all flesh" (27:16 ESV; cf. Num. 16:22) that points to divine sovereignty over all humanity (Cole 2000, 468). Moses asks God to appoint a man to lead the people who will "go out before them and come in before them, who shall lead them out and bring them in" (27:17 ESV). These expressions are frequently military in nature, reflecting the primary task that Moses's successor will undertake (Deut. 31:2–3; Josh. 14:11; 1 Sam. 18:13, 16; Ashley 1993, 551). Numbers 27:17b concludes with Moses asking for the appointment of this leader so that the congregation of YHWH will not be like sheep without a shepherd. Israel was prone to wander even with Moses as God's voice. The absence of a similar voice could have disastrous effects (Cole 2000, 468).

This concern for the next generation links the two episodes of this preaching unit. The daughters of Zelophehad belong to the generation who inherit the land as a lasting testimony to God's faithfulness. Moses belongs to the previous generation, and although Israel's next leader does not come directly from his lineage his plea here is a means of securing his legacy among the people. If God is with his successor as he has been with Moses, then Moses's name will also endure in Israel's memory.

27:18a. God responds favorably to Moses's request, singling out Joshua son of Nun. Joshua has been celebrated already for leading Israel to victory against a foreign enemy (Exod. 17:8–16). Along with Caleb, he was one of the two spies who urged Israel to obey God and march to Canaan (Num. 14:6–9). He is also identified on several occasions as Moses's assistant (Exod. 24:13–14; 32:15–20; Num. 11:26–30). Crucially, God identifies him as "a man in whom there is a spirit" (אִישׁ אֲשֶׁר־רוּחַ בּוֹ). This provides a link to verse 16, where Moses appeals to YHWH as the God of the spirits of all flesh. The nature of Joshua's spirit is left indefinite but is best understood as "divine endowment for leadership" (Ashley 1993, 552). Deuteronomy 34:9 later declares that Joshua is "full of the spirit of wisdom," which echoes God's evaluation here.

27:18b–20. God further instructs Moses to make a public display of this appointment. Moses is first to lay his hand on Joshua (27:18b). This is a commonly known means of transferring authority throughout the ancient world (Cole 2009, 388). Then, Moses is to present Joshua before Eleazar and the whole congregation (27:19a). This provides public confirmation of Joshua's succession. The people and the priestly representative can observe this procedure and understand that it has divine approval. Next, God instructs Moses to commission Joshua in their presence (27:19b). The verb used here (וְצִוִּיתָה) often means "to command," but it is also used to appoint certain leaders and prophets to their stations (2 Sam. 7:7, 11; 1 Kings 1:13; Levine 2000, 351).

Finally, Moses must "delegate some of your authority to him" (Num. 20:20a NET). This elevates Joshua but does not confer upon him all of Moses's prerogatives. God spoke to Moses face to face (Num. 12:6–8), while Joshua's interactions will be mediated through Eleazar (Wenham 2008, 217). However, this transference is sufficient for the Israelites to begin to obey Joshua. Starting this process now while Moses remained alive would make for a smoother transition when Moses died (Allen 2012, 375).

27:21. A further marker of Joshua's authority is the appearance of the Urim (a shorthand for the Urim and Thummim). These were stones attached to the high priestly vestments (Exod. 28:30; Lev. 8:8) and were used to make inquiries of God (1 Sam. 28:6; Ezra 2:63; Neh. 7:65). The scarcity of references to them precludes any certainty as to how this procedure worked. One suggestion is that the stones would light up to reflect a "yes" or "no" answer from God (Cole 2000, 469). Another is that these two words form a hendiadys meaning "dazzling light," and that they would blaze to confirm the priest's speech in response to the question posed by Israel's leaders (Allen 2012, 376). The significance here is that Joshua's access to the Urim and Thummim through Eleazar the priest further signifies that he is God's appointed successor to Moses. God does not speak to Joshua in exactly the same manner as Moses, but the Urim and Thummim provide evidence that he is God's appointed successor.

27:22–23. This episode concludes with an account of Moses's obedience. It reflects Moses's generally exemplary conduct, even in a passage that recalls his greatest failure. Moses's concern for Israel was genuine, and by publicly following God's directions to present Joshua before the congregation and commission him for his forthcoming duties, Moses takes an important step to secure his legacy. Israel will not become sheep without a shepherd; they will have a leader whom God has visibly approved.

THEOLOGICAL FOCUS

The exegetical idea (The daughters of Zelophehad preserve their father's name, and Joshua inherits Moses's legacy) leads to the following theological focus: *God responds graciously to the concerns of his people.* Both episodes involve God's answer to a situation that his people bring before him. The daughters find it unjust for their father's name to disappear from Israel. God hears their plea and instructs Moses to give them their due. It is possible to use this passage to talk about issues of justice related to prioritizing patrilineal inheritance, but biblical law is embedded within a cultural context foreign to the modern reader. Instead, the text focuses upon how God responds to a potentially unjust situation by bending legal expectations toward fairness and equity (Sprinkle 2015, 373–74).

The response to the daughters of Zelophehad are one of many examples where God listens to the cry of the "least of these" for mercy or justice. In biblical narrative, Hannah's plea for a son (1 Samuel 1), Elijah's provision for the widow of Zarephath (1 Kings 17:7–24), Jesus's compassion for a bleeding woman (Luke 8:42–49), and response to the appeals of a blind beggar (Luke 18:35–43) all demonstrate God's receptiveness. Within the legal material of the Old Testament, God commands the Israelites not to infringe upon the rights of the disadvantaged or they will face divine judgment (Exod. 22:22–24; cf. Prov. 22:22–23). This ability to cry out to God is even available to all. Paul instructs the Philippians to bring their prayers and petitions before God and receive his peace (Phil. 4:6–7). All of these examples reveal that God hears and responds to his people's concerns.

The second episode reveals that God listens to the cries of his people for suitable leadership. Centuries after Moses and Joshua, God chose David to be Israel's shepherd despite his seemingly lesser physical qualities because God looks at the heart (1 Sam. 16:7). In the New Testament, Jesus looked upon the descendants of these Israelites and had compassion on them because they were sheep without a shepherd (Matt. 9:36). This episode also demonstrates that the most crucial quality is that the leader be equipped with the proper spirit. The early church looked for men full of the Spirit and wisdom when filling administrative functions (Acts 6:3–6; Gane 2004, 742–43). This spirit—more than competency, eloquence, or other external gifts—is the key marker of a God-appointed leader.

This passage calls upon the metaphor of shepherd for God's appointed leadership which resonates throughout Scripture. Ultimately, God himself is our shepherd (Ps. 23:4) but he desires to give his people shepherds after his own heart (Jer. 3:15) to guide and protect them. It is no coincidence that God summons David from protecting the flock to be his anointed ruler over Israel. The qualities of the shepherd-leader are hard to attain. They must exemplify self-sacrificing humility for the benefit of the flock. They must use authority benevolently, not seeking personal gain or power. Timothy S. Laniak notes that "Authority without compassion leads to harsh authoritarianism. Compassion without authority leads to social chaos" (Laniak 2006, 247). Ultimately, they must remember that they are undershepherds, working in the service of the great Shepherd of the sheep (1 Peter 5:2–4). Just as Moses desired that Israel not become like sheep without a shepherd, so God's people can appeal to him to provide shepherds endowed with his Spirit and who faithfully and humbly lead his people.

PREACHING AND TEACHING STRATEGIES

Exegetical and Theological Significance

Texts are written, read, and interpreted in cultural, subcultural, and individual contexts. One of the challenges for the expositor when faced with the type of material found in Numbers 27 is that, although it resonates with contemporary contexts, it is not necessarily concerned with our culture's sensibilities and priorities. Numbers 27:1–11 is not part of an egalitarian, feminist agenda (although it has been read that way), but neither is it endorsing patriarchy or complementarianism. Those modern issues are just not found in the worldview of the actors and original audience of this text. Zelophehad's daughters are not protesting that they should receive an equal inheritance with their brothers; they are asking for their father's name to continue despite the fact that he had no son. If Zelophehad had a son, the daughters would not have asked for the inheritance.

The absence of a son for Zelophehad is the driving concern of the text. The theological concerns of the *author* (which may be very different than the concerns of the contemporary *reader*) have to do with name, land, and inheritance in Canaan. Note that the Lord's instructions in 27:8–11 repeatedly mention the father, but only once mentions his daughters. If he has sons, this issue does not arise. If he has no daughters, the inheritance goes to his uncles (not his aunts). This law is given to keep together the bond of name and land. It is about lasting possession. As the name lives on, the individual achieves a type of immortality in God's Promised Land. That, of course, foreshadows the fullness of immortality in the new heaven and new earth that all of God's children—of both genders—will enjoy.

Putting ourselves back into the situation of the original readers, it is also the case that Numbers 27:12–23 was far more significant to the majority of people in Israel than 27:1–11. Comparatively few would face a similar situation to Zelophehad's daughters, but all of them had known nothing but the leadership of Moses ever since they left Egypt. The transition from Moses to Joshua is taken for granted by people familiar with the Bible today, but when it was actually happening, the momentous significance could not be exaggerated.

Taking the two passages together, the overall thrust of Numbers 27 is that God is taking care of his people and will ensure that their name will live on in his Promised Land. He does this by raising up and equipping leaders to be the undershepherds of the flock.

Preaching Idea
God takes care of his flock and gives them a good shepherd.

Contemporary Connections

What does it mean?
What does it mean that God takes care of his flock and gives them a good shepherd? Zelophehad's daughters have concerns about their inheritance because of their concern for their father's name. Moses listens to them, takes their case to God, and the Lord of heaven and earth answers them and upholds their cause. Imagine the sovereign, transcendent, and holy God taking the time to hear the concerns of a few Bronze Age women in a desert. He listens, cares for them, reassures them, vindicates them, and issues a statute to protect them and their father's name. The God of the universe cares about the details of their lives. He is glorious and transcendent, but also immanent and intimate.

There is no lamb too small (i.e., socially insignificant, powerless, or marginalized) to be overlooked or ignored by God. He put the tabernacle into the middle of the camp, surrounded by all of his people, regardless of their power, wealth, or status. Manna was given to all equally. The sacrifices of atonement were for all of the people. God takes care of his people.

In order to care for the nation of Israel, God knew that they needed a good shepherd. Moses had faithfully led them through the wilderness for forty years, but he could not enter the Promised Land. Knowing the needs of his desert flock, God appointed a successor to the mantle of Moses's leadership. Joshua was not given the exact authority of Moses, but he was equipped to lead the people into their next stage of life.

The ultimate fulfillment of these motifs—that God cares for all of his sheep, and that he gives them good shepherds to lead them—is found in Jesus Christ. From God's care of Zelophehad's daughters and his care for Zelophehad's name, through the selection of Joshua in Moses's place, we can chart a biblical trajectory to Jesus Christ.

Is it true?
Is it true that God takes care of his flock and gives them a good shepherd? Numbers 27 provides fairly clear proof of this claim, but Scripture is filled with passages that exemplify these themes. In the end, however, nothing proves the veracity of this claim more than the fact that God sent his Son to be the Good Shepherd, and the Good Shepherd laid down his life so that his sheep could be saved (John 10:11). Jesus's life, death, and resurrection are the greatest proofs of the love of God for his people that we could ever have.

There is also a note of intertextuality with these themes that directly tie them to Jesus. Numbers 27:17 says that there needs to be a replacement for Moses, so that "the Lord's sheep will not be like sheep without a shepherd." In Matthew 9:36, we read of Jesus: "When he saw the crowds, he had compassion on them, because they were harassed and helpless, like sheep without a shepherd." Jesus is the one greater than Moses and greater than Joshua; he is the one who ensures that God's people are not left as sheep without a shepherd.

It is also through Jesus that we are given the fulfillment of immortality in God's land. Zelophehad's daughters were given the type and shadow, but in Christ we are given the substance and fullness. God ultimately takes care of his people by giving them his Son the Good Shepherd, and it is through Christ that we learn of his love and receive our eternal inheritance.

Now what?
In light of the care of God for us, mediated and fulfilled through Jesus Christ the Good Shepherd: "Humble yourselves, therefore, under God's mighty hand, that he may lift you up in due time. Cast all your anxiety on him because he cares for you" (1 Peter 5:6–7 NIV). Notice the reason for casting our cares and anxiety upon him: it is not because he is powerful, but because he *cares*. When we care *about* someone, we try our best to care *for* them and we will do all that we can to take care *of* them. Our Good Shepherd cares for us and loves us *so much* that he laid down his life for us and took it up again. No one is more loving and caring. No one is wiser or stronger.

Take your worries and anxieties and bring them before God. He takes care of Zelophehad's name, as well as his daughters Mahlah, Noah, Hoglah, Milkah, and Tirzah. Moses passes away, but God appoints Joshua to shepherd his people. Joshua passes away. David passes away. Jesus dies, but dies victoriously, defeating death, and is raised from the dead. We have an everlasting Shepherd who loves us and cares for us. Follow closely behind him and respond to his every word.

Creativity in Presentation

There is a huge range in what Christians find to be acceptable content in shows and movies, so preachers need to be very careful about using illustrations from movies and making movie recommendations. The 2021 movie adaptation of the award-winning play *Dear Evan Hansen* deals with some mature themes and is not suitable for everyone. There are moral complexities all through the plot, and the storyline deepens and deepens as it unfolds. It deals with issues of mental health, belonging, suicide, loss, friendship, compassion, understanding, community, care, and truth. The song "You Will Be Found" speaks poignantly to our need to be cared for and accepted. If appropriate in your context, referencing this movie and song may tie in to the themes of this message. But always, always be careful with these kinds of things.

God cares for both Zelophehad's name and for his daughters. Jesus cared for the poor, the sick, the lepers, the outcasts. He cared for the tax collectors, prostitutes, and sinners. Precisely because we have Jesus as our Good Shepherd, we are to care for the lost, the hurting, and the marginalized. James highlighted the need to care for the vulnerable, such as widows and orphans (James 1:27). Who are the marginalized today? Who are most vulnerable in our social contexts? We need to work, but like Joshua, we need to work through the empowering gifts of God.

Our capacity to minister to others is not infinite. *Dear Evan Hansen* is a call to care and a cry for faithful shepherding and compassionate leadership, but none of us individually and collectively can meet everyone's needs. More than anything, we need the forgiveness of sins and the gift of eternal life. Through Numbers 27 and the biblical-theological fulfillment of its themes in Jesus, we can point people to the

Good Shepherd. God takes care of his people by giving them a leader who surpasses Joshua in every way. God's flock is taken care of by Jesus, the Good Shepherd. As the preacher of this text—as the undershepherd of the Good Shepherd—lead people to Jesus.

The exposition of this text could be shaped by the following outline:

- God protects the name and legacy of his people (27:1–11).

- God provides shepherd leadership to care for his people (27:12–23).

DISCUSSION QUESTIONS

1. Why do you think that Zelophehad's daughters are mentioned by name in the text? What does that convey about God and his concern for his people?

2. What do we learn about God in seeing him shape his law according to situations raised by his people?

3. Why is Joshua suitable as a successor to Moses? How does God demonstrate the continuity between these leaders?

4. What legacies do we hope to leave behind as followers of Christ? How do we want our names to be remembered by our families? Our places of worship? Our communities?

forthcoming sacrifice. Taking the bread and the cup, he commanded the disciples to consume them in memory of him (Luke 22:17–19). Paul focuses on the rhythm of worship this creates, noting "whenever you eat this bread and drink this cup, you proclaim the LORD's death until he comes" (1 Cor. 11:26 NIV). Although believers no longer offer bulls, rams, and lambs as burnt offerings, they are called to remember the sacrifice of the true Passover Lamb who made lasting atonement. Again, the author of Hebrews notes that Christ's sacrifice was made once for all, fulfilling the burnt offerings and purification offerings of the old covenant (Heb. 10:1–10). However, even though one sacrifice accomplished redemption from sin for all time, it merits regular remembrance through the worship rhythms of the believing community.

The world of the believers of the New Testament had many competing allegiances. Idols and their feasts were omnipresent outside of Judea, the emperor demanded reverence and obedience, and questions lingered about what observances from Judaism were applicable to Gentile converts. However, regular rhythms of worship including daily prayer, communal gathering, and celebrating Christ's death and resurrection provided reorientation, shaping the lives of the believers around worship of the true and living God.

PREACHING AND TEACHING STRATEGIES

Exegetical and Theological Significance

As Numbers 26–27 looks forward to the occupation of the Promised Land, Numbers 28–29 looks forward to the organization of Israel's calendar. In his law, God revealed to Israel the when, where, how, and why of their worship. Daily, weekly, monthly, and yearly cycles were established. God knows that we are temporal beings, and in his wisdom he knows how to structure the cadences and rhythms of our lives. These cycles in Numbers 28–29 were for Israel's good and ultimately pointed to God's glory.

Every one of these sacrifices and feasts is overflowing with practical, physical, spiritual, typological, and theological realities. The exposition done in the previous section explains the meaning of each one, and each one also drives the reader to Christ as he fulfills the purposes of the entire sacrificial system. One incredible presupposition of the text is that God desires to remain in relationship with Israel despite its propensity to sin. Through the sacrificial system, God in his holiness could be with them, forgiving their sin, blessing them abundantly, and inviting them into the holy joy of worship and celebration.

The expositor of Numbers cannot help but note that various passages bring up similar themes. There is a great deal of overlap in certain chapters and literary units throughout the book. None of the material is identical, however, and none is redundant. The sacrifices, offerings, and feasts are multifaceted, and they are worth holding up like a gem, turning them and letting the light's reflection and refraction be seen from different angles. If God's revelation repeats themes, we should not be afraid to repeat them as well.

Preaching Idea
We need regular times of worship, but we also need special times of worship.

Contemporary Connections

What does it mean?
What does it mean that we need regular times of worship, but we also need special times of worship? Perhaps the meaning of this principle can be best explicated by an analogy to *true love*. Think of people who truly, *deeply* love each other. They marry in freedom and build their home and lives together. Each day they express their mutual love for one another in a variety of ways. They establish a daily rhythm of life, and

they can turn even the most mundane things into magical adventures. They are thrilled together, but also comfortable. They fit. They are at home. They are king and queen, Adam and Eve, in the garden.

Such a couple would be incredibly blessed. Their daily life would be a life of love. But, precisely because their lives are so overflowing with bounty, they also take special times to be together. There would be special days and nights of celebration. They would follow their hearts and explore their favorite interests. The daily rhythm would make them look forward to special times: the special times would draw them back into deeper appreciation of their daily lives. Loving each other would make them excited to go on vacation, but then their vacation would increase their appreciation for their daily lives. There would be a spiral of love, joy, and gratitude.

We are to love God with all of our heart, mind, soul, and strength. Given our nature, this means that our daily love and worship should lead us excitedly to special times of worship, and those special times of worship will lead us back into a deeper appreciation of God in our daily worship. How we worship God during the weekdays makes a huge difference in how we join in corporate worship on Sundays. But, being drawn into worship on Sundays fuels us for our own Bible reading, prayer, and singing during the week. The more we prepare for Easter, the more meaningful Easter can be. The more Easter impacts us, the more we will long to draw closer to God in our daily lives.

Is it true?
Is it true that we need regular times of worship as well as special times of worship? Since we are finite, temporal beings, our experiences in time are always very limited. Mentally, we cannot process everything at once. We also cannot perpetually live in the sphere of intense, special experiences: we need balance.

Christmas is wonderful, but we cannot live, give, eat, and act every day of the year like we do on Christmas Day. We need daily, familiar love, and also special, intense expressions of love. Then, fascinatingly, over time even the special expressions become part of the familiar rhythm of life. Once you have experienced several or more decades of Christmas, Easter, and Thanksgiving celebrations, they become a "special" part of your "normal" yearly experience.

In church ministry, pastors sometimes refer to "Christmas Eve and Easter Sunday Christians." These are people who show up at church twice per year and who usually do not seem to have any interest in living for God in between those services. Such attendees should be welcomed and celebrated since their presence in church, however rare, is an opportunity for the Spirit to work. However, attending these special worship occasions does not make up for the absence of participating in daily and weekly rhythms of worship. A family that spends no time together for 364 days and then hopes that Christmas Day will bind it together is living under a delusion.

In Numbers 28–29, the daily, weekly, monthly, and yearly cycles are highly instructive. They focus on great, general theological themes, but also focus on special aspects of God, his redemptive work, and the covenant blessings that he freely bestows. The thrust of Passover was not identical to the theme of the Festival of Tabernacles, even though there was a doctrinal overlap between them. For contemporary Christians, daily, weekly, monthly, and yearly cycles of reflection and praise are still necessary for spiritual health.

Now what?
Since it is true that we need both regular and special times of worship, what should we do? Without any doubt, the most important thing is to ensure that we are healthy in our daily walk with God, and also that we are regularly

engaged in weekly corporate worship with God's people. The daily and weekly rhythms are foundational to the special dates on the yearly calendar.

If you want to get something out of the sermon on Sunday morning, make sure you are prayerfully studying your Bible during the week. If you want to worship while participating in the Lord's Supper, prepare your heart ahead of time. If you want to praise instead of just sing—or worship instead of being reduced to the status of a spectator at a Sunday morning concert—then sing songs of praise in your daily life. If you want to worship God for the incarnation, do so all year round, and not just for one evening out of the year. Matthew and Luke did not write their "Christmas narratives" with our Christmas holiday in mind! They wrote their Gospels to tell us what we need to know about Jesus—they were not writing lines for Sunday school pageants. Saturate your daily life with the great truths of the gospel, and then let the special occasions draw you into even higher spheres of praise.

Creativity in Presentation
Numbers 28–29 is not about Christmas, Good Friday, and Easter Sunday directly (although there are connections with the some of them). A faithful exposition will need to set forth the principles of this text and exegete the significance of these feasts for Israel. Then, the typological connections can be identified that lead to Christ and his work of fulfillment. There will be certain obvious connections with the ordinance of the Lord's Supper, gathering to worship, etc.

Living in the era of fulfillment and the new covenant, there is nothing wrong with connecting our contemporary special days with the finished work of Christ. If these feasts call for repentance and reflection on our sin, they also call for joyful, holy celebration and worship for atonement, redemption, and all of our covenant blessings. They call us to focus on God in our daily, weekly, and yearly rhythms.

Huge redemptive developments took place in the incarnation, on Good Friday, and on Easter Sunday. Many churches recognize the special significance of such times and decorate their auditoriums for Christmas and Easter. (Many also decorate for Thanksgiving, although the latter is more historical and generally related to biblical principles than it is tied to a specific redemptive event.) To help our people grasp how significant the details in Numbers 28–29 were to the Israelites, it may help to set up sections at the front of the auditorium with traditional Christmas, Easter, and Thanksgiving displays. Since we share the cultural and traditional framework in which a cornucopia, a cross, a picture of the tomb with a stone rolled away, mistletoe, a Christmas tree, etc., make sense, we can see them and know immediately what they signify. The same was true in Israel when it came to their special occasions. They understood the meaning of these rituals, and they understood the significance of the details.

In the same way that Numbers 28–29 actually presents an interlinking story about God's nature and work (i.e., the feasts are like chapters in one book), so Christmas, Good Friday, and Easter are coherent only when considered together. Why did the Son of God become incarnate? Why did he die on the cross? Why was he resurrected from the dead? Why did he ascend into heaven? These realities are all part of one package; they form a consistent theological set. Let the story of feasts and special days reveal God's plan, and let his people respond in worship. Highlighting these special occasions builds upon the foundation of regular daily and weekly rhythms of worship.

Although it is a challenge to exposit this entire text in one sermon, a possible outline could be:

The Sacral Calendar (28:1–29:40)

- God ordains regular rhythms of worship to maintain relationship with his people (28:1–15).

- Special times of worship commemorate what God has done for his people (28:16–29:11).

- Worshipping God should be done with a generous spirit and a thankful heart (29:12–40).

DISCUSSION QUESTIONS

1. How did the sacrificial system of ancient Israel orient its life around God?

2. Why did God institute daily, weekly, monthly, and annual observances?

3. What rhythms and routines can we build that help us to orient our lives around God?

4. What are appropriate sacrifices that we can bring before God to show our reverence and devotion?

Numbers 30:1–16

EXEGETICAL IDEA
Vows and pledges sworn to God must be upheld, but those offered by women are subject to the approval of their father or husband.

THEOLOGICAL FOCUS
Speech invoking God must be considered carefully.

PREACHING IDEA
Because God's Word is trustworthy, our words should be trustworthy.

PREACHING POINTERS
For the contemporary Western expositor, this text bristles with potential obstacles. Cultural issues always need to be handled with sensitivity, but the preacher must be faithful to the message of every text in God's Word. The concern of the passage is with social cohesion and harmony in its variety of interpenetrating relationships, and that unity requires a profound commitment to truth. In our contemporary society—as in ancient ones—if human communication cannot be trusted, human community breaks down. Words matter. Anyone who makes a vow to God will be held accountable for their words. As a result, this passage underscores the vital importance of truthfulness in speech, especially when it comes to making special vows to the Lord. Religious vows could be overridden if they disrupted God's design and order for interpersonal relationships, but if they didn't, the vows were binding and could not be annulled.

We know what it is like to live in a society where words are cheap and where lies and propaganda are part of the common milieu in which we all live. Scripture is very clear that our words are to be honest, transparent, and true. When we tell someone we will do something, we must honor our word. When we tell God we will do something, we must fulfill our commitment. Our example and standard for our speech is God himself. Because God's Word is trustworthy, our words should be trustworthy.

MAKING VOWS TO GOD (30:1–16)

LITERARY STRUCTURE AND THEMES

A discussion of vows follows the festal calendar in Numbers 28–29. There is no specific incident that occasions this discussion, but the mention of votive offerings in 29:39 may set the stage since vows could be concluded on holy days (Sprinkle 2015, 398). The focus of the regulations is on vows made by women, which may reflect its proximity to the issues of inheritance raised by the daughters of Zelophehad (Cole 2000, 482). This passage also offers a parallel to the Nazirite vow (Numbers 6), which is found shortly after the first census.

The passage begins with a general statement of the inviolability of vows sworn to YHWH (30:1–2).[1] It then works through a series of hypothetical cases involving women. This likely reflects a codification of judgments surrounding this issue over time (Allen 2012, 395). The first case considers a woman who makes a vow while still in her father's house (30:3–5), followed by the case where she gets married after having sworn her vow (30:6–8). The third case is that of a divorced or widowed woman (30:9), concluding with the case of a woman who swears a vow after her marriage (30:10–15). Finally, Numbers 30:16 summarizes the preceding material.

The theme of this passage is the seriousness of making vows before God. As exemplified in the Nazirite vow, failing to uphold the obligations that an individual has taken before God has profound consequences.

- *General Regulations for Vows (30:1–2)*
- *The Vow of an Unmarried Young Woman (30:3–5)*
- *The Vow of a Recently Married Woman (30:6–8)*
- *The Vow of a Divorced or Widowed Woman (30:9)*
- *The Vow of a Married Woman (30:10–15)*
- *Conclusion (30:16)*

EXPOSITION

Vows are serious business. The individual compels themselves before God to carry out what they have promised to do. On the nature of vows, God later declares, "If you make a vow to the LORD your God, do not be slow to repay it, for the LORD your God will certainly demand it of you and you will be guilty of sin" (Deut. 23:21 NIV). Complicating this standard is the relationship that women in ancient Israel had with male authority figures. This preaching unit reveals that vows and pledges sworn to God must be upheld, but those offered by women are subject to the approval of their father or husband.

> **House of the Father**
> The main unit of kinship organization is known as the "house of the father" (בֵּית אָב; cf. Num. 30:4) which consisted of a patriarch and his spouse(s), male children and their spouses, unmarried female children, and any subsequent generations (Bendor 1996, 48). A woman would be part of

---

[1] There is a minor difference in versification between the Hebrew text and English versions. Numbers 30:1 in the Hebrew text is equivalent to Numbers 29:40 in English versions. Consequently, Numbers 30:1–16 in English versions equals Numbers 30:2–17 in the Masoretic text. Verse numbers in this preaching unit refer to the English versions.

her father's house until she married and then she would join that of her husband. This typically involved physically relocating to where her husband's family lived.[2] Israelite families were patrilineal, patrilocal, and patriarchal. The leading father was at the center of the arrangement, with the other family members placed in orbit around him (Block 2003, 40). Although in healthy arrangements the father was "neither despot nor dictator" (Block 2003, 43), the authority granted to the male head of the family is undeniable. This framework lies behind the guidelines placed on women's vows in this chapter.

General Regulations for Vows (30:1–2)

30:1–2. The discussion of vows begins by establishing an overarching principle that vows must be upheld. Moses speaks to leaders of the tribes, declaring that these instructions come from YHWH. These verses declare that when a man makes a vow or "swears an oath to bind himself by a pledge" (Num. 30:2 ESV), he must not break his word. The use of "man" (אִישׁ) here may be generic, establishing the general principle before discussing the qualifications that apply to women's vows. Two key words are introduced here and repeated throughout the chapter: "vow" (נֶדֶר) and "pledge" (אִסָּר). The text does not differentiate between them, but likely a vow refers to a commitment to do or give something in response to an answer to petitionary prayer, while a pledge reflects a commitment to refrain from something (Ashley 1993, 573–74; Cartledge 1992, 25; Cole 2009, 390).

There is no discussion of what might prompt a vow, but a study of vows in the ancient Near Eastern world suggests that they were often related to physical illness, the desire for protection in war, safety in travel, or the desire for a spouse or a child. They would frequently require gifts of gold, silver, animals, or agricultural goods to redeem (Cartledge 1992, 135).

Vows and pledges create serious obligations since they involve YHWH, just as vows in other ancient cultures involved a deity or deities. Breaking a vow sworn before God likely breaches the commandment not to take God's name in vain (Exod. 20:7; Pressler 2017, 267). Consequently, the discussion of vows and pledges begins by reiterating their solemnity.

The Vow of an Unmarried Young Woman (30:3–5)

30:3–4. The text then transitions to discuss vows and pledges made by women in various life circumstances. It works through four different scenarios: 1) an unmarried woman in her father's house, 2) a newly married woman, 3) a divorced or widowed woman, and 4) a woman in a longstanding marriage. The discussion begins with the presumably young unmarried woman. The basic principle is that if she makes a vow or pledge and her father "remains silent about her" (Num. 30:4 NET) then she is bound by what she has sworn. Therefore, the default situation is for the young woman to have the capacity to make a vow or pledge.

30:5. However, the father has the authority to override his daughter's vows and pledges, so long as he does it immediately upon hearing of them.[3] If he remains silent, he gives tacit consent (Gane 2004, 762). The father thus acts as a safeguard against a vow that could in some way jeopardize the welfare of the larger family unit (Block 2003, 55). His actions also permit YHWH to release her from the vow. The text uses a verb from the root סלח, which also refers to forgiveness from sin (Num. 14:19, 20; 1 Kings 8:30, 34, 36). If the woman failed to uphold what she had sworn before YHWH, she would be in

---

2 See Rebekah's journey to join Isaac in Genesis 24:55–61.
3 The Hebrew idiom here is "in the day of his hearing" (בְּיוֹם שָׁמְעוֹ) which refers to the time when he becomes aware of the vow.

error, but the father's intervention removed any guilt for not fulfilling the vow or pledge.

The Vow of a Recently Married Woman (30:6–8)

30:6–8. The second case resembles the first. It considers a woman who gets married "while under a vow" (Num. 30:6 NET). The implication is that she had made a vow or pledge but its conditions remained unfulfilled at the time of her marriage. The underlying question is whether her husband, as the leader of her new kinship identity group, has the authority to weigh in on her prior obligations (Ashley 1993, 580). The answer is affirmative, subject to the same restrictions as those imposed on the father in the previous case. If the husband remains silent, the vow or pledge remains in force. The husband must declare his intention to override her vow upon hearing of it (Num. 30:8). As before, his actions would release the woman from any guilt before YHWH for failing to uphold what she declared.

This case also introduces a slight shift in terminology. Numbers 30:6, 8 refer to the woman's vow (נֶדֶר) but also to her "rash promise" (NIV) or "thoughtless utterance" (ESV). These translate the expression מִבְטָא שְׂפָתֶיהָ which is only found in this passage. The first noun (מִבְטָא) derives from a root that denotes rash or foolish speech (Lev. 5:4; Ps. 106:32; Prov. 12:18; Ashley 1993, 580). This phrase may introduce a more pejorative sense to the woman's vow or pledge, suggesting that it was not in her best interest, or perhaps bound her and her new family to commitments that would be imprudent (Allen 2012, 394). It is also possible that the phrase is intended to be neutral, focusing on the woman's inability to foresee how her commitments could adversely affect her married life (Gane 2004, 762). These could have been financial in nature, requiring an unwise outlay of the family's resources (Pressler 2017, 269). This regulation then provided an escape clause, permitting a new marriage to begin without prior obligations.

The Vow of a Divorced or Widowed Woman (30:9)

30:9. The third case addresses a divorced or widowed woman. There is no commentary on what might have led to her divorce. In both situations the woman has been under a husband's authority but is no longer. In these situations, one would expect the woman to return to her father's house (Gen. 38:11; Ruth 1:8) or be cared for by a son. The text is unclear if either of those possibilities has happened here. Instead, it addresses the woman as autonomous. It is possible that she possessed a greater degree of legal independence even if she returned to her father's house (Ashley 1993, 581). This verse announces that the divorced or widowed woman must uphold any vows and pledges she makes. This puts her on the same footing as a man (Num. 30:1–2). Although this appears to reflect more gender equity, it is important to note that a woman who was not under the authority of a husband or father was "socially anomalous and economically at risk" (Pressler 2017, 269). Any vow or pledge she might make before God could not be countermanded, but she would be making them from a very precarious position.

The Vow of a Married Woman (30:10–15)

30:10–12. The fourth case addresses a woman in a longstanding marriage. In the second case, the woman had a vow or pledge prior to her marriage that her husband had to confirm or revoke. In this case, the woman makes the vow or pledge while living with her husband, and thus being part of his kinship unit. The same regulations apply in this case. If the husband says nothing about his wife's vows, then they are confirmed. However, he has the authority to countermand them when he hears about them. Again, this may reflect a concern to maintain the husband's authority over the family's economic resources (Pressler 2017, 269). The wife cannot obligate them to be used in service of her vow or pledge without his permission.

30:13–14. The text then adds some additional nuance. First, it expands on the terminology of the pledge (אִסָּר) to include language related to self-denial. The woman's pledge is to "afflict herself" (30:13 ESV), reflecting the expression לְעַנֹּת נָפֶשׁ. This frequently refers to fasting (Lev. 16:29, 31; 23:27; Num. 29:7; Isa. 58:3, 5) but may also involve other elements of self-denial, including sexual abstinence (Gane 2004, 762). As with other pledges, the husband has the authority to permit or annul these commitments. Secondly, Numbers 30:14 explicitly lays out the timeframe of the husband's response. If her husband is silent "from day to day" (מִיּוֹם אֶל־יוֹם), then the woman's vows and pledges will stand. This confirms that the husband's sole opportunity to weigh in on his wife's commitments is when he hears of them. He does not have the authority to revoke his tacit approval if he has remained silent. This prevents the husband from wielding his authority arbitrarily or indecisively.

30:15. The final verse exploring this fourth case appears to reflect the consequences of the husband's delay in denying his wife's vow or pledge. It comments on what happens if the husband annuls them "after he heard" (אַחֲרֵי שָׁמְעוֹ) about them. The length of time specified by אַחֲרֵי is unclear, but read in context with the preceding verse it reflects a delay beyond the established timeframe for the husband to confirm or revoke his wife's obligations. If the husband does this, then he will bear her iniquity (וְנָשָׂא אֶת־עֲוֹנָהּ). The expression "bear iniquity" has both negative and positive connotations. It can refer to "bearing away" sin and guilt, reflecting forgiveness (Gen. 50:17; Exod. 10:17; 1 Sam. 15:25; 25:28) or it can reflect carrying one's own guilt for transgressions (Exod. 28:42; Lev. 5:1, 17; 7:18; 17:16; 19:8; Ezek. 14:10; 23:49; 44:10, 12; Eichler 2021, 320). English translations and most modern commentators read the negative nuance here, suggesting that the penalty that should fall on the wife for failing to meet her obligations before YHWH now falls on the husband. He permitted his wife to incur these commitments and thus bears responsibility for her inability to meet them.[4] The wife is thus protected against an improper use of her husband's authority.

Conclusion (30:16)

30:16. The passage concludes by stating that YHWH gave these regulations to Moses to address this aspect of husband-wife and father-daughter relationships.

THEOLOGICAL FOCUS

The exegetical idea (Vows and pledges sworn to God must be upheld, but those offered by women are subject to the approval of their father or husband) leads to the following theological focus: *Speech invoking God must be considered carefully*. To swear a vow or pledge before God is to draw in the name and reputation of the Creator of the universe. Consequently, it is not speech that should be uttered lightly or frivolously. Ecclesiastes 5:4–5 reminds its audience that it is better not to make a vow than to make one and not uphold its obligations before God. The overarching principle of Numbers 30:1–2 further conveys this seriousness: the one who makes a vow or pledge must fulfill it. The rest of

---

[4] Eichler proposes an alternative reading, suggesting that Numbers 30:15 is simply a summary of 30:13–14. This suggests reading the phrase וְנָשָׂא אֶת־עֲוֹנָהּ with its positive nuance and an indefinite subject, leading to the translation "her guilt will be lifted up" (Eichler 2021, 323). The verse then explicitly declares that when the husband annuls his wife's obligations, there is no guilt on her. Eichler takes the expression אַחֲרֵי שָׁמְעוֹ ("after he hears") as an equivalent of בְּיוֹם שָׁמְעוֹ ("in the day [that] he hears"), meaning that there is no delay in the husband's response. This proposal responds to the oddity of including a new subcase right before the conclusion of a highly patterned chapter. However, since English translations follow the understanding that guilt falls on the husband for a delay in annulling his wife's vows, it is probably best for the expositor not to get sidetracked by such a technical discussion.

the chapter takes that general principle and applies appropriate nuance given the arrangement of family structure in ancient Israel.

A famous example of a woman who was aware of the obligations of her vow is Hannah. In 1 Samuel 1:11 she vowed that if YHWH hears her prayer and granted her a son, she would devote him to YHWH for his whole life. This came from her deep distress and difficult family situation. For Hannah, YHWH alone could be her source of restoration. Her husband Elkanah did not object to her vow, preserving its obligations. His commentary is simply "May the LORD make good his word" (1 Sam. 1:23 NIV), which reflects a prayer for God to uphold his end of the arrangement (Arnold and Choi 2018, 75). The story concludes with Hannah bringing Samuel to Eli along with animal and grain offerings (1 Sam. 1:24–28) which fulfilled her obligations. Hannah made a vow that reflected her devotion to YHWH and carried it through, recognizing the seriousness of her commitment.

Jesus warns against foolishly swearing vows, declaring, "Let what you say be simply 'Yes' or 'No'; anything more than this comes from evil" (Matt. 5:37 ESV; cf. James 5:12). This is unlikely to be a blanket condemnation against vows, given the presence of oath formulations or other invocations of God's name by Paul (Rom. 1:9; 2 Cor. 1:23; Gal. 1:20; 1 Thess. 2:5; Sprinkle 2015, 390). Instead, Jesus compels his followers to be judicious with their speech and to be so forthright and honest that a simple "yes" or "no" has the force of an oath sworn in God's name. He also condemns those who manipulate oaths and commitments to God. He articulates a scenario in Mark 7:9–13 in which the motive for devoting resources to God is to avoid fulfilling one's duties to one's parents. He condemns the use of apparent religious commitment as a means of undercutting filial duty, drawing God's name into their deception (Stubbs 2009, 227). He declares that misusing speech that invokes God in this way nullifies the word of God (Mark 7:13) and does not reflect the reverence that should attend discourse that invokes his name.

PREACHING AND TEACHING STRATEGIES

Exegetical and Theological Significance

For audiences in the contemporary Western world, this text has additional barriers to understanding that simply would not have been shared by the original audience (see the Sidebar above). As with the material on Zelophehad's daughters in Numbers 27:1–11, the expositor needs to be careful in bridging the cultural contexts from Numbers to today. It won't do to say *nothing* of such concerns, but it is important to anchor the exposition and application in the theological principles of the text itself. Our cultural context is very different than that of Numbers 30, but the principle of honest speech and being careful when making promises applies as much today as it ever has.

Although the contemporary reader may be distracted by what seems to be the discriminatory nature of these provisions, in the original social context this was one way of ensuring that the social, marital, familial, and religious domains of life were not set in opposition to one another. Vows, speech, truth, and responsibility all had to flow together in harmony. One's relationship with God was not hermetically sealed off from one's responsibility in human relationships.

As God's special revelation was progressively unfolded, the importance of speech, vows, and truth was emphasized, not minimized (see the Theological Focus above). Every word spoken by God is trustworthy and true, and this is to be the standard for the speech of God's children. Our speech is to reflect the speech of our Father.

Preaching Idea

Because God's Word is trustworthy, our words should be trustworthy.

Contemporary Connections

What does it mean?
What does it mean that because God's Word is trustworthy, our words should be trustworthy? This is one element of a wider connection between a person's character and the character of their speech. Our characters and our words go together. A kind person speaks kind words. A godly person speaks godly words. A mean person speaks hurtful words. The things that we say are rooted in our characters.[5] The same thing is true for God—what God says is a reflection of his character. Note the following connections between God's Word and his character:

> Attribute #1: Authority. God is the supreme authority in heaven and on earth. As a result, nobody can say anything that carries more authority than God's Word.
>
> Attribute #2: Goodness. Good actions and good words flow out of a good heart. God alone is supremely good, and so all of his deeds and words are good.
>
> Attribute #3: Truth. God is too good to lie, so he will never knowingly deceive us. But God also knows everything, so he can never be mistaken. As a result, every word from his mouth is true.
>
> Attribute #4: Power. When God said, "Let there be light," there was light! His word formed our universe. God's Word has the power to give us life and to change our lives and the whole world.
>
> Attribute #5: Righteous. Everything God does is right and just. Every word that he speaks measures up to the perfect, righteous standard of his own character.
>
> Attribute #6: Necessary. Without God, nothing would exist. His independent existence is necessary for our dependent existence. God's Word is necessary—without it, we wouldn't know about the gospel of Jesus Christ, and we wouldn't know how to walk with God.
>
> Attribute #7: Life-Giving. God's word created our physical universe and all of life. God's Word creates spiritual life through the gospel and strengthens our hearts and souls as we grow.
>
> Attribute #8: Delightful. We are to rejoice in the Lord, find our joy in him, and delight in all that he is and does. We are to cultivate our tastes so that we also love and delight in his word.
>
> Attribute #9: Sufficient. God is all that we need. Nothing can be added to him and nothing can be taken away. He is perfect as he is. The same is true of the Bible: it is exactly what it ought to be, and it is entirely sufficient for the purposes for which God has given it.
>
> Attribute #10: Better. This is not a pure attribute, but it is a fitting descriptor. God is better than everything. So is his word. God's Word is better than food, fortune, fame, power, or pleasure. It is better than all the wisdom of the world and all of the knowledge in academia. It cannot be surpassed or equalled. No matter what you put up against it, God's Word is better.

---

5 It is, of course, possible to mask our character through deceitful words. People can speak kindly to others, then conspire against them behind their backs, or seek to wound them from the anonymity of online discourse. However, after taking such malicious actions into account, it is reasonable to link a person's speech to their character.

Because we are created to bear the image of God, our speech is to be righteous, true, pure, and good. When it comes to promises, because God speaks the truth and fulfills his promises, so should we.

Is it true?
Is it true that because God's Word is trustworthy, our words should be trustworthy? In debates and philosophical argumentation, one way to establish the truth of a principle is by showing the impossibility of the contrary, or the absurdity of the negation of the principle under consideration. For example, the claim that "human beings have knowledge" can be supported by showing the absurdity of maintaining that "human beings do not have knowledge." (You cannot argue for that latter proposition if it's true, because if it *is* true it invalidates any thought or speech that you could use to reason your way to it. Furthermore, if it is true and you know that it is true, it is self-referentially incoherent and refutes itself.) Applying that principle, try to argue for the proposition that human speech should be untrustworthy. What kind of society would we live in if we could never trust someone's word?

On the positive side, we have God's great and precious promises, and we can have full confidence that he will fulfill each and every one of them. God is not unreliable or untrustworthy. What God has said he will do. This is an anchor for our souls, and a source of great comfort, hope, and encouragement. Since we can always trust the word of the Lord, let us be people whose words are trustworthy, too.

Now what?
Given this text, there are a few responses that are called for. First, we may need to repent of hasty, careless, and broken vows. How many Christians get in a tough spot and make a quick, unplanned, desperate vow to God that they never bother to fulfill? If we do, it is time to stop this practice. Second, there may be things we need to do to fulfill promises we have made. Third, we need to listen to Jesus and let our yes be yes and our no, no (Matt. 5:37). Fourth, we need to praise God that his every word is trustworthy, and his every promise will be fulfilled! Fifth, we need to pray that God will help us be truthful in our speech, judicious in our vows, and to reflect his character in every word that comes out of our mouths.

Creativity in Presentation
It can be little more than shooting fish in a barrel to talk about the broken promises of politicians, or to look at false claims in advertising, but it is also an illustration of this principle that people understand. Today, we talk about misinformation and disinformation. (Apparently our society is so corrupt in speech that we needed to come up with that latter term to designate a new category of organized lying for nefarious purposes.) Trust in our societal institutions is plummeting. Who really trusts politicians and the media? Who doesn't think that we are being subjected to a ceaseless cycle of propaganda and spin? How many people really trust educators anymore?[6]

The truth is that today we have a society that is so dishonest we need pages-long written contracts for virtually everything. We do not trust the word of the person we're doing business with, so we each sign the contract and are ready to litigate. Think about this: If Jesus's words were actually followed, we could still get along with a verbal agreement and a handshake. A person would be as good as their word. The reason we

---

6   If the expositor builds off this example, they need to be careful here not to fall into the trap of our polarized age and suggest that media/politicians who agree with our preconceptions are trustworthy while those who disagree are corrupt and misleading. Jesus's caution to be wary of the planks in our own eyes (Matt. 7:3–5) also applies to media consumption.

don't trust someone's word is that their word is only as good as the person who spoke it.

Although Matthew 5 and James 5 provide didactic teaching on this subject, a very helpful picture is given to us in Ephesians 4:25: "Therefore each of you must put off falsehood and speak truthfully to your neighbor, for we are all members of one body" (NIV). The rationale here is that the person we are deceiving is a member of our own body. Imagine the eye being upset with the stomach and choosing to deceive it to cause it harm. The eye sees the skull and crossbones symbol on the bottle but does not communicate that message. The hand reaches out and brings the bottle to the mouth. As the poison is swallowed, the eye rejoices in its cleverness (like Peter Pan exclaiming, "Oh, the cleverness of me!"). But what happens? What is the result of the deceit? Because the eye and the stomach all belong to the same body, the eye ends up destroying itself.

God's words are life, and his Word is truth. Satan is a liar from the beginning, and those who lie reflect Satan's nature rather than God's (John 8:44). So, because God's words are trustworthy, our words should be trustworthy, too.

One possible outline for this text could be:

- Speech that invokes God is serious business (30:1–2).

- All followers of God have the ability to make commitments to him, but must also consider their effect on human relationships (30:3–16).

DISCUSSION QUESTIONS

1. What sort of circumstances might call people to make vows to God? Why might people be tempted to swear foolish vows?

2. Why is swearing a vow to God such serious business? What could happen if a person failed to uphold their vow to God?

3. How should this discussion of the seriousness of speech made to God inform how we speak and act in different facets of our lives?

4. Imagine this scenario: at a spiritual retreat or conference, you pledge to devote yourself to God by quitting your job and pursuing ministry training. Upon returning home, your spouse has significant concerns. How should you navigate your commitment to God and your commitment to your spouse?

Numbers 31:1–54

EXEGETICAL IDEA
At God's command, Israel seeks vengeance against the Midianites and shares the spoils of conquest with him.

THEOLOGICAL FOCUS
Vengeance and victory belong to God.

PREACHING IDEA
"Unless you repent, you too will all perish" (Luke 13:3, 5).

PREACHING POINTERS
Anyone who teaches the Old Testament knows that there are hard texts and difficult themes, and some passages raise ethical issues that do not sit well with modern sensibilities and intuitions. Sometimes a careful, nuanced, sensitive, and duly humble apologetic is needed to place a hard text in context so that it can be preached faithfully. It is essential to see that this is not genocide. God already punished Israel for their sin in the event of Baal Peor, and now the Midianites receive the consequences for their sin. Moab and the Midianites had tried to destroy Israel, and thus now they experience reciprocal justice. They had proclaimed war on Israel through subtle seduction and idolatry, and now they reap the bitter fruit of their attempt to kill the souls of the Israelites.

It may be somewhat uncomfortable for us today, but Jesus used tragic events to warn his hearers that they all needed to repent and be prepared to stand before God. When we see the death of 24,000 Israelites because of this event, and see the death of the Midianites, one of the lessons we are to learn is that *we* need to repent. If we remove ourselves from God, we will die. In many churches today, the pendulum has swung so far from hellfire and brimstone preaching that one might be in church services for years without hearing that there is a day of judgment coming. An honest exposition of Scripture, however, requires dealing with the truth that God blesses and gives life, but also judges sin and punishes those who reject him. Scripture is filled with sober warnings that drive people to Christ. As the preacher deals with the historical, ethical, and theological principles of the text, one thing to tell the congregation is that, in the words of our Lord Jesus Christ, "Unless you repent, you too will all perish" (Luke 13:3).

WAR WITH THE MIDIANITES (31:1–54)

LITERARY STRUCTURE AND THEMES

This passage abruptly shifts away from the preceding discussion of vows. Instead, it builds upon God's command in Numbers 25:17 to attack the Midianites on account of the incident at Baal Peor. The reason for the gap between the command and its execution is unknown. One possibility is that structurally, the text uses the incidents with Midian in Numbers 25:16–18 and 31:1–54 as an envelope around Numbers 26–30, which is divided into three pairs of stories that also address the relationship between divine command and human response (Grossman 2007, 61).[1]

This preaching unit can be divided into two mirroring panels: Numbers 31:1–24 and 31:25–54. Each one has three shared elements, but there is a fourth unrepeated element in the first. The structure can be represented as ABC-D-A'B'C' (Brown 2015, 69). The first panel begins with (A) instructions from YHWH and Moses (31:1–4), followed by (B) an account of Israel's obedience (31:5–12). There is then (C) an extension to the narrative, focusing on Moses and the officers of the army (31:13–18). It concludes with (D) a discussion of the need for purification after battle (31:19–24). The second panel begins with (A') instructions from YHWH (31:25–30), followed by (B') an account of Israel's obedience (31:31–47). It concludes with (C') an unexpected extension relating to the commanders of the army (31:48–54).

The most noteworthy theme is the role of divinely sanctioned violence. Israel seeks vengeance at God's command, leading to a military conflict. This raises issues related to the role of violence in achieving God's will, the treatment of Israel's enemies, and the proper use of wealth captured in battle. The passage also explores how the Israelites can remain holy before God even in the presence of so much death.

- ***First Panel: Conflict with the Midianites (31:1–24)***
  - *Instructions from YHWH and Moses (31:1–4)*
  - *Israel's Obedience (31:5–12)*
  - *Extension: Moses and the Army Commanders (31:13–18)*
  - *Regulations for Purification (31:19–24)*
- ***Second Panel: Disposition of the Plunder (31:25–54)***
  - *Instructions from YHWH (31:25–30)*
  - *Israel's Obedience (31:31–47)*
  - *Extension: Moses and the Army Commanders (31:48–54)*

EXPOSITION

This passage contains many elements that resurface the conquest of Canaan, including a divine command to fight, a representative contingent of troops from each tribe, and the presence of YHWH through symbols and a priestly representative (Pressler 2017, 275). It also focuses more on the procedures surrounding war than the conflict itself (Cole 2000, 488). Expositing this text raises uncomfortable issues, especially concerning the

---

1 Grossman pairs the census (Numbers 26) with the daughters of Zelophehad (Num. 27:1–11), Moses's imminent death (Num. 27:12–14) with the appointment of Joshua (Num. 27:15–23), and the instructions for festal sacrifices (Numbers 28–29) with the discussion of women's vows (Numbers 30).

disposition of the captive noncombatants (31:13–18).[2] However, its primary message is clear: at God's command, Israel seeks vengeance against the Midianites and shares the spoils of conquest with him.

First Panel: Conflict with the Midianites (31:1–24)

Instructions from YHWH and Moses (31:1–4)

31:1–2. The passage begins with YHWH instructing Moses to take vengeance on the Midianites on behalf of the Israelites. Although not mentioned here, this command responds to the participation of the Midianites in drawing Israel into idolatry at Baal Peor. Afterward, Moses will be gathered to his people, an idiom repeated from Numbers 27:13 that points to the end of Moses's tenure.

31:3–4. Moses relays God's instructions to the Israelites and directs them to gather an army to "enact the LORD's vengeance on Midian" (31:3 ESV, NET).[3] When applied to God, the Hebrew term for avenge (נְקָמָה) reflects his means of deliverance for his people and punishment on "the immoral, idolatrous, and unjust" (Cole 2000, 494).

The battle plan is for each tribe to contribute one thousand men (31:4). This is a rather small percentage of the available fighting men, according to the census of Numbers 26.[4] The purpose is symbolic, demonstrating that the tribes equally participate. Further, selecting only a representative portion of the army provides a reminder that YHWH brings victory, not Israel's own military strength (cf. Exod. 15:1–22; 17:8–16; Judges 6–7).

Israel's Obedience (31:5–12)

31:5–6. Israel does exactly what Moses instructs and dispatches a force of twelve thousand men. Crucially, this detachment has multiple signs of God's favor. The presence of Phinehas, recently celebrated for his zeal for YHWH, gives this endeavor a sacral nature (cf. Deut. 20:2). He serves as the priestly envoy instead of his father Eleazar the high priest, presumably to prevent Eleazar from becoming unclean due to contact with dead bodies (31:19–20). Further, Phinehas carries "vessels of the sanctuary and the trumpets for the alarm" (31:6 ESV). The trumpets are those that God instructed Moses to make in Numbers 10:1–8 and were used for both military and sacral purposes. The nature of the "vessel of the sanctuary" is unknown. If the ark itself were present, it would be surprising for it not to be named specifically. One suggestion is that the term refers to the Urim and Thummim, but that seems unlikely since they were part of the high priest's vestments (Ashley 1993, 593). A reasonable alternative is that the vessels are the trumpets themselves. The text could then

---

[2] See the excursus below.

[3] Some have noted a minor distinction between God's instruction in 31:2, where the Israelites are to take vengeance *from* the Midianites (מֵאֵת הַמִּדְיָנִים) and Moses's conveyance where he instructs the army to take vengeance *against* Midian (בְּמִדְיָן). The former is thought to reflect a redress of past wrongs, while the latter points to exacting retribution (Milgrom 1990, 255). This is used to drive a wedge between the intentions of God and Moses, suggesting that Moses desires more violent retribution than God (cf. 31:15–18; Brown 2015, 74–75). Although there have been divergences between God and Moses beginning with the incident of water from the rock (Num. 20:1–13), there is no conclusive evidence of that here. If Moses exceeded "the vengeance of YHWH" (Num. 31:3), it is reasonable to presume that YHWH would intervene to prevent a misuse of his name.

[4] See the excursus in Numbers 1 for further discussion of how to read the numbers in the censuses. As mentioned there, it is also possible to read the word for thousand (אֶלֶף) as "military unit." It is thus possible that each tribe contributes a "unit" of soldiers. These units may not have been of the same size, but the focus is still on the equality of participation of all the tribes (Ashley 1993, 591).

be translated "the vessels of the sanctuary, that is, the trumpets for the alarm." Even if the trumpets were not anointed like other sanctuary items, it is reasonable that they were stored there during Israel's travels (Cole 2000, 496).

31:7–8. Israel's attack was a complete success, reflecting its obedience to God's commands. The text declares that they killed every man. This does not entail the complete destruction of the Midianites (cf. Judges 6–8), but rather a complete victory against the portion of the Midianite tribal confederacy that opposed them (Allen 2012, 400; Milgrom 1990, 257). Numbers 31:8 then lists specific foes whom Israel defeated. These include five Midianite rulers, most notably Zur—likely the father of Cozbi, the Midianite woman whom Phinehas killed alongside her Israelite paramour (Num. 25:15). Further, Balaam is included among the slain. He had been absent from the text since his departure from Balak (Num. 24:25) but is now found among the Midianites. The revelation that he masterminded the plan to entice Israel into idolatry (31:16) provides a final evaluation of his character. Previously, he oscillated between announcing what YHWH commanded and angling for his own advantage. His last act is to try to bring down Israel, accomplishing what he could not through his manipulation of the divine realm (Gane 2004, 769). On this occasion, Balaam does not escape his fate.

31:9–12. Israel's victory is only discussed briefly before the text moves to the disposition of the plunder. The army captured a number of women and children, along with animals and material wealth (31:9). As a further sign of their conquest, the Israelites burned the cities and dwelling places of the Midianites (31:10). Given their seminomadic nature, these were likely not major permanent inhabitations (Cole 2000, 497). The victorious force brought the plunder back to the main Israelite encampment where it was presented to Moses, Eleazar the high priest, and the rest of the community. This provided tangible evidence of Israel's victory, secured through YHWH's power and presence.

> **History and Numbers 31**
> There are challenges in associating this campaign with the rest of Israel's wilderness sojourn. Critical scholars are quick to dismiss any possible historical value to this chapter, identifying its purpose as the elevation of the priesthood over matters of war (Budd 1984, 333; Noth 1968, 228). The totality of Israel's victory, including the complete destruction of the Midianites (Num. 31:7–8) and the complete absence of Israelite casualties (Num. 31:49) is "unrealistically absolute" (Pressler 2017, 274). Further, taking the view that Numbers reflects a postexilic compilation, this chapter is seen as a retrojection of attitudes from the Achaemenid Persian era (Levine 2000, 474). Putative parallels to supposedly older biblical passages are also drawn, including Gideon's war against the Midianites (Judges 6–8), the law of war in Deuteronomy 20, and David's regulations for the division of plunder (1 Sam. 30:24; Pressler 2017, 274). However, questions of literary dependence are always fraught. It is possible to reverse these supposed relationships and suggest that the other texts draw from Numbers 31 (Cole 2000, 490).
>
> Further, although the history and organization of the Midianites is impossible to pin down, it is reasonable to follow the biblical presentation of the evidence and accept that they exercised significant authority over the Transjordan region at the time of Israel's sojourn. Milgrom concludes that "Midian was the most powerful and menacing enemy that Israel had to encounter during its migration to Canaan" (Milgrom 1990, 491). While some of the details of the campaign may reflect the hyperbolic language common to battle reports, the text is best read as referring to an actual event, even if it is otherwise unattested.

War with the Midianites (31:1–54)

Extension: Moses and the Army Commanders (31:13–18)

31:13. This verse clarifies that Moses, Eleazar, and the tribal leaders met the returning army outside of the actual encampment. This detail confirms that the returning army did not render the camp ceremonially unclean because of its contact with dead bodies. Instructions for how to remedy that situation follow in 31:19–24.

31:14–16. Somewhat surprisingly, Moses responds with anger to the leaders of the victorious force. His displeasure centers on the presence of captive Midianite women. Moses blames them for Israel's descent into idolatry in Numbers 25, declaring that they followed Balaam's advice to entice Israel to abandon YHWH and worship Baal (31:16). The consequences of that included a devastating plague. The law of war established in Deuteronomy 20:13–14 instructed Israel to spare the women and children of non-Canaanite enemies. They could also claim their livestock as plunder. However, the culpability that Moses assigns to the Midianite women gives him the grounds to push for a harsher response.

31:17–18. Moses instructs the Israelites to kill all of the male children and the women who are sexually mature. Women who had not yet had sexual relations were permitted to live. This represents something of a halfway point between the instructions of Deuteronomy 20:13–14 for war against non-neighboring nations and the total destruction required of the Canaanites in Deuteronomy 20:16–18. Eliminating the male children lessens the possibility of reprisals when that generation matures, while the sexually mature women receive a penalty of collective guilt for the incident at Baal Peor. The absence of sexual activity permits the young women to have their identity shifted to the Israelite community, and thus they are permitted to live (cf. Deut. 21:10–14).

Holy War

Moses's commands are shocking to read in a modern context. In particular, the command to kill women and children is extremely harsh, even though it prefigures the even greater destruction required upon entry into the Promised Land. Further, the idea that young women could be spared because they lack an identity prior to being "claimed" by a man is challenging (Niditch 1993, 51). An expositor needs great care and sensitivity in addressing this topic, especially since it is quite possible that congregants will have participated in wars or been traumatized by them. A thorough discussion of the ethics of divinely sanctioned violence cannot be achieved here, but it is necessary to offer a framework to address the issue as it relates to this text.

We begin with a note of exegetical caution. We must be careful not to divide Scripture between a judging and violent God in the Old Testament and a compassionate and merciful one personified by Jesus in the New Testament. God's mercy and compassion is established in the Old Testament (Exod. 34:6–7) and has been evident in his dealings with Israel throughout Numbers. Further, warnings of God's wrath can be found throughout the New Testament (Rom. 1:18–2:16; Heb. 10:26–31; Rev. 16:1–21). Jesus himself is depicted in Revelation 19:11–21 as a rider on a white horse with a sword coming out of his mouth that strikes down the nations and hostile spiritual powers. Jesus, who fellowshipped with sinners and heard the cries of the poor, weak, and forgotten, also returns "to render judgment, violent judgment against all who resist him" (Longman 2019, 196). New Testament writers further use stories of God's judgment from the Old Testament as warnings and examples for their audiences (1 Cor. 10:6–10; 2 Peter 3:3–7; Jude 11). Consequently, any discussion of God and violence cannot be solved by saying that it is only a problem for the Old Testament (Wright 2008, 76–81).

With that in mind, we can put forward a few considerations. First, it is important to read this narrative against its ancient Near Eastern backdrop. Violent, hyperbolic language was quite common in battle reports, including the mistreatment of captured women. Evidence suggests that captured women may have been subjected to repeated sexual assault, scenes of which were depicted in the visual iconography of the conqueror (Webb and Oeste 2019, 110). Victorious kings also claimed total destruction of their enemies, quite likely claiming to have killed orders of magnitude more men than participated in the battle (Webb and Oeste 2019, 140–41). In that light, the declaration that the Israelites killed "every man" (Num. 32:7–8) can be read as a claim of victory, fitting the rhetoric of the day. The treatment of the sexually immature captured women also appears to be less harsh than possible alternatives. Deuteronomy 21:10–14 supplements this text and requires Israelites to formally marry captive women rather than condemn them to sexual servitude. This would give the women a place within the Israelite community. It is still difficult to read in a modern light, but it reflects more stringent limitations on the behavior of victorious soldiers than in parallel cultures.

Secondly, Moses declares that the Midianite women share collective guilt for leading Israel into idolatry. The women's actions at Balaam's instigation can be read as a way for Balaam to finally manage to curse Israel by separating the nation from its God (Walton and Walton 2017, 48–49). From this framework, the text does not view the women as noncombatants but rather as participants in Israel's downfall. At least a portion of these women "seduced the Israelite men into orgiastic adultery as well as Baal worship" (Copan 2011, 180). At the very least, it indicates that the punishment meted out here was not arbitrary.[5] It is also noteworthy that the concept of collective identity applies to Israel as well. This is evident when Achan's sin prompted the whole of Israel to be defeated at Ai (Josh. 7:1–5) and eventually led to the destruction of his whole family (Josh. 7:6–26).

Thirdly, we should recognize the commands to enact this kind of violence

---

5   Wright's comments on the conquest of Canaan are also applicable here. "There is a huge moral difference between violence that is arbitrary and selfish and violence that is inflicted under strict control within the moral framework of punishment" (Wright 2008, 93).

are limited in time and space. Israel's purpose was to be a kingdom of priests and a holy nation, reflecting the glory of God and calling the nations to worship him (Exod. 19:3–5). To accomplish this, God promised to give Israel a land in which they were to destroy idols and revere him alone. The Israelites were to drive out foreign nations that opposed this because they were devoted to their gods and their own wicked practices (Num. 33:50–53).[6] In the words of God's promises to Abraham, the time had now come when "the iniquity of the Amorites" (Gen. 15:15 ESV) had reached completion.[7] The actions of the Midianites called that divine purpose into question by tempting the Israelites into the practices that God condemned.

However, moving beyond that specific time and place, it is important to recognize that the people of God and the promises of God are not now located in a particular geographical location. They are found wherever people confess the name of Christ. This means that there is no warrant to use violence to clear a geographical space for worshipping God, and attempts to do so in God's name should be denounced (Longman 2019, 198). Instead, believers work within their political settings so that their nation's "laws and statutes might reflect the fullness of justice, righteousness, and ethical quality that derive from the nature of God" (Cole 2000, 492). This does not fully resolve the question of divine violence in the past, but it does provide warrant for not continuing to use God's name as a cover for conquest and power.

Finally, our wrestling with these questions needs to be done from a position of humility before God. Although passages like this may "cause us to shriek with inner tension" (Allen 2012, 404), they do not give us the authority to subject God to our judgment. Our questions and concerns about divine violence spring from our image-bearing of the God who created all life. As such, they are worthy of deep reflection. However, ultimately, God's holiness requires judgment and justice on those who do not submit to him. We must tread carefully since humanity must answer to God, and not him to us.

---

6   Canaanite religion of the time appears to have celebrated the bloodthirsty attributes of warrior deities, involved immoral sexual activity, and permitted child sacrifice (Lev. 18:21). Scripture makes it clear that these practices cannot coexist in space where YHWH is to be worshipped, and failure to express full devotion to YHWH brings serious consequences (Judg. 2:1–5). This sets the stage of Israel's interactions with the Midianites, and later the Canaanites at the end of their wilderness sojourn (Copan 2011, 159–60).

7   It is worth noting that it was possible for non-Israelites to avoid destruction by submitting to YHWH's authority. Rahab (Josh. 2:9–11) provides the most striking example, but faithful Caleb is identified as a Kenizzite (Num. 32:12), a people-group whose land God promised to Israel (Gen. 15:19). His family appears to have been brought into the tribe of Judah (cf. Num. 13:6; 34:19). The Gibeonites submit to Israel, though not specifically to YHWH, and are spared destruction but reduced to servitude (Joshua 9). Later, the piety of Uriah the Hittite was even used to put David to shame (2 Sam. 11:11).

War with the Midianites (31:1–54)

Regulations for Purification (31:19–24)

31:19–20. The final element of the first panel concerns the reentry of the soldiers into the Israelite camp. It builds upon the regulations established in Numbers 19:16–19 for purity after encountering a dead body. These include ceremonial washing with the mixture containing the ashes of the red cow on the third and seventh days. Regular purification did not require expulsion from the camp, presumably because contact with the dead body was inadvertent or had already happened within the camp (Cole 2000, 499). However, a military engagement outside the camp would lead nearly every member of the fighting force to encounter dead bodies. Since this happened in Midianite territory, purifying the unclean outside the boundaries of Israel's sanctified encampment is wise. Notably, the requirement for purification applies to all of the fighters, the remaining captives, every garment, along with everything made from animal skin, goat hair, or wood. Thus, both bodies and everything covering them had to undergo this process.

31:21–23. Eleazar the high priest then breaks in with additional regulations. As Moses ends his tenure as Israel's leader, the priestly voice comes more to the forefront (Gane 2004, 770). Here, Eleazar relays instructions from God given to Moses that require an additional step to the purification process for material goods and precious metal. These do not have a precursor in Numbers 19. Eleazar announces that anything that can withstand flames must "pass through the fire" (31:23 ESV) to be clean. Further, these items also had to be washed in the purification water of Numbers 19. Anything that could not withstand burning was to be cleansed in the water alone. No reason for this extra layer of purification is given, but it seems suitable to apply it to metallic objects that could withstand it (Cole 2000, 499).[8]

31:24. Eleazar concludes by restating the command to wash garments on the seventh day, which completes the purification process. Afterward, the fighters (and remaining female captives) are permitted to enter the camp.

Second Panel: Disposition of the Plunder (31:25–54)

Instructions from YHWH (31:25–30)

31:25–27. The second panel begins with instructions from God on how to divide the plunder from the Midianite conquest. Moses, along with Eleazar and the tribal leaders, were to count the captured people and animals.[9] God then instructs them to divide the spoils into two portions: one for those who went out to fight and one for the rest of the community. Since fewer than half of the Israelites participated in the campaign, their share is proportionally greater. This reflects the greater risks taken by the fighters in obeying God's commands. David institutes a similar policy in 1 Samuel 30:25, emphasizing that the whole community should benefit from victories given by YHWH (Milgrom 1990, 262).

31:28–29. God then requires an offering from each half of the plunder. This acknowledges his power in securing the victory. First, those who fought the Midianites are required to give Eleazar the high priest 1/500th of their spoils, whether people or animals. This is YHWH's portion (תְּרוּמַת יהוה), an expression also used in relationship with the ending of the Nazirite vow (Num. 6:20) and the food offerings given to the

---

8   This is the only place where fire is used in purification rituals. In other texts, purification by fire is either symbolic or eschatological (Isa. 5:6–7; Jer. 6:29; Ezek. 22:20–21; Mal. 3:2; Wright 1985, 222).

9   Numbers 31:26 uses the same idiom "lift up the head" (שְׂא אֶת רֹאשׁ) that is also used of the censuses in Numbers 1 and 26.

priests and Levites (Num. 18:8–30; Cole 2000, 502). This portion would support the priests who served under Eleazar.

31:30. God also requires an offering from the portion be given to the remaining Israelites. They were to give one-fiftieth of the plunder to the Levites who served at YHWH's sanctuary. This is roughly ten times what was required from the fighters. It recognizes that there were many more Levites than Aaronide priests. Further, it is fair that those who did not risk their lives should give more back to YHWH (Ashley 1993, 597). These offerings thus acknowledge God as the source of victory as he calls the Israelites to give a share of the plunder back to his service.

Israel's Obedience (31:31–47)
31:31. In keeping with the tenor of this chapter, Moses and Eleazar follow God's instructions. Israel has obeyed God in seeking vengeance on the Midianites, and their obedience continues as they give him his due.

31:32–35. The remainder of this subsection details the division of the plunder with mathematical precision. It demonstrates that Israel did what God required and did not withhold his portion. It first gives the totals to be divided: "675,000 sheep, 72,000 cattle, 61,000 donkeys, and 32,000 persons in all, women who had known man by lying with him" (31:32b–35 ESV). This is an incredibly vast quantity of plunder.[10] The number of animals devoted to the priests and Levites massively outstrips those given by the tribes in their initial offerings to the sanctuary (Num. 7:87–88). It even exceeds the plunder recorded by an Egyptian pharaoh in a roughly contemporaneous campaign (Cole 2009, 392).[11] It is possible that these numbers reflect hyperbolic inflation that expresses the totality of victory. Alternatively, they can be taken as is, reflecting the vast rewards available to Israel if it obeys YHWH. If this is what God gives for a punitive campaign, the Israelites should anticipate even greater bounty when they enter Canaan (Allen 2012, 407).

31:36–41. The text then looks at the portion given to the fighting men. It divides the total plunder in half (337,500 sheep, 36,000 cattle, 30,500 donkeys, 16,000 young women), then gives 1/500th of that total to YHWH through the priests. This works out to 675 sheep, seventy-two cattle, sixty-one donkeys, and thirty-two young women. The animals could join with the sanctuary herd to be used in worship. There is no statement of what became of the women but they likely performed tasks under priestly supervision and possibly eventually were married into the Israelite community (Allen 2012, 408; Ashley 1993, 598). This part of the account concludes with the declaration that Moses gave the tribute to Eleazar, just as God commanded.

31:42–47. Focus then shifts to the portion given to the rest of the Israelite community. It restates the totals of their portion and then declares that Moses gave one-fiftieth of it to the Levites. The text does not do the calculations, but this would result in the Levites receiving 6,750 sheep, 720 cattle, 610 donkeys, and 320 young women (Cole 2000, 503). These first two parts of the second panel thus provide God's instructions for the plunder and show that the Israelites obeyed.

Extension: Moses and the Army Commanders (31:48–54)
31:48–49. Moses and the commanders of the army again interact after the description of

---

10 More sheep are captured in this campaign than there are men of fighting age according to either census (Gane 2004, 770).

11 In the Karnak temple account, Pharaoh Thutmose III claimed to have captured 1,929 cattle, 2,000 goats, 20,500 sheep, and 2,503 slaves.

Israel's obedience. On this occasion, the interaction is entirely positive. The commanders acknowledge Moses's authority by referring to themselves as "your servants" (31:49a). The reason for this humility is the evidence of a miracle happening in their midst. After counting up the fighters after the campaign, the commanders learn that not a single one has been lost. This underscores YHWH's ability to protect his people and provide victory. It also throws the fears of the wicked spies and the unfaithful first generation into sharp relief (cf. Numbers 13–14). If God can give such total victory over the Midianites, then Israel should not have been afraid to enter Canaan.

31:50. In response to this miracle, the army commanders wish to make an additional offering to YHWH. The stated reason for this offering is to "make atonement for ourselves" (ESV, NET). It is unclear why atonement is needed here, although many have speculated that is on account of the census taken after the battle that God had not specifically authorized (Ashley 1993, 599–600; Cole 2000, 504; Pressler 2017, 278).[12] Further, Exodus 30:11–16 declares that a half-shekel ransom should be assigned to every Israelite counted in a census. The Israelite commanders bring an offering comprised of various items of jewelry and personal adornment that supplements the animal gifts mentioned earlier.

31:51–52. The total amount of this offering is 16,750 shekels. This is more than double what would have been required by the census regulations in Exodus.[13] The generosity of the gift matches the beneficial protection that God had provided. In this military campaign, God demonstrates his power by preserving his people, and they respond with abundant thanksgiving.

31:53–54. The passage concludes with the announcement that Moses and Eleazar brought this gold into the Tent of Meeting where it would serve as a memorial before YHWH. Its presence would be a reminder of what God had done and how Israel should respond in turn.

THEOLOGICAL FOCUS

The exegetical idea (At God's command, Israel seeks vengeance against the Midianites and shares the spoils of conquest with him) gives rise to the following theological focus: *Vengeance and victory belong to God.* The Israelites engage in battle here because God commands it. The Midianites face God's judgment because of their efforts to lead the Israelites into idolatry. God's vengeance does not stem from unjustified anger or emotional outbursts, but rather "vindicates the righteous and punishes the sinner as an essential part of his ethical, moral, and just character" (Cole 2000, 494). Moses's final song calls for rejoicing that God avenges his servants and takes vengeance on his enemies (Deut. 32:43). Similar celebrations of God's vengeance are found in the prophets. Isaiah promises divine vengeance on sinful Israelites so that Jerusalem can be restored (Isa. 1:24–26), while Jeremiah, Ezekiel, and Nahum announce God's vengeance against foreign nations including Egypt (Jer. 46:10), Edom (Ezek. 25:12–15), Philistia (Ezek. 25:15–17), and Assyria (Nah. 1:2–8). Notably, while on the run, David foreswears vengeance against Saul but asks God to redress the matter (1 Sam. 24:12–13).

The New Testament further announces that vengeance is a divine prerogative. In Romans 12:19, Paul cites Deuteronomy 32:35 and calls his audience to leave vengeance and retribution to God. Jesus institutes a similar ethic in his command not to retaliate with "eye for eye, and tooth for tooth" (Matt. 5:38). Instead, his

---

12 The classic example of the danger of an unauthorized census is found in David's actions in 2 Samuel 24:15–17.
13 If each counted Israelite required a redemption of a half shekel, then the twelve thousand fighters would require a gift of six thousand shekels (Cole 2009, 393).

followers are to turn the other cheek. God did establish the principle of talionic justice for Israel (Exod. 21:24; Lev. 24:20; Deut. 19:21). This was a means of balancing retributive actions to avoid escalating cycles of violence in individual confrontations. However, it can be argued that this teaching reflects a concession to human hardened hearts that Jesus demonstrates that "godly kindness should transcend retaliation in personal disputes" (Turner 2008, 174). The church, as an institution, can also model kindness and restraint, secure in the belief that vengeance belongs to a perfectly just God, who will bring full justice in his time.

Further, victory belongs to God. Israel's military success in this chapter is a testimony to God's power. The total absence of casualties is a clear miracle. God is portrayed as giving the victory throughout Scripture as part of his covenant commitment to Israel (Deut. 28:7). Moses and Miriam sing his praises after he drowns pharaoh in the Red Sea (Exodus 15). God brings down the walls of Jericho after Israel follows his instructions (Joshua 6) and his power sustains Israel's conquest of Canaan. God reduces the size of Gideon's army so that there can be no question that he is responsible for the victory (Judges 6–7). The angel of God defeats the Assyrian army besieging Hezekiah, preserving Jerusalem (2 Kings 19).

God's power even wins the ultimate victory over sin, evil, and death. This victory was not accomplished through military strength but by the obedience of Jesus to his Father's will, manifested at the cross. On account of this, those held captive to the ruler of this world have been released and made alive in Christ (Eph. 2:1–5). His victory is secure, as no power on earth or in the heavens is capable of separating God from his redeemed people (Rom. 8:38–39). Jesus himself is portrayed as a heavenly warrior on a white horse, trampling down the forces of evil symbolized by the great beast and his prophet (Rev. 19:11–21). Consequently, even when God's people face enemies who are more than flesh and blood (Eph. 6:12), they must remember that the victory has already been won through Christ and that they never are left reliant on their own strength.

PREACHING AND TEACHING STRATEGIES

Exegetical and Theological Significance

Before examining some of the ways that this chapter is heard in the present day, it is necessary to understand what the passage is saying. Egypt had been struck with a fearful judgment on the first Passover as an act of justice because they were killing God's firstborn son Israel (by killing the male infants). In reciprocal justice, what the Egyptians were doing to Israel was returned upon themselves. Likewise—whether our immediate intuition is to agree that this is fair or not—Midian receives the fate that they were trying to mete out upon Israel. The Midianites and Moabites were trying to curse Israel so that they could be destroyed, and when that strategy failed, they lured Israel into idolatry along with spiritual and physical adultery. In Numbers 25, the Israelites who were guilty in that event had been subjected to death through divine judgment. The text presumes that as a collective, the women of Midian were not innocent—they had been spiritual combatants who were trying to destroy the nation of Israel. Midian had been the aggressors in this war, and their desire was to eradicate the people of God. In defeating the Midianites, God protected his people from their assault. Note well, though, that earlier it was the guilty Israelites who had died for their egregious act of rebellion; now it was the Midianites who suffered the consequences for their sin. Both Israel and Midian were punished by God for what they did.

If we persist in rebellion against God, we will likewise be destroyed, for the wages of sin is death (Rom. 6:23). In one sense, the Midianites—as well as the 24,000 Israelites who died in the plague-judgment—illustrate this fundamental truth of the universe. Life is found in God, and those who sever themselves from God will die. Christ offers eternal life, and those who reject him choose to forgo life in favor of eternal death. This truth must never be preached callously, but it is part of the biblical revelation; faithful teaching requires declaring the whole counsel of God.

Preaching Idea
"Unless you repent, you too will all perish" (Luke 13:3, 5).

Contemporary Connections

What does it mean?
What does it mean that "unless you repent, you too will all perish"? This quotation is from Jesus in Luke 13:3, and he repeats it in Luke 13:5. In context, he is talking about people who had died in catastrophic ways. Rather than weigh their merits against the merits of others, Jesus denies that they were worse than anyone else, but then draws the lesson of repentance directly to the living members of his audience. If we do not repent, we will also perish. Whether Israelites in Korah's rebellion, the Hebrew men sinning at Baal Peor, the Midianite women, Balaam, the armies of Sihon and Og, or Pharaoh, if there is no repentance and faith there will be destruction.

There is no doubt that this text is challenging, but before we weigh it on the basis of our own conscience and wisdom, we need to heed the lesson of Jesus. The Midianites—and the Israelite men who sinned with them—perished because of their rebellion and sin. No one is good enough or righteous enough on their own to escape the wages of sin: "unless you repent, you too will all perish."

This text also shows us that God will fight to protect his people from those who are trying to destroy them. Earlier in Numbers, we examined the themes of God defeating his enemies and how Christ defeated all of the powers of darkness. This passage points to something essential and rooted in the gospel itself: every sinner will die. The great question is whether we will die for our own sins, or whether we will die vicariously in Christ. In union with Christ, his death is our death. His death pays for our sins, since he substitutes himself to die in our place. The death of the rebellious Israelites and Midianites is terrifying, but they died for their own sin. Jesus didn't. Jesus had no personal sins to pay for. When he died, he died for the sins of other people, taking their penalty upon himself. In Christ's death, there is life.

Is it true?
Is it true that "unless you repent, you too will all perish"? Since Jesus said this, its truth value is not up for debate. It is as applicable today as it was when he originally said those words. The Midianites had their own religion and culture; they had their god Baal. But worshiping Baal was not acceptable to the Lord God, and neither were their religious practices. Today, many people believe that as long as they believe in something, or as long as they are sincere, they will be fine with God. Jesus, however, taught very differently, as did the apostles. Today, we need to repent so that we are not numbered among those who will perish.

Now what?
When Jesus said, "unless you repent, you too will all perish," he was not advancing a philosophical proposition: he was calling people to repentance and faith. Although a legacy of fire and brimstone preaching has caused a pendulum swing in most churches to the other extreme, it is biblical to warn people judiciously of God's wrath. If you have any doubt about this, look up the word "wrath" in any concordance of a good Bible translation. The concept is found throughout Scripture; the inspired writers did not shy away from it.

Creativity in Presentation

We cannot compromise fidelity to the text, but we also need incredible sensitivity to our cultural context in preaching this passage. This may be a time to engage in some level of apologetics, but apologetics must be done with both competence and compassion. Triumphalistic apologetics, insensitivity, and *schadenfreude* must be completely absent from preaching this kind of text. For a helpful resource that frames many of the issues in a reasonable way, Paul Copan's book *Is God a Moral Monster?* is a fair place to start.

Nevertheless, a sermon is not an exercise in apologetics, and an exposition of this text should not be focused on defending God's actions here. This passage may be better suited for a time when discussion and critical reflection on the issues it raises can be accommodated (like an adult Sunday school class or seminar). It may even be worth having a special night where the pastor engages in a discussion of the "hard texts of Scripture" (or brings in a speaker who is competent and trustworthy in these areas). One word of warning: bad answers to such questions do more harm than good. Such conversations require the speaker to avoid both inconsiderate triumphalism on one hand, and embarrassment about what is in Scripture on the other.

So, the preacher should not duck the issues that will occur to the contemporary hearer, but the preacher has the job of moving people from the text to the need for repentance and faith in Christ. That God will defeat his enemies is one theme, and that God will give his people the victory is the other side of the coin. Victory ultimately comes through *Christus victor*, so turn from sin and turn to the living God through faith in Jesus Christ.

It is worth reemphasizing that in approaching this text, the preacher must demonstrate tremendous sensitivity. Some may have experienced war and personal traumas. Some may have committed violent acts that they now regret in the service of their country. Some may hear this text as a confirmation of the Bible's inherent bloodthirstiness and unsuitability to a modern age. Some may have grown up in the church, but passages like this have led them to rethink their faith and question the goodness of God. Some self-righteous types may be pleased with themselves and see this text as a foretaste of God "giving all those people what they deserve in hell." The presence of these, and undoubtedly many other perspectives in the congregation, means that there cannot be a one-size-fits-all approach. Be open to the cues given in your specific context and be willing to hear the concerns and questions of your people with grace and humility.

Finally, as Paul instructed Timothy, the expositor must "Preach the word" (2 Tim. 4:2 NIV) even when it is challenging and uncomfortable. Defending a text and preaching a text are not identical exercises. Apologetics can be a component part of a sermon, but a defense of the text is not the same as preaching its message. Although the specifics of this text are deeply challenging, ultimately it reminds its hearers that "Unless you repent, you too will all perish" (Luke 13:3, 5).

One possible outline for approaching this text could be:

- God can authorize vengeance on those who wrong his people (31:1–12).

- Those who entice people into sin face judgment (31:13–18).

- The impurity of death must be cleansed before entering God's presence (31:19–22).

- Offering a portion of the plunder back to God is a reminder that God gives the victory (31:23–47).

- God is capable of miraculously preserving his people (31:48–54).

DISCUSSION QUESTIONS

1. What challenges do we face when wrestling with violent texts in Scripture? What considerations should we keep in mind as we put chapters like this into our understanding of the character of God?

2. How does this chapter serve as an example of how Israel's entry into the Promised Land should have gone?

3. If someone came to you and said something like "passages like this are why I cannot accept that God is good or that the Bible is true," how would you respond?

Numbers 32:1–42

EXEGETICAL IDEA
Tribes that wish to claim an inheritance in the Transjordan region must help their fellow Israelites conquer the Promised Land.

THEOLOGICAL FOCUS
God's people should sacrificially serve their community.

PREACHING IDEA
God's people must be united and work in harmony.

PREACHING POINTERS
In the lens of biblical history, this text marks an important transition. Incredibly, what seems like a threat to the unity of the nation is turned into a unifying event, and what seems like a potential division actually turns into an expansion of their territory. This chapter represents a wise leadership handling a sensitive situation, and an amazing gift of the grace of God. Even though the tribes of Israel will occupy unique geographic locations, they must all work together, serving and helping each other in the conquest of the land. They may be spread out in one way, but they must be united in their God-given tasks.

When we receive the gifts of God's grace, they are not to be used to promote laziness or self-indulgence. Spiritual gifts are given to individuals so that they can work hard to edify others. In the church, the unity of the body of Christ is essential, and maintaining and strengthening that unity must be a priority. We must serve others and ride together side by side along the paths where God calls us to go. Until we all receive our inheritance, God's people must be united and work in harmony.

THE TRANSJORDANIAN TRIBES (32:1–42)

LITERARY STRUCTURE AND THEMES

Numbers 32 addresses a potential complication in Israel's entry into the Promised Land. The tribes of Gad and Reuben, later joined by half of the tribe of Manasseh (32:33, 39–42) express a desire to remain east of the Jordan River.[1] This prompts a harsh response from Moses, and a back-and-forth dialogue ensues. The structure of the text is established by the shifts in speaker. It begins with the request from the Gadites and Reubenites (32:1–5), followed by Moses's initial response (32:6–15). The Gadites and Reubenites propose a compromise (32:16–19), which Moses amends slightly (32:20–24). The Gadites and Reubenites accept Moses's revisions (32:25–27), and so Moses brings this proposal to Israel's tribal leaders (32:28–32). The text then concludes with a general survey of the land granted to these tribes (32:33–42).

One key theme from this passage is identity. What does it mean to be an Israelite outside of the anticipated boundaries of the Promised Land? Does this request betray a lack of commitment from the Transjordanian tribes to YHWH and his promises for Israel? Although the text lands in a place of tribal harmony, this potential geographical division has ongoing repercussions (cf. Josh. 22:8–34; Judg. 12:4–6). A related theme is sacrificial service. The Transjordanian tribes begin by looking out for their own interests. However, through Moses's cajoling, they recall their responsibilities to their fellow Israelites and agree to put the needs of the whole community above their own.

- *The Request (32:1–5)*
- *Moses's Response (32:6–15)*
- *The Gadites and Reubenites Offer a Compromise (32:16–19)*
- *Moses Amends the Compromise (32:20–24)*
- *The Gadites and Reubenites Accept Moses's Revisions (32:25–27)*
- *Moses Brings the Proposal to Israel's Tribal Leaders (32:28–32)*
- *The Division of the Land (32:33–42)*

EXPOSITION

After the defeat of the Midianites in the previous chapter removed an external threat, an internal complication arises. God has promised to give Israel the land he promised to its forefathers, but now the Gadites, Reubenites, and half of the Manassehites appear to spurn it. These tribes wish to claim land that comes from victories won with God's power against Sihon and Og (Num. 21:23–35). This provides some justification for their request. However, Moses's reaction suggests that it reflects poorly on these tribes. Through dialogue and discussion, the parties achieve a compromise that both secures tribal unity and gives these tribes the land they desire: the tribes that wish to claim an inheritance in the Transjordan region must first help their fellow Israelites conquer the Promised Land.

The Request (32:1–5)

32:1. The story begins with the declaration that the Gadites and Reubenites possessed significant herds and flocks and have seen "that the lands of Jazer and Gilead were ideal for cattle"

---

[1] This region is known as the Transjordan, while the Promised Land itself is the Cisjordan.

(NET). This refers to land in the northern Transjordan that possessed "highland grassy regions for grazing" and "valleys and hillsides suitable for grain and fruit orchards" (Cole 2009, 393). It no doubt made a stark contrast to the arid regions through which Israel had been wandering.

32:2–4. These tribes then come before Moses, Eleazar, and the leaders of the community with their request. They introduce it by mentioning a number of locations within the broader region, and repeat the claim that they are suitable for livestock. They further acknowledge that this is land that YHWH has subdued for Israel (32:4). This is a theologically correct assessment of who is responsible for Israel's military success.

32:5. This leads to the request itself. It begins with "If we have found favor in your eyes" (NIV), a common entreaty formula attested in other diplomatic correspondence from the ancient Near East (Cole 2009, 395). Their desire is for this land to be given to them as a possession (לַאֲחֻזָּה). This is the same term used in Numbers 27:5 for the request of the daughters of Zelophehad (Levine 2000, 486). It indicates that these tribes seek their permanent inheritance outside of the expected borders of the Promised Land.

This first statement of the request can be read as neutral. The Gadites and Reubenites acknowledge that YHWH has permitted them to conquer this region and ask to settle there. However, the final statement in 32:5b is problematic: "Do not make us cross the Jordan" (NIV). Although this could simply reflect a desire to settle where they are, it also suggests that these tribes do not wish to participate in the upcoming campaign against the Canaanites west of the Jordan (Ashley 1993, 608; Pressler 2017, 285).

Moses's Response (32:6–15)

32:6–7. Moses's response begins with a pair of incredulous questions, first asking "Must your brothers go to war while you remain here?" (32:6 NET). He accuses them of deserting the tribal alliance right as the conquest is supposed to begin. Secondly, Moses asks why these tribes would discourage their brothers from going to the land that God has given them.[2] Perhaps seeing the Gadites and Reubenites claim territory with no further conflict would prompt the other tribes to make similar requests. Moses's response may be colored by his memory of the rebellion against his leadership led by the Reubenites Dathan and Abiram in Numbers 16 (Gane 2004, 784).

32:8–9. Moses elevates the potential negative consequences of this request by comparing it to the report of the spies in Numbers 13–14. Upon viewing the Promised Land, they discouraged the rest of the Israelites by declaring that the inhabitants were too strong to overcome.[3] The Gadites and Reubenites have not attempted to directly dissuade the other tribes, but granting their request may open up an alternative to crossing the Jordan. Again, the land that YHWH has given to Israel lies just across the river. After forty years of wandering, Moses is extremely sensitive to anything that could derail God's intentions.

32:10–13. Moses continues his history lesson, recalling that God's anger came against Israel, leading to a lingering death sentence upon all of the men twenty years and older (except for Caleb and Joshua). The generation that came out of Egypt would not see the fulfillment of God's promises to Israel's forefathers: Abraham, Isaac, and Jacob (32:11). Instead, YHWH made Israel wander in the wilderness until that whole generation perished.

---

2   The verbal root translated as "discourage" in 32:7 is נוא. It is also found in Numbers 30:5, 8 in the discussion of overriding vows made by women. The nuance is slightly different here, since the Gadites and Reubenites have no authority over the other tribes.

3   Again, the root נוא is used.

32:14–15. Moses's speech returns to the present. He addresses the Gadites and Reubenites in harsh terms, comparing them to the previous generation and calling them "a brood of sinners" (32:14 NET, NIV). The word translated "brood" (תַּרְבּוּת) is unique in biblical literature but is probably derived from the root I-רבה, which sometimes means "to rear/raise children" in the piel stem (Levine 2000, 488). Here, its sense is clearly pejorative. Moses then issues a dire warning: if these tribes turn away from YHWH by pursuing this plan, YHWH will abandon Israel. The Gadites and Reubenites would then bear the responsibility for the destruction of the nation. This is the "hidden horror in Numbers" (Allen 2012, 416). God's plan of redemption through his covenant with Israel could be derailed again by human disobedience. The spy episode is thus a "paradigmatic narrative" that can be used to warn the next generation (Artus 2013, 375).[4] The potential consequences reflect another example of collective responsibility in Numbers. The deleterious actions of two tribes threaten the entire nation.[5]

The Gadites and Reubenites Offer a Compromise (32:16–19)

32:16. The Gadites and Reubenites respond to Moses's invective by offering a compromise. First, they wish to construct pens (גְּדֵרֹת) for their livestock. These would likely be "V shaped stone enclosures" used to protect animals from various threats (Cole 2009, 395). They also want to build cities (עָרִים), defensible locations for the noncombatants to inhabit.

TRANSLATION ANALYSIS
Those who will remain in the cities are identified as "our little ones" (טַפֵּנוּ). The noun טַף typically refers to children but contextually here it must include the women who would care for the children. English translations either use the literal translation "little ones" (ESV, KJV, NASB, NKJV) or a more dynamic translation such as "women and children" (NIV), "wives and children" (NLT), "families" (NET), or "dependents (CSB).

32:17. Once the animals and noncombatants have some measure of protection, the Gadite and Reubenite fighters will "take up arms, ready to go before the people of Israel" (32:17 ESV). This phrasing suggests more than just a willingness to participate. Rather, the Gadites and Reubenites volunteer to lead Israel's armies in their conquest of Canaan (Ashley 1993, 611; Cole 2000, 510; Milgrom 1990, 493).[6] This reflects a full commitment to help the remaining tribes secure the territory God has promised. Joshua 4:13 declares that forty thousand men from these tribes crossed the Jordan, which reflects approximately a third of their fighting strength from the census in Numbers 26. The remaining fighters presumably defended the livestock and noncombatants. This arrangement apparently was acceptable, given the hearty commendation that Joshua offers at the end of the campaign (Josh. 22:1–5).

---

4 Artus writes from a critical perspective that views 32:7–15 as a postexilic addition to the text "aimed at preventing the disobedience of the next generations of the Jews within the Promised Land as well as in the diaspora" (Artus 2013, 375). However, it can also be profitably read as Moses's own words that have continuing relevance as they are remembered and transmitted throughout Israel's history.
5 There is a kind of symmetry between this narrative and the account of the spies in Numbers 13–14. Here, the evaluation of two tribes is negative while the other ten are presumably positive. In the spy story, ten spies were negative while two were positive (Milgrom 1990, 268).
6 Some commentators try to put this level of commitment to leading the attacks into their translation of the phrase וַאֲנַחְנוּ נֵחָלֵץ ("we will take up arms" [ESV]). They use the expression "shock-troops" to capture it (Marquis 2013, 423–24; Milgrom 1990, 270).

32:18–19. The tribes continue to display their willingness to participate. They promise not to return to the land they desire until all Israel has received its inheritance. Further, they guarantee that they will not seek further inheritance in the Cisjordan, alleviating concerns that they would seek additional rewards for their efforts. Their inheritance from God will be in the Transjordan and they will be satisfied with it.

This compromise dramatically shifts the situation. It is unclear whether the Gadites and Reubenites actually intended to abandon the rest of Israel (though "do not make us cross the Jordan" in 32:5 is suggestive!), but their willingness to participate in the conquest of Canaan avoids the worst-case scenario.

Moses Amends the Compromise (32:20–24)
32:20–22. Moses responds to this proposal with two minor amendments. He invokes the name of YHWH five times in order to make this a sacred commitment (32:20, 21, 22 [3x]). He also uses language that recalls covenant stipulations by adding a curse for noncompliance to go along with the blessing for participation (Cole 2009, 395; Milgrom 1990, 271). He begins with the blessing. If the tribes participate in battle and "cross over the Jordan before the Lord" (32:21 NIV), they will receive the land that they desire. Further, they will be "free of obligation to the Lord and to Israel" (32:22 ESV). This phrase reflects a fulfillment of military service (cf. Deut 24:5) and here also suggests that the tribes have discharged their responsibilities (Ashley 1993, 613).

32:23–24. Moses also adds a curse for failing to uphold their obligations. If the tribes do not cross over, they have sinned against God, and he warns them "be sure your sin will find you out" (32:23 ESV). This is reminiscent of the warning given to Cain in Genesis 4:7, where sin crouched at his door. Sin is thus personified as an entity that will track down the guilty (Ashley 1993, 613). Moses thus ensures that the tribes know that there are serious, though unspecified, consequences if they fail to honor their pledge. He concludes with language repeated from 32:16, instructing the tribes to build their cities and sheep pens but then fulfill their commitments.

The Gadites and Reubenites Accept Moses's Revisions (32:25–27)
32:25. The prospective Transjordanian tribes accept Moses's requirements. They position themselves under his authority, calling themselves "your servants" (עֲבָדֶיךָ) and addressing Moses as "my lord" (אֲדֹנִי).[7]

32:26–27. They then restate their commitments. They will leave behind their livestock and families, and their fighting men will cross the Jordan River to fight in YHWH's service. The crisis has been averted. The Israelite tribal coalition remains intact; the people have not departed from God's commands.

Moses Brings the Proposal to Israel's Tribal Leaders (32:28–32)
32:28. The negotiations between the Reubenites, Gadites, and Moses then need to be ratified by the larger Israelite community. Moses brings the arrangement to Eleazar the high priest, Joshua (Moses's successor), and the leaders of the tribes. Their anticipated affirmation provides a final seal of approval.

32:29–30. As before, Moses presents the arrangement with both positive and negative framing. Positively, if the Reubenites and Gadites cross the Jordan and fight until the land is subdued and brought under Israel's control, then the other tribes must grant them their desired regions in the Transjordan (32:29). This makes

---

7 The suffix here is singular even though the speakers are a collective whole. This perhaps reflects the Transjordanian tribes speaking with one voice (Milgrom 1990, 272).

acquiring their desired land contingent upon total commitment to Israel's victory. Negatively, if they do not cross the Jordan prepared to fight, they will not receive their requested inheritance. Instead, they will have to take an inheritance with their fellow Israelites across the Jordan.

The negative consequence here is different than the rest of the passage. It is much less threatening than the total destruction of the nation suggested in 32:15 or the ominous warning that their sin will find them (32:23). Some have used this to suggest that this chapter is the combination of multiple sources (Marquis 2013, 411). However, it also reflects the covenantal framing established in the previous verses. The threat of utter destruction came in response to the initial request not to cross the Jordan, but now that the Gadites and Reubenites have announced their intentions to cross, that threat has dissipated. Consequently, Moses reduces the punishment. If their fighters do not cross willingly, the whole of Gad and Reuben will be forced (presumably by the other tribes) to cross the Jordan and settle on the western side (Cole 2000, 514).

32:31–32. The Reubenites and Gadites affirm their commitment one more time. They will cross into Canaan armed for battle. In return, they will inherit the land they desire.

The Division of the Land (32:33–42)

32:33. The chapter concludes as Moses awards land to the Transjordanian tribes. This anticipates the fulfillment of their pledge since Israel did not cross the Jordan until after his death. These initial land claims come from territory acquired when Israel defeated the Sihon and Og in conflicts that began when Sihon would not grant Israel peaceful passage through his territory (Num. 21:21–35).

An unexpected development in this verse is the appearance of the half-tribe of Manasseh. They also receive an inheritance in the Transjordan and are typically attested as a Transjordanian tribe (Deut. 3:12–15; 4:43; 29:7–8; Josh. 12:6; 13:29). Their presence is discussed further in 32:39–42.

32:34–36. The text then lists the places in which the Gadites settled. Although it claims that they "built" (וַיִּבְנוּ) these locations, contextually it makes more sense that they rebuilt or fortified them after capturing them. Their territory consisted of "a narrow strip of land in the Jordan River plain extending from the Jabbok River to the Sea of Galilee" (Cole 2009, 395; cf. Josh. 13:24–28).

32:37–38. The Reubenites settled in the territory south of the Gadites, including Heshbon, the former capital of Sihon (Num. 21:26; cf. Josh. 13:15–23). This suggests that they have staked a strong claim to the region.

32:39–42. The text concludes with the Manassehites, who have been mostly absent from this story. It declares that the Makirites, one of major clans of Manasseh, defeated and drove out the Amorites of Gilead (32:39). This may not have happened at the same time as the defeat of Sihon and Og, but since this portion of Manasseh settled in the Transjordan, the text recounts this episode here (Ashley 1993, 617). The region of Gilead is well attested as an Israelite possession throughout the Old Testament (Deut. 34:1; Josh. 17:1; Judg. 10:8; 2 Sam. 2:9), with occasion reference made to the fruitfulness of the area (Song 6:5; Jer. 8:22; 46:11).

As the narrative concludes, harmony has been restored among the Israelite tribes. Moses has approved the request of the Transjordanian tribes on the condition that they fully participate in the conquest of Canaan so that their fellow Israelites can lay claim to the land that YHWH has promised.

THEOLOGICAL FOCUS

The exegetical idea (Tribes that wish to claim an inheritance in the Transjordan region must help their fellow Israelites conquer the Promised

Land) points to the following theological focus: *God's people should sacrificially serve their community*. The presentation of this story suggests that the Transjordanian tribes were first looking out for themselves rather than considering the well-being of the entire community. Even if Moses responded more harshly than the situation warranted, he rightly noted how pursuing selfish interests could take Israel away from God's intentions (Sprinkle 2015, 404). Further, the settlement of these tribes beyond the Jordan introduced a potential fracture point among the Israelite tribes. Although these tribes are commended for their service (Josh. 22:1–5), their geographical displacement from the rest of Israel threatened to devolve into civil war (Josh. 22:10–34) and is the subject of mixed evaluations (Wray Beal 2017, 466–68).[8]

This theme of sacrificial service applies to Israel's leaders. When Samuel rebukes Israel for asking for a king, he warns the people that their king will take from them, enriching himself at their expense (1 Sam. 8:10–18). Even David, the shepherd-king, who comes onto the scene risking his life for YHWH's name and for the preservation of Israel, succumbs to the temptation to put his own desires and lusts above service to his people. This trajectory continues through the reign of Solomon his son, whose commitment to God was less than total (1 Kings 11:4, 6). He greatly enriched himself at the expense of the rest of the kingdom, eventually leading to an irreparable division (Stubbs 2009, 236).

As the church begins its ministry as God's people, Paul strongly calls it to sacrificial service. In Philippians 2:3–4, he calls the believers to "Do nothing out of selfish ambition or vain conceit. Rather, in humility value others above yourselves, not looking to your own interests but each of you to the interests of others" (NIV). Similarly, in Romans 12:10, he calls his audience to be "devoted to one another in love. Honor one another above yourselves" (NIV). This manifests itself in further virtues such as patience, joy, and sharing with those in need (Rom. 12:11–12). The metaphor of the body in 1 Corinthians 12 is also appropriate here. The whole of the people of God must work together without pride, jealousy, or selfish desires for the body to function as it should. Just like Israel's tribes could not pursue their own aims without weakening the whole nation, so the head, hands, and feet of the church body must submit and serve each other.

The ultimate exemplar of self-sacrificial service is of course found in Christ. Jesus did not stand on his innate equality with God but humbled himself to become a servant and die a criminal's death so that God's people may achieve the promise of an eternal dwelling (Phil. 2:6–8). In washing his disciples' feet, Jesus further modeled the expectations he placed upon his followers (John 13:12–14). The people of God must emulate this commitment to the well-being of our brothers and sisters, even at the expense of our own desires and comforts.

PREACHING AND TEACHING STRATEGIES

Exegetical and Theological Significance

There are a surprising number of theological and pragmatic principles in this text. In

---

8   The Joshua 22 story is fascinating. Upon returning home, the Transjordanian tribes set up an altar where they crossed the Jordan. The Cisjordan tribes view it as potentially idolatrous and mount a punitive expedition, led by Phinehas who is known for his zealotry (Josh. 22:13). The Transjordanian tribes plead innocence, claiming that the intention of the altar was to remind the other nine-and-a-half tribes that they still belong to Israel even though they have settled across the Jordan (Josh. 22:26–28). The situation is resolved amicably but reveals the underlying tension in the choices of the Transjordanian tribes.

an analogous way to how Israel is going to straddle the Jordan in their settlements, this text has one foot in the past and one foot in the future. It occupies an important and transitional location in biblical history. Promises are about to be fulfilled, but past rebellions and judgments remind the people that individuals can still forfeit the blessings of God.

The text contains lessons in leadership and flexibility. It shows the importance of unity among God's people and the necessity of serving others. It reminds us that sins of omission are equally deadly. In God's eyes, if certain tribes had failed to help Israel conquer the Promised Land, their passivity and inaction would have constituted treason.

What is crucial for Israel is that they remain united, even if they are physically and geographically separated by the Jordan. Amazingly, God gifts his people with even more land than what was promised in Canaan; his grace overflows. Gifts of grace are not to be taken and turned to lazy, selfish ends. Receiving the rich land in the Transjordan expands the territory of the nation, but the ones who settle in it are just as responsible to do the hard work that their compatriots are called to do.

Israel, like the church, is to function as a whole. There are different members, but they all must work together. No one is to put their feet up until everyone has received their allotted inheritance.

Preaching Idea
God's people must be united and work in harmony.

Contemporary Connections

What does it mean?
What does it mean that God's people must be united and work in harmony? It is important to realize that the success of Israel—like the success of the church—is not due to their natural wisdom, strength, and virtue. God is the one who must do the work, and the victory belongs to him. Nevertheless, his people are to cooperate with him, follow his instructions, and walk in faith. They are to fight the battle, trusting God with the outcome.

In the local church, Paul's analogy of the body applies. There are different members, and each must work together for the good of the whole organism. If different parts of the body go to war with each other, they will destroy themselves in destroying one another. If there is a battle to fight and one leg refuses to walk into the fray, the entire body is compromised. God calls his people to walk in his power and see him accomplish great things, but it is our responsibility to walk *together*. If we do not act to keep each other safe, and if we do not ride out side by side to battle together, we are not doing God's will.

To help forge a contemporary connection, one song that memorably and movingly expresses the feeling that goes with people standing together come what may, is Lord Huron's "Brother." It is an excellent expression of part of the ethos of this text, conveyed in contemporary language. If you need to stand with someone you love through a time when you're facing dragons, listen to this together. It can help steel resolve and express commitment. It breathes of *phileo* ("brotherly love"), and sometimes we need to breathe together with those we love so that we have mutual strength for the uncertain days that lie ahead. What we can know for sure is that we have each other's backs when we have each other in our hearts.

Is it true?
Is it true that God's people must be united and work in harmony together? Two instructions from Paul are very helpful when it comes to this principle.

"Let all things be done for edification" (1 Cor. 14:26 NIV). The first verse is given in the context of spiritual gifts and the function of the body. Spiritual gifts are given to us so that we can serve others in love. In love, the giving and receiving are part of a mutual, beautiful spiral. Similarly, Paul calls his audience to "Make every effort to keep the unity of the Spirit through the bond of peace" (Eph. 4:3 NIV). This is an interesting verse. The unity is objective, created by the Spirit in Christ. Our job is to keep that unity intact, tied securely in peace.

Israel in Numbers 32 provides a real, historical example of this principle. God in grace may give special gifts to certain tribes or people, but that unique gift does not exempt them from service. In fact, quite the opposite is true. Those who receive special gifts from God have a great responsibility to respond with humility and service for the common good.

Now what?

Nobody today stands at the end of a retributive wilderness wandering, ready to go into the Promised Land and receive their tribal allotment of land. Today, the people of God—the church of Jesus Christ—is transnational, transgeographic, translinguistic, and transcultural. Nevertheless, the church around the world is to be united in the gospel of Jesus Christ, in the power of the Spirit, and in their relationship to God the Father. At the local level, churches are to demonstrate union with Christ and unity with each other. As Israel needed all of the tribes working together, so the church needs every member of the body to care for and edify one another.

Since we live with sin, fractures develop in relationships. We all know of churches that have had horrific internecine conflicts that have torn them apart. Church splits are common—why not church healings? Some may need to repent of their selfishness and sinful disregard of the needs of others. Some may need to acknowledge that they have put self ahead of the good of God's people. If anyone has "settled in the Transjordan" without helping their brothers and sisters in the tasks they've been given, it is time to roll up their sleeves and get to work.

Creativity in Presentation

There are a variety of ways in which these principles can be illustrated. Paul himself provides the very memorable (and comic) picture of what life would be like if the whole body were an eye or an ear (1 Cor. 12:17). It is not hard to imagine what life would be like if the body was at war with itself. (There are actually some medical conditions where this is a reasonably accurate depiction of what is happening in the subject's body. Some of these conditions could be used as examples, but only with great tact and sensitivity.)

Depending on the country and the cultural, historical context, there may be events that are part of the cultural fabric that can be used as illustrations. In America, the Civil War is one such reality. The principle that a house divided against itself cannot stand is intuitively obvious and also very powerful. One could also draw an illustration from the realm of athletics, talking about what happens when certain team members are more interested in padding their own stats than in sacrificing for the good of the whole.

Focusing on the threat of disunity, however, would distort the significance of this passage. This text does show a threat to Israel's unity, but that threat was overcome. The outcome of this chapter is actually very positive and encouraging. A potential crisis was diverted, unity maintained, and the people worked together to do God's will.

It is common knowledge that projects like the pyramids or Gothic cathedrals took incredibly large numbers of coordinated workers, as well as brilliant engineers and architects who rolled up their sleeves and envisioned something incredible. Teamwork is necessary in all kinds of areas of life, including business, sports, and community-building. The preacher may be able to draw on local examples of how teamwork and cooperation have benefitted their church or community. This principle of unity and service applies in the church, and without working together the body will be unhealthy and unproductive. Whether you are the project manager or the intern sharpening pencils, everyone has a role to play. God's people must be united and work in harmony.

One possible outline for expositing this text could be:

- God's people cannot put selfish desires ahead of the good of the community (32:1–15).

- Submission to God's will brings unity (32:16–33).

- God can graciously extend his promises if he so desires (32:34–42).

DISCUSSION QUESTIONS

1. Should the request from the Gadites and Reubenites be read as neutral or negative? What evidence does the text provide for either alternative?

2. Why does Moses foresee such dire consequences coming from this request?

3. What can we learn from the responses of the Gadites and Reubenites to Moses's concerns?

4. How do we combat the temptation to put our own interests ahead of the good of our faith community? What forms of sacrificial service can we engage in?

Numbers 33:1–49

EXEGETICAL IDEA
Moses preserves the account of Israel's journey.

THEOLOGICAL FOCUS
God's people endure because of his sustaining presence.

PREACHING IDEA
Every believer has a path on which God leads them through their pilgrimage.

PREACHING POINTERS
Having nearly completed their entire time in the wilderness, the Israelites are now told to look back on the places they have been and the things they have experienced. Some of the locations evoke the most significant events in Israel's redemptive history up to that point, whether they were good or bad. Aaron dies and is gathered to his people, ending the era of the first high priest and bearing witness to the fact that God will allow no exceptions to his decree about who would enter the Promised Land.

Remembering what happened at these locations (at least the ones we can collate with recorded events in Scripture), provides us with an extremely important hermeneutical lens for interpreting the important events in Israel's journey. Although we are not aware of the significance of many of these places, they were stopping places in Israel's wilderness wandering, and the names meant something to the people who camped there. Today, believers pass through a variety of experiences and live in a variety of places, and every person has their own life's journey. As believers, it can be very helpful to look back on the key events of our lives, to see what God has brought us through, and to prepare ourselves for his continued leading in the future. We will not recapitulate the route of Israel, but every believer has a path on which God leads them through their pilgrimage.

THE WILDERNESS JOURNEY
(33:1–49)

LITERARY STRUCTURE AND THEMES

The account of the Transjordanian tribes leads into an itinerary of Israel's travels through the wilderness. Israel's arrival on the Plains of Moab provides the opportunity to recount the stages of its journey (Sprinkle 2015, 406). This is incredibly difficult ground for an expositor since the text consists largely of place names, many of which are not mentioned anywhere else. Forty-two locations are mentioned in total, and no obvious structural arrangement is evident. Some propose dividing them into six cycles of seven names, which is reasonable given the significance of seven in Hebrew patterns (Cole 2009, 396–98; Wenham 2008, 243).[1] Since seven often signifies completion, this arrangement is one cycle short. Presumably, it anticipates the future entry and conquest of the Promised Land. This suggestion is plausible and will be used to frame the discussion of the text, but it remains speculative.[2]

The underlying theme of the text is God's presence with Israel. At God's command, Moses recorded these stages of journey (33:2). God receives credit for delivering Israel from Egypt (33:3–4) and is mentioned as the text recalls the death of Aaron (33:38–39). God decreed that Israel would wander for forty years. This itinerary confirms that it did, with the understanding that God never abandoned the people.

- *Cycle 1 (33:1–10)*
- *Cycle 2 (33:11–17)*
- *Cycle 3 (33:18–24)*
- *Cycle 4 (33:25–31)*
- *Cycle 5 (33:32–41)*
- *Cycle 6 (33:42–49)*

EXPOSITION

This preaching unit is highly repetitious, consisting mostly of the verbs "they left" (וַיִּסְעוּ) and "they camped" (וַיַּחֲנוּ). A few expansions can be found in this list, noting significant events. The text marks the progression of Israel's march from Egypt to the eastern side of the Jordan River, just across from the Promised Land. With this list, Moses preserves the account of Israel's journey for posterity.

> **Israel's Journey Through the Wilderness**
> A challenging question that emerges from this chapter is how closely it accords with historical events. In terms of genre, it compares with Egyptian and Assyrian travel itineraries that often listed conquered cities to celebrate the power of a ruler, or listed economic activity to track the accumulation of wealth (Cole 2009, 396). Another scholar identifies itineraries as "archival documents," describing royal campaigns which lends a certain level of historical credence (Davies 1983, 9). However, such historical parallels do not necessarily guarantee reliability. Roskop argues that the ancient itinerary genre moved beyond

---

1 Stubbs divides the place names into seven cycles of six names. This reflects a view that this stage of Israel's journey is complete. It is now in a period of rest before entry into the Promised Land (Stubbs 2009, 237).
2 Another option is to eliminate the first and last locations, yielding a total forty encampments along the way. This number also conveys a sense of completion (Allen 2012, 423).

simple reports to produce an "ideological narrative . . . that communicates the king's mastery over territory and the geographical contiguity of his empire" (Roskop 2011, 135). That is, the purpose of the itinerary genre was not to provide a straightforward record, but to communicate that the ruler had authority over the places that are mentioned. The itinerary in Numbers 33 is not the account of a ruler, but Roskop suggests that it serves a similar ideological purpose. She argues that its author sought to make this account the authoritative record of Israel's putative journey to advance a priestly agenda that the author represented (Roskop 2011, 236). It is thus of limited or no value in tracing Israel's journey. Others reflect even greater skepticism, calling the entire saga of the journey through the wilderness "a brilliant product of the human imagination" (Finkelstein and Silberman 2001, 1).

This perspective is challenging for those with an evangelical commitment to biblical authority. It also reflects a more skeptical attitude to the biblical text than to comparable ancient literature (Hoffmeier 2014, 48). Identifying this chapter as a later creation undercuts the claims in the initial declaration that YHWH instructed Moses to record this account (Num. 33:2). Further, the underlying historicity of the Exodus event and wilderness sojourn are essential for biblical theology. God's covenant with Israel is founded on the repeated refrain, "I am the Lord who brought you out of the land of Egypt" (Exod. 20:2; Lev. 19:36; Num. 15:31; Ps. 81:10). This declares that "Israel was on a real, historical, flesh-and-blood journey" (Stubbs 2009, 238). Additionally, Israel's festivals (Passover and the Feast of Booths most notably) create collective memory that looks back on its deliverance from Egypt and preservation in the wilderness for its corporate identity. Historical retrospectives, Israel's hymnody, and prophetic remembrances all build upon the reality of the exodus experience (Hoffmeier 2012, 99–134). Difficulties in identifying the place names mentioned or fitting them onto a map are not sufficient reasons to discredit its underlying historicity (Allen 2012, 423).

This commitment to the testimony of the text does not eliminate the difficulties it poses. The issues raised in tracing Israel's sojourn "are some of the most intractable that are faced by biblical scholars" (Wenham 2008, 246). Consequently, this chapter requires a great deal of interpretive humility. As mentioned above, the itinerary is likely stylized rather than comprehensive. The absence of the length of stay for each location makes it challenging to establish a precise chronology. Ultimately, the purpose of the itinerary is to ground God's provision for Israel into its recollection of its journey (Allen 2012, 423). Further discussion and study may yield new discoveries about Israel's exact course, but we take the approach that this itinerary reflects a faithful account of Israel's journey from Egypt to the Promised Land.

Cycle 1 (33:1–10)

33:1–2. A brief introduction frames the text. It declares that what follows is a list of the stages of the journey when Moses and Aaron led Israel out of Egypt. Notably, 33:2 is one of the few places where the text directly states that Moses wrote something. It declares "At the LORD's command Moses recorded all the stages in their journey" (NIV).

33:3–4. The first stage of Israel's journey is its departure from Rameses on the day after the Passover. This city is thought to be named after Rameses II, a thirteenth-century Egyptian ruler. Exodus 1:11 declares that it is a storage city built by Israelite forced labor. It may reflect scribal updating (cf. Gen. 47:11), so that Israelite audiences link the departure of their forefathers with a renowned Egyptian ruler (Cole 2009, 396).

These verses also strongly contrast the status of Israel and Egypt at this time. The Israelites depart "triumphantly" (33:3 ESV) or "defiantly" (33:3 NET, NIV). These are translations of the Hebrew idiom בְּיָד רָמָה ("with a high hand"), used in Numbers 15:30 to express flagrant sin against YHWH. Here, it demonstrates that the Israelites are no longer under Egyptian authority; they can boldly defy their former masters because YHWH has acted for them. Meanwhile, the Egyptians are engaged in burying their firstborn on account of the tenth plague. YHWH's actions "executed judgments" (33:4 ESV) against the gods of the Egyptians. This is a third-person report of YHWH's self-declaration from Exodus 12:2 (Ashley 1993, 627). Pharaoh, the earthly representative of the Egyptian deity Horus, and the rest of the pantheon have been weighed and found wanting.

33:5–6. The Israelites' journey then took them from Rameses to Succoth (33:5) and from Succoth to Etham (33:6). A brief explanation places Etham at the edge of the wilderness. This probably reflects a border region across from the Sinai wilderness (Hoffmeier 2014, 72).

33:7. In the next phase, the itinerary recalls that the Israelites "turned back" (וַיָּשָׁב) to a location called Pi Hahiroth. The reason for such a turn is unstated, but Exodus 14:2 attributes it to God's instructions. This turn most likely delayed departure from Egypt and brought Israel into more treacherous, marshy territory closer to the Nile Delta. One possibility is that God intended this move to tempt Pharaoh into pursuing Israel, thinking the nation was wandering aimlessly (Exod. 14:3–4). However, this pursuit soon led to Pharaoh's own demise (Hoffmeier 2014, 74).

33:8. The itinerary omits the account of the miraculous sea crossing, simply stating that Israel traversed it and traveled three days into the wilderness before camping at Marah. The exact location of the crossing is unknown, though reasonable speculation places it in the region of the Bitter Lakes which in ancient times could have been directly connected to the Gulf of Suez (Hoffmeier 2014, 70; Wenham 2008, 250). At Marah, God made bitter water drinkable, though that story is not recalled here (Exod. 15:23).

33:9–10. The first cycle then moves to Elim, keeping the same description of its bounty as Exodus 15:27. It concludes with an encampment at the Red Sea (יַם־סוּף). This is a rather unspecific term since it refers to a large body of water, but here must point to a location along its eastern shore where Israel stopped after escaping Egypt (Cole 2009, 396).

Cycle 2 (33:11–17)

33:11–13. This cycle begins with three further locations: the wilderness of Sin (33:11),[3]

---

[3] "Sin" here is simply a transliteration of the Hebrew word סִין. It carries no theological implications.

Dophkah (33:12), and Alush (33:13). The wilderness of Sin is where Israel received manna for the first time (Exod. 16:1–15). The other two locations are otherwise unattested.

33:14. The next location is Rephidim. Its mention here includes a brief historical note that it was one of the places where the Israelites had no water to drink (Exod. 17:1). Presumably this concise statement would prompt memory of the entire grumbling narrative that followed.

33:15. The next stop is the wilderness of Sinai. Surprisingly, there is no further elaboration on the place where Israel remained from Exodus 19 to Numbers 10.[4] The exact location of Mount Sinai is not known conclusively, but its traditional placement in the southern region of the Sinai peninsula remains the most likely option (Hoffmeier 2014, 85).

33:16–17. After Sinai, the itinerary records some places that have been mentioned in earlier narratives in Numbers. The first two are Kibroth Hattaavah (33:16) and Hazeroth (33:17). The text omits the complaint and punishment stories that occurred at these locations.[5]

Cycle 3 (33:18–24)
33:18–24. None of the locations mentioned in this cycle are attested elsewhere in Scripture and they do not have any clear geographical identification. Presumably, an ancient audience would recall them as stages of the journey undertaken by their forebearers.

Cycle 4 (33:25–31)
33:25–31. This cycle again consists mostly of unknown and otherwise unattested locations. The sixth (Moseroth in 33:30) and seventh (Bene Jaakan in 33:31) appear in Deuteronomy 10:6 as part of a brief digression in Moses's account of his reception of the Sinai covenant.

Cycle 5 (33:32–41)
33:32–35. This cycle begins with unidentified locations, though Hor Haggidgad (33:32) and Jotbathah (33:3) have parallels in Deuteronomy 10:7.[6] The next location, Abronah (33:34), is otherwise unattested. Ezion Geber (33:35) is thought to be on the eastern side of the Sinai peninsula, on the Gulf of Aqaba (Allen 2012, 428). First Kings 9:26 states that Solomon had ships built there.

33:36. The fifth location in this cycle is Kadesh. There is a distance of fifty miles between its likely location and Ebion Gezer. It could not be covered in a single march, again providing a reminder that this itinerary is not intended to be comprehensive (Milgrom 1999, 281). Kadesh plays a pivotal role in Israel's wilderness journey, although none of that is recounted here. It is typically located close to the southern border of the Promised Land. Numbers 13:26 identifies Kadesh as the place where the spies gave their disastrous report, while Deuteronomy 1:46 says that Israel remained there for many days. The accounts of Numbers place Israel at Kadesh twice, once as the launching group for the spies, then again at 20:1 at the end of the wilderness wandering. It is hard to reconcile this with an itinerary that only lists Kadesh once. Does 33:26 reflect Israel's first or second encampment at Kadesh? Some commentators associate it with the first (Allen 2012, 428; Wenham 2008, 254), while others connect it to the second (Cole 2009, 398; Gane 2004, 786; Sprinkle 2015, 409).

---

[4] Further, the fact that Sinai falls in the middle of this second cycle, rather than at a beginning or end point is a reminder of the speculative nature of this proposed framing.

[5] Kibroth Hattaavah is where the Israelites complained about manna, leading to a devastating plague (Num. 11:33–34), while Hazeroth is the place where Miriam and Aaron challenged Moses's leadership (Num. 12:1–16).

[6] Hor Haggidgad is identified with Gudgodah in Deuteronomy 10:7.

Conclusive resolution of this issue is unlikely, though it is suggestive that the next location mentioned is Mount Hor (33:38) where Aaron died in the fortieth year of wandering. This points to the second encampment which means that the itinerary omits Israel's first sojourn.[7]

33:37–40. The mention of Mount Hor comes with a couple of historical notes. First, Aaron died at the age of 123 (33:39). This indicates that the itinerary has reached the final year of wandering. Further, there is a brief mention of the Canaanite king of Arad whom Israel defeated in Numbers 21:1–3.

33:41. The final location in this cycle is Zalmonah. It is otherwise unattested.

Cycle 6 (33:42–49)

33:42–43. The final cycle reflects Israel's journey around Edom and Moab until it reaches its staging ground across the Jordan River from Jericho. Punon (33:42) is otherwise unattested, but Oboth (33:43) is mentioned in 21:10 and is likely near Moabite territory (Allen 2012, 432).

33:44–47. The remaining places on the itinerary can be identified with the Transjordan region. Iye Abarim (33:44) is mentioned in the account of Israel's journey around Moab in 21:11.

33:48–49. This cycle concludes with Israel on the Plains of Moab. The nation has reached the necessary location for God to fulfill his covenant promises. Notably, this entire account has not mentioned Israel's many rebellions, apart from an oblique reference in 33:14 and the mention of Aaron's death in 33:38–39. The emphasis is thus on the continuity of Israel's relationship with God (Allen 2012, 433). He demonstrated his power by bringing them out of Egypt and now stands on the verge of bringing them into Canaan.

THEOLOGICAL FOCUS

The exegetical idea (Moses preserves the account of Israel's journey) points to the following theological focus: *God's people endure because of his sustaining presence*. Direct references to God are notably rare in this text. It begins by remembering that YHWH delivered Israel from the Egyptians through mighty acts that displayed his authority over the gods of Egypt (33:4). Thereafter, YHWH is only mentioned in the recollection of Aaron's death (33:38). However, reading this itinerary alongside of the narratives of Exodus and Numbers calls to mind all that God did to preserve them as they wandered through harsh, inhospitable terrain. As Israel moved from encampment to encampment, God provided water, food in the form of daily manna, deliverance from enemies, along with visible reminders of his presence through the ark. Further, God did not let Israel perish in the wilderness even when it rebelled against him at some of the places mentioned in this itinerary. Recalling the stages of the journey was likely a mnemonic device, reminding later generations of God's presence as his people waited for the fulfillment of his promises.

God's sustaining presence is found throughout the testimony of Scripture, providing hope for both the collective and individuals. God delivered his people from their enemies and brought them into the land that he promised (Joshua 1–12). Even when sin brought about exile, he did not forget his people, but preserved a community who would acknowledge his presence when he brought them back (Ezra 8:21–32). He preserved the life of David when he was on the run from Saul (1 Sam. 23–24, 26) and

---

[7] Identifying Kadesh with the first encampment would require it to cover the thirty-eight years between the spy episode and Aaron's death. This is possible if Kadesh was used as central base for the thirty-eight years of subsequent wandering. Again, conclusive resolution of this question eludes the interpreter.

sustained Elijah from the wiles of Ahab and Jezebel (1 Kings 17–19). As the biblical story transitions into the New Testament, Jesus instructs his disciples to pray to God for their daily bread (Matt. 6:11), recognizing him as their source of strength. In the same sermon, he encourages his followers to consider the birds and flowers, recognizing how God has clothed and sustained them. If he will do such things for the birds and flowers, how much more should his people trust him (Matt. 6:25–34)?

This recognition of God's sustaining presence does not negate the possibility of evil and suffering. The Israelites faced many hardships in the wilderness, and Christ-followers have endured persecution, torment, and even death for the sake of their faith. However, in all of these situations, God is at work, and even if his hand is not made visible, he remains the source of strength and endurance for those who call upon his name.

PREACHING AND TEACHING STRATEGIES

Exegetical and Theological Significance
As Israel prepares to finish its time in the wilderness and enter the Promised Land, God commands that a retrospective look be taken at their journey. Not for the first time, Israel must remember where it has come from in order to be ready for where God is taking them next.

Although we do not know much about many of these locations, each and every one of them would have brought up memories and associations for the people who were about to enter Canaan. Even if nothing momentous in terms of historical perspective happened at a particular place, for the Israelites who camped there, there would be a set of personal stories that would have been reminisced about over time and become part of the shared memory-bonds of family and friends. Shared experiences—good or bad—matter in human relationships.

Some locations were highly significant in the life of the nation. Saying *Rameses* would bring up the glory and awe of their Passover redemption. *Marah* was a place with bitter water that God made sweet. *Elim* was a complete oasis with springs of water and trees; it was a place of peace and rest. *Sinai* was the place of theophany and covenant revelation, as well as the place of idolatry with the golden calf. *Kibroth Hattaavah* (i.e., "graves of craving") was where the people complained about their food, and many died. *Kadesh* was where the nation listened to the ten spies and rejected God's promise to win them the land. *Mount Hor* was where Aaron—the only high priest the people had ever known—died and was buried.

These places are freighted with biblical, theological, and historical importance. Multifaceted lessons of grace, love, faithfulness, sin, rebellion, wrath, judgment, forgiveness, holiness, life, death, and providence are all exemplified. Through it all, the covenant God of Abraham, Isaac, and Jacob is guiding his people toward the Promised Land. Through it all, the Lord God is with his people. Despite the multiple times when Israel deserved to be cast aside in judgment, God's mercy and grace triumphed over their sin. After all of these years of wandering, and despite all of their sin, God was about to bring the next generation of his people into the land of promise.

Preaching Idea
Every believer has a path on which God leads them through their pilgrimage.

Contemporary Connections

What does it mean?
What does it mean that every believer has a path on which God leads them through their pilgrimage? Every Christian's journey has commonalities, but every believer also walks on their own unique path. In the most fundamental and important sense, there is only one road of life and

only one way to the Father, and so every Christian must take this one and only way in God's one and only Son. There is no access to God, no road to the heavenly kingdom, and no way to eternal life apart from the Lord Jesus Christ.

The above paragraph is fundamentally important, but we must also remember that the followers of Jesus have very diverse life experiences. Whereas Israel had a shared list of geographical locations in the desert, the vast majority of Christians in the world today have never lived in the same places. Abraham's faith journey was not identical to Joseph's; Peter's was not identical to Paul's. The faith journeys of expositors and their congregations also have unique elements. God takes his servants through an incredible variety of experiences, but through it all God is present.

Every child of God has their own story of providence and conversion. Every child of God has been led by God to unique camping places and stages throughout their life. Before this momentous event of moving forward, God had the people take a long, careful look at where they had come from and where they had been. That principle is just as applicable today as it was back then.

Is it true?
Is it true that every believer has a path on which God leads them through their pilgrimage? There are different lenses through which life and providence can be viewed. Numbers 33 looks at life from a fairly wide-angled lens, taking in the pathway of the entire nation of Israel as a corporate whole. Reading Exodus–Deuteronomy also shows us how God guided the life of Moses; it lets us zoom in and focus on God's relationship with an individual. It does not take much concentration to see that even though all of Israel was on the same journey in one sense, that journey was not identical for Moses, Aaron, the Levites, Joshua, Korah, Miriam, and the ones who died in the incident at Baal Peor.

Hebrews 11 makes it very clear that God's people are all on a pilgrimage to the heavenly country. On their journey, some struggle through poverty, rejection, persecution, imprisonment, or martyrdom. Others are leaders, kings, or prophets. Some are poor and uneducated; some are powerful, rich, and philosophical. The destination is the same, the road is walked by faith, the way is Christ, but the individual life experiences and callings that God's children have are as diverse as life itself.

Esther may be taken as a fine example of this phenomenon. There have been many discussions in Judaism and Christianity about the status of the book of Esther in the canon of Scripture. There have been questions about the book's theology and ethics.[8] However, one purpose of the book is to consider God's providential care of his postexilic people *who did not return to Jerusalem* and remained living outside of the boundaries of the Promised Land (Jobes 1999, 27). Esther's path was very different from Nehemiah's, but both were called to their positions "for such a time as this" (Esther 4:14).

Now what?
What do we do in light of the fact that every believer has a path on which God leads them through their pilgrimage? Without any doubt, we want to be sure that we are on the one road that leads to glory; we want to make sure that we have entered the narrow gate that leads to life (Matt. 7:14). As we continue following the Lord, Numbers 33 instructs us in the importance of sometimes taking stock and intentionally remembering when and where we were when God rescued us.

Stemming from our redemption, we can then reflect on the significant milestones of our

---

8 There is no space here for defense of the following position, but the authors of this commentary take Esther as fully God-breathed and canonical.

lives. What lessons do we learn? Where are their moments of victory? Are there shameful events? Where do we most clearly see God's grace, patience, kindness, and love? When did we feel the sting of well-deserved discipline or rebuke? Was there a time when we were attacked by our enemies, struck down but then delivered? Where have we seen God's glory?

The backward gaze in Numbers 33 is not an exercise in self-absorbed reflection. On the contrary, it is a humbling look back on the history of God's sustaining presence. It is also designed not as an end in itself, but as a preparation for continuing forward to the next stage and era of life. Christians should sometimes look back in order to confidently move forward. In the words of the old hymn:

> Be still, my soul, thy God doth undertake,
> To guide the future as He has the past.[9]

Looking prayerfully at the past can strengthen our faith in our faithful God.

Creativity in Presentation

Everyone loves a pop quiz. Who knows the significance of the following places in the context of these groupings?

1. Poland, Dunkirk, Dresden, Arnhem, Auschwitz

2. Fort Sumter, Bull Run, Chancellorsville, Gettysburg, Cold Harbor

3. Sarnia, Peterborough, Kawartha Lakes, Madoc, Guelph, Madoc[10]

4. Entebbe, Kampala, Gulu, Kitgum, Pader[11]

It's not likely that anyone in your congregation is going to know the significance of the last two lists, although many will know the connections in the first two. (Obviously lists #3 and #4 could be changed for your own context. *Nobody* in your church should know the significance of the last two lists I [Steve] wrote out! If they do, kindly call the police.)

Ask people to consider what lists they would make. For some, it may be less about different cities than it is about important dates on the calendar, their educational pathway, job and career changes, or ministry involvement. Instruct people to spend time engaged in personal reflection on the way the Lord has led them, as well as on how they have responded in various situations. Can they discern personal growth? Can they see God's faithfulness? How can their past experiences with God prepare them for whatever they're about to face?

Here is another list: Bethlehem, Egypt, Nazareth, the Jordan, the wilderness, Capernaum, the Gadarenes, Jerusalem, Temple, Mount of Olives, the upper room, the garden of Gethsemane, Pilate, Calvary, Joseph of Arimathea's Tomb.

Many more items could be added to that list, but the trajectory is clear. What is essential to note is that the tomb is not the last stop on Jesus's journey. The grave gave way to victory as Jesus conquered death and rose to life. He left the tomb behind, made post-resurrection appearances to certain people, and then ascended to glory. His "last stop" is everlasting life! In this

---

9 Kathrina von Schlegel, "Be Still My Soul" (1855), https://amazinghymns.com/be-still-my-soul. I (Joel) might be betraying my age and musical preferences, but the lyrics from the song "Road to Zion" by Petra are also fitting here; https://www.azlyrics.com/lyrics/petra/roadtozion.html.

10 Although the reader will recognize the significance of the first two sets (or can find out with a quick internet search), this third set might be more challenging. It lists places where I (Steve) have lived, and that are significant to me even if others have never heard of them.

11 The itinerary of locations I (Steve) went to during my first trip to Africa, which was in Uganda.

world, wherever our path meanders, there will eventually be a grave. In Christ, the grave is not our final destination. Jesus conquered death; he defeated *our* death. One day, in resurrected glory, all of God's children will meet again in the new heaven and new earth. In all our diversity of experience and locations, we are reminded that every believer has a path on which God leads them through their pilgrimage.

Crafting an outline for expositing this text is extremely challenging, but the following is given as a suggestion. The focus is on the beginning of the chapter in order to avoid being bogged down by a list of obscure names:

- God commands his people to remember his leading (33:1–2).

- God frees his people from their enemies (33:3–4).

- God preserves his people on their pilgrimage (33:5–49).

DISCUSSION QUESTIONS

1. Why do you think that God instructed Moses to compile this record of Israel's encampments during its wilderness sojourn?

2. What purpose do the additional historical vignettes serve in this account?

3. Could you come up with a list of "key places" or "key events" that could be used as shorthand for your own journey of faith?

Numbers 33:50 – 34:29

EXEGETICAL IDEA
Israel is commanded to drive out the Canaanites so that it can receive its full inheritance.

THEOLOGICAL FOCUS
God intends to give his people a place where they can flourish.

PREACHING IDEA
Hear the word of the Lord, rid yourselves of idols, and live in the boundaries established by God.

PREACHING POINTERS
This preaching unit is built around the word of the Lord to Moses and the necessity of following his commands. Once again, Israel is called to faithful obedience to the word of the Lord, and once again they are faced with challenges beyond their own strength. They have to trust that God will empower them to take the land, and they have to trust in him exclusively. They are going into an environment that is filled with snares and pitfalls, and their track record is abysmal. Nevertheless, their faithful covenant God is determined to fulfill his promises, and he will not swerve from his divine plan.

When the people of God moved into the Promised Land, they were commanded to uproot and destroy every false god and every type of idol. This spiritual principle applies today just as much as it applied then. If we are going to flourish in the land of blessing, we must be a people marked by deep, rigorous obedience. Now is a time to recommit ourselves to faithful and full obedience to every word that proceeds from the mouth of God. It is also a time to identify the false gods, idols, and religious practices of our society, and search our own hearts for the same. We must surrender everything to God and follow him alone. Only then will we excel in the glory of his blessings. Now is the time to hear the word of the Lord, rid ourselves of idols, and live in the boundaries established by God.

THE PROMISED LAND (33:50–34:29)

LITERARY STRUCTURE AND THEMES

Numbers now moves from recounting Israel's journey to anticipating its long-awaited destination. This is the first of three preaching units that conclude the book and share the presumption that Israel will be established in the Promised Land. It consists of three sections, each marked by "The LORD said to Moses." The first (33:50–56) instructs Israel to drive out the Canaanites so that they will not lead Israel away from following YHWH. The second (34:1–15) traces the boundaries of the land that God is giving them, while the final section (34:16–29) lists the tribal leaders who are commissioned to divide the land.

An important theme is the need to obey God to fully experience his blessings. God promised to Abraham, Isaac, and Jacob that their descendants would inherit the Promised Land. Now that Israel learns about its boundaries and anticipates its inheritance, God calls the nation to full obedience. Its failure has consequences that reverberate throughout Israel's history. A related theme is the necessity of worshipping God alone. Unsurprisingly, God's commands for Israel's entry into the land concern the destruction of idols. These false gods cannot be left to draw Israel away from the God who has given his covenant to them.

- *Instructions to Drive Out the Canaanites (33:50–56)*
- *The Boundaries of Canaan (34:1–15)*
- *Leaders Who Help Divide the Land (34:16–29)*

EXPOSITION

This preaching unit has a logical progression through its three sections, since the second and third depend upon the success of the first. If Israel drives out the Canaanites, it will secure the inheritance that God has promised. Describing the land's borders and assigning men to oversee its division is contingent upon this initial step. Together, these three sections reveal this core truth: Israel is commanded to drive out the Canaanites so that it can receive its full inheritance.

Instructions to Drive Out the Canaanites (33:50–56)

33:50. Again, Israel is encamped on the Plains of Moab. It has been there since the taking of the second census (Num. 26:3). The frequent mention of this location in Numbers 26–36 is a reminder that Israel is on the brink of ending its forty-year period of wandering and experiencing the fullness of God's promises.

33:51–52. Divine instructions follow, establishing what Israel should do when it crosses the Jordan. YHWH commands Israel to "drive out" (וְהוֹרַשְׁתֶּם) the inhabitants of the land (33:52a ESV). This directive does not specify what is required to drive them out, but Deuteronomy 7:2–6 calls for the complete destruction of the people and their idols.[1] This is a task that Israel can accomplish only with God's help (Milgrom 1990, 283).

Along with driving out the land's inhabitants, God further directs the Israelites to remove all traces of idolatry among the nations. This verse uses three expressions to describe idol worship. First, the Hebrew word מַשְׂכִּית is

---

[1] See the discussion of the Midianite campaign in Numbers 31 for further reflections on divine commands to engage in holy war.

translated as "carved images" (33:52b NET) and likely refers to a representation of deity carved from wood or stone (Cole 2009, 398). Secondly, the expression צַלְמֵי מַסֵּכֹתָם can be translated as "molten images" (33:52b NET) and refers to images of deities made by melting and pouring copper or bronze into a mold (Cole 2009, 398). Thirdly, God directed the Israelites to destroy the "high places" (בָּמוֹת), which could refer to a variety of cultic worship centers. Later in Israel's history, the removal of the high places (or the failure to do so) was part of the evaluation formula of the kings.[2]

The presence of three expressions of idol worship reflects the comprehensive nature of God's instructions. Everything that pointed to worship of some other deity was to be destroyed.

33:53–54. The destruction of the idols prepares Israel to take possession of the land.[3] God first reminds the people that he is giving it to them (33:53). He then gives instructions for how it is to be divided (33:54). The basic idea is that it is to be proportional, with larger tribes receiving larger shares, and smaller tribes acquiring smaller shares. Further, the division is to happen "by lot" (בְּגוֹרָל), so that no tribe receives preferential treatment. It also implies that God directs this process, which means that divine will rather than random chance governs its results (Allen 2012, 434).

33:55–56. This section ends with a warning. If the Israelites do not drive out the nations and destroy their idols, there will be consequences. These nations will become "barbs in your eyes and thorns in your sides" (33:55 CSB, ESV, NIV). The image here is that of small objects that cause tremendous irritation and damage (Ashley 1993, 637). The continuing presence of Canaanites in the land will derail Israel's promised blessings. Joshua issues a similar warning at the end of his life, calling upon the Israelites to finish the task of claiming the Promised Land (Josh. 23:11–13). The section ends on an ominous note with God announcing that he will do to Israel what he intended for the nations if it does not destroy the idols (33:56). Israel's subsequent history bears witness to the truth of this warning. God lamented Israel's failure to remove the nations and their idols (Judg. 2:1–5) which ultimately led to its removal from the land during the period of the exile.

The Boundaries of Canaan (34:1–15)

34:1–2. The instruction to drive the Canaanites from the land leads into a description of its boundaries. Canaan as a geographical entity with roughly the same parameters is mentioned in contemporaneous Egyptian sources (Cole 2009, 399; Milgrom 1990, 501). This was the land where God's covenant promises to Israel's forefathers would be fulfilled (Gen. 15:18–21). The theological significance of the land is much more important for the expositor than having a detailed grasp of specific geographical markers.

Further, the borders established in this text also reflect an idealized version of Israel's territory. Israel only came close to exercising sovereignty over this full region during the time of David and Solomon. Even then, peoples like the Philistines and Phoenicians were not fully subdued (Stubbs 2009, 244). This gap between ideal Israel and actual Israel reflects Israel's failures to fully obey God's instructions to remain free

---

2   Notably, Hezekiah and Josiah are credited with removing the high places (2 Kings 18:4; 23:5–20). However, some otherwise "good kings" like Azariah and Jotham did not remove them (2 Kings 15:3; 16:35).
3   The verb וְהוֹרַשְׁתֶּם translated "you shall drive out" (ESV) in 33:52 also occurs in 33:53 but is translated as "you shall take possession" (ESV). The underlying root ירש can point to either taking possession or dispossessing someone else, depending on the perspective of the text (Cole 2000, 530). These senses do have a logical link, in that one means of taking possession is to dispossess the previous inhabitants.

from idolatry. The borders mentioned here also resemble those given in Ezekiel's hopeful vision of a restored Israel after captivity (Ezek. 47:5–10). Only through God's redemption could Israel encompass all that it was intended to be (Stubbs 2009, 244).

At this moment, God reminds Israel that this land is its inheritance and then describes the land's boundaries in detail. The precision and order in the descriptions creates a "liturgy of geography" (Allen 2012, 436). Israel is called to worship as it considers the fullness of what God has promised.

34:3–5. The text begins with Israel's southern border. It does not form a straight line but branches up to the east and west from Kadesh Barnea as its most southern point. This had been the staging ground for the mission of the spies in Numbers 13–14 and presumably would be a memorable landmark for the next generation. On the eastern side, this southern boundary runs up against the Dead Sea which is the modern name for the Hebrew יָם־הַמֶּלַח or "Salt Sea." This also abuts territory associated with Edom (34:3). From there, it moves westward through rugged terrain along the "Scorpion Pass" (מַעֲלֵה עַקְרַבִּים) just south of the Dead Sea before arriving at Kadesh Barnea (34:4). From there, the boundary proceeds northeastward, following the Wadi of Egypt (נַחְלָה מִצְרַיִם), a watercourse that met the Mediterranean Sea and separated Canaan from Egypt (Allen 2012, 437).

34:6. The western boundary is the Mediterranean, or the Great Sea (הַיָּם הַגָּדוֹל). The continuous presence of the Philistines along the southern coast and city-states like Tyre and Sidon further north indicates that Israel did not fully control this western boundary.

34:7–9. The northern boundary mentioned here and the eastern border that follows almost certainly reflect an idealized picture. The northern border extended from the sea to Mount Hor (34:7). This must refer to a different location than where Aaron died in Numbers 20:22–25. It is likely a mountain peak in the area of Lebanon (Cole 2009, 400). From there, it ran eastward to Lebo Hamath (34:8). This was also the northernmost point to which the spies journeyed in their exploration of the land (13:21). It appears to have been even further north than the tribal allotments given after the conquest (Josh. 19:28–29; Na'aman 2006, 360–61) and became the northern boundary of Solomon's kingdom (1 Kings 8:65) which contracted swiftly after his death. The border then continued east into regions where Israel rarely exercised dominion, running to places called Zedad (34:8), Ziphron, and Hazar Enan (34:9). Wenham suggests that Zedad can be identified with Sadad in modern Syria, but the other two places are unknown (Wenham 2008, 258).

34:10–12. The eastern border is extremely difficult to trace. Shepham, Riblah, and Ain (34:11) have not been located with any degree of certainty, but it appears that the border traverses through territory controlled by the Arameans during the period of Israel's kingdoms. Eventually the border narrows and works back toward the top of the Jordan Valley around the eastern side of the Sea of Galilee, which is the modern appellation for the Sea of Chinnereth (יָם־כִּנֶּרֶת; Cole 2009, 401). From there, it follows the Jordan River down to the Dead Sea (34:12a).

The tracing of the borders concludes in Numbers 34:12b with a statement that this will encompass Israel's land. As mentioned previously, Israel never fully had dominion over this territory, but it represented the ideal of what God intended to give them (Allen 2012, 440).

34:13–15. A brief addendum follows that acknowledges the reality that the Transjordanian tribes are not included within the boundaries above. Moses directs the Israelites to divide the land as their inheritance and explicitly awards it to the nine and a half tribes (34:13). He notes that Gad, Reuben, and half of Manasseh have claimed their inheritance in the land east of the Jordan River, discussed in detail in Numbers 32:33–42. This provides a further indication of the potential for division between the Transjordanian tribes and the rest of Israel. Although God and Moses have granted them the land they desired, it does not fall within the borders of Canaan that God articulated to Moses.

Leaders Who Help Divide the Land (34:16–29)

34:16–17. After articulating the boundaries of Canaan, God provides leaders to assist in the process of dividing it into tribal allotments. There is an anticipatory element to this task. Until the land is conquered, inheritances for the tribes cannot be allocated. Although it is framed here as instructions from God to Moses, Moses will not participate in the actual division of the land since it takes place in Joshua 13–19. It is therefore fitting that the first two names mentioned are Joshua, Moses's successor, and Eleazar the high priest, the son of Aaron. The division of the land thus falls under the authority of Israel's next generation of military and spiritual leaders.

34:18. God also commands Moses to appoint one leader from each tribe to assist. This means that every tribe in Israel has a voice in the process. Notably, only ten names are given. This is because Reuben, Gad, and half of Manasseh have already received and claimed their desired allotments across the Jordan River (Num. 32:33–42).

34:19–28. The list of helpers begins with Caleb, son of Jephunneh, from the tribe of Judah (34:19). Caleb is also the only name mentioned elsewhere in the Bible. His faithfulness to God in the catastrophe of Numbers 13–14 qualifies him for this position. As the only member of Judah from the first generation, it is fitting that he has a part to play in seeing Judah established in the Promised Land.[4]

The remaining tribal leaders are not listed in the order identified for the two censuses. Instead, the guiding principle seems to be geography, starting with the tribes that settle in the south and working northward from there (Cole 2000, 540). Although nothing is known of these individuals, it is reasonable to assume that they demonstrated similar devotion to God.

There is a slight addition given in Numbers 34:23–24, discussing the leaders of Manasseh and Ephraim.[5] These leaders are also identified as "the son of Joseph." This is another reminder that Joseph receives two shares in Israel's inheritance in Canaan, indicative of his elevated status within the family of Jacob.

Beyond this, the listing of these leaders follows the same pattern with minimal variation. The key concern is to have a record that every tribe had a representative for this process. Individual qualities and characteristics are not a concern.

34:29. The text concludes with a summary statement that these were the men assigned to help create the tribal allotments for Israel's inheritance in Canaan. Since this section is framed as God's instructions to Moses, these men have divine authorization for the role that they play.

THEOLOGICAL FOCUS

The exegetical idea (Israel is commanded to drive out the Canaanites so that it can receive its full inheritance) yields the following theological

---

4 The biblical narrative reveals that Caleb was much more than a passive participant in dividing the land. The account of the division of Cisjordan territory begins with Caleb asking for the right to drive the fearsome Anakites out of Hebron. The presence of this same group caused his fellow spies to persuade Israel not to enter the Promised Land back in Numbers 13:28–29. Caleb successfully takes on this task himself (Josh. 14:6–15).

5 This must refer to the half of Manasseh that did not settle in the Transjordan.

focus: *God intends to give his people a place where they can flourish.* The anticipation of the Promised Land has been with Israel for forty years of wandering and centuries of servitude in Egypt before that. Now, as Israel approaches the borders, God articulates the fullness of his intended gift of the land. Far from being a simple exercise in cartography, this passage reveals God's faithfulness to his promises and his provision of a place for his people to worship him. The gap between the ideal borders of the Promised Land and what Israel actually governed is instructive. A theological reading of this passage reveals that because Israel did not turn from idols as commanded in Numbers 33:50–56, the boundaries described in chapter 34 remained unrealized. God's promise of a place for his people to flourish is marred by human failure and weakness.

This recalls the situation in the garden of Eden, where God had created a perfect place for Adam and Eve, his image-bearers, to reflect his glory. They were to tend God's perfect creation, eat from good plants, and grow in their relationship with him. However, sin and evil tarnished that arrangement, leading to their departure into a land that brought toil and pain (Gen. 3:17–19). However, the biblical story of redemption does not end there, but continues through Abraham and his descendants (Gen. 12:1–3). Israel's imminent entry into the Promised Land reflects a partial redemption as God leads the people through a barren land and shows them a land that he has set aside for them.

In the New Testament, the place where God's people flourish is not limited to a specific location on the earth. Instead, God's redemptive story moves out to every tribe, tongue, and nation and points them forward to time where they dwell eternally in a place that God has prepared. The author of Hebrews captures this in his reflections on Abraham, who left his homeland to go where God called him. Abraham's journey into Canaan reflected that "he was looking forward to the city with foundations whose architect and builder is God" (Heb. 11:10 NIV). As believers persist in faith, they come to "Mount Zion, to the city of the living God, the heavenly Jerusalem" (Heb. 12:22 NIV). Idolatry may have prevented Israel from possessing the full borders of Canaan, but the hope of God's people is rooted in a new heavens and a new earth, where believers will flourish in his presence forever (Rev. 21:1–4).

PREACHING AND TEACHING STRATEGIES

Exegetical and Theological Significance

As mentioned in the exposition, this unit is structured around the Lord's speech to Moses (Num. 33:50, 34:1, 34:16). Additionally, Numbers 34 is framed by an inclusio that references the Lord's commands (Num. 31:1, 29). Since one of the major themes in Numbers is that disobeying the word of the Lord leads to destruction, and obedience to God's word leads to life and blessing, it is not surprising to hear this theme being loudly and prominently proclaimed at this critical juncture in Israel's journey. This truth, of course, is just as significant for our lives as it was for theirs.

The wilderness generation was lost because they did not have enough faith in YHWH to enter the Promised Land. They failed to trust God when they made the golden calf, and they were easily lured into idolatry, immorality, and destruction by the Moabites and Midianites. Now they were about to enter Canaan, a place saturated with false gods, pagan worship, immoral practices, and unspeakable religious rituals. They had already failed to obey God *outside* of this environment. What would they do when they were *inside* of it?

Their only hope was found in God, but they had to walk faithfully with him and obey his word. To be faithful to God's covenant stipulations, they had to remove sources of temptation. They needed to rigorously destroy every vestige of false religion, and they needed to drive out those who would tempt them away from the Lord their God. When the land was devoid of idolatry, it would be ready for them to dwell in the boundaries that the Lord had marked out for them. The land was an incredible gift from God, but it was filled with both an abundance of blessings and an abundance of dangers. The only way to navigate these rapids was to trust God to steer them through. Absolute obedience was crucial, and the same is true today.

Preaching Idea

Hear the word of the Lord, rid yourselves of idols, and live in the boundaries established by God.

Contemporary Connections

What does it mean?

What does it mean that we are to hear the word of the Lord, rid ourselves of idols, and live in the boundaries established by God? The importance of the Word of God cannot be exaggerated. As Christians, we are saved by the *logos*, the "Word" who was with God and is God (John 1:1). The Bible, God's written Word, is indispensable for our lives. Positively, we must study the Scriptures to know what it is that God would have us to do. Negatively, we must also know his Word so that we know what displeases him and to know what we ought not avoid.

Part of God's revelation is that he is the only God, and he will not tolerate the worship of false gods. Idols usurp his glory, and false religion debases and destroys his image-bearers. Every society has idols, and every sinful human heart manufactures and adores personal idols. As regenerate believers in Christ, we must kill idols before they kill us. Hearing and obeying the word of the Lord is essential, and the Lord commands that we root out idols so that we can live safely in the good boundaries he has established for us. God is a God of blessing, but turning to false gods ruins lives and destroys nations. We must obey God with pure hands and a clean heart, and we must not lift our hands to any idol or false god. Only then can we live in security and peace.

Is it true?

Is it true that we are to hear the word of the Lord, rid ourselves of idols, and live in the boundaries established by God? We cannot exaggerate the importance of walking in faith and obedience, submitting to the Word of God. Even in a multicultural, pluralistic society, Scripture cannot be relativized or minimized, as if it is merely one option at the contemporary religious buffet. God does not present himself as a *better* deity, he presents himself as the *only* deity. Every other god is false, and every false god must be eradicated.

The logic behind the destruction of false gods is that only the Lord is worthy of worship, and people can only flourish as they worship him exclusively. When human beings invent gods and religious practices, they invariably rob God of his due and inadvertently impoverish their own lives. False religion causes us to literally miss the entire point of being alive in the universe.

It is critical to understand that God does not require us to destroy idols and avoid false religion because he is irrationally envious or trying to limit us. He gives us these commands for the glory that his name deserves, and also because he loves us infinitely. God is love; he calls us to live in love. We become like what we worship, and thus worshipping God is the only path to blessing. In grace, God lifts us up, whereas false gods tear us apart and try to drag us into the grave. We were created by God and designed to flourish under his hand of blessing, but this requires obeying his word.

Now what?

How should we respond, knowing that we are to hear the word of the Lord, rid ourselves of idols, and live in the boundaries established by God? The imperatives in this preaching idea are clear!

It is not difficult to understand their meaning, but it takes a lifetime of carefully walking with the Spirit to increase our practice.

What we must do is:

1. hear the word of the Lord.
2. rid ourselves of idols.
3. live in the boundaries established by God.

When you open your Bible, open your mind and open your heart. Hearing the Word of the Lord is not a passive exercise but an active one. Hearing means obeying and doing. Pray to God that his Holy Spirit will show you any areas of hidden idolatry and any places where we are trusting in other things rather than God. Allow him to set the parameters for your life and walk with Jesus, trusting him to lead you to the fulfillment of the Promised Land where no sin or false gods will ever be found.

Creativity in Presentation

There are times when a service can be greatly enhanced through the testimony of a wise and godly missionary. Depending on the makeup of the congregation, it would be worthwhile considering having a missionary talk about the false gods or religious practices of the people they are trying to reach with the gospel. Note that this does not have to involve animism, carved figures of deities, and witchdoctors. Highly secular societies have their own pantheon of false gods and idols that need to be identified and rejected. A survey of some major world religions may also be helpful, making sure the details are accurate and helping people understand the theological and doctrinal distinctives of the Christian faith in point of contrast. The logic behind this rejection of false gods and false religious practices should be spelled out so that people understand the reason for God's commands.

This is a time to renew a commitment to hearing and obeying the Word of the Lord. It is also a time to identify personal idols, repent, and destroy them. Are there unclean practices? Pornography? Anger? Arrogance? Give it to God and get rid of it. Are you trusting in false gods? Education? Money? Power? Possessions? Religious works? Humble yourself and turn away from these idols. God always receives those who genuinely repent, and he is quick to forgive and establish his people in the land of his blessing.

This would have to be done with discretion, but it may be meaningful to have people jot down a word on a piece of paper that identifies a temptation or idol, and then have ushers collect the papers. They could be consecrated to destruction before the Lord. This text called Israel to serious action, and the standards are not lower for us today than they were back then. We too are called to hear the word of the Lord, rid ourselves of idols, and live in the boundaries established by God.

A possible outline for this passage is:

- God alone is to be worshipped (33:50–56).

- God is generous in his provision for his people (34:1–15).

- God equips his people to obey his commands (34:16–29).

DISCUSSION QUESTIONS

1. Why does removal of idols go hand in hand with the delineation of the boundaries of the Promised Land?

2. Why does God provide such detail about the boundaries of the Promised Land?

3. What sorts of things do we need to remove so that they do not become "barbs in our eyes and thorns in our sides" (Num. 33:55)?

Numbers 35:1–34

EXEGETICAL IDEA
Upon entry into the Promised Land, the Israelites must assign cities to the Levites, six of which will become cities of refuge.

THEOLOGICAL FOCUS
Human life is sacred in the eyes of the God who created it.

PREACHING IDEA
God is a God of life, and the standard of justice comes from his nature.

PREACHING POINTERS
Contemporary judicial systems have quite different organizational structures than what we find in this text, but there are abiding principles that teach us about how God views justice, mercy, life, and death. Life is sacred, and life cannot be taken without due penalty. No human court is infallible, however, and there are times when it is difficult to know if a killing was premeditated or a tragic accident. In the ancient world, cycles of revenge killing could quickly escalate into blood feuds, and this text guards against that possibility.

At a fundamental level, this passage can be used to remind people that God is a God of justice, and that human laws are to reflect his character. Many cultures have been rightly described as cultures of death, but God desires every society to have a culture of life. God's image-bearers are precious to him, and he cares for their lives. As a result, his image-bearers are to have their lives protected from murderers, but they are also to be protected against execution if they accidentally kill someone. Deep down, at the heart of this text, is the principle that God is a God of life, and the standard of justice comes from his nature.

CITIES OF REFUGE (35:1–34)

LITERARY STRUCTURE AND THEMES

After tracing Israel's promised inheritance, this chapter allots some of the territory for special use. God requires the Israelites to give forty-eight cities to the Levites, six of which become cities of refuge that provide sanctuary for those who commit the ancient equivalent of manslaughter (Num. 35:6–7). This preaching unit begins by assigning cities to the Levites (35:1–8). It then addresses the creation of cities of refuge and regulations for both intentional and unintentional killing (35:9–29). This second section has three constituent parts: the locations of the cities of refuge (35:9–15), a differentiation between deliberate and accidental homicide (35:16–24), and the requirement for the killer to remain in the city of refuge (35:25–29). It concludes with a reflection on death and the sanctity of the land (35:30–34).

A key theme of this passage is the value of life. Spilling blood, even if done unintentionally, calls for response. This is rooted in the understanding that human beings carry the image of God. Taking the life of an image-bearer requires recompense (Gen. 9:5–6). This passage establishes parameters so that justice can be accomplished and the sanctity of life preserved. Another key theme is the value of priestly service. Previous chapters saw gifts given to the sanctuary and awards portions of sacrifices to priests and Levites. Assigning cities to the Levites provides a physical reminder for the Israelites that they are the covenant people of YHWH.

- **Cities for the Levites (35:1–8)**
- **Cities of Refuge (35:9–29)**
  - *Locations of the Cities (35:9–15)*
  - *Deliberate and Accidental Homicide (35:16–24)*
  - *Remaining in the City of Refuge (35:25–29)*
- **Death and the Sanctity of the Land (35:30–34)**

EXPOSITION

This passage is somewhat clinical to start. It is concerned with making sure that the Levites get their full allotment and with differentiating between various kinds of killing. However, underneath the surface there are some deep reflections on what it means to live in God's presence and to cherish life as God does. It gives instructions that upon entry into the Promised Land, the Israelites must assign cities to the Levites, six of which will become cities of refuge.

Cities for the Levites (35:1–8)

35:1–3. The text again reminds its audience that Israel is on the Plains of Moab, just across the Jordan River from Jericho (cf. 26:3; 33:50). From that location, God tells Moses to instruct the Israelites to set aside cities for the Levites along with their associated pasturelands (35:2). This is a reminder that God's intention for the Levites is for them to be scattered throughout Israel as living reminders for Israel to remember him and be faithful (Cole 2000, 544). The Israelites must give cities and pasturelands to the Levites because the Levites do not have their own inheritance within the land. Instead, YHWH promises to be their inheritance (18:20). However, they still require places to live and grazing areas to support their livestock (35:3). God thus instructs the other tribes to donate a portion of their inheritances for the Levites to use. The special status of the Levites is also evident when the text avoids the vocabulary used to describe the other tribes' claims to the land (Ashley 1993, 645).[1] They do not have inheritances, but rather places to live.

The presence of the Levites throughout Israel's territory facilitates the reception of the tithes they were due once the nation entered the land (18:21–24, 30–32). From there, they could offer their tithe-of-the-tithe to the priests as required by God's instructions (18:25–29). The Levites thus were living reminders to the Israelites of what they owed to the God who had delivered them and called them his people.

35:4–5. The text then gives the dimensions of the allotted pastureland for the Levitical cities. Some confusion arises here as 35:4 gives a measurement of one thousand cubits (roughly 1,500 feet) from the city walls, while 35:5 allots two thousand cubits (three thousand feet). The simplest solution is to measure one thousand cubits from the city walls in each direction. This yields a frontage of two thousand cubits for each of the four sides of the pastureland (Ashley 1993, 646; Cole 2009, 402; Milgrom 1990, 503). These are relatively modest dimensions, but likely fit the ancient context in which many so-called cities consisted of only a few adjoined dwellings (Wenham 2008, 261). This allotment also reflects the reality of ancient living, where even those living in somewhat urban settings relied on local agriculture for their continued survival.

35:6–7. Six of the allotted cities become cities of refuge for those who kill another person (35:6).[2] Since the land awarded to the Levites stood apart from Israel's tribal inheritances, it could fittingly provide sanctuary for the manslayer until a legal process took place. These six cities are added to forty-two others, giving the Levites a total allotment of forty-eight cities. This gave them a small but evident presence in the land.[3]

35:8. The final command is for the allotment to be proportional. Larger tribes were to provide more cities, while smaller tribes provided fewer. This reflects a basic standard of fairness also present in the allotment of the land (Num. 33:53–54).

Cities of Refuge (35:9–29)

Locations of the Cities (35:9–15)

35:9–12. Upon entering Canaan, God instructs Moses to set aside the cities of refuge. These were places "to which a person who has killed someone accidentally may flee" (35:11b NIV). The presence of the Levites in these locations gave them a sacral status, making them fitting sanctuaries from the prospect of violence.[4] Such asylum was necessary to hold off retribution from the deceased's family through the figure known as the גֹּאֵל, commonly translated in this context as "avenger" (CSB, ESV, NASB, NET, NIV). The avenger was the next-of-kin male (i.e., a brother, uncle, cousin, or other closely related individual) whose responsibility was to "uphold the rights of a family or restore its losses"

---

1   These include the verb "inherit" (נָחַל) along with the nouns "inheritance" (נַחֲלָה) and "portion" (חֵלֶק).
2   The discussion of who qualifies for sanctuary dominates 35:9–29.
3   The total share of territory allotted to the Levites consisted of 0.1 percent of Canaan (Wenham 2008, 259). However, the number of cities suggests that the other Israelites should be aware that the Levites were in their midst. Joshua 21:1–42 details the fulfillment of these instructions.
4   A similar principle is at work when Adonijah, Solomon's half-brother, fled retribution and grasped the horns of the sacrificial altar (1 Kings 1:50–51; 2:28).

(Stubbs 2009, 246). This involved a wide range of responsibilities such as standing in for levirate marriage (Ruth 3:13), receiving debts owed to a deceased kinsman (Num. 5:8), redeeming a family member from debt slavery (Lev. 25:48), and purchasing back their lost inheritance (Lev. 25:25, 48; Milgrom 1990, 291). This passage adds enacting retribution for a family member's untimely death to the list of responsibilities.

Notably, the intentionality of the killing is not a consideration for the avenger. Their task is to ensure that the death of their slain relative is answered. However, the rest of the passage differentiates between premeditated murder and accidental killing. Seeking asylum in one of the cities of refuge also allowed for a public legal proceeding to adjudicate the matter and declare the appropriate penalty (35:12).

35:13–15. In the interests of balance, three of the six cities were to be on each side of the Jordan River. Joshua 20:7–8 later names the cities and identifies their geographical locations. Essentially, the cities were spread evenly throughout Israel's territory, giving every Israelite the same opportunity to seek sanctuary (Cole 2000, 550).

Deliberate and Accidental Homicide (35:16–24)

35:16–18. The next step is to identify who is eligible to find sanctuary in a city of refuge. The underlying principle is that any deliberate killing remains a capital crime and requires the death of the perpetrator. They will not receive lasting asylum in the city of refuge. These verses give examples of various means of killing, including iron implements (35:16), heavy stones (35:17), and wooden implements (35:18). Striking another person with one of these potential weapons demonstrates an intent to commit violence and indicates that the perpetrator is a murderer.

> **Degrees of Culpability in Killing**
> Hebrew vocabulary has some of the same challenges as English when describing degrees of culpability in killing. The main word for the killer is רֹצֵחַ and it is used in two main contexts throughout this passage. It is used of the one who commits accidental homicide (35:11, 25, 26, 27, 28) as well as the one who commits intentional murder (35:16, 17, 18, 19, 21, 30, 31). English translations must translate this word and its associated phrases in different ways to convey these nuances. For example, the ESV uses "manslayer" for the one who commits unintentional homicide (35:11, 25, 26, 27, 28), while using "murderer" for cases of deliberate homicide (35:16, 17, 18, 19, 21, 30, 31).

35:19. The penalty for these intentional homicides is for the avenger of blood (גֹּאֵל הַדָּם) to kill the perpetrator. Deuteronomy 19:12 adds that the killer shall be removed from the city of refuge and returned to the place of the crime to face judgment. This incorporates the role of the avenger into the justice apparatus of the community. The avenger has the duty of seeking retribution for a slain family member, but limits are placed on their pursuit of vengeance (Kislev 2020, 255).

35:20–21. The text then considers additional scenarios that merit capital punishment. These situations focus more on the question of intent, stating that the violence occurs out of "hatred" (35:20 CSB, ESV, NET)[5] or "enmity" (35:21 ESV, NET, NIV). The means of killing here include hurling something from ambush (35:20b) and direct physical assault (35:21), covering both clandestine and overt

---

5   The underlying Hebrew word is בְּשִׂנְאָה. A literal rendering is "with hatred," but the NIV uses "malice aforethought," a more juridical rendering.

murders (Ashley 1993, 653). These crimes merit the intervention of the avenger of blood, who will kill the perpetrator.

35:22–24. The passage then shifts to the opposite scenario, in which the killing occurred without intent. These scenarios are rough equivalents of manslaughter and merit different consequences. The means of killing are the same (throwing an object, dropping a heavy stone), but the absence of enmity makes the difference. This passage does not detail how to adjudicate the question of intent, but Joshua 20:4 requires the manslayer to appear at the gate of the city of refuge where that city's leadership considered a variety of legal proceedings (Deut. 21:18–21; Ruth 4:1–11; 2 Sam. 15:2; 2 Chron. 18:9–10; Amos 5:15). Since these were also cities of Levites they had a deeper connection to God, which should have ensured fairness and justice at these hearings (Cole 2000, 553).

Remaining in the City of Refuge (35:25–29)
35:25–28. If the killing is ruled an unintentional homicide, then the manslayer is granted lasting sanctuary at the city of refuge. However, this asylum is only valid so long as the manslayer remains within the city's boundaries. If they leave, the avenger is permitted to enact retribution without penalty (35:27). This situation holds until the death of the high priest, at which point presumably the killer can return home free from fear of death (35:28). The rationale for this standard is not explained, but the death of a high priest was a major demarcation point in Israel's religious experience. One suggestion is that the death of this anointed leader redeemed the death of the victim, balancing the scales and permitting the manslayer to resume normal life (Cole 2009, 402). If the manslayer died while residing in the city of refuge, that also brought equilibrium to the situation, with their death matching the death of the one killed unintentionally.

35:29. This discussion concludes with the assertion that this legislation is binding upon Israel throughout its existence, wherever it lived. Dealing with situations of death was serious business, and following these divinely ordained instructions permitted Israel to demonstrate its commitment to the God who created life.

Death and the Sanctity of the Land (35:30–34)
35:30. The passage concludes with a series of clarifying regulations. The first sets a high standard of evidence for capital crimes, declaring that the accused cannot be put to death on the testimony of only one witness. This would hopefully forestall malicious personal vendettas. Relatedly, Deuteronomy 17:6 requires two or three witnesses to sentence a guilty party to death. This standard is also found in other ancient legal contexts such as the laws of Hammurabi (Cole 2009, 402). It could be abused if multiple people engaged in a conspiracy against an innocent person, but the intended purpose was to protect the accused.[6]

35:31–32. The second and third regulations address the possibility of ransom for those who kill another human being. Neither the murderer (35:31) nor the manslayer living in the city of refuge (35:32) can make monetary payments to escape the consequences of their actions. The murderer must die, and the manslayer must remain in the city of refuge until the death of the high priest. This sets a rigorous standard of fairness, not permitting the wealthy to have access to options unavailable to poorer Israelites (Allen 2012, 451). It also reinforces the incomparable worth of human life; no monetary or sacrificial substitute is possible (Cole 2000, 555). Only the

---

[6] In 1 Kings 21:8–14, Jezebel finds two immoral individuals willing to testify against the innocent Naboth. This episode reveals the depths of her wickedness, as she twists God's appointed law to serve her unjust ends.

death of the murderer, the death of the manslayer while in exile, or the death of an anointed substitute (the high priest) was sufficient to balance the situation.

35:33–34. The final regulations provide the theological foundation for the preceding discussion. In essence, all of this is necessary because "bloodshed pollutes the land" (35:33 NIV). This is serious because God dwells among the Israelites in this land. Impurity and pollution from bloodshed is incompatible with his holiness and can lead to serious consequences, including exile from the land (Lev. 18:28). Again, only the death of the manslayer (or the high priestly substitute) could remediate this impurity. This builds upon the idea that blood is the means of expiation that underlies the entire sacrificial system. For most transgressions, the blood of animal sacrifices could make atonement, but in the case of intentional or unintentional killing, a different standard applied (Hadad 2017, 166).

> **2 Samuel 21**
> This principle leads to a challenging story in 2 Samuel 21. David learns that Saul's unjust killing of Gibeonites polluted the land, resulting in a three-year famine (2 Sam. 21:1). Since Saul was long dead, his blood could not be used to remediate the situation. Instead, David permitted expiation to be made (21:3) by allowing the Gibeonites to kill some of Saul's descendants. The purity of the land had to be restored for God to hear prayers and restore its fruitfulness, but the means required to do this are inexplicable apart from understanding the standard established in this passage (Gane 2004, 796).

THEOLOGICAL FOCUS

The exegetical idea (Upon entry into the Promised Land, the Israelites must assign cities to the Levites, six of which will become cities of refuge) leads to the following theological focus: *Human life is sacred in the eyes of the God who created it*. The underlying principle of this chapter is the inestimable worth of human life. Taking a life is a matter of grave consequence, leading the killer to forfeit their own since "Whoever sheds the blood of man by man shall his blood be shed, for God made man in his own image" (Gen. 9:6 ESV). Further, the land itself can cry out with the injustice. The first example of this is Cain's murder of Abel, after which the earth would no longer yield its bounty to him (Gen. 4:12). As Israel prepared to enter the Promised Land, God reminds the nation that human lives are valuable in his sight.

The sacredness of life is also apparent in the provisions for accidental killing. Although human life has been taken, the accidental nature of the killing does not warrant further bloodshed. Instead, God institutes a policy of sanctuary, providing a refuge that stops the potential for a growing cycle of retaliatory bloodshed. Although the avenger of blood has the right to take the life of the involuntary manslayer, God limits their freedom in the interests of greater preservation of life. This same ethic infuses Jesus's commands in Matthew 5:38–42 to avoid "eye-for-an-eye" retribution. Although balancing the scales and achieving fairness is a worthwhile goal, followers of Christ ultimately trust in him to bring appropriate judgment. As mentioned earlier in this commentary, Paul cautions the church in Rome not to take vengeance themselves but to leave such matters to God. He includes a citation of Deuteronomy 32:35, "It is mine to avenge; I will repay" (Rom. 12:19 NIV). The role of avenger in securing justice attested in Numbers 35 is thus given an eternal view in which the followers of Christ submit to his wisdom and timing for bringing justice.

The provision that the manslayer must remain in the city of refuge until the death of the high priest also reinforces the sanctity of life. The penalty for accidental death shifts to this servant of God, anointed to stand between God and the people. The high priest does not have to lay down his own life in place of the manslayer.

However, God graciously uses his natural death as a means of justice by fulfilling the principle of life for a life and as a demonstration of mercy by releasing the unintentional killer from their exile (Stubbs 2009, 247). Of course, substitutionary death reaches its apex in the sacrifice of Jesus Christ, our great High Priest whose sacrifice covered sins for all time (Heb. 7:27). This fulfillment of the divine redemptive plan for humanity reveals God's commitment to the sacredness of human life. Allowing people to dwell eternally in God's presence was worth the price paid by God's own son.

PREACHING AND TEACHING STRATEGIES

Exegetical and Theological Significance

Israel was to have no doubt that God was interested in justice, fairness, the protection of the innocent, the punishment of the guilty, and the integrity of the judicial process. Starting in earnest in Exodus 20, God gave the nation numerous statutes, laws, directives, and principles. There were apodictic commands as well as examples and casuistic laws to help Israel understand God's moral and judicial will. Although God's revealed law covered many topics, issues of life and death were of the utmost importance.

There can be no denying that God prescribed capital punishment for a number of crimes in his law. He also commanded that the innocent be exonerated and the guilty punished accordingly. Justice matters to God. Since human systems of justice are imperfect and fallible, God established safeties in the judicial processes in Israel. One such safety is seen in the cities of refuge.

In these cities—evenly spread throughout the land—those who had killed someone without culpable intention could flee for refuge. As Israel moved into the Promised Land, they would need stability in their judicial system, and these cities helped to provide that. The logic behind the cities was that in questionable cases there needed to be a mechanism to prevent immediate, irrevocable action. Cycles of revenge killings, which could easily become intergenerational blood feuds, were to be avoided at all costs.

The principles we see at work in these laws include God's protection of the innocent and his desire to ensure that people are not executed unless they are guilty of a capital crime. Even in the old covenant law, not every instance where a human life was taken was considered murder. There were cases where there was no doubt that someone had killed another person, but it was difficult to determine their intention: sometimes it is hard for human beings to determine what is accidental versus intentional. God's will for his people was that in these cases, the sacredness of the life that had been ended demanded that the killer flee to a city of refuge. The sacredness of life also demanded that their life be spared from the avenger of blood, since their full guilt was not demonstrable.

Preaching Idea

God is a God of life, and the standard of justice comes from his nature.

Contemporary Connections

What does it mean?
What does it mean that God is a God of life, and the standard of justice comes from his nature? That God has the attribute of aseity (self-existence, independence) is a biblical axiom: he is the God who has life in himself (John 5:26). He is also the God who creates and gives life to all things. It is equally axiomatic that he is a God of justice and righteousness. Justice is not external to God: it is something that is rooted in his nature and applied in the world he has made.

Since life is his gift, and since human beings are his image-bearers, it is important that people honor, defend, and protect the sanctity of life. Although there are various legal codes and statutes around the world—to say nothing of how legal systems and laws evolve over time—the principles of justice are grounded in God himself. Human justice is to reflect God's nature and will. It cannot be archetypal; it is derivative, but can still be genuine in its correspondence to God. In the context of this passage in Numbers, this means that we have a moral responsibility to care for life in a way that honors its Giver. Legal principles and procedures are to separate the innocent, accidental killing of an individual from an act of premeditated murder. Since all of life is sacred, issues of life and death are to be carefully monitored in our judicial systems.

Is it true?
Is it true that God is a God of life, and that the standard of justice comes from his nature? The biblical storyline from Genesis through Revelation is incoherent apart from the truth of this claim. Even accepting this claim, however, does not logically necessitate that human justice systems have done a good job in reflecting God's nature and standards. From a relativistic perspective, all human judicial systems can arguably be reduced to systems of coercion, power, and control. Michel Foucault has subjected the history of Western judicial systems to a severe critique (Foucault 1995), showing if nothing else that much of what has been termed "justice" has been nothing of the kind. While his critiques come from a certain ideological perspective, they are reminders that the institutions of justice created by flawed, sinful human beings cannot be perfect. We need God in order to have genuine justice and to know the value of human lives. Apart from him, ethics, morality, and law will be built on shifting opinions and relativistic standards. Without the life-giving Law-Giver—who is also the Judge—human judicial systems will invariably fall short of what they ought to be.

Now what?
What do we do with the knowledge that God is a God of life, and the standard of justice comes from his nature? It is important that we build our principles on the basis of God's, and in this case, we have to do our best to ensure that our society's laws on issues of life and death conform to God's revealed will.

Modern Christians live in diverse cultures and societies, not under the theocratic governance of ancient Israel. They cannot simply appeal to the revealed truths of Scripture to establish a legal system that binds every member of their nations. Further, countries have different laws and different avenues available for pursuing change. For example, discussing a Christian response to abortion in China is not the same as discussing it in Texas. Very permissive euthanasia laws exist in Canada and Belgium, but there are other countries in which it is completely illegal. Debates about capital punishment exist in some places, but not in others. Yet, regardless of social norms and values, Christians are to assess issues of life and death according to the Scriptures. The pragmatic approaches will vary, but the fundamental ethic of life should be constant and universal. God is concerned with justice, and his people should be as well.

Creativity in Presentation
We have to be so careful when we talk about issues of life and death. With a larger congregation, it is almost certain that someone has been to a funeral recently. There may be people who have lost loved ones to the kind of unintentional accidents this passage has in view (today, that might be because of motor vehicles or careless driving).

Contemporary society has many concerns about inequities in law, and this text points to the principle that everyone is to be treated equally under the law. If someone commits premeditated murder, they should not be able buy their way out of their punishment. Rich and poor, educated and uneducated, native-born and foreigner, all should be treated the same.

Cities of Refuge (35:1–34)

After setting the principles of this passage before the people, the preacher can apply them to their own contemporary context. For those who can preach philosophical principles in an accessible way, drawing people's attention to the presupposition of God's nature and its relationship to various iterations of human judicial systems may be worth doing. This text can also be appropriately applied to issues involving how our societies approach punishing the guilty and protecting the innocent.

At the risk of approaching something akin to allegorizing, both the city of refuge itself and the significance of the death of the high priest in the release of those who killed someone unintentionally can at least remind people of roles played by Christ. Where do we flee for refuge from the avenger of blood? Whose death allows us to go free? We don't want to strain the text, but these details do remind the believer of their Savior. Incredibly, even the serial killer can be forgiven through the blood of Christ. Through Jesus, all can be forgiven, even though some who are guilty may still need to bear the judicial consequences of their crimes in their society's legal system.

One possible outline for this passage could be like the following:

- God uses his servants to reflect his presence among his people (35:1–8).

- Life is sacred to God, and unwarranted vengeance is not permitted (35:9–15).

- Deliberate taking of life is a grave offense against God (35:16–21).

- Accidental taking of life still requires a recompense (35:22–29).

- The sacredness of life cannot be diminished or dismissed (35:30–34).

DISCUSSION QUESTIONS

1. What purpose would it serve to have enclaves of Levites scattered throughout Israel's territory? Why does God want the other tribes to give them places to dwell?

2. How do the cities of refuge reflect God's character as one who values each human life? How is this balanced with God's justice in cases of deliberate homicide?

3. Why does bloodshed "pollute the land" (35:33)?

4. How can contemporary believers model God's concern for each human life?

5. Taking into account the very different socio-historical and covenantal contexts, does this text give us any principles that could shape a just response to murder or manslaughter?

Numbers 36:1–13

EXEGETICAL IDEA
To preserve their tribe's full allotment, God instructs the daughters of Zelophehad to marry within the tribe of Manasseh.

THEOLOGICAL FOCUS
God responds to his people's concerns about his promises.

PREACHING IDEA
"For the Lord is good and his love endures forever; his faithfulness continues through all generations" (Ps. 100:5).

PREACHING POINTERS
This last chapter in the book of Numbers ties up some loose ends but is transparently oriented to the future rather than the past. After all of this time and after all of the things Israel did and failed to do, God has remained a God of steadfast love and covenant faithfulness. His people *will* enter the Promised Land, and he *will* take care of them; he *will* bless them and fulfill all of his covenant promises. This book is not a record of human faithfulness, but an incredible testimony to the gracious and holy character of the living God. No reader can reach this finishing chapter without the conviction that it is only because of the patience and longsuffering of God that the story can continue.

The last verse of the book points the reader to the commands and regulations of the Lord. Numbers is part of God's inspired Word, and it self-referentially directs the reader's gaze to the law of the Lord. There are times when stepping back to observe the contours and development of God's entire special revelation in the Bible is worth doing, and this chapter provides an opportunity not only to unfold the significance of this particular text but also to connect it to God's unfolding plan of redemption. In other words, this passage can be located as the fitting conclusion to Numbers, but also as a springboard for expositing the flow of revelation from the beginning of the Bible to the end. From creation to the new heaven and new earth, it is only because of God's character, and only because of the redemption that was accomplished through Jesus Christ our Lord, that we can be saved. This message will echo down to the end of time, so surely with the psalmist we can joyfully exclaim: "For the Lord is good and his love endures forever; his faithfulness continues through all generations" (Ps. 100:5 NIV).

INHERITANCE AND MARRIAGE: THE DAUGHTERS OF ZELOPHEHAD (36:1–13)

LITERARY STRUCTURE AND THEMES

Numbers concludes by returning to the daughters of Zelophehad from chapter 27. Granting them their father's share in the land raises a question of inheritance rights once it passes down to their children. This passage thus focuses on a small story with wider implications for what it means for Israel to live in the land of Canaan. It may seem like an anticlimactic way to end the book, but it reflects Israel's imminent entry into the land and the expectation that God's people will soon see the fulfillments of God's promises.

This story has a simple tripartite structure. First, the clan leaders of Manasseh bring to Moses a concern about what will happen to Zelophehad's inheritance when his daughters get married (36:1–4). Secondly, God gives Moses a verdict to address the situation (36:5–9). Finally, the daughters of Zelophehad obey God's instructions (36:10–12). A final summary verse then concludes the entire book (36:13).

Key themes of this passage include the fulfillment of God's promises and the necessity of obedience. God promises a proportional share in the Promised Land to each of Israel's tribes. This passage raises and resolves a potential complication that could have caused the tribe of Manasseh to be shortchanged. However, because Zelophehad's daughters follow God's instructions, his promises are fulfilled.

- *The Issue (36:1–4)*
- *The Verdict (36:5–9)*
- *The Obedient Response (36:10–12)*
- *Conclusion to the Book (36:13)*

EXPOSITION

One final issue arises that requires the people to seek God's direction. God awarded to the daughters of Zelophehad their father's share so that his name and lineage would not disappear from Israel. However, the overarching patrilineal system of inheritance remains. The leaders of Manasseh foresee a potential diminution of their tribal allotment should these women marry outside of the tribe, since their children would carry the tribal identity of their fathers. Consequently, to preserve their tribe's full allotment, the daughters of Zelophehad must marry within the tribe of Manasseh.

The Issue (36:1–4)

36:1. The introduction sets up the interested parties. The petitioners on this occasion are "the heads of the fathers' houses of the clan of the people of Gilead, son of Machir, son of Manasseh" (36:1 ESV). The Gileadites are one of the clans in the tribe of Manasseh, and Zelophehad belonged to that clan. Therefore, the Gileadites as a sociological unit have an interest in what happens to the property allotted to Zelophehad's daughters. They approach Moses and an assembly of Israelite elders with their query. The setting is somewhat different than the daughters' initial request. There is no mention of a location (such as the Tent of Meeting) and there is no priestly representative.[1] However,

---

[1] The Septuagint adds "and before Eleazar the priest" after Moses. This is likely an attempted harmonization with Numbers 27:2 (Milgrom 1990, 296).

their question similarly merits a divinely ordained response (36:5).

Mahlah, Noah, Hoglah, Milcah, and Tirzah do not speak in this scene even though it affects them. It is possible to read this as a restriction of rights previously obtained by these women (Sakenfeld 1988, 182), but it also mirrors the account in Numbers 27 where the Gileadite clan leaders did not have a voice in the daughters' request.

36:2–3. The Gileadite elders detail the crux of the situation. They remind Moses that YHWH ordered him to award Zelophehad's inheritance to his daughters (36:2). However, this raises a potential problem: that share of Israel's inheritance will be passed down to the children of these women. If their husbands are non-Manassehites, those children would carry the tribal identity of their fathers, following the principle of patrilineal descent. This would create a scenario in which pockets of non-Mannasehite territory crop up in the middle of Manasseh's allotment. This diminishes the overall share of the land awarded to the tribe (Ashley 1993, 659). It further violates the principle of fairness used to allot the land, leading the Manassehites to fear being shortchanged (26:52–56). Essentially, the legal precedents of territorial integrity and female inheritance are set against each other (Cole 2000, 559). This leads to another example of biblical law adapting general principles to address thorny situations. There is also a certain irony in the possibility that preserving the name of one Manassehite (Zelophehad) could result in the diminishment of his ancestral tribe.

36:4. The petitioners then refer to the Year of Jubilee. One of its key provisions is the return of land to the ancestral families to whom it was awarded (Lev. 25:10, 28). However, they note that the Jubilee provisions do not cover the problem created by this situation. Since the land has not been sold but simply inherited by children whose fathers were from different tribes, there is no mechanism to return the land to Manasseh (Cole 2009, 403). Consequently, the share of the land allotted to the tribes of the women's potential husbands would grow, while that of Manasseh diminishes. Reasonably enough, the current elders of Manasseh are looking out for the tribe's future self-interest by raising this issue.

The Verdict (36:5–9)

36:5. Moses first acknowledges the veracity of the complaint. Notably, this verse refers to the petitioners as "the tribe of the descendants of Joseph" (NIV), rather than descendants of Manasseh. This is another reminder that Joseph received the firstborn double-share of Jacob's inheritance. Joseph's sons Manasseh and Ephraim both lead tribes within Israel.

Unlike Numbers 27, there is no recorded dialogue between him and YHWH, but Moses still responds to the situation "At the Lord's command" (NIV). This provides an implicit assumption that Moses consulted with YHWH and returned to the people with YHWH's verdict.

36:6. Moses then conveys YHWH's verdict regarding the petitioners' request. It strikes a balance between freedom and constraints upon the marriage prospects of Zelophehad's daughters. The first half of the judgment is "Let them marry whomever they think best" (36:6a NET). The idea that a woman could choose her marriage partner is rare in ancient Israel, but the death of their father and the absence of brothers removes the male figures who would have selected spouses for these women (Pressler 2017, 314). Further, their status as propertied women may give them greater standing in this matter (Allen 2012, 454).

The second half of YHWH's judgment places limits on their freedom. It reads "only they must marry within the family of their father's tribe" (36:6b NET). This phrase begins with the Hebrew word אַךְ, whose primary purpose is to restrict the content of a preceding utterance (van der Merwe, Naudé, and Kroeze 2017, 389). Here, the limitation is that the women must marry within the tribe of Manasseh. This prevents their share of the land from passing to another tribe once they bear children. Although this ruling limits their prospective marriage pool, the daughters of Zelophehad still possess greater freedom than most ancient Israelite women. Further, it addresses the values of both individual autonomy and corporate responsibility. Within these parameters, the women should be able to avoid undesirable marriages while preserving their father's name and inheritance within Manasseh.

36:7–9. The verdict concludes by enshrining its requirements into inheritance law. The general principle is that allotments in the Promised Land shall not pass from tribe to tribe. They must remain within the tribe to whom they were given. Again, this upholds the principles of fairness and justice by preventing certain tribes to expand at the expense of others. YHWH has made a covenant with Israel to give them this land just as he promised their forefathers. He now declares that Israelites throughout their generations will have a place in the land. Ultimately, the land belongs to YHWH. He has the authority to determine how it will be apportioned.

Numbers 36:8 also extrapolates an enduring principle from the experience of Zelophehad's daughters. Future women who inherit according to the legislation in 27:8–11 are subject to the same limitations on their prospective marriages. They must also select husbands within their ancestral clan so that their property does not go to another tribe. This preserves "tribal territorial sovereignty" within the land and would help to ensure harmony between the tribes as Israel settled in the land (Cole 2000, 562).

The Obedient Response (36:10–12)
36:10–12. Mahlah, Tirzah, Hoglah, Milkah, and Noah remain commendable characters. These daughters of Zelophehad "did just as the LORD commanded Moses" (36:10 NIV). Their obedience contrasts with Israel's propensity to reject God's instructions throughout the book. There is no grumbling or attempt to circumvent the limitations placed upon them for the good of tribal unity. They use their God-given freedom to follow God's commands. Their boldness in securing the preservation of their father's name is matched by their humility in responding obediently to God's commands (Stubbs 2009, 247).

Numbers 36:11–12 announces that they married people who belonged to their father's tribe. Their husbands came from the tribe of Manasseh, which guaranteed that their inheritance remained within the tribe. This preserved tribal harmony and made these women exemplars of how people should respond to God's direction. Just as the book of Numbers began with obedient response to God's command to take a census, it concludes with otherwise insignificant women hearing and responding faithfully to God's voice.

TRANSLATION ANALYSIS
The phrase identifying the marriage partners of these women is לִבְנֵי דֹדֵיהֶן. This is challenging to define precisely, since the underlying noun in the second word (דּוֹד) has several definitions including "uncle," "beloved," or "relative." English translations tend to work off the "uncle" gloss. Thus, the daughters of Zelophehad marry "the sons of their uncles" (NET), "their uncles' sons" (NASB), "the sons of their father's brothers" (ESV), or "cousins on their father's side" (CSB, NIV, NLT). The precise relationship is less important than the indication that these men were fellow Manassehites, thus obeying YHWH's command.

Conclusion to the Book (36:13)

36:13. The final verse is a summary and conclusion for the book as a whole. It declares, "These are the commands and regulations the LORD gave through Moses to the Israelites on the plains of Moab by the Jordan across from Jericho" (NIV). Although the book consists of many things other than commands and regulations, it does instruct Israel in how it should follow God and provides examples of blessing when it does, and judgment when it does not.

Further, this final verse reinforces that this book is first and foremost the word of YHWH for Israel, with Moses as the intermediary. This is a reminder of the book's divine foundation, making it more than a collection of laws and fanciful stories. It reflects God's relationship with his covenant people and his work to form them in the wilderness as he guided them from Sinai to the borders of the Promised Land.

The book concludes with one final mention of Israel's geographical location. It has traversed through the wilderness and now camps just across the Jordan River from Jericho. God's faithful preservation of Israel, despite its many failings, now awaits a final consummation as Israel stands on the border of seeing his promises fulfilled.

THEOLOGICAL FOCUS

The exegetical idea (To preserve their tribe's full allotment, God instructs the daughters of Zelophehad to marry within the tribe of Manasseh) leads to the following theological focus: *God responds to his people's concerns about his promises.* The elders of Manasseh approach Moses with a legitimate concern about the future of their tribe: God's response to the efforts of Zelophehad's daughters to preserve their father's name opens the door for a later diminution of Manasseh's allotment within the land. As this narrative unfolds, God works through Moses to reassure the petitioners that their inheritance is secure and that their concerns have been addressed. God is neither silent nor hostile in response to a faithful, honest question.

God's responsiveness to his people is attested throughout Scripture. When Abram wondered how God would fulfill his promises of land and descendants through a childless, elderly couple, God made Abram fall asleep and took upon himself an oath to fulfill his promises (Gen. 15:17–21). Later, when Jacob fled from Esau, God appeared to him at Bethel, promising to watch over him wherever he went and to bring him back to the land in due course (Gen. 28:10–15). Upon his return, Jacob went back to Bethel to acknowledge God's faithfulness (Gen. 35:1–7). When Israel was in slavery in Egypt, God answered Moses's questions about the worsening situation for the Israelites with assurances that he would deliver his people (Exod. 6:6–8). The next several chapters of the book detail God's commitment to that promise. In very different circumstances, God even responded to Gideon's doubts about whether God would help him defeat the Midianites by performing the signs Gideon requested (Judg. 6:33–40). The plan of redemption unfolds with God as an active agent who hears his people's worries and responds in a fitting manner.

God's commitment to respond to his people continues into the New Testament. The disciples and other followers frequently misunderstand Jesus, but he remains in fellowship with them, guiding them through their misperceptions and doubts. This culminates after the resurrection when two unnamed followers are returning dejectedly to the village of Emmaus. As far as they can tell, God's plan and promises have failed; Jesus is not the prophesied deliverer, and darkness seems to reign. However, as they unknowingly express their concerns to the resurrected Christ, he rebukes them and explains that the whole story of Scripture was pointing to the crucifixion and resurrection (Luke 24:25–27). This one small story is no doubt a stand-in for the many who wondered if the cross marked the end. Instead, the Evangelist records that Jesus actively responded to these concerns and demonstrated that the story of Scripture and God's plan of redemption continued to unfold. Similarly, at the ascension, Jesus's followers anticipate a fulfillment of God's promises through a physical restoration of God's reign on the earth (Acts 1:6). However, Jesus responds to this by promising a different kind of strength through the Holy Spirit (Acts 1:7–8), which was fulfilled at the Pentecost event (Acts 2:1–4). Again, concerns about the nature of God's kingdom are answered by God's active presence to secure his promises.

PREACHING AND TEACHING STRATEGIES

Exegetical and Theological Significance
This passage can be viewed through a variety of hermeneutical horizons. At one level, it is a self-contained unit. At another level, it functions as an appendix or completion of Numbers 27:1–11. It is the conclusion of Numbers as a book, and it is the literary introduction to Deuteronomy. It completes the thematic section of 33:50–36:12, since this material deals "with matters of property and land *within the land of promise*" (Ashley 1993, 659).[2] In other words, this ending represents a ratification of the promises of God for his people. The logic of the text rests on the presupposition of God's faithfulness to his covenant and looks forward to its future fulfillment.

At this point, the reader has been on a long journey through Numbers, just like Israel had been on a long journey ever since they left Egypt. At times, it seemed like Israel would never make it to the land. It seemed like the people were too rebellious, and that the Holy One would have to end this story with an outpouring of divine wrath and judgment. There were moments of glory, but many moments of shame. One whole generation died in the wilderness. Aaron died; Moses will not lead the people into the Promised Land.

Nevertheless, this follow-up with Zelophehad's daughters points forward to the time when the people will be finally brought into the land. It is a testimony to God's patience, love, care, providence, holiness, and covenant faithfulness. No reader of Numbers can reach this spot and conclude that anything less than the grace and glory of God is responsible for the continuation of the story.

The word of the Lord is a crucial theme in Numbers, and the last verse of the book draws attention once again to the commands and regulations God gave the people through Moses. As the people prepare to enter the Promised Land, and as Moses prepares to be gathered to his ancestors, the last note is on God's word. When the people disobey the word of the Lord, they die; when they obey, they experience the blessing of God. The past narrative has not been one about their stellar faithfulness, but rather serves as a reminder of God's perfection. What the next era holds is hinted at in the future-oriented regulations in this last chapter, but the people's history of sinful rebellion makes the reader cautious. What will Israel do? And what will the contemporary reader do when they hear the Word of the Lord?

Preaching Idea
"For the Lord is good and his love endures forever; his faithfulness continues through all generations" (Ps. 100:5 NIV).

Contemporary Connections

What does it mean?
What does it mean that the Lord is good and his love endures forever, and that his faithfulness continues through all generations? In context, Psalm 100:5 reaches the climax of praise of that particular psalm, but also brings

---
2 Italics in original.

to completion the previous set of Psalms 93–99, which focuses on the Lord's justice and kingly reign. It is a fitting summary of God's gracious character, covenant love, and everlasting faithfulness.

The ending of Numbers shows us that God is making provision for the future of his people in the Promised Land. As he cared for generations past, and aids his covenant people in the present, so he is looking out for their future. Although there are all kinds of lessons in Numbers, the ending of the book also provides a macro-lesson when it is viewed in its relation to the whole sweep of the book (and the rest of God's unfolding revelation).

Numbers makes it clear that God is holy, just, and good. The last chapter is about justice and fairness, both in their present and with a promise for the future. Today, thousands of years later, God's faithfulness to his people is continuing. He is immutable in his nature, so his character doesn't change. The Lord was good and faithful in Numbers; he is good and faithful now. The Lord God will be good and faithful for every generation while the earth endures. And then, he will be good and faithful eternally, blessing his people with his holy presence forever.

Is it true?
Is it true that the Lord is good and his love endures forever, and that his faithfulness continues through all generations? Since Psalm 100:5 is true, this statement is true. However, it is known not only through revelation but also through the experiences that come with walking with God by faith. Through every generation of the church, people have extolled the divine faithfulness of God. In fact, the love and faithfulness of God are dominant themes in Scripture, as is demonstrated in proper systematic theology and also in the legacy of musical worship that the church has engaged in over time. God's people love to testify to his faithfulness as well as celebrate it in joyful song.

Now what?
What do we do with the fact the Lord is good and his love endures forever, and that his faithfulness continues through all generations? *Praise the Lord*. In light of this truth, the only proper response is praise. Joined to praise, there must be deep trust in God. Since he is good, loving, and faithful, we can have faith that he will fulfill every one of his promises. More than the Israelites in Moses's day could have dreamed about, we see the faithfulness of God displayed in his Son, the Lord Jesus Christ. When we have eyes to see, we will praise when we clearly see Jesus, and seeing Jesus leads us into a spiral of ever-deepening love and trust.

Creativity in Presentation

It would be interesting to know how many sermons have been preached on Numbers 36 in the last year in Christian churches. For that matter, it would be interesting to know what percentage of Christian sermons this last year were preached on *any* section of Numbers! How can a preacher creatively present this material? There are the standard sorts of forms that could be used: parallel Scripture verses and readings, stories of incredible faithfulness and fidelity, testimonies, hymn expositions, etc.

Sometimes the most creative thing we can do is simply and clearly unfold the great theological doctrines of the faith. No bells and whistles—simply declare the truth of God. For this section, the preacher may want to consider moving through the horizons of interpretation: immediate context; section-within-the-book; how Numbers 36 ends the whole of Numbers; how it relates to the Pentateuch, and then Joshua, etc., until we reach the end not only of Numbers but of the Bible. The theological theme of God's faithfulness through all generations can be expounded and illustrated. Give the people the meat of the Word; let them feast on God. His beauty and holiness are enough to captivate; his unadorned faithfulness is enough to celebrate. So, for creativity in presentation for

Inheritance and Marriage: The Daughters of Zelophehad (36:1–13)

Numbers 36, set yourself the task to preach the Word. Declare the whole counsel of God. Let God amaze his people afresh. Let God's Spirit pull hearts into the panorama of his truth, so that they are left saying, "Hallelujah!"

God is infinitely creative, and the Bible is a divinely inspired work of genius. Feed God's people with the Word, the whole Word, and nothing but the Word. Take your people by the hand, and as you keep in step with the Spirit, lead them through the canon, showing how Numbers 36 is related to the whole of God's message from Genesis to Revelation. No presentation can be more creative than the presentation given to us by God himself. In doing so, the preacher points God's people to this doxology: "For the Lord is good and his love endures forever; his faithfulness continues through all generations" (Ps. 100:5).

A possible outline of this passage could be:

- God hears the concerns of his people (36:1–4).

- God responds justly to the concerns of his people (36:5–9).

- Obedience to God's commands brings harmony to God's people (36:10–12).

- This whole book is a reminder that God graciously preserves and instructs his people (36:13).

DISCUSSION QUESTIONS

1. How do the daughters of Zelophehad model a proper response to God's commands?

2. Why were property rights and inheritance laws so important to leaders of the tribe of Manasseh?

3. Can you imagine a scenario in which potential conflict arises between two groups in your faith community, both of whom have good points? How could such an impasse be resolved in a manner pleasing to God?

REFERENCES

Adamo, David Tuesday. 2018. "A Silent Unheard Voice in the Old Testament: The Cushite Woman Whom Moses Married in Numbers 12:1–10." *In Die Skriflig* 52(1): 1–8.

Ajah, Miracle. 2010. "An Assessment of the Priestly Emolument in Numbers 18:8–32." *Scriptura* 103: 107–21.

Albright, W. F. 1957. *From the Stone Age to Christianity*. Garden City, NY: Doubleday Anchor.

———. 1963. "Jethro, Hobab and Reuel in Early Hebrew Tradition." *Catholic Biblical Quarterly* 25: 1–11.

Alexander, T. Desmond. 2012. *From Paradise to the Promised Land: An Introduction to the Pentateuch*. 3rd ed. Grand Rapids: Baker.

Allen, Ronald B. 2012. "Numbers." In *The Expositor's Bible Commentary*, edited by Tremper Longman III and David E. Garland, 2:23–456. Grand Rapids: Zondervan.

Amzallag, Gérard Nissim, and Shamir Yonah. 2017. "The Kenite Origin of the Sotah Prescription (Numbers 5.11–31)." *Journal for the Study of the Old Testament* 41(4): 383–412.

Arnold, Bill T., and John H. Choi. 2018. *A Guide to Biblical Hebrew Syntax*. 2nd ed. Cambridge: Cambridge University Press.

Artus, Olivier. 2013. "Numbers 32: The Problem of the Two and a Half Transjordanian Tribes and the Final Composition of the Book of Numbers." In *Torah and the Book of Numbers*, Edited by Christian Frevel, Thomas Pola, and Aaron Schart, 367–82. Tübingen: Mohr Siebeck.

Ashley, Timothy R. 1993. *Numbers*. New International Commentary on the Old Testament. Grand Rapids: Eerdmans.

Awabdy, Mark A. 2018. "The Holiness Composition of the Priestly Blessing." *Biblica* 99(1): 29–49.

Baden, Joel S. 2013. "The Structure and Substance of Numbers 15." *Vetus Testamentum* 63(3): 351–67.

Bailey, Lloyd R. 2005. *Leviticus—Numbers*. Smyth & Helwys Biblical Commentary. Macon, GA: Smyth & Helwys.

Bancroft, Charitie Less. 1863. "Before the Throne of God Above." Public Domain. https://hymnary.org/text/before_the_throne_of_god_above_i_have_a_.

Barkay, Gabriel, Bruce Zuckerman, Kenneth Zuckerman, Marilyn J. Lundberg, and Andrew G. Vaughn. 2003. "The Challenges of Ketef Hinnom: Using Advanced Technologies to Reclaim the Earliest Biblical Texts and Their Context." *Near Eastern Archaeology* 66(4): 162–71.

Beck, John A. 2003. "Why Did Moses Strike Out? The Narrative-Geographical Shaping of Moses's Disqualification in Numbers 20:1–13." *The Westminster Theological Journal* 65(1): 135–41.

Beitzel, Barry J. 2009. *The Moody Atlas of the Bible*. Chicago: Moody.

Bendor, Shunya. 1996. *The Social Structure of Ancient Israel: The Institution of the Family (Beit 'ab) From the Settlement to the End of the Monarchy*. Jerusalem Biblical Studies 7. Jerusalem: Simor.

Berlin, Adele. 2008. *The Dynamics of Biblical Parallelism*. Revised and expanded. Grand Rapids: Eerdmans.

Blenkinsopp, Joseph. 2012. "The Baal Peor Episode Revisited (Num 25,1–18)." *Biblica* 93(1): 86–97.

Block, Daniel I. 2003. "Marriage and Family in Ancient Israel." In *Marriage and Family in the Biblical World*, edited by Ken M. Campbell, 33–102. Downers Grove, IL: InterVarsity Press.

References

Boda, Mark J. 2009. *A Severe Mercy: Sin and Its Remedy in the Old Testament*. Siphrut 1. Winona Lake, IN: Eisenbrauns.

———. 2017. *The Heartbeat of Old Testament Theology: Three Creedal Expressions*. Grand Rapids: Baker.

Brichto, H. C. 1975. "The Case Law of the SŌTĀ and a Reconsideration of Biblical 'Law.'" *Hebrew Union College Annual* 45: 55–70.

Briggs, Richard S. 2018. *Theological Hermeneutics and the Book of Numbers as Christian Scripture*. Notre Dame, IN: University of Notre Dame Press.

Brown, Ken. 2015. "Vengeance and Vindication in Numbers 31." *Journal of Biblical Literature* 134(1): 65–84.

Brown, Raymond. 2002. *The Message of Numbers*. Bible Speaks Today. Downers Grove, IL: InterVarsity Press.

Browning, Daniel C., Jr. 1996. "The Strange Search for the Ashes of the Red Heifer." *The Biblical Archaeologist* 59(2): 74–89.

Budd, Philip J. 1984. *Numbers*. Word Biblical Commentary 5. Waco, TX: Word Books.

Burnside, Jonathan P. 2017. "Why Was Moses Banned from the Promised Land? A Radical Retelling of the Rebellions of Moses (Num. 20:2–13 and Exod. 2:11–15)." *Zeitschrift Für Altorientalische Und Biblische Rechtsgeschichte* 22: 111–59.

Cartledge, Tony W. 1992. *Vows in the Hebrew Bible and the Ancient Near East*. Journal for the Study of the Old Testament Supplements 147. Sheffield: JSOT Press.

Chavel, Simeon. 2009. "The Second Passover, Pilgrimage, and the Centralized Cult." *Harvard Theological Review* 102(1): 1–24.

Cole, R. Dennis. 2000. *Numbers*. New American Commentary 3B. Nashville: Broadman & Holman.

———. 2009. "Numbers." In *Zondervan Illustrated Bible Background Commentary*, edited by John W. Walton, 1:338–417. Grand Rapids: Zondervan.

Collins, John J. 1995. *The Scepter and the Star: The Messiahs of the Dead Sea Scrolls and Other Ancient Literature*. New York: Doubleday.

———. 2003. "The Zeal of Phinehas: The Bible and The Legitimation of Violence." *Journal of Biblical Literature* 122(1): 3–21.

Condie, Keith. 2001. "Narrative Features of Numbers 13–14 and Their Significance for the Meaning of the Book of Numbers." *The Reformed Theological Review* 60(3): 123–37.

Copan, Paul. 2011. *Is God a Moral Monster? Making Sense of the Old Testament God*. Grand Rapids: Baker.

Davies, Eryl W. 1995. *Numbers*. New Century Bible Commentary. Grand Rapids: Eerdmans.

Davies, Graham I. 1983. "The Wilderness Itineraries and the Composition of the Pentateuch." *Vetus Testamentum* 33: 1–13.

Douglas, Mary. 2004. *In the Wilderness: The Doctrine of Defilement in the Book of Numbers*. Oxford: Oxford University Press.

Driver, G. R. 1956. "Two Problems in the Old Testament Examined in Light of Assyriology." *Syria* 33: 70–78.

Eichler, Raanan. 2021. "A Sin Is Borne: Clearing Up the Law of Women's Vows (Numbers 30)." *Vetus Testamentum* 71: 317–28.

Emmrich, Martin. 2003. "The Case against Moses Reopened." *Journal of the Evangelical Theological Society* 46 (1): 53–62.

Falk, David A. 2018. "The Egyptian Sojourn and the Exodus." In *Behind the Scenes of the Old Testament: Cultural, Social, and Historical Contexts*, edited by Jonathan S. Greer, John W. Hilber, and John H. Walton, 194–200. Grand Rapids: Baker.

Feinstein, Eve Levavi. 2012. "The 'Bitter Waters' of Numbers 5:11–31." *Vetus Testamentum* 62 (3): 300–306.

Finkelstein, Israel, and Neil Asher Silberman. 2001. *The Bible Unearthed: Archaeology's New Vision of Ancient Israel and the*

Origin of Its Sacred Texts. New York: Free Press.

Foucault, Michel. 1995. *Discipline and Punishment: The Birth of the Prison*. New York: Vintage.

Fouts, David M. 1997. "A Defense of the Hyperbolic Interpretation of Large Numbers in the Old Testament." *Journal of the Evangelical Theological Society* 40(3): 377–87.

Frame, John M. 2002. *The Doctrine of God*. Phillipsburg, NJ: P&R.

Frevel, Christian. 2013. "Purity Concepts in the Book of Numbers in Context." In *Purity and the Forming of Religious Traditions in the Ancient Mediterranean World and Ancient Judaism*, edited by Christian Frevel and Christophe Nihan, 369–411. Leiden: Brill.

Frick, Frank S. 2002. "Ritual and Social Regulation in Ancient Israel: The Importance of the Social Context for Ritual Studies and a Case Study—The Ritual of the Red Heifer." In *"Imagining" Biblical Worlds: Studies in Spatial, Social and Historical Constructs in Honor of James W. Flanagan*, edited by David M. Gunn and Paula M. McNutt, 219–32. Journal for the Study of the Old Testament Supplements 359. London: Sheffield Academic.

Frymer-Kensky, Tikva. 1984. "The Strange Case of the Suspected Sotah (Numbers V 11–31)." *Vetus Testamentum* 34(1): 11–26.

Gane, Roy E. 2004. *Leviticus, Numbers*. NIV Application Commentary. Grand Rapids: Zondervan.

———. 2005. *Cult and Character: Purification Offerings, Day of Atonement, and Theodicy*. Winona Lake, IN: Eisenbrauns.

———. 2016. "Innovation in the Suspected Adulteress Ritual (Num 5:11–31)." In *Ritual Innovation in the Hebrew Bible and Early Judaism*, edited by Nathan MacDonald, 113–27. BZAW 468. Berlin: de Gruyter.

———. 2017. *Old Testament Law for Christians: Original Context and Enduring Application*. Grand Rapids: Baker.

Garlington, Don B. 2011. "The Salt of the Earth in Covenantal Perspective." *Journal of the Evangelical Theological Society* 54(4): 715–48.

Goldstein, Aaron J. 2012. "Large Census Numbers in Numbers: An Evaluation of Current Proposals." *Presbyterion* 38(2): 99–108.

Graf, David F. 2016. "Arabia and the Arabians." In *The World around the Old Testament*, edited by Bill T. Arnold and Brent A. Strawn, 417–66. Grand Rapids: Baker.

Graves, Michael. 2021. *How Scripture Interprets Scripture: What Biblical Writers Can Teach Us about Interpreting the Bible*. Grand Rapids: Baker.

Grossman, Jonathan. 2007. "Divine Command and Human Initiative: A Literary View on Numbers 25–31." *Biblical Interpretation* 15(1): 54–79.

Gruber, Mayer I. 1983. "The Many Faces of Hebrew Nāśāʾ Pānîm 'Lift up the Face.'" *Zeitschrift Für Die Alttestamentliche Wissenschaft* 95(2): 252–60.

Hadad, Eliezer. 2017. "'Unintentionally' (Numbers 35:11) and 'Unwittingly' (Deuteronomy 19:4): Two Aspects of the Cities of Refuge." *Assocation for Jewish Studies Review* 41(1): 155–73.

Hahn, Christine. 2011. "The Understanding of the Nazirite Vow." In *A God of Faithfulness: Essays in Honour of J. Gordon McConville on His 60th Birthday*, edited by Jamie A. Grant, Alison Lo, and Gordon J. Wenham, 46–60. The Library of Hebrew Bible/Old Testament Studies. New York: T & T Clark.

Hamilton, James M., Jr. 2022. *Typology: Understanding the Bible's Promise-Shaped Patterns*. Grand Rapids: Zondervan.

Harrison, R. K. 1990. *Numbers*. Wycliffe Exegetical Commentary. Chicago: Moody.

Hartley, J. E. 2003. "Holy and Holiness, Clean and Unclean." In *Dictionary of the Old*

Testament: Pentateuch, edited by T. Desmond Alexander and David W. Baker, 420–31. Downers Grove, IL: InterVarsity Press.

Heiser, Michael S. 2015. *The Hidden Realm: Recovering the Supernatural Worldview of the Bible*. Bellingham, WA: Lexham.

Hoffmeier, James K. 2012. "'These Things Happened': Why a Historical Exodus Is Essential for Theology." In *Do Historical Matters Matter to Faith? A Critical Appraisal of Modern and Postmodern Approaches to Scripture*, edited by James K. Hoffmeier and Dennis Robert Margary, 99–134. Wheaton, IL: Crossway.

———. 2014. "The Exodus and Wilderness Narratives." In *Ancient Israel's History: An Introduction to Issues and Sources*, edited by Bill T. Arnold and Richard S. Hess, 46–90. Grand Rapids: Baker.

Howe, Bonnie. 2005. *Because You Bear This Name: Conceptual Metaphor and the Moral Meaning of 1 Peter*. Biblical Interpretation Series 81. Atlanta: SBL.

Humphreys, Colin J. 1998. "The Number of People in the Exodus from Egypt: Decoding Mathematically the Very Large Numbers in Numbers I and XXVI." *Vetus Testamentum* 48(2): 196–213.

Hurowitz, Victor. 2004. "Healing and Hissing Snakes: Listening to Numbers 21:4–9." *Scriptura* 87: 278–87.

Hurtado, Larry W. 2016. *Destroy of the Gods: Early Christian Distinctiveness in the Roman World*. Waco, TX: Baylor University Press.

Janzen, J. Gerald. 2006. "What Does the Priestly Blessing Do?" In *From Babel to Babylon: Essays on Biblical History and Literature in Honour of Brian Peckham*, edited by Joyce Rilett Wood, John E. Harvey, and Mark Leuchter, 26–37. The Library of Hebrew Bible/Old Testament Studies 455. New York: T&T Clark.

Jenson, Philip Peter. 1992. *Graded Holiness: A Key to the Priestly Conception of the World*. Journal for the Study of the Old Testament Supplement Series 106. Sheffield: Sheffield Academic.

Jeon, Jaeyoung. 2015. "The Zadokites in the Wilderness: The Rebellion of Korach (Num 16) and the Zadokite Redaction." *Zeitschrift Für Die Alttestamentliche Wissenschaft* 127(3): 381–411.

Jobes, Karen H. 1999. *Esther*. NIV Application Commentary. Grand Rapids: Zondervan.

Keil, C. F. and F. Delitzsch. 1983. *Commentary on the Old Testament*. Grand Rapids: Eerdmans.

Kislev, Itamar. 2013. "The Census of the Israelites on the Plains of Moab (Numbers 26): Sources and Redaction." *Vetus Testamentum* 63(2): 236–60

———. 2020. "The Cities of Refuge Law in Numbers 35:9–34: A Study of Its Sources, Textual Unity and Relationship to Deuteronomy 19:1–13." *Zeitschrift Für Altorientalische Und Biblische Rechtsgeschichte* 26(1): 249–63.

Klawans, Jonathan. 2000. *Impurity and Sin in Ancient Judaism*. New York: Oxford University Press.

Knierim, Rolf P., and George W. Coats. 2005. *Numbers*. Forms of Old Testament Literature IV. Grand Rapids: Eerdmans.

Konyndyk DeYoung, Rebecca. 2009. *Glittering Vices: A New Look at the Seven Deadly Sins and Their Remedies*. Grand Rapids: Baker.

Kugel, James L. 1981. *The Idea of Biblical Poetry: Parallelism and Its History*. New Haven, CT: Yale University Press.

Laniak, Timothy S. 2006. *Shepherds after My Own Heart: Pastoral Traditions and Leadership in the Bible*. New Studies in Biblical Theology. Downers Grove, IL: InterVarsity Press.

Lee, Won. 2003a. "The Exclusion of Moses from the Promised Land: A Conceptual Approach." In *The Changing Face of Form Criticism for the Twenty-First Century*, edited by Marvin A. Sweeney and Ehud Ben Zvi, 217–39. Grand Rapids: Eerdmans.

———. 2003b. *Punishment and Forgiveness in Israel's Migratory Campaign*. Grand Rapids: Eerdmans.

Leveen, Adriane B. 2002. "Variations on a Theme: Differing Conceptions of Memory in the Book of Numbers." *Journal for the Study of the Old Testament* 27(2): 201–21.

Levine, Baruch. 1993. *Numbers 1–20*. Anchor Bible Commentary 4A. New York: Doubleday.

———. 2000. *Numbers 21–36*. Anchor Bible Commentary 4B. New York: Doubleday.

Levison, John R. 2003. "Prophecy in Ancient Israel: The Case of the Ecstatic Elders." *Catholic Biblical Quarterly* 65(4): 503–21.

Lewis, C. S. 1956. *The Last Battle*. New York: HarperTrophy.

Lindquist, Maria. 2011. "King Og's Iron Bed." *Catholic Biblical Quarterly* 73(3): 477–92.

Lioy, Dan. 2020. "Who Is to Blame for God's Prohibition against Moses Entering the Promised Land?" *Conspectus* 30: 35–57.

Longman, Tremper, III. 2019. *Confronting Old Testament Controversies: Pressing Questions about Evolution, Sexuality, History, and Violence*. Grand Rapids: Baker.

MacDonald, Nathan. 2012. "The Hermeneutics and Genesis of the Red Cow Ritual." *Harvard Theological Review* 105(3): 351–71.

Magonet, Jonathan. 1982. "The Korah Rebellion." *Journal for the Study of the Old Testament* 24: 3–25.

Marquis, Liane M. 2013. "The Composition of Numbers 32: A New Proposal." *Vetus Testamentum* 63(3): 408–32.

Martínez, Florentino García, and Eibert J. C. Tigchelaar, eds. 1997. *The Dead Sea Scrolls Study Edition: Volume 1*. Leiden, Brill.

McAffee, Matthew. 2014. "Covenant and the Warnings of Hebrews: The Blessing and the Curse." *Journal of the Evangelical Theological Society* 57(3): 537–53.

McKeown, J. 2003. "Blessing and Cursing." In *Dictionary of the Old Testament: Pentateuch*, edited by T. Desmond Alexander and David W. Baker, 83–87. Downers Grove, IL: InterVarsity Press.

Meyer, Esias E. 2017. "Ritual Innovation in Numbers 18?" *Scriptura* 116(2): 133–47.

Milgrom, Jacob. 1981. "The Paradox of the Red Cow." *Vetus Testamentum* 31: 62–73.

———. 1990. *Numbers*. JPS Torah Commentary. Philadelphia: Jewish Publication Society.

———. 1998. *Leviticus 1–16*. Anchor Bible Commentary 3A. New Haven, CT: Yale University Press.

———. 1999. "On Decoding Very Large Numbers." *Vetus Testamentum* 49(1): 131–32.

Miller, J. Maxwell. 1989. "The Israelite Journey through (around) Moab and Moabite Toponymy." *Journal of Biblical Literature* 108(4): 577–99.

Miller, Patrick D. 1975. "The Blessing of God: An Interpretation of Numbers 6:22–27." *Interpretation* 29(3): 240–51.

Mirguet, Françoise. 2008. "Numbers 16: The Significance of Place—An Analysis of Spatial Markers." *Journal for the Study of the Old Testament* 32(3): 311–30.

Moberly, R. W. L. 1999. "On Learning to Be a True Prophet: The Story of Balaam and His Ass." In *New Heaven and New Earth—Prophecy and the Millennium: Essays in Honor of Anthony Gelston*, edited by P. J. Harland and Robert Hayward, 1–17. Vetus Testamentum Supplements 77. Leiden: Brill.

———. 2020. *The God of the Old Testament: Encountering the Divine in Christian Scripture*. Grand Rapids: Baker.

Monroe, Lauren A. S. 2012. "Phinehas' Zeal and the Death of Cozbi: Unearthing a Human Scapegoat Tradition in Numbers 25:1–18." *Vetus Testamentum* 62(2): 211–31.

Moshavi, Adina. 2009. "Two Types of Argumentation Involving Rhetorical Questions in Biblical Hebrew Dialogue." *Biblica* 90(1): 32–46.

Na'aman, Nadav. 2006. "Lebo-Hamath, Sub-at-Hamath and the Northern Boundary." In *Ancient Israel's History and Historiography: The First Temple Period*, 3:357–85. Winona Lake, IN: Eisenbrauns.

Niditch, Susan. 1993. "War, Women, and Defilement in Numbers 31." *Semeia* 61: 39–57.

Noonan, Benjamin J. 2020. "High-Handed Sin and the Promised Land: The Rhetorical Relationship between Law and Narrative in Numbers 15." *Journal for the Study of the Old Testament* 45(1): 79–92.

Noth, Martin. 1968. *Numbers*. Translated by James D. Martin. Interpretation. Philadelphia: Westminster.

Olson, Dennis T. 1996. *Numbers*. Interpretation. Louisville: John Knox.

Organ, Barbara E. 2001. "Pursuing Phinehas: A Synchronic Reading." *The Catholic Biblical Quarterly* 63(2): 203–18.

Oswalt, John N. 2011. "Is Balaam's Donkey the Real Prophet (Numbers 24:1–4)?" In *Presence, Power, and Promise: The Role of the Spirit of God in the Old Testament*, edited by David G. Firth and Paul D. Wegner, 208–19. Downers Grove, IL: InterVarsity Press.

Petra. 2006. "Road to Zion." Capitol CMG Publishing. https://www.azlyrics.com/lyrics/petra/roadtozion.html.

Pettit, David P. 2018. "Expiating Apostasy: Baal Peor, Moses, and Intermarriage with a Midianite Woman." *Journal for the Study of the Old Testament* 42: 457–68.

Pressler, Carolyn. 2017. *Numbers*. Abingdon Old Testament Commentaries. Nashville: Abingdon.

Pritchard, James B., ed. 1969. *Ancient Near Eastern Texts Relating to the Old Testament*. 3rd ed. Princeton, NJ: Princeton University Press.

Reis, Pamela Tamarkin. 2005. "Numbers XI: Seeing Moses Plain." *Vetus Testamentum* 55(2): 207–31.

Roskop, Angela R. 2011. *The Wilderness Itineraries: Genre, Geography, and the Growth of the Pentateuch*. History, Archaeology, and Culture of the Levant 3. Winona Lake, IN: Eisenbrauns.

Ross, Allen P. 2002. *Holiness to the Lord: A Guide to the Exposition of the Book of Leviticus*. Grand Rapids: Baker.

Routledge, Robin L. 2015. "The Nephilim: A Tall Story? Who Were the Nephilim and How Did They Survive the Flood?" *Tyndale Bulletin* 66(1): 19–40.

Sakenfeld, Katharine Doob. 1988. "In the Wilderness, Awaiting the Land: The Daughters of Zelophehad and Feminist Interpretation." *The Princeton Seminary Bulletin* 9(3): 179–96.

———. 1995. *Numbers: Journeying with God*. International Theological Commentary. Grand Rapids: Eerdmans.

Schneider, Stanley. 2019. "Moses in Cush: Development of the Legend." *Jewish Bible Quarterly* 47(2): 113–19.

Schnittjer, Gary Edward. 2006. *The Torah Story: An Apprenticeship on the Pentateuch*. Grand Rapids: Zondervan.

Schreckenberg, Heinz, and Kurt Schubert. 1992. *Jewish Traditions in Early Christian Literature. Volume 2: Jewish Historiography and Iconography in Early and Medieval Christianity*. Compendia Rerum Iudaicarum ad Novum Testamentum 3/2. Leiden: Brill.

Sklar, Jay. 2012. "Sin and Atonement: Lessons from the Pentateuch." *Bulletin for Biblical Research* 22(4): 467–91.

Smoak, Jeremy D. 2017. "From Temple to Text: Text as Ritual Space and the Composition of Numbers 6:24–26." *The Journal of Hebrew Scriptures* 17: 1–26.

Sprinkle, Joe M. 2015. *Leviticus and Numbers*. Teach the Text. Grand Rapids: Baker.

Stone, Lawson G. 2014. "Early Israel and Its Appearance in Canaan." In *Ancient Israel's History: An Introduction to Issues and Sources*, edited by Bill T. Arnold and Richard S. Hess, 127–64. Grand Rapids: Baker.

Stubbs, David L. 2009. *Numbers*. Brazos Theological Commentary on the Bible. Grand Rapids: Brazos.

Trever, John C. 1962. "Coriander Seed." In *Interpreter's Dictionary of the Bible*, I:681–82.

Turner, David L. *Matthew*. Baker Exegetical Commentary of the New Testament. Grand Rapids: Baker, 2008.

Ulrich, Dean R. 1998. "The Framing Function of the Narratives about Zelophehad's Daughters." *Journal of the Evangelical Theological Society* 41(4): 529–38.

van der Merwe, Christo H., Jacobus A. Naudé, and Jan H. Kroeze. 2017. *A Biblical Hebrew Reference Grammar*. 2nd ed. New York: Bloomsbury.

von Schlegel, Kathrina. 1855. "Be Still My Soul." Public domain. https://amazinghymns.com/be-still-my-soul.

Waite, Jerry. 2010. "The Census of Israelite Men After Their Exodus from Egypt." *Vetus Testamentum* 60: 487–91.

Walton, John H. 2003. "Exodus, Date Of." In *Dictionary of the Old Testament: Pentateuch*, edited by T. Desmond Alexander and David W. Baker, 258–72. Downers Grove, IL: InterVarsity Press.

Walton, John H., and D. Brent Sandy. 2013. *The Lost World of Scripture: Ancient Literary Culture and Biblical Authority*. Downers Grove, IL: IVP Academic.

Walton, John H., and J. Harvey Walton. 2017. *The Lost World of the Israelite Conquest: Covenant, Retribution, and the Fate of the Canaanites*. Downers Grove, IL: IVP Academic.

Way, Kenneth C. 2011. *Donkeys in the Biblical World: Ceremony and Symbol*. History, Archaeology, and Culture of the Levant 2. Winona Lake, IN: Eisenbrauns.

Webb, William J., and Gordon K. Oeste. 2019. *Bloody, Brutal, and Barbaric? Wrestling with Troubling War Texts*. Downers Grove, IL: IVP Academic.

W'Ehusha, Lubunga. 2010. "The Budding of Aaron's Staff: An Ethic of Non-Violent Conflict Resolution in Numbers 17." *Africa Journal of Evangelical Theology* 29(2): 123–35.

Wenham, Gordon J. 2008. *Numbers*. Tyndale Old Testament Commentary. Leicester: InterVarsity Press.

Wesley, Charles. 1742. "Arise, my Soul, Arise." Public domain. https://hymnary.org/text/arise_my_soul_arise_shake_off_thy_guilty.

Wray Beal, Lissa M. 2017. "The Past as Threat and Hope: Reading Joshua with Numbers." *Bulletin for Biblical Research* 27(4): 461–83.

Wright, Christopher J. H. 2008. *The God I Don't Understand: Reflections on Tough Questions of Faith*. Grand Rapids: Zondervan.

Wright, David P. 1985. "Purification from Corpse-Contamination in Numbers 31:19–24." *Vetus Testamentum* 35(2): 213–23.

KERUX COMMENTARY SERIES

―――――

Numbers: A Commentary for Biblical Preaching and Teaching
Joel Barker & Steven D. West

1 & 2 Kings: A Commentary for Biblical Preaching and Teaching
David B. Schreiner & Lee Compson

Psalms, Volume 1: The Wisdom Psalms: A Commentary for Biblical Preaching and Teaching
W. Creighton Marlowe & Charles H. Savelle Jr.

Jeremiah and Lamentations: A Commentary for Biblical Preaching and Teaching
Duane Garrett & Calvin F. Pearson

Zephaniah–Malachi: A Commentary for Biblical Preaching and Teaching
Gary V. Smith & Timothy D. Sprankle

Acts: A Commentary for Biblical Preaching and Teaching
John D. Harvey & David Gentino

Ephesians: A Commentary for Biblical Preaching and Teaching
Gregory S. MaGee & Jeffrey D. Arthurs

Philippians: A Commentary for Biblical Preaching and Teaching
Thomas S. Moore & Timothy D. Sprankle

Colossians and Philemon: A Commentary for Biblical Preaching and Teaching
Adam Copenhaver & Jeffrey D. Arthurs

Hebrews: A Commentary for Biblical Preaching and Teaching
Herbert W. Bateman IV & Steven Smith

1 Peter: A Commentary for Biblical Preaching and Teaching
Timothy E. Miller & Bryan Murawski